NTA UGC NET

Management (Paper I & II)

Latest Edition
Practice Kit

10 Tests
10 Mock Test

Based On Real Exam Pattern

✓ Thoroughly Revised and Updated
✓ Detailed Analysis of all MCQs

Title	: NTA UGC NET Management (Paper I & II)
Author Name	: Mr. Rohit Manglik
Published By	: EduGorilla Community Pvt. Ltd.
Publishers Address	: 12/651, First Floor Opp. Arvindo Park, Near Jama Masjid, Indira Nagar, Lucknow, Uttar Pradesh-226016, India

Copyright EduGorilla

ISBN : 978-93-90257-10-2

Second Edition

Disclaimer EduGorilla

Compiled and created by EduGorilla Community Pvt. Ltd

Printed By EduGorilla Community Pvt. Ltd.

ROHIT MANGLIK
CEO, EduGorilla

Dear Applicants,

People say *"Success comes to those who work hard."* But I've seen people working hard for their exams day in and day out for marginal success. While others succeed in their examinations by putting in just half the work. So are they God Gifted? No! I believe that it's because they work *smart* and not just *hard*. Similarly, for your exams, you should strategize your preparation so as to increase the likelihood of success. Well with EduGorilla get ready to increase your *chances of selection* in your exam by *16x*.

EduGorilla helps you in not only working *hard* but also working in a *smart and strategic* manner. With EduGorilla's preparation package, you get a chance to make your exam preparation easy, and a fun learning path towards selection. Finding the right path to your preparations can be difficult if you don't know in which direction to head. Don't worry, we have you covered! EduGorilla will be your guide to success in your journey. With our Preparation Package, you can prepare strategically and beat the exam in just one attempt.

EduGorilla's Preparation Package includes-

- **Test Series**
- **Books**

Our preparation package is handcrafted as per the latest changes, expert opinions, and students' discretion. Thus, enabling you to get through each stage of the selection process for your exam.

Our Books are designed by the teachers and experts of the respective exam with a combined 150+ years of experience; to provide you with easy, efficient, and effective learning. Our books are smart, in the sense that not only do they give you the answers to the questions but also provide similar questions for practice.

EduGorilla's competent Test Series gives you real-time experience and confidence through which you can clear your offline or online exam in just one attempt. We currently host 83,000+ mock tests for 1,440+ competitive and academic exams.

Thus, EduGorilla misses no chance to assist you in your preparation and covers all stages of the exam, so that you don't have to look anywhere else.

We provide complete preparation packages for defense, banking, teaching, and other National & State-Level exams. Hence, it doesn't matter which exam you aspire to because you will reach your success.

ALL THE BEST !
Let EduGorilla be your Guide to Success.

Rohit Manglik,
Founder and CEO, EduGorilla

INTRODUCTION

EduGorilla focuses on guiding students to succeed in their examinations. With that in mind, our book, titled "NTA UGC NET : Management (Paper I & II)", has been drafted through the collective efforts of our distinguished experts with 150+ years of combined experience. This book consists of questions that are created following the latest changes in the syllabus and exam pattern. We compiled the book on the basis of questions that are most likely to appear in the UGC NET Management. Through EduGorilla's "NTA UGC NET : Management (Paper I & II)" your chances of success will increase 16x.

EduGorilla does this through our Complete Preparation Package. This package consists of well-conceptualized and structured content in the form of questions that are tailor-made according to your needs and will help you practice for exams in a smart way by pinpointing all the necessary information. It also provides hints and solutions, along with a smart answer sheet for your self-evaluation. You can assess your shortcomings and work accordingly on areas that may require more of your attention.

EduGorilla promises to help you succeed in your examination and accomplish your dream goals. We believe in our aspirants and see them at the top of the merit list. And the first step towards the top is to start preparing with us. EduGorilla's "NTA UGC NET : Management (Paper I & II)" includes the following attributes.

➤ Well-Researched Content

➤ Top-Notch Quality

➤ Detailed Answers and Analysis

➤ Smart Answer Sheet

➤ Exam Relevant Questions

Therefore, EduGorilla fortifies your preparation and makes it durable enough to help you stand tall and beat the examination.

UGC NET Management
Scan QR code for Eligibility, Exam Pattern, Syllabus and more.

Book ID: 0185

TABLE OF CONTENTS

Paper-I

Q.1 Good leadership exhibits:

A. Uniform behaviour and excellent personality

B. High morale and feelings of dedication

C. Partisan of the group

D. Lack of motivation in the group

Q.2 Which of the following learner characteristics is highly related to effectiveness of teaching?

A. Prior experience of the learner

B. Educational status of the parents of the learner

C. Peer groups of the learner

D. Family size from which the learner comes.

Q.3 In the two sets given below Set – I indicates methods of teaching while Set – II provides the basic requirements for success/ effectiveness. Match the two sets and indicate your answer by choosing from the code:

Set – I

(Method of teaching)

1) Lecturing

2) Discussion in groups

3) Brainstorming

4) Programmed Instructional

Set – II

(Basic requirements for success/ effectiveness)

i. Small step presentation with feedback provided

ii. Production of large number of ideas

iii. Content delivery in a lucid language

iv. Use of teaching- aids

v. Theme based interaction among participants

Code:

A-i B-ii C-iii D-iv

A. A-i B-ii C-iii D-iv

B. A-ii B-iii C-iv D-v

C. A-iii B-v C-ii D-i

D. A-iv B-ii C-I D-iii

Q.4 From the list of evaluation procedures given below identify those which will be called 'formative evaluation'. Indicate your answer by choosing from the code:

1) A teacher awards grades to students after having transacted the course work.

2) During interaction with students in the classroom, the teacher provides corrective feedback.

3) The teacher gives marks to students on a unit test.

4) The teacher clarifies the doubts of students in the class itself.

5) The overall performance of a students is reported to parents at every three months interval.

6) The learner's motivation is raised by the teacher through a question-answer session.

Code:

A. 1, 2 and 3

B. 2, 3 and 4

C. 1, 3 and 5

D. 2, 4 and 6

Q.5 Assertion (A): All teaching should aim at ensuring le learning.

Reason (R): All learning results from teaching.

A. Both (A) and (R) are true, and (R) is the correct explanation of (A).

B. Both (A) and (R) are true, but (R) is not the correct explanation of (A).

C. (A) is true, but (R) is false.

D. (A) is false, but (R) is true.

Q.6 Match the following:-

List I	List II
A) Fundamental research	1) Find out the extent of the perceived impact of an intervention
B) Applied research	2) Developing an effective explanation through theory building
C) Action research	3) Improving an existing situation through use of interventions
D) Evaluative research	4) Exploring the possibility of theory for use in various situations

A. A-ii B-iv C-iii D-i

B. A-v B-iv C-iii D-ii

C. A-I B-ii C-iii D-iv

D. A-ii B-iii C-iv D-v

Q.7 Which of the sets of activities best indicate the cyclic nature of action research strategy?

A. Reflect, Observe, Plan, Act

B. Observe, Act, Reflect, Plan

C. Act, Plan, Observe, Reflect

D. Plan, Act, Observe, Reflect

Q.8 Which of the following sequences of research steps is nearer to scientific method?

A. Suggested solution of the problem, Deducing the consequences of the solution, Perceiving the problem situation, Location of the difficulty and testing the solutions.

B. Perceiving the problem situation, Locating the actual problem and its definition, Hypothesizing, Deducing the consequences of the suggested solution and Testing the hypothesis in action.

C. Defining a problem, Identifying the cause of the problem, defining a population, drawing a sample, collecting data and Analysing results.

D. Identifying the causal factors, Defining the problem, developing a hypothesis, selecting a sample, collecting data and arriving at generalizations and Conclusions.

Q.9 The problem of 'research ethics' is concerned with which aspect of research activities?

A. Following the prescribed format of a thesis
B. Data analysis through qualitative or quantitative techniques
C. Defining the population of research
D. Evidence based research reporting

Q.10 In which of the following activities, potential for nurturing creative and critical thinking is relatively greater?
A. Preparing research summary
B. Presenting a seminar paper
C. Participation in research conference
D. Participation in a workshop

Ques (11-15):Direction: Read the following passage carefully and answer questions.

If India has to develop her internal strengths, the nation has to focus on the technological imperatives, keeping in mind three dynamic dimensions: the people, the overall economy and the strategic interests. These technological imperatives also take into account a 'fourth' dimension, time, an offshoot of modern day dynamism in business, trade, and technology that leads to continually shifting targets. We believe that technological strengths are especially crucial in dealing with this fourth dimension underlying continuous change in the aspirations of the people, the economy in the global context, and the strategic interests. The progress of technology lies at the heart of human history. Technological strengths are the key to creating more productive employment in an increasingly competitive market place and to continually upgrade human skills. Without a pervasive use of technologies, we cannot achieve overall development of our people in the years to come. The direct linkages of technology to the nation's strategic strengths are becoming more and more clear, especially since 1990s. India's own strength in a number of core areas still puts it in a position of reasonable strength in geo-political context. Any nation aspiring to become a developed one needs to have strengths in various strategic technologies and also the ability to continually upgrade them through its own creative strengths. For people-oriented actions as well, whether for the creation of large-scale productive employment or for ensuring nutritional and health security for people, or for better living conditions, technology is the only vital input. The absence of greater technological impetus could lead to lower productivity and wastage of precious natural resources. Activities with low productivity or low value addition, in the final analysis hurt the poorest most. The technological imperatives to lift our people to a new life, ad to a life they are entitled to is important. India, aspiring to become a major economic power in terms of trade and increase in GDP, cannot succeed on the strength of turnkey projects designed and built abroad or only through large-scale imports of plant machinery, equipment and know how. Even while being alive to the short-term realities, medium and long-term strategies to develop core technological strengths within our industry are vital for envisioning a developed India.

Q.11 According to the above passage, which of the following are indicative of the fourth dimension?
1) Aspirations of people
2) Modern day dynamism

3) Economy in the global context
4) Strategic interests
Code:

A. 1, 2 and 3 only   B. 2, 3 and 4 only
C. 1, 3 and 4 only   D. 1, 2 and 4 only

Q.12 More productive employment demands:
A. Pervasive use of technology
B. Limiting competitive market place
C. Geo-political considerations
D. Large industries

Q.13 Absence of technology would lead to:
1) Less pollution
2) Wastage of precious natural resources
3) Low value addition
4) Hurting the poorest most
Code:

A. 1, 2 and 3 only   B. 2, 3 and 4 only
C. 1, 2 and 4 only   D. 1, 3 and 4 only

Q.14 The advantage of technological inputs would result in:
A. Unbridled technological growth
B. Importing plant machinery
C. Side lining environmental issues
D. Lifting our people to a life of dignity

Q.15 Envisioning a developed India requires:
A. Aspiration to become a major economic player
B. Dependence upon projects designed abroad
C. Focus on short-term projects
D. Development of core technological strengths

Q.16 Differentiation between acceptance and non-acceptance of certain stimuli in classroom communication is the basis of:
A. selective expectation of performance
B. selective affiliation to peer groups
C. selective attention
D. selective morality

Q.17 Assertion (A): The initial messages to students in the classroom by a teacher need not be critical to establish interactions later.
Reason (R): More control over the communication process means more control over what the students are learning.
Code:

A. Both (A) and (R) are true, and (R) is the correct explanation of (A)
B. Both (A) and (R) are true, but (R) is not the correct explanation of (A).
C. (A) is true, but (R) is false.
D. (A) is false, but (R) is true.

Q.18 Assertion (A) : To communicate well in the classroom is a natural ability.
Reason (R) : Effective teaching in the classroom demands knowledge of the communication process.
Code:

A. Both (A) and (R) are true, and (R) is the correct explanation of (A).

B. Both (A) and (R) are true, but (R) is not the correct explanation of (A).

C. (A) is true, but (R) is false.

D. (A) is false, but (R) is true.

Q.19 Assertion (A) : Classroom communication is a transactional process.

Reason (R) : A teacher does not operate under the assumption that students' responses are purposive.

Select the correct code for your answer:

A. Both (A) and (R) are true, and (R) is the correct explanation of (A).

B. Both (A) and (R) are true, but (R) is not the correct explanation of (A).

C. (A) is true, but (R) is false.

D. (A) is false, but (R) is true.

Q.20 Which of the following set of statements is correct for describing the human communication process?

1) Non-verbal communication can stimulate ideas.

2) Communication is a learnt ability.

3) Communication is not a universal panacea.

4) Communication cannot break-down.

5) More communication means more effective learning by students.

6) Value of what is learnt through classroom communication is not an issue for students.

Code:

A. 1, 3, 5 and 6   **B.** 2, 4, 5 and 6

C. 1, 2, 3 and 4   **D.** 1, 4, 5 and 6

Q.21 The next term in the series- 1, 5, 15, 29, __?__, ...is:

A. 36   **B.** 47   **C.** 59   **D.** 63

Q.22 The next term in the series ABD, DGK, HMS, MTB, SBL, __?__, ... is:

A. ZKU   **B.** ZCA   **C.** ZKW   **D.** KZU

Q.23 If VARANASI is coded as WCUESGZQ, then the code of KOLKATA will be:

A. LOQOZEH   **B.** HLZEOOQ

C. ZELHOQO   **D.** LQOOFZH

Q.24 Introducing Rakesh to her husband a woman said, "His brother's father is the only son of my grandfather". The woman is related to Rakesh as:

A. Aunt   **B.** Mother

C. Sister   **D.** Daughter

Q.25 Two numbers are in the ratio 2: 5. If 16 is added to both the numbers, their ratio becomes 1 : 2. The numbers are:

A. 16, 40   **B.** 20, 50   **C.** 28, 70   **D.** 32, 80

Q.26 Superiority of intellect depends upon its power of concentration on one theme in the same way as a concave mirror collects all the rays that strike upon it into one point.

What type of reasoning is entailed in the above statement?

A. Mathematical   **B.** Psychological

C. Analogical   **D.** Deductive

Q.27 Given below are two premises (A and B). Four conclusions are drawn from them. Select the code that states validly drawn conclusion (s) (taking the premises individually or jointly).

Premises:

A) Most of the dancers are physically fit.

B) Most of the singers are dancers.

Conclusions:

1) Most of the singers are physically fit.

2) Most of the dancers are singers.

3) Most of the physically fit persons are dancers.

4) Most of the physically fit persons are singers.

Code:

A. 1 and 2   **B.** 2 and 3   **C.** 3 and 4   **D.** 4 and 1

Q.28 Which one among the following is a presupposition in inductive reasoning?

A. Law of identity

B. Unchangeability in nature

C. Harmony in nature

D. Uniformity of nature

Q.29 If the proposition 'domestic animals are hardly ferocious' is taken to be false, which of the following proposition/propositions can be claimed to be certainly true? Select the correct code:

Prepositions:

1) All domestic animals are ferocious.

2) Most of the domestic animals are ferocious.

3) No domestic animal is ferocious.

4) Some domestic animals are non-ferocious.

Code:

A. 1 and 2   **B.** 1 only   **C.** 3 and 4   **D.** 2 only

Ques (30-34): Year-wise Production, Exports and Per Capita Consumption of Rice:-

Year	Production (in million kg)	Exports (in million kg)	Per Capita Consumption (in kg)
2012	186.5	114	36.25
2013	202	114	35.2
2014	238	130	38.7
2015	221	116	40.5
2016	215	88	42

Q.30 In what year did the maximum percentage increase in the consumption of rice compared to the previous year?

A. 2013   **B.** 2014   **C.** 2015   **D.** 2016

Q.31 What is the population of the country in the year 2014 (in million)?

A. 2.64   B. 2.72   C. 2.79   D. 2.85

Q.32 In which year the ratio of export to consumption was maximum?

A. 2012   B. 2013   C. 2014   D. 2015

Q.33 In which year, the population of the country was the highest?

A. 2013   B. 2014   C. 2015   D. 2016

Q.34 What is the average consumption of rice (in million kg) over the years 2012-2016?

A. 104   B. 102.1   C. 108   D. 100.1

Q.35 Which of the following statements, regarding the term ICT is/are TRUE?

P: ICT is an acronym that stands for Indian Classical Technology.

Q: Converging technologies that exemplify ICT include the merging of audio-visual, telephone and computer networks through a common cabling system.

A. P only   B. Q only
C. P and Q   D. Neither P nor Q

Q.36 A new Laptop has been produced that weighs less, is smaller and uses less power than previous Laptop models. Which of the following technologies has been used to accomplish this?

A. Universal Serial Bus Mouse
B. Faster Random-Access Memory
C. Blu Ray Drive
D. Solid State Hard Drive

Q.37 Given the following email fields, which of the email addresses will 'swami' be able to see when he receives the message?

To....... ram@test.com

Cc...... rai@test.com; ravi@test.com

Bcc.... swami@test.com; rama@test.com

A. ram @ test.com
B. ram @ test.com; raj @ test.com; ravi @ test.com
C. ram @ test.com; rama @ test.com
D. ram @ test.com; rama @ test.com; raj @ test.com; ravi @ test.com

Q.38 Put the following units of storage into the correct order, starting with the smallest unit first and going down to the largest unit:

1) Kilobyte
2) Byte
3) Megabyte
4) Terabyte
5) Gigabyte
6) Bit

Give your answer from the following code:

A. 6, 2, 1, 3, 4, 5   B. 6, 2, 1, 4, 5, 3
C. 6, 2, 1, 3, 5, 4   D. 6, 2, 1, 4, 3, 5

Q.39 With regard to computer memory, which of the following statements(s) is/are TRUE?

P) Read Only Memory (ROM) is 'volatile' memory.

Q) Random Access Memory (RAM) is 'volatile' memory.

R) Secondary Memory is 'volatile' memory.

A. P only   B. Q only
C. P and Q only   D. P and R only

Ques (40-50):Choose the correct answer from the code given below:

Q.40 'Fly ash' produced in thermal power plants is an eco-friendly resource for use in:

1) agriculture as micro-nutrient
2) wasteland development
3) dam and water holding structures
4) brick industry

Choose the correct answer from the code given below:

A. 1,2 and 4 only   B. 2,3 and 4 only
C. 1,3 and 4 only   D. 1,2,3 and 4

Q.41 Which of the following types of natural disasters has no definite beginning and end?

A. Earthquakes   B. Landslides
C. Hurricanes   D. Droughts

Q.42 Assertion (A): Indoor air pollution is a serious health hazard.

Reason (R): The dispersal of air pollutants is rather limited in indoor environment.

A. Both (A) and (R) are true and (R) is the correct explanation of (A).
B. Both (A) and (R) are true but (R) is not the correct explanation of (A).
C. (A) is true and (R) is false.
D. Both (A) and (R) are false.

Q.43 In terms of their contribution to the total power generation in India, identify the correct sequence of energy sources-Thermal power plants (TPP), Large Hydropower projects (LHP), Nuclear Energy (NE) and Renewable Energy (RE) which includes solar energy, wind energy, biomass and small hydropower projects.

A. TPP>RE>LHP>NE   B. TPP>LHP>RE>NE
C. LHP>TPP>RE>NE   D. LHP>TPP>NE>RE

Q.44 Which of the following is considered as major source of pollution in rivers of India?

A. Unregulated small-scale industry
B. Untreated sewage
C. Agricultural run-off
D. Thermal power plants

Q.45 India has the largest Higher Education System in the World after:

1) The United States of America
2) Australia
3) China
4) United Kingdom (U.K.)

Select the correct answer from the code given below:

A. 1, 2, 3 and 4
B. 1, 2 and 3 only
C. 1, 3 and 4 only
D. 1 and 3 only

Q.46 Prime Minister Research Fellowship is for students pursuing Ph.D programme in:

A. State and Central Universities
B. Central Universities, IISc, IITs, NITs, IISERs and IIITs
C. IISc, IITs, NITs, IISERs, IIITs, State and Central Universities
D. IITs and IISc

Q.47 Leader of the Opposition is a member of committees which select:

1) the Central Information Commissioner
2) the Central Vigilance Commissioner
3) the Chairperson of National Human Rights Commission
4) the Chairperson of National Commission for Women

Select the correct answer from the code given below:

A. 1, 2, 3 and 4
B. 1, 2 and 3 only
C. 1, 3 and 4 only
D. 1, 2 and 4 only

Q.48 Which of the following statements are correct about gender budgeting?

1) It is separate budget addressing the specific needs of women.
2) It assesses the impact of government budget on women.
3) It is an accounting exercise.
4) It is another budgeting innovation.

Select the correct answer from the code given below:

A. 2 and 4 only
B. 1 and 4 only
C. 1, 3 and 4 only
D. 2, 3 and 4 only

Q.49 Which of the following are the barriers to citizen-centric administration in India?

1) Wooden and inflexible attitude of the civil servants
2) Ineffective implementation of laws and rules
3) Awareness of rights and duties of citizens
4) Lack of job opportunities for the youth

Select the correct answer from the code given below:

A. 1, 2, 3 and 4
B. 1, 2, and 3 only
C. 1, 2, and 4 only
D. 1 and 2 only

Q.50 Which one of the following statements is not correct in the context of Venn diagram method?

A. It is a method of testing the validity of arguments.
B. It represents both the premises of a syllogism in one diagram.
C. It requires two overlapping circles for the two premises of a standard-form categorical syllogism.
D. It can be used to represent classes as well as propositions.

Paper-II

Q.51 _________________ is the combination of various promotion mix tools employed by the company for the advancement of the product in the market, raising market shares etc.

A. Competitive parity in advertising
B. Pulsing advertising
C. Optimum promotion
D. None of the above.

Q.52 Branded unleaded petrol is an example of which of the following Pricing decisions?

A. Economy Pricing
B. Penetration Pricing
C. Premium Pricing
D. Skimming Pricing

Q.53 Which of the following statements is/are correct with reference to factors influencing the span of control?

a) Nature of work
b) Size of organisation
c) Type of work
d) Type of personnel
e) Location of personnel

Choose the correct option/code from the following:

A. a,c,d,e
B. a,d,e
C. a,b,c,d
D. a,b,d

Q.54 Statement I: The Smoot-Hawley Act altered US tariffs to be in compliance with the GATT.

Statement II: Geneva Round of negotiations led to the formation of WTO.

Choose the correct option from those below:

A. Statement I is correct, Statement II is incorrect.
B. Statement I is incorrect, Statement II is correct.
C. Both Statement I and Statement II are correct.
D. Both Statement I and Statement II are incorrect.

Q.55 Under which stage of Product Life Cycle, promotion is aimed at innovators and the company seeks to build product awareness and attract customers.

A. Decline stage
B. Maturity stage
C. Introduction stage
D. Growth stage

Q.56 Who among the following provided the first definition of personnel engagement?

A. Saks
B. Kahn
C. Lewin
D. Crim

Q.57 National income equilibrium is at the level where:

A. Aggregate investment equals aggregate savings
B. Aggregate expenditure equals aggregate income
C. Inflationary and deflationary gaps are absent
D. All of these

Q.58 Which of the following is defined as a pricing method wherein a fixed percentage of the total cost of production is added to the cost of product to set its price?

A. Demand based pricing
B. Cost based pricing
C. Competition based pricing
D. None of the above

Q.59 Assertion (A): Commercial banks should formulate a rigorous monitoring system to prevent sickness in small scale industries

Reason (R): This would minimize the uncertainty in the recovery of money lent

A. Both (A) and (R) are correct, and (R) is the correct explanation of (A).

B. Both (A) and (R) are correct, but (R) is not the correct explanation of (A).

C. (A) is correct., but (R) is not correct.

D. (A) is wrong, and (R) is correct.

Q.60 Liberalization of geographic markets is considered as which of the following factors under SWOT analysis?

A. Internal factor, strength

B. External factor, Opportunity

C. Internal factor, Weakness

D. External factor, Threat

Q.61 Which of the following are the determinants of working capital?

a) Inventory

b) Cash

c) Price level changes

d) Market and demand conditions

e) Nature of business

f) Operating efficiency

Choose the correct option from those below:

A. (a), (b), (d), (e)   **B.** (b), (d), (e), (f)

C. Only d   **D.** All of the above

Q.62 Z Theory of motivation is propounded by:

A. Douglas McGregor   **B.** A H Maslow

C. Frederick Herzberg   **D.** Dr William Ouchi

Q.63 _________ refers to any direct or indirect interaction customers have with a brand, product, service etc.

A. Retailers touch point

B. Customers touch point

C. Company touch point

D. All of the above

Q.64 Statement-I. The commodity whose demand is not attached/connected with the demand of other commodities is said to have_____ demand.

Statement-II. FMCG and consumer durables are examples of ______ demand.

A. Individual demand and short term demand

B. Autonomous demand and long term demand

C. Independent demand and durable goods demand

D. Free demand and industry demand

Q.65 Statement I: Conciliation is one of the alternative dispute resolution methods in which both the conflict parties meet the conciliator separately and resolve the issue legally.

Statement II: Arbitration is a way to resolve disputes outside the courts. An arbitration award is provided, which is legally binding on both sides and enforceable in the courts.

Choose the correct option from those below:

A. Statement I is correct., Statement II is incorrect.

B. Statement I is incorrect, Statement II is correct.

C. Both Statement I and Statement II are correct.

D. Both Statement I and Statement II are incorrect.

Q.66 The particular task performance in CPM is

A. Dummy   **B.** Event   **C.** Activity   **D.** Contrary

Q.67 Which of the following is not the primary objective of the operations management?

A. Quality improvement

B. Time schedule

C. Services and facilities

D. Cost reduction

Q.68 _________ are the collection of our social, communication and self-management behavior.

A. Conceptual Skills   **B.** Soft Skills

C. Political Skills   **D.** Hard Skills

Q.69 Assertion (A): If brand awareness is in the building stage, the brand extension requires many efforts.

Reason (R): When the organizations try to build brand extensions without any value addition to the customer, they will definitely fail.

A. Both (A) and (R) are correct, and (R) is the correct explanation of (A).

B. Both (A) and (R) are correct, but (R) is not the correct explanation of (A).

C. (A) is correct., but (R) is not correct.

D. (A) is wrong, and (R) is correct.

Q.70 Which of the following is not the function of the distribution channel?

A. Bridging the Gap between production and consumption

B. Time-saving

C. Promoting the product

D. Storage as well as the distribution of goods

Q.71 Assertion (A): The kinky demand curve hypothesis predicts sticky prices in the market.

Reason (R): The demand curve of oligopoly firms is not perfectly elastic.

A. (A) is correct., but (R) is incorrect.

B. Both (A) and (R) are correct, but (R) is not the right explanation of (A).

C. Both (A) and (R) are correct, (R) is the right explanation of (A).

D. Both (A) and (R) are incorrect.

Q.72 Who pointed out that increased exports lead to inflation and higher prices criticising the theory of Mercantilism?

A. Michael Porter   **B.** David Hume

C. David Ricardo   **D.** Adam Smith

Q.73 In which of the following stages of the consumer buying behaviour process does cognitive dissonance occur?

A. Need Recognition

B. Information search

C. Evaluation of alternatives

D. Post-purchase evaluation

Q.74 Assertion (A): Career planning is the process of enhancing an employee's future value.

Reason (R): Career planning and development is an on-going process to help an employee manage his or her work.

A. (A) is correct., but (R) is incorrect.

B. Both (A) and (R) are correct, but (R) is not the right explanation of (A).

C. Both (A) and (R) are correct, (R) is the right explanation of (A).

D. Both (A) and (R) are incorrect.

Q.75 ________________is the emotional or feeling segment of an attitude whereas behavioural component describes an intention to behave in a certain way towards someone or something.

A. Affective Component

B. Behavioural Component

C. Cognitive Component

D. None of the above

Q.76 Statement I: In the performing phase, all the team members will accomplish the tasks effectively.

Statement II: In the norming stage, there will be differences of opinions among team members.

Choose the correct option from those below:

A. Statement I is correct., Statement II is incorrect.

B. Statement I is incorrect, Statement II is correct.

C. Both Statement I and Statement II are correct.

D. Both Statement I and Statement II are incorrect.

Q.77 Which of the following statements is/are correct with reference to factors of goal-setting theory?

a) Goal Commitment

b) Task characteristics

c) Manpower requirements

d) Culture bound

e) location

f) Self-efficacy

Choose the correct option/code from the following:

A. a,b,d,f **B.** a,b,c,d **C.** a,b,c,d,e **D.** b,c,d,e

Q.78 Assertion (A): Because of selective perception, the individuals develop a fear of the unknown and they resist change.

Reason (R): Selective perception starts when people perceive a change differently. They get disturbed because of new habits and new patterns of work.

A. Both (A) and (R) are correct, and (R) is the correct explanation of (A).

B. Both (A) and (R) are correct, but (R) is not the correct explanation of (A).

C. (A) is correct., but (R) is not correct.

D. (A) is wrong, and (R) is correct.

Q.79 If the sample size is larger than 30, the student's t distribution tends to which of the following distribution?

A. Normal distribution

B. Chi-square distribution

C. Poisson distribution

D. Binomial distribution

Q.80 Statement 1: Demand is the wholesome amount of goods and services demanded by a particular society at a particular point of time.

Statement 2: Demand is an economic principle referring to a consumer's desire to purchase goods and services and the willingness to pay the price for a specific good or service.

Which of the above statements are correct?

A. Statement 1 is correct, Statement 2 is incorrect.

B. Statement 2 is correct, Statement 1 is incorrect

C. Both Statement I and Statement II are correct.

D. Both Statement I and Statement II are incorrect.

Q.81 ________________can be defined as one in which three or more people decide, perhaps on an ad hoc basis, to meet on a regular or semi-regular schedule for the purpose of discussing subjects of common interest.

A. Formal group **B.** Informal group

C. Secondary group **D.** Reference group

Q.82 Which one of the following is not the internal factor affecting the weighted average cost of capital of a firm?

A. Investment policy of the firm

B. Capital structure of the firm

C. Dividend policy followed

D. Market risk premium for the firm

Q.83 Which of the following statements are true?

I. National income at market price is equal to NNP at factor cost.

II. Value of production for self-consumption should not be added to national income.

III. Transfer payments are included while calculating national income by income method.

IV. Disposable income is personal income after payment of direct taxes.

Choose the correct option from those below:

A. I, II, III **B.** II, III, IV

C. I, II, IV **D.** I, III, IV

Q.84 Which of the following is not covered under the EXIM policy in India?

A. Special Economic Zones

B. Export Promotion Schemes

C. Duty Exemption Schemes

D. Finance Assistance

Q.85 If the modal value is not clear in a distribution, it can be ascertained by the method of

A. Grouping **B.** Summarising

C. Trial and error **D.** Guessing

Q.86 Statement I: Breakthrough Innovation is rare and a difficult innovation as it requires the introduction of completely new technology or a new business model.

Statement II: Breakthrough Innovation involves low risk and requires greater investment.

Choose the correct option from the following:

A. Statement I is correct, Statement II is incorrect.

B. Statement I is incorrect, Statement II is correct.
C. Both Statement I and Statement II are correct.
D. Both Statement I and Statement II are incorrect.

Q.87 Company's mission statement, information about the team and key employees, location of business are all included in which of the following elements of a Business plan?
A. Appendix
B. Company description
C. Management
D. Executive summary

Q.88 A group of position involving the same duties, skills, knowledge and responsibilities is called________.
A. Personnel **B.** Product
C. Job **D.** None of the above

Q.89 Which of the following is not a knowledge management technique
A. Data Mining
B. Artificial Intelligence
C. Big data
D. Information and Communication Technology

Q.90 Who popularised the term Equal employment opportunity?
A. Lyndon Johnson **B.** Robertson
C. Burke **D.** Richard Beckhard

Q.91 The job description consists of:
A. Job summary
B. Job duties
C. Job identification
D. All a. , b. and c. are correct

Q.92 Assertion (A): An ethical issue is an unidentifiable problem and an identifiable situation.
Reason (R): An ethical issue requires a person to choose several actions which are to be evaluated and involve conflict between moral imperatives.
A. Both (A) and (R) are correct, and (R) is the correct explanation of (A).
B. Both (A) and (R) are correct, but (R) is not the correct explanation of (A).
C. (A) is correct, but (R) is not correct.
D. (A) is wrong, and (R) is correct.

Q.93 Which of the following is not a method of inventory management?
A. ABC analysis
B. EOQ model
C. VED analysis
D. Regression analysis method

Q.94 Graphically partition values can be determined with the help of
A. Histogram **B.** Bar diagram
C. Frequency polygon **D.** Ogive curve

Q.95 Statement I: The bumper strike is a strike that is meant to affect the whole industry.
Statement II: In the lightning strike, the workers go on a strike without any notice or sometimes after giving short notice.
Choose the correct option from those below:
A. Statement I is correct., Statement II is incorrect.
B. Statement I is incorrect, Statement II is correct.
C. Both Statement I and Statement II are correct.
D. Both Statement I and Statement II are incorrect.

Q.96 In international HRM, Training and development depends on:
I. The degree to which management is centralized.
II. The cultural expectations of training.
III. The kind of employees engaged in subsidiaries or joint ventures.
IV. External factors including cultural distance and institutional factors.
V. The influence of branding and the extent to which human resource are expected to reflect the brand.
Choose the correct code:
A. I, II, III, IV **B.** II, III, IV, V
C. I, III, IV, V **D.** I, II, III, V

Q.97 A test designed to determine a person's ability in a particular skill or field of knowledge is called__________.
A. Achievement test
B. Achievement test
C. Aptitude test
D. All a. , b. and c. are correct

Q.98 What is the default block size in a Hadoop distributed file system(HDFS)?
A. 128 MB **B.** 200 MB **C.** 187 MB **D.** 56 MB

Q.99 Arrange in the right sequence of decisions in manufacturing enterprises:
(A) Making of forecasts
(B) Determination of key factors
(C) Consideration of alternative combination of forecasts
(D) Preparation of budgets
(E) Combination of factors
Choose the correct answer from the options given below.
A. $(A), (B), (C), (E), (D)$
B. $(C), (A), (E), (B), (D)$
C. $(B), (A), (C), (E), (D)$
D. $(A), (C), (B), (E), (D)$

Q.100 What is the main purpose of the critical success factors framework?
A. To ensure the growth of the firm
B. To guide the analysis of the firm's strengths and weaknesses
C. To overcome organizational issues
D. To preserve market share

Q.101 Under which of the following Consumer Sales Promotion techniques, a booklet is added separately to a local newspaper for delivery?
A. Checkout dispensers
B. Price deal
C. Free-standing insert
D. Trade allowances

Q.102 Statement I: In the behavior modeling under social learning theory, an individual tries to follow the behavior which has favorable outcomes.

Statement II: In the learning behavior consequences under social learning theory, the cognitive process has no role to play in learning the new behavior.

Choose the correct option from those below:
A. Statement I is correct, Statement II is incorrect.
B. Statement I is incorrect, Statement II is correct.
C. Both Statement I and Statement II are correct.
D. Both Statement I and Statement II are incorrect.

Q.103 Match the following:-

(A) Debt securities without any explicit interest rate	i) Floating Rate Bonds
(B) Company issuing such bonds experiences less financial distress	(ii) Zero-coupon bonds
(C) Coupon rate quoted as mark-up on the given rate	(iii) Income Bonds
code: (A) (B) (C)	

A. (iii) (ii) (i)   **B.** (i) (iii) (ii)
C. (ii) (iii) (i)   **D.** All of the above

Q.104 Which of the following is not a dimension of organizational climate stated by Likert?
A. Leadership   **B.** Motivation
C. Affiliation   **D.** Decisions

Q.105 Which of the following marketing concepts deals with the exchange of products between the seller and the buyer?
A. Societal concept   **B.** Exchange concept
C. Product concept   **D.** Production concept

Q.106 Suppose there are two goods, rice and meat. Which of the following are true if the price of rice is increasing continuously with the given income?
1) the demand for meat increases and rice decreases
2) the demand for rice increases and meat decreases
3) the demand for rice increases and meat is constant
4) the demand for rice increases and eventually it falls
Which of the following statements are correct?
A. 1&3   **B.** only 2   **C.** 2&4   **D.** only 4

Q.107 Assertion (A): Opportunity cost of good is to produce an additional quantity of a good.
Reason (R): It is the amount of other goods that is sacrificed to produce an additional quantity of that particular good.
A. Both (A) and (R) are correct, and (R) is the correct explanation of (A).
B. Both (A) and (R) are correct, but (R) is not the correct explanation of (A).
C. (A) is correct., but (R) is not correct.
D. (A) is wrong, and (R) is correct.

Q.108 Which of the following are the three categories of entrepreneurs as identified by Arthur H Cole?
A. Innovative, Imitative, Drone
B. Private, Public, Rational
C. Empirical, Rational, Cognitive
D. Innovative, Cognitive, Empirical

Q.109 Select the correct answer in the context of the principles of Corporate Governance?
a) Transparency
b) Fairness
c) Accountability
d) Commitment
e) Responsibility
Choose the correct option from those below:
A. a,b,c,d   **B.** a,b,c,e   **C.** a,c,d,e   **D.** b,c,d,e

Q.110 Statement I: The small sector policy which was introduced in the year 1991, permitted large undertakings to hold twenty-four percent equity in small undertakings.
Statement II: This initiative was taken to decrease ancillarisation, sub-contracting and to bring modern technology to small units.
Choose the correct option from those below:
A. Statement I is correct., Statement II is incorrect.
B. Statement I is incorrect, Statement II is correct.
C. Both Statement I and Statement II are correct.
D. Both Statement I and Statement II are incorrect.

Q.111 _________________works on the concept that all the targeted marketing communications should be accounted for in terms of the result or output they generate.
A. Accountable marketing
B. Relationship marketing
C. Reactive Marketing
D. None of the above.

Q.112 Which of the following is not a type of Grapevine?
A. Cluster chain   **B.** Probability chain
C. Single strand chain   **D.** Network chain

Q.113 Assertion (A): In Law of Marginal utility, money is considered an exception.
Reason (R): Marginal utility of money is always zero or negative.
A. (A) is correct., but (R) is incorrect.
B. Both (A) and (R) are correct, but (R) is not the right explanation of (A).
C. Both (A) and (R) are correct, (R) is the right explanation of (A).
D. Both (A) and (R) are incorrect.

Q.114 Which of the following techniques permits the complainant to remain anonymous?
A. The exit interview
B. The gripe-box system

C. The opinion survey

D. None of the above

Q.115 Assertion(A): Delegatee must have a clear idea about his tasks and how they will fit in the overall plan.

Reason(R): Any ambiguity in defining the authority can produce poor results.

A. Both (A) and (R) are correct, and (R) is the correct explanation of (A).

B. Both (A) and (R) are correct, but (R) is not the correct explanation of (A).

C. (A) is correct, but (R) is not correct.

D. (A) is wrong, and (R) is correct.

Q.116 Statement I: A temporary sales decline should not be interpreted as a sign of product decline.

Statement II: Product Strategy under growth stage is to create product awareness and attract the customers to buy the product.

Choose the correct option from the following:

A. Statement I is correct, Statement II is incorrect.

B. Statement I is incorrect, Statement II is correct.

C. Both Statement I and Statement II are correct.

D. Both Statement I and Statement II are incorrect.

Q.117 In the Boston Consulting Group (BCG) approach, the company classifies its different businesses on a two-dimensional growth-share matrix. What does the horizontal and vertical axis represent?

Statement I: The horizontal axis represents a relative market share.

Statement II: Vertical axis represents the market growth rate.

Choose the correct option from those below:

A. Statement I is correct., Statement II is incorrect.

B. Statement I is incorrect, Statement II is correct.

C. Both Statement I and Statement II are correct.

D. Both Statement I and Statement II are incorrect.

Q.118 Which of the following is not part of Brand identity prism?

A. Brand Personality

B. Customer culture

C. Customer Reflection

D. Customer Self-image

Q.119 Which of the following is(are) true regarding the process layout?

a) There is only a qualitative method available for process layout

b) Process layout is also known as functional layout

c) This has implications in all the organizations

d) It minimizes material handling costs

Choose the correct option from those below:

A. a and b only

B. b and c only

C. a, b and c only

D. b,c and d only

Q.120 According to the Government of India, "any industry located in a rural area, village or town with a population of

______and below and an investment of Rs.______in plant and machinery is classified as a village industry."

A. 30000, 1 crore

B. 25000, 3 crore

C. 35000, 2 crore

D. 20000, 3 crore

Q.121 The process through which individuals attempt to determine the causes behind others' behaviour is known as:

A. Perception

B. Attribution

C. Attitude

D. None of the above

Q.122 Which of the following statement(s) is(are) true according to quality circles?

Statement I: Improve the overall competitiveness of the organization

Statement II: Enhances the work-life of employees by avoiding rework and providing job satisfaction.

Choose the correct option from those below:

A. Statement I is correct., Statement II is incorrect.

B. Statement I is incorrect, Statement II is correct.

C. Both Statement I and Statement II are correct.

D. Both Statement I and Statement II are incorrect.

Q.123 Match the Following:-

(A) Leveraged buyout	(i) Management buyout
(B) Financing for merger	(ii) Cash offer
(C) Accounting for merger	(iii) Greenmail
(D) Preventing hostile takeover	(iv) Pooling of interest

A. (i) (ii) (iv) (iii)

B. (i) (iii) (ii) (iv)

C. (ii) (i) (iv) (iii)

D. (i) (iv) (ii) (iii)

Q.124 Arrange the steps of identifying business opportunities in the correct order.

a) Screening of business opportunities

b) Selecting a business opportunity and preparing a business plan

c) Generate ideas

d) Scanning the environment

A. (a), (b), (c), (d)

B. (c), (d), (a), (b)

C. (a), (d), (c), (b)

D. (c), (a), (d), (b)

Q.125 Which of the following provides the distribution cache in hadoop

A. Name node in Hadoop

B. Job tracker

C. Map-reduce framework

D. Artificial intelligence

Q.126 Who wrote"A Behavioral Theory of the Firm"?

A. J. M. Juran

B. Elwood S. Buffa and Rakesh K. Sarin

C. Richard M. Cyert and James G. March

D. None of the above

Q.127 Statement I. In ______ role, the manager must communicate with internal and external contacts.

Statement II. In ______ role, the manager communicates potentially useful information to colleagues.

Statement III. In _______ role, the manager is involved in solving problems and generating new ideas.

Choose the correct option from those below:

A. Leader, Entrepreneurial, Monitor

B. Resource allocator, Disseminator, Monitor

C. Liaison, Disseminator, Entrepreneurial

D. Disseminator, Liaison, Disturbance handler

Q.128 Which of the following statement is true?

(A) Profit-sharing is an agreement freely entered into by which the employees receive share fixed in advance from the organization's profits.

(B) An experiment in profit shares on a wide scale would, therefore, be definitely undertaking a voyage of an unchartered sea.

(C) Profit distribution under a profit-sharing plan are used to fund employee retirement plans.

A. Only A

B. Only C

C. Only B

D. All of these A, B , C

Q.129 A company XYZ employs a competent and experienced person of their rival company ABC by offering him an attractive pay-package and other benefits. What is this kind of practice known as?

A. Cross Networking

B. Headhunting

C. Poaching

D. Stealing

Q.130 Arrange the following steps taken by the Government to encourage the exports of agricultural products in chronological order.

a) The government exempted Indian exporters from paying service taxes laid on road, railways and ports

b) The announcement of the inclusion of dairy, poultry and minor forest produce in special agriculture plan

c) The announcement of a plan to encourage private companies to export agricultural products

d) Government liberalised the export of plant products and extracts of various herbs

Choose the correct option from those below:

A. a,b,c,d   **B.** d,c,b,a   **C.** c,d,b,a   **D.** b,a,d,c

Q.131 Performance appraisal includes:

A. Check reviews done by the supervisors.

B. Review his performance in relation to the objectives and other behaviours.

C. Promote employees for self-appraisal.

D. All of the above.

Q.132 Which of the following is not one of the characteristics of Innovation as described by E.M Rogers?

A. Compatibility

B. Complexity

C. Rationality

D. Observability

Q.133 Under whose leadership, the Great Bombay textile strike was called in the year 1982?

A. Dutta Samant

B. Joseph Baptista

C. NM Joshi

D. Lokhande

Q.134 Match the following:-

(A) The probability of occurring single event	(i) Conditional Probability
(B) The probability revised in the light of additional information	(ii) Marginal probability
(C) The probability of two events occurring together or in succession	(iii) Joint Probability
(D) The probability of occurring one event given that another event has happened	(iv) Posterior probability

A. (ii) (iv) (iii) (i)   **B.** (i) (iv) (iii) (ii)

C. (i) (ii) (iii) (iv)   **D.** (iv) (iii) (i) (ii)

Q.135 Statement I: The Republic of Nauru was the last country to join the IMF.

Statement II: The resources for IMF loans are provided by member countries mostly through their quotas payments.

Choose the correct option from those below:

A. Statement I is correct, Statement II is incorrect.

B. Statement I is incorrect, Statement II is correct.

C. Both Statement I and Statement II are correct.

D. Both Statement I and Statement II are incorrect.

Q.136 Which one of the following items is not a part of a job description?

A. Location

B. Title

C. Emotional characteristics

D. Working Conditions

Q.137 Which of the following is correct. in context to different forms of Non-Verbal communication?

a) Paralanguage

b) Kinesics

c) Touch

d) Eye-movements

e) Email

Choose the correct option from those below:

A. a,b,c,e   **B.** a,b,c,d   **C.** b,c,d,e   **D.** a,c,d,e

Q.138 Assertion (A): Continuous analysis of the behavior of the organization avoids the win-lose situation.

Reason (R): Analysis of organizational behavior helps in finding the gaps in the skill set.

A. Both (A) and (R) are correct, and (R) is the correct explanation of (A).

B. Both (A) and (R) are correct, but (R) is not the correct explanation of (A).

C. (A) is correct, but (R) is not correct.

D. (A) is wrong, and (R) is correct.

Q.139 Assertion (A): To market a good or a service, the 4Ps of marketing are adequate.

Reason (R): In the service market, the customers act as co-producers and end-users.

A. Both (A) and (R) are correct, and (R) is the correct explanation of (A).

B. Both (A) and (R) are correct, but (R) is not the correct explanation of (A).

C. (A) is correct., but (R) is not correct.

D. (A) is wrong, and (R) is correct.

Q.140 Consider the following statements

Statement 1: Both regression coefficients have the same sign.

Statement 2: Correlation coefficients and regression coefficients have opposite sign.

Select the correct option

A. Both statement 1 and statement 2 are correct

B. Statement 1 is correct but statement 2 is not correct

C. Statement 2 is correct but statement 1 is not correct

D. Both statement 1 and statement 2 are not correct

Q.141 Assertion (A): Business ethics is not just a code of conduct but code of ethics.

Reason (R): Code of conduct should be externalized as a normative value and can bring suitable code of ethics.

A. Both (A) and (R) are correct, and (R) is the correct explanation of (A).

B. Both (A) and (R) are correct, but (R) is not the correct explanation of (A).

C. (A) is correct, but (R) is not correct.

D. (A) is wrong, and (R) is correct.

Q.142 Read the two statements of Assertion (A) and Reasoning (R) suggest the correct code :

Assertion (A) : The equilibrium price is decided at the level where the quantity demanded equals the quantity supplied.

Reasoning (R) : At this level excess of demand and excess of supply both remain zero.

A. (A) is correct but (R) is incorrect.

B. (A) is incorrect but (R) is correct.

C. (A) and (R) both are correct but (R) is not right explanation of (A).

D. (A) and (R) both are correct and (R) is right explanation of (A).

Q.143 Read the two statements of Assertion (A) and Reasoning (R) suggest the correct code :

Assertion (A) : Low initial price regarded as the principal means for entering into mass market for some new products.

Reasoning (R) : Firms generally enter into production of new products with excess capacity of the plant initially.

Code :

A. (A) is correct but (R) is not correct.

B. (A) is not correct but (R) is correct.

C. (A) and (R) both are correct and (R) is right explanation of (A).

D. (A) and (R) both are correct but (R) is not right explanation of (A).

Q.144 Assertion (A) : Under stressful situations, a person is unable to listen to and understand the message correctly.

Reasoning (R) : During stressful situations, the psychological frame of mind changes and the message gets distorted due to the beliefs, experiences, goals and values held by the receiver of the message.

Code :

A. (A) and (R) both are correct and (R) is the correct explanation of (A).

B. (A) and (R) both are correct but (R) is not the correct explanation of (A).

C. (A) is correct whereas (R) is incorrect.

D. (R) is correct whereas (A) is incorrect.

Q.145 Assertion (A) : Risk analysis of capital investment is the most complex and controversial area in finance.

Reasoning (R) : Capital investment decisions are based on estimates of future cash inflows.

Code :

A. (A) is incorrect but (R) is correct.

B. (A) is correct but (R) is incorrect.

C. (A) and (R) both are correct and (R) is right explanation of (A).

D. (A) and (R) both are correct but (R) is not right explanation of (A).

Q.146 Assertion (A) : Invertors in capital market now have higher inclination for investment in debentures.

Reasoning (R) : Debentures have active secondary markets now.

Code :

A. Both (A) and (R) are correct ; and (R) is the right explanation of (A).

B. Both (A) and (R) are correct ; but (R) is not the right explanation of (A).

C. (A) is correct but (R) is incorrect.

D. Both (A) and (R) are incorrect.

Q.147 Assertion (A) : When an industrial unit falls sick, those who depend on it have to face an uncertain future.

Reasoning (R) : The sick units continue to operate below the break-even point and are, thus, forced to depend on external sources for funds of their long-term survival.

Code :

A. (A) and (R) both are correct ; and (R) is the right explanation of (A).

B. Both (A) and (R) are correct ; but (R) is not the right explanation of (A).

C. Both (A) and (R) are incorrect.

D. (A) is correct but (R) is incorrect.

Q.148 Data taken from the Publications Division(PD)(National Portal of India) will be considered as

A. Primary data

B. Secondary data

C. It can be called primary and secondary data both

D. It will not be primary and secondary data

Q.149 Assertion (A) : Companies should measure the profitability of their products, territories, customer groups, segments, trade channels and order sizes.

Reasoning (R) : Measure of profitability helps companies determine whether to expand, reduce, or eliminate any product or marketing activities to ensure profitability control.

Code :

A. Both (A) and (R) are correct and (R) is the right explanation of (A).

B. Both (A) and (R) are correct but (R) is not the right

explanation of (A).
C. (A) is correct but (R) is incorrect.
D. (R) is correct but (A) is incorrect.

Q.150 Which of the following constitute market lifespan stages in which the product goes through sequentially and simultaneously in the international markets?
A. The international product life cycle
B. Competitive advantage
C. Absolute advantage
D. International marketing

// Smart Answer Sheet //

Correct Percentage of students who answered correctly.   **Skipped** Percentage of students who skipped.

Q.	Ans.	Correct / Skipped	Q.	Ans.	Correct / Skipped	Q.	Ans.	Correct / Skipped	Q.	Ans.	Correct / Skipped	Q.	Ans.	Correct / Skipped
1	B	51.93 % / 30.15 %	17	D	16.08 % / 37.02 %	33	D	19.43 % / 37.19 %	49	D	11.39 % / 39.03 %	65	B	20.94 % / 40.03 %
2	A	56.45 % / 22.44 %	18	D	18.93 % / 38.69 %	34	D	17.59 % / 33.83 %	50	C	28.98 % / 38.52 %	66	C	26.97 % / 37.18 %
3	C	49.58 % / 33.84 %	19	C	15.75 % / 38.35 %	35	B	40.54 % / 36.85 %	51	C	21.78 % / 38.19 %	67	C	26.47 % / 36.68 %
4	D	24.29 % / 29.81 %	20	C	17.92 % / 28.31 %	36	D	22.61 % / 36.52 %	52	C	27.3 % / 31.66 %	68	B	37.86 % / 39.86 %
5	C	35.85 % / 34.5 %	21	B	35.85 % / 36.34 %	37	B	35.01 % / 36.01 %	53	B	11.06 % / 39.02 %	69	B	17.42 % / 40.2 %
6	A	32.33 % / 36.01 %	22	C	45.9 % / 35.84 %	38	C	44.72 % / 37.36 %	54	D	9.21 % / 37.69 %	70	B	25.29 % / 24.79 %
7	D	52.09 % / 32.16 %	23	D	49.41 % / 38.03 %	39	B	36.52 % / 36.85 %	55	C	24.79 % / 41.88 %	71	B	27.14 % / 34.67 %
8	B	15.75 % / 35.51 %	24	C	47.74 % / 29.48 %	40	D	15.08 % / 38.52 %	56	B	22.11 % / 40.7 %	72	B	21.11 % / 32.32 %
9	D	30.82 % / 34.34 %	25	D	33.67 % / 38.52 %	41	D	30.82 % / 37.69 %	57	D	25.8 % / 38.35 %	73	D	17.25 % / 41.04 %
10	C	21.61 % / 35.34 %	26	C	34.17 % / 38.53 %	42	A	24.46 % / 36.18 %	58	B	46.06 % / 39.53 %	74	B	28.48 % / 27.3 %
11	C	26.47 % / 38.19 %	27	B	30.15 % / 38.02 %	43	A	12.9 % / 38.02 %	59	A	35.68 % / 39.36 %	75	A	16.92 % / 41.87 %
12	A	40.87 % / 36.52 %	28	D	29.98 % / 34.34 %	44	B	41.37 % / 36.69 %	60	B	38.86 % / 40.37 %	76	A	17.09 % / 39.86 %
13	B	43.38 % / 37.69 %	29	A	20.6 % / 38.03 %	45	D	20.94 % / 38.52 %	61	D	31.49 % / 38.19 %	77	A	21.11 % / 40.36 %
14	D	33.17 % / 36.01 %	30	B	34.84 % / 36.85 %	46	D	22.28 % / 35.34 %	62	D	26.8 % / 37.35 %	78	A	41.37 % / 31.49 %
15	D	36.18 % / 37.69 %	31	C	21.27 % / 37.52 %	47	B	27.3 % / 38.86 %	63	B	31.32 % / 39.87 %	79	A	16.92 % / 41.37 %
16	C	30.82 % / 33.67 %	32	A	12.73 % / 37.86 %	48	A	12.23 % / 38.02 %	64	B	33.0 % / 33.33 %	80	B	19.77 % / 32.83 %

Q.	Ans.	Correct / Skipped	Q.	Ans.	Correct / Skipped	Q.	Ans.	Correct / Skipped	Q.	Ans.	Correct / Skipped	Q.	Ans.	Correct / Skipped
81	B	33.0 % / 37.52 %	95	C	27.47 % / 40.7 %	109	B	25.46 % / 40.37 %	123	A	18.09 % / 39.87 %	137	B	28.64 % / 42.72 %
82	D	24.12 % / 37.69 %	96	D	16.42 % / 34.84 %	110	A	16.08 % / 37.35 %	124	B	33.0 % / 42.38 %	138	B	16.92 % / 41.37 %
83	C	14.24 % / 37.52 %	97	C	28.98 % / 40.53 %	111	A	18.93 % / 38.86 %	125	C	16.08 % / 40.2 %	139	D	13.4 % / 42.21 %
84	D	26.97 % / 32.83 %	98	A	28.64 % / 38.19 %	112	D	13.57 % / 42.21 %	126	C	23.28 % / 43.72 %	140	B	19.1 % / 41.54 %
85	A	10.72 % / 40.37 %	99	D	21.11 % / 41.37 %	113	A	18.93 % / 40.03 %	127	C	30.15 % / 40.54 %	141	C	11.73 % / 41.7 %
86	A	20.77 % / 37.86 %	100	B	31.16 % / 42.04 %	114	B	28.81 % / 41.88 %	128	D	18.26 % / 42.04 %	142	D	24.79 % / 41.54 %
87	D	21.61 % / 37.52 %	101	C	25.96 % / 40.54 %	115	A	29.98 % / 40.87 %	129	C	22.95 % / 41.71 %	143	D	10.05 % / 42.21 %
88	C	29.98 % / 40.71 %	102	A	28.31 % / 37.18 %	116	A	14.91 % / 41.54 %	130	C	20.1 % / 34.0 %	144	A	40.2 % / 39.2 %
89	C	13.9 % / 39.03 %	103	C	22.78 % / 37.86 %	117	C	29.48 % / 40.2 %	131	D	42.88 % / 37.86 %	145	C	24.46 % / 41.2 %
90	A	20.1 % / 40.7 %	104	C	27.3 % / 41.21 %	118	B	23.12 % / 41.54 %	132	C	14.07 % / 35.85 %	146	D	5.03 % / 42.37 %
91	D	47.91 % / 40.2 %	105	B	32.33 % / 39.53 %	119	D	25.46 % / 40.54 %	133	A	15.41 % / 39.87 %	147	B	21.27 % / 41.21 %
92	D	27.47 % / 34.34 %	106	C	11.89 % / 38.19 %	120	D	17.09 % / 41.37 %	134	A	19.77 % / 42.71 %	148	B	31.49 % / 41.54 %
93	D	29.82 % / 40.2 %	107	D	23.79 % / 41.37 %	121	B	19.26 % / 41.71 %	135	C	20.94 % / 42.54 %	149	A	34.84 % / 42.38 %
94	D	22.95 % / 36.85 %	108	C	14.91 % / 41.87 %	122	C	38.36 % / 31.66 %	136	C	35.34 % / 42.38 %	150	A	28.64 % / 39.03 %

//Hints and Solutions//

1. Good leadership exhibits high morale and feelings of dedication.

A leader should possess a high level of integrity and honesty. He should be a role model to others regarding ethics and values. A good leader must possess feelings of dedication towards their goals. He should not wait for opportunities come to his way, rather he should grab the opportunity and use it to the advantage of the organization.

Hence, the correct option is (B).

2. Prior knowledge of learner is highly related to effectiveness of teaching in the following ways:

a) If students do not get correct information, or did not understand the study material in previous classes, they may have some trouble learning the recent material.

b) As, the students who understand the correct information, has a better chance of success learning the recent material. Hence, option A is correct.

3. •Lecturing – It is the process of delivering lectures in understandable languages.

•Discussion in groups -It is the action or process of talking about a theme in groups in order to reach a conclusion or to exchange ideas.

•Brainstorming - Brainstorming is a group creativity technique through which efforts are made to find a conclusion for a particular problem by colecting a list of relevant ideas contributed by its members.

•Programmed instruction - Programmed instruction is a method of presenting new subject matters to students in a graded sequence of controlled steps

4. Formative evaluation helps students in the following ways:

•It provides constant feedback to both teacher and student concerning learning successes and failure while instruction is in process.

•It often happens during the course of instruction. Teacher clarifies the doubts of students in the class itself.

•Feedback to candidates reinforces successful learning and locates the particular learning errors that need correction.

•The teacher raises learner's motivation through a question-answer session. Hence, option D is correct.

5. Teaching ensures positive transformation in students because with the help of teaching a student acquires good habits, knowledge and attitudes.Hence option C is correct.

6. Fundamental Research is concerned with the generalizations and with the formulation of theory building.

Applied Research is a socially useful application of knowledge generated to social concern. It is a form of systematic inquiry involving practical application.

Action Research is used by teachers, supervisors etc. to improve the quality of decision and actions. It lays stress on developing the present situations to make these better.

Evaluative Research determines the impact of social intervention. It analyses the effect of a particular program on a certain problem the program is trying to solve. So, option A is correct.

7. Action research strategy is a strategy to solve an immediate problem through various steps.

The cyclical process of research has the following sequence:

Plan Ã Act Ã Observe Ã Reflect

(To remember, Use the acronym PAOR) . Hence option D is correct.

8. The correct sequence of scientific research is as follows:

a) Perceiving the problem situation – First we represent, what is the problem or what problem we want to study.

b) Locating the actual problem and its definition – Define the problem with locating its causes.

c) Hypothesizing – Formulate the hypothesis. Hypothesis is a proposed explanation on the basis of some limited evidence.

d) Deducing the consequences of the suggested solution.

e) Testing the hypothesis in action. Hence option B is correct.

9. Options A, B and C represents mainly the guidelines for research, but evidence-based research reporting is a part of research ethics in which consent should be taken from the participants, and proper evidence & sources should be mentioned in research. If it's not followed, then there can be a problem which is against ethics. Hence option D is correct.

10. The research conference is a meeting for researchers to present and discuss their creative ideas and work at a large level. The conference inculcates creativity and critical thinking among the participants more than the seminars, workshop, research summary. Hence option C is correct.

11. As mentioned in the passage, "We believe that technological strengths are especially crucial in dealing with this fourth dimension underlying continuous change in the aspirations of the people, the economy in the global context, and the strategic interests." Thus, the highlighted elements are indicative of the fourth dimension. Option 2 is incorrect as the passage states that the fourth dimension is an offshoot or an extension of "modern day dynamism" and not one of its indicators. Thus, option C is the correct answer.

12. According to the passage, "Technological strengths are the key to creating more productive employment in an increasingly competitive market place and to continually upgrade human skills." Thus, option A is the correct answer.

13. According to the passage, "The absence of greater technological impetus could lead to lower productivity and wastage of precious natural resources." which will hurt the poorest most. Hence, option B is the correct answer.

14. According to the passage, "For people-oriented actions as well, whether for the creation of large-scale productive

employment or for ensuring nutritional and health security for people, or for better living conditions, technology is the only vital input." From this sentence, it can be inferred that the advantage of technological inputs will enhance the living standard of the people, hence lifting people to a life of dignity. Thus, option D is the correct answer.

15. According to the last few lines of the passage, "Even while being alive to the short-term realities, medium and long-term strategies to develop core technological strengths within our industry are vital for envisioning a developed India." Thus, option D is the correct answer. The other options are irrelevant in the context of the passage.

16. Differentiation between acceptance and non-acceptance of certain stimuli in classroom communication is the basis of selective attention. Selective attention is the process of focusing on a specific object in the environment for some period of time. Hence option C is correct.

17. The fundamental aspect to teacher and student's success is the teacher's ability to communicate with students, parents and colleagues. Teachers must have quality communication skills to assist their students achieve success in their academic studies. More control over the communication process means more control over what the students are learning. Hence option D is correct.

18. Effective teaching demands knowledge of the communication in the following ways:

•Effective communication can be maintained using different audio video techniques in classroom.

•Effective communication demands careful use of nonverbal cues in the classroom.

•Using an honest and tactful tone, will also add to the effective communication in the classroom. Hence option D is correct.

19. Classroom communication is a transactional process. This model requires continuous change and transformation in which every component is variable such as the people, their environment and the medium. Due to this model, it presumes the communicators to be independent and act the way they wish to. Since both the sender and receiver are essential to keep the communication going in transactional model, the communicators are also interdependent to each other. Hence option C is correct.

20. Human communication is the process of creating a meaning between two or more people. Following are the statement that describes human communication process:

•Non-verbal communication can stimulate ideas.

•Communication is a learnt ability.

•Communication is not a universal panacea.

•Communication cannot break-down or stop working. Hence option C is correct.

21.
$$\rightarrow -1 + 6 = 5 \text{ (We have to add } '6' \text{ to get } '5' \text{ from } '-1')$$
$$\rightarrow 5 + 10 = 15 (6 + 4 = 10) \text{ (We have to add } '10' \text{ to get } '15' \text{ from } '5')$$
$$\rightarrow 15 + 14 = 29(10 + 4 = 14)$$
$$\left(\text{ We have to add } '14' \text{ to get } '29' \text{ from } '15'\right)$$
$$\rightarrow 29 + 18 = 47(14 + 4 = 18)$$

Hence, next term in the series is '47".

22. The pattern followed here is:

$\Rightarrow$ A + 1 = B; B + 2 = D

$\Rightarrow$ D + 3 = G; G + 4 = K

$\Rightarrow$ H + 5 = M; M + 6 = S

$\Rightarrow$ M + 7 = T; T + 8 = B

$\Rightarrow$ S + 9 = B; B + 10 = L

Similarly,

$\Rightarrow$ Z + 11 = K; K + 12 = W

Hence, next term in the series is "ZKW". Hence option C is correct.

23. If VARANASI is coded as WCUESGZQ,

V + 1 = W

A + 2 = C

R + 3 = U

A + 4 = E

N + 5 = S

A + 6 = G

S + 7 = Z

I + 8 = Q

Similarly,

K + 1 = L

O + 2 = Q

L + 3 = O

K + 4 = O

A + 5 = F

T + 6 = Z

A + 7 = H

Hence, KOLKATA is coded as "LQOOFZH". Hence option D is correct.

24.

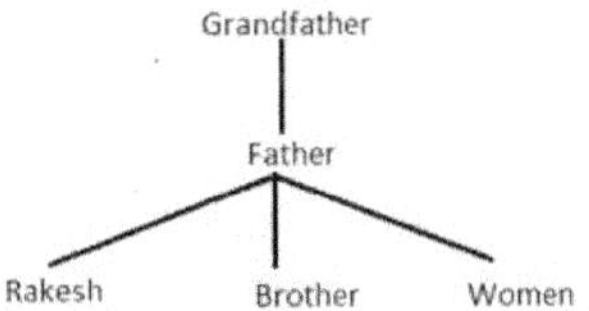

As shown in above diagram, Women is sister of Rakesh.

The woman is related to Rakesh as a sister. So option C is right.

25. $\dfrac{A}{B} = \dfrac{2}{5}$

$5A = 2B \rightarrow 1$

$\dfrac{A+16}{B+16} = \dfrac{1}{2}$

$2A + 32 = B + 16 \rightarrow 2$

From 1 $A = 2B/5$

Now, Put value of A in 2,

$2(2B/5) + 32 = B + 16 - \cdots - \cdots 3$

$4B/5 + 32 = B + 16 - \cdots - 4$

Solve 4, to get $B = 80$ And, $A = 2B/5 = 2*80/5 = 32$

Hence, value of A and B is 32 and 80..

26. It is the analogical reasoning. Analogy here is:

Intellect superiority: Concentration Power :: Concave Mirror: Rays Concentration at one point. Hence option C is correct.

27. Options 2 and 3 seem to be more valid than the other two options 1 and 4. We can draw conclusions 2 and 3 from the premises up to some extent.

Statement a) Most of the dancers are physically fit.

Statement b) Most of the singers are dancers.

It can be concluded that most of the dancers are singers. (From statement 2).

Now if we consider Statement (a) then we can draw that most of the physically fit are dancers. So, conclusions 2 and 3 follows. Hence option C is correct.

28. Inductive Reasoning refers to generalizing about properties for the class of objects based on number of observations.

It presupposes that a sequence of events in future will occur as it always has in the past. This phenomenon is known as uniformity of nature. Hence option D is correct.

29. The proposition 'domestic animals are hardly ferocious' implies Domestic animals are not ferocious. It is false, then statement having No will also be false. This eliminates the option 3 & 4 straight away. The opposite of this statement would be domestic animals are ferocious. Only option 1 & 2 can be claimed to be certainly true. Hence option A is correct.

30. Consumption = Production - Export

$2012,$ consumption $= 186.5 - 114$ million $kg = 72.5 million kg$

$2013,$ consumption $= 202 - 114$ million $kg = 88$ million kg

$2014,$ consumption $= 238 - 130$ million $kg = 108$ million kg

$2015,$ consumption $= 221 - 116$ million $kg = 105$ million kg

$2016,$ consumption $= 215 - 88$ million $kg = 127$ million kg

Now, find out the percentage increase,

% increase in 2013 = (previous year value - recent year value)

$= \dfrac{88-72.5}{72.5} * 100\% = 21.38\%$

% increase in $2014 =$ (previous year value - recent year value)

$= \dfrac{108-88}{88} * 100\% = 22.72\%$

% increase in $2015 =$ (previous year value - recent year value)

$= \dfrac{105-108}{105} * 100\% = $ Decrease $(So,$ discard $)$

% increase in $2016 =$ (previous year value - recent year value)

$= \dfrac{127-105}{105} * 100\% = 20.95\%$

Thus, percentage increase was highest in 2014 .

31. Per capita consumption $= \dfrac{\text{Consumption}}{\text{Population}}$

$$\text{Population} = \dfrac{\text{Consumption}}{\text{Per capita consumption}}$$

$$\text{Population} = \dfrac{108}{38.7} = 2.79 million$$

So , option C is right.

32. Consumption = Production - Export

$2012,$ consumption $= 186.5 \cdot 114$ million $kg = 72.5$ million kg

$2013,$ consumption $= 202 \cdot 114$ million $kg = 88$ million kg

$2014,$ consumption $= 238 \cdot 130$ million $kg = 108$ million kg

$2015,$ consumption $= 221 - 116$ million $kg = 105$ million kg

$\dfrac{2012, \text{Exports}}{\text{Consumption}} = \dfrac{114}{72.5} = 1.57$

$\dfrac{2013 \text{ Exports}}{\text{Consumption}} = \dfrac{114}{88} = 1.3$

$2014 \dfrac{\text{Exports}}{\text{Consumption}} = \dfrac{130}{108} = 1.2$

$\dfrac{2015 \text{ Exports}}{\text{Consumption}} = \dfrac{116}{105} = 1.1$

Thus for 2012 ratio is maximum. So, option A is right.

33. Consumption = Production - Export

2013, consumption $= 202 \cdot 114$ million kg $= 88$ million kg

2014, consumption $= 238 - 130$ million kg $= 108$ million kg

2015, consumption = 221 - 116 million kg = 105 million kg

$2016,$ consumption $= 215 - 88$ million kg $= 127$ million kg

$\text{Population} = \dfrac{\text{Consumption}}{\text{Per Capita consumptior}}$

$2013,$ Population $= \dfrac{88}{35.2} = 2.5$ million

$2014,$ Population $= \dfrac{108}{38.7} = 2.79 million$

$2015,$ Population $= \dfrac{105}{40.5} = 2.59 million$

2016, Population $= \dfrac{127}{42} = 3$ million

Thus, Population in 2016 is max. Option D is correct.

34. Consumption = Production - Export

Consumption in the following years are as following:

2012: 72.5 million Kg

2013: 88 million kg

2014: 108 million Kg

2015: 105 million Kg

2016: 127 million Kg

Average = (72.5 + 88 + 108 + 105 + 127) 500.5 / 5 = 100.1 million kg

35. ICT stands for Information and Communications Technology.

The converging technologies that exemplify Information and Communications Technology include the merging of audio-visual, telephone and computer networks through a common cabling system. Hence option B is correct.

36. A new Laptop has been produced that weight less, is smaller and uses less power than previous Laptop models that might be using solid state hard drive. This device store data on the flash memory. Hence option D is correct.

37. As bcc stands for blind carbon copy and cc stands for carbon copy. So, we will receive all the sender's details and the persons attached in cc (carbon copy). The email ids of bcc are not visible to everyone. So, option B is correct.

38. Smallest to Largest unit of storage:

Bit – Smallest unit of storage

Byte – 8 bits

Kilobyte – 1000 bytes

Megabyte – 1000000 bytes

Gigabyte – 10^9 bytes

Terabyte - 10^{12} bytes

So, the correct order is 6,2,1,3,5,4. Hence option C is correct.

39. Read Only Memory (ROM) is a non-volatile memory.

Random Access Memory (RAM) is 'volatile' memory.

Secondary Memory is 'non-volatile' memory. Hence option B is correct.

40. Fly ash can be used in:

•Construction of the Roman structure.

•Manufacturing of building bricks.

•Manufacture of cement.

•Used as fertilizers.

•In a dam and water holding structures.

•As a replacement of white cement.

•Used in road construction. Hence option D is correct.

41. Among the Earthquakes, Landslides, Hurricanes and Droughts, only Droughts has no definite beginning and end. No one can define when it began and when it ended. Rest all the other disasters might not have a specific beginning but have a definite end. Hence option D is correct.

42. Indoor Air pollution causes serious health problems such as respiratory problems and even cancer. There, it is a serious hazard. The dispersal of air pollutants is limited because it does not get space in the indoor environment. Hence option A is correct.

43. The contribution of energy sources (as per official sources):

Energy source	MW	\%of total
Thermal Power Plants	2,21,803	64.3%
Renewable Energy	70,649	20.5%
Hydropower	45,457	13.2%
Nudear Energy	6780	2.0%

So, Thermal Power Plant $>$ Renewable Energy $>$ Hydropower $>$ Nuclear Energy.

So, option A is correct.

44. The major concern of pollution in rivers of India is water pollution. Untreated sewage is the largest source of water pollution in India. Other different sources of pollution include agricultural runoff and unregulated small-scale industry. Hence option B is correct.

45. The higher education system of India is the third-largest in the world after China and the United States of America. So, option D is correct.

46. Prime Minister Research Fellowship has been promoting research and cutting-edge technologies. This scheme has been designed particularly for those who are willing to pursue Ph.D. course in Indian Institute of Technology (IIT) and Indian Institute of Science (IISc). Hence option D is correct.

47. •The Committee for appointment of Chief Information Commissioner is headed by the Prime Minister; comprises of leader of the Opposition, a Cabinet Minister (nominated by the Prime Minister).

•The Central Vigilance Commissioner shall be appointed by the President on recommendation of a Committee consisting of the Prime Minister, the Minister of Home Affairs and the Leader of the Opposition.

•The Chairperson of NHRC is appointed by the President of India, on the recommendation of a committee consisting of Prime Minister, Home Minister, Leader of Opposition, Speaker of Lok Sabha and other members.

•The Chairperson of National Commission for Women is appointed by the Central Govt. on the recommendation of committee. The committee is headed Minister-in Charge of the Ministry of Women and Child Development along with other members. Hence option B is correct.

48. Gender Budgeting is a powerful and innovative tool for achieving gender mainstreaming to safeguard that the benefits of development should reach women. It is not a separate budget for women. The reason behind this is budget is women lags behind man, so they warrant special attention. It is not and accounting exercise. Hence option A is correct.

49. Following are the main barriers to Citizen Centric Administration:

•Attitudinal Problems of the Civil Servants

•Lack of Accountability

•Redtapism

•Low levels of Awareness of the Rights and Duties of Citizens

•Ineffective Implementation of Laws and Rules

Hence option D is correct.

50. In categorical syllogism using Venn Diagram, an argument consists of three categorical propositions in which there are two premises and one is conclusion, in which there appear a total of exactly three terms, each of which is used exactly twice.

E.g. All trees are white

All white is black

Some black is dull

So, there are three terms used twice in this type of syllogism. Hence option C is correct.

51. Optimum promotion mix is the combination of various promotion mix tools employed by the company for the advancement of the product in the market, raising market shares etc. There is an optimal way of allocating budgets for different elements within the promotional mix to achieve best marketing results. Marketers have to find right mix of all promotional tools. This way each promotional tool of media is mixed such that it gives optimal results and every time marginal equivalence is more.

So, option C is correct.

52. Premium Pricing involves setting a price higher than the competitor in the hope that customers will perceive it as a product of higher quality. Branded unleaded petrol, luxury brands are all examples of Premium pricing.

Thus, Option C is correct.

53. Factor affecting span of control are:

• Nature of work - repetition of work leads to a wider span of control.

• Type of personnel - the better managers and personnel leads to a wider span of control

• Location of personnel - more widely spread personnel narrow the span of control.

Thus, Option B is correct.

54. • The Smoot-Hawley Act raised the US tariffs on hundreds of products at the start of the 1930s.

• Uruguay Round of negotiations (1986-1994) led to the formation of the WTO.

Thus, Option D is correct.

55. Under the Introduction stage of Product Life Cycle, a company tries to build awareness about the newly introduced product in the minds of customers, thereby attracting them to buy the same. Promotion under this stage is aimed at innovators and early adopters.

Thus, Option C is correct.

56. • Employee engagement reveals the relationship between employees and the organization.

• William Kahn was the first person who defined personnel engagement.

Thus, Option B is correct.

57. When production is equal to the demand, it means that a stage where neither some of the goods remain unsold nor there should be any shortage of goods.

Therefore, when aggregate demand is equal to aggregate supply or investment is equal to savings than we have the national income equilibrium. And when aggregate demand is equal to aggregate supply than there is an absence of inflationary and deflationary gap. But it is not necessary for National income equilibrium that aggregate consumption should be constant. So, option D is correct.

58. • Demand based pricing is a pricing method wherein the price of the product is determined on the basis of its demand.

• Cost based pricing is a method wherein a fixed percentage of the total cost of production is added to the cost of product to set its price.

• Competition based pricing is a method wherein a company sets the price of its product after comparing the price of its competitor's product.

Thus, Option B is correct.

59. • Commercial banks should formulate a rigorous monitoring system to prevent sickness in small scale industries.

• This would minimize the uncertainty in the recovery of money lent.

• The banks can proceed with the rehabilitation programs in the initial stages.

Thus, Option A is correct.

60. The following factors are considered as External factors, Opportunities in SWOT analysis:

• Changing customer tastes

• Liberalization of Geographic markets

• Technological advances

• Changes in government policies

• Lower personal taxes

● Change in population age structure

● New distribution channels

Thus, Option B is correct.

61. Determinants of working capital include: Inventory, cash, receivables, Price level changes, operating efficiency, nature of the business, market and demand conditions etc.

Thus, Option D is correct.

62. • Dr William Ouchi - Z Theory

• Douglas McGregor- X Theory

• Frederick Herzberg- Hygiene Theory

• A.H. Maslow- Need Hierarchy Theory

Thus, Option D is correct.

63. Customer Touchpoint refers to any direct or indirect interaction customers have with a brand, product, service etc.

Thus, Option B is correct.

64. • Autonomous demand- It is also called direct demand; it arises on its own out of a natural desire to purchase. It is independent of demand for any other commodity like demand for food, cloth, home etc.

• Long-run demand refers to demand which exists for a long period of time. Most generic food like FMCG and other consumer durables have long-run demand.

Thus, Option B is correct.

65. • Conciliation is one of the alternative dispute resolution methods in which both the conflict parties meet the conciliator separately and resolve the issue. It has no legal stand.

• Arbitration is a way to resolve disputes outside the courts. An arbitration award is provided, which is legally binding on both sides and enforceable in the courts.

Thus, Option B is correct.

66. The particular task performance is called activity.

An event represents a point in time acting as a milestone for the completion of any activities and starting of a new one.

Thus, Option C is correct.

67. • Primary objectives of operations management include the following:

1) Cost reduction

2) Quality improvement

3) Time schedule

• Secondary objectives of operations management include the following:

1) Machine and equipment

2) Material management

3) Services and facilities

Thus, Option C is correct.

68.

● Hard skills are related professional knowledge, tools or techniques that allow us to work within our professions whereas

● Soft skills are the collection of our social, communication and self-management behavior. It is the ability to understand, communicate with, motivate and support other people, both individually and group.

● Conceptual skills are the skills that allow people to visualize the entire thing and work with ideas and the relationships between abstract concepts. It is not related to the question and therefore it is not correct answer.

● Political skills are about using politics at workplace and to motivate or support other people. Therefore it is also incorrect answer.

69. • If brand awareness is in the building stage, the brand extension requires many efforts

• Equal marketing efforts are required for the brand extension also.

• When the organizations try to build a brand extension without any value addition to the customer, they will definitely fail.

• Both the statements are true but the reason does not explain the brand awareness aspect.

Thus, Option B is correct.

70. Time-saving is not a function but an advantage of the distribution channel. Distribution channels help in reducing the time of delivery with the help of channel members.

Thus, Option B is correct.

71. • The Kinky hypothesis assumes that when a firm raises prices, all customers would not shift as few of them are intimately attached to the product because of product differentiation, so prices and output once determined, tend to remain the same even if there is a considerable change in cost.

• The demand curve of oligopoly firms is not perfectly elastic. There is a difference in elasticity between the upper half and lower half of the kink due to a particular competitive reaction pattern assumed by the kinky hypothesis. Thus, both the statements are true but R is not a perfect reason for A.

Thus, Option B is correct.

72. David Hume criticised the theory of Mercantilism by stating that increased exports lead to inflation and higher prices.

Thus, Option B is correct.

73. • The post-purchase decision is the last step in the consumer buying process. Customers at this stage evaluate their decision and decide whether they are satisfied with the decision made by them or not.

• Cognitive dissonance occurs at this stage where customers experience feelings of post-purchase tension or anxiety as to whether they have made the right choice or not.

Thus, Option D is correct.

74. Career planning encourages individuals to explore and gather information, which enables them to gain competencies, make decisions, set goals and take action. It is an ongoing process which helps individuals develop skills required to fulfill different career roles.

Thus, Option B is correct.

75. Evaluative statements or judgments concerning objects, people or event is called Attitudes. There are three components of attitudes.

1. Cognitive Component
2. Affective component
3. Behavioural Component

Cognitive component talks about the opinion or belief segment of an attitude. Affective Component is the emotional or feeling segment of an attitude whereas behavioural component describes an intention to behave in a certain way towards someone or something. So, option A is correct.

76. • In the forming phase, all the team members introduce each other.

• In the storming phase, the difference of opinions arise.

• In the norming stage, the differences begin to settle down.

• In the performing stage, all the team members work collectively.

Thus, Option A is correct.

77. The factors affecting the goal-setting theory of motivation are -

• Goal Commitment - how much employees are committed to attaining goals.

• Task characteristics - what task is to be done is attainable or not.

• Culture bound - from which culture employees belong.

• Self-efficacy - when the individual believes that he/she is capable of doing a task.

Thus, Option A is correct.

78. • Because of selective perception, the individuals develop a fear of the unknown and they resist change.

• Selective perception starts when people perceive a change differently. They get disturbed because of new habits and new patterns of work.

• This happens when people prefer regular routine actions.

Thus, Option A is correct.

79. Limiting property of t distribution: The t-distribution has a greater dispersion(skewness) than the standard normal distribution. And as the sample size increases, it assumes the normal distribution. The sample size is said to be large when n ≥ 30.

Thus, Option A is correct.

80. • Demand is the consumer's desire and ability to purchase a good or service. It's the direct force that drives economic growth and expansion.

• Even the people demand a good, if they don't have the suitable purchasing power, they will not buy goods, and that is not considered as a demand.

Thus, Option B is correct.

81. An informal group can be defined as one in which three or more people decide, perhaps on an ad hoc basis, to meet on a regular or semi-regular schedule for the purpose of discussing subjects of common interest, or for the purpose of engaging in a particular activity of common interest. Hence, option B is correct.

82. The market risk premium for the firm:

• The market risk premium is an additional return the investor can expect to receive from holding on to a risky market portfolio instead of a risk-free asset.

• In other words, it is the difference between the expected return on a market portfolio and a risk-free rate.

• It is not a part of an internal factor that would affect the WACC of the firm.

Therefore, the Market risk premium for the firm is not the internal factor affecting the weighted average cost of capital of a firm.

Hence, the correct option is (D).

83. While calculating national income by income method, transfer payments are not included such as pension, unemployment allowance, subsidies, scholarships are not included.

Thus, Option C is correct.

84. EXIM policy deals in provisions related to duty exemption schemes, SEZ programs, import provisions and export promotion and schemes and measures.

Thus, Option D is correct.

85. The value of mode is determined by grouping in the following situation:

• If the maximum frequency is repeated

• If the maximum frequency occurs in the very beginning or at the end of the distribution

• If there are irregularities in the distribution(if the distribution is not clear)

Thus, Option A is correct.

86. • Breakthrough Innovation is defined as making changes to an existing product, service or process. It is rare and a difficult innovation as it requires the introduction of completely new technology or a new business model.

• Breakthrough Innovation involves high risk because it requires greater investment in terms of capital, time and resources.

Thus, Option A is correct.

87. • Executive summary in the business plan includes the company's mission statement, information about the team and key employees, location of the business.

• Company description includes its target market, competitive advantage, product awards or recognition.

Thus, Option D is correct.

88.

- Job is a group of position involving the same duties, skills, knowledge and responsibilities.
- The nature, conditions of work, skill, knowledge and some basic qualifications through the job analyst has selected a person for doing work in his organisation is called job.
- In job duties and responsibilities are given selected person in organisation.
- Hence, option C is correct.

89. Liao (2003) classifies KM technologies using seven categories

• KM Framework

• Knowledge-Based Systems (KBS)

• Data Mining

• Information and Communication Technology

• Artificial Intelligence (AI)/Expert Systems (ES)

• Database Technology (DT)

• Modeling

Thus, Option C is correct.

90. • Equal employment opportunity refers to the provision of equal opportunities in employment.

• President Lyndon Johnson popularised the concept of equal employment opportunity by signing an executive order on it.

Thus, Option A is correct.

91. The job description is a detailed description of the job. The main elements are job title, job code, job activities, job duties, job summary, and department, etc. Hence, option D is correct.

92. • A situation in which an individual is provided with many alternatives in which more than one option appears to be correct results in an ethical dilemma.

• While Business issues are straightforward , Ethical issues are an identifiable problem, situation or opportunity.

• It involves conflict between moral imperatives.

Thus, Option D is correct.

93. Regression analysis method is used for capital management.

Thus, Option D is correct.

94. Ogive curve: Statisticians use plots to illustrate data in pictorial form to make it easier to understand. ... An ogive graph is a plot used in statistics to show cumulative frequencies. It allows us to quickly estimate the number of observations that are less than or equal to a particular value.

Thus, Option D is correct.

95. • The bumper strike is meant to affect a major part of a particular industry.

• In the lightning strike, the workers go on a strike without any notice or sometimes after giving short notice. It is also known as a wild cat strike.

Thus, Option C is correct.

96. In international HRM, Training and development depends on all the factors except external factors such as cultural and institutional factors.

Thus, Option D is correct.

97.

- Test means to check that individuality level of ability, knowledge, Personality, interest, and aptitude for the job.
- Aptitude test: A test designed to determine a person's ability in a particular skill or field of knowledge
- Achievement test: An achievement test is a test of developed skill or knowledge. The most common type of achievement test is a standardized test developed to measure skills and knowledge learned in a given grade level, usually through planned instruction, such as training or classroom instruction.
- Personality test: A personality test is a questionnaire or other standardized instrument designed to reveal aspects of an individual's character or psychological makeup.
- Therefore, for the recruitment and selection different test were conducted in organisation. So, option C is correct.

98. The Blocks are of fixed size (128 MB in Hadoop 2), so it is very easy to calculate the number of blocks that can be stored on a disk. The main reason for having the HDFS blocks in large size, i.e., 128mb is to reduce the cost of seek time.

Thus, Option A is correct.

99. The following are the right sequence of decisions in manufacturing enterprises:

1. Making of forecasts: Forecasting refers to the practice of predicting what will happen in the future by taking into consideration events in the past and present.

2. Consideration of alternative combination of forecasts: It simply means 'available as another choice'.

3. Determination of key factors: A key factor is defined as the factor in activities of an undertaking which, at a particular point of time or over a period, will limit the volume of output.

4. Combination of factors: The optimum factors combination or the least cost combination refers to the combination of factors

with which a firm can produce a specific quantity of output at the lowest possible cost.

5. Preparation of budgets: A production budget is the amount of product that will have to be manufactured or produced. In order to estimate this, you have to begin first with a sales budget, a per debt projection of how many units you'll probably sell given the budget period.

Hence, the correct option is (D).

100. Managers commonly use two frameworks to guide the analysis of the firm's strengths and weaknesses. They are as follows:

1. CSF (Critical Success Factors)

2. The value chain analysis

Thus, Option B is correct.

101. Free-standing insert is a consumer sales promotion technique wherein a piece of paper (leaflet, brochure, etc.) is added separately to a local newspaper for delivery.

Thus, Option C is correct.

102. ● In behavior modeling, an individual tries to follow the behavior which has favorable outcomes.

● In learning behavior consequences, the cognitive process plays an important role in learning new behavior. The individuals actively analyze all the surrounding situations.

● In self-reinforcement, a person tries to learn the behaviors which have a positive impact on him.

Thus, Option A is correct.

103.

- A debt security without any explicit interest rate is called Zero-coupon bonds

- Income bond is a type of debt security in which issuer is required to pay interest only when they earned interest otherwise they just have to pay face value of the bond. Thus, company experiences less financial distress in case of issuing income bonds.

- A type of bond in which coupon rate quoted as mark-up on the given rate is called Floating rate bonds. Hence, option C is correct.

104. Likert stated six dimensions of organizational climate. They are as follows:

● Leadership

● Motivation

● Communication

● Decisions

● Goals

● Control

Thus, Option C is correct.

105. ● Exchange Concept is the traditional Concept of marketing where the central idea of marketing involves the exchange of products between the seller and the buyer

Thus, Option B is correct.

106. ● Meat is luxurious when compared to rice, so when the price of rice is increasing, the consumption of meat decreases.

● But, if the price of rice increases continuously, the demand increases and eventually it falls as it becomes more costly where people cannot afford it.

Thus, Option C is correct.

107. Opportunity cost of any commodity is the amount of other good which has been given up in order to produce that commodity. It is referred to as the marginal opportunity cost of a particular good.

Thus, Option D is correct.

108. Arthur H Cole classifies entrepreneurs as:

1) Empirical Entrepreneurs: These entrepreneurs do not introduce or discover anything new but follow the rules of thumb.

2) Rational Entrepreneurs: These entrepreneurs are well informed about the market trends and introduce changes accordingly.

3) Cognitive Entrepreneurs: These entrepreneurs take the advice and services of experts and introduce changes.

Thus, Option C is correct.

109. Transparency, Fairness, Accountability and Responsibility are the foremost principles of Corporate Governance.

Thus, Option B is correct.

110. ● Ancillarisation refers to the process of making a small scale industry as a supporting unit for the large scale industries. The small scale industries will produce one of the intermediate products and contribute to the manufacturing process.

● This will prevent the small scale industries from closing down.

● The small sector policy which was introduced in the year 1991, permitted large undertakings to hold twenty-four percent equity in small undertakings.

● This was done to promote ancillarisation, sub-contracting and to bring modern technology to small units.

● All these measures were taken to improve the employment opportunities in the small scale industries.

Thus, Option A is correct.

111. Accountable marketing expects to see a purpose, result and return on every piece of marketing communication. It aligns marketing with a cost and makes marketing efforts accountable for leads and sales in the same way a sales person is accountable.

Accountable marketing works on the concept that all the targeted marketing communications should be accounted for in terms of the result or output they generate. In other words every act of communication should concentrate on a unique selling or a benefit driven point related to the product which ultimately

results in motivating the customer and adding on to the brand image of a brand or the product on a whole. So, option A is correct.

112. • There are four types of Grapevine namely Single strand chain, Gossip chain, Probability chain and Cluster chain.

• Single Strand Chain involves the flow of information through a line of persons to the last person concerned. For instance- Person A tells B, who tells C, who tells D, and so on, till the information has reached most of the persons involved or concerned.

• Gossip Chain occurs when one person seeks and tells the information to everyone.

• Probability Chain also is known as the random process is a process when someone tells the information to others in accordance with the laws of probability.

• Cluster Chain occurs when a person tells the information to the selected persons who are likely to pass the information to other selected persons.

Thus, Option D is correct.

113. According to the law of marginal utility, money can be put to various uses for satisfying different wants and needs, so its marginal utility can never reach zero or negative. So, money is considered as an exception in this law.

Thus, Option A is correct.

114. GRIPE BOXES: These are the boxes in which the employees can drop their anonymous complaints. OPINION SURVEY: The management can be proactive by conducting group meetings, periodical interviews with employees, collective bargaining sessions etc through which one can get information about employees dissatisfaction. Hence, option B is correct.

115. Delegatee must have a clear idea about his tasks and how they will fit in the overall plan. As any ambiguity can lead to poor results. Also, the manager must know the people working under and above him.

Thus, Option A is correct.

116. Product Strategy under growth stage is to improve the features of products and introduce additional features. Product awareness is done in the Introduction stage and not in the Growth stage.

Thus, Option A is correct.

117. • The vertical axis represents the market growth rate and provides a measure of market attractiveness.

• The horizontal axis represents relative market share and serves as a measure of company strength in the market.

Thus, Option C is correct.

118. The six aspects of Brand Identity Prism are as follows:

• Physical Facet

• Brand Personality

• Brand Culture

• Brand Relationships

• Customer Reflection

• Customer Self Image

Thus, Option B is correct.

119. • The process layout is also known as the functional layout.

• Grinding, milling or finishing operations are carried out.

120. According to the Government of India, "any industry located in a rural area, village or town with a population of 20000 and below and an investment of Rs. 3 crore in plant and machinery is classified as a village industry."

Thus, Option D is correct.

121. Attribution is the process of inferring the causes of events or behaviors. The attributions you make each and every day has an important influence on your feelings as well as how you think and relate to other people. Option B is correct,.

122. • Quality circle is a small team of employees who determines, analyzes and resolves work-related problems and aim to achieve a common goal.

Thus, Option C is correct.

123.

- **Preventing hostile takeover- Green mail:** Green mail is the money paid to stop the aggressive behavior of the in mergers or acquisition. It is the premium paid to take its own stocks back.

- **Leveraged buyout- Management Buy Out:** Management buyout is the part of leverage Buyout as LBO is the external company take over or purchasing equity of company to control it whereas MBO is the internal management controlling.

- **Accounting for merger-Pooling of interest.** Pooling of interest is a method of accounting in which the balance sheet of both the companies is being added together during merger.

- **Financing for merger- Cash offer:** Value of the firm to be acquired has been determined then the most straight forward method of making the payment could be by way of offer for cash payment. So, option A is correct.

124. Identification of business opportunities involves four major steps:

1) The first step is to generate ideas about business

2) Scanning the environment: It involves gathering information about the external and internal environment to be used for business.

3) Screening of business opportunities: The next step is to screen or evaluate the markets that offer the greatest opportunities.

4) Selecting a business opportunity and preparing a business plan: After the screening, the last step is to select the best opportunity and prepare a business plan as to how to go with it (selected opportunity) ahead.

Thus, Option B is correct.

125. Distributed Cache is a feature provided by the MapReduce framework. When a person wants to share some files across all nodes in a Hadoop Cluster, Distributed Cache is used.

Thus, Option C is correct.

126. The behavioral theory of the firm first appeared in the 1963 book A Behavioral Theory of the Firm by Richard M. Cyert and James G. March. The work on the behavioral theory started in 1952 when March, a political scientist, joined Carnegie Mellon University, where Cyert was an economist. So, option C is correct.

127. ● Liaison role- In this role the manager communicates with external and internal contacts, to make the network effective on behalf of the organization.

● Disseminator role- In this role manager passes some of his privileged information directly to his subordinates who would otherwise have no access to it.

● Entrepreneurial role- In this role manager constantly looks for new ideas and seeks to improve his unit by adapting it to changing conditions in the environment. He is also involved in problem-solving.

Thus, Option C is correct.

128. Profit-sharing is an agreement freely entered into by which the employees receive share fixed in advance from the organization's profits.

An experiment in profit shares on a wide scale would, therefore, be definitely undertaking a voyage of an unchartered sea.

Profit distribution under a profit-sharing plan are used to fund employee retirement plans.

All Statements are true. So, option D is correct.

129. Poaching is a practice where companies approach a competent and experienced employee of their rival company and offer him a lucrative pay-package in order to fill their vacancies. It is often seen as an unethical practice.

Thus, Option C is correct.

130. Due to liberalisation of trade, there is a threat to the domestic market, and even it also affects the balance of payments negatively. So to promote the exports of a country, the government took some measures.

• Option C was announced on January 2004

• Option D was announced on September 2004

• Option B was announced on 2008 April

• Option A is in 2007.

Thus, Option C is correct.

131. (A) Check reviews done by the supervisors.

(B) Review his performance in relation to the objectives and other behaviours.

(C) Promote employees for self-appraisal. So, option D is correct.

132. According to E.M Rogers, there are five characteristics of Innovation that help to describe the rate at which innovations are adopted: Compatibility, Complexity, Observability, Relative Advantage, Trialability.

Thus, Option C is correct.

133. ● The mill workers of Mumbai called for the Great Bombay textile strike in the year 1982.

● It was headed by Dutta Samant.

● The purpose of that strike was to obtain a bonus and increase in wages.

Thus, Option A is correct.

134.

● Marginal approach of probability is the probability of occurring single event. Conditional approach of probability is the probability of occurring one event given that another event has occurred.

● Point probability is the probability of occurring two events together or in succession. Posterior probability is the probability revised in the light of additional information.

● Hence, option A is correct.

135. ● The Republic of Nauru was the last country to join the IMF as the 189th member in 2016.

● The resources for IMF loans are provided by member countries mostly through their quotas payments.

Thus, Option C is correct.

136. • Job specifications are the characteristics or skills required in the candidate to effectively comply with the respective tasks in a job.

• Job description, on the other hand, is the key information about the job.

137. ● There are two forms of communication-Verbal and non-verbal communication.

● Emailing is an example of verbal communication.

● Various forms of Non-verbal communication are paralanguage, eye movements, gestures, kinesics, touch, physical appearance, facial expressions.

Thus, Option B is correct.

138. ● Continuous analysis of the behavior of the organization avoids the win-lose situation.

● Organizational behavior helps the organization to achieve group co-operation and total group objectives. This will avoid win-lose situations.

● Analysis of organizational behavior helps in finding the gaps in the skill set.

● The reason did not explain the assertion.

Thus, Option B is correct.

139. • The traditional 4Ps of marketing are not adequate to market service.

• In the service market, the customers are involved in the process and act as co-producers as well. This was not considered by the traditional 4Ps of marketing.

Thus, Option D is correct.

140. • The sign of both the regression coefficients will be the same, i.e. they will be either positive or negative. Thus, it is not possible that one regression coefficient is negative while the other is positive.

• The coefficient of correlation will have the same sign as that of the regression coefficients, such as if the regression coefficients have a positive sign, then "r" will be positive and vice-versa.

Thus, Option B is correct.

141. • Business ethics is not just a code of conduct but is code of ethics.

• The Code of conduct should be internalized as a normative value.

• The Code of conduct cannot be an external instrument of control.

• The Code of ethics brings a defined and suitable code of conduct.

Thus, Option C is correct.

142. At this price level, market is in equilibrium. Quantity supplied is equal to quantity demanded (Qs = Qd). Surplus and shortage: If the market price is above the equilibrium price, quantity supplied is greater than quantity demanded, creating a surplus. (A) and (R) both are correct and (R) is right explanation of (A).

143. Price is the value that is put to a product or service and is the result of a complex set of calculations, research and understanding and risk taking ability. A pricing strategy takes into account segments, ability to pay, market conditions, competitor actions, trade margins and input costs, amongst others. It is targeted at the defined customers and against competitors.

(A) and (R) both are correct but (R) is not the right explanation of (A).

144. Most people want to avoid conflict and potentially stressful situations – this is human nature.

People often find it easier to avoid communicating something that they think is going to be controversial or bad, putting off the communication and letting the situation fester.

(A) and (R) both are correct and (R) is the correct explanation of (A).

145. Capital investment analysis is a budgeting procedure that companies and government agencies use to assess the potential profitability of a long-term investment. Capital investment analysis assesses long-term investments, which might include fixed assets like equipment, machinery or real estate. The goal of this process is to identify the option that can yield the highest return on invested capital. Businesses may use techniques such as net present value (NPV) analysis, discounted cash flow (DCF) analysis, risk-return analysis and risk-neutral valuation in a capital investment analysis.

(A) and (R) both are correct and (R) is right explanation of (A).

146. The capital markets are a source of financing for companies around the world. The most famous of the capital markets are the stock market and bond market.

Investors want investment options that manage liquidity and risks while offering substantial returns. Debentures are long-term financial instruments issued by a company for specified tenure with a promise to pay fixed interest to the investor.

Both (A) and (R) are incorrect.

147. One of the adverse trends observable in the corporate private sector of India is the growing incidence of sickness. It is causing considerable concern to planners and policymakers. It is also putting a severe strain on the economic system, particularly on the banks.

There are various criteria of sickness. According to the criteria accepted by the Reserve Bank of India "a sick unit is one which has reported cash loss for the year of its operation and in the judgment of the financing bank is likely to incur cash loss for the current year as also in the following year."

A major symptom of sickness is a steady fall in debt-equity ratio and an imbalance in the financial position of the unit. Simply put, a sick unit is one which is unable to support itself through the operation of internal resources (that is, earnings plough-back). As a general rule, the sick units continue to operate below the break-even point (at which total revenue = total cost) and are, thus, forced to depend on external sources for funds of their long-term survival.

Industrial sickness creates various socio-economic problems. When an industrial unit falls sick those who depend on it have to face an uncertain future. They fear loss of jobs. Even if they do not lose jobs they do not get their wages and compensation in time and are, thus, forced to live in extreme hardship.Both (A) and (R) are correct ; but (R) is not the right explanation of (A).

148. • Primary data: Data collected by an investigator or agency or institution for a specific purpose and these people are the first to use these data.

• Secondary data: Data gathered by an investigator or agency or institution from an existing source. The Publication division of National Portal of India is an existing source to collect data.

Thus, Option B is correct.

149. Management accounting systems often focus on products, departments, or geographic regions, but not on customers. As a result, companies are often unable to produce reliable per-customer profitability figures, which leads to keeping unprofitable customers, decreasing company's potential to make profits.

The "why?" of Customer Profitability Analysis can be reduced to the simple statement that each dollar of revenue does not contribute equally to profit. Differences in customer profitability can arise from either differences in revenues and/or differences in costs. In other words, customer profitability depends not only on the revenue resulting from sold units of a product or service, but also on the 'back end' services provided, including marketing, distribution, and customer service. Both (A) and (R) are correct and (R) is the right explanation of (A).

150. ● Competitive advantage: It is based on lower costs, technological innovation, and product differentiation. It determines the pattern and direction of international trade.

● Absolute advantage: Production of more quantity of goods with a given amount of resources than another country.

● International marketing: Business activities that direct the flow of a company's goods and services to customers.

Thus, Option A is correct.

Paper-I

Q.1 The term 'Yellow journalism' refers to:

A. sensational news about terrorism and violence

B. sensationalism and exaggeration to attract readers/viewers.

C. sensational news about arts and culture

D. sensational news prints in yellow paper.

Q.2 In the classroom, the teacher sends the message either as words or images. The students are really:

A. Encoders

B. Decoders

C. Agitators

D. Propagators

Q.3 Media is known as:

A. First Estate

B. Second Estate

C. Third Estate

D. Fourth Estate

Q.4 The mode of communication that involves a single source transmitting information to a large number of receivers simultaneously, is called:

A. Group Communication

B. Mass Communication

C. Intrapersonal Communication

D. Intrapersonal Communication

Q.5 A smart classroom is a teaching space which has
i. Smart portion with a touch panel control system. ii. PC/Laptop connection and DVD/VCR player. iii. Document camera and specialized software. iv. Projector and screen **Select the correct answer from the codes given below:**

A. i and ii only

B. ii and iv only

C. i, ii and iii only

D. i, ii, iii and iv

Q.6 Digital Empowerment means
i. Universal digit literacy ii. Universal access to all digital resources. iii. Collaborative digital platform for participative governance. iv. Probability of all entitlements for individuals through cloud. **Choose the correct answer form the codes given below:**

A. i and ii only

B. ii and iii only

C. i, ii and iii only

D. i, ii, iii and iv

Q.7
Look at this series: 2, 1, (1/2), (1/4), ... What number should come next?

A. 1/8

B. 1/7

C. 1/5

D. 1/9

Q.8 Look at this series: 53, 53, 40, 40, 27, 27, ... What number should come next?

A. 18

B. 14

C. 16

D. 15

Q.9 In a certain code language COMPUTER is written as RFUVQNPC. How will MEDICINE be written in that code language?

A. EOJDEJFM

B. MFEDJJOE

C. MFEJDJOE

D. EOJDJEFM

Q.10 In a certain code language,
'134' means 'good and tasty';
'478' means 'see good pictures' and
'729' means 'pictures are faint'.
Which of the following digits stands for 'see'?

A. 6

B. 5

C. 9

D. 8

Q.11 If Z= 2197 and R= 729. How would J be written in that code?

A. 128

B. 126

C. 130

D. 125

Q.12 The marked price of an article is 60% more than its cost price. If the article is sold for Rs 300 after offering a discount of Rs 20, then what will be the profit percentage?

A. 50%

B. 40%

C. 60%

D. 30%

Ques (13-17):Direction: Read the following passage carefully and answer questions:

The literary distaste for politics, however, seems to be focused not so much on the largely murky practice of politics in itself as a subject of literary representation but rather more on how it is often depicted in Literature, i.e., On the very politics of representation. A political novel often turns out be not merely a novel about politics but a novel with a politics of its own, for it seeks not merely to show us how things are but has fairly definite ideas about how things should be, and precisely what one should think and do in order to make things move in that desired direction. In short, it seeks to convert and enlist the reader to a particular cause or ideology; it often is (in an only too familiar phrase) not literature but propaganda. This is said to violate the very spirit of literature which is to broaden our understanding of the world and the range of our sympathies rather than to narrow them down through partisan commitment. As John Keats said, 'We hate poetry that has a palpable design upon us'. Another reason why politics does not seem amenable to the highest kind of literary representation seems to arise from the fact that politics by its very nature is constituted of ideas and ideologies. If political situations do not lend themselves to happy literary treatment, political ideas present perhaps an even greater problem in this regard. Literature, it is argued, is about human experiences rather than about intellectual abstractions; it deals in what is called the 'felt reality' of human flesh and blood, and in sap and savour (rasa) rather than in arid and lifeless ideas. In an extensive discussion of the matter in her book Ideas and the Novel, the American novelist Mary McCarthy observed that 'ideas are still today felt to be unsightly in the novel' though that was not so in 'former days', i.e., in the 18th and 19th centuries. Her formulation of the precise nature of the incompatibility between ideas on the one hand and the novel on the other betrays perhaps a divided conscience in the matter and a sense of dilemma shared by many writers and readers: 'An idea cannot have loose ends, but a novel, I almost think, needs them. Nevertheless, there is enough in common for the novelists to feel ... the attraction of ideas while taking up arms against them – most often with weapons of mockery.'

Q.13 According to the passage, a political novel often turns out to be a:
A. Literary distaste for politics
B. Literary representation of politics
C. Novel with its own politics
D. Decpiction of murky practice of politics

Q.14 A political novel reveals
A. Reality of the things
B. Writer's perception
C. Particular ideology of the readers
D. The spirit of literature

Q.15 The constructs of politics by its nature is
A. Prevalent political situation
B. Ideas and Ideologies
C. Political propaganda
D. Understanding of human nature

Q.16 Literature deals with
A. Human-experiences in politics
B. Intellectual abstractions
C. Dry and empty ideas
D. Felt reality of human life

Q.17 The observation of the novelist, Mary McCarthy reveals:
A. unseen felt ideas of today in the novel
B. dichotomy of conscience on political ideas and novels
C. compatibility between idea and novel
D. endless ideas and novels

Q.18 The coding or scrambling of data so that humans cannot read them, is known as _____.
A. Compression
B. Encryption
C. Ergonomics
D. Biometrics

Q.19 In a certain coding language, iF GO = 32 & SHE = 49 then SOME will be equal to?
A. 56   B. 50   C. 58   D. 60

Q.20 Odometer is to mileage as compass is to.
A. speed   B. needle   C. hiking   D. direction

Q.21 Look at this series: 1.5, 2.3, 3.1, 3.9, ... What number should come next?
A. 4.6   B. 4.4   C. 4.7   D. 4.9

Q.22 Look at this series: 80, 10, 70, 15, 60, ... What number should come next?
A. 20   B. 25   C. 10   D. 30

Q.23 By which of the following proposition, the proposition 'wise men are hardly afraid of death' is contradicted?
A. Some wise men are afraid of death.
B. All wise men are afraid of death.
C. No wise men is afraid of death.
D. Some wise men are not afraid of death.

Q.24 The present age of Aradhana and Aadrika is in the ratio 3:4. 5 years back, the ratio of their ages was 2:3. What is the present age of Aradhana?
A. 8 years   B. 15 years   C. 25 years   D. 16 years

Q.25 Identify the correct sequence of control cycle:
A. Feedback -> Evaluation -> Adjustment -> Action.
B. Action -> Evaluation -> Feedback -> Adjustment.
C. Action -> Feedback -> Evaluation -> Adjustment.
D. Adjustment -> Action -> Feedback -> Evaluation.

Q.26 A father is twice as old as his daughter. If 20 years ago, the age of the father was 10 times the age of the daughter, what is the present age of the father?
A. 45 years   B. 35 years   C. 25 years   D. 55 years

Q.27 A builder appoints three construction workers Akash, Sunil and Rakesh on one of his sites. They take 20, 30 and 60 days respectively to do a piece of work. How many days will it take Akash to complete the entire work if he is assisted by Sunil and Rakesh every third day?
A. 25 days   B. 15 days   C. 12 days   D. 18 days

Q.28 Dev completed the school project in 20 days. How many days will Arun take to complete the same work if he is 25% more efficient than Dev?
A. 18 days   B. 26 days   C. 16 days   D. 15 days

Q.29 By interchanging which two signs the equation will be correct?
$16 + 31 - 3 \times 93 \div 11 = 966$
A. + and −   B. − and ÷   C. ÷ and ×   D. × and +

Q.30 If in a certain language, NOIDA is coded as OPJEB, how is DELHI coded in that language?
A. FGNJK   B. EFMIJ   C. IHLED   D. CDKGH

Q.31 Pointing to a photograph, a man said, "I have no brother, and that man's father is my father's son." Whose photograph was it?
A. His son   B. His nephew
C. His father   D. His own

Q.32 In a row of persons, the position of Sakshi from the left side of the row is 26th and position of Sakshi from the right side of the row is 35th. Find the total number of students in the row?
A. 30   B. 40   C. 50   D. 60

Q.33 MOOC stands for:-
A. Media Online Open Course
B. Massachusetts Open Online Course
C. Massive Open Online Course
D. Myrind Open Online Course

Q.34 Binary equivalent of decimal number 25 is:
A. 11001   B. 10001   C. 11010   D. 10111

Q.35 MPG, . MP2, . MPEG, . MPE, . MPV. are used as extensions for files which store

A. audio data   **B.** image data

C. video data   **D.** text data

Q.36 Which of the anthropogenic activity accounts for more than 2/3rd of global water consumption?

A. Agriculture

B. Hydropower generation

C. Industry

D. Domestic and Municipal usage

Q.37 The substance or mixture of substances used to prevent, destroy, repel, attract, sterilize, mitigate any insects is called:

A. Cement industry   **B.** Fertiliser industry

C. Foam industry   **D.** Pesticide industry

Q.38 In terms of total CO_2 emissions from a country, identify the correct sequence:

A. U.S. A>China>India>Russia

B. China>U.S. A>India>Russia

C. China>U.S. A>Russia>India

D. U.S. A>China>Russia>India

Q.39 Which is the World Ozone Day?

A. 11th July   **B.** 16th September

C. 7th April   **D.** 1st December

Q.40 The cyclone 'Hudhud' hit the coast of which State?

A. Andhra Pradesh   **B.** Karnataka

C. Kerala   **D.** Gujarat

Q.41 Which of the following is a renewable natural resource?

A. Clean air   **B.** Fresh water

C. Fertile soil   **D.** All of these

Q.42 The maximum number of fake institutions/ universities as identified by the UGC in the year 2014 are in the State/ Union territory of:-

A. Bihar   **B.** Uttar Pradesh

C. Tamil Nadu   **D.** Delhi

Q.43 Arrange the words given below in a meaningful sequence.
1.Presentation 2.Recommendation 3.
Arrival 4.Discussion 5.Introduction

A. 5, 3, 4, 1, 2   **B.** 3, 5, 4, 2, 1

C. 3, 5, 1, 4, 2   **D.** 5, 3, 1, 2, 4

Q.44 What was the day on 15th august 1947 ?

A. Friday   **B.** Monday   **C.** Sunday   **D.** Saturday

Q.45 In an election between two candidates, one got 55% of the total valid votes, 20% of the votes were invalid. If the total number of votes was 7500, the number of valid votes that the other candidate got, was :

A. 2800   **B.** 3700   **C.** 2700   **D.** 2900

Q.46 The interval between two sessions of parliament must not exceed:-

A. 3 months   **B.** 6 months

C. 4 months   **D.** 100 days

Q.47 Right to Privacy as a Fundamental Right is implied in:-

A. Right to Freedom

B. Right to Life and Personal Liberty

C. Right to Equality

D. Right against Exploitation

Q.48 Which of the following organizations deals with 'capacity building program' on Educational Planning?

A. NCERT   **B.** UGC   **C.** NAAC   **D.** NUEPA

Q.49 "Education is the manifestation of perfection already in man" was stated by which personality?

A. M.K. Gandhi   **B.** R.N. Tagore

C. Swami Vivekanand   **D.** Sri Aurobindo

Q.50 Which of the following is prescribed level of teaching?

A. Memory   **B.** Understanding

C. Reflective   **D.** All of the above

Paper-II

Q.51 There are different phases in the Operations Research Project. They are:

(i) Research phase

(ii) Action phase

(iii) Judgment phase

The correct sequence of these phases is:

A. (i), (ii), (iii)   **B.** (iii), (i), (ii)

C. (ii), (iii), (i)   **D.** (iii), (ii), (i)

Q.52 In economics, _________________ are inputs to production that a firm uses closely together.

A. Market ability of products

B. Complementarity of inputs

C. Specificity of inputs

D. Substitutability of inputs

Q.53 The Graphical method can be used to solve:

(A) A Linear Programming Problem (LPP) with all integer data.

(B) A LPP with two decision variables.

A. Only A   **B.** Only B

C. Neither A nor B   **D.** Either A or B

Q.54 Which moral philosophy seeks the greatest good for the greatest number of people?

A. Consequentialism   **B.** Utilitarianism

C. Egoism   **D.** Ethical formalism

Q.55 If the EOQ for an item of inventory in a firm is 4000 units, the estimated demand for the term next year gets doubled, what shall be the revised EOQ next year, all other relevant costs remaining unchanged?

A. 4000   **B.** 5000

C. 5656   **D.** None of the above

Q.56 Macroeconomics is concerned with______________and______ level of the economy as it is a macro aspect of the economy.

A. Industry, Trade and Commerce

B. Agriculture, Industry & Trade

C. Employment, Inflation & Growth

D. Population, Income and Economic Planning

Q.57 Which of the following industries comes under the category of threshold resources in the strategic resources?

A. Pharma industry

B. Automobile industry

C. Food industry

D. Agro-industry

Q.58 Chi-square distribution has a number of applications which are enumerated below:

a) To test if the population has a specified value of the variance σ^2

b) Chi-square test of goodness of fit.

C) Chi-square test for independence of attributes.

A. Either a or b

B. Only a

C. Only b

D. All of these

Q.59 The world conference of the United Nations Decade for Women at Copenhagen on July 30, 1980 focused on which of the following?

A. To provide financial assistance to women entrepreneurs to carry on business.

B. To remove social, institutional barriers in industrial activities.

C. To promote equal opportunities and treatment of women in employment.

D. To provide counselling and coaching to women entrepreneurs.

Q.60 Assertion (A): Inflation is a state of increasing price but not high price.

Reason (R): Inflation is a rise in the general level of prices of goods and services in an economy over a period of time.

A. (A) is correct., but (R) is incorrect.

B. Both (A) and (R) are correct, but (R) is not the right explanation of (A).

C. (A) is incorrect, but (R) is correct.

D. Both (A) and (R) are incorrect.

Q.61 How many types of Agriculture Business?

A. 7   **B.** 3   **C.** 4   **D.** 6

Q.62 Assertion (A): The essence of every strategy formulation is coping with competition in the market.

Reason (R): Multinationals and large organizations clash directly on every level of product and service.

A. Both (A) and (R) are correct, and (R) is the correct explanation of (A).

B. Both (A) and (R) are correct, but (R) is not the correct explanation of (A).

C. (A) is correct., but (R) is not correct.

D. (A) is wrong, and (R) is correct.

Q.63 Pichot suggested which of the following three roles for the Intrapreneur in promoting Innovation?

A. Inventor, Innovator, Sponsor

B. Developer, Inventor, Marketer

C. Innovator, Developer, Change agent

D. Inventor, Product Champion, Sponsor

Q.64 'XYZ Pvt LTD.' never uses its products on animals and also focuses on raising funds so as to promote awareness about global issues like HIV etc.

Which of the following strategies of Green Marketing is highlighted in the above example?

A. Green Pricing   **B.** Green Design

C. Green Logistics   **D.** Green Positioning

Q.65 Which of the following layouts is suitable when a large variety of products are needed in small volumes?

A. Office layout

B. Group layout

C. Fixed-position layout

D. Storage layout

Q.66 Which of the following is a type of cognitive bias and is the opposite of the Horn Effect?

A. Leniency effect

B. Halo effect

C. Central tendency error

D. Recency effect

Q.67 Which of the following points describing the difference between Entrepreneur and Intrapreneur is/are not true?

a) An entrepreneur is free and is the leader of his organization, whereas Intrapreneur is an employee of the organization.

b) Entrepreneurship is restorative in nature, whereas Intrapreneurship is intuitive in nature.

c) An Entrepreneur arranges and uses his own resources, whereas an Intrapreneur uses the resources provided by the company.

d) An Intrapreneur bears all the risk involved in the company, whereas an Entrepreneur does not have to bear any risk.

A. Only b and d   **B.** Only A

C. Only c and d   **D.** Only a, b and c

Q.68 Identify who among the following introduced the concept of social marketing and societal marketing?

A. Adam Smith   **B.** Philip Kotler

C. Edward Deming   **D.** Joseph M Juran

Q.69 Strategic human resource management is facing the major issues, challenges and notable trends in the current changing environment, which among the following are part of it?

I. Cross-cultural factors

II. Internationalization of market integration

III. Significant technological change

IV. Workforce diversity

Choose the correct code:

A. I, II, III   **B.** II, III, IV

C. I, III, IV   **D.** I, II, IV

Q.70 Statement I: Planning bridges the gap from where we are to where we want to go.

Statement II: To organise means to provide it with everything useful to its functioning.

Choose the correct option from the following:

A. Statement I is correct, Statement II is incorrect.

B. Statement I is incorrect, Statement II is correct.

C. Both Statement I and Statement II are correct.

D. Both Statement I and Statement II are incorrect.

Q.71 Assertion (A): In international economic integration, FDI plays an important role.

Reason (R): FDI can play a strategic role in the development of enterprises.

A. Both (A) and (R) are correct, and (R) is the correct explanation of (A).

B. Both (A) and (R) are correct, but (R) is not the correct explanation of (A).

C. (A) is correct, but (R) is not correct.

D. (A) is wrong, and (R) is correct.

Q.72 In the context of an organization engaged in strategy formulation and implementation, substantive dimension deal with?

A. Puts strategy into operation

B. Executes long-run direction

C. Determination of strategy

D. Performance of an organization

Q.73 Statement I: Modigliani and Miller (MM) Approach to Capital Structure states that the valuation of a firm is unrelated to the capital structure of a company. Being highly leveraged or having a low debt component does not in any way affect its market value.

Statement II: This approach assumes that the cost of borrowing is different for investors and companies.

Choose the correct option from those below:

A. Statement I is correct., Statement II is incorrect.

B. Statement I is incorrect, Statement II is correct.

C. Both Statement I and Statement II are correct.

D. Both Statement I and Statement II are incorrect.

Q.74 When does the process of communication get completed?

A. When a message enters the channel

B. When receiver decodes the message

C. When the receiver sends feedback

D. When the sender encodes the message

Q.75 Which of the following industrial approaches was developed by John Dunlop?

A. Pluralistic approach

B. Systems approach

C. Unitary approach

D. Psychological approach

Q.76 For 'make or buy decision', which cost is to be considered?

(A) Marginal cost

(B) Total cost

A. Only A

B. Only B

C. Either A or B

D. None of these

Q.77 According to Guthman and Dougal, Financial management is the activity concerned with planning, raising, controlling and _________of funds used in the business.

A. Administering

B. Organizing

C. Directing

D. Utilization

Q.78 Which of the following is the purpose of the supply chain?

A. To provide customer satisfaction

B. To improve product quality

C. To increase sales

D. To integrate supply and demand management

Q.79 Which of the following usually require the smallest sample size

A. Cluster sampling

B. Two-stage sampling

C. Simple random sampling

D. Quota sampling

Q.80 Which of the following is not a major component of the Non-monotonic reasoning system (NMRS)?

A. Knowledgebase

B. Inference engine

C. Truth maintenance system

D. Closed world assumption system

Q.81 Any revenue expenses for which a separate fund is available will be:

A. Debited to the Separate Fund

B. Debited to the Income and Expenditure Account

C. Capitalized and shown in the Balance Sheet

D. Credited to the Separate Fund

Q.82 In an organization, managers have to perform various functions. They are responsible for decision-making, planning, organizing, leading and controlling. For each of these functions, they have to be trained accordingly. What kind of training is this known as?

A. Skills Training

B. Functional Training

C. Versatility Training

D. Role Specific Training

Q.83 Which type of event includes all the possibilities associated with the same trial?

A. Mutually exclusive events

B. Independent events

C. Exhaustive events

D. Dependent events

Q.84 Statement I: The blind area under the Johari window consists of information that is known to others but unknown to the self.

Statement II: The unknown area under the Johari window consists of information that is not known to self and others.

Choose the correct option from those below:

A. Statement I is correct, Statement II is incorrect.

B. Statement I is incorrect, Statement II is correct.

C. Both Statement I and Statement II are correct.

D. Both Statement I and Statement II are incorrect.

Q.85 Statement I: Renuka Sugars Ltd setting up a sugar facility in Cuba is an example of brownfield investment.

Statement II: H&M, a famous apparel brand from Sweden entered India via Joint Venture.

Choose the correct option from those below:

A. Statement I is correct, Statement II is incorrect.

B. Statement I is incorrect, Statement II is correct.

C. Both Statement I and Statement II are correct.

D. Both Statement I and Statement II are incorrect.

Q.86 Which among the following is/are not false statements?

I. Potential assessment evaluates the capabilities of employees for taking higher positions with greater and more critical responsibilities.

II. In the performance appraisal programme, evaluation is done by supervisors and HR consultants only.

III. Decision-making skills and Interpersonal skills are developed by managers in management development programmes.

IV. In the recency effect, rater gives greater weightage to recent incidents than earlier performance.

Choose the correct code:

A. I, II, III   **B.** I, III, IV

C. I, II, IV   **D.** II, III, IV

Q.87 Which of the following characteristic contain random information developed on a case to case basis?

A. External source   **B.** Adhocness

C. Subjectiveness   **D.** Unexpectedness

Q.88 Non-governmental organizations(NGOs), Voluntary Organizations(VOs), Self-help Groups(SHGs) form part of which type of Rural Entrepreneurship?

A. Group Entrepreneurship

B. Individual Entrepreneurship

C. Cooperatives

D. Cluster Formation

Q.89 The group of positions involving the same duties, skills, knowledge and responsibilities is called______________.

A. Management   **B.** Personnel

C. Job   **D.** Product

Q.90 The Following figures are provided to you:

Opening Stock- 10,000

Closing Stock- 11,000

Purchase- 70,000

The goods are sold at a profit of 30% on cost. The amount of sales will be:

A. 21,000   **B.** 91,000   **C.** 1,04,000   **D.** 89,700

Q.91 Acceptance sampling plans are given by

A. Neyman fisher   **B.** Neyman Pearson

C. Rao Blackwell   **D.** Wadge & poring

Q.92 In the law of decreasing returns:

A. Marginal productivity of variable input increases

B. Marginal productivity of variable input declines

C. Marginal productivity of fixed input increases

D. Marginal productivity of fixed input increases

Q.93 Assertion (A): Employee engagement occurs when the attitude of the employees is positive towards their job.

Reason (R): Employee engagement rate will be high when the employees are not underpaid.

A. Both (A) and (R) are correct, and (R) is the correct explanation of (A).

B. Both (A) and (R) are correct, but (R) is not the correct explanation of (A).

C. (A) is correct., but (R) is not correct.

D. (A) is wrong, and (R) is correct.

Q.94 Statement I: Niche Marketing concentrates on small numbers of customers in a market.

Statement II: Companies that have highly specific goods often use this strategy.

Choose the correct option from the following:

A. Statement I is correct, Statement II is incorrect.

B. Statement I is incorrect, Statement II is correct.

C. Both Statement I and Statement II are correct.

D. Both Statement I and Statement II are incorrect.

Q.95 Which of the following categories of women entrepreneurs involves women who are educated and take the risk of establishing an Enterprise with or without experience, with the help of financial institutions and commercial banks?

A. Affluent Entrepreneurs

B. Self employed Entrepreneurs

C. Push factors

D. Pull factors

Q.96 The histogram is useful to determine graphically the value of

A. Harmonic Mean   **B.** Median

C. Mode   **D.** Arithmetic Mean

Q.97 According to the Zinger model, how many aspects should a manager follow to achieve good results through employee engagement?

A. 8   **B.** 10   **C.** 12   **D.** 14

Q.98 An entrepreneurial person employed by a corporation and encouraged to be innovative and creative is referred to as:

A. Competitor   **B.** Entrepreneur

C. Intrapreneur   **D.** None of the above

Q.99 The quantitative approach using quantitative techniques in Management is called:

A. Scientific Method

B. Operations Research

C. Quantitative Approach

D. None of these

Q.100 Statement I: First-mover advantages can help a firm dominate global trade in that product.

Statement II: Porter's diamond of competitive advantage includes first-mover advantages.

Choose the correct option from those below:

A. Statement I is correct, Statement II is incorrect.

B. Statement I is incorrect, Statement II is correct.

C. Both Statement I and Statement II are correct.

D. Both Statement I and Statement II are incorrect.

Q.101 Assertion (A): The actual performance will be less than the potential performance because of social loafing.

Reason (R): The size of groups is kept small to reduce social loafing.

A. Both (A) and (R) are correct, and (R) is the correct explanation of (A).

B. Both (A) and (R) are correct, but (R) is not the correct explanation of (A).

C. (A) is correct, but (R) is not correct.

D. (A) is wrong, and (R) is correct.

Q.102 Which one of the following is not a part of the four basic principles stated by N.Q.Herrick and M.Maccoby, which will humanize work and improve the Quality of Work-Life?

A. The Principle of Security

B. The Principle of Equity

C. The Principle of Freedom

D. The Principle of Democracy

Q.103 Which of the following are the objectives of financial management?

a) To ensure a regular and adequate supply of funds to the enterprise.

b) To plan a sound and fair capital structure.

c) To make sure that funds are invested in safe ventures.

d) To see that funds are utilized in the best possible way at the least cost.

Choose the correct option from those below:

A. a,b and c

B. a,c and d

C. Only d

D. All of the above

Q.104 Debt security without any explicit interest rate is known as:

A. income bonds.

B. Floating rate bonds.

C. Zero-coupon bonds

D. None of these

Q.105 Which of the following is incurred due to the failure of not adopting the most favourable course of action or strategy?

A. Payoff

B. Opportunity loss

C. Profit

D. Courses of action

Q.106 What does T stand for in OCTAPACE Values?

A. Talent

B. Technology

C. Trust

D. Team

Q.107 Assertion (A): Wealth maximisation is the appropriate objective of an enterprise.

Reason (R): Financial theory asserts that wealth maximisation is the single substitute for a stockholder's utility.

A. Both (A) and (R) are correct, and (R) is the correct explanation of (A).

B. Both (A) and (R) are correct, but (R) is not the correct explanation of (A).

C. (A) is correct., but (R) is not correct.

D. (A) is wrong, and (R) is correct.

Q.108 Which of the following approaches of Capital Structure assumes that the rate of interest on the debt remains the same for a certain period, and it increases with an increase in leverage.

A. MM Approach

B. Traditional Approach

C. Net Income Approach

D. Net Operating Income Approach

Q.109 Which of the following is considered as documentation as per the requirement of the importing country?

A. Commercial invoice

B. Customs invoice

C. Inspection certificate

D. Packing list

Q.110 Which among the following are the individual evaluation techniques of performance appraisal?

I. Checklists, Graphical rating scale

II. Essay evaluation, Confidential report

III.The critical incident method, Ranking method

IV. Behaviorally anchored rating scale, Forced choice method

Choose the correct code:

A. I, II, III

B. II, III, IV

C. I, III, IV

D. I, II, IV

Q.111 Which of the following tasks is not performed under technical feasibility study?

A. Ascertaining whether the current resources and technology can be upgraded or added in the software.

B. Determining whether the solution suggested by the software development team is acceptable.

C. Determining whether the relevant technology is stable as well as established.

D. Ascertaining that the technology that has been chosen for software development has a large number of users.

Q.112 A formal document of what the entrepreneur intends to do to sell enough of the firm's product or service to make a satisfactory profit is called:

A. Long-range plan

B. Strategic plan

C. Business plan

D. None of the above

Q.113 Which of the following feasibility studies would prove to be successful when dealing with issues such as business expansion, product development, and starting up a business.

A. Resources Feasibility

B. Technical Feasibility

C. Market Feasibility

D. Economic Feasibility

Q.114 The definition of the strategy includes:

Statement I: Determination of very short term goals and objectives.

Statement II: Adoption of courses of action.

Choose the correct option from those below:

A. Statement I is correct., Statement II is incorrect.
B. Statement I is incorrect, Statement II is correct.
C. Both Statement I and Statement II are correct.
D. Both Statement I and Statement II are incorrect.

Q.115 The number of subordinates a superior can effectively handle is called:

A. Organising people **B.** Direction
C. Coordination **D.** Span of control

Q.116 Statement I: Product Innovation includes changes in the equipment and technology used in manufacturing, improvement in the tools etc.

Statement II: Process Innovation includes technological advancement, changes in customer requirements.

Choose the correct option from the following:

A. Statement I is correct, Statement II is incorrect.
B. Statement I is incorrect, Statement II is correct.
C. Both Statement I and Statement II are correct.
D. Both Statement I and Statement II are incorrect.

Q.117 When there is perfect substitutability between two factors of production, what does it imply?

A. L shaped isoquant **B.** Convex isoquant
C. Kinked isoquant **D.** Linear isoquant

Q.118 Statement I: Encoding and decoding of messages are not influenced by emotions.

Statement II: Semantic problems arise from expression and transmission of meaning.

Choose the correct option from those below:

A. Statement I is correct, Statement II is incorrect.
B. Statement I is incorrect, Statement II is correct.
C. Both Statement I and Statement II are correct.
D. Both Statement I and Statement II are incorrect.

Q.119 Mr X is the supervisor of a new employee Mr Y. Due to his busy schedule and other reasons, Mr X could not pay sufficient attention to the latter's performance. When at the end of the quarter, he is asked to evaluate his junior's performance, he plays it safe by rating him 'average' in most of the aspects instead of choosing the outer ends. What kind of error is this known as?

A. Halo Error
B. Leniency Error
C. Central Tendency Error
D. Mid-value Error

Q.120 Assertion (A): New entrants are always a powerful source of competition.

Reason (R): The new capacity and the product range, they bring in may increase competitive pressure.

A. Both (A) and (R) are correct, and (R) is the correct explanation of (A).
B. Both (A) and (R) are correct, but (R) is not the correct explanation of (A).
C. (A) is correct., but (R) is not correct.
D. (A) is wrong, and (R) is correct.

Q.121 Assertion (A): CRM systems reduce wastage in the marketing efforts of the organization.

Reason (R): CRM systems help the organization to identify the buying patterns of the customers and segment them accordingly.

A. Both (A) and (R) are correct, and (R) is the correct explanation of (A).
B. Both (A) and (R) are correct, but (R) is not the correct explanation of (A).
C. (A) is correct., but (R) is not correct.
D. (A) is wrong, and (R) is correct.

Q.122 A marketing effectiveness review is part of ______ control.

A. Annual Plan **B.** Proficiency
C. Strategic **D.** Profitability

Q.123 Assertion (A): While establishing the talent reservoir, the supervisor is responsible for final evaluation and recommendations

Reason (R): The talent management plan stems in a formal way when top-level management includes data related to employee assessment.

A. Both (A) and (R) are correct, and (R) is the correct explanation of (A).
B. Both (A) and (R) are correct, but (R) is not the correct explanation of (A).
C. (A) is correct., but (R) is not correct.
D. (A) is wrong, and (R) is correct.

Q.124 Strategies formulated to convert a sick unit to healthy is referred to:

(A) Turnaround
(B) Expansion

A. Only A **B.** Only B
C. Either A or B **D.** None of these

Q.125 ______ is a process of measuring or identifying and applying best practices to improve a specific task.

A. Quality circle **B.** Outsourcing
C. Bench marking **D.** Strategy

Q.126 Emerging market economies are:

(A) A part of developed countries
(B) Newly industrializing countries

A. Only A **B.** Only B
C. Either A or B **D.** None of these

Q.127 Quality Control Handbook theory has given by:

A. Martin K. Starr and D. W. Miller
B. Elwood S. Buffa and Rakesh K. Sarin
C. J. M. Juran
D. None of the above

Q.128 Assertion (A): TVC (Total Variable Costs) is the sum of marginal costs since total fixed costs remain the same.

Reason (R): MC (Marginal Cost) is an addition to the total variable cost when an additional unit is produced.

A. Both (A) and (R) are correct, and (R) is the correct

explanation of (A).

B. Both (A) and (R) are correct, but (R) is not the correct explanation of (A).

C. (A) is correct., but (R) is not correct.

D. (A) is wrong, and (R) is correct.

Q.129 The term "Grapevine Communication" is related to:

(A) Formal Communication

(B) Informal Communication

A. Only A

B. Only B

C. Neither A nor B

D. Both A or B

Q.130 Assertion (A): Concept of elasticity of price expectation is very useful in formulating future pricing policy.

Reason (R): Price expectation elasticity refers to the expected changes in current price as a result of the change in the future price of a good.

A. (A) is correct., but (R) is incorrect.

B. Both (A) and (R) are correct, but (R) is not the right explanation of (A).

C. Both (A) and (R) are correct, (R) is the right explanation of (A).

D. Both (A) and (R) are incorrect.

Q.131 Which among the following statements defines the state of Hyperinflation?

A. Situation created by increase in price of input, such as raw material, labour.

B. Situation when economy faces accelerating, high and increasing rate of inflation.

C. Situation when aggregate demand of an economy exceeds aggregate demand.

D. Situation caused by continuous rise in inflation and rise in unemployment.

Q.132 The Economic Order Quantity (EOQ) is calculated as:

A. Product range

B. Product line length

C. Product mix width

D. Product mix depth

Q.133 The five different schemes for rewarding merchandise exports now have been merged into a single scheme known as Merchandise Export from India Scheme (MEIS). The five schemes were-

a) Focus Product Scheme

b) Market Linked Focus Product Scheme

c) Focus Market Scheme

d) Agri. Infrastructure Incentive Scrip

e) Standard Market Linked Scheme

f) Product Scheme

Choose the correct option from those below:

A. a,b,c,d,f   **B.** b,c,d,e,f   **C.** a,c,d,e,f   **D.** a,b,c,e,f

Q.134 Which of the following components is not a part of Carroll's CSR Pyramid?

A. Social

B. Philanthropic

C. Ethical

D. Economic

Q.135 Who is the father of Administrative Management Theory?

A. Max Weber

B. Henry Fayol

C. Frank Gilbraith

D. None of the above

Q.136 Which institution focuses on the promotion of cross-border investment by providing guarantees to investors and lenders?

A. MIGA   **B.** IFC   **C.** OECD   **D.** ICSID

Q.137 Assertion(A): Product line deletion is done when a firm's product does not perform well

Reason(R): If a product is not performing it is considered to be wasting a firm's money and resources.

A. Both (A) and (R) are correct, and (R) is the correct explanation of (A).

B. Both (A) and (R) are correct, but (R) is not the correct explanation of (A).

C. (A) is correct, but (R) is not correct.

D. (A) is wrong, and (R) is correct.

Q.138 Works committees in the establishments promote the participation of workers in the management. What is the minimum number of workers required to form a works committee in an establishment under the industrial disputes act, 1947?

A. 100   **B.** 250   **C.** 500   **D.** 1000

Q.139 An Entrepreneur adds value to an existing organization by improving the products, services or methods.

Which of the following characteristics of Intrapreneurship is highlighted above?

A. Diversification

B. Mutual Benefit

C. Restoration Concept

D. Innovative Approach

Q.140 Statement I: Maslow's hierarchy needs theory is based on the assumption that a person moves to the next higher level of need only when the lower level need is satisfied.

Statement II: Hierarchy of needs theory was proposed by Alfred Maslow in his 1990 Paper 'A Theory of Human Motivation'.

Choose the correct option from the following:

A. Statement I is correct, Statement II is incorrect.

B. Statement I is incorrect, Statement II is correct.

C. Both Statement I and Statement II are correct.

D. Both Statement I and Statement II are incorrect.

Q.141 Which of the following types of budgets can be adopted in case of a labour-intensive industry wherein the production of the company rests on or is dependent upon the availability of labour?

A. Fixed Budget

B. Flexible Budget

C. Production Budget

D. Factory overhead Budget

Q.142 Assertion (A): In the distributive bargaining, settlement always gets resolved within settlement range.

Reason (R): In the distributive bargaining, the settlement range is the range between resistance points of both the employee and the employer.

A. Both (A) and (R) are correct, and (R) is the correct explanation of (A).

B. Both (A) and (R) are correct, but (R) is not the correct explanation of (A).

C. (A) is correct., but (R) is not correct.

D. (A) is wrong, and (R) is correct.

Q.143 Benefits provided for temporary and permanent disability disfigurement, medical expenses and medical rehabilitation is referred to as:

A. Financial incentives

B. Workers' compensation

C. Fringe benefits

D. None of these

Q.144 The following two statements of Assertion (A) and Reasoning (R) suggest the correct code :

Assertion (A) : Low initial price regarded as the principal means for entering into mass market for some new products.

Reasoning (R) : Firms generally enter into production of new products with excess capacity of the plant initially.

Code :

A. (A) is correct but (R) is not correct.

B. (A) is not correct but (R) is correct.

C. (A) and (R) both are correct and (R) is right explanation of (A).

D. (A) and (R) both are correct but (R) is not right explanation of (A).

Ques (145-149):Read the assertion and reason both carefully:-

Q.145 Assertion (A) : Under stressful situations, a person is unable to listen to and understand the message correctly.

Reasoning (R) : During stressful situations, the psychological frame of mind changes and the message gets distorted due to the beliefs, experiences, goals and values held by the receiver of the message.

Code :

A. (A) and (R) both are correct and (R) is the correct explanation of (A).

B. (A) and (R) both are correct but (R) is not the correct explanation of (A).

C. (A) is correct whereas (R) is incorrect.

D. (R) is correct whereas (A) is incorrect.

Q.146 Assertion (A) : Risk analysis of capital investment is the most complex and controversial area in finance.

Reasoning (R) : Capital investment decisions are based on estimates of future cash inflows.

A. (A) is incorrect but (R) is correct.

B. (A) is correct but (R) is incorrect.

C. (A) and (R) both are correct and (R) is right explanation of (A).

D. (A) and (R) both are correct but (R) is not right explanation of (A).

Q.147 Assertion (A) : Invertors in capital market now have higher inclination for investment in debentures.

Reasoning (R) : Debentures have active secondary markets now.

Code :

A. Both (A) and (R) are correct ; and (R) is the right explanation of (A).

B. Both (A) and (R) are correct ; but (R) is not the right explanation of (A).

C. (A) is correct but (R) is incorrect.

D. Both (A) and (R) are incorrect.

Q.148 Assertion (A) : When an industrial unit falls sick, those who depend on it have to face an uncertain future.

Reasoning (R) : The sick units continue to operate below the break-even point and are, thus, forced to depend on external sources for funds of their long-term survival.

Code :

A. (A) and (R) both are correct ; and (R) is the right explanation of (A).

B. Both (A) and (R) are correct ; but (R) is not the right explanation of (A).

C. Both (A) and (R) are incorrect.

D. (A) is correct but (R) is incorrect.

Q.149 Assertion (A) : One of the trends to build a sustainable competitive advantage are innovations and innovations management.

Reasoning (R) : Human Resource Management has to be able to connect innovations with the traditional change management to design a true powerful weapon against competitors in the market.

Code :

A. Both (A) and (R) are correct ; and (R) is the right explanation of (A).

B. Both (A) and (R) are correct ; but (R) is not the right explanation of (A).

C. (A) is correct but (R) is incorrect.

D. (R) is correct but (A) is incorrect.

Q.150 Select the correct code of the Assertion (A) and Reasoning (R) :-

Assertion (A) : Companies should measure the profitability of their products, territories, customer groups, segments, trade channels and order sizes.

Reasoning (R) : Measure of profitability helps companies determine whether to expand, reduce, or eliminate any product or marketing activities to ensure profitability control.

Code :

A. Both (A) and (R) are correct and (R) is the right explanation of (A).

B. Both (A) and (R) are correct but (R) is not the right explanation of (A).

C. (A) is correct but (R) is incorrect.

D. (R) is correct but (A) is incorrect.

// Smart Answer Sheet //

Correct — Percentage of students who answered correctly.   **Skipped** — Percentage of students who skipped.

Q.	Ans.	Correct / Skipped	Q.	Ans.	Correct / Skipped	Q.	Ans.	Correct / Skipped	Q.	Ans.	Correct / Skipped	Q.	Ans.	Correct / Skipped
1	B	56.88 % / 5.51 %	17	A	35.78 % / 23.85 %	33	C	66.06 % / 23.85 %	49	C	46.79 % / 23.85 %	65	B	52.29 % / 22.94 %
2	B	69.72 % / 17.44 %	18	B	60.55 % / 23.85 %	34	A	42.2 % / 23.86 %	50	D	51.38 % / 23.85 %	66	B	53.21 % / 22.94 %
3	D	66.06 % / 17.43 %	19	A	33.03 % / 22.93 %	35	C	37.61 % / 22.94 %	51	B	22.94 % / 15.59 %	67	A	43.12 % / 22.94 %
4	B	77.06 % / 17.44 %	20	D	60.55 % / 22.94 %	36	A	39.45 % / 22.94 %	52	B	39.45 % / 22.02 %	68	B	41.28 % / 22.94 %
5	D	54.13 % / 18.35 %	21	C	65.14 % / 22.93 %	37	D	42.2 % / 22.02 %	53	B	31.19 % / 22.02 %	69	A	17.43 % / 22.94 %
6	D	33.03 % / 20.18 %	22	A	63.3 % / 23.86 %	38	B	30.28 % / 23.85 %	54	B	37.61 % / 23.86 %	70	C	38.53 % / 23.86 %
7	A	68.81 % / 20.18 %	23	B	53.21 % / 23.85 %	39	B	53.21 % / 23.85 %	55	C	23.85 % / 22.94 %	71	B	36.7 % / 23.85 %
8	B	69.72 % / 20.19 %	24	B	63.3 % / 24.77 %	40	A	55.05 % / 23.85 %	56	C	38.53 % / 22.94 %	72	C	18.35 % / 23.85 %
9	D	64.22 % / 21.1 %	25	C	23.85 % / 24.77 %	41	D	45.87 % / 23.85 %	57	B	35.78 % / 22.94 %	73	A	33.94 % / 23.86 %
10	D	70.64 % / 21.1 %	26	A	49.54 % / 25.69 %	42	B	55.05 % / 23.85 %	58	D	35.78 % / 22.94 %	74	C	52.29 % / 23.86 %
11	D	50.46 % / 22.02 %	27	B	47.71 % / 25.68 %	43	C	51.38 % / 23.85 %	59	C	42.2 % / 22.94 %	75	B	37.61 % / 23.86 %
12	A	33.03 % / 22.02 %	28	C	24.77 % / 24.77 %	44	A	43.12 % / 23.85 %	60	B	39.45 % / 22.94 %	76	A	21.1 % / 23.85 %
13	C	54.13 % / 22.93 %	29	B	28.44 % / 25.69 %	45	C	45.87 % / 23.85 %	61	C	33.03 % / 22.93 %	77	A	17.43 % / 23.85 %
14	B	31.19 % / 23.86 %	30	B	64.22 % / 23.85 %	46	B	57.8 % / 23.85 %	62	D	17.43 % / 22.94 %	78	D	54.13 % / 23.85 %
15	B	50.46 % / 23.85 %	31	A	28.44 % / 22.94 %	47	B	61.47 % / 23.85 %	63	D	22.02 % / 22.93 %	79	C	45.87 % / 23.85 %
16	D	35.78 % / 23.85 %	32	D	57.8 % / 22.93 %	48	D	33.03 % / 23.85 %	64	D	43.12 % / 22.94 %	80	D	22.02 % / 24.77 %

Q.	Ans.	Correct / Skipped	Q.	Ans.	Correct / Skipped	Q.	Ans.	Correct / Skipped	Q.	Ans.	Correct / Skipped	Q.	Ans.	Correct / Skipped
81	A	11.93 % / 24.77 %	95	D	22.02 % / 25.69 %	109	B	44.04 % / 28.44 %	123	C	18.35 % / 29.36 %	137	A	42.2 % / 29.36 %
82	D	23.85 % / 24.77 %	96	C	15.6 % / 25.68 %	110	D	20.18 % / 28.44 %	124	A	33.03 % / 28.44 %	138	A	24.77 % / 29.36 %
83	C	25.69 % / 24.77 %	97	D	11.01 % / 25.69 %	111	B	33.03 % / 28.44 %	125	C	42.2 % / 28.44 %	139	C	19.27 % / 29.35 %
84	C	29.36 % / 24.77 %	98	C	49.54 % / 25.69 %	112	C	30.28 % / 29.35 %	126	B	33.94 % / 28.45 %	140	A	32.11 % / 29.36 %
85	D	17.43 % / 24.77 %	99	C	25.69 % / 25.69 %	113	C	31.19 % / 29.36 %	127	C	30.28 % / 29.35 %	141	B	41.28 % / 29.36 %
86	B	41.28 % / 24.78 %	100	A	31.19 % / 25.69 %	114	B	40.37 % / 29.35 %	128	A	32.11 % / 28.44 %	142	A	40.37 % / 29.35 %
87	B	33.94 % / 24.78 %	101	B	26.61 % / 24.77 %	115	D	39.45 % / 29.36 %	129	B	58.72 % / 28.44 %	143	B	43.12 % / 29.36 %
88	D	20.18 % / 24.77 %	102	C	19.27 % / 26.6 %	116	D	23.85 % / 29.36 %	130	A	21.1 % / 28.44 %	144	D	15.6 % / 30.27 %
89	C	41.28 % / 25.69 %	103	D	42.2 % / 26.61 %	117	D	22.02 % / 29.36 %	131	B	50.46 % / 28.44 %	145	A	49.54 % / 32.11 %
90	D	24.77 % / 25.69 %	104	C	37.61 % / 26.61 %	118	B	41.28 % / 29.36 %	132	C	12.84 % / 28.44 %	146	C	34.86 % / 30.28 %
91	D	22.02 % / 25.69 %	105	B	60.55 % / 26.61 %	119	C	32.11 % / 29.36 %	133	A	24.77 % / 28.44 %	147	D	11.93 % / 31.19 %
92	B	58.72 % / 25.68 %	106	C	29.36 % / 27.52 %	120	A	45.87 % / 29.36 %	134	A	21.1 % / 28.44 %	148	B	29.36 % / 30.27 %
93	B	45.87 % / 26.61 %	107	A	26.61 % / 28.44 %	121	A	53.21 % / 28.44 %	135	B	49.54 % / 28.44 %	149	A	33.03 % / 31.19 %
94	C	40.37 % / 25.69 %	108	B	47.71 % / 28.44 %	122	C	30.28 % / 28.44 %	136	A	25.69 % / 28.44 %	150	A	50.46 % / 31.19 %

//Hints and Solutions//

1. Yellow journalism refers to the sensationalism and exaggeration to attract readers/viewers. It is the type of journalism that does not report complete real news, instead of that, it exaggerates the real issue. Hence, option B is correct.

2. In the classroom, the teacher sends the messages either as words or images. The students are decoders. Hence, option B is correct.

3. Media is also known as the fourth estate. Fourth estate refers to the press and news media. Hence, option D is correct.

4. Mass communication is the communication mode in which a single source is transmitting information to the large number of students. E.g. Teacher is the transmitter and students are the receivers. Hence, option B is correct.

5. A smart classroom is a teaching space which has smart portion with a touch panel control laptop, it also has laptop connection and DVD player with camera and specialized software. A smart classroom is installed with projector and screen too. Hence, option D is correct.

6. Digital empowerment includes digital literacy, universal access to all digital resources. It also gives digital platform for participative governance and provides probability of all entitlements for individuals through cloud. Hence, option D is correct.

7. In other terms to say, the number is divided by 2 successively to get the next result.

4/2 = 2

2/2 = 1

1/2 = 1/2

(1/2)/2 = 1/4

(1/4)/2 = 1/8 and so on.

8. In this series, each number is repeated, then 13 is subtracted to arrive at the next number.Hence, option B is correct.

9. Answer: D) EOJDJEFM

- There are 8 letters in the word.

- The coded word can be obtained by taking the immediately following letters of word, expect the first and the last letters of the given word but in the reverse order. That means, in the coded form the first and the last letters have been interchanged while the remaining letters are coded by taking their immediate next letters in the reverse order.

10. Answer: D) 8

Justification:

In the first and second statements, the common code digit is '4' and the common word is 'good'.

So, '4' stands for 'good'.

In the second and third statements, the common code digit is '7' and the common word is 'pictures'.

So, '7' means 'pictures'.

Thus, in the second statements, '8' means 'see'.

11. Answer: D
Explanation:

$$Z \text{ Code} \Rightarrow 26 \Rightarrow \frac{26}{2} \Rightarrow 13 \Leftrightarrow (13^3) = 2197$$

$$R \text{ Code} \Rightarrow 18 \Rightarrow \frac{18}{2} \Rightarrow 9 \Leftrightarrow (9^3) = 729$$

Similarly, $J \text{ Code} \Rightarrow 10 \Rightarrow \frac{10}{2} \Rightarrow 5 \Leftrightarrow (5^3) = 125$

12. LET THE COST BE Rs 100X

MARKED PRICE = Rs160X

SOLD -= Rs 300

160X -20 = 300

160X =320

X =2

100X =200

So profit = Rs 100

Profit % = 100/200 x 100 =50% ANSWER

13. According to the passage, a political novel often turns out to be a novel with its own politics. (Reference line in passage: A political novel often turns out be not merely a novel about politics but a novel with a politics of its own.)

14. A political novel only talks about writer's perception.

15. The constructs of politics by its nature is all about the ideas and ideologies.(Reference line in passage: Another reason why politics does not seem amenable to the highest kind of literary representation seems to arise from the fact that politics by its very nature is constituted of ideas and ideologies.)

16. Literature deals with the felt reality of human life. (Reference line in passage: Literature, it is argued, is about human experiences rather than about intellectual abstractions; it deals in what is called the 'felt reality' of human flesh and blood, and in sap and savour (rasa) rather than in arid and lifeless ideas.)

17. The observation of the novelist, Mary McCarthy reveals unseen felt ideas of today in the novel. (Reference line in passage: In an extensive discussion of the matter in her book Ideas and the Novel, the American novelist Mary McCarthy observed that 'ideas are still today felt to be unsightly in the novel' though that was not so in 'former days', i.e., in the 18th and 19th centuries.)

18. Answer: B) Encryption

Explanation:

The coding or scrambling of data so that humans cannot read them is known as encryption.

19. Answer: A) 56

If we count letters till the end of the alphabet including that letter in reverse order then

Here the values are nothing but the values corresponding to the alphabets when taken in a reverse order,i.e,A=26 ,B=25...,Z=1

G = 20 and O = 12 totaling 32

S = 8, H = 19 and E = 22 totaling 49

SOME = 8 + 12 + 14 + 22 = 56.

20. Answer: Option D

An odometer is an instrument used to measure mileage. A compass is an instrument used to determine direction. Choices a, b, and c are incorrect because none is an instrument.

21. Option C

In this simple addition series, each number increases by 0.8.

22. Option A

This is an alternating addition and subtraction series. In the first pattern, 10 is subtracted from each number to arrive at the next. In the second, 5 is added to each number to arrive at the next.

23. The Proposition 'All wise men are afraid of death' is contradicted because in the question it is mention that wise man are hardly afraid of death, here hardly means difficult. So, from this all wise man are not afraid of death, 'some' can be possible, 'no' can also be possible. Option B contradicts.

24. Answer: (2) 15 years

Solution

Let the present age of Aradhana be 3x

Let the present age of Aadrika be 4x

5 years back, Aradhana's age = (3x-5) years

5 years back, Aadrika's age = (4x-5)

According to the question, (3x-5) : (4x-5) = 2:3

$\Rightarrow$(3x-5) ÷ (4x-5) = 2/3

$\Rightarrow$3(3x-5) = 2(4x-5)

$\Rightarrow$9x-15 = 8x-10

$\Rightarrow$x = 5

Therefore, Aradhana's current age = 3×5 = 15 years

25. Action -> Feedback -> Evaluation -> Adjustment is correct sequence.

26. Let the present age of the father be $2x$

So, the present age of the daughter $= x$

According to the question,

$$\Rightarrow 2x - 20 = 10(x - 20)$$
$$\Rightarrow 2x - 20 = 10x - 200$$
$$\Rightarrow 8x = 180$$
$$\Rightarrow x = 22.5$$

Thus, the present age of father $= 22.5 \times 2 = 45$ years

27. Answer: (2) 15 days
Solution:
Total work done by Akash, Sunil and Rakesh in 1 day $=$
$$\{(1/20) + (1/30) + (1/60)\} = 1/10$$
Work done along by Akash in 2 days $= (1/20) \times 2 =$

$1/10$
Work Done in 3 days
$(1 \text{ day of all three together } + 2$
$\text{ days of Akash's work}) = (1/10) + (1/10) = 1/5$
So, work done in 3 days $= 1/5$
Time taken to complete the work $= 5 \times 3 = 15$ days

28. Answer: (3) 16 days

Solution:

Let the days taken by Arun to complete the work be x

The ratio of time taken by Arun and Dev = 125:100 = 5:4

5:4 :: 20:x

$\Rightarrow$ x = {(4×20) / 5}

$\Rightarrow$ x = 16

29. On checking option A;

16 + 31 − 3 × 93 ÷ 11 = 966

After changing the sign:

16 - 31 + 3 × 93 ÷ 11 = 966

93 is not completely divided by 11

On checking option B;

16 + 31 − 3 × 93 ÷ 11 = 966

After changing the sign

16 + 31 ÷ 3 × 93 − 11 = 966

16 + 31 × 31 − 11 = 966

16 + 961 − 11 = 966

961 + 5 = 966

966 = 966

No need to check other options.

Hence, the correct option is (B).

30. Answer: B

Each letter in the word NOIDA is moved one step forward to form the code OPJEB. So, in DELHI, D will be coded as E, E as F, L as M, H as I, I as J. Thus, the code becomes EFMIJ.

31. Answer: A

The narrator has no brother, so he is the only son of his father, and his father's son is he himself. Hence, the narrator is the father of the man in the photograph, so the man in the photograph is his son.

32. Answer: (4) 60; {26+35-1 = 61-1 = 60}

33. MOOC stands for Massive Open Online Course. It is an online course that aims at unlimited participation and access through internet or web. It helps to reach to the students who are in remote areas.

34. 25 / 2 = 12 with 1 remainder

12 / 2 = 6 with 0 remainder

6 / 2 = 3 with 0 remainder

3 / 2 = 1 with 1 remainder

1 / 2 = 0 with 1 remainder

Then, when we put the remainders together in reverse order, we get the answer. The decimal number 25 converted to binary is therefore: 11001

35. In summary, the most common video file types are:

WEBM.

MPG, . MP2, . MPEG, . MPE, . MPV.

OGG.

MP4, . M4P, . M4V.

AVI, . WMV.

MOV, . QT.

FLV, . SWF.

AVCHD. hence, option C is correct.

36. Worldwide, agriculture accounts for around 67% of all water consumption, compared to 23% for industry and 10% for domestic use.

37. Pesticides are defined as the substance or mixture of substances used to prevent, destroy, repel, attract, sterilise, mitigate any insects. Generally pesticides are used in three sectors viz. agriculture, public health and consumer use. Hence, option D is correct.

38. China: 10,641,789 kt
USA: 5,172,338 kt India: 2,454,968 kt Russia: 1,760,895 kt China > U.S.A > India > Russia

39. World Health Day: 7th April
World Population Day: 11th July World Ozone Day: 16th September World AIDS Day: 1st December

40. Cyclone 'hudhud' hits coast of Andhra Pradesh. Hence, option A is correct.

41. Renewable resources include biomass energy (such as ethanol), hydropower, geothermal power, wind energy, and solar energy. Biomass refers to organic material from plants or animals. This includes wood, sewage, and ethanol (which comes from corn or other plants). Hence, option D is correct.

42. Uttar Pradesh tops the list with 10 fake universities. Hence, option B is correct.

43. Answer: C) 3, 5, 1, 4, 2

The correct order is :

Arrival Introduction Presentation Discussion Recommendation

44. Odd days in 1600 years = 0

Odd days in 300 years = 1

46 years = (35 ordinary years + 11 leap years) = (35 x 1 + 11 x 2)= 57 (8 weeks + 1 day) = 1 odd day

Jan. Feb. Mar. Apr. May. Jun. Jul. Aug

(31 + 28 + 31 + 30 + 31 + 30 + 31 + 15) = 227 days = (32 weeks + 3 days) = 3 odd days.

Total number of odd days = (0 + 1 + 1 + 3) = 5 odd days.

Hence, as the number of odd days = 5 , given day is Friday.

45. Answer: B) 2700

Total number of votes = 7500

Given that 20% of Percentage votes were invalid

 => Valid votes = 80%

 Total valid votes = 7500*(80/100)

1st candidate got 55% of the total valid votes.

Hence the 2nd candidate should have got 45% of the total valid votes

=> Valid votes that 2nd candidate got = total valid votes x (45/100)

7500*(80/100)*(45/100) = 2700

46. The maximum gap is 6 months between 2 parliament sessions. Parliament has 3 sessions: Budget, Monsoon session, winter session.

47. According to Supreme Court privacy is a fundamental right as it is intrinsic to the right to life.Right to Privacy is an integral part of Right to Life and Personal Liberty guaranteed in Article 21 of the Constitution. Hence, option B is correct.

48. The National University of Educational Planning and Administration (NUEPA) is a premier organization dealing with capacity building and research in planning and management of education in India as well as in South Asia also.

49. "Education is the manifestation of perfection already in man" –this is the very famous quotation by Swami Vivekanand. Hence, option C is correct.

50. The article is about the levels of teaching. We have three levels of teaching that are

1. memory level of teaching

2. understanding level

3. reflective level. Hence, option D is correct.

51. There are different phases in the Operations Research Project. They are:

Judgment phase

Research phase

Action phase

Above these are the correct sequences. So, option B is correct.

52. In economics, complementary inputs are inputs to production that a firm uses closely together.

The economic effect of their complementary nature is that when the price of one of the inputs increases, then the firm will use both inputs less even at constant output. So, option B is correct.

53. The Graphical method can be used to solve an LPP with two decision variables. So, Option B is correct.

54. Utilitarianism is a theory of morality which advocates actions that foster happiness and opposes actions that cause unhappiness. Utilitarianism promotes the greatest amount of good for the greatest number of people.

Hence, the correct option is (B).

55. EOQ is abbreviation of Economic Order Quantity and formulae to find EOQ is $EOQ = \sqrt{2DK/h}$

Whereas $D =$ annual demand Quantity

$K =$ Fixed cost and $h =$ holding cost

Here, $EOQ = 4000$ unit and we have to find EOQ for the next year. In the next year, only demand for quantity is doubled everything else remained constant.

Thus, putting values in a formula we have given two equations.

$$4000 = \sqrt{d}$$
$$x = \sqrt{2d}$$
$$= 1.414 \times 4000$$
$$= 5656,$$ Option C is correct.

56. Macroeconomics deals with aggregate level of output, income and spending for all goods and services. It concerns with whole economy and its sectors and not any individual sector. Therefore, Choice A & B is not correct option as, it just focused on Industrial sectors only.

Choice D also focuses on the population and income area only. Therefore, it is also not correct answer. Macroeconomics is concerned with Inflation & growth and employment level of the economy as it is a macro aspects of economy.

57. ● There is a continuous need to improve the resources to stay in business.

● Threshold resources are inevitable because of competitors and new entrants.

● Some of the threshold resources are automobile, telecom, etc.

Thus, Option B is correct.

58. Applications of the χ^2–distribution

Chi-square distribution has a number of applications which are enumerated below:

a)   To test if the population has a specified value of the variance σ^2.

b)   Chi-square test of goodness of fit.

c)   Chi-square test for independence of attributes. So, option D is correct.

59. The world conference of the United Nations Decade for Women held at Copenhagen on July 30, 1980 focused on promoting equal opportunities and treatment of women in employment.

Thus, Option C is correct.

60. Inflation is an overall increase in price level; it is seen as devaluing the worth of money. It is not the high price but rising price level that constitutes inflation. Both A and R are correct, but R is not the right explanation of A.

Thus, Option B is correct.

61. Types of Agriculture Business:

(a) Crop production: The businesses are engaged in the production and selling of crops like fruits, vegetables, coffee, cotton, maize, tea, flowers, tobacco, etc.

(b) Livestock production: The businesses are engaged in the rearing and selling of different animals for their meat and other products like milk and skins, etc.

(c) Poultry keeping: The businesses concentrate on rearing and selling different types of birds for their meat, eggs, skins and feathers.

(d) Agricultural support businesses: Such businesses provide extension services, inputs like fertilizers, drugs, etc. Hence option C is correct.

62. ● Assertion states that the essence of every strategy is based on competition. This is not true. Some strategies may be formulated for the overall growth of the organization.

● Reason states that multinationals clash directly. This is true in every market.

Thus, Option D is correct.

63. Pichot suggested three roles for the Intrapreneur in promoting Innovation:

1) Inventor: Inventor is the person who actually develops a new idea, product or service.

2) Product champion: A product champion is a middle manager who understands the project and helps organizations to overcome resistance and convinces others to adapt to the innovation.

3) Sponsor: A sponsor is a top-level manager who supports and approves the project.

Thus, Option D is correct.

64. ● Green Positioning is a brand positioning strategy wherein the company positions itself as one that cares.

● It focuses on partnering with green organizations and getting certifications from them as well.

Thus, Option D is correct.

65. ● Office layout provides effective allocation and use of the floor space of the building.

● Group layout is suitable when a large variety of products are needed in small volumes.

● A Fixed-position layout is essential when the products are difficult to move, and it is suitable for large project jobs.

● Storage layout is used to receive inbound shipments from suppliers and outbound orders to customers.

Thus, Option B is correct.

66. ● Leniency effect- It is a rating error wherein the rater rates individuals too positively and goes too easy on them while rating.

● Halo effect- It is a type of cognitive bias where one trait of an individual is used to make an overall judgement about that person. It is the opposite of the Horn Effect, where one negative or bad trait of an individual overshadows other traits. Halo effect is considered as the positive first impression of a person

● Central tendency error-It is a rating error wherein the raters evaluate most of their employees as 'average' while applying a rating scale.

● Recency effect- It is an inaccuracy in a performance appraisal that occurs because the evaluator relies only on the most recent occurrences of the employee's behaviour.

Thus, Option B is correct.

67. ● Intrapreneurship is restorative in nature, whereas Entrepreneurship is intuitive in nature.

● An Entrepreneur bears all the risk involved in the company, whereas an Intrapreneur does not have to bear the full risk (it is borne by the company)

Thus, Option A is correct.

68. Philip Kotler introduced the Concept of social and societal marketing.

Thus, Option B is correct.

69. ● Human Resource managers are facing some challenging issues in current competitive and changing environment which includes performance management of employees carrying varied skills, employee participation in decision making and performance, human resource inflow and outflow in and from the organization, compensation systems and high commitment work systems, globalization and internationalization, rapid technological changes and improvements, new emerging concepts of management, Cross-cultural diversity of employees in the organization etc.

Thus, Option A is correct.

70. These statements are taken from the definitions of management:

● According to Koontz and O'Donnell defines planning is deciding in advance what to do, how to do, when to do, and who is to do it. Planning bridges the gap from where we are to where we want to go. It makes it possible for things to occur, which would not otherwise happen.

● According to Henry Fayol "To organise means to provide it with everything useful to its functioning raw materials, tools, capital and personnel."

Thus, Option C is correct.

71. ● In international economic integration, FDI plays an important role as FDI creates stable and long-lasting relationships between countries.

● FDI can play a strategic role in the development of enterprises as an additional source of funding.

Thus, Option B is correct.

72. There are two dimensions of every action, i.e., substantive and procedural.

● The substantive dimension deals with the determination of strategy or set of strategies.

● The procedural dimension deals with placing a strategy into operation.

Thus, Option C is correct.

73. ● Modigliani and Miller (MM) Approach to Capital Structure states that the valuation of a firm is unrelated to the capital structure of a company. Being highly leveraged or having low debt component does not in any way affect its market value.

● Assumptions of this approach are:

1) There are no taxes

2) There is no corporate dividend tax

3) The cost of borrowing is the same and not different for investors and companies.

Thus, Option A is correct.

74. Process of communication in the two-way process involves the following seven elements:

● Sender

● Encoding

● Message

● Channel

● Receiver

● Decoding

● Feedback

Thus, Option C is correct.

75. ● John Dunlop developed the systems approach to industrial relations.

● It focuses on the following aspects:

1) Environmental forces

2) Participants in the system

3) Outputs

Thus, Option B is correct.

76. The cost to buy an item should include -purchase price of the item or component, transportation cost, sales tax and octopi, procurement cost, carrying cost, receiving and incoming inspection costs. The analysis of these two costs helps take decision whether to make or buy(Marginal cost).

Hence, option A is correct.

77. According to Guthman and Dougal, Financial management is the activity concerned with planning, raising, controlling and administering funds used in the business.

Thus, Option A is correct.

78. Supply Chain management refers to the management of the flow of goods and services and involves movement and storage of raw materials, finished goods. The purpose of the supply chain is to integrate supply and demand management and improve supply chain performance.

Thus, Option D is correct.

79. Simple random sampling requires a small sample size because of its efficiency.

But nowadays, simple random sampling is rarely used. But it is the fundamental sampling scheme in the theory of sampling.

Thus, Option C is correct.

80. ● The knowledgebase contains facts, information relevant to the type of problems that are expected to be solved by the system.

● The inference engine gets facts from Knowledgebase to draw new inferences and send the new facts discovered by it to Knowledgebase.

● TMS (Truth maintenance system) is the new fact inferred by the inference engine and contradicts some of the facts already in the knowledge base.

● The closed world assumption system is another mechanism of handling incompleteness of a knowledge base.

Thus, Option D is correct.

81. ● A special fund is typically established for each of the organisation's various programs as well as it's overhead, general administrative, and fundraising activities.

● They are formed for the specific purpose if a revenue expense of such purpose occurs, it is debited from that separate fund instead of Profit and loss account.

Thus, Option A is correct.

82. Role-specific training is provided to managers to make them efficient in different types of roles that they have to perform from time to time. They have to act as decision-makers, planners, organisers, leaders, and controllers. For each of these roles, they need to be trained.

Thus, Option D is correct.

83. ● For a mutually exhaustive event, P(AUB)=P(A)+(B)

● That means it includes all the possibilities associated with the same trial.

Thus, Option C is correct.

84. ● The open area refers to the information which is known to self and others.

● The hidden area refers to the information which is known to self and is hidden from others.

● The blind area refers to the information which is known to others but not known to self.

● The unknown area consists of information that is not known to self and others.

Thus, Option C is correct.

85. ● Greenfield FDI means investment in order to start a business from scratch.

● Renuka Sugars Ltd setting up a sugar facility in Cuba is an example of Greenfield investment.

● H&M, a famous apparel brand from Sweden entered India via FDI under single-brand retail.

Thus, Option D is correct.

86. Performance is a method of evaluating the behavior of employees in the workplace, evaluating the quantitative and qualitative aspects of job performance in terms of output. The evaluator or appraiser can be Supervisor, peers, subordinates, self-appraisal, HR consultants, users of service.

Thus, Option B is correct.

87. ● External source: Input data required for a strategic information system is obtained from external sources.

● Adhocness: Produced is either periodic information such as balance sheet, income and expenditure statement. It simply contains random information developed on cases to case basis.

● Subjectiveness: Input data used for this is mostly subjective in nature

● Unexpectedness: The system may provide unexpected information

Thus, Option B is correct.

88. Cluster formation rural entrepreneurship is a formal and non-formal group of people in order to achieve a common objective. It includes Non-governmental organizations(NGOs), Voluntary Organizations(VOs), Self-help Groups(SHGs) and networking of all of these.

Thus, Option D is correct.

89.

● Job is a group of position involving the same duties, skills, knowledge and responsibilities.

● The nature, conditions of work, skill, knowledge and some basic qualifications through the job analyst has selected a person for doing work in his organisation is called job.

● In job duties and responsibilities are given selected person in organisation.

90. Cost of goods sold = Opening stock + Purchases – Closing stock

In the given question,

COGS=10,000+70,000-11,000

= 69,000

Profit 30% on cost = 69,000*30% = 20,700

Sales= COGS + Profit

= 69,000 + 20,700

= 89,700.

Thus, Option D is correct.

91. Accepting sampling plans are given by wadge and poring.

Thus, Option D is correct.

92. Theory of marginal productivity of distribution, is based on the law of decreasing returns, in which factors are determined on the basis of marginal product of factors of production, So diminishing law of returns leads to decline in the marginal productivity of variable input.

Thus, Option B is correct.

93. • Employee engagement refers to the enthusiasm of the employees for their work. It occurs when the attitude of the employees is positive towards their job.

• Employee engagement rate is affected not only by the wage rate but also by the other factors such as the nature of work, working environment, opportunities for career growth, etc.

• The reason did not explain the assertion completely.

Thus, Option B is correct.

94. Niche marketing is also called Concentrated Segmentation and is used by companies with highly specific goods to customers with certain similar characteristics.

Thus, Option C is correct.

95. Pull factors is a category of women entrepreneurs that involves women who are educated and take the risk of establishing an Enterprise with or without experience, with the help of financial institutions and commercial banks.

Thus, Option D is correct.

96. The highest peak of the histogram represents the location of the mode of the data set. The mode is the data value that occurs most often in a data set. For a symmetric histogram, the values of the mean, median, and mode are all the same and are all located at the center of the distribution.

Thus, Option C is correct.

97. The aspects of the Zinger model are as follows:

1) Connect

2) Authentic

3) Recognition

4) Engage

5) Esteem Organization

6) Fater community

7) Serve customers

8) Develop career

9) Leverage energies

10) Experience well being

11) Craft strategies

12) Enliven roles

13) Maximize performance

14) Achieve results

Thus, Option D is correct.

98. Intrapreneur is an entrepreneurial person employed by a corporation anti encouraged to be innovative and creative'. Hence, option C is correct.

99. The quantitative approach using quantitative techniques in Management is called Quantitative Approach. The quantitative approach applies statistics, optimization models, information models, computer simulations, and other quantitative techniques to the management process.
Central to the quantitative approach is the principle that organizations are decision-making units. These decision-making units can be made more efficiently using mathematical models that place relevant factors into numerical terms.

The primary branches of quantitative management include:

- Management Science
- Operations Management
- Management Information Systems
- Total Quality Management

Hence, the correct option is (C).

100. • First-mover advantages can help a firm dominate global trade in that product.

• Porter's diamond of competitive advantage includes factor conditions, demand conditions, relating and supporting industries and firm structure, strategy and rivalry.

Thus, Option A is correct.

101. • The actual performance will be less than the potential performance because of social loafing.

• Social loafing starts when the workers think that their contributions are not important.

• It also starts when their individual performances are not readily monitorable.

• The size of the groups is kept small to reduce social loafing.

• The reason is correct but did not explain the assertion.

Thus, Option B is correct.

102. N.Q.Herrick and M.Maccoby stated four basic principles that will humanize work and improve the Quality of Work Life. They are as follows:

1. The Principle of Security

2. The Principle of Equity

3. The Principle of individualism

4. The Principle of Democracy

Thus, Option C is correct.

103. Objectives of financial management include:

1. To see that funds are utilized in the best possible way at the least cost.

2. To ensure a regular and adequate supply of funds to the enterprise.

3. To plan a sound and fair capital structure.

4. To make sure that funds are invested in safe ventures.

5. To ensure adequate returns to the shareholders.

Thus, Option D is correct.

104.

- A debt security without any explicit interest rate is called Zero-coupon bonds

- Income bond is a type of debt security in which issuer is required to pay interest only when they earned interest otherwise they just have to pay face value of the bond. Thus, company experiences less financial distress in case of issuing income bonds.

- A type of bond in which coupon rate quoted as mark-up on the given rate is called Floating rate bonds. Hence, option C is correct.

105. ● Payoff: It is effectiveness associated with a specified combination of action.

● Opportunity loss: Opportunity loss is incurred due to the failure of not adopting the most favourable course of action or strategy.

● Courses of action: Courses of action, sometimes called actions or decision alternatives.

Thus, Option B is correct.

106. The OCTAPACE climate is essential for organizational development. The variables under OCTAPACE are as follows:

● Openness

● Confrontation

● Trust

● Authenticity

● Pro-action

● Autonomy

● Collaboration

● Experimentation

Thus, Option C is correct.

107. When a firm maximises the stockholder's wealth, the individual stockholder can use this wealth to maximise his individual utility. It means by maximising stockholder's wealth the

firm is operating consistently towards maximising stockholder's utility.

Thus, Option A is correct.

108. As per Traditional Approach to Capital Structure there should be a right combination of debt and equity in the capital structure and debt should exist only upto a certain point beyond which an increase in leverage would lead to a reduction on the value of the firm.

Thus, Option B is correct.

109. ● Documentation as per the requirement of importing country are as follows:

1) Customs invoice

2) GSP certificate of origin

● Documentation as per the requirements of the contract are as follows:

1) Commercial invoice

2) Packing list

3) Bill of exchange

4) Certificate of origin

5) Inspection certificate

6) Insurance certificate

Thus, Option B is correct.

110. Individual evaluation techniques include all of the above except ranking method as it is a multivariate technique.

Thus, Option D is correct.

111. Determining whether the solution suggested by the software development team is acceptable is one of the tasks performed under Operational feasibility study.

Thus, Option B is correct.

112. Business plans can help perform a number of tasks for those who write and read them. They're used by investment-seeking entrepreneurs to convey their vision to potential investors. They may also be used by firms that are trying to attract key employees, prospect for new business, deal with suppliers or simply to understand how to manage their companies better. A formal document of what the entrepreneur intends to do to sell enough of the firm's product or service to make a satisfactory profit. Hence, option C is correct.

113. Market Feasibility is one of the important parts of the Feasibility Study. It helps to deal with issues such as business expansion, product development, and starting up a business.

Thus, Option C is correct.

114. The definition of the strategy includes the following:

● Determination of long term goals and objectives

● Adoption of courses of action

● Allocation of resources

Thus, Option B is correct.

115. The number of subordinates a superior can effectively handle is called Spam of control. Hence, option D is correct.

116. ● Product Innovation is defined as the development of new products, changes in product design etc. It includes technological advancement, changes in customer requirements.

● Process Innovation refers to the implementation of a new or improved production or delivery method.

Thus, Option D is correct.

117. When MRTS between two factors remain constant, and output can be produced by substituting factors of production on all the points of the curve, iso-quant takes the shape of linear isoquant.

• When there is zero substitutability isoquant is L shaped.

• When there is limited substitutability, isoquant is Kinked.

• When there is continuous substitutability, isoquant is convex to the origin.

Thus, Option D is correct.

118. ● Emotions play an important role in our life. Both encoding and decoding are influenced by emotions.

● Semantic barriers occur in the following ways:

1) The sender and receiver understand the same message in a different manner.

2) Fault translation.

3) Poor expression and transmission of meaning in communication.

Thus, Option B is correct.

119. ● Central Tendency error is the tendency of a rater to assign some central value to the employee's performance as they may be reluctant to rate them as very high or very low.

● This could be in the cases where they do not want to be disliked by the employee by giving a harsh rating or when they are unfamiliar with some of the subordinates to give a clear rating on their performance.

Thus, Option C is correct.

120. ● Assertion states about the new entrants in the market.

● Reason explains how the new entrants may increase competitive pressure. It explains the assertion.

Thus, Option A is correct.

121. ● The organization can identify the buying patterns of the customers and segment the customers accordingly.

● The customer segmentation will help the organization to implement different strategies for different segments of the customers.

● This will remove the ambiguity in the marketing plan.

Thus, Option A is correct.

122. Marketing effectiveness is the measure of how effective a given marketer's go to market strategy is toward meeting the goal of maximizing their spending to achieve positive results in both the short- and long-term. It is also related to marketing ROI and return on marketing investment (ROMI). A marketing effectiveness review is part of Strategic control. Hence, option C is correct.

123. ● Assertion states about the talent reservoir and the role of the supervisor in building it.

● Reason states that the initial inputs will be given by the top-level management, but it is not true. The initial inputs will be given by the supervisors or managers.

Thus, Option C is correct.

124. Strategies formulated to convert a sick unit to healthy are referred to as turnaround. Hence, option A is correct.

125.

- When group of employees of an organization meet regularly for solving their problems and improving production is called quality circle.

- Strategy is a method or plans used to achieve future goals whereas outsourcing means task or work getting done through outsiders. None of it is matched with the question.

- Bench marking is a process of measuring or identifying and applying best practices to improve specific task. Bench marking gives correct answer to the question.

126. An emerging market economy is the economy of a developing nation that is becoming more engaged with global markets as it grows. Countries classified as emerging market economies are those with some, but not all, of the characteristics of a developed market. Hence, option B is correct.

127.

- Elwood S. Buffa and Rakesh K. Sarin have given a theory of Production and operation management.

- Richard M. Cyert and James E March have given a Behavioural Theory of the Firm.

- Martin K. Starr and D. W. Miller have given a theory Inventory control, its theory and practice.

- J. M. Juran has given Quality Control Handbook theory and Hillier and Leiberman gave Introduction to operations research.

128. TVC is simply the sum of marginal costs as MC is an addition to the total variable cost when an additional unit is produced. Thus, under the assumption of the smooth marginal cost curve, total variable cost (TVC) is equal to the area under the marginal cost curve.

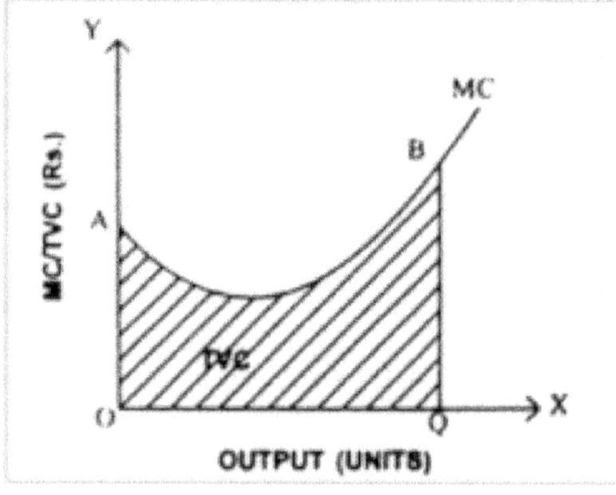

Thus, Option A is correct.

129. Grapevine communication is an informal communication because it is an unauthenticated, person to person communication protocol taking place within the organisation in the form of whispering. Hence, option B is correct.

130.

- Price expectation elasticity refers to the expected changes in future price as a result of the change in the current price. It is important in case of costly and highly valuable goods.

  Thus, Option A is correct.

131. Hyperinflation is a situation when the whole economy faces a very high and accelerating rate of inflation, in which rate of inflation runs into millions and trillions in a short period of time. This causes people to minimize their holding in that currency as they switch to more stable currency.

Thus, Option B is correct.

132. The Economic Order Quantity (EOQ) is calculated as the product mix width. Economic order quantity is one of the techniques of inventory control which minimizes total holding and ordering costs for the year. Hence, option C is correct.

133. The five different schemes, i.e. Focus Product Scheme, Market Linked Focus Product Scheme, Focus Market Scheme, Agri. Infrastructure Incentive Scrip and Product Scheme for rewarding merchandise exports now have been merged into a single scheme known as Merchandise Export from India Scheme (MEIS).

Thus, Option A is correct.

134. • The CSR pyramid with four components was published by Carroll in 1979.

• The four components are in order of rank- Economic, Legal, Ethical and Philanthropic.

• Carroll stated that CSR is the behaviour of firms that is economically sustainable, follows the law, is ethical and caters to social responsibility and charity.

Thus, Option A is correct.

135. The father of administrative management is considered to be Henri Fayol (1841-1925), a Frenchman who worked for a coal-mining company. Hence, option B is correct.

136. • MIGA (Multilateral Investment Guarantee Agency) established in 1988 is a part of the world bank group.

• Its objective is to provide guarantees in the form of political risk insurance and credit enhancement to investors and lenders for the promotion of cross-border investment.

Thus, Option A is correct.

137. Product line deletion or pruning involves removing a product from the product line, and it is necessary to be done if a product becomes unprofitable in order to not waste a firm's money or resources.

Thus, Option A is correct.

138. • Section 3 of the Industrial disputes act, 1947 deals with the Works Committees.

• Works committees are formed in an establishment in which one hundred or more workmen are employed or have been employed on any day in the preceding twelve months.

Thus, Option A is correct.

139. Restoration concept of Intrapreneurship states that an Entrepreneur adds value to an existing organization by improving the products, services or methods.

Thus, Option C is correct.

140. Hierarchy of needs theory was proposed by Abraham Maslow in his 1943 paper 'A Theory of Human Motivation'.

Thus, Option A is correct.

141. A Flexible Budget is a budget which adjusts itself or changes with the change in the level of activity. It shows the expected results for different activity levels. Flexible Budget can be adopted in case of a labour-intensive industry wherein the production of the company rests on or is dependent upon the availability of labour.

Thus, Option B is correct.

142. • The distributive bargaining is also known as win-lose agreement.

• The settlement gets resolved within the settlement range as it indicates the resistance points of both the employee and employer.

Thus, Option A is correct.

143. Benefits provided for temporary and permanent disability disfigurement, medical expenses and medical rehabilitation is referred to as Workers' compensation. Hence, option B is correct.

144. Price is the value that is put to a product or service and is the result of a complex set of calculations, research and understanding and risk taking ability. A pricing strategy takes into account segments, ability to pay, market conditions, competitor actions, trade margins and input costs, amongst others. It is targeted at the defined customers and against competitors. Hence, option D is correct.

145. Most people want to avoid conflict and potentially stressful situations – this is human nature.

People often find it easier to avoid communicating something that they think is going to be controversial or bad, putting off the communication and letting the situation fester. Hence, option A is correct.

146. Capital investment analysis is a budgeting procedure that companies and government agencies use to assess the potential profitability of a long-term investment. Capital investment analysis assesses long-term investments, which might include fixed assets like equipment, machinery or real estate. The goal of this process is to identify the option that can yield the highest return on invested capital. Businesses may use techniques such as net present value (NPV) analysis, discounted cash flow (DCF) analysis, risk-return analysis and risk-neutral valuation in a capital investment analysis. Hence, option C is correct.

147. The capital markets are a source of financing for companies around the world. The most famous of the capital markets are the stock market and bond market.

Investors want investment options that manage liquidity and risks while offering substantial returns. Debentures are long-term financial instruments issued by a company for specified tenure with a promise to pay fixed interest to the investor. Hence, option D is correct.

148. One of the adverse trends observable in the corporate private sector of India is the growing incidence of sickness. It is causing considerable concern to planners and policymakers. It is also putting a severe strain on the economic system, particularly on the banks.

There are various criteria of sickness. According to the criteria accepted by the Reserve Bank of India "a sick unit is one which has reported cash loss for the year of its operation and in the judgment of the financing bank is likely to incur cash loss for the current year as also in the following year."

A major symptom of sickness is a steady fall in debt-equity ratio and an imbalance in the financial position of the unit. Simply put, a sick unit is one which is unable to support itself through the operation of internal resources (that is, earnings plough-back). As a general rule, the sick units continue to operate below the break-even point (at which total revenue = total cost) and are, thus, forced to depend on external sources for funds of their long-term survival.

Industrial sickness creates various socio-economic problems. When an industrial unit falls sick those who depend on it have to face an uncertain future. They fear loss of jobs. Even if they do not lose jobs they do not get their wages and compensation in time and are, thus, forced to live in extreme hardship. Hence, option B is correct.

149. This study examined the innovation that leads to a competitive advantage in the frozen food business in the context of small-sized and medium-sized enterprises (SMEs). The research process consisted of three parts: 1) a literature study; 2) an empirical research study using questionnaires as a data collection tool; and 3) an analysis and conclusion of the research results using exploratory factor analysis (EFA), confirmatory factor analysis (CFA), and structural equation modelling (SEM). The findings showed that innovation enhanced the advantages in competition via external factors. These external factors were divided into two groups: micro-oriented factors and macro-oriented factors. The external factors at the micro level had more influence on the innovation development of the frozen food businesses than those at the macro level. The results showed that entrepreneurs, especially SME entrepreneurs, need to adapt and readily prepare themselves to face upcoming economic changes, which are about to occur not only at the global level but also at the regional and the country levels. In addition to the internal contexts within the organization, external factors are also important, especially those that will lead to the development of innovation. Innovation will become the strategic tool in this important competition for the improvement, creation, and enhancement of business to create competitive advantages equal to or better than those in foreign countries in order to realize sustainable development. Hence, option A is correct.

150. Management accounting systems often focus on products, departments, or geographic regions, but not on customers. As a result, companies are often unable to produce reliable per-customer profitability figures, which leads to keeping unprofitable customers, decreasing company's potential to make profits.

The "why?" of Customer Profitability Analysis can be reduced to the simple statement that each dollar of revenue does not contribute equally to profit. Differences in customer profitability can arise from either differences in revenues and/or differences in costs. In other words, customer profitability depends not only on the revenue resulting from sold units of a product or service, but also on the 'back end' services provided, including marketing, distribution, and customer service. Hence, option A is correct.

Mock Test 03

Paper-I

Q.1 Which of the following is the highest level of cognitive ability?

A. Knowing
B. Understanding
C. Analysing
D. Evaluating

Q.2 Which of the following factors does not impact teaching?

A. Teacher's knowledge
B. Class room activities that encourage learning
C. Socio-economic background of teachers and students
D. Learning through experience

Q.3 Which of the following statements about teaching aids are correct?
1) They help in retaining concepts for longer duration.
2) They help students learn better.
3) They make teaching learning process interesting.
4) They enhance rote learning.
Select the correct answer from the codes given below:

A. 1, 2, 3 and 4
B. 1, 2 and 3
C. 2, 3 and 4
D. 1, 2 and 4

Q.4 Techniques used by a teacher to teach include:
1) Lecture
2) Interactive lecture
3) Group work
4) Self study
Select the correct answer from the codes given below:

A. 1, 2 and 3
B. 1, 2, 3 and 4
C. 2, 3 and 4
D. 1, 2 and 4

Q.5 Achievement tests are commonly used for the purpose of:

A. Making selections for a specific job
B. Selecting candidates for a course
C. Identifying strengths and weaknesses of learners
D. Assessing the amount of learning after teaching

Q.6 A good teacher is one who:

A. gives useful information
B. explains concepts and principles
C. gives printed notes to students
D. inspires students to learn

Q.7 Which of the following statements regarding the meaning of research are correct?
1) Research refers to a series of systematic activity or activities undertaken to find out the solution of a problem.
2) It is a systematic, reasoned and pious process in which hypothesis testing, data analysis, theories can be interpreted and formulated.
3) It is an intellectual enquiry or quest towards truth.
4) It leads to enhancement of knowledge.
Select the correct answer from the codes given below:

A. 1, 2 and 3
B. 2, 3 and 4
C. 1, 3 and 4
D. 1, 2, 3 and 4

Q.8 A good thesis writing should involve:
1) reduction of punctuation and grammatical errors to a minimum.
2) careful checking of references.
3) consistency in the way the thesis is written.
4) a clear and well written abstract.
Select the correct answer from the codes given below:

A. 1, 2, 3 and 4
B. 1, 2 and 3
C. 1, 2 and 4
D. 2, 3 and 4

Q.9 Jean Piaget gave a theory of cognitive development of humans on the basis of his:

A. Fundamental Research
B. Applied Research
C. Action Research
D. Evaluation Research

Q.10 "Male and female students perform equally well in a numerical aptitude test." This statement indicates a:

A. research hypothesis
B. null hypothesis
C. directional hypothesis
D. statistical hypothesis

Q.11 The conclusions/findings of which type of research cannot be generalized to other situations?

A. Historical Research
B. Descriptive Research
C. Experimental Research
D. Causal Comparative Research

Q.12 Which of the following steps are required to design a questionnaire?
1) Writing primary and secondary aims of the study.
2) Review of the current literature.
3) Prepare a draft of questionnaire.
4) Revision of the draft.
Select the correct answer from the codes given below:

A. 1, 2 and 3
B. 1, 3 and 4
C. 2, 3 and 4
D. 1, 2, 3 and 4

Ques (13-18):Read the following passage carefully and answer questions.

Story telling is not in our genes. Neither it is an evolutionary history. It is the essence of what makes us Human.

Human being progress by telling stories. One event can result in a great variety of stories being told about it. Sometimes those stories differ greatly. Which stories are picked up and repeated and which ones are dropped and forgotten often determines how we progress. Our history, knowledge and

"

understanding are all the collections of few stories that survive. This includes the stories that we tell each other about the future. And how the future will turn out depends partly, possibly largely, on which stories we collectively choose to believe.

Some stories are designed to spread fear and concern. This is because some story-tellers feel that there is a need to raise some tensions. Some stories are frightening, they are like totemic warnings : "Fail to act now and we are all doomed." Then there are stories that indicate that all will be fine so long as we heave everything upto a few especially able adults. Currently, this trend is being led by those who call themselves "rational optimists". They tend to claim that it is human nature to compete and to succeed and also to profit at the expense of others. The rational optimists however, do not realize how humanity has progressed overtime through amiable social networks and how large groups works in less selfishness and in the process accommodate rich and poor, high and low alike. This aspect in story-telling is considered by the 'Practical Possibles', who sit between those who say all is fine and cheerful and be individualistic in your approach to a successful future, and those who ordain pessimism and fear that we are doomed.

Q.13 What the future holds for us is which stories we hold on to and how we act on them.

Out knowledge is a collection of:

A. all stories that we have heard during our life-time

B. some stories that we remember

C. a few stories that survive

D. some important stories

Q.14 What the future holds for us is which stories we hold on to and how we act on them.

Story telling is:

A. an art

B. a science

C. in our genes

D. the essence of what makes us human

Q.15 What the future holds for us is which stories we hold on to and how we act on them.

How the future will turn out to be, depends upon the stories?

A. We collectively choose to believe in

B. Which are repeatedly narrated

C. Designed to spread fear and tension

D. Designed to make prophecy

Q.16 What the future holds for us is which stories we hold on to and how we act on them.

Rational optimists:

1) Look for opportunities.

2) Are sensible and cheerful.

3) Are selfishly driven

Identify the correct answer from the codes given below:

A. 1, 2 and 3   **B.** 1 only

C. 1 and 2 only   **D.** 2 and 3 only

Q.17 What the future holds for us is which stories we hold on to and how we act on them.

Humans become less selfish when:

A. they work in large groups

B. they listen to frightening stories

C. they listen to cheerful stories

D. they work in solitude

Q.18 What the future holds for us is which stories we hold on to and how we act on them.

'Practical Possibles' are the ones who:

A. follow Midway Path

B. are doom-mongers

C. are self-centred

D. are cheerful and carefree

Q.19 Effectiveness of communication can be traced from which of the following?

1) Attitude surveys

2) Performance records

3) Students attendance

4) Selection of communication channel

Select the correct answer from the codes given below:

A. 1, 2, 3 and 4   **B.** 1, 2 and 3

C. 2, 3 and 4   **D.** 1, 2 and 4

Q.20 Read the assertion and reason both carefully:-

Assertion (A) : Formal communication tends to be fast and flexible.

Reason (R) : Formal communication is a systematic and orderly flow of information.

A. Both (A) and (R) are correct and (R) is correct explanation of (A)

B. Both (A) and (R) are correct, but (R) is not correct explanation of (A)

C. (A) is correct but, (R) is false

D. (A) is false but, (R) is correct

Q.21 Which of the following are the characteristic features of communication?

1) Communication involves exchange of ideas, facts and opinions.

2) Communication involves both information and understanding.

3) Communication is a continuous process.

4) Communication is a circular process.

Select the correct answer from the codes given below:

A. 1, 2 and 3   **B.** 1, 2 and 4

C. 2, 3 and 4   **D.** 1, 2, 3 and 4

Q.22 The term 'grapevine' is also known as:

A. Downward communication

B. Informal communication

C. Upward communication

D. Horizontal communication

Q.23 Which of the following is not a principle of effective communication?

A. Persuasive and convincing dialogue
B. Participation of the audience
C. One-way transfer of information
D. Strategic use of grapevine

Q.24 In communication, the language is:
A. The verbal code
B. Intrapersonal
C. The symbolic code
D. The non-verbal code

Q.25 The next term in the series is:
2, 5, 9, 19, 37, ?
A. 73   **B.** 75   **C.** 78   **D.** 80

Q.26 In certain code MATHURA is coded as JXQEROX. The code of HOTELS will be:
A. LEQIBP   **B.** ELQBIP   **C.** LEBIQP   **D.** ELIPQB

Q.27 An exam was conducted in a state with over 222 centres. The average number of applicants per centre was found to be 1560. However, it was later realized that in one centre, the number of applicants was counted as 1857 instead of 1747. What was the correct average number of applicants per centre (up to two decimals)?
A. 1557.87   **B.** 1558.20   **C.** 1558.92   **D.** 1559.51

Q.28 A girl introduced a boy as the son of the daughter of the father of her uncle. The boy is related to girl as:
A. Brother   **B.** Uncle
C. NephewSon   **D.** Son

Q.29 In an examination 10,000 students appeared. The result revealed the number of students who have:
Passed in all five subjects = 5583
Passed in three subjects only = 1400
Passed in two subjects only = 1200
Passed in one subject only = 735
Failed in English only = 75
Failed in Physics only = 145
Failed in Chemistry only = 140
Failed in Mathematics only = 200
Failed in Bio-science only = 157
The number of students passed in at least four subjects is:
A. 6300   **B.** 6900   **C.** 7300   **D.** 7900

Q.30 At present a person is 4 time older than his son and is 3 years older than his wife. After 3 years the age of the son will be 15 years. The age of the person's wife after 5 years will be:
A. 42   **B.** 48   **C.** 45   **D.** 50

Q.31 If we want to seek new knowledge of facts about the world, we must rely on reason of the type:
A. Inductive   **B.** Deductive
C. Demonstrative   **D.** Physiological

Q.32 A deductive argument is invalid if:
A. Its premises and conclusions are all false

B. Its premises are true its conclusion is false
C. Its premises are false but its conclusion is true
D. Its premises and conclusions are all true

Q.33 Inductive reasoning is grounded on:
A. Integrity of nature
B. Unity of nature
C. Uniformity of nature
D. Harmony of nature

Q.34 Among the following statements two are contradictory to each other. Select the correct code that represents them:
Statements:
1) All poets are philosophers
2) Some poets are philosophers.
3) Some poets are not philosophers.
4) No philosopher is a poet.
Codes:
A. 1 and 2   **B.** 1 and 4   **C.** 1 and 3   **D.** 2 and 3

Q.35 Which of the codes given below contains only the correct statements? Select the code:
Statements:
1) Venn diagram represents the arguments graphically.
2) Venn diagram can enhance our understanding.
3) Venn diagram may be called valid or invalid.
4) Venn diagram is clear method of notation.
Codes:
A. 1, 2 and 3   **B.** 1, 2 and 4
C. 2, 3 and 4   **D.** 1, 3 and 4

Q.36 When the purpose of a definition is to explain the use or to eliminate ambiguity the definition is called:
A. Stipulative   **B.** Theoretical
C. Lexical   **D.** Persuasive

Q.37 What is the full form of IMF?
A. International Monetary Funds
B. Inflation Management Fund
C. Indian Management Funds
D. International Management Funds

Q.38 Which bank has the most international branches?
A. State Bank of India   **B.** Bank of India
C. Bank of Baroda   **D.** Citibank

Q.39 An accurate clock shows 7 a.m. Through how many degrees will the hour hand rotate when the clock shows 1 p.m.?
A. 280°   **B.** 180°   **C.** 150°   **D.** 170°

Q.40 How many times in a day, the hands of a clock are straight?
A. 55   **B.** 22   **C.** 44   **D.** 32

Ques (41-42):Directions : Refer to the alphanumeric series given below and answer the following questions:

A * 5 9 I N & E @ # U 1 &

Q.41 How many vowels in the above arrangement are preceded by a symbol?

A. one   **B.** two   **C.** three   **D.** four

Q.42 Which is the second element to the left of the sixth element from the right?

A. E   **B.** &   **C.** N   **D.** @

Q.43 __________ is encoding or scrambling data for transmission across a network.

A. Protection   **B.** Detection
C. Encryption   **D.** Decryption

Q.44 Which of the following is not an input device?

A. Printer   **B.** Scanner
C. Mouse   **D.** Keyboard

Q.45 Which of the following represents one billion characters?

A. Kilobyte   **B.** Megabyte
C. Gigabyte   **D.** Terabyte

Q.46 Which of the following is not open source software?

A. Internet explorer
B. Fedora Linux
C. Open office
D. Apache HTTP server

Q.47 What is the full form of IMEI?

A. International Mobile Equipment Information
B. International Mobile Equipment Identity
C. International Mobile Educational Identity
D. International Machine Equipment Identity

Q.48 Which is an instant messenger that is used for chatting?

A. Altavista   **B.** MAC
C. Microsoft Office   **D.** Google Talk

Q.49 In which of the countries per capita use of water is maximum?

A. USA   **B.** European Union
C. China   **D.** India

Q.50 India's contribution to total global carbon dioxide emissions is about:

A. ~ 3%   **B.** ~ 6%   **C.** ~ 10%   **D.** ~ 15%

Paper-II

Q.51 The formula of traffic intensity in a simple queueing model is

A. Mean service time/ mean inter-arrival time
B. Mean service rate /mean arrival rate
C. Mean service rate / mean inter-arrival time
D. Mean service time/ mean arrival rate

Q.52 Which of the following is not a type of decision in decision analysis

A. Subjective decision
B. Strategic decision
C. Administrative decision
D. Operating decision

Q.53 Which of the following brands helps to challenge various business departments for getting their complete employees' commitment?

A. Employee brand   **B.** Employer brand
C. Management brand   **D.** Organization brand

Q.54 Which of the following is generally initiated by the workers?

A. Lockout   **B.** Retrenchment
C. Strike   **D.** Layoff

Q.55 Statement I: _______ is a structured job analysis instrument to measure job characteristics and relate them to human characteristics.

Statement II: _______contains 617 "work elements" designed to yield more specific job information while still capturing work requirements for virtually all occupations.

Choose the correct option from the following:

A. Common Metric Questionnaire, Work Profiling System
B. Work Profiling System, Occupational Analysis Inventory
C. Position Analysis Questionnaire, Occupational Analysis Inventory
D. Position Analysis Questionnaire, Common Metric Questionnaire

Q.56 Statement I: UNCTAD was established in 1965.

Statement II: UNCTAD implemented the GSP.

Choose the correct option from the following:

A. Statement I is correct, Statement II is incorrect.
B. Statement I is incorrect, Statement II is correct.
C. Both Statement I and Statement II are correct.
D. Both Statement I and Statement II are incorrect.

Q.57 Which of the following trade unions is contrary to International labor law?

A. Craft Unions   **B.** Industrial Unions
C. Company unions   **D.** General Unions

Q.58 Statement I: When the degree of financial leverage (DFL) is more than 1, financial Leverage exists.

Statement II: Degree of financial leverage can never be zero or less.

Choose the correct option from those below:

A. Statement I is correct., Statement II is incorrect.
B. Statement I is incorrect, Statement II is correct.
C. Both Statement I and Statement II are correct.
D. Both Statement I and Statement II are incorrect.

Q.59 Statement I: According to Net Income Approach, with taxes, the value of the firm can be increased by decreasing the weighted average cost of capital (WACC), i.e. the overall cost of capital through higher debt proportion.

Statement II: The theory assumes that there are only two sources of finance namely, debt and equity.

Choose the correct option from those below:

A. Statement I is correct., Statement II is incorrect.

B. Statement I is incorrect, Statement II is correct.

C. Both Statement I and Statement II are correct.

D. Both Statement I and Statement II are incorrect.

Q.60 Assertion (A): Performance appraisal indicates how well an individual is fulfilling the job requirement.

Reason (R): Its objective is to evaluate current performance on the job to seek positive results for employees.

A. (A) is correct, but (R) is incorrect.

B. Both (A) and (R) are correct, but (R) is not the right explanation of (A).

C. Both (A) and (R) are correct, (R) is the right explanation of (A).

D. Both (A) and (R) are incorrect.

Q.61 Companies using ___ strategy rely on the fact that if they set the price of their product lower than the product next to theirs on the shelf then it will result in increasing sales of their product.

A. Demand based pricing

B. Cost based pricing

C. Economy pricing

D. Premium pricing

Q.62 In this kind of training, the trainee is presented with a situation where he has to demonstrate his decision-making ability as a manager in his absence. He may have to deal with several phone calls, complaints, meetings and orders that resemble the tasks performed by his manager. What is the name given to this training?

A. Role-Playing

B. In-Basket Training

C. Vestibule Training

D. Job Rotation

Q.63 Which of the following is not a characteristic of a data warehouse?

A. Subject oriented

B. Erasable data

C. Time-dependent data

D. Consolidated data

Q.64 Statement I: System approach under the modern theory of organisation state organisation as a unified system.

Statement II: Contingency approach is an extension of the system theory of organisation.

Choose the correct option from the following:

A. Statement I is correct, Statement II is incorrect.

B. Statement I is incorrect, Statement II is correct.

C. Both Statement I and Statement II are correct.

D. Both Statement I and Statement II are incorrect.

Q.65 For maintaining discipline in the class:

A. Students should be severely punished for acts of indiscipline

B. The teacher should try to make his teaching interesting

C. Non-attending students should be turned out of the class

D. Parents of the indisciplined students should be informed

Q.66 Under ___________, the actual competencies of an entrepreneur are compared with the competencies required to become a successful entrepreneur so as to ascertain the gap in the entrepreneurial competencies.

A. Competency Assessment

B. Competency Mapping

C. Competency Deficiency

D. Competency Management

Q.67 Statement I: ______ is generalizing behaviour of a person on the basis of the mental picture set in the mind of the appraiser.

Statement II: _______ is when the rater's bias is directed towards one negative quality of the ratee.

Choose the correct option among the following:

A. Leniency, Horn effect

B. central tendency, Recency effect

C. Stereotyping, Horn effect

D. Stereotyping, Halo effect

Q.68 Statement I: Greenfield Investment is when a company purchases an existing production facility to launch a new production activity.

Statement II: OLI theory is also known as transaction cost theory.

Choose the correct option from those below:

A. Statement I is correct, Statement II is incorrect.

B. Statement I is incorrect, Statement II is correct.

C. Both Statement I and Statement II are correct.

D. Both Statement I and Statement II are incorrect.

Q.69 Which of the following is not an advantage of the Time Wage System?

A. Better Quality

B. Equality of Wages

C. Less Supervision

D. Simplicity

Q.70 Assertion (A): Emotional restraint makes the communication process more effective.

Reason (R): The sender should defer the communication process for a specific period of time to avoid the negative impact of emotion.

A. Both (A) and (R) are correct, and (R) is the correct explanation of (A).

B. Both (A) and (R) are correct, but (R) is not the correct explanation of (A).

C. (A) is correct., but (R) is not correct.

D. (A) is wrong, and (R) is correct.

Q.71 Audit fees, subscriptions, insurance, postage, telephone, telegrams etc. are examples of which of the following types of Budget?

A. Administrative Expenses Budget

B. Capital Expenditure Budget

C. Research and Development Expense Budget

D. Cash Budget

Q.72 Statement I: Lack of planning or poor planning will cause the organisation to be continually drifting.

Statement II: Controlling avoids confusion and duplication of activities between departments.

Choose the correct option from the following:-

A. Statement I is correct, Statement II is incorrect.

B. Statement I is incorrect, Statement II is correct.

C. Both Statement I and Statement II are correct.

D. Both Statement I and Statement II are incorrect.

Q.73 People who adopt an innovation after the average participants have adopted it and are extremely cautious of the results before buying are referred to as ___________.

A. Late majority

B. Early adopters

C. Laggards

D. Early majority

Q.74 Which of the following is concerned with providing greater freedom, resources, authority, and responsibility to the employees to set their own goals related to their work and make their own decisions.

A. Employee Enrichment

B. Employees Development

C. Employee Empowerment

D. Employee Promotion

Q.75 Assertion (A): Group decisions delay the decision-making process.

Reason (R): In group decision making, nobody takes responsibility and the group is dominated by a few members.

A. Both (A) and (R) are correct, and (R) is the correct explanation of (A).

B. Both (A) and (R) are correct, but (R) is not the correct explanation of (A).

C. (A) is correct, but (R) is not correct.

D. (A) is wrong, and (R) is correct

Q.76 Statement-I. Diamond water paradox establishes the fact that marginal utility can be low, but total utility will be high for ________ goods.

Statement-II. In the case of ________ goods, the price effect is negative on demand.

Choose the correct option from those below:

A. Luxury goods, Giffen's goods

B. Comfort goods, Complementary goods

C. Necessary goods, Giffen's goods

D. Substitute goods, Inferior goods

Q.77 Statement I: Burke-Litwin's model of organizational change explains about the first order and second-order change created in an organization.

Statement II: The first order and second-order changes are also known as transactional and transformational changes, respectively.

Choose the correct option from those below:

A. Statement I is correct., Statement II is incorrect.

B. Statement I is incorrect, Statement II is correct.

C. Both Statement I and Statement II are correct.

D. Both Statement I and Statement II are incorrect.

Q.78 A marketing information system (MIS) caters to the needs of:

A. Marketing decision

B. Databases

C. Safeguard

D. Customized

Q.79 Which of the following types of Business ethics follow a win-win approach?

A. Participatory ethics

B. Transactional ethics

C. Recognition ethics

D. Performance ethics

Q.80 Assertion (A): Implementing a workplace investigation process and enforcing fair employment practices are the two components of an employee relations program.

Reason (R): Strengthening the employer-employee relationship is the sole strategic role of a human resources manager.

A. (A) is correct., but (R) is incorrect.

B. Both (A) and (R) are correct, but (R) is not the right explanation of (A).

C. Both (A) and (R) are correct, (R) is the right explanation of (A).

D. Both (A) and (R) are incorrect.

Q.81 Which of the following methods of determining promotional budget is based on the assumption that other companies have the same marketing objectives and execute them rationally?

A. Percentage of sales method

B. Competitive parity method

C. Objective and task method

D. Affordable method

Q.82 The owner of the asset retains most of the risk, and the term of the lease is substantially lower than the expected useful life of the asset. Identify the source of finance.

A. Finance Lease

B. Operating lease

C. Overdraft

D. Trade credit

Q.83 Which scheme allows for the import of capital goods at zero customs duty for producing quality goods and services to enhance India's export competitiveness?

A. Duty Exemption Goods Scheme

B. Export Oriented Units Scheme

C. EPCG Scheme

D. Customs Free Access

Q.84 Which of the following types of Positioning focuses on the function, features and benefits that a product provides to the customers?

A. Symbolic Positioning

B. Functional Positioning

C. Experimental Positioning

D. Repositioning

Q.85 According to the Government of India, a women entrepreneur is defined as an enterprise owned and controlled by a woman having a minimum financial interest of ___% of the capital and giving at least ___% of the employment generated in the enterprise to women.

A. 49%, 51%

B. 48%, 50%

C. 51%, 51%

D. 50%, 51%

Q.86 Which of the following can be termed as a codified form of generally accepted accounting principles?

A. Accounting Principles

B. Accounting Standards

C. Accounting Concepts

D. Accounting Policies

Q.87 Which of the following statements is/are correct with reference to situational variables?

a) Task structure

b) Relationship behaviour

c) Leader-member relationship

d) Position power

e) Maturity level

Choose the correct option/code from the following:

A. a,c,d,e   **B.** a,b,c   **C.** a,c,d   **D.** b,c,d,e

Q.88 Statement I: The World Bank provides financial and technical assistance to its members.

Statement II: Dispute settlement can take place under the World Bank Group's auspices through MIGA.

Choose the correct option from those below:

A. Statement I is correct, Statement II is incorrect.

B. Statement I is incorrect, Statement II is correct.

C. Both Statement I and Statement II are correct.

D. Both Statement I and Statement II are incorrect.

Q.89 If a constant value 10 is added to each observation of a set, the variance is:

A. Reduced by 25   **B.** Increased by 25

C. increased by 5   **D.** Unaltered

Q.90 Statement 1: Diminishing marginal utility is one of a factor, which result in the downward slope of the demand curve.

Statement 2: Income and substitution effect is responsible for the upward slope of the demand curve.

A. Statement I is correct, Statement II is incorrect.

B. Statement I is incorrect, Statement II is correct.

C. Both Statement I and Statement II are correct.

D. Both Statement I and Statement II are incorrect.

Q.91 Group Entrepreneurship is classified into three types such as Partnership, Public Limited Company and Private Limited Company.

Which of the following characteristics of Partnership is not true?

A. Contractual relation

B. Lawful business

C. Limited liability

D. Non-transferability of interest

Q.92 The Inflation and unemployment specification in PESTLE analysis is under which of the following factors?

A. Social factors   **B.** Economic factors

C. Political factors   **D.** Legal factors

Q.93 There are four different types of products, such as stars, cash cows, question marks and dogs. Which of the following is (are) objective(s) of Dogs?

Statement I: The objective of Build is to increase short term cash flow

Statement II: The objective of Hold is to preserve the market place

Choose the correct option from those below:

A. Statement I is correct., Statement II is incorrect.

B. Statement I is incorrect, Statement II is correct.

C. Both Statement I and Statement II are correct.

D. Both Statement I and Statement II are incorrect.

Q.94 In the Value Chain Analysis, Differentiation comes under which of the following perspective of Blanaced scorecard?

A. Financial perspective

B. Customer perspective

C. Operations perspective

D. Organizational perspective

Q.95 Which of the following entrepreneurial competencies include analytical, systematic and creative thinking ability of the employees to identify and solve the work-related problem or find innovative solutions?

A. Generic management competencies

B. Cognitive competencies

C. Functional competencies

D. Social and interpersonal competencies

Q.96 Which of the following theories is not included in Psychological Entrepreneurship Theories?

A. Locus of control

B. Need for achievement

C. Social network

D. Personality traits

Q.97 Statement I: SEBI amended clause 49 of the listing agreement and included the provision related to whistleblowing policy.

Statement II: SEBI has mandated whistleblowing policy and ordered to make internal whistleblowing provision within the policy of the organization.

Choose the correct option from those below:

A. Statement I is correct., Statement II is incorrect.

B. Statement I is incorrect, Statement II is correct.

C. Both Statement I and Statement II are correct.

D. Both Statement I and Statement II are incorrect.

Q.98 Statement I: In the adult-adult ego states, the transactions proceed in an effective manner.

Statement II: In the adult-child transaction, the manager may warn or appreciate the employees.

Choose the correct option from those below:

A. Statement I is correct, Statement II is incorrect.

B. Statement I is incorrect, Statement II is correct.

C. Both Statement I and Statement II are correct.

D. Both Statement I and Statement II are incorrect.

Q.99 Statement I: Product Development strategy refers to modifying the product in order to meet changing customers needs.

Statement II: Marketing Innovation refers to innovating the market and adopting strategies to attract customers.

Choose the correct option from the following:

A. Statement I is correct, Statement II is incorrect.

B. Statement I is incorrect, Statement II is correct.

C. Both Statement I and Statement II are correct.

D. Both Statement I and Statement II are incorrect.

Q.100 Read the Statements and choose the correct code.

Which of the following is not a characteristic of Business Economics?

A. Normative science

B. Pragmatic

C. Macro in nature

D. Decision making

Q.101 Assertion (A): Transactional analysis contributes to organizational development by valuing autonomy and assertiveness.

Reason (R): With autonomy and assertiveness, an employee may find it easy to fit in the role after training and contributes to the organization.

A. Both (A) and (R) are correct, and (R) is the correct explanation of (A).

B. Both (A) and (R) are correct, but (R) is not the correct explanation of (A).

C. (A) is correct, but (R) is not correct.

D. (A) is wrong, and (R) is correct.

Q.102 Which of the following is not a primary aspect of industrial relations?

A. Co-operation between employees and employers

B. Conflict resolution

C. Profit and loss of the organization

D. The welfare of the employees and employers

Q.103 Assertion (A): Value engineering helps the organization in achieving the lowest total cost with required quality standards

Reason (R): In value engineering, the product designing process is done with the utmost importance and the changes are made in the early stages itself

A. Both (A) and (R) are correct, and (R) is the correct explanation of (A).

B. Both (A) and (R) are correct, but (R) is not the correct explanation of (A).

C. (A) is correct., but (R) is not correct.

D. (A) is wrong, and (R) is correct.

Q.104 The National Alliance of Young Entrepreneurs organized a conference on Women Entrepreneurs in New Delhi in 1989. Which of the following declarations was not made during the conference?

A. Financial assistance as well as consultancy services must be given to women for doing exports.

B. Nation and state government should promote the participation of women in social and economic development programs.

C. Remove social, attitudinal and institutional barriers in industrial activities.

D. Fairs and exhibitions having products made by women entrepreneurs must be widely advertised.

Q.105 Assertion (A): The miscommunication in a cross-cultural organization is directly proportional to the difference between the cultures of the sender and the receiver.

Reason (R): The miscommunication may arise because of the differences in the perceptions, interpretations, and evaluations.

A. Both (A) and (R) are correct, and (R) is the correct explanation of (A).

B. Both (A) and (R) are correct, but (R) is not the correct explanation of (A).

C. (A) is correct., but (R) is not correct.

D. (A) is wrong, and (R) is correct.

Q.106 ___________ is an apex body in India which determines the policy for Entrepreneurship Development.

A. Industrial Development Bank of India

B. National Entrepreneurship Development Board

C. Reserve Bank of India

D. Small Industries Development Bank of India (SIDBI)

Q.107 Assertion (A): Job analysis makes the recruitment and selection process easier.

Reason (R): Job analysis provides data related to specific jobs in terms of duties, responsibilities, skills and knowledge.

A. (A) is correct., but (R) is incorrect.

B. Both (A) and (R) are correct, but (R) is not the right explanation of (A).

C. Both (A) and (R) are correct, (R) is the right explanation of (A).

D. Both (A) and (R) are incorrect.

Q.108 Which of the following is not true regarding the Gandhian approach to industrial relations?

A. Accepted right to strike with the non-violent approach

B. Workers should resort to non-cooperation if they do not get minimum wages

C. Workers should believe in their collective strength

D. The ballot authority of the workers need not be checked for peaceful protests

Q.109 Column heading of the table is called

A. Prefatory notes

B. Captions

C. Titles

D. Stubs

Q.110 According to ____ invisible hands promote public welfare?

A. Ackerman

B. Redman

C. Adam Smith

D. Shea

Q.111 Strategic business units(SBU) provide the right direction to strategic planning. So what are the attributes of SBU?

a) The scientific method of grouping businesses

b) Unrelated business in any group are separated

c) The strategic business unit does not have a distinct set of competitors

d) Each strategic business unit will have a CEO.

Choose the correct option from those below:

A. a, b and c only

B. a, c and d only

C. a, b and d only

D. a, b, c and d

Q.112 Assertion (A): The cross elasticity of demand for a monopoly product is either zero or negative.

Reason (R): Product produced by a monopoly firm has no close substitute in the market.

A. (A) is correct., but (R) is incorrect.

B. Both (A) and (R) are correct, but (R) is not the right explanation of (A).

C. Both (A) and (R) are correct, (R) is the right explanation of (A).

D. Both (A) and (R) are incorrect.

Q.113 Which political system maintains power through the exercise of forceful coercion?

A. Autocracy   **B.** Democracy

C. Liberalism   **D.** Conservatism

Q.114 Statement I: Leader Effectiveness and Adaptability Description (LEAD) data failed to determine the shape of the quadrants in the leadership Johari window of a person.

Statement II: Leader Effectiveness and Adaptability Description (LEAD) aims at finding the discrepancy between self-perception and perception of others.

Choose the correct option from those below:

A. Statement I is correct, Statement II is incorrect.

B. Statement I is incorrect, Statement II is correct.

C. Both Statement I and Statement II are correct.

D. Both Statement I and Statement II are incorrect.

Q.115 Which of the following statements are incorrect regarding TRIMS.

a) It formalised in 1995

b) It offers equal rights to both foreign investors and domestic investors

c) The foreign investment is allowed with a certain ceiling limit

d) Grants permission to import raw materials without any limitation

Choose the correct option from those below:

A. a, b   **B.** a, c   **C.** b, c   **D.** b, d

Q.116 Scatter diagram of the variate values (X, Y) gives the idea about

A. Regression model

B. Distribution of errors

C. Functional relationship

D. Both A and C

Q.117 Which of the following laws is related to wages?

A. Employees State Insurance Act, 1948

B. The Maternity Benefit Act, 1961,

C. The Payment of Gratuity Act, 1972

D. The Equal Remuneration Act, 1976

Q.118 Which of the following refers to a person who, by operating within the organization, focuses on creativity and innovation and transforms an idea into a profitable investment?

A. Intra Entrepreneur

B. Employee Entrepreneur

C. Technopreneur

D. Ultrapreneur

Q.119 Which of the following is not a part of Mckinsey's 7S framework?

A. Structure   **B.** Strategy

C. Supervision   **D.** Style

Q.120 Assertion (A): To get good results, cultural transformation should be a part of the whole system change process.

Reason (R): Employees will get motivated to change when the process includes a change in the underlying processes, structures and systems like payroll, rewards, etc.

A. Both (A) and (R) are correct, and (R) is the correct explanation of (A).

B. Both (A) and (R) are correct, but (R) is not the correct explanation of (A).

C. (A) is correct, but (R) is not correct.

D. (A) is wrong, and (R) is correct.

Q.121 ___________helps a company to manage unpredictable growth as well as the demand and includes three components, i.e. generating ideas, recognizing opportunities and driving opportunities.

A. Opportunity Management

B. Lead Management

C. Customer-centric Relationship Management

D. None of the above

Q.122 Statement I: In Kurt Lewin's change theory, unfreezing refers to ready to change.

Statement II: In Kurt Lewin's change theory, refreeze refers to the continuation of the new change.

Choose the correct option from those below:

A. Statement I is correct., Statement II is incorrect.

B. Statement I is incorrect, Statement II is correct.

C. Both Statement I and Statement II are correct.

D. Both Statement I and Statement II are incorrect.

Q.123 The determination of expenses for an accounting period is based on the concept of:

A. Objectivity   **B.** Materiality

C. Matching   **D.** Periodicity

Q.124 Unstructured or semi-structured data can be stored in?

A. Hadoop   **B.** DBMS

C. Blockchain   **D.** Mongo DB

Q.125 _________refers to a situation wherein a consumer has very little involvement in the purchase and sees very few differences between brands of a product.

A. Variety seeking behavior

B. Habitual buying behavior

C. Dissonance reducing buying behavior

D. Complex buying behavior

Q.126 Which of the following is an assumption of the Net Operating Income (NOI) approach?

A. The levels of debt and equity remain unchanged

B. Increase in dividends at a constant rate

C. The cost of capital remains constant regardless of variation in leverage

D. Taxes and interest expense are included in the calculation

Q.127 Sum of the square of the deviation from _______ is always minimum.

A. Mode

B. Arithmetic Mean

C. Median

D. Geometric Mean

Q.128 The architecture of Business Intelligence does not consist of which of the following components?

A. Data warehouse

B. Data quality

C. Business analytics

D. User interface

Q.129 Special Drawing Rights is defined in a basket of international currencies. Which of the following currencies is not included in the basket of international currencies for SDR?

A. Chinese Renminbi

B. Japanese Yen

C. Pound Sterling

D. Australian Dollar

Q.130 Time value of money is not based on the fact that:

A. people would rather have money today than in the future.

B. time frame is an important determinant of the time value of money.

C. money is more valuable in future than in the present.

D. Time value of money considers interest rate as an important determinant in its formula.

Q.131 Statement I: The statistical discrepancy (SD) is defined as the sum of all the BoP items with their signs reversed.

Statement II: The accounting principles behind BOP transactions are derived from the double-entry bookkeeping system.

Choose the correct option from those below:

A. Statement I is correct, Statement II is incorrect.

B. Statement I is incorrect, Statement II is correct.

C. Both Statement I and Statement II are correct.

D. Both Statement I and Statement II are incorrect.

Q.132 The Intrapreneurial process begins with a new idea or an innovation followed by development, implementation and __________.

A. Retention

B. Execution

C. Modification

D. Invention

Q.133 Statement I: Job Enrichment refers to horizontal enrichment or the addition of tasks to make the job richer.

Statement II: Job Enlargement refers to the vertical expansion of tasks without additional responsibility.

Choose the correct option from those below:

A. Statement I is correct., Statement II is incorrect.

B. Statement I is incorrect, Statement II is correct.

C. Both Statement I and Statement II are correct.

D. Both Statement I and Statement II are incorrect.

Q.134 Which of the following are the entrepreneurial problems faced by women entrepreneurs?

a) Price and availability of raw materials

b) High competition in low technology products

c) Mobility problems

d) Shortage of finance

e) Family responsibilities

f) Shortage of raw material

A. (a), (b), (c), (d)

B. (a), (b), (d), (f)

C. (b), (c), (d), (e)

D. (c), (d), (e), (f)

Q.135 Which of the following is not true regarding the second national labor commission?

A. The commission submitted its report in the year 2002.

B. It recommends the recognition of social security as a fundamental human right.

C. It recommends setting up a social security fund of India and a separate fund for each state.

D. It recommends a social security scheme that is completely non-contributory.

Q.136 Under __________, if the actual and budgeted activity levels differ considerably, then various aspects like cost ascertainment, fixation of price do not give a correct picture.

A. Flexible Budgeting

B. Sales Budgeting

C. Fixed Budgeting

D. Production Budgeting

Q.137 Which of the following is used to describe a framework for analyzing macro-environmental factors?

A. Competitive analysis

B. SWOT analysis

C. PESTLE analysis

D. Value Chain analysis

Q.138 Which of the following doesn't include Green box subsidy?

A. Research fund

B. Subsidy on fertilizers

C. Subsidy of domestic aid

D. Farmer training programme

Q.139 Which of the following statements is/are correct with reference to Esprit de corps principle.

a) It means creating a team spirit or union is strength.

b) Create a sense of belonging among employees

c) One of keenest satisfaction for an intelligent man to experience.

d) It brings loyalty, commitment and dedication in the group.

e) Develop an atmosphere of mutual trust and understanding.

Choose the correct option/code from the following:

A. a,b,c,d,e

B. a,b,c,e

C. a,b,d,e

D. b,d,e

Q.140 Which of the following is true regarding the number of modes in a binomial distribution?

A. One mode

B. Two modes

C. It depends on the value of n and p both

D. It depends only value of n

Q.141 Under which of the following types of Consumer behaviors, consumers are highly involved in the purchase but consider little difference in the brands?

A. Complex buying behavior

B. Variety seeking behavior

C. Dissonance-reducing buying behavior

D. Novelty seeking behavior

Q.142 Read the statements carefully and choose the correct option:-

___________is an autonomous association of people that are united voluntarily so as to achieve a common objective.

A. Group Entrepreneurship

B. Rural Entrepreneurship

C. Partnership

D. Cooperatives

Ques (143-145):Read the reason, assertion carefully and choose the correct option:

Q.143 tatement I: Kumar Mangalam Birla Committee was set up as a replacement to the CII code.

Statement II: CII code was not a statutory but rather a voluntary code for the Indian companies.

Choose the correct option from those below:

A. Statement I is correct., Statement II is incorrect.

B. Statement I is incorrect, Statement II is correct.

C. Both Statement I and Statement II are correct.

D. Both Statement I and Statement II are incorrect.

Q.144 Assertion (A): Brand revitalization focuses on restoring brand relevance in the initial stages.

Reason (R): Restoring brand relevance brings back the loyal customer base which got shifted to the other competitive brand in recent times.

A. Both (A) and (R) are correct, and (R) is the correct explanation of (A).

B. Both (A) and (R) are correct, but (R) is not the correct explanation of (A).

C. (A) is correct., but (R) is not correct.

D. (A) is wrong, and (R) is correct.

Q.145 Assertion (A): The data collected from customer touchpoints is of good quality and help in understanding the buyer behavior.

Reason (R): Customer touchpoints are the survey questions which are aimed at understanding product experiences.

A. Both (A) and (R) are correct, and (R) is the correct explanation of (A).

B. Both (A) and (R) are correct, but (R) is not the correct explanation of (A).

C. (A) is correct., but (R) is not correct.

D. (A) is wrong, and (R) is correct.

Q.146 Read the statements both carefully:-

If x and y are two regression lines then there can be at most

A. An infinite number of regression line

B. One regression line

C. Two regression line

D. Four regression line

Q.147 Assertion(A): The cost of the product is the seller's concern whereas the utility of the product is the buyer's concern.

Reason(R): The cost of the product only provides a basis or standard to determine the price whereas the upper limit of the price range depends upon the utility of the product, i.e. its demand in the market.

A. Both (A) and (R) are correct, and (R) is the correct explanation of (A).

B. Both (A) and (R) are correct, but (R) is not the correct explanation of (A).

C. (A) is correct, but (R) is not correct.

D. (A) is wrong, and (R) is correct.

Q.148 Read the assertion and reason both carefully:-

Which of the following is a collection of data extracted from several groups or applications?

A. User interface

B. DSS database

C. Sensitivity analysis

D. Goal seeking analysis

Q.149 Assertion (A): Organizations decrease the stress levels of the employees by increasing the job decision latitude.

Reason (R): Increasing the job decision latitude will give more authority regarding the selection of work teams, selection of work schedules, etc.

A. Both (A) and (R) are correct, and (R) is the correct explanation of (A).

B. Both (A) and (R) are correct, but (R) is not the correct explanation of (A).

C. (A) is correct., but (R) is not correct.

D. (A) is wrong, and (R) is correct.

Q.150 ___________is used to change behaviour, whereas, ___________is used to form new policies as well as development strategies.

A. Strategic social marketing, Operational social marketing

B. Green marketing, social marketing

C. Operational social marketing, Strategic social marketing

D. Social marketing, Strategic social marketing

// Smart Answer Sheet //

Correct — Percentage of students who answered correctly. **Skipped** — Percentage of students who skipped.

Q.	Ans.	Correct / Skipped
1	D	50.0 % / 7.32 %
2	C	69.51 % / 19.51 %
3	B	47.56 % / 24.39 %
4	A	52.44 % / 25.61 %
5	D	42.68 % / 25.61 %
6	D	54.88 % / 25.61 %
7	D	67.07 % / 25.61 %
8	A	64.63 % / 25.61 %
9	A	29.27 % / 25.61 %
10	B	52.44 % / 25.61 %
11	A	37.8 % / 25.61 %
12	D	56.1 % / 25.61 %
13	C	50.0 % / 25.61 %
14	D	62.2 % / 25.6 %
15	A	53.66 % / 25.61 %
16	A	42.68 % / 25.61 %

Q.	Ans.	Correct / Skipped
17	A	45.12 % / 25.61 %
18	A	34.15 % / 25.61 %
19	B	29.27 % / 25.61 %
20	D	47.56 % / 25.61 %
21	D	59.76 % / 25.61 %
22	B	67.07 % / 25.61 %
23	C	60.98 % / 25.61 %
24	A	52.44 % / 25.61 %
25	B	58.54 % / 24.39 %
26	B	63.41 % / 25.61 %
27	D	26.83 % / 25.61 %
28	A	57.32 % / 25.61 %
29	A	34.15 % / 25.61 %
30	D	48.78 % / 26.83 %
31	A	42.68 % / 25.61 %
32	B	41.46 % / 24.39 %

Q.	Ans.	Correct / Skipped
33	C	51.22 % / 25.61 %
34	C	29.27 % / 26.83 %
35	B	41.46 % / 26.83 %
36	C	29.27 % / 26.83 %
37	A	60.98 % / 26.82 %
38	D	23.17 % / 26.83 %
39	B	52.44 % / 26.83 %
40	C	24.39 % / 26.83 %
41	B	54.88 % / 26.83 %
42	C	50.0 % / 26.83 %
43	C	67.07 % / 26.83 %
44	A	65.85 % / 26.83 %
45	C	51.22 % / 26.83 %
46	A	30.49 % / 26.83 %
47	B	35.37 % / 26.83 %
48	D	67.07 % / 26.83 %

Q.	Ans.	Correct / Skipped
49	B	37.8 % / 26.83 %
50	B	42.68 % / 28.05 %
51	A	24.39 % / 15.85 %
52	A	37.8 % / 18.3 %
53	B	30.49 % / 20.73 %
54	C	60.98 % / 19.51 %
55	C	34.15 % / 20.73 %
56	B	32.93 % / 21.95 %
57	C	26.83 % / 21.95 %
58	A	28.05 % / 21.95 %
59	C	35.37 % / 21.95 %
60	B	25.61 % / 21.95 %
61	C	35.37 % / 21.95 %
62	B	34.15 % / 21.95 %
63	B	58.54 % / 23.17 %
64	C	43.9 % / 23.17 %

Q.	Ans.	Correct / Skipped
65	B	65.85 % / 23.17 %
66	B	51.22 % / 23.17 %
67	C	43.9 % / 23.17 %
68	D	26.83 % / 23.17 %
69	C	24.39 % / 25.61 %
70	B	21.95 % / 24.39 %
71	A	34.15 % / 25.61 %
72	A	30.49 % / 25.61 %
73	A	30.49 % / 25.61 %
74	C	29.27 % / 25.61 %
75	A	50.0 % / 25.61 %
76	C	20.73 % / 25.61 %
77	C	43.9 % / 25.61 %
78	A	39.02 % / 25.61 %
79	B	42.68 % / 25.61 %
80	A	30.49 % / 25.61 %

Q.	Ans.	Correct / Skipped
81	B	50.0 % / 25.61 %
82	B	47.56 % / 25.61 %
83	C	30.49 % / 25.61 %
84	B	42.68 % / 26.83 %
85	C	41.46 % / 26.83 %
86	B	35.37 % / 26.83 %
87	C	20.73 % / 28.05 %
88	A	32.93 % / 28.05 %
89	D	31.71 % / 26.83 %
90	A	34.15 % / 26.83 %
91	C	25.61 % / 26.83 %
92	B	52.44 % / 26.83 %
93	B	28.05 % / 26.83 %
94	B	45.12 % / 28.05 %

Q.	Ans.	Correct / Skipped
95	B	53.66 % / 26.83 %
96	C	29.27 % / 26.83 %
97	A	21.95 % / 26.83 %
98	A	24.39 % / 26.83 %
99	A	15.85 % / 26.83 %
100	C	37.8 % / 26.83 %
101	A	37.8 % / 25.61 %
102	C	41.46 % / 28.05 %
103	A	50.0 % / 26.83 %
104	C	30.49 % / 26.83 %
105	A	54.88 % / 26.83 %
106	B	48.78 % / 26.83 %
107	C	54.88 % / 26.83 %
108	D	41.46 % / 26.83 %

Q.	Ans.	Correct / Skipped
109	B	39.02 % / 26.83 %
110	C	37.8 % / 26.83 %
111	C	37.8 % / 26.83 %
112	C	35.37 % / 25.61 %
113	A	42.68 % / 26.83 %
114	B	32.93 % / 26.83 %
115	B	21.95 % / 28.05 %
116	C	24.39 % / 26.83 %
117	D	46.34 % / 28.05 %
118	B	29.27 % / 29.27 %
119	C	46.34 % / 29.27 %
120	A	42.68 % / 29.27 %
121	A	35.37 % / 28.04 %
122	C	36.59 % / 28.04 %

Q.	Ans.	Correct / Skipped
123	C	23.17 % / 28.05 %
124	A	26.83 % / 28.05 %
125	B	40.24 % / 28.05 %
126	C	26.83 % / 29.27 %
127	B	48.78 % / 28.05 %
128	B	30.49 % / 28.05 %
129	D	19.51 % / 29.27 %
130	C	23.17 % / 28.05 %
131	C	31.71 % / 28.05 %
132	C	25.61 % / 28.05 %
133	D	36.59 % / 28.04 %
134	B	25.61 % / 28.05 %
135	D	32.93 % / 28.05 %
136	C	24.39 % / 28.05 %

Q.	Ans.	Correct / Skipped
137	C	35.37 % / 29.26 %
138	B	35.37 % / 28.04 %
139	C	31.71 % / 28.05 %
140	C	28.05 % / 28.05 %
141	C	20.73 % / 28.05 %
142	D	31.71 % / 28.05 %
143	C	25.61 % / 28.05 %
144	A	36.59 % / 28.04 %
145	C	7.32 % / 28.05 %
146	C	24.39 % / 29.27 %
147	A	28.05 % / 28.05 %
148	B	51.22 % / 28.05 %
149	A	34.15 % / 28.05 %
150	C	23.17 % / 26.83 %

//Hints and Solutions//

1. Evaluation is concerned with the ability to judge the value of material for a given purpose. The judgments are on the basis of specific criteria which may be either internal criteria (organization) or external criteria (relevance to the purpose). Cognitive Ability is ability of an individual to perform the different mental activities mostly linked with learning and problem solving. So, Evaluation is the highest level of cognitive ability.

2. Socio-economic background of teachers and students have nothing to do with the impact on enhancing knowledge of the student. Teacher's knowledge, Classroom activities and learning through experience will have a positive impact on teaching, as it will help in improving the knowledge of students.

3. Teaching aids like charts, boards, projectors etc. make teaching-learning process interesting, which will further help the student to learn better and retain concepts for a longer duration. The student's retention power is increased through these different audio and video teaching aids.

4. Lecture, interactive lecture, Group study are the techniques used by the teacher to teach to give knowledge to students or enhance knowledge. Self-study technique is used by students not by teachers as there is no involvement of teachers.

5. A test of developed skills or knowledge is called an achievement test. It includes assessing the amount of learning after teaching. Standardized tests are developed to measure skills and knowledge acquired in a given grade level. This is the most common type of achievement and test is usually a through planned instruction, such as training or classroom instruction. Achievement tests are often contrasted with tests that measure aptitude, a more general and stable cognitive trait.

6. A good teacher is one who learns how to motivate and inspire students. Students who are not motivated will not learn effectively and in turn, they won't retain information or participate and may even become disruptive.

7. Research is an investigation which comprises creative work undertaken on a systematic and logical basis to increase the stock of knowledge, culture and society. It deals with the verification of hypothesis, data analysis, interpretation and formation of principles and by using this stock of knowledge (research) new applications are being devised. Research is also an intellectual enquiry towards truth.

8. A good thesis writing should have an abstract that should be clear and well written to give a complete overview of the topic with the minimum number of grammatical errors and consistency in writing. Also, references play an important role for thesis writing which should be carefully written with the required format.

9. Piaget's theory of cognitive development is a comprehensive theory about the nature and development of human intelligence. Piaget theory is based on four stages i.e. sensorimotor stage, preoperational stage, concrete operational stage and formal operation stage.

Fundamental Research aims to improve scientific theories for improved understanding of natural phenomena. Piaget's idea is based on his fundamental research.

10. A null hypothesis is a hypothesis used in statistics which refers that no statistical significance difference exists in a set of given observation or populations. So, 'Male and female students perform equally well in a numerical aptitude test' is a case of null hypothesis.

11. The Historical Research is to collect, verify, and synthesize evidence from the past to establish facts that defend the hypothesis. So, the conclusions or results of this research cannot be generalised to other situations.

Descriptive research is used to give characteristics of phenomenon and situation being studied. It addresses the "what" question.

Experimental Research: This type of research method involves the process of manipulation of one variable so as to determine if there are any changes in one variable which affects another variable.

Causal-comparative research attempts to determine the cause or reason of differences that already exist between groups of individuals.

12. The steps which are required to design a questionnaire includes the aim of the study i.e. writing primary and secondary aims of the study, to prepare a draft of questionnaire in which number of questions will be asked related to the topic, review the literature so as to frame the relevant questions and revision of the draft for making it error free.

13. Our knowledge is the collection of few stories that survive.

(Reference Line in 2nd Paragraph: Our history, knowledge and understanding are all the collections of few stories that survive.)

14. From 1st line of the 1st Paragraph, it is clear that Story telling is not in our genes. Neither it is an evolutionary history. It is the essence of what makes us Human.

(Reference Line: Story telling is not in our genes. Neither it is an evolutionary history. It is the essence of what makes us Human.)

15. The future will depend partly, possibly largely, on which stories we collectively choose to believe.

(Reference line in 2nd Paragraph: This includes the stories that we tell each other about the future. And how the future will turn out depends partly, possibly largely, on which stories we collectively choose to believe.)

16. Rational optimist tends to claim that it is human nature to compete and to succeed and also to profit at the expense of others clearly give the idea that they are sensible, cheerful and are selfishly driven and look for opportunities.

(Reference line: Currently, this trend is being led by those who call themselves "rational optimists". They tend to claim that it is human nature to compete and to succeed and also to profit at the expense of others. The rational optimists however, do not realize how humanity has progressed overtime through amiable social networks and how large groups works in less selfishness and in the process accommodate rich and poor, high and low alike.)

17. In the 3rd paragraph, it is given that how large groups work in less selfishness.

(Reference line: The rational optimists however, do not realize how humanity has progressed overtime through amiable social networks and how large groups works in less selfishness and in the process accommodate rich and poor, high and low alike.)

18. Practical Possibles are the ones who follow Midway Path. This aspect in story-telling is considered by the 'Practical Possibles', who sit between those who say all is fine and cheerful and be individualistic, it indicates they follow midway path.

(Reference line: This aspect in story-telling is considered by the 'Practical Possibles', who sit between those who say all is fine and cheerful and be individualistic in your approach to a successful future, and those who ordain pessimism and fear that we are doomed.)

19. Communication is an exchange of feelings, ideas, knowledge and information, either by speaking, writing, signals, or behaviours and for the success of organization, effective communication is an essential component at all levels. This effective communication can be traced or manged through performance records, student's attendance and communication channel.

20. Formal communication, a systematic and orderly flow of information tends to interchange or transmit the information officially in an organization. The flow of the formal communication is more in a controlled way. Formal communication, according to the direction or flow may be of two types-(a) Vertical, and (b) horizontal.

21. Communication is the continuous and circular process which involve an exchange of ideas, knowledge and opinions for understanding. Communication is a circular process because in the first stage it starts when one individual prepares the purpose of conveying a message to another individual and the next step is one in which, the conveying process happens. Finally, the other individuals receive the message and process the information in the correct manner and respond and the process repeats itself.

22. Grapevine communication is also known as informal communication because communication is performed without maintaining the formalities/guidelines prescribed by the organization and moreover, there is no particular route for sharing the relevant information.

23. Effective communication is a way of transferring information, thoughts and ideas to create understanding between sender and receiver. Communication is a persuasive and convincing dialogue which involves the participation of the audience through the strategic use of informal communication, also known as grapevine communication. Communication cannot be possible in one-way because it includes dispensing of information to another person.

24. In communication, the language is verbal code, as verbal communication uses spoken and written words for expressing and transferring views and ideas.

25.

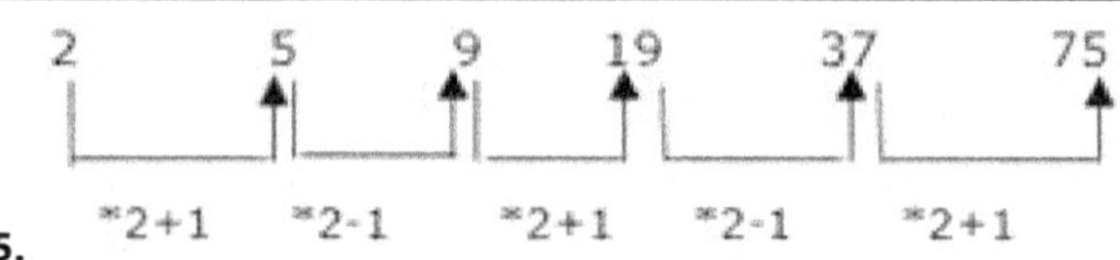

Hence, the next term in the series is 75

26.

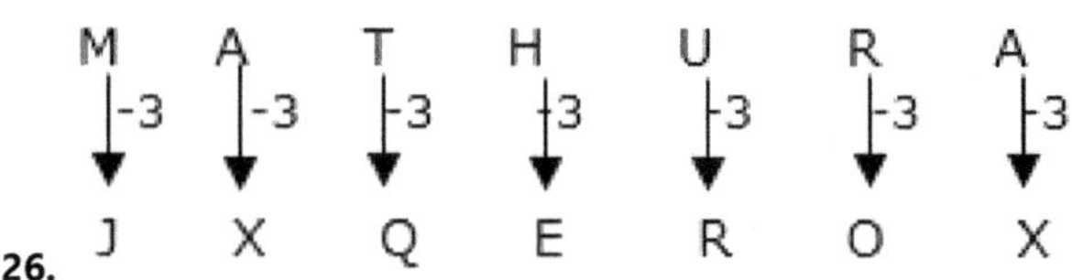

Here in MATHURA,

Place value of M=13 and place value of J=10 so difference in place value is 3.

Place value of A=1 and place value of X=24 so difference in place value is 3.

Therefore, fixed pattern is followed in which coded letter place value is 3 less.

Code of HOTELS is;

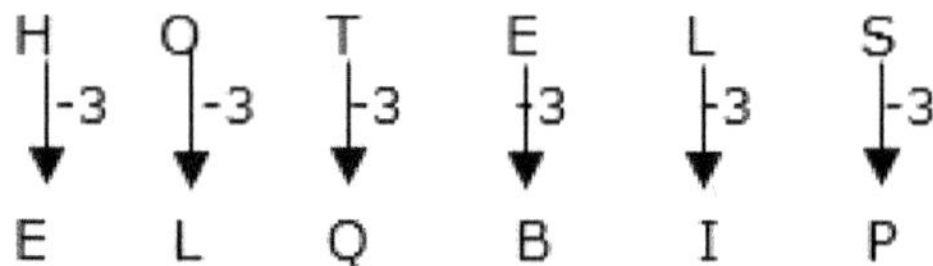

27. Given:

Total number of centers $= 222$

The average number of applicants per center $= 1560$

Total number of applicants $= 222 \times 1560 = 346320$

Number of applicants that have been counted extra $=$ $1857 - 1747 = 110$

The correct number of applicants $= 346320 - 110 = 346210$

New average $= \dfrac{346210}{222}$

$= 1559.505$

$= 1559.51$

Hence, the correct option is (D).

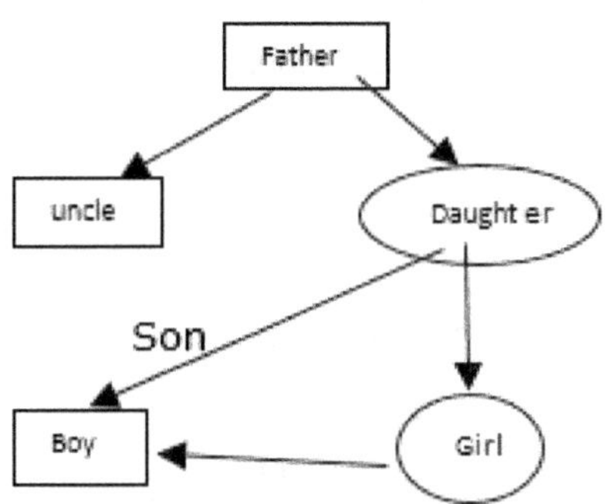

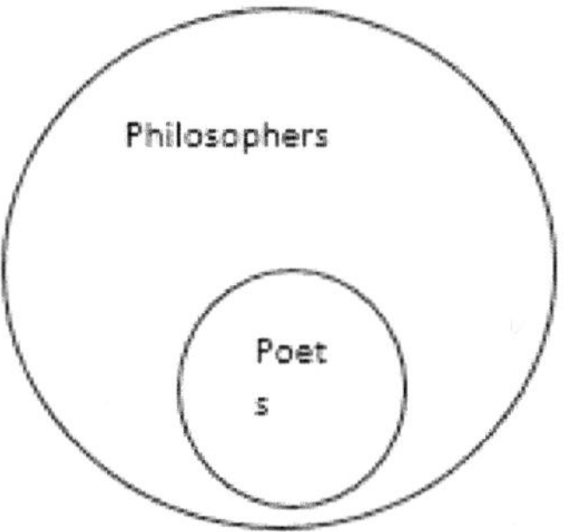

28.

Hence from above figure it is clear that boy and girl are brother and sister.

29. Total no of student=10000
Total number of students passed in all five subjects=5583
Total number of students passed in four subjects = total number of students failed in one subject
only=75+145+140+200+157=717
Therefore, number of students passed in at least four subjects is 5583 + 717 = 6300.

30. 3 years hence, son's age=15
Therefore, present age of son=15-3 =12 years
Person present age= present age of son * 4 =12*4=48 years
Wife present age= Person present age -3 = 48-3=45 years
After 5 years' person wife's age = 45 + 5 = 50 years.

31. Inductive reasoning is the one in which the premises seek to supply strong evidence for the truth of the conclusion. The truth of the conclusion of an inductive argument is probable, based upon the provided evidence. Inductive reasoning is known as hypothesis construction because the conclusions derived are based on the current knowledge and predictions. So, if we want to seek new knowledge of facts about the world, we must rely on inductive reasoning.

32. A deductive argument is invalid if its premises are true and its conclusion is false. A deductive argument is an argument which is given by the arguer to be deductively valid, i.e., to provide a surety of the truth of the conclusion provided that the argument's premises are also true. Premises should provide strong support for conclusion.

33. Inductive reasoning is grounded on the uniformity of nature. This reasoning involves logical process in which multiple premises, all are believed true or found true, are combined together to get a specific conclusion. Inductive reasoning is often used in applications that involves prediction, forecasting, or behaviour.

34. From above figure it is clear that (a) and (c) are contradictory to each other.

35. Venn diagrams are an effective way of representing and analysing sets and performing operations. Problems that are solved by using Venn diagrams are problems based on sets and set operations. Venn diagram represents the arguments graphically.

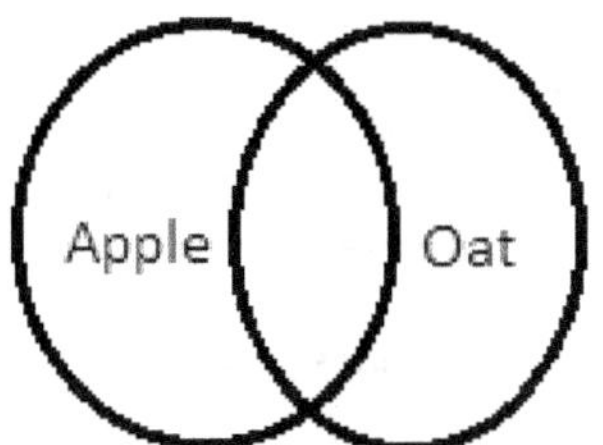

The Venn diagrams include an ideal representation of the standard form to enhance our understanding. They provide a clear method of notation.

36. A lexical definition is the meaning of the term in common usage or it simply reports the way in which a term is used within a language community. Lexical definition is descriptive, which report actual usage of language used by speakers and vary with the usage of the term, rather than prescriptive. When the purpose of a definition is to explain the use or to eliminate ambiguity the definition is called Lexical.

37. The International Monetary Fund (IMF) is an organization of 189 countries, working to foster global monetary cooperation, secure financial stability, facilitate international trade, promote high employment and sustainable economic growth, and reduce poverty around the world. Hence option A is correct.

38. Citibank has perhaps the largest global reach of any major bank, operating in over 30 countries with thousands of branches worldwide. Hence, option D is correct.

39. We know that angle traced by hour hand in 12 hrs. = 360°

From 7 to 1, there are 6 hours.

Angle traced by the hour hand in 6 hours =6*(360/12)=180°

Option B is the correct answer.

40. The hands of clocks make a straight line of 180° about 22 times in 24 hours. Also, the hands coincide 22 times in 24 hours, the coincidence of the hands also forms a straight line. Hence, the total straight lines are 22+22 = 44.

Option C is the correct answer.

41. Answer: (2) Two; "E" is preceded by "&" and "U" is preceded by "#"

42.

Answer: (3) N; Sixth element from the right is E and second to its left is N

43. Encoding or scrambling data for transmission across a network is known as Encryption.

To transfer data securely, encryption is an effective way. In the encryption process, information to be transferred is encoded securely so that only authorized parties can access it. To decrypt information authorized party should have a secret key or password. The data when unencrypted is known a plain text while the encrypted test is called as cipher text.

In Encryption, information is encrypted packet-by-packet basis. There are two types of Encryption: asymmetric encryption (public key) and symmetric encryption (private key). In symmetric encryption same key is used to encrypt and decrypt data in order to keep the key secret. In asymmetric one key is used for encoding and other key is used for decoding.

44. In computing, an input device is a piece of equipment used to provide data and control signals to an information processing system such as a computer or information appliance. Examples of input devices include keyboards, mouse, scanners, digital cameras, joysticks, and microphones.

Hence, option A is correct.

45. 1GigaByte= 2^30 which is nearly one billion characters.

46. Open source refers to something which one can modify, study, reuse, enhance or redistribute and share because it is accessible publicly. Therefore, Open source software (OSS) is software with source code that anyone can inspect, modify, and enhance. So, Linux, open office and apache http server all are open source software.

Major Web browsers like Mozilla Firefox, Google Chrome, Opera and Safari are open-source components. Presently, Internet Explorer is the only one of the big 5 browsers to remain entirely "closed source".

47. The full form of IMEI is International Mobile Equipment Identity.

It refers to a code or number that identifies a specific mobile phone used over a mobile network. Every mobile phone has a unique IMEI number consisting of 15 to 17 digit numbers. Usually, it is printed on the backside of your mobile battery. You can check your mobile phone IMEI number by dialing *#06#.

Hence, the correct option is (B).

48. Google Talk provides an instant messaging service which includes both text and voice communication. The instant messaging service is popularly known as "gtalk", "gchat", or "gmessage" to its users. Hence, option D is correct.

49. The European Union (EU) is a political and economic union of 28-member states that are located primarily in Europe. So, per capita use of water is highest in European Union.

50. In India contribution of Carbon dioxide (CO2) emissions is due to following sources

1) Electricity production: 29% percent gas emissions.

2) Transportation: 27% percent gas emissions.

3) Industry: 21% percent gas emissions.

4) Commercial and Residential: 12% percent gas emissions.

5) Agriculture: 9% percent gas emissions.

6) Land Use and forestry: 11.8% percent gas emissions.

Overall contribution of India is around 6%.

51. Traffic intensity = Mean arrival rate / Mean service rate

= mean service time / mean inter-arrival time

= λ / μ

Thus, Option A is correct.

52. In general decisions can be classified into three categories:

● Strategic decision: These decisions are concerned with the external environment of the organization.

● Administrative decision: This is concerned with structuring and acquisition of the organization's resources so as to optimize the performance of the organization.

● Operating decision: This is primarily concerned with day to day operations of the organization, such as pricing, production scheduling, inventory levels.

Thus, Option A is correct.

53. Features of Bate's brand wheel:

● Employer brand

● It helps employees to become a part of the consolidated winning team.

● It develops the current organizational culture.

Thus, Option B is correct.

54. ● A layoff is the removal of workers from the establishment because of the unavailability of the work.

● Retrenchment is done by an establishment to cut down their expenses.

● Lockout is done by the employers when the workers do not agree upon the rules of employers.

● A strike is a mass protest by the employees to fulfill their demands.

Thus, Option C is correct.

55. ● Position Analysis Questionnaire- It is a technique of structured job analysis which analyze features and requirements pertaining to a job and compare them to employees characteristics and features.

● Occupational Analysis Inventory- This Instrument is used to measure the job requirement and other job related information for virtually various kinds of occupations. Information received, mental exercises, job behavior, work goals, and job context are some of the types of this technique.

Thus, Option C is correct.

56. ● UNCTAD was established in 1964 to facilitate trade, investment and development.

● UNCTAD implemented the Generalised System of Preferences to allow duty-free imports from LDCs to developed countries.

Thus, Option B is correct.

57. • The members of the craft union are the workers in a particular craft or trade.

• The members of industrial unions are the workers of different companies but from the same industry.

• All the workers from different crafts and industries are the members of general unions.

• Company unions are company-level unions and are influenced by employers. These are not independent unions.

Thus, Option C is correct.

58. Degree of financial leverage can never be between zero and one. It can be zero or less than zero or it can be one or more.

Thus, Option A is correct.

59. ● Net Income Approach to Capital Structure was presented by Durand. According to this approach, if the tax information is given, the value of the firm can be increased by decreasing the weighted average cost of capital (WACC), i.e. the overall cost of capital through higher debt proportion.

● Assumptions of Net Income Approach include:

1) There is no flotation cost, no transaction cost as well as no corporate dividend tax.

2) There are only two sources of finance, i.e. debt and equity.

3) All the firms have a uniform dividend payout ratio which is 1

Thus, Option C is correct.

60. It is a continuous process to secure information necessary for making correct and objective decisions on employees. Performance appraisal indicates how well an individual is fulfilling the job requirement by the way of evaluating an employee's performance by various performance appraisal techniques.

Thus, Option B is correct.

61. Economy Pricing is no frills pricing wherein a company keeps the price of its product lower than the brand items with a view to increasing its product sales. Also, economy pricing works well during times of Economic recession.

Thus, Option C is correct.

62. ● In-Basket Training emphasizes the importance of skills needed for decision-making. It helps a trainee in developing those skills that help him make the right decisions in the absence of his manager.

● A manager has to handle several tasks on a typical day. To ensure that his absence does not hamper the work, the executives are trained by assigning them the tasks that they would have to face if they were holding such a position.

Thus, Option B is correct.

63. There are four characteristics of a data warehouse. They are as follows:

● A subject-oriented data warehouse focuses mainly on important subjects like a producer, consumer, manufacturer, etc

● Once data is entered in a Non-erasable data warehouse, it remains static.

● The time-dependent data warehouse not only stores current information but also stores historical information.

● The consolidated data warehouse is capable of retrieving appropriate data from heterogeneous databases.

Thus, Option B is correct.

64. ● The system approach is also called system organisation theory states the organisation as a unified system composed of interrelated or interdependent parts of the subsystem.

● Whereas, contingency theory is an extension of system organisational theory and states that there cannot be one organisational design for all situations it depends upon internal needs and external environment.

Thus, Option C is correct.

65. In order to maintain discipline in the class, the best way is to make learning and teaching interesting in the class. Punishing, Informing parents, eliminating students wouldn't be a feasible and appropriate course of action in this case.

Thus, Option B is correct.In order to maintain discipline in the class, the best way is to make learning and teaching interesting in the class. Punishing, Informing parents, eliminating students wouldn't be a feasible and appropriate course of action in this case.

Thus, Option B is correct.

66. Competency Mapping involves comparing the actual competencies of an entrepreneur with the competencies required to become a successful entrepreneur so as to ascertain the gap in the entrepreneurial competencies.

Thus, Option B is correct.Competency Mapping involves comparing the actual competencies of an entrepreneur with the competencies required to become a successful entrepreneur so as to ascertain the gap in the entrepreneurial competencies.

Thus, Option B is correct.

67. ● Stereotyping- It is generalizing behavior of a person on the basis of the mental picture set in the mind of the appraiser. If the appraiser thinks that the appraisee is lazy, he will rate him according to the image he has in his mind.

● Horn effect- It is when the rater's bias is directed towards one negative quality of the employee. In horns effect even a single negative attribute and characteristic might result in marking low end scale by the appraiser.

Thus, Option C is correct.

68. ● Brownfield Investment is when a company purchases an existing production facility to launch a new production activity.

- OLI theory is also known as the Eclectic Paradigm.

Thus, Option D is correct.

69. Under the Time Wage System, workers are paid on the basis of the amount of time spent by them on the job. It can lead to lower productivity if they are not strictly supervised. Therefore, it requires increased supervision.

Thus, Option C is correct.

70. ● Emotional restraint makes the communication process more effective.

● If the sender receives any negative news while sending a message, the message may miss a few details because of the negative impact of the news.

● Emotional restraint will help the sender to concentrate on the message.

● The sender should defer the communication process for a specific period of time to avoid the negative impact of emotion.

● The reason did not explain the assertion statement.

Thus, Option B is correct.

71. Expenses in an Administrative Budget include: Audit fees, Insurance, Postage, Office supplies, Stationery etc. It is important to keep reviewing these expenses at regular intervals so as to keep them under control.

Thus, Option A is correct.

72. ● Lack of planning or poor planning will cause the organisation to be continually drifting. It will be unable to fulfil its mission, and this will inevitably lead to demise.

● Coordinating avoids confusion and duplication of activities between departments. It involves all resources in the business to work together, effectively and efficiently.

Thus, Option A is correct.

73. Late majority is one of the adopter categories where people adopt an innovation after the average participants have adopted it and are extremely cautious of the results before buying.

Thus, Option A is correct.

74.

- In the context of HRM, employee empowerment is the management strategy that enables employees to fix their own work goals, solve their problems and make better decisions by granting them greater autonomy and responsibility for their tasks.

    Thus, Option C is correct.

75.

- ● Group decisions delay the decision-making process.

    ● In the group decision making, nobody takes responsibility and it delays the process.

● Few members dominate the group and hinder the process.

Thus, Option A is correct.

76. ● According to the diamond water paradox (given by adam smith) marginal utility of necessary goods (example water) will be low while the total utility of necessary goods will be high. This is because, at low consumption, necessary goods have much higher utility then luxury goods (example diamond). People tend to consume water at higher levels than that of the diamond, so its marginal utility is lower compared to diamonds.

● In the case of Giffen's goods, the price effect is negative, which means when there is an increase in the price of such goods, its demand decreases as people switch to substitute goods.

Thus, Option C is correct.

77. ● Burke-Litwin developed a model which examines the organizational change and its performance.

● It explains about the first order and second-order change created in an organization.

● In the first-order change, only a few features of the organization are changed.

● In the second-order change, complete transformation takes place.

● The first order and second-order changes are also known as transactional and transformational changes, respectively.

Thus, Option C is correct.

78. A marketing information system (MIS) caters to the need of marketing decisions.

Marketing Information System refers to the systematic collection, analysis, interpretation, storage, and dissemination of the market information from both internal and external sources, to the marketers on a regular basis.

Hence, the correct option is (A).

79. ● In participatory ethics, all participants follow ethical practices and standards. The level of participation depends on the degree of motivation in society.

● In transactional ethics, man has to react with others through different transactions. It includes a win-win approach, i.e., binds all people for good ethical interests.

● In recognition ethics, people are endowed with the ability to understand the problems of others. The quality of recognition depends on individuals and societies, i.e., learned is helping the lesser learned.

Thus, Option B is correct.

80.

- Strengthening the employer-employee relationship is not the sole strategic role of a human resources manager. There are many other strategic roles of Hr manager, which includes work safety and risk

management, compensation and benefits, developing public relations, employee training and development and recruitment and selection apart from maintaining employee relationships.

- Thus, Option A is correct

81. Under competitive parity method, advertising expenditure of a company is equal to the amount spent by its competitors. It based on the assumption that other companies have the same marketing objectives and execute them rationally.

Thus, Option B is correct.

82. • In the operating lease, the purchaser takes the asset on hire, but he doesn't purchase it. So there is no transfer of ownership in this case.

• However, In the case of a finance lease, the term of the lease will be close to the expected life of the asset.

Thus, Option B is correct.

83. Export Promotion Capital Goods (EPCG) Scheme allows for the import of capital goods at zero customs duty for producing quality goods and services to enhance India's export competitiveness.

Thus, Option C is correct.

84. • Symbolic positioning includes customers' affection, social connection with the product.

• Functional Positioning focuses on the function, features and benefits that a product provides to the customer.

• Experimental Positioning concentrates on the elements of a brand.

• Repositioning refers to altering the position of a brand in the minds of customers.

Thus, Option B is correct.

85.

- According to the Government of India, a women entrepreneur is defined as an enterprise owned and controlled by a woman having a minimum financial interest of 51% of the capital and giving at least 51% of the employment generated in the enterprise to women.

  Thus, Option C is correct.

86.

- Accounting Standards can be termed as a codified form of GAAP because the essence of accounting standards is that they convey the same accounting concepts to all the users of financial statement in the same manner, so as to bring consistency, uniformity and comparability in all the financial statements of every organization.

  Thus, Option B is correct.

87. There are three major situational factors:

- Task structure - the extent to which work is well defined and standardised or ambiguous and vague.

- Leader-member relationship - the amount of trust between subordinate and leader.

- Position power - a formal authority.

Thus, Option C is correct.

88. • The World Bank provides financial and technical assistance to its members.

• Dispute settlement can take place under the World Bank Group's auspices through ICSID.

Thus, Option A is correct.

89.

- Variance is not affected by the change of origin.

  i.e. var(x+c) = var(x)

  Thus, Option D is correct.

90. Diminishing marginal utility:

• The law of diminishing marginal utility states that with the increasing quantity of demand, the marginal utility declines.

• Thus, when the quantity of goods is more, the marginal utility decreases. So, the consumer will not pay more price for the commodity and its demand will decline.

Substitution Effect:

• As Tea and coffee are substitute goods, if the price of tea rises, the demand for coffee increases.

• Thus, the demand curve of tea will slope downwards.

Income Effect:

• Income effect refers to the change in the real income or the purchasing power of the consumers. When the price of a good falls the purchasing power of the consumer's increases, and they buy more goods and vice-versa.

Thus, Option A is correct.

91.

- • A partnership is a contract between two or more persons to carry on lawful business.

  • The members of a Partnership have unlimited. They are individually or collectively responsible for firm's debts or obligations.

  • No partner can transfer his partnership share to any other person to make him a partner without the consent of other partners.

  Thus, Option C is correct.

92.

- The economic factors are as follows:

  • Economy situation and trends

  • Market and trade cycles

  • Customer end-user drivers

  • Interest and exchange rates

  • Inflation and unemployment

  Thus, Option B is correct.

93. The four objectives of Dogs are as follows:

• Build: To increase market share

• Hold: To preserve market share

• Harvest: To increase short term cashflow

• Divest: To sell or liquidate the business

Thus, Option B is correct.

94. The four perspectives of Balanced scorecard are as follows:

• Growth and profitability come from a financial perspective.

• Differentiation, cost and quick response come under the customer perspective.

• Product development, demand management, and order fulfilment come under the operations perspective.

• Leadership, organizational learning and ability to change come under organizational perspective.

Thus, Option B is correct.

95.

- Cognitive competencies comprise of analytical, systematic and creative thinking ability of the employees to identify and solve the work-related problem or find innovative solutions.

  Thus, Option B is correct.

96. Psychological Entrepreneurship Theories emphasize personal characteristics that define entrepreneurship and include Personality traits theory, locus of control and need for theory.

Thus, Option C is correct.

97. • SEBI amended clause 49 of the listing agreement and included the provision related to whistleblowing policy.

• The whistleblowing policy has not been made mandatory for the companies. It is a recommendation by SEBI.

• SEBI advised the companies to develop a mechanism for employees to report their concerns regarding unethical behaviour or fraud or any other violation.

Thus, Option A is correct.

98.

- • In the adult-adult ego states, the transaction proceeds in an effective manner. Both parties work on solutions after data processing.

  • In the adult-child transaction, the manager expects the child ego of the employee to be creative.

  • In the parent-parent transaction, the manager offers rewards, warns or appreciates based on the performance. It may create a competition between the manager and the employee.

  Thus, Option A is correct.

99.

- Marketing Innovation refers to altering the marketing mix, i.e. implementing new marketing methods by altering product, price, place, promotion (marketing mix).

  Thus, Option A is correct.

100.

- Business economics is micro in nature. It is concerned with businesses at a firm level.

  Thus, Option C is correct.

101. • The transactional analysis contributes to organizational development by valuing autonomy and assertiveness.

• With the autonomy and assertiveness, an employee may find it easy to fit in the role after training and contributes to the organization.

• With autonomy, people feel responsible and with assertiveness people express their needs.

• The reason explained the assertion statement.

Thus, Option A is correct.

102. • Profit and loss is an internal matter of the organization.

• The main aspect of industrial relations is

1) To promote the co-operation between employees and employers

2) Conflict resolution

3) To look after The welfare of the employees and employers

Thus, Option C is correct.

103. • In value engineering, the product designing process is done with the utmost importance and the changes are made in the early stages itself.

• This will prevent the extra costs in the latter stages of the production process.

- With this, the quality of the product is not compromised.

Thus, Option A is correct.

104. Remove social, attitudinal and institutional barriers in industrial activities was a declaration made by the United Nations Industrial Development Organization (UNIDO) in a conference at Vienna.

Thus, Option C is correct.

105. ● The miscommunication in a cross-cultural organization is directly proportional to the difference between the cultures of the sender and the receiver.

● The miscommunication may arise because of the differences in the perceptions, interpretations, and evaluations.

● The reason statement explained the assertion statement.

Thus, Option A is correct.

106. National Entrepreneurship Development Board is an apex body in India which determines the policy for Entrepreneurship Development.

Thus, Option B is correct.

107. Job analysis makes the recruitment and selection process easier by the way of the job description and job specification as it provides data related to specific jobs in terms of duties, responsibilities, skills and knowledge making it easier for employees to make the process easier.

Thus, Option C is correct.

108. ● The Gandhian approach accepted the right to strike with the non-violent approach.

● Workers should resort to non-cooperation if they do not get minimum wages.

● Workers should believe in their collective strength.

● The ballot authority of the workers need to be checked for peaceful protests

Thus, Option D is correct.

109. ● Prefatory notes- A statement given below the title and enclosed in brackets usually describes the units of measurement and is called the prefatory notes.

● Captions- The vertical heading and subheading of the column are called columns captions.

● Stubs- The horizontal headings and subheading of the row are called row captions and space where these rows headings are written is called the stub.

● Titles- The title is the main heading written in capitals shown at the top of the table.

Thus, Option B is correct.

110. Adam Smith is the father of the classical economic model. He deduced that the invisible hand promotes public welfare.

Thus, Option C is correct.

111. The attributes of strategic business units are as follows:

- It is is a scientific method of grouping the business

- Task consisting of analyzing and segregating the assortment of businesses

- Unrelated businesses in any group are separated.

- It will have its distinct set of competitors, and it's own distinct strategy.

● Each unit will have a CEO.

Thus, Option C is correct.

112. Cross elasticity measures the change in demand for a commodity due to the change in the price of another commodity. Since in the monopoly market firms have an absolute power to produce and sell a product that has no close substitute in the market, cross elasticity of goods is either zero or negative.

Thus, Option C is correct.

113. Autocracy is the oldest form of government and maintains power through the exercise of forceful coercion.

Thus, Option A is correct.

114. ● Leader Effectiveness and Adaptability Description (LEAD) data can actually determine the shape of the quadrants in the leadership Johari window of a person. This depends on the organizational settings of the person in which he operates.

● Leader Effectiveness and Adaptability Description (LEAD) data, which was developed by Hersey and Blanchard aims at finding the discrepancy between self-perception and perception of others.

Thus, Option B is correct.

115. • TRIMS is an agreement on Trade-related investment measures that are applicable to the domestic regulations a country applies to foreign investors, often as part of industrial policy.

• It was formalised in 1994, was negotiated under the WTO's predecessor, the General Agreement on Tariffs and Trade (GATT), and came into force in 1995. The foreign investment is allowed into a country without any limitation.

Thus, Option B is correct.

116. If the variables in a bivariate distribution are related ,one can find that the points in the scatter diagram will cluster around some curve. For example in the given diagram curve is a straight line.

Basically this helps in knowing the functional relationship between x and y.

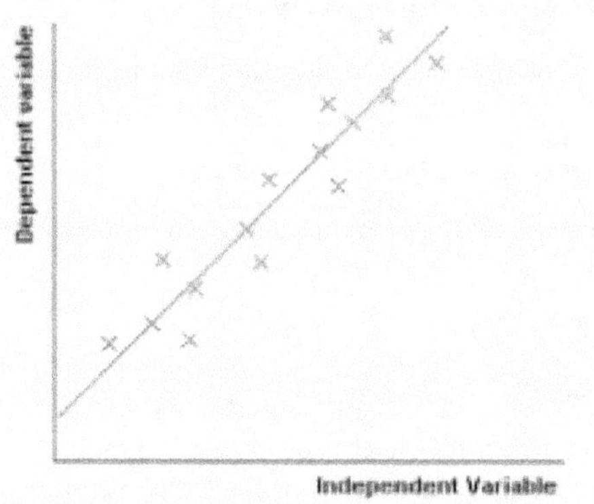

Thus, Option C is correct.

117. • The Equal Remuneration Act, 1976 aims to provide equal remuneration to men and women workers and to prevent discrimination, on the ground of gender, against women in the matter of employment.

Thus, Option D is correct.

118. An Employee Entrepreneur is a person who, by operating within the organization, focuses on creativity and innovation and transforms an idea into a profitable investment.

Thus, Option B is correct.

119. Mckinsey's 7S framework consists of the following super-ordinate goals:

• Structure

• Systems

• Style

• Staff

• Skills

• Strategy

• Superordinate goals

Thus, Option C is correct.

120. • To get good results, cultural transformation should be a part of the whole system change process.

• Employees will get motivated to change when the process includes a change in the underlying processes, structures and systems like payroll, rewards, etc.

• People may resist the change if the process involves only a few departments.

• The reason explained the assertion statement.

Thus, Option A is correct.

121. Opportunity management is a collaborative approach that focuses on Tangibles outcomes. It helps a company to manage unpredictable growth as well as the demand and includes three components, i.e. generating ideas, recognizing opportunities and driving opportunities.

Thus, Option A is correct.

122. In Kurt Lewin change theory,

• Unfreeze refers to ready to change.

• Implementation refers to the movement from one state to another state.

• Refreeze refers to the continuation of the new change.

Thus, Option C is correct.

123. It is referred to as matching of expenses against incomes. It means that all incomes and expenses relating to the financial period to which the accounts relate should be taken into the accounts without regard to the date of receipt or payment.

Thus, Option C is correct.

124. Unstructured and semi-structured data can be stored in Hadoop. Because rest given options are relational database which can only store structure data.

Thus, Option A is correct.

125. Habitual buying behavior occurs when a consumer has very little involvement in the purchase and sees very few differences between brands of a product such as salt, turmeric, pepper etc.

Thus, Option B is correct.

126. Net operating income approach advocates that any change in the level of debt of company does not influence the total value of the company. According to this approach, neither the WACC of a company nor its total value depends upon the capital structure decision or financial leverage.

There are presumptions, which form the basis of net operating income.

1) Corporate tax does not exist

2) The overall cost of capital is not affected by changes in any leverage

3) Cost of capital depends on its business risk

4) Cost of Debt is unvarying

Thus, Option C is correct.

127. It is a property of arithmetic mean, which says that the sum of the square of deviation from mean is always minimum.

Thus, Option B is correct.

128. Components of the architecture of business intelligence are as follows:

• Data warehouse deals with technical staff.

• Business analytics consists of reports, queries, data, text and web mining.

• Business Performance management includes the evolution and architecture of business intelligence.

• The user interface includes dashboards and other information broadcasting tools.

Thus, Option B is correct.

129. The SDR is an international reserve asset, created by the IMF in 1969 to supplement its member countries' official reserves. The value of the SDR is based on a basket of five currencies—the U.S. dollar, the euro, the Chinese renminbi, the Japanese yen, and the British pound sterling.

Thus, Option D is correct.

130. Time value of money is based on the idea that people prefer the same money today rather in the future because of money's potential to grow over time. Thus money is more valuable today rather than in future.

Thus, Option C is correct.

131. • The statistical discrepancy (SD) is defined as the sum of all the BoP items with their signs reversed, i.e. SD = -(CA+KA+FA)

• The accounting principles behind BOP transactions are derived from the double-entry bookkeeping system.

Thus, Option C is correct.

132. The Intrapreneurial process starts with a new idea or an innovation after which, an Intrapreneur begins to develop that idea- be it a product, service, or company. After development, an Intrapreneur assesses the market so as to know if implementing the same will pay off well and Implementation is further followed by modification.

Thus, Option C is correct.

133. • Job Enrichment refers to vertical enrichment or the addition of tasks.

• It involves giving additional responsibilities and expecting more accountability.

• Job Enlargement focuses on the horizontal expansion of related tasks without additional responsibility and accountability.

• It involves the expansion of tasks to be carried out.

Thus, Option D is correct.

134. • Women Entrepreneurs face difficulty due to specific problems such as family responsibilities, lack of support from family etc.

• Entrepreneurial problems faced by women entrepreneurs include: Price and availability of raw materials, High competition in low technology products, Shortage of finance, Shortage of raw material etc.

Thus, Option B is correct.

135. • The second national labor commission submitted its report in the year 2002.

• It recommends the recognition of social security as a fundamental human right.

• It recommends setting up a social security fund of India and a separate fund for each state.

• It recommends three kinds of social security schemes. They are as follows:

1) Social insurance type

2) Subsidized scheme or partly contributory

3) Social assistance scheme which is wholly non-contributory.

Thus, Option D is correct.

136. Under Fixed Budgeting, if the actual and budgeted activity levels differ considerably, then various aspects like cost ascertainment, fixation of price do not give a correct picture. A Fixed Budget is a budget that remains unchanged even if the activity changes. It represents the expected results of a responsibility centre only for a single activity level.

Thus, Option C is correct.

137. • PESTLE analysis is used to describe a framework for analyzing the macro-environmental factors.

• PESTLE is an acronym for:

1) Political

2) Economic

3) Socio-economic

4) Technological

5) Legal

6) Environmental

Thus, Option C is correct.

138. • In WTO terminology, the subsides provided are identified with different colours like green, blue, amber boxes etc.

• The subsidies which don't distort trade are placed in the green box. Option a, c, d are included in the green box.

• The subsidies which distort the International trade by making goods cheaper with comparison to others are placed in Amber box. The subsidies on seeds, fertilizers, irrigation, minimum support prices come under this box.

Thus, Option B is correct.

139. Following are true regarding esprit de corps:

• It means creating a team spirit or union is strength.

• Create a sense of belonging among employees.

• It brings loyalty, commitment and dedication in the group.

• Develop an atmosphere of mutual trust and understanding.

Whereas, in the principle of initiative, it is conceived as thinking out and execution of the plan. It is one of keenest satisfaction for an intelligent man to experience.

Thus, Option C is correct.

140. There are two cases

Case 1: when $(n+1)p$ is not an integer. let $(n+1)p=m+f$, where m is an integer and f is fractional. In this case, there exists a unique modal value for binomial distribution and it is m, the integral part of $(n+1)p$.

Case 2: when (n+1)p is an integer. Let (n+1)p=m (an integer). In this case, the binomial distribution is bimodal and the modal values are m and m-1.

Thus, Option C is correct.

141. • Dissonance-reducing behavior occurs when consumers are highly involved in the purchase but worries for little difference in the brands. Dissonance is seen when a consumer gets worried as to whether he/she has made the right choice.

• Complex buying behavior occurs when consumers are purchasing an expensive, and there is a noteworthy difference between the brands.

• Variety seeking or Novelty seeking behavior occurs when consumers are not particularly involved in the purchase and buy different products because in search of variety.

Thus, Option C is correct.

142. Cooperatives is one of the types of Rural Entrepreneurship. It is an autonomous association of people, usually with limited means, that are united voluntarily so as to achieve a common objective.

Thus, Option D is correct.

143. • CII code was a voluntary code for the Indian companies. Though the code contained detailed provisions and focused on listed companies, it was felt that a statutory code would be more purposeful and meaningful.

• Kumar Mangalam Birla Committee was set up as a replacement to the CII code to raise the standards of good corporate governance.

Thus, Option C is correct.

144. • Brand relevance refers to the comeback of a brand with a few mandatory changes to get back the loyal customers.

• Loyal customers are the last ones to leave the brand. When they come to know that the brand they left is updating, they will be the first set of people to test the product again.

Thus, Option A is correct.

145. • Customer touchpoints are the experiences or interactions that occur between the customer and the organization throughout the journey of the customers.

• This may be customer service experience, social media presence, email marketing, television ads, opinion on review sites, etc.

Thus, Option C is correct.

146. • There are always two lines of regression, one of y on x and the other of x on y.

• The line of regression y on x is used to estimate or predict the value of y for any given value of x. Here, y is the dependent variable and x is the independent variable.

• The line of regression x on y is used to predict the value of x for any given value of y i.e. x is the dependent variable and y is an independent variable.

Thus, Option C is correct.

147. • The cost of the product is the seller's concern whereas the utility of the product is the buyer's concern.

• The cost of the product only provides the seller with a basis or standard to determine the price which makes it a seller's concern whereas the upper limit of the price range depends upon the utility of the product, i.e. its demand in the market making it a buyer's concern.

Thus, Option A is correct.

148. • DSS database is a collection of data extracted from several groups or applications. DSS can be either a small database or a large data warehouse.

• The user interface allows the DSS software tools to work accordingly.

• Sensitivity analysis models test the effect of changing one or more factors on overall profit.

• Goal seeking analysis determines the required data by following a backward solution approach.

Thus, Option B is correct.

149. • Decision latitude refers to the potential control of an employee over their tasks in the working environment.

• Organizations decrease the stress levels of the employees by increasing the job decision latitude.

• Increasing the job decision latitude will give more authority regarding the selection of work teams, selection of work schedules, etc.

• The reason explained the assertion statement.

Thus, Option A is correct.

150. Operational and Strategic social marketing are two types of social marketing. Operational social marketing is used to change behaviour, whereas Strategic social marketing is used to form new policies as well as development strategies.

Thus, Option C is correct.

Paper-I

Q.1 A researcher is interested in studying the prospects of a particular political party in an urban area, What tool should he prefer for the study?

A. Rating scale   **B.** Interview

C. Questionnaire   **D.** Schedule

Q.2 In a research on the effect of child- rearing practices on stress-proneness of children in completing school projects, the hypothesis formulated is that 'child rearing practices do influence stress-proneness'. At the data-analysis stage a null hypothesis is advanced to find out the tenability of research hypothesis. On the basis of the evidence available, the null hypothesis is rejected at 0.01 level of significance. What decision may be warranted in respect of the research hypothesis?

A. The research hypothesis will also be rejected.

B. The research hypothesis will be accepted.

C. Both the research hypothesis and the null hypothesis will be rejected.

D. No decision can be taken in respect of the research hypothesis.

Q.3 In which of the following, reporting format is formally prescribed?

A. Doctoral level thesis

B. Conference of researchers

C. Workshops and seminars

D. Symposia

Q.4 How many 4's are there preceded by 7 but not followed by 3?

5 9 3 2 1 7 4 2 6 9 7 4 6 1 3 2 8 7 4 1 3 8 3 2 5 6 7 4 3 9 5 8 2 0 1 8 7 4 6 3

A. Three   **B.** Four   **C.** Six   **D.** Five

Q.5 The compound interest on Rs.30000 at 7% per annum is Rs.4347. The period is:

A. 1 year   **B.** 3 years   **C.** 2 years   **D.** 4 years

Q.6 A is twice as good a workman as B and is, therefore, able to finish a piece of work in 30 days less than B.In how many days they can complete the whole work; working together?

A. 40 days.   **B.** 30 days.   **C.** 10 days.   **D.** 20 days.

Q.7 In finalizing a thesis writing format which of the following would form part of supplementary pages?

A. List of tables and figures

B. Table of contents

C. Conclusions of the study

D. Bibliography and Appendices

Q.8 _________is the study of structures of consciousness as experienced from the first-person point of view.

A. Educational Sociology

B. Social Psychology

C. Educational Psychology

D. Phenomenology

Q.9 A works twice as fast as B.If B can complete a work in 18 days independently,the number of days in which A and B can together finish the work is:

A. 3 days   **B.** 6 days   **C.** 5 days   **D.** 7 days

Q.10 Fixed Position Layout is used when:

A. the operation requires heavy tools and equipment.

B. the operation requires only hand tools and simple equipments.

C. the continuity of the production process is to be maintained.

D. None of the above

Q.11 Diagnostic evaluation ascertains:-

A. Students performance at the beginning of instructions.

B. Learning progress and failures during instructions.

C. Degree of achievement of instructions at the end.

D. Causes and remedies of persistent learning problems during instructions.

Q.12 Which of the following attributes denote great strengths of a teacher?

a) Full-time active involvement in the institutional management

b) Setting examples

c) Willingness to put assumptions to the test

Select the correct answer from the codes given below:

A. a, b   **B.** b, c   **C.** a, c   **D.** a, b, c

Ques (13-14):Choose the correct answer from the following code:

Q.13 Assertion (A) : Learning is a lifelong process.

Reason (R) : Learning to be useful must be linked with life processes.

A. Both (A) and (R) are true and (R) is the correct explanation of (A)

B. Both (A) and (R) are true, but (R) is not the correct explanation of (A)

C. (A) is true, but (R) is false.

D. (A) is false, but (R) is true.

Q.14 Assertion (A) : All teaching implies learning.

Reason (R) : Learning to be useful must be derived from teaching.

A. Both (A) and (R) are true and (R) is the correct explanation of (A).

B. Both (A) and (R) are true but (R) is not the correct explanation of (A).

C. (A) is true, but (R) is false.

D. (A) is false, but (R) is true.

Q.15 From the list given below identify the learner characteristics which would facilitate teaching-learning system to become effective.

1) Prior experience of learner

2) Learner's family lineage

3) Aptitude of the learner

4) Learner's stage of Development

5) Lerner's food habits and hobbies

6) Learner's religious affiliation

Choose the correct code to indicate your answer.

A. 1, 3 and 4   **B.** 4, 5 and 6

C. 1, 4 and 5   **D.** 2, 3 and 6

Q.16 In a deductive argument, validity is the principle that if all the premises are true, the conclusion must also be true. It is called_________.

A. An argument

B. A valid argument

C. An explanation

D. An invalid argument

Q.17 4 men can repair a road in 7 hours. How many men are required to repair the road in 2 hours ?

A. 14 men.   **B.** 24 men.   **C.** 15 men.   **D.** 18 men.

Q.18 Which one of the following statements is not correct in the context of Venn diagram method?

A. It is a method of testing the validity of arguments.

B. It represents both the premises of a syllogism in one diagram.

C. It requires two overlapping circles for the two premises of a standard-form categorical syllogism

D. It can be used to represent classes as well as propositions.

Q.19 A girl introduced a boy as the son of' the daughter of the father of her uncle. The boy is a girl's :

A. Brother   **B.** Son-in-law

C. Son   **D.** Uncle

Q.20 Inductive reasoning is grounded on:

A. Integrity of nature

B. Unity of nature

C. Uniformity of nature

D. Harmony of nature

Q.21 If in a certain code language " bed" is coded as " $AAGGEE$", then how will " mat" be coded in that code language?

A. $LLCCUU$ **B.** $UUCCLL$

C. $CCLLUU$ **D.** $LCLCUU$

Q.22 If Z= 2197 and R= 729. How would J be written in that code?

A. 130   **B.** 129   **C.** 128   **D.** 125

Q.23 If E = 5 and READ is coded as 7, then what is the code of 'DEAR' ?

A. 6   **B.** 7   **C.** 5   **D.** 10

Q.24 I. Tanya is older than Eric.

II. Cliff is older than Tanya.

III. Eric is older than Cliff.

If the first two statements are true, the third statement is:

A. true   **B.** false

C. uncertain   **D.** none

Q.25 The ___________ is using observation and background to reach a logical conclusion. You probably practice inference every day.

A. inference   **B.** argument

C. An explanation   **D.** A valid argument

Q.26 Which of the following are the tools of good governance?

1) Social Audit

2) Separation of Powers

3) Citizen's Charter

4) Right of Information

Select the correct answer from the codes given below:

A. 1, 3 and 4   **B.** 2, 3 and 4

C. 1 and 4   **D.** 1,2,3 and 4

Q.27 The South Asia University is situated in the city of:

A. Colombo   **B.** Dhaka

C. New Delhi   **D.** Kathmandu

Q.28 The national currency of the United States of America (USA) is ____.

A. Euro   **B.** Yen   **C.** Rand   **D.** Dollar

Q.29 _____ is known as the Sorrow of Bihar.

A. Koshi River   **B.** Son River

C. Bagmati River   **D.** Gandaki River

Q.30 MS-Word is an example of ____.

A. A processing device

B. An operating system

C. Application software

D. An input device

Ques (31-35):Read the following passage carefully.

I did that thing recently where you have to sign a big card – which is a horror unto itself, especially as the keeper of the Big Card was leaning over me at the time. Suddenly I was on the spot, a rabbit in the headlights, torn between doing a fun message or some sort of in-joke or a drawing. Instead overwhelmed by the myriad options available to me, I decided to just write: "Good luck, best, Joel".

It was then that I realised, to my horror, that I had forgotten how to write. My entire existence is "tap letters into computer". My shopping lists are hidden in the notes function of my phone. If I need to remember something I send an e-mail to myself. A pen is something I chew when I'm struggling to think. Paper is something I pile beneath my laptop to make it a more comfortable height for me to type on.

A poll of 1,000 teens by the stationers, Bic found that one in 10 don't own a pen, a third have never written a letter, and half of 13 to 19 years – old have never been forced to sit down and write a thank you letter. More than 80% have never written a lover letter, 56% don't have letter paper at home. And a quarter have never known the unique torture of writing a birthday card. The most a teen ever has to use a pen is on an exam paper.

Bic, have you heard of mobile phones? Have you heard of e-mail, facebook and snap chatting? This is the future. Pens are dead. Paper is dead. Paper is dead. Handwriting is a relic.

"Handwriting is one of the most creative outlets we have and should be given the same importance as other art forms such as sketching, painting or photography."

Q.31 When confronted with signing a big card, the author felt like "a rabbit in the headlight". What does this phrase mean?

A. A state of confusion **B.** A state of pleasure
C. A state of anxiety **D.** A state of pain

Q.32 According to the author, which one is not the most creative outlet of pursuit?

A. Handwriting **B.** Photography
C. Sketching **D.** Reading

Q.33 The entire existence of the author revolves round:

1) Computer
2) Mobile phone
3) Typewriter
Identify the correct answer from the codes given below:

A. 2 only **B.** 1 and 2 only
C. 1, 2 and 3 **D.** 2 and 3 only

Q.34 In S-M-C-R model of communication, what does M stands for?

A. Message **B.** Medium
C. Multimedia **D.** Meaning

Q.35 Communication is considered as meaningful only if some elements are present in the procedure. Which of the following element/s will be appropriate in communication?

A. Process **B.** Interaction
C. Social context **D.** All the above

Q.36 Digital Empowerment means :-

i. Universal digit literacy
ii. Universal access to all digital resources.
iii. Collaborative digital platform for participative governance.
iv. Probability of all entitlements for individuals through cloud.
Choose the correct answer form the codes given below:

A. i and ii only **B.** ii and iii only
C. i, ii and iii only **D.** i, ii, iii and iv

Q.37 The mode of communication that involves a single source transmitting information to a large number of receivers simultaneously, is known as:-

A. Group Communication
B. Mass Communication
C. Intrapersonal Communicatio

D. Intrapersonal Communication

Q.38 Junk e-mail is also called _____.

A. Sniffer script **B.** Spam
C. Spoof **D.** Spool

Ques (39-43):Study the table below to answer these questions.

Rate of Interest, Dividend Payout Ratio and the Retained Earnings of Five Companies

Company	Interest (Rs. 000)	Rate of Interest (\%)	Dividend Payout Ratio (\%)	Retained Earnings (Rs. L akh)
A	234	18	22.50	155
B	576	24	19.60	402
C	129.6	16	8.75	365
D	144	9	32.50	270
E	180	15	28.00	216

Profit earned is either paid out as dividend or ploughed back in business as retained earnings. Interest is paid on borrowings.

Q.39 By how much do the borrowings of Company B exceed that of Company A ?

A. Rs. 1,210,000 **B.** Rs.1,320,000
C. Rs.1,000,000 **D.** Rs.1,100,000

Q.40 By how much does the dividend paid by Company D exceed the dividend paid by Company B ?

A. Rs.23 lakh **B.** Rs.25 lakh
C. Rs.33 lakh **D.** Rs. 32 lakh

Q.41 The profit of E is more/less than that of C by ____ %

A. 64% less **B.** 60% less **C.** 25% less **D.** 50% less

Q.42 What is the sum of profits made by Companies A and B ?

A. ₹9.2 lakh **B.** ₹8.1 lakh
C. ₹7 lakh **D.** ₹6 lakh

Q.43 What is the sum of the borrowings of all five companies ?

A. Rs. 53.1 lakh **B.** Rs. 72.1 lakh
C. Rs. 73.1 lakh **D.** Rs. 63.1 lakh

Q.44 In Government interaction in E-governance G2C stands for:

A. Government to Center
B. Government to Company
C. Government to Citizen
D. Government to Commerce.

Q.45 In a computer, if 7 bits are used to specify address in memory, the total number of addresses will be:

A. 128 **B.** 512 **C.** 216 **D.** 256

Q.46 The First Mechanical Computer Designed by Charles Babbage was called?

A. Super Computer
B. Abacus
C. Calculator
D. Analytical Engine

Q.47 Which of the following indoor plant helps to improve indoor air quality?
A. Areca Palm
B. Lady Palm
C. Dragon Tree
D. All of them

Q.48 The primary source of organic pollution in fresh water bodies is:-
A. run-off urban areas
B. run-off agricultural forms
C. sewage effluents
D. industrial effluents

Q.49 Read the assertion and reason both carefully:-

Assertion (A): The volume of imports tends to be very high when there is a conjecture of high rate of economic growth and a sharp fall in the relative price of imports and vice versa.

Reason (R): High rate of growth, ceteris paribus, is associated with rise in imports and increase in the imports, ceteris paribus, is associated with a fall in the relative price of imports.

A. Both (A) and (R) are correct and (R) is the right explanation of (A).
B. Both (A) and (R) are correct but (R) is not the right explanation of (A).
C. (A) is correct but (R) is not correct.
D. (R) is correct but (A) is not correct.

Q.50 Which of the following is the salient feature of the industrial policy developments since 1991?
A. The scope of the private sector has been enormously expanded.
B. Public sector has been withdrawing partially or fully from several of the enterprises by divestment.
C. The Indian industry is increasingly exposed to foreign competition.
D. All of these

Paper-II

Q.51 Match the items of the following two lists:-

List 1	List 2
(A) Tie-up sales	(i) Oligopoly pricing
(B) Price being non-responsive to changes in demand costs	(ii) Differential pricing
(C) Trade channel discounts	(iii) Product-line pricing
(D) Basing-point pricing	(iv) Locational price differentials

A. (iv) (iii) (ii) (i)
B. (iii) (iv) (i) (ii)
C. (iii) (i) (ii) (iv)
D. (iii) (ii) (iv) (i)

Q.52 Which of the following statements are correct with reference to V.V. Giri approach to Industrial relations?
a) Outside interference must be avoided when there is a difference of opinions
b) Collective bargaining and joint negotiations must be used to solve the disputes
c) Trade unions should use voluntary arbitration in place of compulsory adjudication
d) There should be bipartite machinery in every unit of the industry
Choose the correct option from those below:
A. a, b and c only
B. a, b, c and d
C. a, c and d only
D. b and d only

Q.53 Which of the following is not a part of the operational areas covered under the second schedule of the Participation of workers in management act, 1990?
A. Material supply
B. Housekeeping
C. Review of monthly targets and schedules
D. Pollution control

Q.54 What is the distribution of arrivals
A. Gamma distribution
B. Exponential distribution
C. Poisson distribution
D. Normal distribution

Q.55 Assertion (A): Eustress increases the stress levels above the optimum level.

Reason (R): Eustress provides strength and physical force for short intervals of time which results in peak performance.
A. Both (A) and (R) are correct, and (R) is the correct explanation of (A).
B. Both (A) and (R) are correct, but (R) is not the correct explanation of (A).
C. (A) is correct., but (R) is not correct.
D. (A) is wrong, and (R) is correct.

Q.56 Which of the following statements is/are correct with reference to provisions of CSR policy 135(1) of the companies act 2013 required to contribute to a CSR committee
a) Turnover of Rs 1200 cr or more
b) Net worth of Rs 500 cr or more
c) Net Profit of Rs.5 cr or more
Choose the correct option/code from the following:
A. a,c
B. a,b
C. b,c
D. a,b,c

Q.57 Statement I: Corporate social responsibility does not deal with the environmental principles and anti-corruption practices.
Statement II: Corporate social responsibility is a way of integrating societal demands into business operations.
Choose the correct option from those below:
A. Statement I is correct, Statement II is incorrect.
B. Statement I is incorrect, Statement II is correct.
C. Both Statement I and Statement II are correct.
D. Both Statement I and Statement II are incorrect.

Q.58 Which of the following Ps of marketing mix covers the actual amount the end-user is expected to pay for a product?
A. Product
B. Price
C. Place
D. Promotion

Q.59 _____________theory says that in order to successfully initiate a venture, the social and cultural contexts should be carefully examined and considered.

A. Sociological Entrepreneurship Theory

B. Psychological Entrepreneurship Theory

C. Anthropological Entrepreneurship Theory

D. Resource-based Entrepreneurship Theory

Q.60 Which of the following is not an advantage of Analytical CRM?

A. Improves customer satisfaction as well as loyalty

B. Helps in retaining profitable customers with the help of thorough analysis of customer's information and data

C. Determines, develops and analysis analytical methods to scale and optimize relationships with customers

D. Helps in addressing the needs of the customers thereby improving relationships with them

Q.61 There are seven elements in the process of communication. Rank the following elements in a proper sequence of steps.

a) Ideas

b) Decoding

c) Sender

d) Feedback

e) Communication channel

f) Receiver

g) Encoding

Choose the correct option from those below:

A. a,c,g,e,f,b,d

B. c,a,g,e,b,f,d

C. c,a,e,g,f,b,d

D. c,a,g,e,f,b,d

Q.62 What was the word coined by Mckinsey and Company after a study in 1997?

A. Core competency

B. Talent management

C. Employee engagement

D. Business process re-engineering

Q.63 Statement I: The Royal Commission on Labour is also known as the Whitley Commission.

Statement II: The commission was set up in 1929 to determine the conditions of labor in industries in India.

Choose the correct option from those below:

A. Statement I is correct., Statement II is incorrect.

B. Statement I is incorrect, Statement II is correct.

C. Both Statement I and Statement II are correct.

D. Both Statement I and Statement II are incorrect.

Q.64 _________ tries to duplicate the workplace environment and is used for training personnel for semi-skilled jobs.

A. Programmed instructions

B. Vestibule training

C. Simulation

D. Experiential exercise

Q.65 Which measure(s) of central tendency is/are not affected by outliers

A. Harmonic mean and median

B. Geometric mean and mode

C. Median and mode

D. Arithmetic mean and median

Q.66 Assertion (A): Organisations can discourage unionization by offering the open-door policy to the employees.

Reason (R): If the unionization is regarding the new decisions taken by the organization or regarding grievance management, then the open-door policy may stop them from forming the unions.

A. Both (A) and (R) are correct, and (R) is the correct explanation of (A).

B. Both (A) and (R) are correct, but (R) is not the correct explanation of (A).

C. (A) is correct., but (R) is not correct.

D. (A) is wrong, and (R) is correct.

Q.67 Advantages of the Critical Incident Technique is/ are:-

A. The respondents are not forced into any framework

B. The respondent's perspective is taken into account

C. Many ways to implement the technique like observation, questionnaires and interviews

D. All of these

Q.68 Disadvantages of the Critical Incident Technique is /are:-

A. Many incidents may go unreported or might not be precise as the reporting of incidents relies on memory of the respondent.

B. The respondents are not forced into any framework

C. Many ways to implement the technique like observation, questionnaires and interviews

D. None of the above

Q.69 Generalised conclusion on the basis of a sample is technically known as:

A. Data analysis and interpretation

B. Parameter inference

C. Statistical inference of external validity of the research

D. All of the above

Q.70 For computing earliest event time one may use

A. Latest allowable time

B. Backward pass communication

C. Forward pass communication

D. Critical path

Q.71 A wage that is defined as the goods and services that could be purchased with the help of money wages is known as?

A. Nominal Wage

B. Real Wage

C. Cash Wage

D. Money Wage

Q.72 The PESTLE framework primarily involves which of the following areas?

Statement I: The environmental factors affecting the organization

Statement II: Important factors relevant to the present context

Choose the correct option from those below:

A. Statement I is correct., Statement II is incorrect.

B. Statement I is incorrect, Statement II is correct.

C. Both Statement I and Statement II are correct.

D. Both Statement I and Statement II are incorrect.

Q.73 Under which of the following forms of personal selling, a salesperson communicates directly with potential customers who visit the store on their own to inquire about a product or to purchase one?

A. Business to business selling

B. Trade selling

C. Retail selling

D. None of the above

Q.74 Statement I: Indian rupee was made 100% convertible on current account in 1994.

Statement II: Indian rupee is still partially convertible in the capital account.

Choose the correct option from those below:

A. Statement I is correct, Statement II is incorrect.

B. Statement I is incorrect, Statement II is correct.

C. Both Statement I and Statement II are correct.

D. Both Statement I and Statement II are incorrect.

Q.75 Which of the following countries is not a member of SAARC?

A. India

B. Bangladesh

C. China

D. Pakistan

Q.76 Which of the following is not a characteristic of an Entrepreneur?

A. An entrepreneur is a good leader, motivator, as well as a team builder.

B. An entrepreneur decides the policy of production as to what, how, and how much to produce.

C. An entrepreneur has the ability to persuade others with his communication skills.

D. An entrepreneur is action-oriented and takes risks to achieve goals.

Q.77 Which of the following statements relating to Opportunity-Based Entrepreneurship theory is not true?

A. Opportunity based Theory is anchored by Peter Drucker and Howard Stevenson.

B. It believes that entrepreneurs excel at taking advantage of possibilities that are created by social, cultural and technological changes.

C. This theory argues that entrepreneurs have individual specific resources that make the recognition of new opportunities easier.

D. Stevenson extended Drucker's opportunity based theory to include resourcefulness.

Q.78 Under Neo-Freudian theory of Personality, Which of the following personality types are not much aware of brands and desire independence, self-reliance, etc.?

A. Compliant Personalities

B. Aggressive Personalities

C. Detached Personalities

D. None of the above

Q.79 Billboards, posters, signs are examples of which form of media?

A. Print Media

B. Display Media

C. Network Media

D. Electronic Media

Q.80 Assertion (A): Ethics and Morality are the same and can be used interchangeably.

Reason (R): Ethics is concerned with activities of organizations with professional codes of conduct.

A. Both (A) and (R) are correct, and (R) is the correct explanation of (A).

B. Both (A) and (R) are correct, but (R) is not the correct explanation of (A).

C. (A) is correct., but (R) is not correct.

D. (A) is wrong, and (R) is correct.

Q.81 David A. Aaker outlined the dimensions of a Market Analysis. Which of the following is not one of the dimensions as identified by him?

A. Market Trends

B. Market Profitability

C. Industry cost structure

D. Market Segmentation

Q.82 Which of the following talent development approaches deals with the movement of an employee from one job to another of the same nature?

A. Job monitoring

B. Job rotation

C. Internal posting

D. Career fairs

Q.83 Which among the following is not considered a compensation challenge in the current environment?

A. Wage and salaries policy

B. Government constraints

C. Union power

D. Employment management

Q.84 According to which of the following theories of Entrepreneurship, an entrepreneur has to fill the gaps in the market, in case there are any imperfections (gap filler) and is also required to transform available inputs and improve the efficiency of existing production method (Input Completer)?

A. X-Efficiency Theory

B. Innovation Theory

C. Opportunity-based Theory

D. Resource-based Theory

Q.85 Which among the following of HR practice are part of three important components in aligning business strategy:

I. Business strategy

II. Human resource practices

III. Marketing strategy

IV. Organizational capabilities

V. Organizational structure

Choose the correct code:

A. I, II, III

B. I, II, IV

C. II, III, V

D. I, IV, V

Q.86 Statement I: Adam Smith gave the theory of Absolute Advantage.

Statement II: David Ricardo's theory of Comparative Advantage was illustrated in his book- On the Principles of Political Economy and Taxation.

Choose the correct option from those below:

A. Statement I is correct, Statement II is incorrect.

B. Statement I is incorrect, Statement II is correct.

C. Both Statement I and Statement II are correct.

D. Both Statement I and Statement II are incorrect.

Q.87 In the Value Chain Analysis, which of the following performances come under the operations perspective of the Balanced scorecard?

A. Ability to change

B. Product development

C. Differentiation

D. Profitability

Q.88 Assertion (A): David Ricardo's trading principle focuses on the demand side of the market.

Reason (R): Specialisation results from economies of large scale production.

A. Both (A) and (R) are correct, and (R) is the correct explanation of (A)

B. Both (A) and (R) are correct, but (R) is not the correct explanation of (A)

C. (A) is correct, but (R) is not correct.

D. (A) is wrong, and (R) is correct.

Q.89 An organization encourages its employees to follow and practice the entrepreneurial principles so as to transform the slow growth of the company into high growth. This characteristic of Intrapreneurship states that it is __________in nature.

A. Intuitive **B.** Exhaustive

C. Restorative **D.** Consumptive

Q.90 The consumer will be in equilibrium when the

A. MRS_{xy} is greater than the ratio of commodity prices

B. MRS_{xy} is lesser than the ratio of commodity prices

C. MRS_{xy} is equal to the ratio of commodity prices

D. The slope of MRS_{xy} is greater than the slope of IC curve

Q.91 Which of the following is not a type of artificial intelligence?

A. Reactive machines **B.** Supervised learning

C. Theory of mind **D.** Self-awareness

Q.92 Variables such as age, gender, family size, occupation, income describe which of the following type of market segmentation?

A. Behavioral Segmentation

B. Psychographic Segmentation

C. Demographic Segmentation

D. Geographic Segmentation

Q.93 A company has 5 Product lines and each line has 3 Product variations. Identify which of the following is its correct Product Mix Length and Width?

A. 15,3 **B.** 5,3 **C.** 15,5 **D.** 5,10

Q.94 Which of the following theories of Capital Structure believes that the value of the firm remains the same and is not affected by the change of debt component in the capital structure without tax?

A. Net Operating Income Theory

B. Net Income Theory

C. Modigliani and Miller Theory

D. Traditional Approach

Q.95 Statement I: Decentralisation creates a pool of promotable manpower with skills.

Statement II: Decentralisation helps managers to see their own results of their actions.

Choose the correct option from the following:

A. Statement I is correct, Statement II is incorrect.

B. Statement I is incorrect, Statement II is correct.

C. Both Statement I and Statement II are correct.

D. Both Statement I and Statement II are incorrect.

Q.96 Which of the following programs was launched by NITI Aayog on 8 March,2018 to promote and support established as well as aspiring women entrepreneurs in India?

A. Women Entrepreneurship Platform

B. Women Support Program

C. Women-owned Businesses Program

D. Women Entrepreneur talent program

Q.97 Which of the following methods of performance appraisal is also called bell curve rating?

A. Graphic rating scale

B. Critical incident method

C. Forced distribution method

D. BARS

Ques (98-100): Lovely private limited provided the following information:

Raw Material Storage Period = 80 days

Work-in-Progress conversion Period = 22 days

Finished Stock Storage Period = 30 days

Debtor Collection Period = 50 days

Creditors Payment Period = 90 days

Annual operating costs = Rs 25,00,000

(including depreciation of Rs 3,50,000)

Average Debtors = Rs 4,00,000

[Take 1 year = 365 days]

Q.98 What is the name of the technique of development where a company creates live situations at work (usually one that involves conflicts between people) and invites the trainees to participate in it and handle the situation?

A. Project Assignment

B. Sensitivity Training

C. Role-Playing

D. Management Games

Q.99 Which institution defined FDI as "FDI as a category of international investment that reflects the objective of a resident in one economy (the direct investor) obtaining a lasting interest in an enterprise resident in another economy (the direct investment enterprise)."

A. WTO

B. UNCTAD

C. OECD

D. IMF

Q.100 Assertion (A): Cultural entropy increases the internal cohesion and level of trust.

Reason (R): Cultural entropy involves fear-based decisions of the leaders and it is a measure of friction that employees encounter on a daily basis.

A. Both (A) and (R) are correct, and (R) is the correct explanation of (A).

B. Both (A) and (R) are correct, but (R) is not the correct explanation of (A).

C. (A) is correct, but (R) is not correct.

D. (A) is wrong, and (R) is correct.

Q.101 What is the amount of Annual Credit Sales?

A. Rs 29,20,000

B. Rs 35,00,000

C. Rs 12,80,000

D. Rs 20,00,000

Q.102 Calculate the Operating Cycle Period of the company?

A. 125 days   **B.** 60 days   **C.** 100 days   **D.** 92 days

Q.103 Calculate the number of operating cycles of the company in a year?

A. 8.905   **B.** 7.329   **C.** 3.967   **D.** 1.118

Q.104 What is the amount of working capital required by the company?

A. Rs 2,21,248

B. Rs 8,09,902

C. Rs 3,50,108

D. Rs 5,41,971

Q.105 Company is planning to discontinue sales on credit and start delivering products based on pre-payment. Then what would be the amount of working capital required in this case?

A. Rs 3,42,590

B. Rs 7,02,305

C. Rs 5,80,928

D. Rs 2,47,397

Ques (106-115):Direction: Read the passage and attempt the questions that follow:

Before getting acquired by Softtech company, ABC software company faced many HR issues. The manual performance appraisal was one of the main concerns of the employees as the company was following the essay method for assessing the employees. The essay method involves feedback from the immediate manager and colleagues and takes months to complete.

All the employees started sending emails to the HR team regarding the delay in the appraisal process as it impacts their rewards and promotions. Looking at the large volume of the mails, the HR team started sending the same reply to all the employees. This annoyed the employees.

Some employees argued that the appraisal results were biased and favoured only a few of them. This lasted for a longer period of time, and the employees with more than two years of

experience started leaving the organization. The remaining employees were not at all happy with the decisions of the top-level management and demanded the revision of the appraisal process. The employees who left the company started posting bad reviews regarding the work culture on various portals. This affected the brand value of the company and gradually lost its clients.

Q.106 Which of the following appraisal methods involves assessment from multiple departments within the firm and also from external sources?

A. 360-degree appraisal

B. Ranking method

C. Essay method

D. Grading method

Q.107 Which of the following is not a traditional method of performance appraisal?

A. Forced choice method

B. Field review method

C. Assessment centres

D. Checklist method

Q.108 Who developed Management by Objective (MBO) method of appraisal method?

A. Elton Mayo

B. Kurt Lewin

C. Peter Drucker

D. Mary Parker Follett

Q.109 Who introduced the word "Employer Brand"?

A. Bronisław Malinowski

B. Simon Barrow

C. Sigmund Freud

D. Pierre Janet

Q.110 Which of the following is the last phase of the performance management cycle?

A. Performance planning

B. Performance action

C. Performance monitoring

D. Performance review

Q.111 Legal formalities, lack of technical knowledge, poor quality of products, procurement of raw materials etc. fall under which of the following types of problems in Rural Entrepreneurship?

A. Marketing problems

B. Management problems

C. Human Resources problems

D. Financial problems

Q.112 Statement I: Reserve Bank of India stated that a small-scale unit should be considered as sick if it had accumulated losses equal to or exceeding seventy-five percent of its peak net worth during the previous accounting year

Statement II: The Sick Industrial Companies Act,1985 stated sickness in terms of cash losses for two consecutive financial years and the accumulated losses at the end of the second financial year which are equal to or exceed the net worth of the company

Choose the correct option from those below:

A. Statement I is correct., Statement II is incorrect.
B. Statement I is incorrect, Statement II is correct.
C. Both Statement I and Statement II are correct.
D. Both Statement I and Statement II are incorrect.

Q.113 Choose the correct option from those below:

I. Cross elasticity of demand for complementary goods is negative.

II. Demand curve moves downward due to the law of diminishing marginal utility and income effect.

III. Law of demand establishes a qualitative relationship between demand and price.

IV. If the demand curve is a rectangular hyperbola, the elasticity of demand is zero.

Choose the correct option from those below:

A. I, II, III
B. I, III, IV
C. II, III, IV
D. I, II, IV

Q.114 Statement I: Emotional barriers are closely associated with physical barriers.

Statement II: Authoritarian attitude of management is an example of organizational barriers.

Choose the correct option from those below:

A. Statement I is correct., Statement II is incorrect.
B. Statement I is incorrect, Statement II is correct.
C. Both Statement I and Statement II are correct.
D. Both Statement I and Statement II are incorrect.

Q.115 Assertion (A): Informal organization leads to a faster spread of information and quick feedback.

Reason (R): An organization's development activity is incomplete without proper feedback.

A. (A) is correct, but (R) is incorrect.
B. Both (A) and (R) are correct, but (R) is not the right explanation of (A).
C. Both (A) and (R) are correct, (R) is the right explanation of (A).
D. Both (A) and (R) are incorrect.

Q.116 Veterinary education is related:

A. General Education
B. Medical Education
C. Agricultural Education
D. Technical Education

Q.117 Which of the labour welfare legislative acts is applicable to non-seasonal factories using power and employing 10 or more persons and non-power using 20 or more persons.

A. Factories Act, 1948
B. Employee State Insurance Act, 1948
C. Employee Provident Fund Act, 1952
D. Payment of Gratuity Scheme Act, 1972

Q.118 In which of the following methods of performance appraisal, traits important for effective performance are listed out, and each employee is rated against these traits

A. Paired comparison method
B. Graphic rating scale
C. Behaviorally anchored rating scale
D. Forced distribution

Q.119 Which of the following sampling scheme is generally used in qualitative sampling?

A. Systematic sampling
B. Multistage sampling
C. Quota sampling
D. Multiphase sampling

Q.120 Under which of the following approaches of working capital investment, an organization invests high capital in current assets, keeps inventory level higher and follows liberal credit policies?

A. Moderate approach
B. Conservative approach
C. Aggressive approach
D. Combined approach

Q.121 Assertion(A): Decline stage is reached when the Sales of a product start to fall and it becomes no more profitable to the company(futile).

Reason(R): It often happens because substitute products enter the market and satisfy customer needs better than previous products.

A. Both (A) and (R) are correct, and (R) is the correct explanation of (A).
B. Both (A) and (R) are correct, but (R) is not the correct explanation of (A).
C. (A) is correct, but (R) is not correct.
D. (A) is wrong, and (R) is correct.

Q.122 Which of the following is not an objective of EXIM policy of India?

A. Develop export potential
B. Improve BOT
C. Enhance foreign exchange reserves
D. Increase domestic money circulation

Q.123 Which EU Treaty led to the creation of a single Commission and a single Council to serve the three European Communities?

A. Brussels Treaty
B. Schengen treaty
C. Maastricht Treaty
D. Lisbon Treaty

Q.124 Assertion (A): Branding is a very important feature of a Product

Reason(R): It differentiates itself from other similar products available in the market

A. Both (A) and (R) are correct, and (R) is the correct explanation of (A).
B. Both (A) and (R) are correct, but (R) is not the correct explanation of (A).
C. (A) is correct, but (R) is not correct.
D. (A) is wrong, and (R) is correct.

Q.125 Who developed the concept of the seven-phase model of organization development?

A. Peter Drucker
B. Elton Mayo
C. Warner Burke
D. Kurt Lewin

Q.126 Statement I: In India, the right to strike is not a fundamental right but a legal right.

Statement II: In India, the right to protest is a fundamental right under Article 19 of the constitution of India.

Choose the correct option from those below:

A. Statement I is correct., Statement II is incorrect.

B. Statement I is incorrect, Statement II is correct.

C. Both Statement I and Statement II are correct.

D. Both Statement I and Statement II are incorrect.

Q.127 Assertion (A): Balanced scorecards are used to measure and provide feedback to organizations.

Reason (R): In the balanced scorecard model, customer perspectives are collected to gauge customer satisfaction.

A. (A) is correct., but (R) is incorrect.

B. Both (A) and (R) are correct, but (R) is not the right explanation of (A).

C. Both (A) and (R) are correct, (R) is the right explanation of (A).

D. Both (A) and (R) are incorrect.

Q.128 Which of the following types of Intrapreneurs are independent, prefer working in a less structured environment and are also called big-picture thinkers?

A. Inside Intrapreneurs

B. Doers Intrapreneurs

C. Creator Intrapreneurs

D. Implementers Intrapreneurs

Q.129 Statement I: Free riders are the employees who join the union and are covered by a collective bargaining agreement. These people do not pay for the services they receive.

Statement II: Cheap riders are the employees who are not members of a union but are covered by a collective bargaining agreement. These people pay for the services they receive from the unions.

Choose the correct option from those below:

A. Statement I is correct., Statement II is incorrect.

B. Statement I is incorrect, Statement II is correct.

C. Both Statement I and Statement II are correct.

D. Both Statement I and Statement II are incorrect.

Q.130 Who said that the purpose of business is to increase profits?

A. Milton Friedman

B. Michael Porter

C. C K Prahalad

D. Philips Kotler

Q.131 Which of the following is not a barrier to delegation?

A. Fear of losing power

B. Losing informal relations

C. Personal attitude which stops him from delegating.

D. Inability to direct people efficiently

Q.132 Which of the following refers to entrepreneurs who are very sceptical in experimenting with any new change and adopt new technologies only when they feel that not doing so would result in a heavy loss?

A. Drone entrepreneurs

B. Fabian entrepreneurs

C. Innovative entrepreneurs

D. Imitating entrepreneurs

Q.133 Which of the following is the largest trade union in India?

A. All India Trade Union Congress

B. Hind Mazdoor Sabha

C. All India United Trade Union Centre

D. Bharatiya Mazdoor Sangh

Q.134 According to _________, Innovation distinguishes between a leader and a follower.

A. Bill Gates

B. Steve Jobs

C. Philip Kotler

D. Adam Smith

Q.135 Who developed the theory of Cumulative Causation?

A. Michael Porter

B. Paul Krugman

C. Nicholas Kaldor

D. J M Keynes

Q.136 Statement I. Ranking, classification, factor compensation and point method are main techniques of _________.

Statement II. Tools such as cost of living indicators and salary budget averages are components of _______ used to analyze competitive and appropriate salary of organization's employees.

Statement III. Interviews, questionnaires, and observation are techniques of _________.

Choose the correct option from those below:

A. Salary survey, job analysis, pay structures

B. Job description, job evaluation, job specification

C. Job evaluation, salary survey, job analysis

D. Compensation plan, Human resource planning, pay structure

Q.137 Statement I: Learning refers to a relatively permanent change in behavior.

Statement II: Learning is a continuous process that involves practice and experience and supports normal behavior to meet new challenges.

Choose the correct option from those below:

A. Statement I is correct., Statement II is incorrect.

B. Statement I is incorrect, Statement II is correct.

C. Both Statement I and Statement II are correct.

D. Both Statement I and Statement II are incorrect.

Q.138 Which of the following is the observer of WTO?

A. Iran

B. Tajikistan

C. Srilanka

D. Papua New Guinea

Q.139 An officer or an expert from the HR department comes and interviews the appraiser regarding the performance of each employee and takes notes in his notebook. Name this method of performance appraisal?

A. Confidential Report

B. Essay Method

C. Field Review Method

D. 360-degree appraisal

Q.140 A company asks an employee to relocate to a different location or to another unit that has similar job responsibilities and status. This phenomenon in HRM is known as:

A. Promotion

B. Dislocation

C. Transfer

D. Re-employment

Q.141 Statement I: Functional competencies are also called technical competencies that include professional skills, abilities and technical knowledge required to perform a job.

Statement II: Conceptual competencies are not easily identifiable behaviours but have a strong linkage with entrepreneurial traits.

Choose the correct option from the following:

A. Statement I is correct, Statement II is incorrect.

B. Statement I is incorrect, Statement II is correct.

C. Both Statement I and Statement II are correct.

D. Both Statement I and Statement II are incorrect.

Q.142 Statement I: Strategic Corporate Social Responsibility (CSR) emerged from Management.

Statement II: Transformative CSR is different from strategic CSR as it is focused at the micro-level.

Choose the correct option from those below:

A. Statement I is correct., Statement II is incorrect.

B. Statement I is incorrect, Statement II is correct.

C. Both Statement I and Statement II are correct.

D. Both Statement I and Statement II are incorrect.

Ques (143-144):Read the assertion and reason and choose the correct code:-

Q.143 Which of the following statements is not incorrect?

I. Lower the elasticity, greater the degree of monopoly.

II. Price elasticity of demand in a monopolistic market is large.

III. In the monopolistic market, the point at which the firm covers its fixed cost is called "closing-down point"

IV. A monopolist always charges a price which is greater than marginal cost.

Choose the correct option from those below:

A. I, II, III

B. I, II, IV

C. II, III, IV

D. I, III, IV

Q.144 Porter has defined the business-level strategy as a competitive strategy and classified it into three basic strategies. Which of the following is not a part of the basic strategy?

A. Differentiation

B. Organization's performance

C. Focus

D. Cost leadership

Ques (145-146):Read the assertion and reason both carefully:-

Q.145 _________indicates the degree to which the production facilities have been utilized by comparing it with the expected budgeted capacity.

A. Efficiency Ratio

B. Capacity Ratio

C. Calendar Ratio

D. Activity Ratio

Q.146 Assertion (A): Transactional analysis develops the interpersonal relationship.

Reason (R): Transactional analysis helps an individual in enhancing the positive approach and decision making skills.

A. Both (A) and (R) are correct, and (R) is the correct explanation of (A).

B. Both (A) and (R) are correct, but (R) is not the correct explanation of (A).

C. (A) is correct, but (R) is not correct.

D. (A) is wrong, and (R) is correct.

Q.147 Assertion (A): Money income is the flow of money received for productive activity.

Reason (R): The Monetary values of goods and services are calculated by the expenditure done on it, and the total amount spent by a community depends on its money income.

A. (A) is correct., but (R) is incorrect.

B. Both (A) and (R) are correct, but (R) is not the right explanation of (A).

C. Both (A) and (R) are correct, (R) is the right explanation of (A).

D. Both (A) and (R) are incorrect.

Q.148 Statement I: Borrowings from unrelated parties abroad that are guaranteed by direct investors are classified under FDI.

Statement II: FDI is based on the residency of the direct investor.

Choose the correct option from those below:

A. Statement I is correct, Statement II is incorrect.

B. Statement I is incorrect, Statement II is correct.

C. Both Statement I and Statement II are correct.

D. Both Statement I and Statement II are incorrect.

Q.149 _________is a person within a large corporation who takes direct responsibility to innovate new ideas, products or services.

A. Entrepreneur

B. Intrapreneur

C. Intra Entrepreneur

D. Ultrapreneur

Q.150 Two series having the same mean, median and mode

Statement 1: will have necessarily equal values in the series.

Statement 2: will have necessarily unequal values in the series.

Select the correct option

A. Statement 1 is correct but statement 2 is incorrect

B. Both statement 2 and statement 1 are correct.

C. Both statements 1 and 2 are not correct.

D. Statement 1 is incorrect but statement 2 is correct.

// Smart Answer Sheet //

Correct Percentage of students who answered correctly. **Skipped** Percentage of students who skipped.

Q.	Ans.	Correct / Skipped	Q.	Ans.	Correct / Skipped	Q.	Ans.	Correct / Skipped	Q.	Ans.	Correct / Skipped	Q.	Ans.	Correct / Skipped
1	C	48.21 % / 14.29 %	17	A	32.14 % / 35.72 %	33	B	41.07 % / 41.07 %	49	A	37.5 % / 41.07 %	65	C	44.64 % / 26.79 %
2	B	44.64 % / 32.15 %	18	C	30.36 % / 39.28 %	34	A	37.5 % / 41.07 %	50	D	35.71 % / 41.08 %	66	A	58.93 % / 26.78 %
3	A	46.43 % / 35.71 %	19	A	50.0 % / 39.29 %	35	D	35.71 % / 41.08 %	51	C	50.0 % / 21.43 %	67	D	37.5 % / 26.79 %
4	B	57.14 % / 35.72 %	20	C	50.0 % / 39.29 %	36	D	41.07 % / 41.07 %	52	B	46.43 % / 23.21 %	68	A	51.79 % / 28.57 %
5	C	35.71 % / 35.72 %	21	A	39.29 % / 39.28 %	37	B	53.57 % / 41.07 %	53	D	17.86 % / 23.21 %	69	C	21.43 % / 26.78 %
6	D	26.79 % / 35.71 %	22	D	44.64 % / 39.29 %	38	B	53.57 % / 41.07 %	54	C	55.36 % / 23.21 %	70	C	14.29 % / 26.78 %
7	D	51.79 % / 35.71 %	23	B	53.57 % / 41.07 %	39	D	25.0 % / 41.07 %	55	D	30.36 % / 23.21 %	71	B	30.36 % / 26.78 %
8	D	28.57 % / 35.72 %	24	B	53.57 % / 41.07 %	40	D	28.57 % / 39.29 %	56	C	30.36 % / 25.0 %	72	C	50.0 % / 28.57 %
9	B	44.64 % / 35.72 %	25	A	32.14 % / 41.07 %	41	C	25.0 % / 41.07 %	57	B	50.0 % / 26.79 %	73	C	42.86 % / 28.57 %
10	A	46.43 % / 35.71 %	26	A	23.21 % / 41.08 %	42	C	17.86 % / 41.07 %	58	B	55.36 % / 26.78 %	74	C	35.71 % / 28.58 %
11	D	35.71 % / 35.72 %	27	C	41.07 % / 41.07 %	43	C	26.79 % / 41.07 %	59	C	17.86 % / 26.78 %	75	C	50.0 % / 28.57 %
12	B	30.36 % / 37.5 %	28	D	48.21 % / 41.08 %	44	C	46.43 % / 41.07 %	60	C	23.21 % / 28.58 %	76	B	48.21 % / 28.58 %
13	A	48.21 % / 37.5 %	29	A	41.07 % / 41.07 %	45	A	32.14 % / 41.07 %	61	D	16.07 % / 26.79 %	77	C	25.0 % / 28.57 %
14	C	30.36 % / 37.5 %	30	C	46.43 % / 41.07 %	46	D	28.57 % / 41.07 %	62	B	37.5 % / 26.79 %	78	C	41.07 % / 28.57 %
15	A	51.79 % / 37.5 %	31	A	26.79 % / 41.07 %	47	D	44.64 % / 41.07 %	63	C	44.64 % / 26.79 %	79	B	44.64 % / 28.57 %
16	B	46.43 % / 37.5 %	32	D	19.64 % / 41.07 %	48	C	37.5 % / 41.07 %	64	B	57.14 % / 26.79 %	80	D	30.36 % / 28.57 %

Q.	Ans.	Correct / Skipped	Q.	Ans.	Correct / Skipped	Q.	Ans.	Correct / Skipped	Q.	Ans.	Correct / Skipped	Q.	Ans.	Correct / Skipped
81	D	28.57 % / 28.57 %	95	C	42.86 % / 30.35 %	109	B	37.5 % / 33.93 %	123	A	23.21 % / 33.93 %	137	C	26.79 % / 35.71 %
82	B	51.79 % / 28.57 %	96	A	28.57 % / 30.36 %	110	D	44.64 % / 32.15 %	124	A	50.0 % / 33.93 %	138	A	16.07 % / 33.93 %
83	D	23.21 % / 28.58 %	97	C	19.64 % / 30.36 %	111	B	48.21 % / 32.15 %	125	C	16.07 % / 33.93 %	139	C	21.43 % / 35.71 %
84	A	30.36 % / 30.35 %	98	C	35.71 % / 30.36 %	112	B	37.5 % / 32.14 %	126	C	30.36 % / 33.93 %	140	C	32.14 % / 37.5 %
85	B	16.07 % / 28.57 %	99	D	10.71 % / 32.15 %	113	A	25.0 % / 33.93 %	127	C	23.21 % / 37.5 %	141	C	30.36 % / 35.71 %
86	C	42.86 % / 30.35 %	100	D	23.21 % / 30.36 %	114	B	23.21 % / 35.72 %	128	C	28.57 % / 33.93 %	142	A	21.43 % / 35.71 %
87	B	41.07 % / 30.36 %	101	A	25.0 % / 30.36 %	115	B	41.07 % / 33.93 %	129	B	26.79 % / 33.92 %	143	B	25.0 % / 35.71 %
88	D	21.43 % / 28.57 %	102	D	28.57 % / 30.36 %	116	B	35.71 % / 33.93 %	130	A	23.21 % / 35.72 %	144	B	50.0 % / 35.71 %
89	C	23.21 % / 28.58 %	103	C	32.14 % / 30.36 %	117	B	30.36 % / 33.93 %	131	B	32.14 % / 37.5 %	145	D	21.43 % / 35.71 %
90	C	51.79 % / 30.35 %	104	D	17.86 % / 30.35 %	118	B	32.14 % / 35.72 %	132	B	37.5 % / 35.71 %	146	B	26.79 % / 37.5 %
91	B	23.21 % / 32.15 %	105	D	17.86 % / 30.35 %	119	C	41.07 % / 33.93 %	133	D	19.64 % / 35.72 %	147	B	35.71 % / 37.5 %
92	C	42.86 % / 30.35 %	106	A	41.07 % / 30.36 %	120	B	42.86 % / 33.93 %	134	B	35.71 % / 33.93 %	148	B	21.43 % / 37.5 %
93	C	30.36 % / 30.35 %	107	C	32.14 % / 32.15 %	121	A	44.64 % / 33.93 %	135	C	21.43 % / 35.71 %	149	B	33.93 % / 35.71 %
94	A	32.14 % / 30.36 %	108	C	35.71 % / 32.15 %	122	D	39.29 % / 33.92 %	136	C	39.29 % / 35.71 %	150	C	10.71 % / 33.93 %

//Hints and Solutions//

1. A researcher is interested in studying the prospects of a particular political party in an urban area, Then he should prefer a questionnaire for the study. A questionnaire is a group of printed or written questions with the different choice of answers, devised with the motive for a survey or statistical study. So, the researcher will give multiple choice questions to the people for studying the prospects of a political party in a particular area. Hence C option is correct.

2. In a research on the effect of child-rearing practices on stress-proneness of children in completing school projects, the hypothesis formulated is that 'child rearing practices do influence stress-proneness'. At the data-analysis stage a null hypothesis is advanced to find out the tenability of research hypothesis. On the basis of the evidence available, the null hypothesis is rejected at 0.01 level of significance. In this case research hypothesis will be accepted. Hence B option is correct.

3. Among the following options, doctoral level thesis has a prescribed format. One of the formats could be:

i. Introduction

ii. Literature Review

iii. Objectives

iv. Data Collection and Analysis

v. Findings and Conclusions

vi. References.

Rest of the options do not have a prescribed format. Hence A option is correct.

4. Answer: A) Four

7 4 2

7 4 6

7 4 1

7 4 6

Only at these places 4 is preceded by 7 but not followed by 3

5. Answer: A) 2 years

Amount = Rs.(30000+4347) = Rs.34347

let the time be n years

Then,$30000(1+7/100)^n = 34347$

$(107/100)^n = 34347/30000 = 11449/10000 = (107/100)^2$

n = 2years

6. Ratio of times taken by A and B = 1 : 2.

The time difference is (2 - 1) 1 day while B take 2 days and A takes 1 day.

If difference of time is 1 day, B takes 2 days.

If difference of time is 30 days, B takes 2 x 30 = 60 days.

So, A takes 30 days to do the work.

A's 1 day's work = 1/30

B's 1 day's work = 1/60

(A + B)'s 1 day's work = 1/30 + 1/60 = 1/20

A and B together can do the work in 20 days.

7. The List of tables and figures, Table of contents, Conclusions of the study are the main components of thesis whereas the bibliography and appendices are the supplementary pages.

• Appendices provides the supplementary or additional information to the main thesis and always appear after the bibliography page.

• Bibliography lists down the sources of references used for preparing the thesis.

8. Phenomenology is the study of structures of consciousness as experienced from the first-person point of view. The central structure of an experience is its intentionality, its being directed toward something, as it is an experience of or about some object.

9. Answer: B) 6 days

Ratio of rates of working of A and B =2:1. So, ratio of times taken =1:2

Therefore, A's 1 day's work=1/9

B's 1 day's work=1/18

(A+B)'s 1 day's work= 1/9 + 1/18 = 1/6

so, A and B together can finish the work in 6 days

10. Fixed-Position Layouts. Fixed-Position Layouts are often used when the product is too fragile or too heavy to move through a production or process line. This includes manufacturers that produce items like ships, houses, or aircraft vehicles.

11. Diagnostic evaluation ascertains causes and remedies of persistent learning problems during instructions. Diagnostic assessment is a form of pre-assessment that allows the teacher to determine individual students' strengths, weaknesses, knowledge and skills prior to the instruction

12. Teaching is that guiding force that motive the students to achieve their dreams.Good strength of the teacher includes quoting good examples, willingness to put assumptions to the test and acknowledging mistakes denote of the students that will help in their great overall development and strength.

13. Learning is the acquisition of knowledge, and modification of behavior. According to question both statements are correct because learning is the life long process because whole learning cannot be acquired within certain or specified time but it is acquired by the individual throughout whole life by interacting with different environment and needs. Learning is useful if an individual links it with their life experiences and tries to avoid mistakes by learning from his/her mistakes.

14. All teaching implies learning this statement is absolutely correct because all teachings are the consequences of learning and it is the learning that makes the teaching effective. No teaching takes place without the learning.

Learning to be useful must be derived from teaching this statement is incorrect because learning is the main step of teaching without learning teaching cannot exist. So, it is very wrong to say that learning to be useful must be derived from teaching it is only the learning from which the teaching is derived.

15. Following are the characteristics of learner which facilitates teaching-learning system to become effective are:

a) Prior or previous experience of the learner facilitates the teaching learning process a lot because without students' good previous knowledge or learning a good teaching learning process does not takes place.

b) Aptitude of a learner: Student talent, behaviour or aptitude facilitates the teaching learning process effectively.

c) Stage of development of a learner also affects the teaching learning process if the learners is in preschool level. His/her physical and intellectual development takes place very rapidly in comparison to other stage of development.

16. In a deductive argument, validity is the principle that if all the premises are true, the conclusion must also be true. Also known as formal validity and valid argument.

In logic, validity isn't the same as truth. As Paul Tomassi observes, "Validity is a property of arguments. Truth is a property of individual sentences. Moreover, not every valid argument is a sound argument" (Logic, 1999). According to a popular slogan, "Valid arguments are valid by virtue of their form" (although not all logicians would wholly agree). Arguments that are not valid are said to be invalid.

17. Answer: B) 14 men

M x T / W = Constant

where, M= Men (no. of men)

T= Time taken

W= Work load

So, here we apply

M1 x T1/ W1 = M2 x T2 / W2

Given that, M1 = 4 men, T1 = 7 hours ; T2 = 2 hours, we have to find M2 =?

Note that here, W1 = W2 = 1 road, ie. equal work load.

Clearly, substituting in the above equation we get, M2 = 14 men.

18. In categorical syllogism using Venn Diagram, an argument consists of three categorical propositions in which there are two premises and one is conclusion, in which there appear a total of exactly three terms, each of which is used exactly twice.

E.g. All trees are white

All white is black

Some black is dull

So, there are three terms used twice in this type of syllogism.

19. Answer: A) Brother

Daughter of uncle's father — Uncle's sister — Mother;

Mother's son — Brother

20. Inductive reasoning is grounded on the uniformity of nature. This reasoning involves logical process in which multiple premises, all are believed true or found true, are combined together to get a specific conclusion. Inductive reasoning is often used in applications that involves prediction, forecasting, or behaviour.

21. The logic follows here is:

Given code: " bed" is coded as " $AAGGEE$"

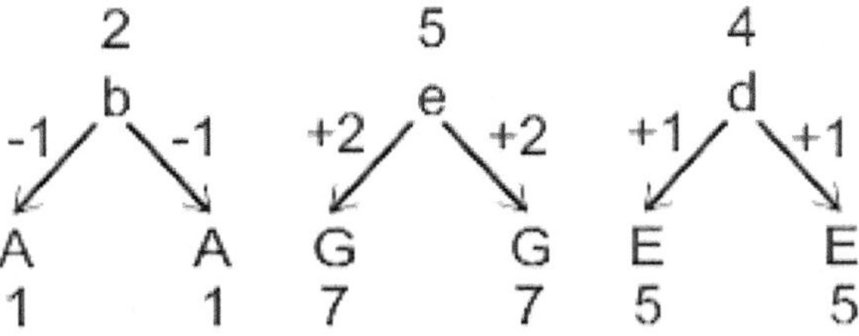

Similarly,

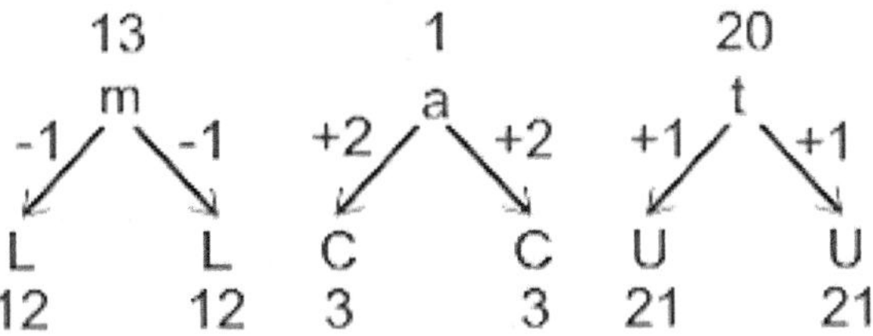

Thus " mat" will be coded as " $LLCCUU$".

Hence, the correct option is (A).

22. Answer: D) 125
Explanation:

$$Z \text{ Code} \Rightarrow 26 \Rightarrow \frac{26}{2} \Rightarrow 13 \Leftrightarrow (13^3) = 2197$$

$$R \text{ Code} \Rightarrow 18 \Rightarrow \frac{18}{2} \Rightarrow 9 \Leftrightarrow (9^3) = 729$$

Similarly, $J \text{ Code} \Rightarrow 10 \Rightarrow \frac{10}{2} \Rightarrow 5 \Leftrightarrow (5^3) = 125$

23. Answer: B) 7

Here E = 5 = 5/1 = 5

=> READ = 18 + 5 + 1 + 4 = 28/4 = 7

=> DEAR = 4 + 5 + 1 + 18 = 28/4 = 7

24. Answer: B) false

Because the first two statements are true, Eric is the youngest of the three, so the third statement must be false

25. The inference is using observation and background to reach a logical conclusion. You probably practice inference every day. For example, if you see someone eating new food and he or she makes a face, then you infer he does not like it. Or if someone slams a door, you can infer that she is upset about something.

26. Separation of powers is not a tool for good governance. Good governance is a process of making and implementing decision. It includes social audit, right to information and citizen's charter.

27. South Asian University (SAU) is an International University established by the eight Member States of the South Asian Association for Regional Cooperation (SAARC) in 2010. The eight countries are: Afghanistan, Bangladesh, Bhutan, India, Maldives, Nepal, Pakistan and Sri Lanka. The University current campus is Akbar Bhawan Campus in Chanakyapuri, New Delhi.

28. The United States dollar (symbol: $; code: USD; also abbreviated US$; referred to as the dollar, U.S. dollar, or American dollar) is the official currency of the United States and its territories per the Coinage Act of 1792.

29. The Koshi River is known as the "Sorrow of Bihar" as the annual floods affect about 21,000 km² (8,100 sq mi) of fertile agricultural lands thereby disturbing the rural economy.

30. Answer: C) Application software

Microsoft Word or MS-Word is an Application software developed by the company Microsoft. It allows users to Type and Save documents.

31. When confronted with signing a big card, the author felt like "a rabbit in the headlight". It was the state of confusion and we can clearly get that after reading the second sentence of the paragraph.

32. According to author, reading is not the most creative outlet of pursuit as mentioned in the last line of the paragraph.

(Reference line: "Handwriting is one of the most creative outlets we have and should be given the same importance as other art forms such as sketching, painting or photography.")

33. The entire existences of author revolve around mobile phone, laptop, computer but not typewriter. So, option (B) is correct.

(Reference line: My entire existence is "tap letters into computer". My shopping lists are hidden in the notes function of my phone. If I need to remember something I send an e-mail to myself. A pen is something I chew when I'm struggling to think. Paper is something I pile beneath my laptop to make it a more comfortable height for me to type on.)

34. S-M-C-R Model of communication was developed by BERLO. S-M-C-R stands for sender-message-channel-receiver.

35. Process is used to exchange information properly between sender and a receiver to achieve the desired result.

Interaction is a process of linking senders and receiver. The concept of interaction is central for understanding the concept of process in the communication.

Social context consists of set of rules which govern the origin, flow and effect of messages.

36. Digital empowerment includes digital literacy, universal access to all digital resources. It also gives digital platform for participative governance and provides probability of all entitlements for individuals through cloud.

37. Mass communication is the communication mode in which a single source is transmitting information to the large number of students. E.g. Teacher is the transmitter and students are the receivers.

38. Junk e-mail is also called Spam.

Sending irrelevant messages or the same message to a large number of users over the internet for the purpose of advertisement or malicious intent is called as spamming and that content is called as SPAM or JUNK.

39. Explanation : Let the borrowing of Company $A = x$

Interest of Company $A = 234000$

Rate of Interest $= 18\%$

$$\therefore x \times \frac{18}{100} = 234000 \quad \Rightarrow x = 1300000$$

Let the borrowing of Company $B = y$

Interest of Company $B = 576000$

Rate of interest $= 24\%$

$$\therefore y \times \frac{24}{100} = 576000 \quad \Rightarrow y = 2400000$$

Required difference $= y - x = 2400000 - 1300000 =$ Rs. 1100000

40. Let the profit of Comapny B = 100%

Dividend Payout ratio(%) of B = 19.60

Remaining percent i.e retained earning = 100 - 19.60 = 80.4%

According to question, 80.4% = Rs.402 lakh

100% = Rs.500 lakh

Therefore, Total dividend paid by Company B = 500 - 402 = Rs. 98 lakh

Let the profit of company D = 100%

Dividend payout ratio (%) of D = 32.50

Remaining percent i.e retained earning = 100 - 32.50 = 67.5%

According to question, 67.5% = Rs. 270 lakh

100% = Rs. 400 lakh

Therefore, Total dividend paid by company D = 400 - 270 = Rs. 130 lakh

Required difference = 130 - 98 = Rs. 32 lakh

41. Let the profit of Company C = 100%

Dividend payout ratio of C = 8.75%

Remaining percent i.e, retained earning = 100 - 8.75 = 91.25

According to question, 91.25% = Rs. 365 lakh

100% = Rs. 400 lakh

Therefore, Profit of C = Rs. 400 lakh

Let the profit of company $E = 100\%$

Dividend payout ratio of $E = 28\%$

Remaining percent i.e retained earning $= 100 - 28 = 72\%$

According to question, $72\% =$ Rs. 216 lakh

$100\% =$ Rs. 300 lakh

Therefore, Profit of $E = Rs.\,300 lakh$

Required percentage $= \dfrac{100}{400} \times 100 = 25\%$ less

42. Profit made by company A = Rs. 200 lakh

Profit made by company B = Rs. 500 lakh

Required Sum = 200 + 500 = Rs. 700 lakh

43. Required Sum = 1300000 + 2400000 + 810000 + 1600000 + 1200000 = 7310000 = Rs. 73.1 lakh

44. The E-governance focuses on the use of new ICT by governments as applied to the full range of government functions. It is the application of information and communication technology which helps to deliver government services, communication, transaction, integration various stands alone systems, exchange of information, and services between government and citizen, government and business as well as back-office process and interaction within the entire government framework.

Types of Government interaction in E-governance.

G2G: Government to Government

G2C: Government to Citizen

G2B: Government to business

G2E: Government to Employee.

Hence, in government interaction in E-governance G2C stands for Government to Citizen. Therefore, the correct options is C.

45. In a computer, if 8 bits are used to specify address in memory, the total number of addresses will be 2^bits = 2^7 = 128 addresses.

46. Answer: D) Analytical Engine

The computer was invented by Charles Babbage.

The First Mechanical Computer Designed by Charles Babbage, a British mathematician was called as Analytical Engine which resembles today's modern machines between 1833 and 1871.

47. A study by NASA confirms that common houseplants are the natural air purifiers. These include aloe Vera, areca palm, lady palm, dragon tree, bamboo among others.

48. The main source of freshwater pollution can be attributed to discharge of untreated waste mainly sewage effluents.

49. High rate of growth, Ceteris paribus (other things equal) means increase in employment rate and purchasing power in a country, thus rise in

demand of imported goods, which will positively increase the imports. And rising imports will result in increased supply of imported goods

which will make imported goods cheaper and thus fall in price of imports and vice versa.

Thus both A and R are correct and R is the right explanation of A.

50. In India, the major LPG (Liberalisation, Privatisation, Globalisation) Reforms, 1991 were:

Liberalisation- To allow private entities to deal in sectors previously owned solely by public entities by waving off license requirements and

easing laws.

Privatisation- Encouraging private investment in government entities by devesting and withdrawing capital from public companies.

Globalisation- Opening national doors to world so that Indian companies can participate in international markets and exposed to foreign

competition.

The industrial reforms of 1991 do not gave monopoly or dominant position to public sector rather it encouraged private entities to grow and

contribute to the national economy.

51.

- Trade channel discounting is a business practice where a company sells products to the retailer at different prices as per their order. If there is bulk order by retailer then they will give more discounts. Thus, differential pricing strategy is used in this case.

- Product line pricing refers to the practice of setting prices for multiple products that a company offers in coordination with one another. If a buyer buys a product separately than buying combo offers provided by company, they are end up paying more. Thus, it attracts customer to buy multiple products at a time. The same strategy is used in tie up sales. One product is tied up with another product to increase sales.

- In oligopoly pricing model, price is not responsive to change in demand cost and thus it matched with it.

- Abasing point pricing is a pricing system in which the buyer pays a base price plus a set of shipping price depending on the distance from a specific location. In this basing point is decided at primary level and distance covered from that location is charged extra as shipping charge. The same is in a case of locational price differentials.

52. VV Giri approach to Industrial relations states the following:

● There should be bipartite machinery in every unit of the industry.

● Collective bargaining and joint negotiations must be used to solve the disputes

● Trade unions should use voluntary arbitration in place of compulsory adjudication to resolve disputes.

● Outside interference must be avoided when there is a difference of opinions.

Thus, Option B is correct.

53. Important operational areas are as follows:

- Evolution of productivity schemes

- Material supply

- Housekeeping

- Review of monthly targets and schedules

- Machine utilization

Thus, Option D is correct.

54. ● Distribution of arrivals is a Poisson process.

● Distribution of service time is exponential.

● Distribution of inter-arrival time is an exponential process

● Distribution of departures is truncated Poisson distribution.

Thus, Option C is correct.

55. ● Eustress refers to healthy stress levels. It improves the performance of an employee by arousing him to action.

● Eustress provides strength and physical force for short intervals of time which results in peak performance.

Thus, Option D is correct.

56. To contribute to a CSR committee following provisions should be fulfilled as written under section 135(1) of the companies act 2013

● Turnover of Rs 1000 cr or more

● Net worth of Rs 500 cr or more

● Net Profit of Rs.5 cr or more

It should spend at least 2% of the average net profits of the company during three immediately preceding financial years.

Thus, Option C is correct.

57. ● Corporate social responsibility encompasses four key issues. They are as follows:

1) Human rights

2) Labor rights

3) Environmental principles

4) Anti-corruption practices

● Corporate social responsibility is an advantage to firms and society.

● It reflects the social, environmental and ethical impact of various activities.

Thus, Option B is correct.

58. ● Product: Product aspect deals with the specification of the actual good or service.

● Price covers the actual amount the end-user is expected to pay for a product.

● Place aspect of marketing Mix talks about how the product will be provided to the customer.

● Promotion: Marketing communication strategies and techniques are all included in the promotion.

Thus, Option B is correct.

59. Anthropological entrepreneurship theory is the study of customs, origin, development and beliefs of a community. It says that in order to successfully initiate a venture, the social and cultural contexts should be carefully examined and considered.

Thus, Option C is correct.

60. Determining, developing and analysing analytical methods to scale and optimize relationships with customers is one of the key features of Analytical CRM and not an advantage.

Thus, Option C is correct.

61. ● There are seven elements in the process of communication.

● The sequence of steps are as follows- Sender, Ideas, Encoding, Communication channel, Receiver, Decoding and lastly Feedback.

Thus, Option D is correct.

62. ● Mckinsey and Company coined the word Talent management after a study in the year 1997.

● It deals with the human capital of an organization.

Thus, Option B is correct.

63. ● The Royal Commission on Labour is also known as the Whitley Commission on Labour.

● It was set up in 1929 to determine the conditions of labor in industries in India.

● The commission submitted its report in 1931.

Thus, Option C is correct.

64. Vestibule training is a kind of off-the-job training which tries to duplicate the workplace environment and is used for training personnel for semi-skilled jobs. Usually used to train clerks, machine operators, typists, filters etc. Duration of such training ranges from few days to few weeks.

Thus, Option B is correct.

65. ● outliers are extreme values (very small and very big).

● Mean is much affected by extreme values as it is based on all observations whereas mode and median are the averages which are not based on all observations so these are not at all affected by extreme values.

Thus, Option C is correct.

66. ● Organizations can discourage unionization by offering the open-door policy to the employees.

● If the unionization is regarding the new decisions taken by the organization or regarding grievance management, then the open-door policy may stop them from forming the unions.

● With the implementation of the open-door policy, the workers will get an opportunity to share their views with the management. This will resolve all the conflicts.

Thus, Option A is correct.

67. Advantages of Critical Incident Technique

A few advantages of critical incident method are:

1. Helps to identify rare events which might be missed by other methods as they focus only on common events.

2. The technique is cost effective and provides rich information

3. The respondent's perspective is taken into account

4. The respondents are not forced into any framework

5. Many ways to implement the technique like observation, questionnaires and interviews

68. Disadvantages of Critical Incident Technique

1. Many incidents may go unreported or might not be precise as the reporting of incidents relies on memory of the respondent.

2. Biasness might creep in towards the incidents that happened recently.

3. The incidents narrated may not be representative of everyday situation that takes place during the job.

69. Generalised conclusion on the basis of a sample is technically known as statistical inference of external validity of the research.

70. For computing earliest event time, one should use forward pass communication method, and for computing latest completion time, one should use backward pass communication.

Thus, Option C is correct..

71. Real Wage refers to the wage expressed in terms of commodities and services that money can buy after taking into account factors like inflation. They are calculated by diving nominal wages by the cost of living or consumer price index.

Thus, Option B is correct.

72. 1) PESTLE framework includes the following factors:

- Political

- Economic

- Sociocultural

- Technological

- Legal

- Environmental

2) PESTLE framework involves the following two areas:

- The environmental factors affecting the organization.

73. • Business to business selling includes companies primary selling goods or services to another business.

• Under Trade selling, a salesperson sells products or services to market distributors such as wholesalers and retailers.

• Under Retail selling, a salesperson communicates directly with potential customers who visit the store on their own to inquire about a product or to purchase a product.

Thus, Option C is correct.

74. • Indian rupee was made 100% convertible on current account in 1994.

• Indian rupee is still partially convertible (40:60) on the capital account transactions.

Thus, Option C is correct.

75. • South Asian Association for Regional Cooperation (SAARC) was founded in 1985.

• The member countries are Afghanistan, Bangladesh, Bhutan, India, Maldives, Nepal, Pakistan and Sri Lanka.

Thus, Option C is correct.

76. 'An entrepreneur decides the policy of production as to what, how and how much to produce' is a function and not the characteristic of an entrepreneur.

Thus, Option B is correct.

77. Financial capital/liquidity theory and not Opportunity-based theory argues that entrepreneurs have individual specific resources that make the recognition of new opportunities easier.

Thus, Option C is correct.

78. • Detached Personality types are not much aware of brands and desire independence, self-reliance etc.

• Compliant Personality types move towards others and desire to be loved and appreciated.

• Aggressive Personality types move against others and desire to win and excel.

Thus, Option C is correct.

79. Advertising includes various media namely, Print media (Newspapers, magazines), Display media (Billboards, posters), Network media (Satellite, telephone), Electronic media (Web page).

Thus, Option B is correct.

80. • Ethics and Morality are not the same and not used interchangeably.

• Ethics are concerned with activities of organizations with professional codes of conduct and Morality, on the other hand, is defined as when individuals conduct their personal and private lives in relation to acceptable standards of interpersonal and lawful behaviour.

Thus, Option D is correct.

81. David A. Aaker outlined the following dimensions of a Market Analysis:

- Market Trends

- Market Size

- Market Profitability

- Industry cost structure

- Key success factors

- Key success details

• Market growth rate

• Distribution channels

Thus, Option D is correct.

82. • Job monitoring: Trainee is placed under the guidance of a supervisor.

• Job rotation: Movement of an employee from one job to another of the same nature.

• Internal posting: Searching for talented individuals within the organization and promoting them.

• Career fairs: Helps the company to search and find the right talent.

Thus, Option B is correct.

83. Human Resource experts in most of the companies have major compensation-related concerns. The challenges they face include Wage and salaries policy, government constraints, Union power, compensation budget and salaries, productivity, prevailing wage rate etc.

Thus, Option D is correct.

84. X-Efficiency Theory was developed by Harvey Leibenstein. It focuses on efficiently using the available inputs to produce outputs. Leibenstein has identified two roles for the entrepreneur:

1) Gap filler, wherein an entrepreneur has to fill the gaps in the market, in case there are any imperfections.

2) Input Completer, wherein an entrepreneur is required to transform available inputs and improve the efficiency of existing production methods.

Thus, Option A is correct.

85. Aligning business strategy with HR helps the business organization in competing with changing environment practices. It has three important components: Business strategy, Human resource practices, and Organizational capabilities.

Thus, Option B is correct.

86. • Adam Smith gave the theory of Absolute Advantage.

• David Ricardo's theory of Comparative Advantage was illustrated in his book- On the Principles of Political Economy and Taxation.

Thus, Option C is correct.

87. The four perspectives of Balanced scorecard are as follows:

• Growth and profitability come under the financial perspective.

• Differentiation, cost and quick response come under the customer perspective.

• Product development, demand management, and order fulfilment come under the operations perspective.

• Leadership, organizational learning and ability to change come under organizational perspective.

Thus, Option B is correct.

88. • David Ricardo's trading principle focuses on the role of comparative costs.

• Specialisation results from economies of large scale production.

Thus, Option D is correct.

89. Intrapreneurship is restorative in nature, which means that an organization encourages its employees to follow and practice the entrepreneurial principles so as to transform the slow growth of the company into high growth.

Thus, Option C is correct.

90. The three conditions of consumer's equilibrium are:

• The Budget line should be tangent to the IC.

• At the point of equilibrium, the slope of the Indifference Curve and of the Budget Line should be the same, which means $MRS_{xy} = P_x / P_y$

Thus, Option C is correct.

91. • Four types of artificial intelligence

a. Reactive machine

b. Limited memory

c. Theory of mind

d. Self-awareness

• Three types of machine learning algorithm

a. Supervised learning

b. Unsupervised learning

c. Reinforcement learning

Thus, Option B is correct.

92. • Behavioral Segmentation: Behavioral segmentation includes consumers attitudes towards the brand, their knowledge about it, brand loyalty etc.

• Psychographic Segmentation: It includes values, interests, lifestyle, opinions etc.

• Demographic Segmentation includes variables such as gender, age, income, occupation etc.

• Geographic Segmentation includes differences in interests, tastes and preferences that vary in different states and cities.

Thus, Option C is correct.

93. • Length relates to the total number of products in a product mix.

• Therefore, the product mix Length in the above example is 15(5×3), i.e. it offers a total of 15 products to the market.

• The width refers to the total number of product lines that a company sells. Therefore, product mix width is 5.

Thus, Option C is correct.

94. Net Operating Income Approach was provided by Durand. It believes that the value of the firm remains the same and is not affected by the change of debt component in the capital structure.

Thus, Option A is correct.

95. ● Decentralisation creates a pool of promotable manpower with skills as it provides exposure to the lower and middle-level managers.

● Decentralisation helps managers to see their own results of their actions. They become more driven and improved morale.

Thus, Option C is correct.

96. NITI Aayog, on March 8, 2018(International Women's Day) launched Women Entrepreneurship Platform(WEP) to promote and support established as well as aspiring women entrepreneurs in India. It includes more than 30 partners from various industries and sectors.

Thus, Option A is correct.

97. The Forced Distribution Method is also called a bell curve rating or stacked ranking. It helps in classifying the performers as best, mediocre and worst.

Thus, Option C is correct.

98. Roleplaying is described as a development technique of creating live situations at workplaces and then having employees participate in the situation by playing a certain part or role. For example, Two trainees may be asked to play the roles of a superior and a subordinate to discuss the conflicts arising between them.

Thus, Option C is correct.

99. According to IMF, "FDI as a category of international investment that reflects the objective of a resident in one economy (the direct investor) obtaining a lasting interest in an enterprise resident in another economy (the direct investment enterprise)."

Thus, Option D is correct.

100. ● Cultural entropy is the degree of dysfunction in an organization which is generated by fear-based decisions of the leaders.

● It is also a measure of the friction that an employee encounters on a daily basis.

● It decreases the internal cohesion and level of trust in an organization.

Thus, Option D is correct.

101. Given,

Debtor Collection Period = 50 days

Average Debtors = Rs 4,00,000

And, Debtor Collection Period = Average Debtors / Annual Credit Sales * 365

So, 50 days = Rs 4,00,000 / Annual credit sales * 365

Annual credit sales = Rs 29,20,000

Thus, Option A is correct.

102. Given,

Raw Material Storage Period (R) = 80 days

Work-in-Progress conversion Period (W) = 22 days

Finished Stock Storage Period (F) = 30 days

Debtor Collection Period (D) = 50 days

Creditors Payment Period (C) = 90 days

Operating cycle period = R + W + F + D - C

Operating cycle period = 80 + 22 + 30 + 50 - 90 days

= 92 days

Thus, Option D is correct.

103. Given,

Operating cycle period = 92 days

And, No. of operating cycles in a year = 365 / operating cycle period

So, No. of operating cycles in a year = 365 / 92 days = 3.967 cycles

Thus, Option C is correct.

104. Given,

Annual operating cost = Rs 21,50,000 (Rs 25,00,000 - Rs 3,50,000)

No. of operating cycles in a year = 3.967

And, Amount of working capital required = Annual operating cost / No. of operating cycles

So, Amount of working capital required = Rs 21,50,000 / 3.967

= Rs 5,41,971

Thus, Option D is correct.

105. Given,

Raw Material Storage Period (R) = 80 days

Work-in-Progress conversion Period (W) = 22 days

Finished Stock Storage Period (F) = 30 days

Creditors Payment Period (C) = 90 days

Annual operating cost = Rs 21,50,000 (Rs 25,00,000 - Rs 3,50,000)

Operating cycle period = R + W + F - C

(debtors will not be considered because company plans to discontinue sales on credit)

Operating cycle period = 80 + 22 + 30 - 90 days

= 42 days

Amount of working capital required = Rs 21,50,000 / 365 * 42 days

= Rs 2,47,397

Thus, Option D is correct.

106. • In the 360-degree appraisal method, an employee is appraised by the supervisors, managers, subordinates, colleagues, clients, and customers.

• It helps an employee to know their capabilities and skills to be attained.

Thus, Option A is correct.

107. • Traditional methods of appraisal methods are as follows:

1) Forced choice method

2) Grading method

3) Essay method

4) Field review method

5) Critical incidents method

6) Grading method

7) Checklist method

8) Paired comparison method

• Modern methods of appraisal methods are as follows:

1) 360-degree appraisal method

2) Behaviourally anchored rating scales

3) Management by objectives

4) Assessment centres

Thus, Option C is correct.

108. • The MBO method of performance appraisal was developed by Peter Drucker.

• It is also known as appraisal by results or evaluation by outcomes method.

• MBO method helps management in planning, defining objectives and strategy formulation.

Thus, Option C is correct.

109. • The term "Employer Brand" was first defined by Simon Barrow.

• It describes the reputation of the employer in terms of working conditions.

Thus, Option B is correct.

110. The steps of the performance management cycle are as follows:

• Performance planning

• Performance action

• Performance monitoring

• Performance review

Thus, Option D is correct.

111. • Rural Entrepreneurs face several problems in day to day work. Management problems face by them involve:

1) Legal formalities: It becomes difficult for them to comply with the legal formalities to obtain licensing due to lack of knowledge.

2) Lack of technical knowledge: Rural entrepreneurs suffer problems of lack of technical knowledge due to absence or lack of training facilities.

3) Procurement of raw materials: procurement of raw materials becomes a tough task for rural entrepreneurs; they also have to face problems of storage and warehousing.

Thus, Option B is correct.

112. • The Reserve Bank of India stated that a small-scale unit should be considered as sick if it had accumulated losses equal to or exceeding fifty percent of its peak net worth during the previous accounting year.

• The Sick Industrial Companies Act,1985 stated sickness in terms of cash losses for two consecutive financial years and the accumulated losses at the end of the second financial year which are equal to or exceed the net worth of the company.

Thus, Option B is correct.

113. If the demand curve is a rectangular hyperbola, elasticity is unity (one). Rectangular hyperbola is a curve under which the total area at all points is the same; it is the case of unitary elasticity of demand when the elasticity of demand is equal to 1.

Thus, Option A is correct.

114. • Emotional barriers are closely associated with personal barriers.

• Organizational barriers are barriers to the information flow among the employees like rules & policies, organizational facilities, hierarchical positions.

• The authoritarian attitude of management is an example of organizational barriers.

Thus, Option B is correct.

115. Informal organization helps employees in better communication, faster delivery of information and quick and timely feedback. Informal communication is important in every organization as it eventually leads to development.

Both the statements are right, but R does not give proper explanation to A.

Thus, Option B is correct.

116. Veterinary education is related to medical education.

A veterinarian, also known as a veterinary surgeon or veterinary physician, is a professional who practices veterinary medicine by treating diseases, disorders, and injuries in non-human animals.

• They diagnose and control animal diseases and treat sick and injured animals.

• They also advise owners on proper care of their pets and livestock.

• Veterinarians provide a wide range of services in private practice, teaching, research, government

service, public health, military service, private industry, and other areas.

- Aspiring veterinarians can earn several types of degrees, differing by country and involving undergraduate or graduate education. In various countries, schools award the Doctor of Veterinary Medicine degree (DVM).

Hence, the correct option is (B).

117. Employee State Insurance Act, 1948 provides medical benefits in form of hospital, treatments, medicines to insured employees and family; It is applicable to non-seasonal factories using power and employing 10 or more persons and non-power using 20 or more persons.

Thus, Option B is correct.

118. • Paired comparison method: It involves a pairwise comparison wherein each employee and job is compared with another employee of a similar job, post.

• Graphic rating scale: This method of performance appraisal lists the traits employees should have, and then each employee is rated against these traits.

• Behaviorally anchored rating scale: It is a measuring system used to rate performance against specific examples of behaviour with scale points ranging from 5 to 9.

• Forced distribution: Under this method of performance appraisal, the raters have to make a forced choice (i.e. the scale does not allow a Neutral, don't know option) between the mentioned characteristics about the employees.

Thus, Option B is correct.

119. Quota sampling scheme: Quota sampling is a non-probability sampling scheme in which the researcher seeks a specific characteristic (quality or attribute) in their respondents.

Thus, Option C is correct.

120. Under the conservative approach of working capital investment, an organization invests high capital in current assets, keeps inventory level higher and follows liberal credit policies.

Thus, Option B is correct.

121. Decline is the last stage in the Product Life Cycle, where the sales of a product start declining or falling down. The reason behind this decline of a product is often the entrance of substitute products in the market.

Thus, Option A is correct.

122. The objectives of EXIM policy of India includes developing export potential, improving BOP and BOT, enhancing foreign exchange reserves, encouraging foreign trade, allowing import of technology and equipment to establish new industries.

Thus, Option D is correct.

123. • Brussels treaty also known as the Merger treaty entered into force in 1967.

• It led to the creation of a single Commission and a single Council to serve the then three European Communities (EEC, Euratom, ECSC).

Thus, Option A is correct.

124. For a Product to be successful in the market, it is very important to communicate its features and benefits. Branding is one of the important features of a product because it helps in differentiating other similar products in the market.

Thus, Option A is correct.

125. • Warner Burke developed the seven-phase model of organization development.

• The seven phases are as follows:

1) Entry

2) Contracting

3) Diagnosis

4) Feedback

5) Planning change

6) Intervention

7) Evaluation

Thus, Option C is correct.

126. • In India, the right to strike is not a fundamental right. It is a legal right.

• In India, the right to protest is a fundamental right under Article 19 of the constitution of India

Thus, Option C is correct.

127. The balanced scorecard model reinforces four separate areas that need to be analyzed, involving learning and growth, business processes, customers, and finance. Customer viewpoints and prospects are collected to analyze customer satisfaction in regard with quality, price, and easy availability of products or services. Customers provide feedback about their satisfaction regarding products and service they use.

Thus, Option C is correct.

128. Creator Intrapreneurs are persons who are independent, generate ideas, prefer working in a less structured environment and are also called big-picture thinkers.

Thus, Option C is correct.

129. • Free riders are the employees who do not join the union but are covered by a collective bargaining agreement. These people do not pay for the services they receive.

• Cheap riders are the employees who are not members of a union but are covered by a collective bargaining agreement. These people pay for the services they receive from the unions.

Thus, Option B is correct.

130. Milton Friedman stated that the purpose of business is to only increase profits.

Thus, Option A is correct.

131. There are three major barriers to delegation -

• Fear of losing power

• Personal attitude which stops him to delegate.

• Inability to direct people efficiently.

Above stated barriers stops a person to delegate, which can lead to inefficiency and increases workload.

Thus, Option B is correct.

132. Fabian entrepreneurs are very sceptical in experimenting with any new change and adopt new technologies only when they feel that not doing so would result in heavy loss.

Thus, Option B is correct.

133. • Bharatiya Mazdoor Sangh is the largest trade union in India.

• It was founded by Dattopant Thengadi in the year 1955.

• BMS is not affiliated with any International Trade Union Confederation.

Thus, Option D is correct.

134. According to Steve Jobs, "Innovation distinguishes between a leader and a follower."

Thus, Option B is correct.

135. Nicholas Kaldor developed the theory of Cumulative Causation by stating a strong causal relationship between GDP growth and manufacturing sector growth.

Thus, Option C is correct.

136. • Job evaluation- It is a process of analyzing the worth of a job/work done by employee in comparison to other job of organization. Job evaluation includes job analysis and job specification. Ranking, classification of job, factor comparison, and point method are few techniques of job evaluation.

• Salary survey - Tools such as cost of living indicators and salary budget averages are components of salary survey used to analyze competitive and appropriate salary of organization's employees. The compensation output from salary survey is result of consideration of industry, residing city of employees, employee's knowledge and capabilities and the size of company.

• Job analysis- The process of analyzing jobs from which job descriptions are developed. Job analysis techniques include the use of interviews, questionnaires, and observation.

Thus, Option C is correct.

137. • Learning refers to a relatively permanent change in behavior.

• Learning is a continuous process that involves practice and experience and supports normal behavior to meet new challenges.

Thus, Option C is correct.

138. • The WTO has 164 members and 23 observer governments. The countries like Iran, Iraq, Sudan, South Sudan etc. are the observers of WTO.

• The purpose of observer status is to enable such organizations to follow discussions, on the matters of direct interest to them.

Thus, Option A is correct.

139. • In the field review method, the supervisors are interviewed by an expert from the HR department, where they are asked questions pertaining to the performance of their subordinates.

• The supervisor gives all the necessary information about the level of the employee's performance, his strengths, and weaknesses, understanding of the work environment, etc. to the HR officer who then makes note of these.

Thus, Option C is correct.

140. Job Transfer means shifting an employee from one job to another or from one place to another without involving a change in the job responsibilities and duties. It is, therefore, a lateral shift of an employee.

Thus, Option C is correct.

141. • Functional competencies are also called job-specific or technical competencies and include a set of professional skills, abilities and technical knowledge required to perform a job.

• Conceptual competencies are competencies that are not easily observable but have a strong linkage with entrepreneurial traits.

Thus, Option C is correct.

142. • Strategic Corporate Social Responsibility (CSR) emerged from Management referring to relating CSR activities to the company's core business.

• Strategic CSR is different from transformative CSR as it is focused at the micro-level, i.e. aligning social and environmental goals with the company's strategy.

Thus, Option A is correct.

143. In a monopolistic market, the firm will continue to produce only if it covers its variable costs. The point at which the firm covers its variable cost is called "closing-down point". If the sale is below this point, firms will bear losses.

Thus, Option B is correct.

144. • The organization's performance is not included in Porter's business-level strategy.

• Porter has defined business-level strategy as a competitive strategy and classified it into Three basic strategies they are as follows.

1) Differentiation

2) Focus

3) Cost leadership

Thus, Option B is correct.

145. Activity Ratio is one of the Control Ratios that represents the degree to which the production facilities have been utilized by comparing it with the expected budgeted capacity. 100% ratio or more indicates a favourable position and a ratio of less than 100% indicates an unfavorable position.

Thus, Option D is correct.

146. ● The transactional analysis develops the interpersonal relationship by enabling them to understand the ego states of the parties and focusing on the complementary transactions.

● The transactional analysis develops positive thinking of the individual by enhancing the positive approach and improving the decision-making skills.

Thus, Option B is correct.

147. ● Money income is a form of income received in the form of money, rather than other forms and benefits in kind.

● Money earned through production of goods and services are speny on buying goods and services to satisfy wants.

● Monetary value is the total currency that is exchanged for the expenditure on goods and services.

Both A and R are true, but R does not give the right explanation of A.

Thus, Option B is correct.

148. ● Borrowings from unrelated parties abroad that are guaranteed by direct investors are not FDI.

● FDI is based on the residency of the investor and not nationality.

Thus, Option B is correct.

149. An Intrapreneur is a person within a large corporation who takes direct responsibility to innovate new ideas, products or services. An entrepreneur runs his own company and has complete freedom and responsibility.

Thus, Option B is correct.

150. Two series having the same mean, median and mode can have equal and unequal values in the series.

Thus, Option C is correct.

Paper-I

Q.1 Supply chain management starts before physical distribution.

A. Yes
B. No
C. Can't say
D. None of the above

Q.2 Which of the following sequences of research steps is nearer to scientific method?

A. Suggested solution of the problem, Deducing the consequences of the solution, Perceiving the problem situation, Location of the difficulty and testing the solutions.

B. Perceiving the problem situation, Locating the actual problem and its definition, Hypothesizing, Deducing the consequences of the suggested solution and Testing the hypothesis in action.

C. Defining a problem, Identifying the cause of the problem, defining a population, drawing a sample, collecting data and Analysing results.

D. Identifying the causal factors, Defining the problem, developing a hypothesis, selecting a sample, collecting data and arriving at generalizations and Conclusions.

Q.3 The supply chain concept can help a company locate:-

A. Superior suppliers
B. Superior distributors
C. Both a and b
D. None of the above

Q.4 A specific, clear, and testable proposition or predictive statement about the possible outcome of a scientific research study based on a particular property of a population, such as presumed differences between groups on a particular variable or relationship between variables. It is called ___________.

A. research hypothesis
B. null hypothesis
C. directional hypothesis
D. statistical hypothesis

Q.5 Which of the following statements defines the main objectives of Research?

A. Research should be highly focused and feasible.
B. Research makes accurate use of concepts.
C. Research is done to find out the hidden truth.
D. All of the above

Q.6 In a bank, an amount of Rs. 20,000 is deposited for one year. The rate of interest is 8% per annum and is compounded semi-annually. What is the effective rate of interest?

A. 5.16 percent.
B. 6.16 percent.
C. 7.16 percent.
D. 8.16 percent.

Q.7 Capital gearing ratio indicates the relationship between:

A. assets and capital
B. equity shareholders fund and long term borrowed funds
C. loans and capital
D. debentures and share capital

Q.8 Bilateral arrangements instituted to restrain the rapid growth of exports of specifically manufactured goods are called:

A. Voluntary export restraints
B. Administered protection
C. Imposed export restraints
D. None of the above

Q.9 The training control system includes:

A. Annual review of years training plans
B. Real-time review of specific projects
C. Monthly review of budget and plans
D. All of these

Q.10 Which is the Principles of Human Relations?

A. Principle of Work Recognition
B. Principle of Participation
C. Principle of Motivation
D. All of the above

Q.11 External sources of recruitment consists:

A. Recommendations of Existing employees
B. Private Employment Agencies
C. Through Employment Exchange
D. All of the above

Q.12 What is the name of the highest body in India that advises the Central and State Governments in the field of education?

A. National Knowledge Commission
B. National Commission for Higher Education and Research
C. Central Advisory Board of Education
D. Both (A) and (B)

Q.13 The kinked demand curve explains:

A. Price rigidity
B. Price flexibility
C. Demand rigidity
D. Demand flexibility

Q.14 Choose the correct answer from the following code:

Assertion (A): The purpose of higher education is to promote critical and creative thinking abilities among students.

Reason (R):These abilities ensure job placements.

A. Both (A) and (R) are true and (R) is the correct explanation of (A)
B. Both (A) and (R) are true but (R) is not the correct explanation of (A)
C. (A) is true but (R) is false
D. (A) is false but (R) is true

Q.15 Imperfect competition was introduced by:

A. Marshall
B. Chamberlin

C. Keynes   **D.** None

Q.16 By which of the following proposition, the proposition 'wise men are hardly afraid of death' is contradicted?

A. Some wise men are afraid of death.
B. All wise men are afraid of death.
C. No wise men is afraid of death.
D. Some wise men are not afraid of death.

Q.17 If $45\%11 = 7, 59\%34 = 7$ then what is the value of $55\%4 = ?$

A. 6   **B.** 7   **C.** 8   **D.** 9

Q.18 The weights of 4 boxes are 30,20,50 and 90 kilograms. Which of the following cannot be the total weight, in kilograms, of any combination of these boxes, and in a combination a box can be used only once?

A. 100   **B.** 200   **C.** 300   **D.** 400

Q.19 Fresh fruit contains 68% water and dry fruit contains 20% water. How much dry fruit can be obtained from 100 kg of fresh fruits ?

A. 30   **B.** 36   **C.** 40   **D.** 42

Q.20 The superiority of intellect depends upon its power of concentration on one theme in the same way as a concave mirror collects all the rays that strike upon it into one point. What type of reasoning is entailed in the above statement?

A. Mathematical   **B.** Psychological
C. Analogical   **D.** Deductive

Q.21 A B C D E F G H I J K L M N O P Q R S T U V W X Y Z

Which letter in this alphabet is the eighth letter to the right of the letter and which is the tenth letter to the left of the last but one letter of the alphabet?

A. X   **B.** W   **C.** Z   **D.** I

Q.22 S L U A Y J V E I O N Q G Z B D R H

What will come in place of question (?) mark in the following series :

LA UJ YI EG ?

A. IB   **B.** NR   **C.** ZH   **D.** QH

Q.23 In a family, there are six members A, B, C, D, E and F.

A and B are a married couple, A being the male member. D is the only son of C, who is the brother of A. E is the sister of D. B is the daughter-in-law of F, whose husband has died. How is E related to C?

A. Cousin   **B.** Daughter
C. Mother   **D.** Sister

Q.24 Pointing to a photograph, a person tells his friend, "She is the granddaughter of the elder brother of my father." How is the girl in the photograph related to his Man?

A. Sister-in-law   **B.** Aunt
C. Nephew   **D.** Niece

Q.25 In a class of 60 students where girls are twice that of boys, Laxmi ranked 27th from the top. If there are 9 boys ahead of Laxmi, how many girls are after her rank ?

A. 15   **B.** 22   **C.** 14   **D.** 23

Q.26 A situation where there is only one buyer is called:-

A. Monopoly   **B.** Oligopoly
C. Monopsony   **D.** None of the above

Q.27 "Education is the manifestation of perfection already in man" was stated by which personality?

A. M.K. Gandhi   **B.** R.N. Tagore
C. Swami Vivekanand   **D.** Sri Aurobindo

Q.28 Factors responsible for creating conditions for emergence and growth of monopoly are:-

A. Control over strategic raw materials
B. Patents
C. Licensing
D. All of the above

Ques (29-34):Direction: Read the following passage carefully and answer questions.

If India has to develop her internal strengths, the nation has to focus on the technological imperatives, keeping in mind three dynamic dimensions: the people, the overall economy and the strategic interests. These technological imperatives also take into account a 'fourth' dimension, time, an offshoot of modern day dynamism in business, trade, and technology that leads to continually shifting targets. We believe that technological strengths are especially crucial in dealing with this fourth dimension underlying continuous change in the aspirations of the people, the economy in the global context, and the strategic interests. The progress of technology lies at the heart of human history. Technological strengths are the key to creating more productive employment in an increasingly competitive market place and to continually upgrade human skills. Without a pervasive use of technologies, we cannot achieve overall development of our people in the years to come. The direct linkages of technology to the nation's strategic strengths are becoming more and more clear, especially since 1990s. India's own strength in a number of core areas still puts it in a position of reasonable strength in geo-political context. Any nation aspiring to become a developed one needs to have strengths in various strategic technologies and also the ability to continually upgrade them through its own creative strengths. For people-oriented actions as well, whether for the creation of large-scale productive employment or for ensuring nutritional and health security for people, or for better living conditions, technology is the only vital input. The absence of greater technological impetus could lead to lower productivity and wastage of precious natural resources. Activities with low productivity or low value addition, in the final analysis hurt the poorest most. The technological imperatives to lift our people to a new life, ad to a life they are entitled to is important. India, aspiring to become a major economic power in terms of trade and increase in GDP, cannot succeed on the strength of turnkey projects designed and built abroad or only through large-scale imports of plant machinery, equipment and know how. Even while being alive to the short-term realities, medium and long-term strategies to develop core technological strengths within our industry are vital for envisioning a developed India.

Q.29 According to the above passage, which of the following are indicative of the fourth dimension?

1) Aspirations of people

2) Modern-day dynamism

3) The economy in the global context

4) Strategic interests

A. 1, 2 and 3 only

B. 2, 3 and 4 only

C. 1, 3 and 4 only

D. 1, 2 and 4 only

Q.30 More productive employment demands:

A. Pervasive use of technology

B. Limiting competitive market place

C. Geo-political considerations

D. Large industries

Q.31 Absence of technology would lead to:

1) Less pollution

2) Wastage of precious natural resources

3) Low-value addition

4) Hurting the poorest most

A. 1, 2 and 3 only

B. 2, 3 and 4 only

C. 1, 2 and 4 only

D. 1, 3 and 4 only

Q.32 The advantage of technological inputs would result in:

A. Unbridled technological growth

B. Importing plant machinery

C. Side lining environmental issues

D. Lifting our people to a life of dignity

Q.33 Envisioning a developed India requires:

A. Aspiration to become a major economic player

B. Dependence upon projects designed abroad

C. Focus on short-term projects

D. Development of core technological strengths

Q.34 If you write down all the numbers from 1 to 100, then how many times do you write 3 ?

A. 30   **B.** 20   **C.** 10   **D.** 40

Q.35 In the question, two statements are given, followed by two conclusions, I and II. You have to consider the statements to be true even if it seems to be at variance from commonly known facts. You have to decide which of the given conclusions, if any, follows from the given statements.

Statement I: No umbrellas are raincoats

Statement II: Some jackets are umbrellas

Conclusion I: All raincoats are jackets

Conclusion II: All jackets are raincoats

A. Only conclusion I follow

B. Only conclusion II follows

C. Both conclusions I and II follow

D. Neither conclusion I nor conclusion II follows

Q.36 If the sequence of the English alphabet is reversed then which letter is 7th to the left of the second vowel from the right of the English alphabet in the new series?

A. V   **B.** U   **C.** L   **D.** M

Q.37 Arun said, "This girl is the wife of the grandson of my mother." Who is Arun to the girl?

A. Father-in-law   **B.** Husband

C. Grandfather   **D.** Father

Q.38 Which of the following features is included in nonverbal communication?

a) Appearance

b) Body language

c) Sound

d) Report

e) Job description

A. (b), (c) and (d)

B. (a), (b) and (c)

C. (a), (c) and (d)

D. (a), (b), (c), (d) and (e)

Ques (39-43): The following table gives the percentage of marks obtained by seven students in six different subjects in an examination.

The Numbers in the Brackets give the Maximum Marks in Each Subject.

Student	Maths	Chemistry	Physics	Geography	History	Computer Science
	(150)	(130)	(120)	(100)	(60)	(40)
Ayush	90	50	90	60	70	80
Aman	100	80	80	40	80	70
Sajal	90	60	70	70	90	70
Rohit	80	65	80	80	60	60
Muskan	80	65	85	95	50	90
Tanvi	70	75	65	85	40	60
Tarun	65	35	50	77	80	80

Q.39 What are the average marks obtained by all the seven students in Physics? (rounded off to two-digit after the decimal)

A. 96.11   **B.** 89.14   **C.** 89   **D.** 77.26

Q.40 The number of students who obtained 60% and above marks in all subjects is?

A. 1   **B.** 2   **C.** 3   **D.** None

Q.41 What was the aggregate of marks obtained by Sajal in all the six subjects?

A. 449   **B.** 448   **C.** 447   **D.** 443

Q.42 In which subject is the overall percentage the best?

A. Chemistry   **B.** Geography

C. Physics   **D.** Maths

Q.43 What is the overall percentage of Tarun?

A. 60%   **B.** 50%   **C.** 63%   **D.** 62%

Q.44 Which feature in Microsoft Word is used for adding 'Table of Contents'?

A. Insert   **B.** Review

C. View   **D.** References

Q.45 Which of the following are the two major categories of the printer?
A.   Impact and Non-Impact Printer
B.   Primary and Secondary Printer
C.   Dynamic and Static Printer
D.   Digital and Analog Printer

Q.46 National Income estimates in India are prepared by:
A.   Central Statistical Organisation
B.   Planning Commission
C.   Reserve Bank of India
D.   None of these

Q.47 The purest form of iron is :-
A. wrought iron
B. steel
C. nickel steel
D. none of the above

Q.48 Ctrl, Shift and Alt are called .... keys.
A. alphanumeric
B. adjustment
C. modifier
D. function

Q.49 Which of the following is not written by Munshi Premchand?
A. Gaban
B. Godan
C. Manasorovar
D. Guide

Q.50 Which one of the following is not an example of 'financing activities' with reference to cash flow statement?
A.   Repayment of bank loan
B.   Interest on debentures/Dividend paid
C.   Cash proceeds from public deposits
D.   Sale of fixed assets

Paper-II

Q.51 When the marginal cost is equal to average cost, the slope of the average cost is :
A. positive
B. negative
C. zero
D. infinite

Q.52 Which of the following dimensions of Service Quality involves the ability and courtesy of employees to inspire knowledge and trust?
A. Reliability
B. Empathy
C. Assurance
D. Tangibles

Q.53 Which amongst the following is a correct description of the inverse demand function?
A. $p=f(D)$
B. $D=f(p)$
C. $D=F\left(\frac{1}{p}\right)$
D. None of the above

Q.54 Which of the following are referred to as the three cardinal features of budgetary control?
A.   Planning, Organizing and Coordination
B.   Organizing, Direction and Control
C.   Planning, Coordination and Control
D.   Planning, Direction and Staffing

Q.55 What is known as a form of negotiated bribery when a commission is paid to the broker/bribe-taker in exchange for services provided?
A. Kickbacks
B. Gifts
C. Payoffs
D. Embezzlement

Q.56 Which of the following competencies include having a minimum requirement of skills, knowledge, motive, traits that are essential to perform a job?
A.   Personal competencies
B.   Threshold competencies
C.   Cognitive competencies
D.   Generic management competencies

Q.57 Which of the following is(are) correct about Big data analysis?
Statement I: Big data businesses can analyze varieties of seeds across numerous fields and climates
Statement II: Big data helps to understand customers profile and needs, keeps centralized data of sales and deliver customized services.
Choose the correct option from those below:
A.   Statement I is correct., Statement II is incorrect.
B.   Statement I is incorrect, Statement II is correct.
C.   Both Statement I and Statement II are correct.
D.   Both Statement I and Statement II are incorrect.

Q.58 Assertion(A): Division of work makes man specialist.
Reason(R): Chain of command helps to specialise in an activity which increases output with perfection.
A.   Both (A) and (R) are correct, and (R) is the correct explanation of (A).
B.   Both (A) and (R) are correct, but (R) is not the correct explanation of (A).
C.   (A) is correct, but (R) is not correct.
D.   (A) is wrong, and (R) is correct.

Q.59 Statement I. Primary focus of _______ is on reducing interpersonal conflict by employing T-Groups assisted by a professional behavioral scientist.
Statement II. Simulations that represent actual business situations which involves two or more hypothetical organizations competing in a given product market to make a profit is _______
Choose the correct option from those below:
A.   Sensitivity training and Understudy
B.   Multiple management and Business game
C.   Sensitivity training and Business game
D.   In basket training and Business game

Q.60 Assertion (A): In the low involvement buying, brand recall is very essential for the organizations.
Reason (R): A buyer finds no risk while purchasing low involvement products and no research is done while buying.
A.   Both (A) and (R) are correct, and (R) is the correct explanation of (A).
B.   Both (A) and (R) are correct, but (R) is not the correct explanation of (A).
C.   (A) is correct., but (R) is not correct.

D. (A) is wrong, and (R) is correct.

Q.61 Assertion (A): Discrimination in treating employees is one of the ethical issues faced by business.

Reason (R): Management can create a workplace environment that supports ethical behavior and act as a role model for employees.

A. Both (A) and (R) are correct, and (R) is the correct explanation of (A).

B. Both (A) and (R) are correct, but (R) is not the correct explanation of (A).

C. (A) is correct, but (R) is not correct.

D. (A) is wrong, and (R) is correct.

Q.62 Which of the following is not the tenets of the CRM formulated by Kutner and Cripps?

A. The customers should be treated as important assets

B. All the customers are equally desirable

C. Customers vary in their needs, preferences, buying behavior and price sensitivity

D. By understanding their customers, companies can tailor their offerings to maximize the overall value

Q.63 Which of the following statements relating to the analysis of operating leverage is not correct?

A. If the breakeven point is higher, then the fixed cost will be lower.

B. If there is no fixed cost no operating leverage will exist in the company.

C. If the breakeven point is higher, then the fixed cost will also be higher.

D. If the operating leverage of a company is positive, then it is said to be operating at a higher level than the breakeven point.

Q.64 Statement I: The three broad components of sustainability are Planet, People and Profits.

Statement II: The three P's of sustainability are often referred to the Bottom of the Pyramid.

Choose the correct option from the following:

A. Statement I is correct, Statement II is incorrect.

B. Statement I is incorrect, Statement II is correct.

C. Both Statement I and Statement II are correct.

D. Both Statement I and Statement II are incorrect.

Q.65 Which of the following benefits are provided by the Employees State Insurance Act, 1948?

a) Sickness benefit

b) Medical Benefit

c) Disablement Benefit

d) Dependant's Benefit

Choose the correct option from those below:

A. a, b and c only   **B.** b and c only

C. a and c only   **D.** a, b, c and d

Q.66 X Theory of motivation is propounded by:

A. Douglas McGregor   **B.** A H Maslow

C. Frederick Herzberg   **D.** Dr William Ouchi

Q.67 In marketing, the process of creating new products or modifying the existing products is known as _______.

A. Branding

B. Product synergies

C. Product–service bundling

D. Product innovation

Q.68 Which among the following is not one of the objectives of career planning and development?

A. To identify positive characteristics of the employees

B. To develop awareness about each employee's uniqueness

C. To train employees towards team-building skills

D. To help the organization in the formulation of strategic planning in Human resource

Q.69 Which of the following is (are) correct in relation to the selection of a site for the plant?

Statement I: In India, the western and central regions are generally the most preferable regions for manufacturing facilities.

Statement II: Customer concentrations become important considerations in selecting a site.

Choose the correct option from those below:

A. Statement I is correct., Statement II is incorrect.

B. Statement I is incorrect, Statement II is correct.

C. Both Statement I and Statement II are correct.

D. Both Statement I and Statement II are incorrect.

Q.70 Who founded the Bombay Mill-Hands Association, the first association of Indian workers?

A. Lokhande   **B.** Joseph Baptista

C. Dutta Samant   **D.** NM Joshi

Q.71 Adaptability, which is a strategic dimension is insignificant in which of the following levels of strategy?

A. Corporate level   **B.** Business level

C. Functional level   **D.** Economic level

Q.72 Which of the following is not a general function of retailers?

A. Provide information to consumers

B. Store merchandise

C. Collect product from manufacturers

D. Conclude transactions with final customers

Q.73 Statement I: Long run objective of financial management is to maximise the value of the firm's common stock

Statement II: Profit maximisation objective ignores the time value of money and does not consider the magnitude and timing of earnings.

Choose the correct option from the following:

A. Statement I is correct, Statement II is incorrect.

B. Statement I is incorrect, Statement II is correct.

C. Both Statement I and Statement II are correct.

D. Both Statement I and Statement II are incorrect.

Q.74 Statement I: Parties involved in corporate governance includes a chief executive officer, board of directors and management.

Statement II: Corporate governance is an internal thing and it does not have any effect on market valuation.

Choose the correct option from those below:

A. Statement I is correct, Statement II is incorrect.
B. Statement I is incorrect, Statement II is correct.
C. Both Statement I and Statement II are correct.
D. Both Statement I and Statement II are incorrect.

Q.75 Which of the following is the highest level of the decision-making body of the WTO?

A. Ministerial Conference
B. Council of trade in goods
C. Dispute Settlement Body
D. Trade Policy Review Body

Q.76 _________is a documented investigation of a market which is used to inform a company's planning activities, around decisions of inventory, purchase, purchases of capital equipment and many other aspects of a company.

A. Market Analysis
B. Market Trends
C. Market Campaign
D. Market Size

Q.77 Which of the following types of Rural Entrepreneurship involves an Entrepreneur who possesses very good skill or craft but has little business savvy.

A. Cluster Entrepreneurship
B. Artisan Entrepreneurship
C. Individual Entrepreneurship
D. Merchant and traders Entrepreneurship

Q.78 Assertion (A): In the storming phase of group formation, the breaking up of the team is done.

Reason (R): In the storming phase, members start competing for leadership and control over the group.

A. Both (A) and (R) are correct, and (R) is the correct explanation of (A).
B. Both (A) and (R) are correct, but (R) is not the correct explanation of (A).
C. (A) is correct, but (R) is not correct.
D. (A) is wrong, and (R) is correct.

Q.79 Before the expiry of which day, the wages to the workers should be paid, if there are less than one thousand employed persons in an establishment?

A. 7
B. 8
C. 10
D. 11

Q.80 Statement I: The human relations school of organizational behavior was developed by Abraham Maslow.

Statement II: The behavioral science school of organizational behavior was developed by Elton Mayo through Hawthorne Experiments.

Choose the correct option from those below:

A. Statement I is correct, Statement II is incorrect.
B. Statement I is incorrect, Statement II is correct.
C. Both Statement I and Statement II are correct.
D. Both Statement I and Statement II are incorrect.

Q.81 Arrange the following steps of Promotion decision process in correct sequence and select the correct code:

a) Determining promotion budget
b) Setting Objectives
c) The appeal
d) Promotion mix
e) Target market

A. (b),(d),(e),(a),(c)
B. (a),(c),(e),(d),(b)
C. (b),(a),(d),(c),(e)
D. (b),(a),(e),(c),(d)

Q.82 Into how many groups did French and Bell Clubb the interventions?

A. 8
B. 6
C. 12
D. 10

Q.83 Statement I: Unilateral transfers include private transfers and public transfers.

Statement II: Net income receipts are a part of a capital account.

Choose the correct option from those below:

A. Statement I is correct, Statement II is incorrect.
B. Statement I is incorrect, Statement II is correct.
C. Both Statement I and Statement II are correct.
D. Both Statement I and Statement II are incorrect.

Q.84 The knowledge, qualification, competency, capability, skills, and expertise of employees of organization is termed as______.

A. Improved competitiveness
B. Knowledge management
C. Human capital
D. Job specification

Q.85 Assertion (A): Raymond Vernon's PLC theory was developed from the viewpoint of developed countries like the United States.

Reason (R): PLC theory puts emphasis on the proportion of factors (advanced & natural) available in a country.

A. Both (A) and (R) are correct, and (R) is the correct explanation of (A).
B. Both (A) and (R) are correct, but (R) is not the correct explanation of (A).
C. (A) is correct, but (R) is not correct.
D. (A) is wrong, and (R) is correct.

Q.86 In TOWS matrix, what does ST indicate?

A. Strength can be used to capitalize on emerging opportunities
B. The firm strives to minimize threats through its strengths
C. Need to overcome organizational weaknesses
D. A firm facing external threats and internal weaknesses may struggle for its survival

Ques (87-95):Direction : Read the passage and attempt the questions that follow:

ABC is one of the successful retail supermarkets in the city. Two years ago, they faced tough competition from e-commerce companies, and there was a significant decline in their daily sales. The management decided to retain and reward their regular customers and finally decided to maintain a database of its customers.

To do this, they adopted software that attached a mobile number to every bill. They thought this would help them to track the buying patterns of their customers, but a lot of customers initially denied giving their mobile number stating privacy issues. The sales and service team resolved the issue by explaining the data policy of the store to the customers. The store clearly mentioned that their phone numbers would be used to communicate the best offers.

Most of the customers gave their mobile numbers. The company started analyzing the buying patterns of the customers on a weekly basis and separated regular and occasional customers. To reward its customers, the store started to send discount codes and the customers can redeem the code by informing it in the billing section. The same procedure is followed for the occasional customers but with less percentage of discount codes and improving the percentage of discount gradually.

Q.87 Which of the following is not a criterion of decision making under uncertainty?

A. Hurwitz criterion

B. Savage criterion

C. Breakeven analysis criterion

D. Laplace criterion

Q.88 Statement I: The production concept assumes that consumers are primarily interested in product availability and low prices

Statement II: The product concept assumes that buyers admire well-made products and appraise quality and performance

Choose the correct option from the following:

A. Statement I is correct, Statement II is incorrect.

B. Statement I is incorrect, Statement II is correct.

C. Both Statement I and Statement II are correct.

D. Both Statement I and Statement II are incorrect.

Q.89 Which among the following is/are the importance of managerial economics?

I. Helpful in business planning

II. Helpful in cost control

III. Helpful in controlling market risks

IV. Useful in demand forecasting

Choose the correct option from those below:

A. I, II, III

B. I, III, IV

C. II, III, IV

D. I, II, IV

Q.90 Statement I: In monolithic organizations, persons from different cultural groups are seen only in the positions of power and leadership.

Statement II: The plural organizations give importance to persons from various cultural backgrounds who are different from the dominant group.

Choose the correct option from those below:

A. Statement I is correct., Statement II is incorrect.

B. Statement I is incorrect, Statement II is correct.

C. Both Statement I and Statement II are correct.

D. Both Statement I and Statement II are incorrect.

Q.91 What is the Annual Sale of Tom limited?

A. Rs 22,20,000

B. Rs 10,53,000

C. Rs 13,70,500

D. Rs 15,23,000

Q.92 Calculate the Degree of Operating Leverage of the firm?

A. 2.3

B. 4.0

C. 5.6

D. 1.1

Q.93 Calculate the Degree of Financial Leverage of the firm?

A. 2.24

B. 3.39

C. 1.63

D. 5.68

Q.94 Calculate the Degree of Combined Leverage of the firm?

A. 8.984

B. 5.152

C. 3.329

D. 1.793

Q.95 If the sale of the company increases by 10%, what would be the percentage (%) change in the earnings per share (EPS) of the company?

A. 17.93%

B. 15.32%

C. 8.98%

D. 3.32%

Q.96 Which of the following processes involves finding the relation between the entities of different databases?

A. Data mining

B. Data warehousing

C. On-demand computing

D. Data strategy

Q.97 Which kind of turnover stores price their products higher than those in the market but not higher than those in similar outlets?

A. Low margin low turnover stores

B. High margin high turnover stores

C. Low margin high turnover stores

D. High margin low turnover stores

Q.98 Which of the following forms of ownership involves combining the financial resources of retailers and agree on common policies?

A. Retail chain

B. Retail co-operatives

C. Retail franchising

D. Seasonal retailer

Q.99 Which of the following attacking strategies was used by the supermarket to challenge e-commerce companies?

A. Leapfrog strategy

B. Flanking attack strategy

C. Encirclement strategy

D. Guerrilla attack strategy

Q.100 Which of the following statements is true regarding retail chain stores?

A. The retail chain will not involve common ownership of multiple units

B. To take a centralized decision

C. They cannot cut prices because of financial constraints

D. To achieve promotional economics

Q.101 Only equity shareholders can be called as

A. Father of the company

B. Shareholders of the company

C. Owners of the company

D. Partners of the company

Q.102 Assertion(A): Financial and Economic Feasibility are both related to each other but are not the same.

Reason(R): Financial Feasibility is only concerned with the financing of the project and not its economic implications.

A. Both (A) and (R) are correct, and (R) is the correct explanation of (A).

B. Both (A) and (R) are correct, but (R) is not the correct explanation of (A).

C. (A) is correct, but (R) is not correct.

D. (A) is wrong, and (R) is correct.

Q.103 Statement I: The difference between the bid and the offer is called the spread.

Statement II: The offer is generally higher than the bid.

Choose the correct option from those below:

A. Statement I is correct., Statement II is incorrect.

B. Statement I is incorrect, Statement II is correct.

C. Both Statement I and Statement II are correct.

D. Both Statement I and Statement II are incorrect.

Q.104 Which of the following statements is not incorrect?

I. Five forces that determine industry attractiveness and long-run industry profitability are the threat of entry of new competitors, the threat of substitutes, the bargaining power of buyers, the bargaining power of suppliers and the degree of rivalry between existing competitors.

II. Economies of scale, Capital requirements and Customer switching costs are some of the entry barriers in some industries.

III. The bargaining power of suppliers will be low when there are many interested buyers and a few dominant suppliers.

IV. The bargaining power of buyers is greater when there are very few dominant buyers and many sellers in the industry.

Choose the correct option from those below:

A. I, II, III

B. I, II,IV

C. I, III, IV

D. II, III, IV

Q.105 Money raised through the small saving schemes, provident fund schemes are held in

A. Consolidated Fund of India

B. Public Accounts of India

C. Contingency fund of India

D. Consolidated Fund or respective states

Q.106 When 'n', the number of trials is very large or infinite and neither 'p' nor 'q' is very small or nearer to equal, then ______ distribution tends to be ______ distribution.

A. Normal, Poisson

B. Binomial, Poisson

C. Normal, Binomial

D. Binomial, Normal

Q.107 Marketing mix of service involves which of the three Ps among the following?

I. People

II. Place

III. Process

IV. Physical evidence

Choose the correct option from those below:

A. I,II,III

B. II,III,IV

C. I,II,IV

D. I,III,IV

Q.108 ______ is one of the financial institutions supporting small businesses which provide machinery on hire-purchase to small scale and ancillary industries for a value between Rs. 60 lakhs and Rs. 75 lakhs.

A. Small Industries Development Bank of India

B. State Small Industries Corporations

C. Small Industry Development Corporations

D. Industrial Development Bank of India

Q.109 If a manager is entitled to a commission of 5% on "profit after deduction of this commission", he will get a commission of Rs.____ on a profit of Rs 12,600.

A. Rs 600

B. Rs 663.065

C. Rs 630

D. None of these

Q.110 Government data, Trade association data and customer surveys are examples of Information sources for determining the __________.

A. Market trends

B. Market growth rate

C. Market size

D. Market profitability

Q.111 Assertion (A): The selection of location is of paramount importance for any manufacturing enterprise.

Reason (R): Appropriate location can provide advantage of effective production and marketing strategies to increase sales and reduce cost.

A. Both (A) and (R) are correct, and (R) is the correct explanation of (A).

B. Both (A) and (R) are correct, but (R) is not the correct explanation of (A).

C. (A) is correct., but (R) is not correct.

D. (A) is wrong, and (R) is correct.

Q.112 Statement I: Five dynamic factors that influence the shape of international business are interdependence of the world economies, the rapid growth of regional free trade areas, increased purchasing power, evolution of large emerging markets and availability of advancement in communication and information technology.

Statement II: Home-country factors that are outside the control of the company and have a direct effect on the success of a foreign company's political factor, legal structure and economic environment are called as foreign uncontrollables.

Choose the correct option from those below:

A. Statement I is correct, Statement II is incorrect.

B. Statement I is incorrect, Statement II is correct.

C. Both Statement I and Statement II are correct.

D. Both Statement I and Statement II are incorrect.

Q.113 Statement I: The main focus of stability strategy is on incremental improvement of functional performance.

Statement II: Divestment, turnaround, liquidation and bankruptcy are the types of a combination strategy.

Choose the correct option from those below:

A. Statement I is correct., Statement II is incorrect.

B. Statement I is incorrect, Statement II is correct.

C. Both Statement I and Statement II are correct.

D. Both Statement I and Statement II are incorrect.

Q.114 Read the statements and choose correct code:-

Statement I: The distance between the third quartile and median and median and first quartile are equal.

Statement II: The point where the curveity of a normal curve changes its direction is termed as the point of inflection.

Choose the correct option from those below:

A. Statement I is correct but Statement II is incorrect

B. Statements I and II are incorrect

C. Both Statement I and Statement II are correct.

D. Both Statement I and Statement II are incorrect.

Q.115 Which of the following forms of research focuses on describing the culture of a group of people?

A. Phenomenology   **B.** Ground Theory

C. Historical Research   **D.** Ethnography

Q.116 Assertion (A): Under perfect competition, Rothschild index equals zero.

Reason (R): The demand curve is vertical for each individual firm in perfect competition.

A. Both (A) and (R) are correct, and (R) is the correct explanation of (A).

B. Both (A) and (R) are correct, but (R) is not the correct explanation of (A).

C. (A) is correct., but (R) is not correct.

D. (A) is wrong, and (R) is correct.

Q.117 Statement I: Foreign Trade policy is announced every 5 five years by the Ministry of Finance.

Statement II: EXIM policy is regulated by the Imports and Exports (Control) Act 1947.

Choose the correct option from those below:

A. Statement I is correct, Statement II is incorrect.

B. Statement I is incorrect, Statement II is correct.

C. Both Statement I and Statement II are correct.

D. Both Statement I and Statement II are incorrect.

Q.118 Statement I. The greater the value of chi-square, lesser will be the discrepancy between observed and expected frequency.

Statement II. Chi-square is used to determine only goodness of fit, not the association between two or more variables.

Choose the correct option from those below:

A. Statement I is correct., Statement II is incorrect.

B. Statement I is incorrect, Statement II is correct.

C. Both Statement I and Statement II are correct.

D. Both Statement I and Statement II are incorrect.

Q.119 Assertion (A): Enterprise Resource Planning makes the information flow between all business functions within the organization easy and manages the organization's connections with its outside stakeholders.

Reason (R): Enterprise Resource Planning integrates all the different departments and functions of an organization into a single computer system.

A. Both (A) and (R) are correct, and (R) is the correct explanation of (A).

B. Both (A) and (R) are correct, but (R) is not the correct explanation of (A).

C. (A) is correct., but (R) is not correct.

D. (A) is wrong, and (R) is correct.

Q.120 Which of the following is not a data mining technique?

A. Classification analysis

B. Association rule learning

C. Sequential pattern

D. Spark

Q.121 Which among the following statements is not incorrect?

I. Inflation is a recurring phenomenon.

II. Keynesian hold the view that the essence of demand-pull inflation is "too much money chasing too few goods".

III. Wage-push inflation and profit-push inflation are important variants of cost-push inflation.

IV. Stagflation is the combination of high inflation with high unemployment.

Choose the correct option from those below:

A. I, II, III, IV   **B.** I, III, IV

C. II, III, IV   **D.** I, II, IV

Q.122 Pie charts represent the components of a factor by:

A. Percentages   **B.** Angles

C. Sectors   **D.** circles

Q.123 In the CSR model, Carroll suggested four possible strategies to companies to respond to social pressure. Which of the following are the strategies as suggested by Carroll?

a) Reaction

b) Proaction

c) Defence

d) Expedient

e) Accomodation

Choose the correct option from those below:

A. a,b,c,e   **B.** a,b,c,d   **C.** a,c,d,e   **D.** b,c,d,e

Q.124 Assertion (A): To attract customers, service providers should attach physical evidence to their service offerings.

Reason (R): The physical evidence or a tangible element serves as a promotional tool for the organizations to market their services.

A. Both (A) and (R) are correct, and (R) is the correct explanation of (A).

B. Both (A) and (R) are correct, but (R) is not the correct explanation of (A).

C. (A) is correct., but (R) is not correct.

D. (A) is wrong, and (R) is correct.

Q.125 Which one of the following is NOT correctly matched?

A. Friedman and Edmund Phelps: Accelerationist Hypothesis

B. J.M. Keynes: Liquidity Trap

C. Findlay Shirras: International Trade Equilibrium

D. R.S. Sayers: Central Bank and Commercial bank

Q.126 Statement I: 'Comply-or-explain' approach is a key characteristic of the UK's corporate governance system.

Statement II: Greenbury Report on Corporate Governance focused specifically on non-executive directors.

Choose the correct option from those below:

A. Statement I is correct., Statement II is incorrect.
B. Statement I is incorrect, Statement II is correct.
C. Both Statement I and Statement II are correct.
D. Both Statement I and Statement II are incorrect.

Q.127 Statement I: CSR can go a long way in improving the social welfare of India.

Statement II: India has become the first country in the world to make CSR mandatory for Indian companies.

Choose the correct option from those below:

A. Statement I is correct., Statement II is incorrect.
B. Statement I is incorrect, Statement II is correct.
C. Both Statement I and Statement II are correct.
D. Both Statement I and Statement II are incorrect.

Q.128 Normally one should resort to simple random sampling as it is bias-free and sampling error can be estimated, but ______ is considered more appropriate when the universe happens to be small, and a known characteristic of it is to be studied intensively.

A. Stratified sampling
B. Sequential sampling
C. Purposive sampling
D. Multi-stage sampling

Q.129 Statement I: In calculating mean deviation, we ignore the minus sign of deviation while taking their total for obtaining the mean deviation.

Statement II: When the average used in finding out the mean deviation is divided by mean deviation, the result we get is the coefficient of mean deviation.

Choose the correct option from those below:

A. Statement I is correct., Statement II is incorrect.
B. Statement I is incorrect, Statement II is correct.
C. Both Statement I and Statement II are correct.
D. Both Statement I and Statement II are incorrect.

Q.130 Analysis of variance (ANOVA) technique was invented by

A. MM Blair
B. RA Fisher
C. WI King
D. AL Bowley

Q.131 Phillips merging into cellular phones, electronic computer peripherals is an example of which kind of diversification?

A. Forward vertical integration
B. Concentric integration
C. Backward vertical integration
D. Conglomerate integration

Q.132 Which of the following includes movement of raw materials to a location at the required time, just before the material is required for the manufacturing process?

A. Inventory Management
B. Just in time Logistics
C. Transportation Management
D. Reverse Logistics

Q.133 C-chart is based on which distribution?

A. Binomial
B. Normal
C. Hypergeometric
D. Poisson

Q.134 ______ is a cost-effective strategy of entering the international market, for reducing cost through allotting a portion of work to outsiders rather than doing it completely internally.

A. Outsourcing
B. Franchising
C. Joint venture
D. Acquisition

Q.135 Statement I: The CSR committee in India should consist of less than three directors and two independent directors.

Statement II: Schedule VI of the Companies Act, 2013 prescribes the CSR projects.

Choose the correct option from those below:

A. Statement I is correct., Statement II is incorrect.
B. Statement I is incorrect, Statement II is correct.
C. Both Statement I and Statement II are correct.
D. Both Statement I and Statement II are incorrect.

Q.136 Which among the following are considered as a part of the scope of operation management?

I. Deciding facility location and layout

II. Human capital planning

III. Capacity planning

IV. Maintenance and replacement

V. Cost reduction

Choose the correct option from those below:

A. I, II, III, IV
B. I, III, IV, V
C. II, III, IV, V
D. I, II, III, V

Q.137 Consider the following advantages. Which layout are these advantages related to?

I. Team attitude and job enlargement tend to occur.

II. Shorter travel distance and smoother flow lines than for process layout.

III. Supports use of general purpose equipment.

IV. Increased machine utilization.

Choose the correct option from those below:

A. Fixed layout
B. Combination layout
C. Product layout
D. Functional layout

Q.138 Which of the following current accounts is also called "our account with you"?

A. Loro account
B. Vostro account
C. Nostro account
D. None of these

Q.139 In Social Marketing, ______ represents putting all the efforts so as to make the change in behavior as easy as possible to a consumer.

A. Product
B. Price
C. Place
D. Promotion

Q.140 A __________occurs when an individual is not able to interpret a stimuli whereas, a ________occurs when an individual manipulates the stimuli as per his needs and experience.

A. Perceptual bias, Stimulus ambiguity
B. Stimulus ambiguity, Dissonance
C. Perceived risk, Perceptual bias
D. Stimulus ambiguity, Perceptual bias

Q.141 Producer's risk means

A. Accepting the bad lot
B. Rejecting the bad lot
C. Accepting the good lot
D. Rejecting the good lot

Q.142 Read the statements and choose the correct code:-

In __________, only a few components of a product are changed, whereas the overall design of the product remains the same.

A. Architectural Innovation
B. Radical Innovation
C. Incremental Innovation
D. Modular Innovation

Q.143 Assertion (A): Marketing a service-based business is non-identical to marketing a product-based business.

Reason (R): Service marketing depends entirely on value and relationship.

A. Both (A) and (R) are correct, and (R) is the correct explanation of (A).
B. Both (A) and (R) are correct, but (R) is not the correct explanation of (A).
C. (A) is correct, but (R) is not correct.
D. (A) is wrong, and (R) is correct.

Q.144 A type of national income measure, in which the final value of all the goods and services produced within the geographical territory of country plus income from abroad is considered is called:

A. Gross National Product
B. Net National Product
C. Gross Domestic Product
D. Net Domestic Product

Q.145 Which of the following forms of Innovation is also known as Stealth Innovation?

A. Radical Innovation
B. Architectural Innovation
C. Sustaining Innovation
D. Disruptive Innovation

Q.146 Assertion(A): Sustaining Innovation exists in the current market and focuses on improving and growing the existing markets.

Reason(R): Sustaining Innovation is the opposite of Disruptive Innovation.

A. Both (A) and (R) are correct, and (R) is the correct explanation of (A).
B. Both (A) and (R) are correct, but (R) is not the correct explanation of (A).
C. (A) is correct, but (R) is not correct.

D. (A) is wrong, and (R) is correct.

Q.147 Select the correct code :

Which of the following are the examples of fall in the volume of the resources?

a) Wear and tear or breakdown of machinery.
b) Saturation of natural resources.
c) Technology has become obsolete.
d) Availability of new equipment.
e) Discovery of new natural resources.

Choose the correct option from those below:

A. a) and d) **B.** a), c) and d)
C. a), b) and d) **D.** a), b) and c)

Q.148 Which of the following are the strategies that will create a competitive advantage through SWOT analysis?

a) Functional level strategy
b) Global strategy
c) Corporate level strategy
d) Business level strategy

Choose the correct option from those below:

A. a, b and c only **B.** a, b and d only
C. b, c and d only **D.** a, b, c and d

Q.149 Statement I: For an enterprise to fall under the category of small scale industry in the manufacturing sector, investment in plant and machinery should be between 10 lakh to two crores.

Statement II: Small scale industries are generally under a partnership.

Choose the correct option from those below:

A. Statement I is correct, Statement II is incorrect.
B. Statement I is incorrect, Statement II is correct.
C. Both Statement I and Statement II are correct.
D. Both Statement I and Statement II are incorrect.

Q.150 Which institution is also a leading mobilizer of third-party resources for projects in developing countries?

A. IFC **B.** IDA **C.** IBRD **D.** MIGA

// Smart Answer Sheet //

Correct — Percentage of students who answered correctly. **Skipped** — Percentage of students who skipped.

Q.	Ans.	Correct / Skipped
1	A	59.52 % / 7.15 %
2	B	21.43 % / 23.81 %
3	C	66.67 % / 26.19 %
4	A	47.62 % / 26.19 %
5	D	61.9 % / 26.2 %
6	D	35.71 % / 26.19 %
7	B	38.1 % / 28.57 %
8	B	23.81 % / 26.19 %
9	D	57.14 % / 26.19 %
10	D	61.9 % / 26.2 %
11	D	64.29 % / 26.19 %
12	C	28.57 % / 26.19 %
13	A	28.57 % / 26.19 %
14	B	35.71 % / 26.19 %
15	D	9.52 % / 26.19 %
16	B	45.24 % / 26.19 %
17	A	28.57 % / 26.19 %
18	B	54.76 % / 26.19 %
19	C	35.71 % / 26.19 %
20	C	52.38 % / 26.19 %
21	B	47.62 % / 26.19 %
22	D	54.76 % / 26.19 %
23	B	52.38 % / 26.19 %
24	D	50.0 % / 26.19 %
25	B	50.0 % / 26.19 %
26	C	50.0 % / 26.19 %
27	C	50.0 % / 26.19 %
28	D	54.76 % / 26.19 %
29	C	28.57 % / 26.19 %
30	A	45.24 % / 26.19 %
31	B	57.14 % / 26.19 %
32	D	47.62 % / 26.19 %
33	D	40.48 % / 26.19 %
34	B	47.62 % / 26.19 %
35	D	30.95 % / 26.19 %
36	C	42.86 % / 28.57 %
37	A	66.67 % / 28.57 %
38	B	45.24 % / 28.57 %
39	B	35.71 % / 28.58 %
40	B	42.86 % / 28.57 %
41	A	33.33 % / 28.57 %
42	D	33.33 % / 28.57 %
43	A	14.29 % / 30.95 %
44	D	11.9 % / 28.58 %
45	A	40.48 % / 28.57 %
46	A	45.24 % / 28.57 %
47	A	35.71 % / 28.58 %
48	C	26.19 % / 28.57 %
49	D	30.95 % / 28.57 %
50	D	14.29 % / 30.95 %
51	C	33.33 % / 14.29 %
52	C	35.71 % / 16.67 %
53	B	47.62 % / 19.05 %
54	C	52.38 % / 19.05 %
55	A	40.48 % / 19.04 %
56	B	30.95 % / 19.05 %
57	C	40.48 % / 19.04 %
58	C	21.43 % / 21.43 %
59	C	47.62 % / 19.05 %
60	A	47.62 % / 19.05 %
61	B	47.62 % / 19.05 %
62	B	47.62 % / 21.43 %
63	A	35.71 % / 19.05 %
64	A	45.24 % / 19.05 %
65	D	28.57 % / 19.05 %
66	A	52.38 % / 21.43 %
67	D	35.71 % / 19.05 %
68	D	40.48 % / 21.42 %
69	C	42.86 % / 19.04 %
70	A	26.19 % / 21.43 %
71	A	23.81 % / 19.05 %
72	C	47.62 % / 19.05 %
73	C	19.05 % / 19.05 %
74	D	16.67 % / 19.04 %
75	A	30.95 % / 19.05 %
76	A	64.29 % / 19.04 %
77	B	45.24 % / 19.05 %
78	D	38.1 % / 21.42 %
79	A	26.19 % / 23.81 %
80	D	23.81 % / 23.81 %

Q.	Ans.	Correct / Skipped	Q.	Ans.	Correct / Skipped	Q.	Ans.	Correct / Skipped	Q.	Ans.	Correct / Skipped	Q.	Ans.	Correct / Skipped
81	D	40.48 % / 23.81 %	95	A	21.43 % / 26.19 %	109	A	26.19 % / 26.19 %	123	A	35.71 % / 26.19 %	137	B	28.57 % / 28.57 %
82	C	30.95 % / 23.81 %	96	A	26.19 % / 23.81 %	110	C	19.05 % / 26.19 %	124	A	52.38 % / 26.19 %	138	C	14.29 % / 35.71 %
83	A	19.05 % / 23.81 %	97	D	9.52 % / 26.19 %	111	A	50.0 % / 26.19 %	125	C	14.29 % / 26.19 %	139	C	9.52 % / 33.34 %
84	C	30.95 % / 21.43 %	98	B	47.62 % / 23.81 %	112	A	21.43 % / 28.57 %	126	A	23.81 % / 28.57 %	140	D	28.57 % / 30.95 %
85	C	21.43 % / 23.81 %	99	D	33.33 % / 23.81 %	113	A	30.95 % / 28.57 %	127	C	45.24 % / 26.19 %	141	D	21.43 % / 30.95 %
86	B	47.62 % / 21.43 %	100	B	23.81 % / 28.57 %	114	C	33.33 % / 26.19 %	128	C	14.29 % / 28.57 %	142	D	21.43 % / 30.95 %
87	C	30.95 % / 21.43 %	101	C	38.1 % / 30.95 %	115	D	26.19 % / 28.57 %	129	A	26.19 % / 26.19 %	143	B	16.67 % / 33.33 %
88	C	33.33 % / 23.81 %	102	A	42.86 % / 26.19 %	116	C	14.29 % / 28.57 %	130	B	42.86 % / 26.19 %	144	A	26.19 % / 33.33 %
89	D	19.05 % / 21.43 %	103	C	35.71 % / 28.58 %	117	D	21.43 % / 28.57 %	131	B	38.1 % / 28.57 %	145	D	16.67 % / 33.33 %
90	B	50.0 % / 23.81 %	104	B	42.86 % / 28.57 %	118	D	16.67 % / 28.57 %	132	B	50.0 % / 26.19 %	146	B	35.71 % / 33.34 %
91	B	26.19 % / 26.19 %	105	B	45.24 % / 28.57 %	119	B	16.67 % / 28.57 %	133	D	21.43 % / 26.19 %	147	D	38.1 % / 30.95 %
92	D	19.05 % / 23.81 %	106	D	26.19 % / 28.57 %	120	D	40.48 % / 26.19 %	134	A	28.57 % / 28.57 %	148	D	21.43 % / 33.33 %
93	C	19.05 % / 23.81 %	107	D	33.33 % / 26.19 %	121	B	19.05 % / 26.19 %	135	D	14.29 % / 28.57 %	149	D	7.14 % / 30.96 %
94	D	14.29 % / 28.57 %	108	B	33.33 % / 28.57 %	122	C	28.57 % / 26.19 %	136	B	35.71 % / 30.96 %	150	A	26.19 % / 28.57 %

//Hints and Solutions//

1. Physical distribution includes all the activities associated with the supply of finished product at every step, from the production line to the consumers. Important physical distribution functions include customer service, order processing, inventory control, transportation and logistics, and packaging and materials. Hence option A is correct.

2. The correct sequence of scientific research is as follows:

a) Perceiving the problem situation – First we represent, what is the problem or what problem we want to study.

b) Locating the actual problem and its definition – Define the problem with locating its causes.

c) Hypothesizing – Formulate the hypothesis. Hypothesis is a proposed explanation on the basis of some limited evidence.

d) Deducing the consequences of the suggested solution.

e) Testing the hypothesis in action.

3. The supply chain concept can help a company locate: Superior suppliers and Superior distributors.

Hence, Option C is correct.

4. A **research hypothesis** is a specific, clear, and testable proposition or predictive statement about the possible outcome of a scientific **research** study based on a particular property of a population, such as presumed differences between groups on a particular variable or relationships between variables.

For example, a study designed to look at the relationship between sleep deprivation and test performance might have a hypothesis that states, "This study is designed to assess the hypothesis that sleep-deprived people will perform worse on a test than individuals who are not sleep-deprived."

5. The objective of Research is to makes accurate use of concepts. The Research can also be done to find out the hidden truth. The Research's objective should be highly focused and feasible.

6. Solution: To calculate the effective rate of interest, we do not need the amount. As per equation (1) above,

$E = (1 + i)^n - 1$ ... where 'E' is the effective rate of interest, 'i' is the actual rate of interest in decimal, and 'n' is the number of conversion periods.

In this problem, we know that,

The actual rate of interest = i = 8% p.a. = 0.08 p.a. = 0.04 per semi-year (6 months).

Number of conversion periods = n = 2 (since we are calculating for one year and compounding happens once every six months)

Therefore, the effective rate of interest is,

$E = (1 + i)^n - 1 = (1 + 0.04)^2 - 1 = 1.0816 - 1 = 0.0816$ or 8.16%.

Hence, the correct answer is option C – 8.16 percent.

7. Capital gearing ratio indicates the relationship between equity shareholders fund and long term borrowed funds.

8. Bilateral arrangements instituted to restrain the rapid growth of exports of specifically manufactured goods are called administered protection.

9. ISA offers comprehensive control systems training across essential areas, including:

Basic continuous control.

Control strategy design and application.

Integration and software.

Instrumentation maintenance and troubleshooting.

Control documentation.

Advanced control.

Automatic controls and robotics.

10. Human relations are good when every worker participates in planning and decision-making. Plans should satisfy various groups and eliminate objections from the workers in a way that the objectives are attained easily and the interests of the workers are well protected.

11. Sources of external recruitment include:

People joining an organization, specifically through recommendations.

Employment agencies(e.g. naukri.com) or employment exchanges.

Advertising.

Institutes like colleges and vocational schools (e.g. campus selection)

Contractors.

Hiring unskilled labor.

List of applications.

12. The Central Advisory Board Of Education (CABE) is the oldest and highest advisory body in India to advise the central and state governments in the field of education.

It was established in 1920 as a realization of the recommendations of the Calcutta university commission (1917-19) but dissolved in 1923 as a measure of the economy. This board consists of nominated members representing various interests in addition to elected members from Lok sabha and Rajya sabha. Its main function is to advise Central and State Govt. in the field of education.

Hence, the correct option is (C).

13. A kinked demand curve occurs when the demand curve is not a straight line but has a different elasticity for higher and lower prices. ... This model of oligopoly suggests that prices are rigid and that firms will face different effects for both increasing price or decreasing price.

14. The purpose of higher education is to promote critical and creative thinking abilities among students so that they can become self-dependent. These abilities will help them to think independently, develops creativity and also ensure job placements. Therefore, both the statements are correct, but the only reason is not the correct explanation of assertion. So, option B is correct.

15. The concept of Imperfect Competition was initially developed by a prestigious English economist, Roy Harrod. In 1933, Joan Robinson of Cambridge University in England and Edward Chamberlin of Harvard University in America, two distinguished economists, complemented this concept with essential contributions.

16. The Proposition 'All wise men are afraid of death' is contradicted because in the question it is mention that wise man are hardlyafraid of death, here hardly means difficult. So, from this all wise man are not afraid of death, 'some' can be possible, 'no' can also be possible. Option B contradicts.

17. The pattern followed is that the sum of digits of second number is subtracted from the sum of digits of first number.
$Eg: 45\%11 = (4+5) - (1+1) = 9 - 2 = 7$
and $59\%34 = (5+9) - (3+4) = 14 - 7 = 7$
Similarly, $55\%4 = (5+5) - (4) = 10 - 4 = 6$
$\Rightarrow Ans - (A)$

18. Weights of 4 boxes $= 30, 20, 50$ and 90 kilograms
(A) $: 200 =$ not possible
(B) $: 190 = 20 + 30 + 50 + 90$
(C) $: 140 = 50 + 90$
(D) $: 160 = 20 + 50 + 90$

Hence, option B is correct.

19. Answer: C) 40

The fruit content in both the fresh fruit and dry fruit is the same.

Given, fresh fruit has 68% water.so remaining 32% is fruit content. weight of fresh fruits is 100kg

Dry fruit has 20% water.so remaining 80% is fruit content.let weight if dry fruit be y kg.

Fruit % in freshfruit = Fruit% in dryfruit

Therefore, (32/100) x 100 = (80/100) x y

we get, y = 40 kg.

20. It is the analogical reasoning. Analogy here is:

Intellect superiority: Concentration Power :: Concave Mirror: Rays Concentration at one point.

21. Answer: B) W

In the given alphabet, last but one letter of alphabet is Y.

10th letter to the left of Y is O

8th letter to the right of O is W

22. Answer: D) QH

The first letter follows +1, +2, +3, +4,

The second letter follows +2, +3, +4, +5,.

23. A is a male and married to B. So, A is the husband and B is the wife. C is the brother of A. D is the son of C. E. who is the sister of D will be the daughter of C. B is the daughter-in-law of F whose husband has died means F is the mother of A.

Clearly. E is the daughter of C.

24. Brother of father — Uncle;

Uncle's granddaughter — daughter of uncle's son — daughter of a cousin — niece.

25. Given number of girls are twice that of boys.

--> G=2B and G+B = 60

Therefore, G=40 and B= 20

Given Laxmi ranked 27th from the top and 9 boys are ahead of Laxmi.

Therefore, There are 17 girls ahead of Laxmi.

Therefore, Number of girls who ranked after Laxmi = 40 - (17+1) = 22.

26. A monopsony is a market condition in which there is only one buyer, the monopsonist. Like a monopoly, a monopsony also has imperfect market conditions.

27. "Education is the manifestation of perfection already in man" –this is the very famous quotation by Swami Vivekanand.

28. The various reasons for emergence of Monopoly are:

Government licensing: ADVERTISEMENTS:

Patent Rights: Certain big private companies are engaged in research and development activities.

Cartel: ADVERTISEMENTS:

Control on raw materials:

29. As mentioned in the passage, "We believe that technological strengths are especially crucial in dealing with this fourth dimension underlying continuous change in the aspirations of the people, the economy in the global context, and the strategic interests." Thus, the highlighted elements are indicative of the fourth dimension. Option 2 is incorrect as the passage states that the fourth dimension is an offshoot or an extension of "modern day dynamism" and not one of its indicators. Thus, option C is the correct answer.

30. According to the passage, "Technological strengths are the key to creating more productive employment in an increasingly competitive market place and to continually upgrade human skills." Thus, option A is the correct answer.

31. According to the passage, "The absence of greater technological impetus could lead to lower productivity and wastage of precious natural resources." which will hurt the poorest most. Hence, option B is the correct answer.

32. According to the passage, "For people-oriented actions as well, whether for the creation of large-scale productive employment or for ensuring nutritional and health security for people, or for better living conditions, technology is the only vital input." From this sentence, it can be inferred that the advantage of technological inputs will enhance the living standard of the people, hence lifting people to a life of dignity. Thus, option D is the correct answer.

33. According to the last few lines of the passage, "Even while being alive to the short-term realities, medium and long-term strategies to develop core technological strengths within our industry are vital for envisioning a developed India." Thus, option D is the correct answer. The other options are irrelevant in the context of the passage.

34. Answer: B) 20

Clearly, From 1 to 100, there are ten numbers with 3 as the unit's digit - 3, 13, 23, 33, 43, 53, 63, 73, 83, 93 and ten numbers with 3 as the ten's digit - 30, 31, 32, 33, 34, 35, 36, 37, 38, 39.

So, required number = 10 + 10 = 20.

35. All raincoats are jackets.

All jackets are raincoats. Both conclusion are justified the statements.

36. The second vowel from the right of the reversed English alphabet is E and 7th letter to the left of E in the new series is L.

37. Answer: Father-in-law

Mother's grandson — Son, Son's wife — Daughter-in.law

38. Non-verbal communication is all about the body language of the speaker. In appearance, it includes clothing, hairstyle, neatness of the speaker. In body language, it consists of facial expressions, gestures and postures. In sound, it includes voice tone, volume and speech rate. Report and job description are part of written communication.

39. Average marks obtained in Physics by all the seven students

$$= \frac{1}{7} \times [(90\% \text{ of } 120) + (80\% \text{ of } 120) + (70\% \text{ of } 120)$$
$$+ (80\% \text{ of } 120) + (85\% \text{ of } 120) + (65\% \text{ of } 120)$$
$$+ (50\% \text{ of } 120)]$$
$$= \frac{1}{7} \times [(90 + 80 + 70 + 80 + 85 + 65 + 50)\% \text{ of } 120]$$
$$= \frac{1}{7} \times [520\% \text{ of } 120]$$
$$= \frac{624}{7}$$
$$= 89.14$$

40. Answer: Option B

From the table, it is clear that Sajal and Rohit have 60% or more marks in each of the six subjects.

41. Aggregate marks obtained by Sajal

$$= [(90\% \text{ of } 150) + (60\% \text{ of } 130) + (70\% \text{ of } 120)$$
$$+ (70\% \text{ of } 100) + (90\% \text{ of } 60) + (70\% \text{ of } 40)]$$
$$= [135 + 78 + 84 + 70 + 54 + 28]$$

$$= 449$$

42. We shall find the overall percentage (for all the seven students) with respect to each subject.

The overall percentage for any subject is equal to the average of percentages obtained by all the seven students since the maximum marks for any subject is the same for all the students.

Therefore, overall percentage for:

(i) Maths $= \left[\frac{1}{7} \times (90 + 100 + 90 + 80 + 80 + 70 + 65)\right]\%$

$$= \left[\frac{1}{7} \times (575)\right]\%$$
$$= 82.14\%$$

(ii) Chemistry $= \left[\frac{1}{7} \times (50 + 80 + 60 + 65 + 65 + 75 + 35)\right]\%$

$$= \left[\frac{1}{7} \times (430)\right]\%$$
$$= 61.43\%$$

(iii) Physics $= \left[\frac{1}{7} \times (90 + 80 + 70 + 80 + 85 + 65 + 50)\right]\%$

$$= \left[\frac{1}{7} \times (520)\right]\%$$
$$= 74.29\%$$

(Iv) Geography $= \left[\frac{1}{7} \times (60 + 40 + 70 + 80 + 95 + 85 + 77)\right]\%$
$$= \left[\frac{1}{7} \times (507)\right]\%$$
$$= 72.43\%$$

(v) History $= \left[\frac{1}{7} \times (70 + 80 + 90 + 60 + 50 + 40 + 80)\right]\%$

$$= \left[\frac{1}{7} \times (470)\right]\%$$
$$= 67.14\%$$

(vi) Comp. Science $= \left[\frac{1}{7} \times (80 + 70 + 70 + 60 + 90 + 60 + 80)\right]\%$
$$= \left[\frac{1}{7} \times (510)\right]\%$$
$$= 72.86\%$$

Clearly, this percentage is highest for Maths.

43. Aggregate marks obtained by Tarun

$$= \quad [(65\% \text{ of } 150) + (35\% \text{ of } 130) + (50\% \text{ of } 120)$$
$$+((77\% \text{ of } 100) + (80\% \text{ of } 60) + (80\% \text{ of } 40)]$$
$$= \quad [97.5 + 45.5 + 60 + 77 + 48 + 32]$$
$$= \quad 360.$$

The maximum marks (of all the six subjects)
=(150+130+120+100+60+40)

$$= 600$$

$\therefore$ Overall percentage of Tarun $= \left(\frac{360}{600} \times 100\right) \% = 60\%$

44. For adding table of contents, click on the tab 'References' to add the 'table of contents. The references tab also helps to add footnotes, citations, and bibliography.

45. Printers can be broadly classified into two categories-Impact and Non-Impact Printers.

Impact printers: It is a printer that strikes a print head against an ink ribbon to mark the paper. Common examples -dot matrix anddaisy-wheel printers.

Non-Impact printers: These printers print the characters without using ribbon. Common examples- Laser and Inkjet Printers.

46. Central Statistical Organisation

According to the first report, the National Income of India for 1948-49 was Rs. 8,710 crore and the per capita income was Rs. 225. Since 1955 the national income estimates are being prepared by Central Statistical Organisation.

47. Wrought Iron:-

Wrought Iron is the purest form of iron. It contains 0.12 to 0.25% carbon and is thus the purest form of iron.

48. Modifier keys include Alt, Ctrl, Shift and the Windows key.

49. Novels include Godaan, Karmabhoomi, Gaban, Mansarovar, Idgah.

50. Cash flow statement, unlike other accounting statements neglects accrual transactions and summaries all transactions with involvement of

cash or cash equivalents. The cash flow statement disintegrate profit under three heads, operating, investing and financing activities.

Operating activities deals with business operational transactions and recordings like depreciation, amortization, account payable etc.

Investing activities concerns with matters related to sale and purchase or capital assets in cash. And financing activities covers transaction

related funds procured by business. It includes debts, equity, loans and short plus long-term borrowings.

51. When marginal cost is equal to the average cost the slope is at zero. Explanation: When the 'marginal cost' is equal to average

cost than the point at which they intersect each other is also the minimum of the AC curve.

52. • SERVQUAL Model is also called RATER Model, which stands for:

1. Reliability: the ability of the firm to perform service accurately.

2. Assurance: ability and courtesy of employees to inspire knowledge and trust.

3. Tangibles: physical facilities, equipment, appearance.

4. Empathy: care and attention paid towards the customers

5. Responsiveness: ability and willingness of the firm to help customers and provide the required service.

Thus, Option C is correct.

53. Inverse odd function means demand is inversely related to price.

P = f(D)

54. The three cardinal features of budgetary control are: Planning, Coordination and Control. It involves objects that are set by preparing budgets. For preparing various budgets, the business is divided into various responsibility centres, and then the actual figures are recorded and compared to the budgeted figures so as to study the performance. Remedial actions are taken if actual performance is less than the budgeted.

Thus, Option C is correct.

55. • Since kickbacks are a form of negotiated bribery when a commission is paid to the broker/bribe-taker in exchange for services provided, it is different from bribes where one party takes money/gifts from the other party in exchange of a favour.

Thus, Option A is correct.

56. Threshold competencies include a basic minimum requirement of skills, knowledge, motive, traits that are essential to perform a job.

Thus, Option B is correct.

57. Important fields on which Big data can be applied are as follows:

• Governance

• Business

• Agriculture

• Marketing

• Human resources

Thus, Option C is correct.

58. Division of work refers to dividing work, job, task or assignment into smaller tasks, which makes man specialists. Division of work but not the chain of command helps to specialise in an activity which increases output with perfection and also avoids wastage.

Thus, Option C is correct.

59. ● Sensitivity training- This is a method of changing behavior through unstructured group interaction. Its primary focus is on reducing interpersonal conflict. The actual technique employed in this training is T-group.

● Business game- Simulations that represent actual business situations are termed as a business game. It involves two or more hypothetical organizations competing in a given product market to make a profit. Participants assume the role of managers, take decisions, evaluate results and find out the outcome.

Thus, Option C is correct.

60. ● Brand recall is very much essential to make the customer purchase a low involvement product.

● As these products pose no risk, the customer does not research much and purchase the product of a particular brand which they recall at that moment.

Thus, Option A is correct.

61. ● The key factors which create ethical issues at the workplace are as follows:

1) Behavior of management

2) Compensation

3) Positive reinforcement for ethical behavior

● Some ethical issues related to the behavior of management are as follows:

1) Hiring and treating employees

2) Dishonest advertisements

● Discrimination in hiring and treating employees can be reduced by creating a workplace environment that supports ethical behavior and act as a role model for employees.

Thus, Option B is correct.

62. The following are the tenets of CRM formulated by Kutner and Cripps:

1) The customers should be treated as important assets.

2) All the customers are not equally desirable.

3) Customers vary in their needs, preferences, buying behavior and price sensitivity.

4) By understanding their customers, companies can tailor their offerings to maximize the overall value.

Thus, Option B is correct.

63. If the breakeven point is higher, then the fixed cost will also be higher and not lower.

Thus, Option A is correct.

64. • The three broad components of sustainability are Planet, People and Profits.

• The three P's of sustainability are often referred to as the Triple Bottom Line.

Thus, Option A is correct.

65. Section 46 of the Act provides the following six social security benefits:

1) Medical Benefit

2) Sickness Benefit

3) Maternity Benefit

4) Disablement Benefit

5) Dependant's Benefit

6) Funeral Expenses

Thus, Option D is correct.

66. • डॉ। विलियम ओची - जेड थ्योरी

• डगलस मैकग्रेगर- एक्स थ्योरी

• फ्रेडरिक हर्ज़बर्ग- हाइजीन थ्योरी

• ए.एच. मास्लो-नीड हायरार्की थ्योरी

67. In marketing, the process of creating new products or modifying the existing products is known as product innovation.

This innovation can be in the form of a product's functionality, or it can be in the form of new technology. Organizations take feedback from customers and try to improve the product by introducing something unique.

Hence, the correct option is (D).

68. The objectives of career planning and development are all of the above except to help the organization in the formulation of strategic planning in Human resource. It has various other objectives like to attract talented employees to the organization, managing healthy ways of resolving conflicts, emotions, and stress of employees etc.

Thus, Option D is correct.

69. ● A thorough evaluation of sites is required when they are potentially similar.

● Customer concentrations become important considerations in selecting a site within a community.

● In India, the western and central regions are generally the most preferable regions for manufacturing facilities.

Thus, Option C is correct.

70. ● The Bombay Mill-Hands Association was the first association of Indian workers.

● It was founded by N.M. Lokhande in the year 1890.

Thus, Option A is correct.

71. The strategic dimension adaptability is

● Insignificant at the corporate level

● Medium at the business level

● Significant at the function level

Thus, Option A is correct.

72. Following are the functions of retailers:

- Provide information to consumers.

- Collect products from wholesalers.

- Store merchandise and marking the prices.

- Conclude transactions with Final customers.

Thus, Option C is correct.

73. Profit maximisation objective ignores the time value of money and does not consider the magnitude and timing of earnings. It treats all earnings as equal though they occur in different periods. But the long term objective of financial management is to maximise the value of the firm's common stock; it means that by maximising common stock the firm is operating consistently towards maximising shareholder's utility.

Thus, Option C is correct.

74. • Parties involved in corporate governance include chief executive officer, the board of directors, management and shareholders.

• Directors, workers, and management receive salaries and benefits. Shareholders receive capital returns.

• Corporate governance protects the interests of investors and ensures the commitment of the board in managing the company.

• Good corporate governance is rewarded with the higher market valuation.

Thus, Option D is correct.

75. Ministerial Conference is the highest level of the decision-making body of the WTO

Thus, Option A is correct.

76. The Market Analysis is also known as a documented investigation of a market which is used to inform a company's planning activities, around decisions of inventory, purchase, purchases of capital equipment and many other aspects of a company.

Thus, Option A is correct.

77. Artisan Entrepreneur is one who possesses very good skill or craft but has little business knowledge. These entrepreneurs focus on personal Selling efforts and use few sources of capital.

Thus, Option B is correct.

78. • In the storming phase of group formation, members start competing for leadership and control over the group.

• In the adjourning phase of group formation, the breaking up of the team is done as the purpose is completed.

Thus, Option D is correct.

79. • Section 5 of the Payment of Wages Act, 1936 deals with the time of payment of wages.

• It states that if there are less than a thousand persons employed in an establishment, the wages should be paid before the expiry of the seventh day.

Thus, Option A is correct.

80. • Abraham Maslow developed the behavioral science school of organizational behavior.

• Elton Mayo developed the human relations school of organizational behavior through Hawthorne Experiments.

Thus, Option D is correct.

81. • Setting objectives: The first step is to set objectives which usually revolves around creating awareness, educating the buyers, persuading them etc.

• Determining promotion budget: It is one of the most crucial steps in promotion decision. Budget is decided after considering all expenditures.

• Target market: A regular study of the target market is very important so as to consider various environmental factors.

• The appeal: Next step is to appeal, to persuade customers to buy the product.

• Promotion mix: Last step is to select the most efficient promotional tool so as to make sure the message is delivered as intended.

Thus, Option D is correct.

82. French and Bell clubbed the interventions into twelve groups. They are as follows:

1) Diagnostic

2) Team building

3) Intergroup activities

4) Survey feedback methods

5) Education and training programs

6) Techno-structural activities

7) Process consultation

8) The management grid

9) Mediation and negotiation activities

10) Coaching and counselling

11) Career planning

12) Planning and goal-setting activities

Thus, Option C is correct.

83. • Unilateral transfers include private transfers like foreign remittances and public transfers such as government aid.

• Net income receipts are a part of a current account.

Thus, Option A is correct.

84. Accumulation of skill, aptitude, ability, expertise, qualification and knowledge of manpower poses in a nation at a point of time is called as human capital.

Thus, Option C is correct.

85. • Raymond Vernon's PLC theory was developed from the viewpoint of developed countries like the United States.

- PLC theory puts emphasis on the timing of innovation and economies of scale.

Thus, Option C is correct.

86. • SO - Strength can be used to capitalize on emerging opportunities.

• ST - The firm strives to minimize threats through its strengths.

• WO - Need to overcome organizational weaknesses.

• WT - A firm facing external threats and internal weaknesses may struggle for its survival.

Thus, Option B is correct.

87. Hurwitz, Savage and Laplace these three are the criteria of decision under uncertainty.

Thus, Option C is correct.

88. • Production Concept assumes that consumers are interested in product availability and low prices and consumers prefer inexpensive products that are widely available.

• Product Concept states that consumers prefer products offering the most quality, features and performance, and it assumes that buyers admire well-made products and appraise quality and performance.

Thus, Option C is correct.

89. Managerial economics is helpful in helping in managing and controlling cost, profit maximization, demand forecasting, business planning, computing economic relationship etc. but it is not helpful in controlling market risk.

Thus, Option D is correct.

90. • In monolithic organizations, persons from different cultural groups are rarely seen in the positions of power and leadership. Even in the workforce, they are less in number.

• The plural organizations give importance to persons from various cultural backgrounds who are different from the dominant group.

Thus, Option B is correct.

91. Given,

Earnings before Interest and Tax (EBIT) = Rs 8,50,000

Fixed costs = Rs 82,100

Variable costs = Rs 1,20,900

And, Annual sales = EBIT + Fixed cost + variable cost

So, Annual sales = Rs 8,50,000 + Rs 82,100 + Rs 1,20,900

= Rs 10,53,000

Thus, Option B is correct.

92. Given,

EBIT = Rs 8,50,000

Fixed costs = Rs 82,100

And, Degree Of Operating Leverage = Contribution / EBIT

Contribution = EBIT + Fixed cost

So, contribution = Rs 8,50,000 + Rs 82,100 = Rs 9,32,100

then, Degree Of Operating Leverage = Rs 9,32,100 / Rs 8,50,000 = 1.1

Thus, Option D is correct.

93. Given,

EBIT = Rs 8,50,000

EBT = Rs 5,20,800

And, Degree Of Financial Leverage = EBIT / EBT

So, Degree Of Financial Leverage = Rs 8,50,000 / Rs 5,20,800 = 1.63

Thus, Option C is correct.

94. Given,

Degree Of Operating Leverage (DOL) = 1.1

Degree Of Financial Leverage (DFL) = 1.63

And, Degree Of Combined Leverage = DOL * DFL

So, Degree Of Combined Leverage = 1.1 * 1.63 = 1.793

Thus, Option D is correct.

95. Given,

Degree Of Combined Leverage (DCL)= 1.793

Percentage change in sales = 10%

And, Percentage (%) change in EPS = DCL * Percentage change in sales

So, % Change in EPS = 1.793 * 10% = 17.93%

Thus, Option A is correct.

96. • Data mining is the process of finding the relation between the common entities of different databases.

• Several statistical methods are used for this purpose.

Thus, Option A is correct.

97. High margin low turnover stores focus on the following:

• On product quality and uniqueness.

• Sold in store but not pre-sold.

• These are located in major shopping centres.

Thus, Option D is correct.

98. • Retail co-operatives are a group of independent retailers who combine financial resources.

• They agree on common policies and effectively control wholesaling needs.

Thus, Option B is correct.

99. • Leapfrog strategy is used to gain an advantage over the competitors by providing more advanced products.

• Flanking attack strategy is used to gain an advantage by providing more features at the same prices with more promotions.

• Encirclement strategy is used when a company is focusing on developing multiple segments at the same time to challenge its competitors.

• Guerilla attack strategy is used to challenge by using a limited number of resources. Promotions or price-cutting are the main tools used in this strategy.

Thus, Option D is correct.

100. • The retail chain involves common ownership of multiple units.

• It involves centralized decision making and purchasing.

• Maintain their prices and increase their margins

• They can cut prices to attract a large volume of sales.

Thus, Option B is correct.

101. • Equity shareholders are called the owners of the company as they get a share of profits at last. All benefits and losses are to be borne by them.

• They have their say in the company's meetings and also possess voting rights as well. They are paid after preference shareholders are paid.

• Preference shareholders can also be called shareholders but not owners of the company.

Thus, Option C is correct.

102. Financial and Economic Feasibility are related to each other but are two different concepts. Financial feasibility is only concerned with the financing of the project, whereas, It does not take into account the project's economic implications.

Thus, Option A is correct.

103. • Spread is the difference between the bid and the offer price of the share.

• The offer is always higher than the bid to make a profit.

Thus, Option C is correct.

104. The bargaining power of suppliers will be high when there are many buyers and few dominant suppliers and there are homogeneous products. If suppliers have high bargaining power over a company, then the company is less attractive.

Thus, Option B is correct.

105. • Public Accounts of India is established under Article 266 (2) of the Constitution.

• All public money received other than those included in the Consolidated Fund of India are held in Public Accounts of India.

• This account mainly consists of money raised through small saving schemes,

• provident fund schemes etc.

• Government is just the custodian of these funds. It has to repay either on the maturity date or whenever claimed by people.

Thus, Option B is correct.

106. When 'n', the number of trials is very large or infinite, and neither 'p' nor 'q' is very small or nearer to equal then binomial distribution tends to be a normal distribution.The perfectly smooth and symmetrical curve, resulting from the expansion of the binomial $(p+q)^n$ when n approaches infinity is known as the normal curve.

Thus, Option D is correct.

107. Marketing mix of service involves three P's including people, process and physical evidence. People who are involved in providing service, Process actual operational activities, and Actual place and infrastructure in which the service is generated and delivered.

Thus, Option D is correct.

108. State Small Industries Corporations provide machinery on hire-purchase to small scale and ancillary industries, whose value is between Rs. 60 lakhs and Rs. 75 lakhs, including the value of machinery and equipment. The hire-purchase value is recovered in thirteen half-yearly instalments and a rebate of 2 per cent is given in some conditions.

Thus, Option B is correct.

109. Commission: 12,600 * 5 / 105 = 600

Thus, Option A is correct.

110. • Market Analysis involves studying various important points such as defining the target market, studying their buying habits, examining the sale and market share outlook of the proposal.

• The elements of Market Analysis include Market size, Market growth rate, Market profitability, Market trends, Distribution channels.

• Market size defines market volume as well as the market potential. Examples of information sources for determining market size are: Government data, Trade association data, customer surveys etc.

Thus, Option C is correct.

111. If an enterprise is located near its potential market, then the organisation can have better and up to date understanding of the market and thus can formulate more effective production and marketing strategies to increase sales and reduce cost.

Thus, Option A is correct.

112. Home-country factors that are outside the control of the company and have a direct effect on the success of a foreign company's political factor, legal structure and economic environment are called Domestic uncontrollables.

Thus, Option A is correct.

113. Divestment, turnaround, liquidation and bankruptcy are the types of retrenchment strategy. This strategy is followed when an organisation substantially reduces the scope of its activity.

Thus, Option A is correct.

114. Equidistance of quartile is one of the properties of a normal curve which states that the distance between the third quartile and median and median and first quartile are equal. Point of inflection is found at the difference between mean and one standard deviation.

Thus, Option C is correct.

115. Ethnography form of research focuses on describing the culture of a group of people.

Thus, Option D is correct.

116. ● Rothschild measure of the degree of monopoly power is the ratio between the slope of a firm's demand curve to the slope of the industry's demand curve. The degree of monopoly power ranges from 0 to 1.

● Under perfect competition, the index is zero because the demand curve is horizontal for each individual firm. Under pure monopoly, the index equals unity as there is no difference between firm and industry.

Thus, Option C is correct.

117. ● Foreign Trade policy is announced every 5 five years by the Ministry of Commerce & Industry.

● EXIM policy is regulated by the Foreign Trade Development and Regulation Act, 1992 which replaced the Imports and Exports (Control) Act 1947.

Thus, Option D is correct.

118. In chi-square, the greater the value of chi-square, the greater will be the discrepancy between observed and expected frequency. Chi-square is used to determine the goodness of fit, the association between two or more variables and test the discrepancy between observed and expected frequencies.

Thus, Option D is correct.

119. Enterprise Resource Planning is a software that handles the needs of an organization, along with meeting an organization's objectives while incorporating all the functions of an organization. This integrated software helps different departments to share information and communicate with each other.

Thus, Option B is correct.

120. Some data mining techniques are mentioned below:

a. Classification Analysis

b. Association Rule Learning

c. Anomaly or Outlier Detection

d. Clustering Analysis

e. Regression Analysis

f. Prediction

g. Sequential Patterns

h. Decision trees

Thus, Option D is correct.

121. Keynesians hold the view that the essence of demand-pull inflation is "too much spending chasing too few goods", while classical economist Coulborn was of the view that "too much money chasing too few goods".

Thus, Option B is correct.

122. Pie chart: A pie chart is a type of graph in which a circle is divided into sectors that each represents a proportion of the whole. Pie charts are a useful way to organize data in order to see the size of components relative to the whole and are particularly good at showing percentage or proportional data.

Thus, Option C is correct.

123. ● In the CSR model, Carroll suggested four possible strategies, i.e. Reaction, Proaction, Defence and Accommodation to companies to respond to social pressure.

● Gray, Owens and Adams gave this strategy on social responsibility.

Thus, Option A is correct.

124. ● To attract customers, service providers should attach physical evidence to their service offerings.

● The physical evidence like television commercials or brochures indicating their behavior or ambiance will attract the new customers.

Thus, Option A is correct.

125. ● Phillips Curve presents a tradeoff between inflation and unemployment rate. Friedman and Phelps revised and formulated the accelerationist theory. They believed a tradeoff exists only to the extent that the public (labour) was fooled while forming inflation expectations, but this would be transitory.

● Keynes' Liquidity trap is a situation in which people hold cash (inactive form) due to very low-interest rate and belief that it will rise soon.

● Findlay Shirras gave "The Science of Public Finance".

● R.S. Sayers: Defined the difference between Central Bank and Commercial bank.

Thus, Option C is correct.

126. ● Comply-or-explain' approach is a key characteristic of the UK's corporate governance system as compliance with the UK Corporate Governance Code is voluntary for public listed companies.

● Higgs Report on Corporate governance focused specifically on non-executive directors.

Thus, Option A is correct.

127. ● India has become the first country in the world to make CSR mandatory for Indian companies.

● CSR can go a long way in improving the social welfare of any country as per a KPMG survey results Indian companies have spent 47% higher on CSR activities than in 2014.

Thus, Option C is correct.

128. Purposive sampling, is a type of non-probability sampling in which researchers depend on their own judgment while choosing samples from the population. It is also known as judgmental and selective sampling. It is best used when the universe happens to be small, and a known characteristic of it is to be studied intensively.

Thus, Option C is correct.

129. When the mean deviation is divided by average used in finding out the mean deviation, the result we get is the coefficient of mean deviation. It is a relative measure of dispersion.

Thus, Option A is correct.

130. ANOVA technique was developed by Sir Ronald Aylmer Fisher, a famous statistician and biologist.

Thus, Option B is correct.

131. Merging with businesses of related or same industry is Concentric integration. Sharing resources or facilities is an example of concentric integration.

Thus, Option B is correct.

132. Just in time Logistics is a management strategy that includes movement of raw materials to a location at the required time, just before the material is required for the manufacturing process.

Thus, Option B is correct.

133. C- chart: Control charts for the number of defects per unit.

In many manufacturing situations and inspection situations, the sample size n, i.e. the area of opportunity is very large, and the probability of p of the occurrence of a defect in any one spot is very much small that np is finite. In such a situation from statistical theory, patterns of variation in data can be represented by Poisson distribution.

Thus, Option D is correct.

134. Outsourcing is adopted by companies to save cost. It is done both domestic and foreign contracting. It helps in concentrating on core processes rather than supporting ones.

Thus, option A is correct.

135. ● The CSR committee in India should consist of more than or equal to three directors, out of which one should be an independent director.

● Schedule VII of the Companies Act, 2013 prescribes the CSR projects.

Thus, Option D is correct.

136. Human capital planning is not considered a part of the scope of operation management. Other scopes include Product selection and design, material procurement, handling and allocation, quality control, maintenance and replacement etc.

Thus, Option B is correct.

137. It is also called a group or combined layout. It is used when production volumes for individual products are not sufficient to justify product layouts. It is a compromise between product layout and process layout, with associate advantages.

Thus, Option B is correct.

138. Three types of main current accounts maintained by the banks in order to facilitate the quick transfer of funds in different currencies are:

● Loro- an account where the bank remits funds in foreign currency to another bank for credit to an account of a third bank (their)

● Vostro- local currency account maintained by a foreign bank with a domestic bank. (your account with us)

● Nostro- foreign currency account maintained by the domestic bank in a foreign country in the foreign currency. (our account with you)

Thus, Option C is correct.

139. Place refers to where the majority of the priority population can be reached. In social marketing, Place represents putting all the efforts so as to make the change in behavior as easy as possible to a consumer.

Thus, Option C is correct.

140. ● Perceptual and Learning Constructs is one of the variables under Howarth Sheth Model of Consumer Behavior. The interpretation, when a consumer receives a stimulus, is influenced by two factors, namely, Stimulus ambiguity and Perceptual bias.

● A Stimulus ambiguity occurs when an individual is not able to interpret a stimulus, and a Perceptual bias occurs when an individual manipulates the stimuli as per his needs and experience.

Thus, Option D is correct.

141. • Producer's risk (alpha) is the probability of rejecting a high-quality lot.

• Consumer's risk (beta) is the probability of accepting a low-quality lot.

Thus, Option D is correct.

142. Modular Innovation is a form of Innovation wherein only a few components of a product are changed, whereas the overall design of the product remains the same. It is the opposite of Architectural Innovation and is also called Component Innovation.

Thus, Option D is correct.

143. In a service-based business, buyers purchases are intangible and perishable which is not the case in product-based business. In the service business, service providers have to look after value, reputation and delivery. Marketing of service depends upon three P's- People, Process and Physical evidence.

Thus, Option B is correct.

144. ● Gross National Product (GNP) is Gross Domestic Product (GDP) plus net factor income from abroad.

• GNP measures the monetary value of all finished goods and services produced by the country's factors of production irrespective of their location.

Thus, Option A is correct.

145. Disruptive Innovation is also known as Stealth Innovation that involves applying new technology or processes to a company's existing market.

Thus, Option D is correct.

146. Sustaining Innovation is a form of Innovation that, instead of creating new value networks, focuses on improving and growing the existing markets by satisfying the needs of a customer. It is the opposite of Disruptive Innovation.

Thus, Option B is correct.

147. • Only three statements out of five are the example of fall in the volume of resources. These include wear and tear or breakdown of machinery, saturation of natural resources, technology becomes obsolete. These examples show underutilisation or inefficient utilisation of resources.

• Whereas examples such as availability of new equipment, and discovery of natural resources are the examples of growth of resources.

Thus, Option D is correct.

148. • Financial level strategy improves the effectiveness of operations within a company.

• Business level strategy enhances the overall competitive theme of the company.

• Global strategy deals with the expansion of operations outside the home country.

• Corporate level strategy answers the primary questions of the business entity.

Thus, Option D is correct.

149. For an enterprise to fall under the category of small scale industry in the manufacturing sector, investment in plant and machinery should be between 25 lakh to 5 crores, whereas in service sector investment should be between 10 lakh to 2 crores. Small scale industries are generally under single ownership, hence it is a mostly sole proprietorship or sometimes a partnership firm.

Thus, Option D is correct.

150. International Finance Corporation (IFC) is a leading mobilizer of third-party resources for projects in developing countries

Thus, Option A is correct.

Mock Test 06

Paper-I

Q.1 _____________is research that is based on observation and measurement of phenomena, as directly experienced by the researcher.

A. Conceptual research

B. Action research

C. Fundamental research

D. Empirical research

Q.2 When planning to do as social research, it is better to:--

A. approach the topic with an open mind

B. do a pilot study before getting stuck into it

C. be familiar with literature on the topic

D. forget about theory because this is a very practical

Q.3 Factors affecting job design are:

A. Behavioral factors

B. Environmental factors

C. Organizational factors

D. All of the above

Q.4 The procedure for determining the duties and skill requirements of a job andthe kind of person who should be hired for it is:

A. Job analysis **B.** Job design

C. Job recruitment **D.** Job description

Q.5 Which of these models is not a rational planning approach:

A. Corporate- level strategic planning

B. Strategic business unit level strategic planning

C. Processual approach

D. Operational level strategic planning

Q.6 The unstructured interview:

A. Infrequently conducted

B. Typically is unbiased

C. Typically is related to future

D. Typically biased job performance

Q.7 Tests that measure traits, temperament, or disposition are examples of:

A. Manual dexterity tests

B. Personality tests

C. Intelligence tests

D. Work sample tests

Q.8 Which one of the following is NOT the advantage of Workforce Diversity?

A. Increased creativity and flexibility

B. Decreased problem-solving skills

C. Multiple perspectives

D. Greater openness to new ideas

Q.9 The best hiring occurs when the goals of which of the following should

consistent to each other?

A. HR managers, Finance managers

B. Head office, Brand

C. Organization, individual

D. Lower managers, Top managers

Q.10 Assertion (A): All teaching should aim at ensuring le learning.

Reason (R): All learning results from teaching.

Choose the correct answer from the following code:

A. Both (A) and (R) are true, and (R) is the correct explanation of (A).

B. Both (A) and (R) are true, but (R) is not the correct explanation of (A).

C. (A) is true, but (R) is false.

D. (A) is false, but (R) is true.

Q.11 Which of the following learner characteristics is highly related to effectiveness of teaching?

A. Prior experience of the learner

B. Educational status of the parents of the learner

C. Peer groups of the learner

D. Family size from which the learner comes.

Q.12 Which of the following role a manager performs as a Resource allocator?

A. Interpersonal role **B.** Decisional role

C. Informational role **D.** Supportive role

Q.13 Is the main source of innovations:

A. Upgraded technology

B. Human mind

C. Competitors' pressure

D. Research & Development

Q.14 AND   FOR   THE   BIG   SUM

If the second alphabet in each of the words is changed to the next alphabet in the English alphabetical order, How many words having two vowels will be formed?

A. One **B.** Two **C.** Three **D.** Four

Q.15 Which one of the following pedagogy approach refers to an approach in which students explores topics in greater depth during class time, and ICT education tools technologies like online videos are used to 'deliver the content' outside of the classroom to students.

A. Flipped Classroom Approach

B. Brainstorming Approach

C. ICT based approach

D. Two-way approach

Ques (16-17):Directions : Based on the alphanumeric series given below, answer the following questions:

Alphanumeric Series: W % ^ K V P 1 I 7 E 0 & 2 9 A F Z N 4 * @ U ? M

Q.16 How many numbers in the series are preceded by a vowel?

A. One
B. Four
C. Two
D. None of the above

Q.17 What is the second element from the right of 7th element from left?

A. V
B. 1
C. K
D. 7

Q.18 In a row of persons, the position of Sakshi from the left side of the row is 26th and position of Sakshi from the right side of the row is 35th. Find the total number of students in the row?

A. 40
B. 55
C. 45
D. 60

Q.19 A family consists of six members Priya, Qureshi, Raj, Xavi, Yusuf and Zain. Qureshi is the son of Raj but Raj is not mother of Qureshi. Priya and Raj are a married couple. Yusuf is the brother of Raj. Xavi is the daughter of Priya. Zain is the brother of Priya. How many children does Priya have?

A. Four
B. Two
C. Three
D. None of the above

Ques (20-22):Refer to the numerical series given below and answer the following questions:

435 224 786 823 902

Q.20 Find the missing element is the series given below:
ABD EFH IJL MNP QRT?

A. XYZ
B. VWY
C. UVX
D. WXZ

Q.21 When all the digits in each of the given numbers are arranged in ascending order, which number becomes the highest?

A. 435
B. 224
C. 786
D. None of these

Q.22 When the digits within the number are multiplied with each other, the product of which number is the lowest?

A. 435
B. 786
C. 902
D. 224

Q.23 Given below are some characteristics of reasoning. Select the code that states a characteristic which is not of deductive reasoning:

A. The conclusion must be based on observation and experiment.

B. The conclusion should be supported by the premise/premises.

C. The conclusion must follow from the premise/premises necessarily.

D. The conclusion must follow from the premise/premises necessarily.

Ques (24-25):Directions: Based on the digit-alphabets-symbols series given below, answer the following questions:

@ 1 8 H L I 6 K * & ? U E

Q.24 How many such consonants are there in the series which are immediately followed by a symbol and preceded by a number?

A. Two
B. One
C. Four
D. Three

Q.25 How many numbers are there in the series which are preceded by a vowel and succeeded by a consonant?

A. Two
B. One
C. Three
D. None of these

Ques (26-30):Read the passage carefully and answer the following question.

Climate change is considered to be one of the most serious threats to sustainable development, with adverse impacts on the environment, human health, food security, economic activity, natural resources and physical infrastructure. Global climate varies naturally. Accordingly to the Inter-governmental Panel on Climate Change (IPCC), the effects of climate change have already been observed, and scientific findings indicate that precautionary and prompt action is necessary. Vulnerability to climate change is not just a function of geography or dependence on natural resources; it also has social, economic and political dimensions which influence how climate change affects different groups. Poor people rarely have insurance to cover loss of property due to natural calamities i.e. drought, floods, super cyclones etc. The poor communities are already struggling to cope with the existing challenges of poverty and climate variability and climate change could push many beyond their ability to cope or even survive. It is vital that these communities are helped to adapt to the changing dynamics of nature. Adaptation is a process through which societies make themselves better able to cope with an uncertain future. Adapting to climate change entails taking the right measures to reduce the negative effects of climate change (or exploit the positive ones) by making the appropriate adjustments and changes. These range from technological options such as increased sea defences or flood – proof houses on stilts to behavioural change at the individual level, such as reducing water use in times of drought. Other strategies include early warning systems for extreme events, better water management, improved risk management, various insurance options and biodiversity conservation. Because of the speed at which climate change is happening due to global temperature rise, it is urgent that the vulnerability of developing countries to climate change is reduced and their capacity to adapt is increased and national adaptation plans are implemented. Adapting to climate change will entail adjustments and changes at every level from community to national and international. Communities must build their resilience, including adopting appropriate technologies while making the most of traditional knowledge, and diversifying their livelihoods to cope with current and future climate stress. Local coping strategies and knowledge need to be used in synergy with government and local interventions. The need of adaptation interventions depends on national circumstances. There is a large body of knowledge and experience within local communities on coping with climatic variability and extreme weather events. Local communities have always aimed to adapt to variations in their climate. To do so, they have made preparations based on their resources and their knowledge accumulated through

experience of past weather patterns. This includes times when they have also been forced to react to and recover from extreme events, such as floods, drought and hurricanes. Local coping strategies are an important element of planning for adaptation. Climate change is leading communities to experience climatic extremes more frequently, as well as new climate conditions and extremes. Traditional knowledge can help to provide efficient, appropriate and time – tested ways of advising and enabling adaptation to climate change in communities who are feeling the effects of climate changes due to global warming.

Q.26 Given below are the factors of vulnerability of poor people to climate change. Select the code that contains the correct answer.

1) Their dependence on natural resources
2) Geographical attributes
3) Lack of financial resources
4) Lack of traditional knowledge

A. 1, 2 and 3
B. 2, 3 and 4
C. 1, 2, 3 and 4
D. 3 only

Q.27 Adaptation as a process enables societies to cope with:

1) An uncertain future
2) Adjustments and changes
3) Negative impact of climate change
4) Positive impact of climate change

A. 1, 2, 3 and 4
B. 1 and 3
C. 2, 3 and 4
D. 3 only

Q.28 To address the challenge of climate change, developing countries urgently require:

A. Imposition of climate change tax
B. Implementation of national adaptation policy at their level
C. Adoption of short-term plans
D. Adoption of technological solutions

Q.29 The traditional knowledge should be used through:

A. Its dissemination
B. Improvement in national circumstances
C. Synergy between government and local interventions
D. Modern technology

Q.30 The main focus of the passage is on:

A. Combining traditional knowledge with appropriate technology
B. Co-ordination between regional and national efforts
C. Adaptation to climate change
D. Social dimensions of climate change

Q.31 The e-content generation for under-graduate courses has been assigned by the Ministry of Human Resource Development to:-

A. INFLIBNET
B. Consortium for Educational Communication.
C. National Knowledge Commission
D. Indira Gandhi National Open University

Q.32 Which of the following are Central Universities?

1. Pondicherry University
2. VIshwa bharati
3. H.N.B. Garhwal University
4. Kurukshetra University

A. 1, 2 and 3
B. 1, 3 and 4
C. 2, 3 and 4
D. 1, 2and 4

Q.33 Education as a subject of legislation figures in the which of the following lists?

A. Union List
B. State List
C. Concurrent List
D. Residuary Powers

Ques (34-35):Direction:- Ravi is the son of Aman's father's sister. Sahil is the son of Divya who is the mother of Gaurav and grandmother of Aman. Ashok is the father of Tanya and grandfather of Ravi. Divya is the wife of Ashok.

Q.34 How is Ravi related to Divya?

A. Nephew
B. Son
C. Grandson
D. Data inadequate

Q.35 How is Gaurav's wife related to Tanya?

A. Sister
B. Niece
C. Sister in law
D. Mother

Q.36 A new Laptop has been produced that weight less, is smaller and uses less power than previous Laptop models. Which of the following technologies has been used to accomplish this?

A. Universal Serial Bus Mouse
B. Faster Random-Access Memory
C. Blu Ray Drive
D. Solid State Hard Drive

Q.37 The dominant source of pollution due to oxides of nitrogen (NOX) in urban areas is:-

A. road transport
B. commercial sector
C. energy use in industry
D. power plants

Q.38 Which of the following is the largest source of water pollution in major rivers of India?

A. Untreated sewage
B. Agriculture run-off
C. Unregulated small scale industries
D. Religious practices

Q.39 Read the assertion and reason both carefully:-

Assertion (A): A high operating ratio indicates a favorable position.

Reasoning (R): A high operating ratio leaves a high margin to meet non-operating expenses.

A. (A) and (R) both are correct and (R) correctly explains (A).
B. Both (A) and (R) are correct but (R) does not explain (A).
C. Both (A) and (R) are incorrect.
D. (A) is correct but (R) is incorrect.

Q.40 8 litres are drawn from a cask full of wine and is then filled with water. This operation is performed three more times. The

ratio of the quantity of wine now left in cask to that of the water is 16 : 65. How much wine the cask hold originally?

A. 34 litres   **B.** 24 litres   **C.** 22 litres   **D.** 44 litres

Ques (41-45):Study the bar chart and answer the question based on it.

Production of Fertilizers by a Company (in 1000 tonnes) Over the Years

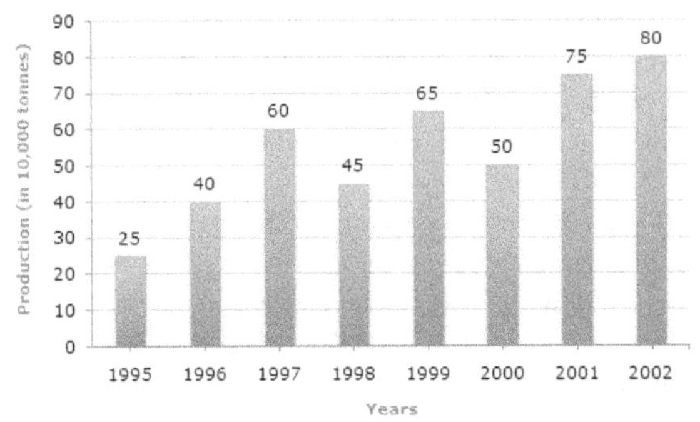

Q.41 What was the percentage decline in the production of fertilizers from 1997 to 1998?

A. 20%   **B.** 50%   **C.** 25%   **D.** 30%

Q.42 The average production of 1996 and 1997 was exactly equal to the average production of which of the following pairs of years?

A. 2000 and 2001   **B.** 1999 and 2000
C. 1998 and 2000   **D.** 1995 and 2001

Q.43 What was the percentage increase in production of fertilizers in 2002 compared to that in 1995?

A. 200%   **B.** 57.62%   **C.** 220%   **D.** 113.12%

Q.44 In which year was the percentage increase in production as compared to the previous year the maximum?

A. 2002   **B.** 2001   **C.** 1997   **D.** 1996

Q.45 In how many of the given years was the production of fertilizers more than the average production of the given years?

A. 1   **B.** 2   **C.** 3   **D.** 4

Q.46 Look at this series: 664, 332, 340, 170, ___, 89, ... What number should fill the blank?

A. 178   **B.** 97   **C.** 109   **D.** 177

Q.47 Look at this series: 8, 43, 11, 41, __, 39, 17, ... What number should fill in the blank?

A. 8   **B.** 14   **C.** 43   **D.** 44

Q.48 In these series, you will be looking at both the letter pattern and the number pattern. Fill the blank in the middle of the series or end of the series.

SCD, TEF, UGH, ___, WKL

A. CMN   **B.** VIJ   **C.** IJT   **D.** UJI

Q.49 Characteristics of Secondary Memory:-

A. It is known as backup memory.
B. Data is permanently stored even if power is switched off.
C. It is volatile memory.

D. Both A and B

Q.50 Positive classroom communication leads to:-

A. Coercion   **B.** Submission
C. Confrontation   **D.** Persuasion

Paper-II

Q.51 Assertion (A): Random sampling ensures the Law of statistical regularity.

Reason (R): Under random sampling, if the sample chosen is a random one, the sample will have the same composition and characteristics as the universe.

A. Both (A) and (R) are correct, and (R) is the correct explanation of (A).

B. Both (A) and (R) are correct, but (R) is not the correct explanation of (A).

C. (A) is correct., but (R) is not correct.

D. (A) is wrong, and (R) is correct.

Q.52 _______ is done to achieve maximum utilization of plant, machinery, workforce and minimize inventory of raw materials and work in progress.

A. Production evaluation
B. Production scheduling
C. Production review
D. Production planning

Q.53 _______ is the technique of determining the degree of correlation between two variables in case of ordinary data and is useful when a group of n individuals is arranged in order of merit or proficiency in possession of two characteristics.

A. Karl Pearson's coefficient of correlation
B. Rank correlation
C. Covariance
D. quartile deviation

Q.54 __________ is the simplest possible measure of dispersion and is defined as the difference between values of the extreme items of s series.

A. Mean deviation   **B.** Range
C. Standard deviation   **D.** Harmonic mean

Q.55 According to _______ model, a consumer has a complex set of deep motives which drive him towards a buying decision and consumers buying action can be influenced by desires and longings.

A. Motivation model
B. Psychoanalytical model
C. Economical model
D. Input-process-output model

Q.56 Which of the following is a part of operations management?

Statement I: Ongoing management of daily works of the company such as technical support, network support, etc.

Statement II: Planning, organization, staffing, control, and co-ordinating of human and material resources.

Choose the correct option from those below:

A. Statement I is correct., Statement II is incorrect.

B. Statement I is incorrect, Statement II is correct.

C. Both Statement I and Statement II are correct.

D. Both Statement I and Statement II are incorrect.

Q.57 Inclusion index and global competitiveness report is given by

A. WEF

B. World bank

C. IMF

D. UNDP

Q.58 ______ divides the area under the probability curve of distribution of test static into the rejection region and acceptance region.

A. Level of significance

B. Hypothesis testing

C. Null hypothesis

D. Critical value

Q.59 Assertion (A): Management helps an organization to achieve efficiency and effectiveness.Reason (R): Management ensures maximum production at minimum cost with optimal usage of resources.

A. (A) is correct., but (R) is incorrect.

B. Both (A) and (R) are correct, but (R) is not the right explanation of (A).

C. Both (A) and (R) are correct, (R) is the right explanation of (A).

D. Both (A) and (R) are incorrect.

Q.60 ______ is the combination of beliefs, ideas and imagination about the brand developed over a period of time and held in the consumer's mind.

A. Brand image

B. Brand perception

C. Brand Loyalty

D. Brand awareness

Q.61 An agriculturist has produced 500 quintals of wheat during a given period of time. He offers for sale 100 quintals of wheat @ 1500 per quintal, 150 quintals @ 1600 per quintal and so on.

What is the stock and supply of wheat in this case?

A. stock is 250 quintals and supply is 500 quintals.

B. stock is different whereas supply is 500 quintals.

C. stock is 500 quintals and supply is different.

D. both stock and supply are the same as 500 quintals.

Ques (62-74):Direction: Read the following passage and answer the questions given at the end by picking up the appropriate answer from the given alternatives.

Knowledge refers to the process of decision making using the existing information and to convert raw data into information; some knowledge is required. The required knowledge in both cases is different. The activities like data gathering, structuring, storing and accessing the information when required, fall under knowledge management. The decisions of an organization depend on the quality of data and the techniques used to structure and analyze the data. Even though it is very expensive to build and maintain knowledge management systems, the new companies are allocating some amount of capital to build customized knowledge management systems because of market instability and growing competition. These systems will

assist the management in the decision-making process and maintain the change process according to the market conditions.

Most of the knowledge in the firms will be tacit in nature after structuring the data, and this is maintained by a set of key people. When a person maintaining the data, leaves the organization, a new person appointed in place of that person can understand the mechanism of the knowledge management system with the minimum amount of training

Q.62 Which of the following statements correctly explain about inferior goods?

a) Income effect is positive, i.e. if income goes up, the demand for such goods also goes up.

b) Inferior goods are a special case of Giffen goods

c) Inferior goods are a special case of normal goods

d) Giffen goods are a special case of inferior goods

e) There is an inverse relationship between income and demand for an inferior good

Choose the correct option from those below:

A. a) and d)

B. d) and e)

C. a), c) and d)

D. a), b), c) and d)

Q.63 Assertion (A): WTO replaced GATT and came into existence in 1995 after the eight years of negotiations in the Uruguay Round.

Reason (R): Matters including intellectual property rights, textile and agricultural agreements were not covered under the GATT rules which lead to the replacement of GATT by WTO.

A. Both (A) and (R) are correct, and (R) is the correct explanation of (A).

B. Both (A) and (R) are correct, but (R) is not the correct explanation of (A).

C. (A) is correct., but (R) is not correct.

D. (A) is wrong, and (R) is correct.

Q.64 Which of the following statement is not true?

A. Law of demand is a qualitative concept.

B. Giffen goods were named after economist Sir Robert Giffen.

C. The elasticity of demand is a qualitative concept.

D. Law of demand holds good when other things remain the same.

Q.65 Arrange the steps of conducting a Feasibility Study in the correct order.

a) Examining the market conditions

b) Outlining the project scope and conducting current analysis

c) Understanding the financial costs

d) Conduct preliminary analysis

e) Reviewing and analyzing data

f) Comparing the proposal with existing products/services

A. (d), (b), (f), (a), (c), (e)

B. (a), (b), (c), (d), (e), (f)

C. (b), (e), (f), (c), (a), (d)

D. (d), (e), (c), (f), (a), (b)

Q.66 Which of the following statements regarding various characteristics of competency are true?

a) Competency refers to the attitude, knowledge, and skill of an individual

b) Motive refers to the reason behind the behaviour of an individual.

c) Competency determines the performance level of an individual.

d) The affective component of attitude deals with opinion and beliefs of an individual.

Choose the correct option from those below:

A. a, c and d only   **B.** a and c only

C. a and b only   **D.** a, b and c only

Q.67 Which of the following will most commonly be a part of zero-level channel, i.e. Producer/Manufacturer to Customer?

A. Mcdonalds   **B.** Tata Automobile

C. Speciality Products   **D.** Nokia

Q.68 ________refers to the set of different human psychological traits that gives consistency to an individual's behaviour to respond in different situations.

A. Lifestyle   **B.** Personality

C. Attitude   **D.** Motivation

Q.69 Statement I: Traits are relatively inconsistent over various situations.

Statement II: Competency refers to the ability of an individual to accomplish the task effectively and efficiently.

Choose the correct option from those below:

A. Statement I is correct., Statement II is incorrect.

B. Statement I is incorrect, Statement II is correct.

C. Both Statement I and Statement II are correct.

D. Both Statement I and Statement II are incorrect.

Q.70 Assertion (A): Managerial economics is conceptual as well as empirical in nature.

Reason (R): Managerial economics aims to analyze business problems on the basis of establishing concepts.

A. (A) is correct., but (R) is incorrect.

B. Both (A) and (R) are correct, but (R) is not the right explanation of (A).

C. Both (A) and (R) are correct, (R) is the right explanation of (A).

D. Both (A) and (R) are incorrect.

Q.71 ________ is a method of data collection which is used by dealers of consumer durables to collect information regarding their products.

________ is a method of data collection which is used to estimate consumption of the basket of goods at the consumer level.

A. Store audits, Consumer panels

B. Consumer panels, Warranty cards

C. Store audits, Pantry audits

D. Warranty cards, Pantry audits

Q.72 Assertion (A): Level of significance is the probability of Type I error.

Reason (R): Significance level is the maximum value of the probability of rejecting the hypothesis when it is true.

A. Both (A) and (R) are correct, and (R) is the correct explanation of (A).

B. Both (A) and (R) are correct, but (R) is not the correct explanation of (A).

C. (A) is correct., but (R) is not correct.

D. (A) is wrong, and (R) is correct.

Q.73 Assertion (A): The modern view on globalization is "Think global, act local".

Reason (R): Globalization may involve the decisions taken at a global perspective is applied to the local markets.

A. Both (A) and (R) are correct, and (R) is the correct explanation of (A).

B. Both (A) and (R) are correct, but (R) is not the correct explanation of (A).

C. (A) is correct., but (R) is not correct.

D. (A) is wrong, and (R) is correct.

Q.74 In the theory of relative advantage, factor endowments are determined by?

a) Geographical features

b) Historical features

c) Political stability

d) Social and demographic issues

Choose the correct option from those below:

A. a and b only   **B.** a, b, c and d

C. a, b and c only   **D.** b and only

Ques (75-109):Direction: Read the following passage and answer the questions given at the end by picking up the appropriate answer from the given alternatives.

Knowledge refers to the process of decision making using the existing information and to convert raw data into information; some knowledge is required. The required knowledge in both cases is different. The activities like data gathering, structuring, storing and accessing the information when required, fall under knowledge management. The decisions of an organization depend on the quality of data and the techniques used to structure and analyze the data. Even though it is very expensive to build and maintain knowledge management systems, the new companies are allocating some amount of capital to build customized knowledge management systems because of market instability and growing competition. These systems will assist the management in the decision-making process and maintain the change process according to the market conditions.

Most of the knowledge in the firms will be tacit in nature after structuring the data, and this is maintained by a set of key people. When a person maintaining the data, leaves the organization, a new person appointed in place of that person can understand the mechanism of the knowledge management system with the minimum amount of training

Q.75 Assertion (A): Non-verbal communication is the same across cultures.

Reason (R): Due to globalisation, there is an exchange of cultures between countries.

A. Both (A) and (R) are correct, and (R) is the correct explanation of (A).

B. Both (A) and (R) are correct, but (R) is not the correct explanation of (A).

C. (A) is correct., but (R) is not correct.

D. (A) is wrong, and (R) is correct.

Q.76 Which of the following types of knowledge is personalized, context-specific, and difficult to communicate?

A. Declarative knowledge

B. Explicit knowledge

C. Procedural knowledge

D. Tacit knowledge

Q.77 Which type of knowledge helps a firm to lead the industry?

A. Core knowledge

B. Advanced knowledge

C. Innovative knowledge

D. Process knowledge

Q.78 In which stage, the implicit knowledge is converted to explicit knowledge?

A. Acquisition

B. Creation

C. Storing

D. Transfer and utilization

Q.79 Text mining is used to discover the information in unstructured repositories. Which of the following is not a layer in core text mining analysis?

A. Linguistic analysis and natural language processing

B. Statistical or co-occurrence analysis

C. Statistical and neural networks clustering

D. Knowledge discovery and retrieval

Q.80 The institutional knowledge evolution cycle consists of five stages. Which of the following is not a part of it?

A. Knowledge development:

B. Knowledge acquisition

C. Knowledge distribution and development

D. Automating routine working knowledge

Q.81 Which among the following statements are not incorrect?

I. According to Atma-nirbhar Bharat Abhiyaan, Rs 3 lakh crore collateral-free automatic loans are provided to MSMEs.

II. Limited Liability Partnership Act, 2008 was introduced to aid early corporatization of MSMEs.

III. In MSMEs, 25% share in procurement by government and government-owned companies.

IV. In case, small scale industries are owned and managed by women entrepreneurs, they must have share capital not less than 49 %.

Choose the correct option from those below:

A. I,II,III   **B.** II,III,IV   **C.** I,III,IV   **D.** I,II,IV

Q.82 Which of the following is not included in the Ten C's model of employee engagement developed by Crim and Seijts?

A. Credibility   **B.** Control

C. Career   **D.** Change

Q.83 Statement (I): Cost Sheet statements break the total costs into various heads such as material cost, labour cost and overhead costs.

Statement (II): Cost Sheet is one of the basic financial statements to be prepared by the companies and thus forms part of the double-entry system.

Choose the correct option from below:

A. Statement I is correct, Statement II is incorrect.

B. Statement I is incorrect, Statement II is correct.

C. Both Statement I and Statement II are correct.

D. Both Statement I and Statement II are incorrect.

Q.84 Assertion (A): Selection is a negative process in contrast to the positive nature of recruitment.

Reason (R): Selection involves the rejection of applicants who are unfit to a job, while recruitment aims at attracting job seekers.

A. (A) is correct, but (R) is incorrect.

B. Both (A) and (R) are correct, but (R) is not the right explanation of (A).

C. Both (A) and (R) are correct, (R) is the right explanation of (A).

D. Both (A) and (R) are incorrect.

Q.85 Statement (I): Amount spent on scientific research is an example of deferred expenditure.

Statement (II): Deferred Expenditures are those expenditures, the benefit of which will last for a period of 3-4 years and thus forms a part of capital expenditures.

Choose the correct option from those below:

A. Statement I is correct, Statement II is incorrect.

B. Statement I is incorrect, Statement II is correct.

C. Both Statement I and Statement II are correct.

D. Both Statement I and Statement II are incorrect.

Q.86 Assertion(A): India follows civil law.

Reason(R): It has a single court system to administer both Central and State Laws.

A. Both (A) and (R) are correct, and (R) is the correct explanation of (A).

B. Both (A) and (R) are correct, but (R) is not the correct explanation of (A).

C. (A) is correct, but (R) is not correct.

D. (A) is incorrect, and (R) is correct.

Q.87 The type of standard that represents the performance under most favourable situations is

A. Basic Standard.   **B.** Normal Standard

C. Expected Standard   **D.** Ideal Standard

Q.88 __________ is the process of evaluating innovative product ideas, strategies as well as marketing trends.

A. Concept development

B. Idea screening

C. Innovation

D. Idea generation

Q.89 The change in the Purchasing Power of currency will be reflected in the exchange rate. The equilibrium exchange rate (ER) can be calculated by:

(Er= exchange rate in the reference period, Pd = domestic price index, Pf= foreign currency price index)

A. Er*(Pd/Pf)
B. Er*(Pf/Pd)
C. Er*(Pd+Pf)
D. Er*(Pf-Pd)

Q.90 Which of the following methods of sales promotion means presenting or displaying the product so as to bring the customers attention towards the product and communicate product information to them?

A. Loyalty cards
B. Point of sale materials
C. Discount vouchers
D. Coupons

Q.91 If the scrap materials are obtained during the manufacturing process, the amount received from the sale of scraps are deducted from the:

A. Prime Cost
B. Factory Cost
C. Cost of Production
D. Cost of goods sold

Q.92 When a particular lot is to be accepted or rejected based on many samples, but the number of samples is certain and decided in advance, that sampling is called as _________.

A. Single sampling
B. Multiple sampling
C. Cross sampling
D. Certain sampling

Q.93 _________ module is used for handling the replenishment of the products helps the organisation to plan the production beforehand and keep a stock of products which go below critical level.

_________ module is integrated with the stock control and production planning modules and supply chain management software and is used for automation

A. Inventory control module, Sales module
B. Accounting module, Finance module
C. Inventory module, Purchasing module
D. Manufacturing module, Purchasing module

Q.94 According to Schumpeter's Innovation Theory, Which of the following is not the type of Innovation as described by him?

A. Launch of a new product
B. New industry structure
C. Acquiring new sources of supply
D. New knowledge

Q.95 Special Drawing Rights (SDRs) issued by the IMF are sometimes referred to as

A. Paper Gold
B. Paper Silver
C. Paper Bullion
D. Cold Money

Q.96 The "twin deficit" problem means a country has:

A. High fiscal deficit and high governance deficit
B. High primary deficit and high fiscal deficit
C. High fiscal deficit and high current account deficit
D. High revenue deficit and high fiscal deficit

Q.97 Interactive display ads which appear on the internet besides the content on website pages or services and promotion coupons which the customer receives through the mail and which can be discounted on store's checkout counter is an example of:

A. Green marketing
B. Direct marketing
C. E-marketing
D. Digital marketing

Q.98 The serv qual model measures customer satisfaction on the basis of the evaluation of five quality parameters. Which among the following includes them?

I. Tangibles
II. Reliability
III. Responsiveness
IV. Communication
V. Empathy
VI. Assurance

Choose the correct option from those below:

A. I,II,III, IV,V
B. II,III,IV,V,IV
C. I,II, III,V,VI
D. II,III,IV,V,VI

Q.99 The coefficient of correlation is 0.3 then the coefficient of alienation is

A. 0.51
B. 0.91
C. 0.71
D. 0.61

Q.100 In _________ all machines performing similar types of operations are grouped at one location and are also known as functional layout.

_________ is the process of maintaining a balance between various activities evolved during production planning in order to minimize cost and minimize wastage of material.

A. Product layout, Production control
B. Mixed layout, Production control
C. Project layout, Production planning
D. Process layout, Production control

Q.101 Assertion (A): The German Model of Corporate Governance specifies two boards with separate members.

Reason (R): The size of the supervisory board cannot be changed by shareholders.

A. Both (A) and (R) are correct, and (R) is the correct explanation of (A).
B. Both (A) and (R) are correct, but (R) is not the correct explanation of (A).
C. (A) is correct., but (R) is not correct.
D. (A) is wrong, and (R) is correct.

Q.102 Which among the following is the correct sequence of service marketing planning?

A. Understanding customer's expectation- Understanding nature of service- developing service market mix- organising delivery channels- Pricing service- promotion- achieving differentiation- measuring service quality- monitoring customer satisfaction.

B. Understanding nature of service- Understanding customer's expectation- developing service market mix- organising delivery channels- Pricing service- promotion- achieving differentiation- measuring service quality- monitoring customer satisfaction.

Understanding customer's expectation- Understanding nature of service- developing service market mix-

C. organising delivery channels- promotion- Pricing service- achieving differentiation- measuring service quality- monitoring customer satisfaction.

Understanding nature of service- Understanding customer's expectation- organising delivery channels-

D. developing service market mix- Pricing service- promotion- measuring service quality- achieving differentiation- monitoring customer satisfaction.

Q.103 Statement I: In domestic marketing, control marketing activities are easier in comparison to international marketing activities because of various factors.

Statement II: In the domestic market, the focus of interest is on strategic emphasis, while in international marketing focus of interest is on general information.

Choose the correct option from those below:

A. Statement I is correct, Statement II is incorrect.
B. Statement I is incorrect, Statement II is correct.
C. Both Statement I and Statement II are correct.
D. Both Statement I and Statement II are incorrect.

Q.104 ___________focuses on the extent to which the proposed development project fits in with the current business environment and objectives related to the development schedule, corporate culture etc.

A. Technical Feasibility Study
B. Scheduling Feasibility Study
C. Operational Feasibility Study
D. Economic Feasibility Study

Q.105 The changes implemented through_____are usually focused on improving an existing product's development efficiency as well as productivity.

A. Radical Innovation
B. Incremental Innovation
C. Architectural Innovation
D. Disruptive Innovation

Q.106 Statement I. Availability of raw material, nearness of potential market, the supply of labour and supply of power, capital and transport are primary factors responsible for plant location decision.

Statement II. Social factors and environmental factors are the secondary factors responsible for plant location decisions.

Choose the correct option from those below:

A. Statement I is correct., Statement II is incorrect.
B. Statement I is incorrect, Statement II is correct.
C. Both Statement I and Statement II are correct.
D. Both Statement I and Statement II are incorrect.

Q.107 Degree of financial leverage refers to the ratio of percentage increase in earnings per share (EPS) to the percentage increase in earnings before interest and taxes (EBIT). A positive degree of financial leverage means that the firm is_____________.

A. operating at a level lower than break-even point and EPS is negative.
B. operating at a level higher than break-even point and EBIT and EPS move in the same direction.
C. at no profit no loss.
D. operating at a break-even point and EBIT and EPS are positive.

Q.108 Which of the following estimators is unique

A. Unbiased estimator
B. Maximum likelihood estimator
C. Consistent estimator
D. Minimum variance unbiased estimator

Q.109
What is the value of β_1 for the chi-square distribution

A. $8/n$ **B.** $12/n$ **C.** $32/n$ **D.** $2/n$

Q.110 Which of the following refers to a product that includes additional features offered by a company compared to its competitors?

A. Basic Product **B.** Augmented Product
C. Core Product **D.** Potential Product

Q.111 Which of the following relies majorly on the internet to organize and communicate?

A. Social movement Unionism
B. Community Unionism
C. Business Unionism
D. Open-source Unionism

Q.112 Long channels are usually used wherein the consumers are widely spread whereas if consumers are confined to a small place, short channels are used.

Which factor affecting the choice of channel of distribution is highlighted here?

A. Geographical concentration
B. Environmental factor
C. Economic Condition
D. Quantity purchased

Q.113 Which of the following is not a part of IMF resources for providing loans to member countries?

A. Gold
B. Special Drawing Rights
C. Quota subscriptions
D. Financial Markets

Q.114 Assertion (A): Direct marketing helps marketers better match a particular consumer's needs.

Reason (R): Direct marketing is often used to obtain instant orders directly from targeted consumers.

A. Both (A) and (R) are correct, and (R) is the correct explanation of (A).
B. Both (A) and (R) are correct, but (R) is not the correct explanation of (A).
C. (A) is correct, but (R) is not correct.
D. (A) is wrong, and (R) is correct.

Q.115 ________refers to the practice of portraying an organization's product or services as environment-friendly than it really is.

A. Greenwashing **B.** Green marketing
C. Green seal **D.** Go green marketing

Q.116 In _____ approach of ERP implementation process, in which all the employees of the company are brought together and prepare for a cutover date which is around a few weeks of plant shutdown.
A. Phased approach
B. Cold turkey approach
C. Integration approach
D. Pilot approach

Q.117 Which of the following is store retailing?
A. Direct selling **B.** Catalogue retailing
C. Hypermarkets **D.** Direct marketing

Q.118 _______ refers to the advertisements that are mostly content-led and marketed on a platform beside other, non-paid content.
A. Native advertising **B.** Market automation
C. Affiliate marketing **D.** Inbound marketing

Q.119 Assertion (A): Low-cost position yields the firm above average returns in the industry.
Reason (R): To be effective, the company should be the cost leader, not just one of several players.
A. Both (A) and (R) are correct, and (R) is the correct explanation of (A).
B. Both (A) and (R) are correct, but (R) is not the correct explanation of (A).
C. (A) is correct., but (R) is not correct.
D. (A) is wrong, and (R) is correct.

Q.120 Statement I: The Industrial Policy Resolution 1956 favored the establishment of Small scale enterprises
Statement II: The Industrial Policy Resolution 1956 believed that small scale industries would ensure equitable distribution of national income and solve unplanned urbanization problems
A. Statement I is correct., Statement II is incorrect.
B. Statement I is incorrect, Statement II is correct.
C. Both Statement I and Statement II are correct.
D. Both Statement I and Statement II are incorrect.

Q.121 A good index number is one that satisfies
A. Unit test
B. Time test
C. Time reversal test and factor reversal test
D. None of these

Q.122 Which of the following factors contribute to higher elasticity of demand?
Statement a: more the number of close substitutes
Statement b: less the proportion of income spent on the goods
Statement c: more the number of uses of the commodity
Choose the correct option from those below:
A. Statement a and b are correct.
B. Statement a, b and c are correct.
C. Statement a and c are correct.
D. Statement b and c are correct.

Q.123 Statement (I): While preparing the fund flow statement, the transactions that increase the funds are known as the application of funds.
Statement (II): Fund Flow Statement prepared on the basis of cash is known as Cash Flow Statement.
Choose the correct option from below:
A. Statement I is correct, Statement II is incorrect.
B. Statement I is incorrect, Statement II is correct.
C. Both Statement I and Statement II are correct.
D. Both Statement I and Statement II are incorrect.

Q.124
If $P(A) = P_1$ and $P(B) = P_2$ and $P(AB) = P_3$ then what is the probability of $P(A \cap \cap B)$

A. $1 - P_3$ **B.** $P_2 - P_3$

C. $1 - P_1 - P_2 + P_3$ **D.** $1 + P_3 - P_1$

Q.125 Statement I: If a company uses its company name for its entire range of products offered, then it is called______.
Statement II: Companies that track other firms including market leaders in an attempt to build market share are called _____.
Choose the correct option from those below:
A. Sponsored branding, Market Influencers
B. Corporate branding, Market Penetrators
C. Marketing automation, Market Developers
D. Goodwill branding, Product Developers

Q.126 Assertion(A): There is little government interference under market economic systems.
Reason(R): Under market economic systems, regulation comes from the relationship between market and supply.
A. Both (A) and (R) are correct, and (R) is the correct explanation of (A).
B. Both (A) and (R) are correct, but (R) is not the correct explanation of (A).
C. (A) is correct, but (R) is not correct.
D. (A) is incorrect, and (R) is correct.

Q.127 There are three broad areas of Ethics. Which of the following areas is not a part of Ethics?
A. Meta-Ethics **B.** Normative Ethics
C. Applied Ethics **D.** Positive Ethics

Q.128 Assertion (A): Sarbanes-Oxley Act was passed in 2002 to restore public confidence in publicly traded corporations by the United States.
Reason (R): Accounting fraud and scandals by companies like Worldcom, Enron raised issues on corporate governance practices in the US.
A. Both (A) and (R) are correct, and (R) is the correct explanation of (A).
B. Both (A) and (R) are correct, but (R) is not the correct explanation of (A).
C. (A) is correct., but (R) is not correct.
D. (A) is wrong, and (R) is correct.

Q.129 Which among the following statements is/are not incorrect?

I. Violation of 'esprit de corps' principle leads to loss of coordination.

II. Violation of 'unity of direction' principle leads to lack of unity of action.

III. Violation of 'unity of command' principle leads to an increase in labour turnover.

IV. Violation of 'social order' principle leads to ease in contact with needed employees.

Choose the correct option from those below:

A. I, II, III　　　　**B.** II, III, IV

C. I, II, IV　　　　**D.** I, III, IV

Q.130 Under which of the following sales promotion tools, a consumer is required to send the proof of purchase to the manufacturer after which a part of the purchase price is returned to him/her?

A. Samples　　　　**B.** Coupons

C. Cash refund　　　　**D.** Cents-off

Q.131 Some customers may, upon the arrival, not join the queue for some reason and decide to return for service later, in Queuing theory it is called ______.

A. Jockeying　　　　**B.** Reneging

C. Balking　　　　**D.** Server idle time

Q.132 ______ is a type of retailer who focuses more on price as their main sales attraction. It includes both hard and soft goods, but assortments are quite limited to the popular goods, colours, and sizes.

A. Warehouse retailers　　　　**B.** Supermarkets

C. Discount retailers　　　　**D.** Chain stores

Q.133 Which of the following statements is/are not wrong?

I. Public relation is included in 7 Ps of marketing.

II. Market segmentation is never the stage in the product development life cycle.

III. Theodore Levitt coined the term marketing myopia.

IV. Selling is a part of marketing.

Choose the correct option from those below:

A. I, III, III　　　　**B.** II, III, IV

C. I, III, IV　　　　**D.** I, II, IV

Q.134 Which of the following types of Innovation includes adding new features to existing products or services or removing features or making small updates to user experience?

A. Disruptive Innovation

B. Radical Innovation

C. Incremental Innovation

D. Architectural Innovation

Q.135 Which of the combinations of the following reflects the scope of Human resource management?

I. Compensation and Motivation

II. Performance appraisal

III. Employee Counseling and Leadership

IV. Social security and medical benefits

Choose the correct option from those below:

A. I, II, III　　　　**B.** II, III, IV

C. I, II, IV　　　　**D.** I, III, IV

Q.136 Statement (I): It is necessary to divide the total costs into fixed costs and variable costs for the computation of marginal cost.

Statement (II): Marginal costing technique does not involve the computation of contribution.

Choose the correct option from those below:

A. Statement I is correct, Statement II is incorrect.

B. Statement I is incorrect, Statement II is correct.

C. Both Statement I and Statement II are correct.

D. Both Statement I and Statement II are incorrect.

Q.137 Statement I: Managing online reviews and comments on a company's personal website or blog are a major role of online PR of a company.

Statement II: Inbound marketing refers to a marketing technique in which companies attract, sustain, and satisfy customers at every stage of their journey.

Choose the correct option from those below:

A. Statement I is correct, Statement II is incorrect.

B. Statement I is incorrect, Statement II is correct.

C. Both Statement I and Statement II are correct.

D. Both Statement I and Statement II are incorrect.

Q.138 Which of the following has primary responsibility for securing the interest of the Unitholder while making sure that the mutual fund complies with all the regulations of SEBI

A. Registrar and Transfer agent

B. Asset Management companies

C. Custodian

D. Trustee

Q.139 Assertion (A): Green marketing highly focuses on safeguarding long-term welfare and wellbeing of customers and society.

Reason (R): It is a marketing philosophy which emphasizes on production and trading of eco-friendly products for promoting ecological balance.

A. Both (A) and (R) are correct, and (R) is the correct explanation of (A).

B. Both (A) and (R) are correct, but (R) is not the correct explanation of (A).

C. (A) is correct, but (R) is not correct.

D. (A) is wrong, and (R) is correct.

Q.140 Assertion (A): Median is not useful where items need to be assigned relative importance and weights.

Reason (R): It is a positional average and is used only in the context of qualitative phenomena.

A. Both (A) and (R) are correct, and (R) is the correct explanation of (A).

B. Both (A) and (R) are correct, but (R) is not the correct explanation of (A).

C. (A) is correct., but (R) is not correct.

D. (A) is wrong, and (R) is correct.

Q.141 ______ refers to Innovation that involves making improvement on a product or process in an already existing market that provides a new value for the customer.

A. Radically Sustaining
B. Incrementally Disruptive
C. Radically Disruptive
D. Incrementally Sustaining

Q.142 Which of the following characterize good corporate board practices?

a) Well-defined roles and responsibilities

b) Emphasize integrity and ethical dealing

c) Strong shareholder rights

d) Well-structured board

e) Effective risk management

Choose the correct option from those below:

A. a,b,c,d   **B.** a,b,d,e   **C.** a,c,d,e   **D.** b,c,d,e

Q.143 The core reason behind using standard costing technique over actual costs is

A. Analyze the variances of standard and actual cost.
B. Actual cost calculation is a time-consuming process.
C. To provide accurate information to stakeholders.
D. To assess the performance and efficiencies.

Q.144 Assertion(A): Decentralised way of working is more about the philosophy of the organisation.

Reason(R): It is a way of approaching the decision-making process in the organisation.

A. Both (A) and (R) are correct, and (R) is the correct explanation of (A).
B. Both (A) and (R) are correct, but (R) is not the correct explanation of (A).
C. (A) is correct, but (R) is not correct.
D. (A) is wrong, and (R) is correct.

Q.145 _______ is a quality control chart which is used to monitor the total count of defects in fixed samples of size n.

The purpose of a _________ is to maintain good relationships with employees, resulting in increased quality, productivity and cost reduction.

A. Pareto chart, cause and effect diagram
B. Checksheets, Stratification
C. Scatter diagram, Total quality management
D. C chart, Quality circle

Q.146 Issue of Debentures will result in:

A. Cash inflow
B. Increase in working capital
C. Cash outflow
D. Decrease in working capital

Q.147 Assertion(A): A feasibility study is just the same as a business plan.

Reason(R): Feasibility Study determines the risks associated with the idea and a Business plan explains the management of how to deal with the risks.

A. Both (A) and (R) are correct, and (R) is the correct explanation of (A).
B. Both (A) and (R) are correct, but (R) is not the correct explanation of (A).

C. (A) is correct, but (R) is not correct.
D. (A) is wrong, and (R) is correct.

Q.148 Which theory of Corporate Governance has a more social-oriented perspective on Corporate Governance and focuses on the behaviour of executives?

A. Agency Theory
B. Stakeholder Theory
C. Resource Dependence Theory
D. Stewardship Theory

Q.149 Which among the following is not a type of projective techniques of data collection?

A. Word association test
B. Verbal projection tests
C. Pictorial technique
D. Content analysis

Q.150 Read the assertion and reason both carefully:-

_______ becomes necessary to introduce when different processes, equipment or technology is introduced or there is a significant change in demand or throughput volume.

A. Capacity planning
B. Production scheduling
C. Facility layout
D. Facility location

// Smart Answer Sheet //

Correct Percentage of students who answered correctly.　　**Skipped** Percentage of students who skipped.

Q.	Ans.	Correct / Skipped	Q.	Ans.	Correct / Skipped	Q.	Ans.	Correct / Skipped	Q.	Ans.	Correct / Skipped	Q.	Ans.	Correct / Skipped
1	D	56.1 % / 2.44 %	17	D	65.85 % / 29.27 %	33	C	36.59 % / 34.14 %	49	D	39.02 % / 31.71 %	65	A	34.15 % / 29.26 %
2	C	21.95 % / 21.95 %	18	D	48.78 % / 29.27 %	34	C	56.1 % / 34.14 %	50	D	34.15 % / 31.7 %	66	D	34.15 % / 29.26 %
3	D	56.1 % / 29.27 %	19	B	60.98 % / 29.26 %	35	C	56.1 % / 34.14 %	51	A	36.59 % / 21.95 %	67	A	43.9 % / 29.27 %
4	A	48.78 % / 29.27 %	20	C	60.98 % / 29.26 %	36	D	36.59 % / 34.14 %	52	B	21.95 % / 26.83 %	68	B	53.66 % / 29.27 %
5	C	26.83 % / 29.27 %	21	C	53.66 % / 29.27 %	37	A	36.59 % / 34.14 %	53	B	53.66 % / 29.27 %	69	B	34.15 % / 31.7 %
6	D	31.71 % / 29.27 %	22	C	26.83 % / 29.27 %	38	A	53.66 % / 31.71 %	54	B	43.9 % / 29.27 %	70	C	26.83 % / 29.27 %
7	B	65.85 % / 29.27 %	23	A	26.83 % / 29.27 %	39	C	9.76 % / 31.7 %	55	B	34.15 % / 31.7 %	71	D	21.95 % / 29.27 %
8	B	36.59 % / 29.26 %	24	B	53.66 % / 29.27 %	40	D	9.76 % / 31.7 %	56	A	29.27 % / 31.71 %	72	A	39.02 % / 29.27 %
9	C	36.59 % / 29.26 %	25	B	48.78 % / 29.27 %	41	C	60.98 % / 31.7 %	57	A	24.39 % / 31.71 %	73	A	41.46 % / 29.27 %
10	C	56.1 % / 29.27 %	26	A	29.27 % / 29.27 %	42	D	58.54 % / 31.7 %	58	D	17.07 % / 29.27 %	74	B	46.34 % / 29.27 %
11	A	65.85 % / 29.27 %	27	A	14.63 % / 31.71 %	43	C	48.78 % / 31.71 %	59	C	41.46 % / 29.27 %	75	C	21.95 % / 29.27 %
12	B	41.46 % / 29.27 %	28	B	48.78 % / 31.71 %	44	D	41.46 % / 31.71 %	60	A	39.02 % / 29.27 %	76	D	34.15 % / 29.26 %
13	B	36.59 % / 29.26 %	29	C	34.15 % / 31.7 %	45	D	48.78 % / 31.71 %	61	C	24.39 % / 29.27 %	77	C	19.51 % / 34.15 %
14	B	41.46 % / 29.27 %	30	C	24.39 % / 34.15 %	46	A	41.46 % / 31.71 %	62	B	41.46 % / 29.27 %	78	B	48.78 % / 29.27 %
15	A	26.83 % / 29.27 %	31	B	26.83 % / 34.15 %	47	B	51.22 % / 31.71 %	63	A	43.9 % / 29.27 %	79	D	14.63 % / 29.27 %
16	C	34.15 % / 29.26 %	32	A	26.83 % / 34.15 %	48	B	65.85 % / 31.71 %	64	C	26.83 % / 31.71 %	80	D	41.46 % / 29.27 %

Q.	Ans.	Correct	Skipped
81	A	53.66 %	29.27 %
82	D	26.83 %	31.71 %
83	A	39.02 %	29.27 %
84	C	34.15 %	29.26 %
85	A	29.27 %	29.27 %
86	D	17.07 %	29.27 %
87	D	36.59 %	31.7 %
88	B	46.34 %	29.27 %
89	A	31.71 %	29.27 %
90	B	56.1 %	29.27 %
91	B	41.46 %	29.27 %
92	B	26.83 %	29.27 %
93	C	34.15 %	29.26 %
94	D	17.07 %	31.71 %

Q.	Ans.	Correct	Skipped
95	A	41.46 %	29.27 %
96	C	19.51 %	29.27 %
97	B	29.27 %	29.27 %
98	C	26.83 %	29.27 %
99	B	36.59 %	29.26 %
100	D	36.59 %	29.26 %
101	A	21.95 %	29.27 %
102	B	24.39 %	31.71 %
103	A	21.95 %	29.27 %
104	C	34.15 %	31.7 %
105	B	39.02 %	31.71 %
106	A	29.27 %	31.71 %
107	B	56.1 %	29.27 %
108	D	17.07 %	31.71 %

Q.	Ans.	Correct	Skipped
109	D	26.83 %	31.71 %
110	B	43.9 %	29.27 %
111	D	34.15 %	31.7 %
112	A	51.22 %	29.27 %
113	D	26.83 %	31.71 %
114	B	17.07 %	31.71 %
115	C	9.76 %	29.26 %
116	B	31.71 %	31.7 %
117	C	31.71 %	31.7 %
118	D	26.83 %	31.71 %
119	A	51.22 %	31.71 %
120	C	21.95 %	29.27 %
121	C	36.59 %	29.26 %
122	C	36.59 %	29.26 %

Q.	Ans.	Correct	Skipped
123	B	24.39 %	31.71 %
124	C	19.51 %	31.71 %
125	B	26.83 %	31.71 %
126	A	26.83 %	31.71 %
127	D	31.71 %	29.27 %
128	A	36.59 %	31.7 %
129	C	19.51 %	36.59 %
130	C	39.02 %	29.27 %
131	C	14.63 %	29.27 %
132	C	31.71 %	29.27 %
133	B	26.83 %	29.27 %
134	C	19.51 %	29.27 %
135	C	17.07 %	31.71 %
136	A	34.15 %	29.26 %

Q.	Ans.	Correct	Skipped
137	C	24.39 %	39.02 %
138	D	17.07 %	31.71 %
139	A	46.34 %	31.71 %
140	A	29.27 %	34.14 %
141	A	26.83 %	31.71 %
142	B	31.71 %	31.7 %
143	B	24.39 %	31.71 %
144	A	51.22 %	31.71 %
145	D	19.51 %	31.71 %
146	A	36.59 %	31.7 %
147	D	21.95 %	34.15 %
148	D	7.32 %	34.14 %
149	D	26.83 %	34.15 %
150	D	4.88 %	34.14 %

//Hints and Solutions//

1. Empirical research is research that is based on observation and measurement of phenomena, as directly experienced by the researcher. The data thus gathered may be compared against a theory or hypothesis, but the results are still based on real life experience.

2. When planning to do as social research, it is better to be familiar with literature on the topic.

3. Answer: Option D

Factors affecting job design are Behavioral factors, Environmental factors and Organizational factors.

Behavioral factors have to do with human needs and the necessary to satisfy them. Higher-level needs are more significant in this context.

Environmental elements affect all activities of HRM, and job design is no exception. The external factors that have a bearing on job design are employee abilities and availability, and social and cultural expectations.

Organizational factors include characteristics of task, work flow, ergonomics, and work practices.

4. Answer: Option A

The procedure for determining the duties and skill requirements of a job and the kind of person who should be hired for it is Job analysis. A job analysis is a process used to collect information about the duties, responsibilities, necessary skills, outcomes, and work environment of a particular job.

5. Answer: Option C

The processual approach is not a rational planning approach. The processual approach states that change is continuous and without a finite endpoint. Change is also a "messy" process that is shaped by an organization's history, culture, and internal politics.

6. Answer: Option D

The unstructured interview is typically biased job performance. An unstructured interview is an interview in which there is no specific set of predetermined questions, although the interviewers usually have certain topics in mind that they wish to cover during the interview.

7. Answer: Option B

Tests that measure traits, temperament, or disposition are examples of Personality tests. A personality test is a method of assessing human personality constructs. Most personality assessment instruments are in fact introspective self-report questionnaire measures or reports from life records such as rating scales.

8. Answer: Option B

Decreased problem-solving skills is NOT the advantage of Workforce Diversity. Workforce diversity can bring about an increase in productivity and competitive advantages. Workplace diversity also increases employee morale and causes employees to desire to work more effectively and efficiently.

9. Answer: Option C

The best hiring occurs when the goals of Organisation and individual should be consistent to each other. Employee relations specialists in HR help the organization achieve high performance, morale and satisfaction levels throughout the workforce, by creating ways to strengthen the employer-employee relationship.

10. Teaching ensures positive transformation in students because with the help of teaching a student acquires good habits, knowledge and attitudes

Hence option C is correct.

11. Prior knowledge of learner is highly related to effectiveness of teaching in the following ways:

a) If students do not get correct information, or did not understand the study material in previous classes, they may have some trouble learning the recent material.

b) As, the students who understand the correct information, has a better chance of success learning the recent material.

12. Answer: Option B

A manager performs decisional role as a Resource allocator. The resource allocator role is one of the four decisional managerial roles because its primary focus is on making and implementing decisions. Familiarity with the resource allocator and other managerial roles allows both new and seasoned supervisors to understand a manager's job.

13. Answer: Option B

Human mind is the main source of innovations. In business, innovation often results when ideas are applied by the company in order to further satisfy the needs and expectations of the customers.

14. Given:

AND   FOR   THE   BIG   SUM

When the second alphabets in each of the words are changed to the next alphabet in the English alphabetical order, we have,

AOD   FPR   TIE   BJG   SVM

Clearly, there are two words having two vowels. These words are AOD and TIE.

Hence, the correct option is (B).

15. Flipped classroom approach is a modern approach that deals with students are asked to do some homework before the class and then they learn that topic in depth with live examples with the help of the instructor.

16. Answer: (3) Two; 1 is preceded by I and 0 is preceded by E

17. Answer: (4) 7; the Seventh element from left is 1 and 2nd element to the right of 1 is 7

18. Answer: (4) 60; {26+35-1 = 61-1 = 60}

19. Answer: (2) Two; Qureshi and Xavi are children of Priya.

20.

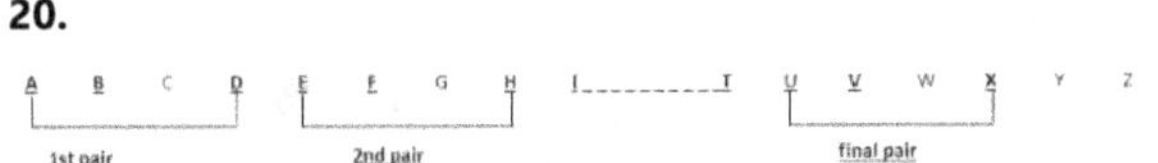

Hence, option C is correct.

21. Answer: (3)786

Solution: When the digits are arranged in ascending order within the number, the new numbers formed are:

435 – 345

224 – 224

786 – 678

823 – 238

902 – 092

22. Answer: (C)902; any number multiplied with 0 with give the answer 0, which is the least.

23. In deductive reasoning, the conclusion is supported by the premises and must follow the premises is true. It is not based on observations and experiments. The argument may be valid or invalid is also true. Therefore, option A is correct.

24. K is followed by "*" and preceded by "6"

Hence, option B is correct.

25. Answer: (B) **One**; 6 is preceded by "I" and succeeded by "K"

26. The given paragraph mentions the first three points as the factors of vulnerability of poor people to climate change: "Vulnerability to climate change is not just a function of geography or dependence on natural resources; it also has social, economic and political dimensions which influence how climate change affects different groups. Poor people rarely have insurance to cover loss of property due to natural calamities..."

So, besides geography and natural resources, lack of money plays a major role increasing the vulnerability of the poor. Thus, option A is the correct answer.

27. According to the given passage, "Adaptation is a process through which societies make themselves better able to cope with an uncertain future. Adapting to climate change entails taking the right measures to reduce the negative effects of climate change (or exploit the positive ones) by making the appropriate adjustments and changes."

Hence, all the alternatives are correct with reference to the question asked and option A is the correct answer.

28. According to the given passage, "Because of the speed at which climate change is happening due to global temperature rise, it is urgent that the vulnerability of developing countries to climate change is reduced and their capacity to adapt is increased and national adaptation plans are implemented". Thus, option B is the correct answer.

29. According to the given passage, "Communities must build their resilience, including adopting appropriate technologies while making the most of traditional knowledge... Local coping strategies and knowledge need to be used in synergy with government and local interventions." Thus, the author suggests that traditional knowledge should be used through cooperation between government and local interventions. Thus, option C is the correct answer.

30. The given passage begins by stating how Climate Change poses threat to sustainable development and how the poor people are the worst affected in the process. The passage gives a resolution to the problem by suggesting that "It is vital that these communities are helped to adapt to the changing dynamics of nature". Also, this change must not only occur at the individual or community level, but at the national and international level.

Hence, the passages focus on the concept of adaptation to climate change and option C is the correct answer.

31. The e-content generation for under-graduate courses has been assigned by the Ministry of Human Resource Development to Consortium for Educational Communication. E-content is launched on seven subjects Anthropology, English, Hindi, Mathematics, Photography, Environmental Studies and History.

32. Pondicherry university, Viswa Bharati and HNB Garhwal university all come under central universities. A Central University in India is established by Act of Parliament and are under the purview of the Department of Higher Education in the Union Human Resource Development Ministry. Universities in India are recognized by the University Grants Commission (UGC). The number of central universities published by the UGC includes 43 central universities as on April 2015.

33. Education as a subject of legislation figures in the Concurrent List. The Concurrent List is a list of 52 items given in the Seventh Schedule of the Constitution of India. It includes the power to be considered by both the central and state government.

34. Solution: There is no requirement for drawing a family tree to solve this question. Since Divya is the grandmother of Aman and Aman and Ravi are cousins (from the first statement). Ravi should be a grandson to Divya.

Hence, option C is the correct answer.

35. Since Divya is the wife of Ashok and Ashok is the father of Tanya. We already know the Divya is also the mother of Gaurav and Sahil, Gaurav and Tanya should be siblings. Hence Gaurav's wife will be Sister in law to Tanya.

36. A new Laptop has been produced that weight less, is smaller and uses less power than previous Laptop models that might be using solid state hard drive. This device store data on the flash memory.

37. NOx is produced from the reaction of nitrogen and oxygen gases in the air during combustion, especially at high temperatures. In areas of high motor vehicle traffic, such as in large cities, the number of nitrogen oxides emitted into the atmosphere as air pollution can be significant. The dominant source of pollution due to oxides of nitrogen (NOX) in urban areas is road transport.

38. Untreated sewage is the largest source of water pollution in major rivers of India. Untreated sewage also poses a lot of diseases.

39. Operating ratio = operating expenses / net sales

That is how efficient the company management in managing expenses with respect to its net sales.

High operating ratio means increasing expenses while sales is decreasing, which shows the inefficiency of management. And low or downfall in operating ratio means decreasing expenses with increasing sales which implies efficient and favorable position of the firm.

Therefore low operating ratio leaves a high margin to meet non-operating expenses.

40. Answer: B) 24 litres
Explanation:
Let the quantity of the wine in the cask originally be x litres
Then, quantity of wine left in cask after 4 operations $=$

$$\left[x \left(1 - \frac{8}{x} \right)^4 \right] \text{ litres}$$

$$\therefore \left[\frac{x\left(1-\frac{8}{x}\right)^4}{x} \right] = \frac{16}{81}$$

$$\Rightarrow \left[1 - \frac{8}{x} \right]^4 = \left(\frac{2}{3} \right)^4$$
$$\Rightarrow x = 24$$

41. Answer: Option C
Explanation:

Required percentage $= \left[\frac{(45-60)}{60} \right] \% = -25\%$

$\therefore$ There is a decline of 25% in production from 1997 to 1998.

42. Answer: Option D
Explanation:
Average production (in 10000 tonnes) of 1996 and

$$1997 \frac{40+60}{2} = 50$$

We shall find the average production (in 10000 tonnes) for each of the given alternative pairs:

2000 and $2001 = \frac{50+75}{2} = 62.5$

1999 and $2000 = \frac{65+50}{2} = 57.5$

1998 and $2000 = \frac{45+50}{2} = 47.5$

1995 and $1999 = \frac{25+65}{2} = 45$

1995 and $2001 = \frac{25+75}{2} = 50$

$\therefore$ The average production of 1996 and 1997 is equal to the average production of 1995 and 2001.

43. Answer: Option C

Required percentage $= \left[\frac{(80-25)}{25} \times 100 \right] \% = 220\%$

44. Answer: Option D
Explanation:
The percentage increase in production compared to previous year for different years are:

$$\ln 1996 = \left[\frac{(40-25)}{25} \times 100 \right] \% = 60\%$$
$$\ln 1997 = \left[\frac{(60-40)}{40} \times 100 \right] \% = 50\%$$

In 1998 there is a decrease in production.

$$\ln 1999 = \left[\frac{(65-45)}{45} \times 100 \right] \% = 44.44\%$$

In 2000 there is a decrease in production.

$$\ln 2001 = \left[\frac{(75-50)}{50} \times 100 \right] \% = 50\%$$
$$\ln 2002 = \left[\frac{(80-75)}{75} \times 100 \right] \% = 6.67\%$$

Clearlyl, there is maximum percentage increase in production in 1996 .

45. Answer: Option D
Explanation:
Average production (in 10000 tonnes) over the given years

$$= \frac{1}{8}(25 + 40 + 60 + 45 + 65 + 50 + 75 + 80) = 55$$

$\therefore$ The productions during the years 1997,1999,2001 and 2002 are more than the average production.

46. This is an alternating division and addition series: First, divide by 2, and then add 8.

Hence, option A is correct.

47. Answer: Option B

This is a simple alternating addition and subtraction series. The first series begins with 8 and adds 3; the second begins with 43 and subtracts 2.

48. There are two alphabetical series here. The first series is with the first letters only: STUVW. The second series involves the remaining letters: CD, EF, GH, IJ, KL.

Hence, option B is correct.

49. Characteristics of Secondary Memory:-

•It is known as backup memory.

•It is non-volatile memory.

•Data is permanently stored even if power is switched off.

•It is used for storage of the data in the computer.

•Computer may run without secondary memory.

•Slower than primary memories.

•These are magnetic and optical memories.

50. • Coercion refers to the action or practice of persuading someone to do something by using force or threats.

• Submission is a state of mind in which people cannot no longer do what they want to do because they have been influenced by someone else.

• Confrontation is a situation in which people or groups with opposing ideas or opinions disagree angrily:

• Persuasion is the act to influence someone to do something or to change their mind.

Therefore, positive classroom communication leads to persuasion.

51. Under random sampling, every item of the universe has an equal chance of inclusion in the sample, this is why random sampling is considered as the best technique of selecting a representative sample, and it ensures the Law of statistical regularity.

Thus, Option A is correct.

52. Production Scheduling is the process of arranging, controlling and optimizing workloads under the production process. It is done to achieve maximum utilization of plant, machinery, workforce and minimize inventory of raw materials and work in progress.

Thus, Option B is correct.

53. Rank correlation helps to determine the correlation between two variables where ranks are given to different values of the variables. The main objective of this coefficient is to determine the extent to which the two sets of ranking are similar or dissimilar.

Thus, Option B is correct.

54. Range is equal to the highest value of an item in a series minus the lowest value of an item in a series. Its value is never stable as it is based on the only two values of the variable.

Thus, Option B is correct.

55. This model is drawn from the psychological theory of Freud, according to which personality has three parts- ID, superego and ego. Every consumer has motives and desires which influence his buying behaviour.

Thus, Option B is correct.

56. • Operations management refers to the ongoing management of daily works of a company such as technical or network support. It will ensure the smooth functioning of all the activities.

• Production management includes planning, organization, staffing, leading, control and coordination of human and material resources for execution of facility in a specific function to meet determined objectives.

Thus, Option A is correct.

57. World Economic Forum (WEF) publishes the report on inclusion index and global competitiveness report. Apart from these, WEF also publishes various other reports like global risks report etc.

Thus, Option A is correct.

58. Critical values obtained using the sampling distribution of test static and prefixed level of significance. Size of the critical region is the same as the level of significance.

Thus, Option D is correct.

59. Efficiency means performing activities with minimum wastage of resources and optimum utilization of resources. Effectiveness means the capacity of management to achieve desired targets in a specified time. Management helps organizations to achieve efficiency as it ensures maximum utilization of resources with minimum cost.

Thus, Option C is correct.

60. Brand image is made and maintained through social and traditional communication and marketing media such as advertising, word of mouth, packaging, online promotions and social media advertising etc.

Thus, Option A is correct.

61. • In this case, stock of wheat is 500 quintals but supply is different (100 quintals or 150 quintals, etc.) at different prices. Therefore, supply is defined as that part of the stock of a commodity which is offered for sale at a particular price during a period of time.

• For perishable commodities like fish and fruit supply and stock are the same because whatever is the stock must be disposed off.

Thus, Option C is correct.

62. Only two statements are correct above all of the statements.

• Income effect of inferior goods is negative as when income increases the demand for such good decreases. For instance, with an increase in income, a consumer may start using wheat in place of barley.

• Giffen goods are a special category of inferior goods.

Thus, Option B is correct.

63. GATT was formed to liberalize international trade by reducing the trade and tariffs, which allows the smooth flow of trade. Since GATT didn't mention the rules regarding intellectual property rights, agriculture and textile, dispute settlement measures, various negotiations were held to revise the GATT policies, which subsequently resulted in the creation of WTO.

Thus, Option A is correct.

64. Giffen goods was named after the 19th-century economist (Sir Robert Giffen) and are those goods whose demand falls even when the real income of the consumer rises. The elasticity of demand is a quantitative concept.

Thus, Option C is correct.

65. • Conduct preliminary analysis: The first step to conduct a feasibility study is to conduct a preliminary analysis of the proposed action. It examines if the feasibility assessment is worth time and money.

• Outlining the project scope and conducting current analysis: It involves the analysis of the five elements of feasibility study which are: technical, economic, legal, operational and scheduling analysis.

• Comparing the proposal with existing products/services: Next step is to examine the viability of the proposed idea or action. It involves comparing the proposed product or service with other similar items available in the market.

• Examining the market conditions: It involves studying various important points, such as defining the target market, studying their buying habits, examining the sale and market share outlook of the proposal.

- Understanding the financial costs: Next step is to calculate the financial costs related to the proposal.

- Reviewing and analyzing data: The final step is to review the feasibility study carefully and examine the findings.

Thus, Option A is correct.

66. • Attitude consists of three components. They are as follows:

○ The cognitive component deals with the opinions, beliefs, and thoughts of an individual.

○ Affective component deals with the emotional aspect of an individual.

○ The behavioural component is the way of behaviour of an individual towards a particular situation.

Thus, Option D is correct.

67. Zero level channel is a direct channel involving no intermediaries. Mcdonalds, therefore, is a zero level channel without involving any middlemen and is the shortest mode of distribution.

Thus, Option A is correct.

68. Personality refers to the set of different human psychological traits that gives consistency to an individual's behaviour to respond in different situations.

Thus, Option B is correct.

69. • Trait refers to the distinguishing quality of an individual. Traits remain constant over a period of time and are relatively consistent over various situations.

- Traits determine the behaviour of an individual. Self-control, sincerity, determination, impatience, courageous, etc. are some examples of traits.

- Competence refers to the ability of an individual to accomplish the tasks efficiently and effectively.

- Competency deals with behavioural characteristics along with work-related abilities. It determines the performance level of an employee in an assigned job.

Thus, Option B is correct.

70. Managerial economics is based on the framework of economics concepts. Its main aim is to analyze business problems on the basis of established concepts. So it is conceptual in nature.

Thus, Option C is correct.

71. Warranty cards are used to seek information from the questions which are placed inside the package along with the product with a request to the consumer to fill in the card and post it back to the dealer. Pantry audit data is recorded from the examination of consumer's pantry.

Thus, Option D is correct.

72. Significance level implies that the hypothesis is rejected when the sampling result or the observed evidence has a probability of occurring if hypothesis is true. For example, the level of significance is 5%, which means researchers are willing to take as

much as 5% risk of rejecting the null hypothesis when the hypothesis happens to be true, which is the case of type I error.

Thus, Option A is correct.

73. • The modern view on globalization is "Think globally, act locally"

- Because on the one hand markets are becoming global, there is also a trend towards customization. Customization means treating customers individually or locally.

- So while thinking of a global perspective, actions or operations should be done in a customized manner as per the modern view on globalization.

Thus, Option A is correct.

74. Factor endowments are determined by:

- Geographical features such as climatic conditions and natural resources

- Historical development

- Political stability

- Economic development, size and quality of the workforce

- Social and demographic issues

- Entrepreneur skills and freedom to pursue entrepreneurial activities

Thus, Option B is correct.

75. • Non-verbal communication varies across cultures. For instance- A nod of the head means a yes in some cultures and no in others.

- Due to globalisation, there is an increase in the exchange of cultures and tastes between countries.

Thus, Option C is correct.

76. • Declarative knowledge enables a person to know factual aspects of a concept or an idea.

- Explicit knowledge can be easily accessed and communicated.

- Procedural knowledge enables a person to understand how an activity can be performed.

- Tacit knowledge is personalized, context-specific, and difficult to communicate.

Thus, Option D is correct.

77. • Core knowledge refers to the process-related knowledge that is required to do daily operations.

- Advanced knowledge helps the firm to be in the competition.

- Innovative knowledge helps the firm to lead the industry with new products.

Thus, Option C is correct.

78. • In the acquisition stage, the data is collected from various sources.

• In the creation stage, new knowledge is created by converting implicit knowledge into explicit knowledge.

• In the storing stage, new knowledge is coded and stored for easy access.

• In the transfer and utilization stage, the processed knowledge is transferred throughout the firm electronically. This data is used for various purposes.

Thus, Option B is correct.

79. • Text mining is used to discover the information in unstructured repositories.

• The core text mining analysis consists of the following layers:

1- Linguistic analysis and natural language processing.

2- Statistical or co-occurrence analysis.

3- Statistical and neural networks clustering.

4- Visualization.

Thus, Option D is correct.

80. • The institutional knowledge evolution cycle consists of five stages. They are as follows:

1- Knowledge development.

2- Knowledge acquisition.

3- Knowledge refinement.

4- Knowledge distribution and development.

5- Knowledge leveraging.

Thus, Option D is correct.

81. If small scale industries owned and managed by women entrepreneurs, then Women entrepreneurs must have share capital not less than 51 % (individual or jointly).

Thus, Option A is correct.

82. Ten C's of employee engagement developed by Crim and Seijts are as follows:

• Connect

• Credibility

• Convey

• Control

• Contribute

• Congratulate

• Confidence

• Collaborate

• Clarity

• Career

Thus, Option D is correct.

83. Cost sheet is a statement prepared to provide detailed information on the total costs of a particular product or job. It is only a memorandum statement and thus does not form part of the double-entry system

Thus, Option A is correct.

84. Selection is considered as negative in nature while recruitment as positive. Recruitment aims at increasing the job seekers and attracting the applicants who are fit for the job, and Selection is a process in which applicants who are not qualified according to job specification are rejected.

Thus, Option C is correct.

85. Deferred revenue expenditures are a part of revenue expenditures, the benefit of which will last for more than 1 year but maximum to a period of 5 years. But the benefits of capital expenditures will be enjoyed for many years.

Thus, Option A is correct.

86. • India follows common law.

• It has a single court system to administer both Central and State Laws.

Thus, Option D is correct.

87. • Basic standards are fixed standards kept as a base for comparing the performance. They will be constant for an indefinite period of time.

• Normal standards are those standards used under normal circumstances without any fluctuations in the operations.

• Expected standards are those standards determined on the basis of current conditions and compared with the actual performance.

• Ideal standards are standards set under the most favourable conditions like high efficiency, proper utilisation of resources etc.

Thus, Option D is correct.

88. Idea screening is the process of evaluating innovative product ideas, strategies as well as marketing trends.

Thus, Option B is correct.

89. The purchasing power parity theory was developed by Sir Gustav Cassel in the year 1918. According to this theory, when exchange rates are fluctuating in nature, then the rate of exchange between the two currencies will be fixed by their respective purchasing power in the long run in their own nations.

The new equilibrium exchange rate (ER) = Er * (Pd/Pf)

Thus, Option A is correct.

90. Point of sale materials is one of the methods of sales promotion which includes presenting or displaying the product so as to bring the customers attention towards the product and communicate product information to them. For example, posters etc.

Thus, Option B is correct.

91. Scrap materials can either be deducted from the material costs or overhead cost. When scrap is obtained during the raw material stage, it is deducted from the material costs and when the scrap is obtained during the manufacturing process, it is deducted from the factory cost.

Thus, Option B is correct.

92. In sequential sampling when acception or rejection decision of sample is based on a single sample it is called single sampling, when acception or rejection decision of sample is based on two samples it is called double sampling, and when acception or rejection decision of sample is based on two samples it is called multiple sampling.

Thus, Option B is correct.

93. • Inventory Control Module: This module is used for handling the replenishment of the goods and maintenance of the stock levels of the products. It helps the organisation to plan the production beforehand.

• Purchasing Module: It is integrated with the stock control and production planning modules and supply chain management software. It automates the identification of potential suppliers. It is used for automation and purchase management.

Thus, Option C is correct.

94. Schumpeter divided Innovation into the following five types:

1) Launch of a new product

2) New industry structure

3) Acquiring new sources of supply

4) Application of new methods

5) Opening of a new market

Thus, Option D is correct.

95. Special Drawing Rights (SDRs) are units of accounts maintained by the IMF to provide financial assistance to its members. They are not currencies, but their value can be expressed in currencies. They help in offsetting the imbalances in the balance of payments like gold and other assets.

Thus, Option A is correct.

96. Double deficit or twin deficit occurs when a nation has both a budget deficit and a current account deficit.

Thus, Option C is correct.

97. Direct marketing involves targeting potential customers, through conventional face-to-face marketing to online selling via the internet. Source of media used in Direct Marketing includes Email Marketing, Online Marketing, Mobile texting, Telemarketing, Voicemail Marketing, coupons etc.

Thus, Option B is correct.

98. The serv qual model was developed by Parsuraman provides a reliable methodology for measuring customer satisfaction on the basis of evaluating Tangibles, reliability, responsiveness, assurance and empathy.

Thus, Option C is correct.

99. Coefficient of alienation: The coefficient of alienation (a.k.a., coefficient of non-determination) represents the proportion of variance in the dependent variable that is not accounted for by the independent variable(s). It is the coefficient of determination's counterpart. It is estimated by $1 - r^2$.

So as r= 0.3

Coefficient of alienation = $1 - 0.3^2 = 1-0.09 = 0.91$

Thus, Option B is correct.

100. In process layout, all machines performing similar types of operations are grouped at one location. The process rather than the product has a dominating role in deciding the layout design of plant setup. Production control also involves monitoring of performance to achieve planned quality standards.

Thus, Option D is correct.

101. • The German Model of Corporate Governance specifies two boards (management and supervisory board) with separate members since the two boards are distinct, and the same person will not be able to serve simultaneously on two boards.

• The size of the supervisory board cannot be changed by shareholders and is set by law

Thus, Option B is correct.

102. Marketing a service-based business is intangible, inseparable, variable and perishable, unlike product-based business. The steps in service marketing planning involve Understanding nature of service- Understanding customer's expectation- developing service market mix- organising delivery channels- Pricing service- promotion- achieving differentiation- measuring service quality- monitoring customer satisfaction.

Thus, Option B is correct.

103. As the market is much more homogeneous and has different segments, in the domestic, market focus of interest is on general information, while in the international marketing market is different or diverse fragmented in nature, the focus of interest is on strategic emphasis.

Thus, Option A is correct.

104. Operational Feasibility Study measures how well a proposed software solves the problems. It focuses on the extent to which the proposed development project fits in with the current business environment and objectives related to the development schedule, corporate culture etc.

Thus, Option C is correct.

105. • Incremental Innovation involves adding or removing features to an existing product.

• The changes implemented through Incremental Innovation are usually focused on improving an existing product's development efficiency as well as productivity.

Thus, Option B is correct.

106. Natural factors, Political factors, infrastructure facilities and personal factors are secondary factors responsible for plant location decisions.

Thus, Option A is correct.

107. A positive degree of financial leverage means that the firm is operating at a level higher than break-even point and EBIT and EPS move in the same direction.

Thus, Option B is correct.

108. Minimum variance unbiased estimator: In the class of unbiased estimators, the estimator which has the smallest variance, is called minimum variance unbiased estimator.

Thus, Option D is correct.

109.

$$\beta_1 = \frac{\mu_3^2}{\mu_2^3}$$
$$\beta_1 = (8n)^2/(2n)^3 = 8/n$$

Thus, Option A is correct.

110. Augmented products refer to the products that provide additional benefits offered by a company in comparison to their competitors.

Thus, Option B is correct.

111. • Social movement Unionism works for human rights, social issues and other contemporary issues apart from issues of the workers.

• Community Unionism takes the help of non-labor groups and works for the fulfilment of common goals.

• Business Unionism emphasizes that unions should work like business units.

• Open source Unionism is a new model of unionism in which the entire process of communication, organizing and decision making are done over the internet.

Thus, Option D is correct.

112. Geographical concentration affects the choice of channel of distribution in such a way that if consumers are widely spread, long channels are used, and consumers are confined to a small place, short channels are used.

Thus, Option A is correct.

113. IMF resources for providing loans consists of Gold, SDR, Quotas and other borrowing arrangements but not Financial Markets.

Thus, Option D is correct.

114. Direct marketing aids sellers and marketers to concentrate efficiently on minimarkets which offer better match targeted consumer needs. Direct marketing also helps in the selection of commodities through a catalogue, ordering goods via mail and delivery in a similar way.
Thus, Option A is correct.

115. Greenwashing refers to the practice of portraying an organization's product or services as environment-friendly than it really is.

Thus, Option A is correct.

116. In a cold turkey approach during implementation of ERP, the whole company is brought onto the new system and prepares for the cutover date, which is normally during a plant shutdown of one to two weeks. It is done after document policy and procedure.

Thus, Option B is correct.

117. • It is a special kind of combination store and it integrates economy supermarkets with a discount department store.

• It attracts the family as a whole.

• Offers products at less than market prices.

Thus, Option C is correct.

118. Native ads are mostly seen on social media feeds or posts, or as recommended content on a web page. Examples can be BuzzFeed-sponsored posts on social media sites.

Thus, Option A is correct.

119. Cost leadership is a strategy that focuses on making an organisation more competitive by producing its products at a cheaper cost than competitors cost. To be effective, the company should be the cost leader, not just one of several players. Low cost may enable firms to reinvest and improve further its position in the industry, Thus, Both A and R are correct and R is the correct explanation of A.

Thus, Option A is correct.

120. • The Industrial Policy Resolution 1956 favored the establishment of Small scale enterprises.

• The policy stated the following aspects regarding small scale industries:

1) Small scale industries ensure equitable distribution of national income.

2) They would solve unplanned urbanization problems.

3) They would facilitate the effective mobilization of resources and provide immediate large scale employment.

Thus, Option C is correct.

121. Good index number should satisfy the time-reversal and factor reversal test.

Thus, Option C is correct.

122. • More the number of close substitutes, more will be the elasticity of demand. For example: demand for coca-cola, pepsi are highly elastic because of availability of close substitutes.

• Statement b is not correct since more the more the proportion of income spent on the goods, then more will be the elasticity. Demand for a commodity is inelastic if the amount spent on the product constitutes a very small proportion of small expenditure, e.g. demand for salt.

• Statement c is correct. as more the number of uses of a commodity more is the elasticity. Thus demand for a commodity which has many uses is generally elastic, e.g. demand for electricity, milk etc.

Thus, Option C is correct.

123. • Fund Flow Statements shows the movement of the working capital in the financial year.

• The 2 parts of the statements are sources of funds and application of these funds.

• Sources of funds represent those transactions that increase the funds while application of funds represent the use of these funds and thus decrease the funds.

Thus, Option B is correct.

124.

$$\cdot P(A \cap B) = P(B) - P(A \cap B)$$
$$\cdot P\left(A \cap \underline{B}\right) = P(A) - P(A \cap B)$$

Thus, Option B is correct.

125. Market penetration is essential for a business growth strategy which is extracted from the Ansoff matrix. It refers to the selling of a product or service in a specific market. Corporate branding is promoting the brand name of a company, and not to specific products or services. The scope of corporate branding is quite broader.

Thus, Option B is correct.

126. • There is little government interference under market economic systems.

• Under market economic systems, regulation comes from the relationship between market and supply.

Thus, Option A is correct.

127. • There are three broad areas of Ethics namely Meta-ethics, Normative ethics and Applied ethics.

• Meta-ethics focuses on the meaning of ethical terms and how ethical knowledge is obtained. For example-What is goodness?

• Normative ethics focuses on questions of what people ought to do, and on how people can decide what moral decisions to take.

• Applied ethics focuses on how people can achieve moral results in specific situations.

Thus, Option D is correct.

128. • Accounting fraud and scandals by companies like Worldcom, Enron raised issues on corporate governance practices in the US.

• Hence, the Sarbanes-Oxley Act was passed in 2002 to restore public confidence in publicly traded corporations by the United States.

Thus, Option A is correct.

129. • Violation of unity of command principle leads to undermined authority, disturbing discipline and order, conflict among superiors etc.

• Violation of remuneration to employee principle leads to labour turnover as unfair and unreasonable remuneration may lead to lack of satisfaction and motivation.

Thus, Option C is correct.

130. Cash refund is a Consumer Promotion Tool wherein a consumer is supposed to send the proof of purchase to the manufacturer after which a part of the purchase price is returned to him/her. Therefore, price reduction occurs after the purchase.

Thus, Option C is correct.

131. Blacking is when the customer decides not to enter the waiting line. Balking occurs particularly, when there are limits on the time and extent of storage capacity available to hold waiting customers.

Thus, Option C is correct.

132. Discount retailers focus more on price as their main sales attraction. It includes both hard and soft goods, but assortments are quite limited to the popular goods, colours, and sizes. Traditional stories of discounted retailers are generally large, self-service, free parking and with simple fixtures. Online discount retailers have accumulated products which are gold at heavy discounts.

Thus, Option C is correct.

133. The 7 Ps of Marketing is used by companies to continually evaluate and reevaluate your business activities. The seven Ps are product, price, promotion, place, packaging, positioning and people.

Thus, Option B is correct.

134. Incremental Innovation is a process of making small improvements or updates in the existing products or services.

Thus, Option C is correct.

135. Scope of Human Resource Management includes Human resource planning, performance appraisal, compensation, motivation, employee relations, Social security and medical benefits but not leadership and counseling.

Thus, Option C is correct.

136. • Marginal costing technique is used to compute the additional cost incurred on additional units of input.

• All the elements of costs are divided into fixed costs and variable costs as marginal costing requires the computation of variable cost incurred in the production process.

• While computing the marginal cost, the variable costs are deducted from total sales to arrive at contribution. Hence, marginal costing involves the computation of contribution.

Thus, Option A is correct.

137. Online PR is much like traditional PR. It is done in the online space by securing the online image of a company with blogs, and other content-based websites. Inbound marketing is a business technique that attracts customers by creating valuable content customized for them.

Thus, Option C is correct.

138. Trustees are responsible for securing the interest of the unitholders; they are vested with the power of direction and superintendence over AMC.

Thus, Option D is correct.

139. Green marketing focuses on welfare and wellbeing of customers and society by producing quality products which don't have any adverse effect on the environment. It encourages the production of pure products, conservation of energy, the safety of the environment, use of natural ingredients in production.

Thus, Option A is correct.

140. Median is considered only in qualitative phenomena context, for example, in estimating intelligence, which is often encountered in sociological fields. It is not frequently used in sampling statistics.

Thus, Option A is correct.

141. Radically Sustaining Innovation refers to making improvement in a product or process in an already existing market which provides a new value for the customer.

Thus, Option A is correct

142. • Good corporate board practices include well-defined roles and responsibilities, emphasize integrity and ethical dealing, well-structured board, effective risk management, best remunerations practices.

• Strong shareholder rights lead to conflict with other stakeholders.

Thus, Option B is correct.

143. Standard costing technique is used when it is difficult to calculate the actual costs of many transactions. Thus, standard costs can be a close approximation in finding the total cost incurred in the business.

Thus, Option B is correct.

144. Decentralised way of working is more about the philosophy of the organisation. It is not about handing over the power of authority to subordinate, but it is a way of approaching the decision-making process in the organisation.

Thus, Option A is correct.

145. • Control charts are used to find non-conformities and defects from a fixed size of sample. Its formats are fully customizable. It is used to predict the expected range of outcomes.

• Quality circles originated in Japan, this tool has many benefits for the work environment like improvement of quality, effective company communication, using employee problem-solving capabilities and job involvement.

Thus, Option D is correct.

146. The issue of debentures will result in the inflow of cash into the company. They would not influence the working capital as the issue of debentures are treated as a non-current liability.

Thus, Option A is correct.

147. Feasibility Study and a Business Plan are two different concepts and are not the same. A business plan is conducted only after it is identified that the business idea is viable.

Thus, Option D is correct.

148. • Stewardship theory has a more social-oriented perspective on Corporate Governance and focuses on the behaviour of executives.

• The theory further states that managers are good stewards who will act in the best interest of the owners.

Thus, Option D is correct.

149. Content analysis is not a part of projective techniques. Other types of the projective technique include sentence completion, play technique, sociometry etc.

Thus, Option D is correct.

150. Facility layout refers to the specific arrangement of physical facilities. It becomes necessary when a new facility is constructed, a new good/service is introduced to the customer benefit package, different processes, equipment or technology is introduced or there is a significant change in demand or throughput volume.

Thus, Option C is correct.

Paper-I

Q.1 Using the central point of the classroom communication as the beginning of a dynamic pattern of ideas is referred to as:-

A. Systemisation

B. Problem – orientation

C. Idea protocol

D. Mind mapping

Q.2 Effective communication pre- supposes:-

A. Non-alignment

B. Domination

C. Passivity

D. Understanding

Q.3 Read the assertion and reason both carefully, choose the correct option:-

Assertion (A) : Formal communication tends to be fast and flexible.

Reason (R) : Formal communication is a systematic and orderly flow of information.

A. Both (A) and (R) are correct and (R) is correct explanation of (A)

B. Both (A) and (R) are correct, but (R) is not correct explanation of (A)

C. (A) is correct but, (R) is false

D. (A) is false but, (R) is correct

Q.4 Most often, the teacher – student communication is:

A. Spurious

B. Critical

C. Utilitarian

D. Confrontational

Q.5 Assertion (A): The initial messages to students in the classroom by a teacher need not be critical to establishing interactions later.

Reason (R): More control over the communication process means more control over what the students are learning.

Choose the correct code:-

A. Both (A) and (R) are true, and (R) is the correct explanation of (A).

B. Both (A) and (R) are true, but (R) is not the correct explanation of (A).

C. (A) is true, but (R) is false.

D. (A) is false, but (R) is true.

Ques (6-10):Study the following table and answer the questions.

Classification of 100 Students Based on the Marks Obtained by them in Physics and Chemistry in an Examination.

Marks out of 50

Subject	40 and above	30 and above	20 and above	10 and above	0 and above
Physics	9	32	80	92	100
Chemistry	4	21	66	81	100
Average (Aggregate)	7	27	73	87	100

Q.6 What is the difference between the number of students passed with 30 as cut-off marks in Chemistry and those passed with 30 as cut-off marks in aggregate?

A. 3 **B.** 4 **C.** 5 **D.** 6

Q.7 If at least 60% marks in Physics are required for pursuing higher studies in Physics, how many students will be eligible to pursue higher studies in Physics?

A. 31 **B.** 32 **C.** 37 **D.** 41

Q.8 The percentage of number of students getting at least 60% marks in Chemistry over those getting at least 40% marks in aggregate, is approximately?

A. 31% **B.** 28% **C.** 29% **D.** 17%

Q.9 The number of students scoring less than 40% marks in aggregate is?

A. 14 **B.** 24 **C.** 31 **D.** 27

Q.10 If it is known that at least 23 students were eligible for a Symposium on Chemistry, then the minimum qualifying marks in Chemistry for eligibility to Symposium would lie in the range?

A. 40-45 **B.** 30-40

C. 20-30 **D.** Below 20

Q.11 Which of the following set of statements reflects the basic characteristics of teaching?

(i) Teaching is the same as training.

(ii) There is no difference between instruction and conditioning when we teach.

(iii) Teaching is related to learning.

(iv) Teaching is a 'task' word while learning is an 'achievement' word.

(v) Teaching means giving information.

(vi) One may teach without learning taking place.

A. (i), (ii) and (iii) **B.** (iii), (iv) and (vi)

C. (ii), (iii) and (v) **D.** (i), (iv) and (vi)

Q.12 Which combination of methods of teaching is likely to optimize learning?

A. Lecturing, discussions and seminar method

B. Interactive discussions, planned lectures and PowerPoint based presentations

C. Interactive lecture sessions followed by buzz sessions, brainstorming and projects

D. Lecturing, demonstrations and PowerPoint based presentations

Q.13 Read the assertion, reason both carefully and Choose the correct answer from the codes given below:

Assertion (A): Teaching aids have to be considered as effective supplements to instruction.

Reason (R): They keep the students in good humor.

A. Both (A) and (R) are true and (R) is the correct explanation of (A).

B. Both (A) and (R) are true, but (R) is not the correct explanation of (A).

C. (A) is true, but (R) is false.

D. (A) is false, but (R) is true.

Q.14 Which of the following learner characteristics are likely to influence the effectiveness of teaching aids and evaluation systems to ensure positive results?

A. Learner's family background, age and habitation.

B. Learner's parentage, socio-economic background and performance in learning of the concerned subject.

C. Learner's stage of development, social background and personal interests.

D. Learner's maturity level, academic performance level and motivational dispositions.

Q.15 Which statement about Ultrabook computers is false?

A. Ultrabooks are equipped with SSD drives for fast start-up

B. Ultrabooks do not offer HDMI video output ports

C. Ultrabooks typically weigh less than 3 pounds

D. Ultrabooks have the fastest optical drives

Q.16 Which of the following teaching methods involves a group of experts coming together for the discussion and learning of specific techniques and topics?

A. Demonstration Method

B. Lecture Method

C. Discussion Method

D. Seminar Method

Q.17 Which among the following is best advantage of Choice Based Credit System?

A. Reducing examination anxiety among students

B. Helping teacher to complete syllabus on time

C. Shift in focus from teacher-centric education

D. Improving classroom attendance

Q.18 Among the following which one is not an instructional material?

A. printed study guide

B. Overhead projector

C. Audio podcast

D. You tube video

Q.19 The Telephone Model of Communication was first developed in the area of:-

A. Technological theory

B. Dispersion theory

C. Minimal effects theory

D. Information theory

Q.20 Which of the following statements, regarding the term ICT is/are **TRUE**?

P: Converging technologies that exemplify ICT include the merging of audio-visual, telephone and computer networks through a common cabling system.

Q: ICT is an acronym that stands for Indian Classical Technology.

A. P only

B. Q only

C. P and Q

D. Neither P nor Q

Q.21 _________ is a form of computer data storage which stores frequently used program instructions to increase the general speed of a system.

A. Arithmetic Logic Unit

B. Integrated Circuit

C. Random Access Memory

D. Portable Document Format

Q.22 SMTP in computer science stands for?

A. Simple Markup Transfer Protocol

B. Systems Mail Transfer Protocol

C. Simple Mail Transfer Protocol

D. Systems Memory Transfer Protocol

Q.23 Who wrote the book "Five Point Someone: What Not to Do at IIT"?

A. Jhumpa Lahiri

B. Kiran Bedi

C. Amish Tripathi

D. Chetan Bhagat

Q.24 If any Fundamental Right of a citizen is breached then under Article 226 of Indian Constitution he can move to _____.

A. President of India

B. High Court of State

C. Chief Justice of India

D. Prime Minister of India

Q.25 There are four kinds of factors that influence the environment – topographic, climatic, edaphic, and biotic. Out of these, which is also known as physiographic factors?

A. Topographic

B. Climatic

C. Edaphic

D. Biotic

Q.26 According to the Sustainable Development Goal (SDG) India Index 2019-2020, which state among the following has the highest SDG Index score?

A. Kerala

B. Goa

C. Andhra Pradesh

D. Gujarat

Q.27 Books in electronic formats are called _______.

A. e-library

B. i-books

C. e-books

D. none of these

Q.28 _____________, also known as program evaluation.

A. Evaluation Research

B. Fundamental Research

C. Action Research

D. Applied Research

Q.29 Author, A, & Author, B (year). Title of book. DOI/URL/Publisher location: Publisher Name

Which style of referencing has been used in the above illustration?

A. APA   **B.** MLA   **C.** Harvard   **D.** Oxford

Q.30 Writing style and format for academic documents such as scholarly journal articles and books, in which of the following formats?
A. APA style format
B. Chicago style format
C. MLA style format
D. Harvard style format

Q.31 The ______________ is the variable the experimenter changes or controls.
A. Confounding variable
B. Control variable
C. Dependent variable
D. Independent variable

Q.32 Which of the following is not a method of a survey?
A. Personal Interview
B. Archives
C. Mailing questionnaires
D. Schedule

Q.33 Which of the following is susceptible to the issue of research ethics?
A. Inaccurate application of statistical techniques
B. Inaccurate application of statistical techniques
C. Choice of sampling techniques
D. Reporting of research findings

Q.34 Given below are four statements. Among them two are related in such a way that they can both be true but they cannot both be false. Select the code that indicates those two statements:
Statements:
a) Honest people never suffer.
b) Almost all honest people do suffer.
c) Honest people hardly suffer.
d) Each and every honest person suffers.
A. (a) and (b)   B. (a) and (c)
C. (a) and (d)   D. (b) and (c)

Q.35 If A + B means A is the mother of B; A - B means A is the brother B; A % B means A is the father of B and A x B means A is the sister of B, which of the following shows that P is the maternal uncle of Q?
A. Q - N + M x P   B. P + S x N - Q
C. P - M + N x Q   D. Q - S % P

Q.36 A person crosses a 600 m long street in 5 minutes. What is his speed in km per hour?
A. 5.2 km/hr.   B. 5.0 km/hr.
C. 6.2 km/hr.   D. 7.2 km/hr.

Q.37 If STREAMERS is coded as UVTGALDQR, then KNOWLEDGE will be coded as:-
A. MQPYLCDFD   B. MPQYLDCFD
C. PMYQLDFCD   D. YMQPLDDFC

Q.38 In a certain code, "COVALENT" is coded as BWPDUOFM. The code of "ELEPHANT" will be:-

A. MFUIQRTW   B. QMUBIADH
C. QFMFUOBI   D. EPHNTEAS

Q.39 In the following question, a matrix of certain characters is given. These characters follow a certain trend, row-wise or column-wise. Find out this trend and choose the missing character accordingly.

$$\begin{array}{ccc} B & G & N \\ D & J & R \\ G & N & ? \end{array}$$

A. U   B. W   C. V   D. X

Q.40 A party was held in which a grandmother, father, mother, four sons, their wives and two son and two daughters to each of the sons were present. The number of females present in the party is:-
A. 12   B. 18   C. 14   D. 24

Q.41 Which number replaces 'x' in the below figure ?

$$\begin{array}{ccc} 7 & 370 & 3 \\ 6 & 224 & 2 \\ X & 730 & 1 \end{array}$$

A. 7   B. 9   C. 8   D. 6

Q.42 If we want to seek new knowledge of facts about the world, we must rely on reason of the type:
A. Inductive   B. Deductive
C. Demonstrative   D. Physiological

Q.43 Consider the following statement and select the correct code stating the nature of the argument involved in it:
To suppose that the earth is the only populated world in the infinite space is as absurd as to assert that in an entire field of millet only one grain will grow.
A. Astronomical   B. Anthropological
C. Deductive   D. Analogical

Ques (44-48):Read the passage carefully and answer the following questions:-

In terms of labour, for decades the relatively low cost and high quality of Japanese workers conferred considerable competitive advantage across numerous durable goods and consumer electronics industries (eg. Machinery, automobiles, televisions, radios). Then labour-based advantages shifted to South Korea, then to Malaysia, Mexico and other nations. Today, China appears to be capitalizing best on the basis of labour. Japanese firms still remain competitive in markets for such durable goods, electronics and other products, but the labour force is no longer sufficient for competitive advantage over manufacturers in other industrializing nations. Such shifting of labour-based advantage is clearly not limited to manufacturing industries. Today, a huge number of IT and service jobs are moving from Europe and North America to India, Singapore, and like countries with relatively well- educated, low - cost workforces possessing technical skills. However, as educational levels and technical skills continue to rise in other countries, India, Singapore, and like nations enjoying labour-based competitive advantage today are likely to find such advantage cannot be sustained through emergence of new competitors.

In terms of capital, for centuries the days of gold coins and later even paper money restricted financial flows. Subsequently regional concentrations were formed where large banks, industries and markets coalesced. But today capital flows internationally at rapid speed. Global commerce no longer requires regional interactions among business players. Regional capital concentrations in places such as New York, London and Tokyo still persist, of course, but the capital concentrated there is no longer sufficient for competitive advantage over other capitalists distributed worldwide. Only if an organization is able to combine, integrate and apply its resources (eg. Land, labour, capital, IT) in an effective manner that is not readily imitable by competitors can such an organization enjoy competitive advantage sustainable overtime. In a knowledge-based theory of the firm, this idea is extended to view organizational knowledge as a resource with atleast the same level of power and importance as the traditional economic inputs. An organization with superior knowledge can achieve competitive advantage in markets that appreciate the application of such knowledge. Semiconductors, genetic engineering, pharmaceuticals, software, military warfare, and like knowledge-intensive competitive arenas provide both time-proven and current examples. Consider semiconductors (e.g. computer chips), which are made principally of sand and common metals. These ubiquitous and powerful electronic devices are designed within common office buildings, using commercially available tools, and fabricated within factories in many industrialized nations. Hence, land is not the key competitive resource in the semiconductor industry.

Q.44 Which country enjoyed competitive advantages in automobile industry for decades?

A. South Korea

B. Japan

C. Mexico

D. Malaysia

Q.45 Why labour-based competitive advantages of India and Singapore cannot be sustained in IT and service sectors?

A. Due to diminishing levels of skill.

B. Due to capital-intensive technology making inroads.

C. Because of new competitors.

D. Because of shifting of labour- based advantage in manufacturing industries.

Q.46 How can an organization enjoy competitive advantage sustainable overtime?

A. Through regional capital flows.

B. Through regional interactions among business players.

C. By making large banks, industries and markets coalesced.

D. By effective use of various instrumentalities.

Q.47 What is required to ensure competitive advantages in specific markets?

A. Access to capital

B. Common office buildings

C. Superior knowledge

D. Common metals

Q.48 The passage also mentions the trend of:-

A. Global financial flow

B. Absence of competition in manufacturing industry

C. Regionalisation of capitalists

D. Organizational incompatibility

Q.49 The prices used between traders, usually company treating their own subsidiaries as separate entity use transfer pricing to trade goods between there units. It is called:-

A. Transfer pricing

B. Going Rate pricing

C. Product bundling

D. Full cost pricing

Q.50 When labour is plotted on X-axis and capital is plotted on Y-axis and an iso-quant is prepared, then which of the following statements is/are false?

(a) Marginal rate of technical substitution of labor for capital is equal to the slope of the iso quant.

(b) Marginal rate of technical substitution of labor for capital is equal to change in the units of capital divided by the change in the units of labor.

(c) Marginal rate of technical substitution of labor for capital is the ratio of marginal productivity of capital to marginal productivity of labor.

A. (a) and (b) statements

B. Only (c) statement

C. Only (a) statement

D. Only (b) statement

Paper-II

Q.51 Who among the following is/are considered as corporate level members?

a) CEO

b) Board of Directors

c) Corporate staff

d) Divisional manager

Choose the correct option from those below:

A. a and d only

B. a,b and d only

C. a, b and c only

D. b and c only

Q.52 _______ model of consumer buying behaviour is based on four essential components named as Decision-making process, environment influence, information processing and central control unit.

The _______ model of consumer buying behaviour deals with exposure faced by consumers while making purchase decisions and it is divided into four fields.

A. Economic model, Pavlovian Model

B. Psychological model, Sociological model

C. Engel-Blackwell-Kollat model, Nicosia model

D. Industrial buying model, Family decision-making model

Q.53 Assertion (A): EXIM policy is also known as Foreign Trade Policy.

Reason (R): The objective is to facilitate sustained growth in exports from India and import in India.

A. Both (A) and (R) are correct, and (R) is the correct explanation of (A).

B. Both (A) and (R) are correct, but (R) is not the correct

explanation of (A).

C. (A) is correct, but (R) is not correct.

D. (A) is wrong, and (R) is correct.

Q.54 Assertion (A): While calculating the fund from operations, the amount of preliminary expenses should be deducted from the closing value of profit and loss account.

Reason (R): Preliminary Expenses are non-operating expenses which do not form part of the usual trading operations of the business.

A. Both (A) and (R) are correct, and (R) is the correct explanation of (A).

B. Both (A) and (R) are correct, but (R) is not the correct explanation of (A).

C. (A) is correct, but (R) is not correct.

D. (A) is wrong, and (R) is correct.

Q.55 P-charts is based on which distribution

A. Binomial

B. Normal

C. Hypergeometric

D. Poisson

Q.56 International Product Life Cycle theory was propounded by:

A. Adam Smith

B. David Ricardo

C. Antonio Serra

D. Raymond Vernon

Q.57 _______ involves the consumer's visit to the website or social media accounts, buying products by choosing a mode of payment, product delivery by the retailer and at last the customer's review or feedback.

A. Augmented reality

B. Non-store retailing

C. Catalog retailing

D. E-tailing

Q.58 Which among the following is/are the primary function of managerial economics?

I. Pricing problem

II. Investment problem

III. Profit analyzing

IV. Identifying business problem related to resource allocation

Choose the correct option from those below:

A. I, II, III

B. I, II, IV

C. I, III, IV

D. II, III, IV

Q.59 Assertion (A): Operations management always tries to reduce the investment cost of the product by making use of different tools and techniques.

Reason (R): The variable cost is reduced with the help of new and advanced machines. The fixed cost is reduced by increasing the quality of production.

A. Both (A) and (R) are correct, and (R) is the correct explanation of (A).

B. Both (A) and (R) are correct, but (R) is not the correct explanation of (A).

C. (A) is correct, but (R) is not correct.

D. (A) is wrong, and (R) is correct.

Q.60 Which of the following reference groups includes people that an individual would not like to be associated with?

A. Associative group

B. Dissociative group

C. Primary reference group

D. Aspirational group

Q.61 Assertion (A): Brand equity can be analysed by measuring premium price that the brand charges over unbranded goods.

Reason (R): Brand equity is also reflected in the way consumers look, feel, and react towards the brand.

A. Both (A) and (R) are correct, and (R) is the correct explanation of (A).

B. Both (A) and (R) are correct, but (R) is not the correct explanation of (A).

C. (A) is correct, but (R) is not correct.

D. (A) is wrong, and (R) is correct.

Q.62 According to Keller's brand equity model, _______ arises out of brand associations, that can be either imagery-related or function-related.

Brand loyalty, attitudinal attachment, sense of community and active engagement are categories of _______

A. Brand salience, Brand relationships

B. Brand meaning, brand response

C. Brand identity, Brand resonance

D. Brand meaning, Brand relationships

Q.63 Statement I: The analytic inventory approach of evaluating inventory management options involve the utilization of mathematical and probabilistic model of the logistics operating environment.

Statement II: The simulation inventory approach of evaluating inventory management options involve the utilization of functional relationships which determine desired service level

Choose the correct option from those below:

A. Statement I is correct., Statement II is incorrect.

B. Statement I is incorrect, Statement II is correct.

C. Both Statement I and Statement II are correct.

D. Both Statement I and Statement II are incorrect.

Ques (64-65):Direction: Read the following passage and answer the questions given at the end by picking up the appropriate answer from the given alternatives.

Different companies use different steps in performance benchmarking, but the main aim of this process is to improve the overall performance of the organization. For a new company, the main task is to maintain the quality of the product and to acquire customers. If the company achieves a target in six months, which is to be achieved in four months, then it implies that the departments of the organization are not in complete coordination. For the next six months, the company should set its benchmarks in such a way that they should complement the existing processes and cover the mistakes which were done in the first half of the year.

Although, benchmarking involves the comparison with the competitors, the resources, and the opinions of the employees should be considered. They should not have a counter effect on the human and financial resources. The collected data should be analyzed well to identify the qualitative and quantitative gaps, and this should lead to the action plan. To achieve the objectives, the purpose of the benchmarking should be

explained to the employees, and their opinions and suggestions should be taken into account. This will create a sense of ownership among employees and acts as a motivational factor.

Q.64 Which of the following involves benchmarking between functions within the same group of companies?

A. Internal benchmarking
B. Competitive benchmarking
C. Functional benchmarking
D. Generic benchmarking

Q.65 Which of the following is a traditional form of benchmarking?

A. Informal benchmarking
B. Functional benchmarking
C. Generic benchmarking
D. Internal benchmarking

Ques (66-68):Direction: Read the following passage and answer the questions given at the end by picking up the appropriate answer from the given alternatives.

Different companies use different steps in performance benchmarking, but the main aim of this process is to improve the overall performance of the organization. For a new company, the main task is to maintain the quality of the product and to acquire customers. If the company achieves a target in six months, which is to be achieved in four months, then it implies that the departments of the organization are not in complete coordination. For the next six months, the company should set its benchmarks in such a way that they should complement the existing processes and cover the mistakes which were done in the first half of the year.

Although, benchmarking involves the comparison with the competitors, the resources, and the opinions of the employees should be considered. They should not have a counter effect on the human and financial resources. The collected data should be analyzed well to identify the qualitative and quantitative gaps, and this should lead to the action plan. To achieve the objectives, the purpose of the benchmarking should be explained to the employees, and their opinions and suggestions should be taken into account. This will create a sense of ownership among employees and acts as a motivational factor.

Q.66 In which of the following, 'identifying the gaps in various aspects' is the main objective?

A. Functional benchmarking
B. Diagnostic benchmarking
C. Process benchmarking
D. Internal benchmarking

Q.67 Taguchi developed a technique for quality improvement. As per this technique, the factors which cannot be controlled are known as?

A. Design factors
B. Signal factors
C. Noise factors
D. Cost factors

Q.68 Six sigma approach is used to analyze the root cause of business problems and to find different ways to solve them. What is the main target of the six sigma approach?

A. To achieve less than 3.4 defects or errors per million opportunities
B. To achieve less than 3.6 defects or errors per million opportunities
C. To achieve less than 3.8 defects or errors per million opportunities
D. To achieve less than 4.4 defects or errors per million opportunities

Q.69 Statement I: Selective Perception is the process in which an individual only perceives what he desires and ignores other perceptions.

Statement II: A low level of perception is known as perceptual defence, and a high level of perception is known as perceptual vigilance.

Choose the correct option from the following:

A. Statement I is correct, Statement II is incorrect.
B. Statement I is incorrect, Statement II is correct.
C. Both Statement I and Statement II are correct.
D. Both Statement I and Statement II are incorrect.

Q.70 Statement I: Corporate strategy ensures the growth of the firm.

Statement II: Corporate strategy ensures the correct alignment of the firm.

Choose the correct option from those below:

A. Statement I is correct., Statement II is incorrect.
B. Statement I is incorrect, Statement II is correct.
C. Both Statement I and Statement II are correct.
D. Both Statement I and Statement II are incorrect.

Q.71 Which of the following statements is/are not wrong:

I. People, process and physical evidence are the 3 Ps of the service marketing mix.

II. When a customer derives more satisfaction from a product/service than his expectation is known as customer delight.

III. The 7ps of the service marketing mix are product, price, place, promotion, plan, process, physical evidence

IV. Green marketing refers to being environmentally friendly.

Choose the correct option from those below:

A. I, III, III
B. II, III, IV
C. I, III, IV
D. I, II, IV

Q.72 Which of the following statements related to Disruptive Innovation is not true?

A. The Disruptive Innovation concept was popularized by Clayton Christensen.
B. Disruptive Innovation creates a new market and value network and ultimately overtakes an existing market.
C. The risk associated with disruptive Innovation is lower other forms of Innovation.
D. Disruptive Innovations have lower performance in the beginning.

Q.73 Statement (I): The Berne Convention was created for the Protection of Industrial Property, and the Paris Convention was created for the protection of Literary and Artistic Works.

Statement (II): The TRIPs agreement is also known as Berne and Paris -plus agreement.

Choose the correct option from below:

A. Statement (I) is correct., while statement (II) is incorrect.

B. Statement (I) is incorrect, while statement (II) is correct.

C. Both statements are correct.

D. Both statements are incorrect.

Q.74 Statement I: Product line filling is the addition of items in the current line of products

Statement II: Product line pruning is the elimination or removal of futile products from the product line

Choose the correct option from the following:

A. Statement I is correct, Statement II is incorrect.

B. Statement I is incorrect, Statement II is correct.

C. Both Statement I and Statement II are correct.

D. Both Statement I and Statement II are incorrect.

Q.75 The concept of purchasing power parity is developed by:

A. Gottfried Haberler

B. Sidney Alexander

C. Gustav Cassel

D. William Taussig

Q.76 Assertion (A): Cost minimisation policy cannot work as the primary goal of financial management.

Reason (R): Market value is not a function of cost, minimising cost will not result in the highest price for the company's shares.

A. Both (A) and (R) are correct, and (R) is the correct explanation of (A).

B. Both (A) and (R) are correct, but (R) is not the correct explanation of (A).

C. (A) is correct, but (R) is not correct.

D. (A) is wrong, and (R) is correct.

Q.77 Statement I: Rejection of hypothesis when it is true is considered as Type I error

Statement II: Accepting a hypothesis when it is false is considered as Type II error.

Choose the correct option from those below:

A. Statement I is correct., Statement II is incorrect.

B. Statement I is incorrect, Statement II is correct.

C. Both Statement I and Statement II are correct.

D. Both Statement I and Statement II are incorrect.

Q.78 __________ is the process of systematically searching for new approaches, creating and communicating ideas which may be abstract, concrete or visual.

A. Idea screening

B. Idea generation

C. Environmental scanning

D. Radical Innovation

Q.79 Which of the following promotional tools is a customized, non-public, immediate and interactive promotional tool?

A. Sponsorship

B. Advertising

C. Direct marketing

D. Sales Promotion

Q.80 __________ is a quasi-judicial body to deal effectively with the problem of sick industrial companies.

A. Reserve Bank of India

B. Board for Industrial and Financial Reconstruction (BIFR)

C. Sick industries companies Act

D. Federation of Indian Chambers of Commerce and Industry

Q.81 Statement I: Personal income, expectation about future income, liquid asset position and standard of living are considered as Sociological factors influencing consumer behaviour.

Statement II: Motivation, perception, learning and attitudes are considered as Psychological factors influencing consumer behaviour.

Choose the correct option from those below:

A. Statement I is correct, Statement II is incorrect.

B. Statement I is incorrect, Statement II is correct.

C. Both Statement I and Statement II are correct.

D. Both Statement I and Statement II are incorrect.

Q.82 Which of the following is not a factor of Sirota's three-factor model of employee engagement?

A. Prioritize

B. Camaraderie

C. Achievement

D. Equity

Q.83 Calculating the number of man-hours required for various jobs with reference to a planned output is termed as____.

A. Job analysis

B. Workload analysis

C. Workforce analysis

D. Simulation

Q.84 The philosophy of __________ is to identify market segments, select one or more, and develop products and marketing mixes tailored to each selected segment.

A. Mass marketing

B. Product-variety marketing

C. Macro marketing

D. Target Marketing

Q.85 A feasibility study is an assessment of the viability of a proposed project. TELOS refers to the five areas of feasibility. What does the acronym TELOS stand for?

A. Technical, Economic, Legal, Operational and Scheduling.

B. Tenure, Economic, Lawful, Optimum and Scheduling.

C. Technical, Enforced, Legal, Operational and Social.

D. Tenure, Economic, Legal, Objective and Society

Q.86 Which among the following characteristics about binomial distribution is not wrong?

I. For binomial distribution, the variance is less then mean

II. It is a discrete distribution.

III. If 'p' is equal to 'q' and if 'n' is increased, the value of mean and standard deviation will decrease

IV. If 'p' is not equal to 'q', the distribution will be skewed.

Choose the correct option from those below:

A. I, II, III

B. II, III, IV

C. I, II, IV

D. I, III, IV

Q.87 Peter Drucker listed seven sources of Innovative Opportunity in his book 'Innovation and Entrepreneurship'. Which of the following is not one of the sources as listed by Peter Drucker?

A. Industry and market disparities

B. Demographic shifts

C. New industry structure

D. The unexpected

Q.88 Assertion (A): In hypothesis testing, we initially assume that the null hypothesis is true, and we process to try to reject the null hypothesis using the sample.

Reason (R): In case we cannot reject the null hypothesis it means that the parametric statement under the alternative hypothesis is true.

A. Both (A) and (R) are correct, and (R) is the correct explanation of (A)

B. Both (A) and (R) are correct, but (R) is not the correct explanation of (A).

C. (A) is correct., but (R) is not correct.

D. (A) is wrong, and (R) is correct.

Q.89 Assertion (A): Discipline facilitates smooth and systematic functioning of the business.

Reason (R): Discipline is required not only for workers but also on part of management.

A. (A) is correct., but (R) is incorrect.

B. Both (A) and (R) are correct, but (R) is not the right explanation of (A).

C. Both (A) and (R) are correct, (R) is the right explanation of (A).

D. Both (A) and (R) are incorrect.

Q.90 Assertion (A): Investment decisions and Financing decisions are interrelated.

Reason (R): Investment decision is influenced by financing decisions because only that investment proposal is accepted which is expected to generate return more than the cost of financing.

A. Both (A) and (R) are correct, and (R) is the correct explanation of (A).

B. Both (A) and (R) are correct, but (R) is not the correct explanation of (A).

C. (A) is correct, but (R) is not correct.

D. (A) is wrong, and (R) is correct.

Q.91 "Cisco decided to co-brand with the Fujitsu brand of japan to leverage Fujitsu's reputation in Japan for IT equipment while still retaining the Cisco name to benefit from Cisco's global reputation". This is an example of:

A. Acquisition   **B.** Greenfield venture

C. Strategic alliance   **D.** Franchising

Q.92 Statement I: When a company's marketing activities may be criticized for false or misleading advertising, it is termed as green washing.

Statement II: Donation of a ratio of a company's sales proceeds for environment protection like tree planting can also be termed as green marketing.

Choose the correct option from those below:

A. Statement I is correct, Statement II is incorrect.

B. Statement I is incorrect, Statement II is correct.

C. Both Statement I and Statement II are correct.

D. Both Statement I and Statement II are incorrect.

Q.93 _______ is an SBU category in the BCG matrix, which requires large amounts of cash to support their rapid and significant growth.

_______ is an SBU category in the BCG matrix, which barely supports themselves or they may even drain cash resources that other SBU's have generated. _______ is an SBU category in the BCG matrix, which has a high market share in a slowly growing market.

A. Stars, Dogs, Question mark

B. Cash cow, Stars, Dogs

C. Stars, Dogs, Cash cows

D. Dogs, Question mark, Star

Q.94 Which of the following elements of a firm are assessed in financial analysis?

a) Profitability

b) Solvency

c) Price

d) Stability

e) Volume

f) Liquidity

g) Range

A. (a), (b), (c), (d)   **B.** (a), (b), (d), (f)

C. (d), (e), (f), (g)   **D.** (c), (d), (e), (f)

Q.95 Which of the following concepts were introduced in the Companies Act, 2013?

a) Class Action suits

b) Women Directorship

c) Small Shareholder Director

d) Dormant company

e) Business Responsibility Report

Choose the correct option from those below:

A. a,b,d,e   **B.** a,c,d,e   **C.** b,c,d,e   **D.** a,b,c,d

Q.96 Identify the three equivalent goals of financial management from the following:

A. Maximising - value of the firm, shareholders' value and share price

B. Maximising - value of the firm, stakeholders' value and market price

C. Maximising - market share, profit and the current value of the company's stock

D. Maximising - market share, shareholders' value and profit

Q.97 Statement I: Wealth maximisation boosts the net present value of a course of action to shareholders

Statement II: Benefits of wealth maximisation are measured in terms of cash flows.

Choose the correct option from those below:

A. Statement I is correct, Statement II is incorrect.

B. Statement I is incorrect, Statement II is correct.

C. Both Statement I and Statement II are correct.

D. Both Statement I and Statement II are incorrect.

Q.98 Statement I: An organisation can experience heavy cost if its ERP system is not implemented carefully.

Statement II: The ERP is designed to focus on four main areas in an organisation including financial, human resources, marketing and supply chain management.

Choose the correct option from those below:

A. Statement I is correct., Statement II is incorrect.

B. Statement I is incorrect, Statement II is correct.

C. Both Statement I and Statement II are correct.

D. Both Statement I and Statement II are incorrect.

Q.99 Which among the following sentences about transportation models are correct?

I. It assumes total supply equals total demand.

II. The unbalanced problem is changed into a balanced problem by introducing a dummy plant or warehouse.

III. North west corner rule considers only the cost of transportation not demand and supply factor in allocating route.

IV. Vogel's approximation model is also called Unit cost penalty method.

Choose the correct option from those below:

A. I, II, IIII

B. I, III, IV

C. I, II, IV

D. II, III, IV

Q.100 India is an original member nation of IMF with 2.76% of quota. Say, the percentage quota of the Republic of Nauru, which has joined the IMF as its 189th member in 2016 is 2.84%. Then which of these two will have higher voting rights under the IMF?

A. India

B. The Republic of Nauru

C. Data is insufficient

D. Both will have the same voting rights as per IMF directories

Q.101 Assertion (A): Small scale industries support per capita income and resource utilization in the economy.

Reason (R): These units are mostly labour-intensive industries which help in the creation of employment.

A. Both (A) and (R) are correct, and (R) is the correct explanation of (A).

B. Both (A) and (R) are correct, but (R) is not the correct explanation of (A).

C. (A) is correct, but (R) is not correct

D. (A) is wrong, and (R) is correct.

Q.102 Statement I: Fixed cost curve is parallel to x-axis whereas Variable cost curve is downward sloping.

Statement II: Fixed cost curve does not increase or decrease with increase or decrease in the level of production whereas the variable cost curve rises or falls accordingly.

Choose the correct option from those below:

A. Statement I is correct., Statement II is incorrect.

B. Statement I is incorrect, Statement II is correct.

C. Both Statement I and Statement II are correct.

D. Both Statement I and Statement II are incorrect.

Q.103 Assertion (A): In the organizational diagnosis process, the output desired at the individual level is an improvement in the performance level.

Reason (R): In the organizational diagnosis process, organizational design and workgroup design are focused at the individual level. This will improve the performance levels of the employees.

A. Both (A) and (R) are correct, and (R) is the correct explanation of (A).

B. Both (A) and (R) are correct, but (R) is not the correct explanation of (A).

C. (A) is correct., but (R) is not correct.

D. (A) is wrong, and (R) is correct.

Q.104 Sampling error is reduced if:

A. Sample size decreases

B. Sample size increase

C. Sample size is fixed

D. It is not affected by the sample size

Q.105 Which one of the following is not a type of control chart for variable?

A. x -chart

B. R-chart

C. P-chart

D. σ -chart

Q.106 Japanese industrial groups linked by trading relationships as well as cross-shareholdings of debt and equity are known as?

A. Keiretsu **B.** Chaebol **C.** Zaibatsu **D.** Kaisha

Q.107 Statement I: Creative salesmanship is a type of personal selling, in which people are educated in an innovative way that they begin to demand new products.

Statement II: In changing technology and changing lifestyle, competition is becoming intense, salespeople resort to competitive salesmanship of selling approach.

Choose the correct option from those below:

A. Statement I is correct, Statement II is incorrect.

B. Statement I is incorrect, Statement II is correct.

C. Both Statement I and Statement II are correct.

D. Both Statement I and Statement II are incorrect.

Q.108 Two unbiased dice are thrown then what is the probability that the total of the numbers on the dice is greater than 8?

A. 1/6 **B.** 5/36 **C.** 5/18 **D.** 8/25

Q.109 Which among the following sentences is/are correct about Retail Marketing?

I. The four decisions of retail marketing are Product, Place, Price and Physical evidence.

II. Vending machines and point-of-sale kiosks are examples of non-store retailing.

III. Attractiveness, accessibility and affordability are the key contributions of retailing marketing.

IV. Demographic and sociological changes, availability of adequate store space, Information technologies and healthy communication channels are some of the key factors influencing the retail industry.

Choose the correct option from those below:

A. I, II, III   **B.** II, III, IV
C. I, II, IV   **D.** I, III, IV

Q.110 Statement I: Z test is used when the size of the sample is more than 30, and t-test is used when the size of the sample is less than 30.

Statement II: There is one sample(1-Z), two independent samples (2-Z) and two paired samples (3-Z) in the z test for mean.

Choose the correct option from those below:

A. Statement I is correct., Statement II is incorrect.
B. Statement I is incorrect, Statement II is correct.
C. Both Statement I and Statement II are correct.
D. Both Statement I and Statement II are incorrect.

Q.111 Statement I. A brief write-up about the job done at the workplace is termed as________.

Statement II. A brief description about the position, designation, and code of the position held by the employee is termed as _________ and gives an idea about the position in the organizational hierarchy.

Choose the correct option from those below:

A. Job specification, job analysis
B. Job summary, job title
C. Job title, Job summary
D. Job activities, job analysis

Q.112 Which among the following is not incorrect?

I. It is a continuous distribution

II. When two variables change values in the opposite direction, it has a negative correlation.

III. Covariance can take value from 0 to infinity.

IV. Karl Pearson's coefficient of correlation is not affected by change in scale or by change in location.

Choose the correct option from those below:

A. I, II, III   **B.** II, III, IV
C. I, III, IV   **D.** I, II, IV

Q.113 Assertion (A): Retailing is surviving and coping up with the changing times in the new marketing era.

Reason (R): Retailers are changing their business composition, outlet designs, methods of communication with stakeholders and mode of marketing.

A. Both (A) and (R) are correct, and (R) is the correct explanation of (A).
B. Both (A) and (R) are correct, but (R) is not the correct explanation of (A).
C. (A) is correct, but (R) is not correct.
D. (A) is wrong, and (R) is correct.

Q.114 Which among the objectives of the facility layout is correct.?

I. Proper and efficient utilization of available floor space

II. Use labour and space effectively

III. Proper utilization of production capacity

IV. Minimize cost of production

Choose the correct option from those below:

A. I, II, IIII   **B.** I, III, IV
C. I, II, IV   **D.** II, III, IV

Q.115 Statement I: In the internal marketing of the service triangle, the employee is prepared to serve the customers with the commitment.

Statement II: In the interactive marketing of the service triangle, the customer is prepared to receive the service in the right perspective.

Choose the correct option from those below:

A. Statement I is correct., Statement II is incorrect.
B. Statement I is incorrect, Statement II is correct.
C. Both Statement I and Statement II are correct.
D. Both Statement I and Statement II are incorrect.

Q.116 Measures that are taken to protect against risks linked to food safety, animal health & plant protection:

A. Testing standards
B. VERs
C. Labelling
D. Sanitary & Phytosanitary

Q.117 Among the below-mentioned statements, which statement about the mean is correct.?

I. It is the simplest and most widely used measure of central tendency.

II. Mean is also called a synonym of average.

III. When the data set has one or more extreme values, the magnitude of mean is affected.

IV. When the data set has one or more extreme values, and when the mean is used to represent the whole data set, it provides an absolute impression of other values.

Choose the correct option from those below:

A. I, II, III   **B.** II, III, IV
C. I, II, IV   **D.** I, III, IV

Q.118 A market situation when there is a single buyer of a product or service is know

A. Monopoly   **B.** Bilateral Monopoly
C. Monopsony   **D.** None of the above

Q.119 Below mentioned statements are about the advantages of one of the measures of central tendency/ measure of dispersion. Which of the following are these advantages related to?

I. It is regarded as a very satisfactory measure and is mostly used in research studies.

II. It is less affected by fluctuations of sampling

III. It is popularly used in the context of estimation and testing of hypotheses.

Choose the correct option from those below.

A. Mean deviation   **B.** Median
C. Standard deviation   **D.** Mean

Q.120 Assertion (A): Today's customers are becoming harder to please.

Reason (R): Key to customer loyalty is customer value and customer equity.

A. Both (A) and (R) are correct, and (R) is the correct explanation of (A).

B. Both (A) and (R) are correct, but (R) is not the correct explanation of (A).

C. (A) is correct, but (R) is not correct.

D. (A) is wrong, and (R) is correct.

Q.121 Assertion (A): Post-purchase behaviour of consumers is very crucial for a marketer.

Reason (R): A well-satisfied buyer is a silent advertiser.

A. Both (A) and (R) are correct, and (R) is the correct explanation of (A).

B. Both (A) and (R) are correct, but (R) is not the correct explanation of (A).

C. (A) is correct, but (R) is not correct.

D. (A) is wrong, and (R) is correct.

Q.122 Which among the following sentences is/are correct about PERT and CPM technique?

I. CPM shows the sequence of events and activities within a PERT network that requires the longest periods of time to complete.

II. PERT is deterministic in nature, while CPM is probabilistic in nature.

III. In PERT, events marking the start of activities are called tail events.

IV. CPM network analysis is done with the objective of determining the completion time for the project.

Choose the correct option from those below:

A. I, II, IIII   **B.** I, III, IV

C. I, II, IV   **D.** II, III, IV

Q.123 Which of the following information does the financial viability of a project provide?

a) Full details of the assets as well as how liquid are those assets.

b) Funding potential of a project and repayment terms.

c) How easily can the assets be converted into cash

d) Type and amount of resources required as well as developmental procedures.

A. a and b   **B.** a, b and c

C. c and d   **D.** a, b and d

Q.124 Statement I: IBRD loans are to be repaid in SDRs only while IDA loans are repayable in local currency as well.

Statement II: The interest rates on loans provided by IDA are higher than IBRD.

Choose the correct option from those below:

A. Statement I is correct, Statement II is incorrect.

B. Statement I is incorrect, Statement II is correct.

C. Both Statement I and Statement II are correct.

D. Both Statement I and Statement II are incorrect.

Q.125 Which of the following is the correct step in production planning and control?

A. Planning-Routing-Scheduling-Dispatching-Expediting-Inspection

B. Planning-Expediting-Scheduling-Dispatching-Routing-Inspection

C. Planning-Scheduling-Routing-Dispatching-Expediting-Inspection

D. Planning-Routing-Dispatching-Scheduling-Expediting-Inspection

Q.126 __________is a type of advertising technique that tries to convince customers to join a group of people who already have bought a particular product.

A. Promotional Advertising

B. Bandwagon Advertising

C. Patriotic Advertising

D. Surrogate Advertising

Q.127 ut the following steps of Personal Selling process in the correct sequence and select the correct code:

a) Approach

b) Prospecting

c) Pre-Approach

d) Handling objections

e) Presentation and demonstration

f) Closing the sales

g) Follow up

A. (c),(a),(e),(d),(b),(f),(g)

B. (c),(a),(b),(e),(d),(f),(g)

C. (b),(c),(a),(e),(d),(f),(g)

D. (b),(a),(c),(d),(e),(f),(g)

Q.128 Statement I: Grapevine is an internal documented person-to-person method of spreading information.

Statement II: Proxemics is a communication term for distance and personal space.

Choose the correct option from those below:

A. Statement I is correct., Statement II is incorrect.

B. Statement I is incorrect, Statement II is correct.

C. Both Statement I and Statement II are correct.

D. Both Statement I and Statement II are incorrect.

Q.129 Statement I: Strata are purposely formed and are usually based on past experience and personal judgement.

Statement II: For the selection of items for a sample from each stratum, convenient sampling is used.

Choose the correct option from those below:

A. Statement I is correct., Statement II is incorrect.

B. Statement I is incorrect, Statement II is correct.

C. Both Statement I and Statement II are correct.

D. Both Statement I and Statement II are incorrect.

Q.130 Statement I: Structured interview involves a predetermined and highly standardised technique of recording, as against it, Unstructured interview does not involve a system of predetermined questions and standardised technique of recording information.

Statement II: A focused interview is concerned with broad underlying feelings or motivations or with the course of an individual's life experience. Whereas, in a non-directive interview, the interviewer acts as a catalyst to a comprehensive expression of the respondent's feelings and beliefs.

Choose the correct option from those below:

A. Statement I is correct., Statement II is incorrect.

B. Statement I is incorrect, Statement II is correct.

C. Both Statement I and Statement II are correct.

D. Both Statement I and Statement II are incorrect.

Q.131 Amount set aside to meet probable losses on account of bad debts is:

A. Liability

B. Reserve

C. Provision

D. Contingent Liability

Q.132 Which of the following is not a type of blockchain?

A. Public

B. Consortium

C. Private

D. Divison

Q.133 Select the Instruments of fiscal policy:

(1) Statutory liquidity ratio

(2) Direct action

(3) Taxation policy

(4) Government expenditure policy

(5) Public debt policy

(5) Deficit financing

Choose the correct option from those below:

A. (1), (4), (5), (6)

B. (1), (2), (4), (5)

C. (2), (3), (4), (5)

D. (3), (4), (5), (6)

Q.134 Read the assertion and reason both carefully:-

According to the Diffusion of Innovation Theory, which of the following are the three main aspects that affect the distribution of a new idea or Innovation?

A. Time, Space and Money

B. Time, Communication and Social systems

C. Society, Business and Communication Channels

D. Social systems, Money and Space

Q.135 Read the statement I and Statement II carefully, choose the correct code:-

Input-output analysis is used

A. To analyze intra industry relationships and deal with technical problems of consumption.

B. To analyze issues related to demand in the economy.

C. To analyze inter-industry relationships and deal with the technical problems of consumption.

D. To analyze inter-industry relationships and deal with technical problems of production.

Q.136 Which among the following are the right assumptions of F-test?

I. For two sets of populations, there has to be a set of two samples.

II. Populations should have the same variance.

III. Parent population from which samples are drawn should be normal in nature.

IV. Samples should be random and independent.

Choose the correct option from those below:

A. I, II, IIII

B. I, III, IV

C. I, II, IV

D. II, III, IV

Q.137 Which of the following is not a type of digital marketing?

A. E-marketing

B. Media marketing

C. Print advertisements

D. Internet marketing

Q.138 Direction: Read the following passage and answer the questions given at the end by picking up the appropriate answer from the given alternatives.

Understanding the behavior of the consumers is very much essential for a firm to be in the competition. The purchasing behavior of consumers undergoes certain changes over a period of time. Some have the habit of following the regular buying pattern while others follow the changing trends. Some take the help of social media and review sites while others take the help of their friends and relatives. The purchasing power, which depends on the economy and the hierarchy of needs of the buyers will have an impact on the buying pattern.

The psychological state of the buyer may not allow him to go for the products that satisfy his esteem and self-actualization needs if the savings and income levels are very low. This buying pattern leaves the industries that produce such types of goods in huge losses, and it further results in unemployment. This is not the case for the products that are related to physiological, safety needs, and social needs. The purchasing behavior of these products is influenced by the concept of utility, environmental conditions, and societal compulsions.

___________in green marketing means when a firm develops a green brand in addition to its other brands.

A. Tactical greening

B. Strategic greening

C. Quasi-strategic greening

D. Eco-marketing

Ques (139-143):Direction: Read the following passage and answer the questions given at the end by picking up the appropriate answer from the given alternatives.

Understanding the behavior of the consumers is very much essential for a firm to be in the competition. The purchasing behavior of consumers undergoes certain changes over a period of time. Some have the habit of following the regular buying pattern while others follow the changing trends. Some take the help of social media and review sites while others take the help of their friends and relatives. The purchasing power, which depends on the economy and the hierarchy of needs of the buyers will have an impact on the buying pattern.

The psychological state of the buyer may not allow him to go for the products that satisfy his esteem and self-actualization needs if the savings and income levels are very low. This buying pattern leaves the industries that produce such types of goods in huge losses, and it further results in unemployment. This is not the case for the products that are related to physiological,

safety needs, and social needs. The purchasing behavior of these products is influenced by the concept of utility, environmental conditions, and societal compulsions.

Q.139 Buyers consider brands while making a purchase. Which of the following refers to the brand image?

A. What consumers interpret and understand about the brand

B. It is a unique set of brand associations

C. It is the value proposition that is to be communicated to the target audience

D. It is the set of brand assets and liabilities linked to a brand

Q.140 Which of the following is a form of the market with many sellers of a differentiated product?

A. Perfect competition

B. Monopoly

C. Oligopoly

D. Monopolistic competition

Q.141 Which of the following types of consumer goods do people buy frequently with the least possible time and effort?

A. Specialty goods

B. Convenience goods

C. Shopping goods

D. Non-durable goods

Q.142 Which of the following is an environmental factor that influences organizational buying behavior?

A. Persuasiveness

B. Policies

C. Risk attitude

D. Infrastructure

Q.143 Which of the following functions protects consumers against internal and external anxieties and the environment?

A. Ego defensive function

B. Value expressive function

C. Utilitarian function

D. Utility function

Ques (144-146): Rama Limited has Rs 1,00,000 as Earnings before interest and tax (EBIT). It has Rs 8,00,000,10% debentures. The equity capitalisation rate of the company is 10%.

Q.144 Calculate the earning available for equity shareholders (EAES)?

A. Rs 2,50,000

B. Rs 1,00,000

C. Rs 20,000

D. Rs 50,000

Q.145 Calculate market value of equity?

A. Rs 2,00,000

B. Rs 1,50,000

C. Rs 5,50,000

D. Rs 7,90,000

Q.146 Calculate the value of the company under Net Income approach?

A. Rs 8,50,000

B. Rs 2,90,000

C. Rs 5,98,500

D. Rs 10,00,000

Q.147 According to Black Scholes model, purchaser can borrow fraction of security at risk free interest rate which is:

A. short term

B. long term

C. transaction cost

D. no transaction cost

Q.148 Input call parity relationship, put option minus call option in addition with stock is equal to:

A. exercise price present value

B. exercise price future value

C. time line value

D. time value of bond

Q.149 Stocks which has lower book for market ratio are considered as:

A. pessimistic

B. optimistic

C. less risky

D. more risky

Q.150 A _____________ sets target to cover all major aspects of the economy.

A. Partial plan

B. Comprehensive plan

C. All of the above

D. Question does not provide sufficient data or is vague

// Smart Answer Sheet //

Correct — Percentage of students who answered correctly. **Skipped** — Percentage of students who skipped.

Q.	Ans.	Correct / Skipped
1	D	34.62 % / 3.84 %
2	D	61.54 % / 15.38 %
3	D	73.08 % / 19.23 %
4	C	65.38 % / 19.24 %
5	D	34.62 % / 19.23 %
6	D	26.92 % / 19.23 %
7	B	30.77 % / 23.08 %
8	C	15.38 % / 23.08 %
9	D	19.23 % / 23.08 %
10	C	26.92 % / 23.08 %
11	B	38.46 % / 23.08 %
12	C	50.0 % / 23.08 %
13	B	15.38 % / 23.08 %
14	D	50.0 % / 23.08 %
15	D	19.23 % / 23.08 %
16	D	42.31 % / 23.07 %
17	C	38.46 % / 23.08 %
18	B	38.46 % / 23.08 %
19	B	34.62 % / 23.07 %
20	A	65.38 % / 23.08 %
21	C	57.69 % / 23.08 %
22	C	61.54 % / 23.08 %
23	D	38.46 % / 23.08 %
24	B	42.31 % / 23.07 %
25	A	19.23 % / 23.08 %
26	A	30.77 % / 23.08 %
27	C	50.0 % / 23.08 %
28	C	26.92 % / 23.08 %
29	A	26.92 % / 23.08 %
30	A	23.08 % / 23.07 %
31	D	23.08 % / 23.07 %
32	B	38.46 % / 23.08 %
33	D	34.62 % / 23.07 %
34	D	15.38 % / 23.08 %
35	C	42.31 % / 23.07 %
36	D	46.15 % / 23.08 %
37	B	65.38 % / 23.08 %
38	C	46.15 % / 23.08 %
39	B	61.54 % / 23.08 %
40	C	57.69 % / 23.08 %
41	B	57.69 % / 23.08 %
42	A	50.0 % / 23.08 %
43	D	42.31 % / 23.07 %
44	B	69.23 % / 23.08 %
45	C	34.62 % / 23.07 %
46	D	26.92 % / 23.08 %
47	C	34.62 % / 23.07 %
48	A	26.92 % / 23.08 %
49	A	38.46 % / 23.08 %
50	B	30.77 % / 23.08 %
51	C	34.62 % / 7.69 %
52	C	38.46 % / 11.54 %
53	A	46.15 % / 15.39 %
54	D	11.54 % / 15.38 %
55	A	34.62 % / 15.38 %
56	D	42.31 % / 15.38 %
57	D	53.85 % / 15.38 %
58	B	50.0 % / 15.38 %
59	A	34.62 % / 15.38 %
60	B	65.38 % / 15.39 %
61	B	23.08 % / 15.38 %
62	D	15.38 % / 15.39 %
63	D	23.08 % / 15.38 %
64	A	34.62 % / 15.38 %
65	A	11.54 % / 15.38 %
66	B	69.23 % / 15.39 %
67	C	42.31 % / 15.38 %
68	A	42.31 % / 15.38 %
69	A	19.23 % / 15.39 %
70	C	34.62 % / 15.38 %
71	D	30.77 % / 15.38 %
72	C	23.08 % / 15.38 %
73	B	42.31 % / 15.38 %
74	C	57.69 % / 15.39 %
75	C	53.85 % / 15.38 %
76	A	30.77 % / 15.38 %
77	C	42.31 % / 15.38 %
78	B	65.38 % / 15.39 %
79	C	50.0 % / 15.38 %
80	B	69.23 % / 15.39 %

Q.	Ans.	Correct	Skipped
81	B	61.54 %	15.38 %
82	A	11.54 %	15.38 %
83	B	42.31 %	15.38 %
84	D	46.15 %	19.23 %
85	A	30.77 %	15.38 %
86	C	26.92 %	15.39 %
87	C	30.77 %	15.38 %
88	C	26.92 %	15.39 %
89	B	50.0 %	15.38 %
90	A	53.85 %	15.38 %
91	C	50.0 %	15.38 %
92	C	15.38 %	15.39 %
93	C	38.46 %	15.39 %
94	B	53.85 %	15.38 %

Q.	Ans.	Correct	Skipped
95	D	23.08 %	15.38 %
96	A	34.62 %	15.38 %
97	C	38.46 %	15.39 %
98	C	38.46 %	15.39 %
99	C	46.15 %	15.39 %
100	B	57.69 %	15.39 %
101	A	65.38 %	15.39 %
102	B	30.77 %	15.38 %
103	C	15.38 %	15.39 %
104	B	57.69 %	15.39 %
105	C	23.08 %	19.23 %
106	A	30.77 %	15.38 %
107	C	50.0 %	15.38 %
108	C	7.69 %	15.39 %

Q.	Ans.	Correct	Skipped
109	B	34.62 %	15.38 %
110	A	38.46 %	15.39 %
111	B	50.0 %	15.38 %
112	D	15.38 %	15.39 %
113	A	34.62 %	15.38 %
114	A	30.77 %	15.38 %
115	A	19.23 %	15.39 %
116	D	30.77 %	15.38 %
117	A	61.54 %	15.38 %
118	C	30.77 %	15.38 %
119	C	34.62 %	15.38 %
120	B	38.46 %	15.39 %
121	A	46.15 %	15.39 %
122	B	23.08 %	15.38 %

Q.	Ans.	Correct	Skipped
123	B	50.0 %	15.38 %
124	A	26.92 %	15.39 %
125	A	42.31 %	15.38 %
126	B	57.69 %	15.39 %
127	C	19.23 %	15.39 %
128	B	46.15 %	15.39 %
129	A	23.08 %	15.38 %
130	A	15.38 %	15.39 %
131	C	30.77 %	15.38 %
132	D	19.23 %	15.39 %
133	D	23.08 %	15.38 %
134	B	61.54 %	15.38 %
135	D	42.31 %	15.38 %
136	D	7.69 %	15.39 %

Q.	Ans.	Correct	Skipped
137	C	53.85 %	15.38 %
138	C	19.23 %	15.39 %
139	A	46.15 %	15.39 %
140	D	38.46 %	15.39 %
141	B	69.23 %	15.39 %
142	D	23.08 %	15.38 %
143	A	19.23 %	15.39 %
144	C	26.92 %	15.39 %
145	A	38.46 %	15.39 %
146	D	23.08 %	15.38 %
147	A	26.92 %	15.39 %
148	A	15.38 %	15.39 %
149	C	15.38 %	15.39 %
150	B	73.08 %	11.54 %

//Hints and Solutions//

1. The central point of classroom communication as the beginning of a dynamic pattern is known as mind mapping. It captures information and ideas, helping us to improve our brainstorming sessions and become more organized and productive.

2. Effective communication pre-supposes understanding. The understanding of the subject and concept will help the students to understand better and assist the teacher to function the class smoothly. So, option D is correct.

3. Formal communication, a systematic and orderly flow of information tends to interchange or transmit the information officially in an organization. The flow of the formal communication is more in a controlled way. Formal communication, according to the direction or flow may be of two types-(a) Vertical, and (b) horizontal.

4. The teacher – student communication is Utilitarian. Utilitarian is the practice which states that best action is the one that maximizes utility, which produces the well being for the greater number of people.

5. The fundamental aspect to teacher and student's success is the teacher's ability to communicate with students, parents and colleagues. Teachers must have quality communication skills to assist their students achieve success in their academic studies. More control over the communication process means more control over what the students are learning.

6. Answer: Option D

Required difference = (No. of students scoring 30 and above marks in Chemistry) - (Number of students scoring 30 and above marks in aggregate)

= 27 - 21

= 6.

7. Answer: Option B

We have 60% of $50 = \left(\frac{60}{100} \times 50\right) = 30$

∴ Required number

= No. of students scoring 30 and above marks in Physics

$= 32$

8. Answer: Option C

Number of students getting at least 60% marks in Chemistry
= Number of students getting 30 and above marks in Chemistry

$= 21$

Number of students getting at least 40% marks in aggregate
= Number of students getting 20 and above marks in aggregate

$= 73$

Required percentage $= \left(\frac{21}{73} \times 100\right)\%$

$= 28.77\%$
$\approx 29\%$

9. Answer: Option D

We have 40% of $50 = \left(\frac{40}{100} \times 50\right) = 20$

∴ Required number

= Number of students scoring less than 20 marks in aggeagate

$= 100 -$ Number of students scoring 20 and above marks in aggregate

$= 100 - 73$
$= 27$

10. Answer: Option C

Since 66 students get 20 and above marks in Chemistry and out of these 21 students get 30 and above marks, therefore to select top 35 students in Chemistry, the qualifying marks should lie in the range 20-30.

11. As we all know that teaching is a process where a teacher imparts hi/her knowledge to the students in order to make students learn.

Teaching is related to learning here is the correct alternative because all the teaching is related with learning. Teaching can be acquired only by learning and teaching can be done to make the students learn.

Teaching is a 'task' word while learning is an 'achievement' word – this statement is also correct because teaching is a task and it can be performed in order to make the student learn and improve their behavior while learning is an achievement because an individual or students acquire a number of behavior and knowledge in order to modify their behavior so it is an achievement for the student.

One may teach without learning taking place- This statement also corrects because teaching may occur without the learning takes place. It is the work of a teacher to teach but learning depends upon the students if they are not ready to acquire knowledge then learning cannot be happen.

12. Interactive lectures are the lecture where a teacher can at least break the lecture once in order to engage the student in teaching learning process. To make the interactive lectures interesting a teacher should employ the buzz session in between the lecture in order to discuss or give the feedback to the students.

If brainstorming and projects employed with the interactive lecture then it can be an icing on the cake. Brain storming is a method of teaching where efforts are made for finding conclusion by gathering lots of ideas by the students and then the project is given to the students so that student will learn by doing under the guidance of the teacher.

13. Option b is absolutely correct because according to (A) assertion teaching aids have to be considered as effective supplements to instruction because with the help of teaching aids teaching can be imparted in a best possible manner without making much effort with teaching skills of a teacher.

Reason(R): yes, it is right that teaching keeps the students in good humor the mind of the student diverted in observing the various teaching aids like projector, slides, tapes etc. and their irrelevant activities controlled up to an extent. But Reason (R) is

not the correct explanation of Assertion (A) as both the sentences are different but the topics are same.

14. Yes, it is rightly said that the leaners maturity level, academic performance and motivational disposition all have a big influence in the effectiveness of teaching aids and evaluation system in the following ways:

i) If the maturity level of the learner is low to the extent of teacher employs teaching aid during his/her then it will hinder the effectiveness of teaching and learning and vice-versa.

ii) If the learner is low or weak in his/her academic learning then it also hinders the effectiveness of teaching because a weak learner find himself/herself difficult to understand the teaching aid which influences the effectiveness of teaching.

iii) Motivational nature or behavior of students also influences the effectiveness of teaching aid because if the learner is low motivated then he feels difficult to understand the teaching which is delivered with the helps of teaching aid and if a learner is highly motivated then he accepts the teaching through teaching aids easily.

15. Answer: D) Ultrabooks have the fastest optical drives

Ultrabooks have the fastest optical drives is the false statement in the given options about Ultrabook computers.

16. Seminar Method involves the exchange of information by the experts on specific techniques and concepts. It also provides guidance to a group working on a research project.

Demonstration Method is where the instructor actually performs an operation /task and shows the students what to do, how to do it.

Lecture Method is a formal or a semi-formal method in which the instructor gives overview about the topic just by dictating.

Discussion Method is a method in which solutions are developed by discussing within a group

17. Choice Based Credit System is the method in which the student can choose his/her course from the prescribed curriculum. The advantage of Choice Based Credit System is to shift in focus from teacher-centric education. In this, the student can opt for the elective course based upon his/her interest.

18. Printed study guide has an instructional material in the form of notes from a particular topic. Audio podcast is the material which contains the useful information in audio form. YouTube video is the medium through which the instructional material is provided in the form of audio as well as video. So, option B Overhead projector is not an instructional material.

19. First theory of model of communication was given by Shannon and Weaver. It includes design to mirror the function of latest radio and telephone technologies. It consists of three main part first sender where person spoke into, second channel which is telephone itself and third receiver is the person who hear to other person. This technology basically includes transmission of information through telephone or radio.

20. ICT stands for Information and Communications Technology.

The converging technologies that exemplify Information and Communications Technology include the merging of audio-visual, telephone and computer networks through a common cabling system.

21. Answer: C) Random Access Memory is a form of computer data storage that stores frequently used program instructions to increase the general speed of a system.

22. Answer: C) Simple Mail Transfer Protocol

Stands for "Simple Mail Transfer Protocol." This is the protocol used for sending e-mail over the Internet. Your e-mail client (such as Outlook, Eudora, or Mac OS X Mail) uses SMTP to send a message to the mail server, and the mail server uses SMTP to relay that message to the correct receiving mail server.

23. Answer: D) Chetan Bhagat

'Five Point Someone: What Not To Do at IIT' is the debut narrative by renowned author Chetan Bhagat. The plot rotates around 3 friends Hari, Ryan and Alok at IIT.

24. Answer: B) If any Fundamental Right of a citizen is breached then under Article 226 of the Indian Constitution he can move to the High Court of State.

25. Topographic factors can also be known as physiographic factors which include altitude, direction of mountain chains, plateaus, plains, lakes, rivers, sea level, and valleys etc.

26. Kerala, Himachal Pradesh, Andhra Pradesh, Tamil Nadu and Telangana have topped the list of states on the sustainable development goals index 2019-20. While Uttar Pradesh, Odisha and Sikkim have shown maximum improvement, states like Gujarat have not shown any improvement vis-a-vis first ranking in 2018.

27. Books in electronic formats are called e-books

Hence, option C is correct.

28. Evaluation research, also known as program evaluation, refers to research purpose instead of a specific method. Evaluation research is the systematic assessment of the worth or merit of time, money, effort and resources spent in order to achieve a goal.

Examples of evaluation research:-

Evaluation research questions lay the foundation of a successful evaluation. They define the topics that will be evaluated. Keeping evaluation questions ready not only saves time and money, but also makes it easier to decide what data to collect, how to analyze it, and how to report it.

Evaluation research questions must be developed and agreed on in the planning stage, however, ready-made research templates can also be used.

29. APA (American Psychological Association) uses brackets around year of publication. It also uses place of publication before the publisher name. Full stops after initials are used in APA . All this is not true for other style of referencing.

30. APA style is a writing style and format for academic documents such as scholarly journal articles and books. It is

commonly used for citing sources within the field of behavioral and social sciences.

31. The variable that is changed in an experiment is called the manipulated variable. Sometimes, it is also called an independent variable. The independent variable is the variable the experimenter changes or controls and is assumed to have a direct effect on the dependent variable. Two examples of common independent variables are gender and educational level.

32. Surveys can be done in various ways. Some of the methods of conducting surveys are personal interviews, telephonic interviews, mailing questionnaires, through schedules, etc. Whereas archive is a historical record of an event which can be utilised for data collection but it is not appropriate for a survey.

33. Research ethics is specifically related to the analysis of ethical issues that are raised when people are involved as participants in research.

The reporting of research findings is susceptible to the issue of research ethics, as there cannot be any distortion with the findings.

Whereas the other three options are not susceptible to the issue of research ethics because these are not influenced by research ethics.

34. The rule of square of opposition (AEIO Rule) implies here:

Four types of propositions, are, say for instance.

A: All S are P

E: No S areP

I: Some S are P.

O: Some S are not P.

• The two statements are related in such a way that they can both be true but they cannot both be false are said to be sub contrary.

• According to the rule, I and O propositions are sub contrary.

• Therefore, Statement B and Statement C are sub contrary.

35. Answer: Option C

P - M → P is the brother of M

M + N → M is the mother of N

N x Q → N is the sister of Q

Therefore, P is the maternal uncle of Q.

36. Answer: Option D

$$\text{Speed} = \left(\frac{600}{5 \times 60}\right) m/sec$$
$$= 2 m/sec$$

Converting m/sec to km/hr (see important formulas section)

$$= \left(2 \times \frac{18}{5}\right) km/hr$$
$$= 7.2 km/hr$$

37. The first four word is coded by adding 2 in the alphabetical series, middle word is same, last four word is coded by subtracting 1.

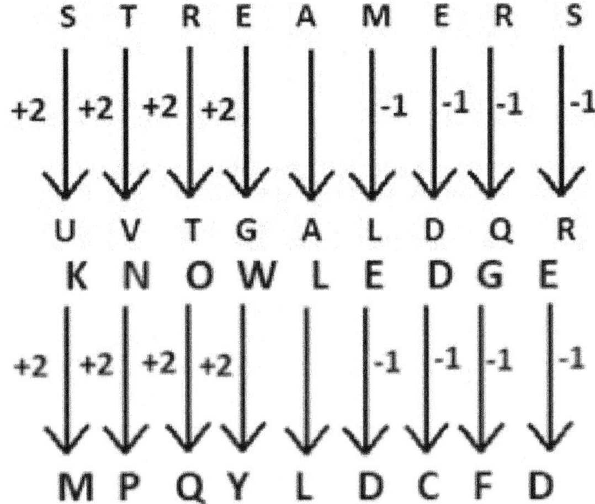

38.

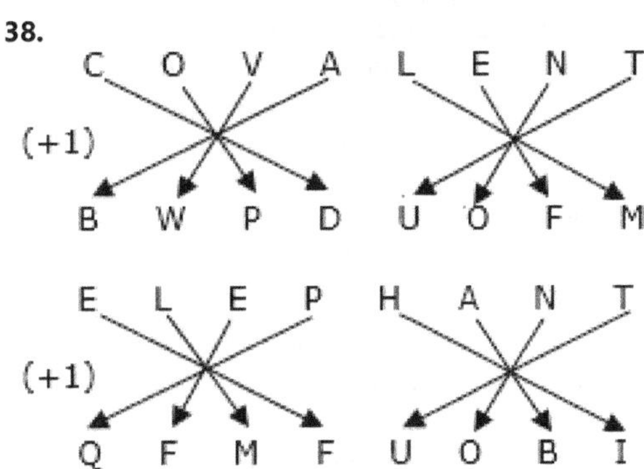

Hence, option C is correct.

39. The letters in the first row follow the sequence +5, +7.

The letters in the second row follow the sequence +6, +8.

In the third row, the first letter G moves 7 steps forward to give the second letter N.

Clearly, the missing letter will be 9 steps ahead of N i.e. W.

40. 1 grandmother (1) + 1 mother (1) + 4 son's wife (4) + 2 daughters to every son (8) = 14. So, total number of females = 14

41. Here in 2nd column if you add the individual digits

we get 3 + 7 + 0 =10 , 2 + 2 + 4 = 8 , 7 + 3 + 0 = 10

7 10 3 --> 7+3 =10

6 8 2 --> 6+2 =8

x 10 1 --> x+1 =10

Here we can observe that by adding 1st and 3rd column elements we get 2nd column elements

--> x = 9

42. Inductive reasoning is the one in which the premises seek to supply strong evidence for the truth of the conclusion. The truth of the conclusion of an inductive argument is probable, based upon the provided evidence. Inductive reasoning is known as hypothesis construction because the conclusions derived are based on the current knowledge and predictions. So, if we want to seek new knowledge of facts about the world, we must rely on inductive reasoning.

43. Here, we have given a comparison between one thing and other. Infinite space: Earth :: Millet Field: One grain. Infinite space has been compared to Millet field and Earth has been compared to a single grain.

So, the nature of argument is Analogical.

44. According to the first sentence of the passage, "In terms of labour, for decades the relatively low cost and high quality of Japanese workers conferred considerable competitive advantage across numerous durable goods and consumer electronics industries (e.g. Machinery, automobiles, televisions, radios)." This clearly states that the automobile industry was one of those countries which enjoyed competitive advantages in automobile industry for decades. Thus, option B is the correct answer.

45. According to the second paragraph of the passage, "However, as educational levels and technical skills continue to rise in other countries, India, Singapore, and like nations enjoying labour-based competitive advantage today are likely to find such advantage cannot be sustained through emergence of new competitors." This segment states that since the competitors in the technical field are growing, the labour-based competitive advantages of India and Singapore cannot be sustained in IT and service sectors. Thus, option C is the correct answer.

46. According to the second last paragraph of the passage, "Only if an organization is able to combine, integrate and apply its resources (e.g. Land, labour, capital, IT) in an effective manner that is not readily imitable by competitors can such an organization enjoy competitive advantage sustainable overtime." This sentence means that if the resources are efficiently used by organizations, in a way which is not harnessed by the competitors, they can enjoy competitive advantage overtime.

47. According to the second last paragraph of the passage, "An organization with superior knowledge can achieve competitive advantage in markets that appreciate the application of such knowledge." Hence, to ensure competitive advantages in specific markets, superior knowledge is required.

48. The first paragraph of the given passage discusses the considerable competitive labour- based advantage Japan has. It also states this advantage is now being taken by several other countries like India and Singapore. The second paragraph goes on to discuss the international capital flows. Thus, option A is the correct answer and the other options have not been dealt with in the passage.

49. Transfer pricing - the prices used between traders, usually company treating their own subsidiaries as separate entity use transfer pricing to trade goods between there units. Going Rate pricing - this means following the leader or whatever is going on in market, it is suitable for homogeneous products. Product bundling - in this method, the company bundles multiple products and offers the bundle at a price.

Full cost pricing - under full pricing, direct material, labour and overhead costs are added up along with administrative and

selling expenses and prices are fixed after adding particular margin percentage to total cost. Highly substitute goods are better priced over going pricing rates instead of other options as other pricing strategies will either compromises profits (low pricing then market) or consumers will simply shift to substitute goods (if priced high then market).

50. When in order to produce an output, two inputs are required, isoquant or is product is the curve which shows all the possible combinations of

input required to achieve same level of output. Reason for isoquant curve to be convex to origin is it's diminishing marginal rate of technical

substitution (MRTS). In this question the increase in units of labour in lieu of decrease in units of capital are MRTS of labour for capital, thus

forming the slope of curve convex to origin. MRTS isn't associated with ratio but of sacrifice of one input in place of other.

51. ● A large organization has separate self-contained divisions to manage different divisions.

● There are three main levels of management. They are as follows:

1) Corporate level - CEO, Board of Directors and Corporate staff

2) Business level - Divisional manager and staff

3) Functional level - Functional managers

Thus, Option C is correct.

52. In the Nicosia model, the output of the first field is the input of the second field and so on. Subfield one consists of product and firm attributes and sub filed two consists of the existing attitude of the consumer towards product and attributes exhibited by organisations whose products are to be purchased.

Thus, Option C is correct.

53. EXIM policy i.e.Export (ex) and import (im) is also known as Foreign Trade Policy as the main objective is to facilitate sustained growth in exports from India and import in India.

Thus, Option A is correct.

54. While calculating the fund from operations, the non-operating expenses already debited to the profit and loss account should be added back to net profits and non-operating incomes already credited should be deducted from the net profits. Thus, preliminary expenses that are part of non-operating expenses should be added to the net profits.

Thus, Option D is correct.

55. P - chart: control chart for fraction defective

If d is the number of defectives in a sample of size n then the sample proportion defectives p= d/n. Hence, d is a binomial variate with parameter n and p.

Thus, Option A is correct.

56. International product life cycle was propounded by Raymond Vernon in 1960s and it explains about the cycle that products go through when exposed to an international market.

Thus, Option D is correct.

57. E-tailing is also called E-Retailing. It is the process of selling or buying the products and services using the Internet for B2B or B2C transactions. It does not require any outlets, stores or floor space to showcase products.

Thus, Option D is correct.

58. Solving profit analyzing is not a primary function of managerial economics rather, solving pricing problem, Investment problem and Identifying business problem related to resource allocation is.

Thus, Option B is correct.

59. ● Assertion states the concept of operations management.

● Reason supports the assertion by giving the facts about operations cost.

Thus, Option A is correct.

60. Dissociative group is a reference group and includes people that an individual does not wish to be linked to.

Thus, Option B is correct.

61. Brand equity is referred to as the total value that the brand holds, which measures the financial value of the business. Brand awareness, brand loyalty, brand association and perceived quality makes brand equity. If the brand value is good consumers are ready to pay a premium price for it.

Thus, Option B is correct.

62. Brand meaning is essential to create a brand image and features. The imagery-related associations show the satisfaction of the social and psychological needs of the consumer. The function-related is what the consumer looks at as a priority. Brand relationships are also called brand resonance. It is when a consumer has good psychological bonding with the brand.

Thus, Option D is correct.

63. ● The simulation inventory approach of evaluating inventory management options involves the utilization of mathematical and probabilistic models of the logistics operating environment.

● The analytic inventory approach of evaluating inventory management options involves the utilization of functional relationships that determine the desired service level.

Thus, Option D is correct.

64. ● Internal benchmarking involves benchmarking between functions within the same group of companies.

● Competitive benchmarking involves a comparison between direct competitors.

● Functional benchmarking refers to the measurement of functional similarities of the organizations.

● Generic benchmarking measures various similar aspects of the organizations.

Thus, Option A is correct.

65. ● Informal benchmarking is a traditional form of benchmarking. In this, companies visit other companies to get help in improving the existing processes.

● The types of formal benchmarking are as follows:

1- Internal benchmarking.

2- Competitive benchmarking.

3- Functional / Generic benchmarking.

Thus, Option A is correct.

66. ● Functional benchmarking refers to the measurement of functional similarities of the organizations.

● In diagnostic benchmarking, one firm is measured against another superior company of the same industry to identify the gaps in various aspects.

● In process benchmarking, effective practices followed by various companies in carrying out the same process are determined.

● Internal benchmarking involves benchmarking between functions within the same group of companies.

Thus, Option B is correct.

67. ● As per Taguchi's quality improvement technique, the behavior of a process is grouped into two factors. They are as follows:

1- Controllable factors or design factors.

2- Uncontrollable factors or noise factors.

● Controllable factors are further classified as follows:

1- Target control factors or signal factors.

2- Variability control factors.

3- Cost factors.

Thus, Option C is correct.

68. ● Six sigma approach is used to analyze the root cause of business problems and find different ways to solve them.

● The main target of the six sigma approach is to achieve less than 3.4 defects or errors per million opportunities.

● It is an enterprise-wide strategy to improve overall performance.

Thus, Option A is correct.

69. A low level of perception is known as perceptual vigilance whereas, a high level of perception is known as perceptual defence.

Thus, Option A is correct.

70. ● Corporate strategy is basically the growth design of the firm.

- It is a set of goals and priorities. It ensures:

1) Growth of the firm and

2) Correct alignment of the firm

Thus, Option C is correct.

71. The 7ps of the service marketing mix are product, price, place, promotion, people, process, physical evidence

Thus, Option D is correct.

72. The risk associated with disruptive Innovation is higher and not lower other forms of Innovation. Although the risks are big, there is a huge growth potential if the strategy goes as planned.

Thus, Option C is correct.

73. The Berne and Paris Convention were a part of the TRIPS agreement. The Berne Convention was established for the protection of Literary and Artistic Works, and the Paris Convention was established for the Protection of Industrial Property.

Thus, Option B is correct.

74. • Line filling decisions include adding items in the current product line. This is done to increase profits, utilise capacity.

• Product line pruning refers to eliminating those products or items that are no more profitable to the company.

Thus, Option C is correct.

75. • Purchasing power parity theory, propounded by Prof. Gustav Cassel, states that the rate of exchange of two countries depends upon the relative purchasing power of the respective countries.

• Gottfried Harbeler is the propounder of opportunity cost theory.

• The concept of absorption approach to the balance of trade is given by Sidney Alexander.

• William Taussig has introduced the concept of Net Barter Terms of Trade.

Thus, Option C is correct.

76. Cost minimisation implies making the products or services available at a minimum cost. Such a policy may not always result in the highest sales revenue or highest profit. Since market value is not a function of cost, minimising cost will not result in the highest price for the company's shares. Hence, cost minimisation policy can not work as the primary goal of financial management.

Thus, Option A is correct.

77. Type I error means rejecting a hypothesis which should have been accepted, and Type II error means accepting the hypothesis which should have been rejected.

Thus, Option C is correct.

78. Idea generation refers to the process of systematically searching for new approaches, creating and communicating ideas which may be abstract, concrete or visual.

Thus, Option B is correct.

79. Direct marketing is a customized, non-public, immediate and interactive promotional tool that includes catalogue, direct emails, telemarketing etc.

Thus, Option C is correct.

80. BIFR is an agency of Government of India and a part of the Department of Financial Services of the Ministry of Finance, established under the Sick Industrial Companies (Special Provisions) Act, 1985.

Thus, Option B is correct.

81. Personal income, expectation about future income, liquid asset position and standard of living is considered as Economic factors influencing consumer behaviour. While reference groups, opinion leaders, family, social class and caste and culture are considered as sociological factors influencing consumer behaviour.

Thus, Option B is correct.

82. • Sirota's three-factor model of employee engagement is as follows:

1) Achievement

2) Camaraderie

3) Equity

• This model states that an engaged employee performs with a greater level of commitment.

Thus, Option A is correct.

83. Workload analysis is a technique of demand forecasting in which the number of man-hours are calculated for a variety of jobs in regard to demand analysis. a tool used to predict and plan future work and skill requirements based on historical performance to set the baseline for specific jobs.

Thus, Option B is correct.

84. • Mass Marketing- Marketing product to everybody. Example, Tata Salt.

• Target Marketing- Only Targeting special segments. Example, Targeting the age group of 18-24 years boys for funky watches production.

Thus, Option D is correct.

85. TELOS refers to the five areas of feasibility, namely, Technical, Economic, Legal, Operational and Scheduling Study.

Thus, Option A is correct.

86. In binomial distribution, if 'p' is equal to 'q' and if 'n' is increased, the value of mean and standard deviation will also increase.

Thus, Option C is correct.

87. The seven sources of Innovative Opportunity as listed by Peter Drucker include: Industry and market disparities, demographic shifts, the unexpected, incongruities, process vulnerabilities, changes in perception and new knowledge.

Thus, Option C is correct.

88. In case we cannot reject the null hypothesis it only means that the sample has insufficient information to reject the null hypothesis at the given level of significance, it does not mean that the parametric statement under the alternative hypothesis is true.

Thus, Option C is correct.

89. It is one of the principles of Fayol's principle of management. Discipline is necessary for the smooth running of the organization. It is required at all levels of management. Both sentences are right, but R is not an explanation to A.

Thus, Option B is correct.

90. Investment decision is influenced by financing decisions because only that investment proposal is accepted which is expected to generate return more than the cost of financing. Acceptance of those proposals of which return is more than the cost of financing will increase the return to equity shareholders and thus, maximizes their wealth.

Thus, Option A is correct.

91. Cisco entered into a strategic alliance with Fujitsu to develop routers for Japan. A strategic alliance or partnership is a contractual agreement between two or more companies with conditions that the agreeing parties will cooperate in a particular way for a particular period of time to achieve a common goal.

Thus, option C is correct.

92. If green marketing activities of any company are not substantiated by investments or operational changes, they may be criticized for misleading marketing, which is called green washing. Few companies may market their image as being environmentally-friendly companies by planting a tree or so, it is also included in green marketing.

Thus, Option C is correct.

93. Stars is an SBU category in the BCG matrix having a high share in a high growth market; they have additional growth potential and more intense potential. Dogs are the categories that have a relatively small share of a low growth market. Cash cows are the units which provide a lot of cash for the firms which were former stars in the growing market.

Thus, Option C is correct.

94. ● The financial analysis assesses the following elements of a firm: Profitability, Solvency, Stability and Liquidity.

● Volume, Price and Range are the elements of Technical analysis.

Thus, Option B is correct.

95. ● The new concepts introduced in Companies Act 2013 are class action suits, one-person company, small shareholder director, women director, dormant company, key managerial person.

● The Business Responsibility Report was introduced in 2012 by SEBI.

Thus, Option D is correct.

96. Value maximisation implies maximising value of the firm, shareholders' value and share price. The goal is to maximise shareholders' wealth. Wealth maximisation means maximising the Net Present Value of a course of action. The wealth of owners of a company is reflected by the market value of the company's shares in the long run.

Thus, Option A is correct.

97. The primary objective of financial management is wealth maximisation i.e., maximising the NPV (or wealth) of a course of action to shareholders. It refers to the shareholders' wealth as reflected by the price of their shares in the share market. Its benefits are measured in terms of cash flows.

Thus, Option C is correct.

98. Enterprise resource planning are software systems for business management, which support various functional areas such as planning, manufacturing, sales, marketing, accounting, finance, human resource management, stock management, research and development etc. But it focuses on four major areas including financial, human resources, marketing and supply chain management.

Thus, Option C is correct.

99. North west corner rule considers only the demand and supply factor in allocating routes not cost of transportation, while LCM and VAM consider the cost of transportation to start with the least cost cell.

Thus, Option C is correct.

100. Voting rights of member nations in the IMF are in proportion to their quotas. Hence the member with the highest quota = higher say.

Thus, Option B is correct.

101. In developing countries like India, micro and small scale industries are considered as the lifeline of the economy. These are generally labour-intensive industries and they are an essential sector of the economy from a financial and social viewpoint.

Thus, Option A is correct.

102. Statement II is correct. whereas Statement I is wrong. The variable cost curve is an upward sloping curve whereas Fixed cost curve is parallel to x-axis which represents that cost does not increase or decrease with the level of production.

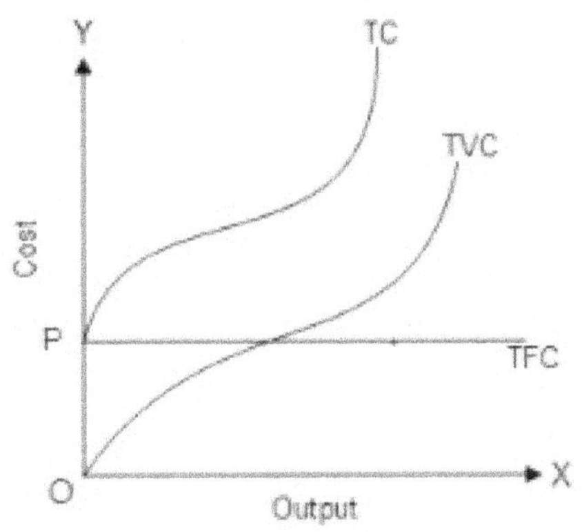

Thus, Option B is correct.

103. ● In the organizational diagnosis process, the output desired at the individual level is an improvement in the performance level.

● In the organizational diagnosis process, task identification, skill variety, and task significance are focused at the individual level. This will improve the performance levels of the employees.

Thus, Option C is correct.

104. Increase in the number of units in the sample usually results in a decrease in sampling error. In fact, in many situations, this decrease in sampling error is inversely proportional to the square root of the sample size.

Thus, Option B is correct.

105. ● P-chart(control chart for fraction defective)- While dealing with attributes, a process will be adjudged in statistical quality control if all the samples or sub groups are ascertained to have the same population proportion p.

● The Remaining three are the control charts for the variables.

Thus, Option C is correct.

106. ● Keiretsu refers to a group of enterprises structured along with a horizontal or vertical integration model

● Japanese industrial groups linked by trading relationships as well as cross-shareholdings of debt and equity are known as Keiretsu.

Thus, Option A is correct.

107. In creative salesmanship, a salesman uses imagination and originality in making sales presentations and it requires creative thinking. When a salesman is pitching on the product's advantage in relation to the substitute or competitor's product, he is using competitive salesmanship.

Thus, Option C is correct.

108. In a random throw of two dice, since each of the six faces of one dice can be associated with each of six faces of the other dice, the total no of cases is 6 * 6 =36

The cases favourable to getting a total of more than 8:

(3,6),(6,3),(4,5),(5,4),(5,5),(6,5),(5,6),(6,6),(4,6),(6,4)

i.e. m=10

The probability that the total of numbers on two dice is greater than 8 = 10/36 = 5/18

Thus, Option C is correct.

109. For the success of retail business and marketing, proper implementation of the components of the traditional marketing mix i.e. product, place, price and promotion are essential as these form the basis of decision making for retailers.

Thus, Option B is correct.

110. There is one sample (1-t), two independent samples (2-t) and two paired samples (3-t) in t-test for Mean. While in z test for mean there are only one sample(1-Z), two independent samples(2-Z).

Thus, Option A is correct.

111. ● Job summary- Brief write-up and a general statement about the job done at the workplace is termed as a job summary. It is a statement of more important function and responsibilities of a job.

● Job title- a brief description of the position held by the employee and gives an idea about the position in the organizational hierarchy. The job title is the name given to a position held by an employee in an organization.

Thus, Option B is correct.

112. Covariance can take value from negative infinity(-∞) to positive infinity (+∞). Negative values indicate negative relationships while positive relationships indicate positive relationships between variables.

Thus, Option D is correct.

113. In today's era, to survive and grow retailers have to keep pace with changing requirements and needs and demands of consumers to beat the tough competition. For which modern retailers are adapting to new technology, forward-thinking retailers are marketing their business on social media, companies are keeping healthy communication with the consumers, opening online retail stores and using augmented reality.

Thus, Option A is correct.

114. Minimize cost of production is the objective of facility location. Other objectives of facility layout include providing for volume and product flexibility, reducing accidents, providing for volume and product flexibility etc.

Thus, Option A is correct.

115. ● The service triangle was developed by Christian Gronross.

● In the internal marketing of the service triangle, the employee is prepared to serve the customers with the commitment.

● In external marketing, the customer is prepared to receive the service from the right perspective.

● In interactive marketing, positive and satisfactory experiences are created between customers and employees.

Thus, Option A is correct.

116. ● Labelling and testing measures insist upon ensuring good quality of the goods seeking access to the domestic market. Such measures are complex and discriminatory measures for international trade.

● VERs (Voluntary Export Restraints) are voluntary bilateral agreements instituted to restrain the rapid growth of exports of specific kinds.

● Sanitary & Phytosanitary measures to protect against risks linked to food safety, animal health & plant protection

Thus, Option D is correct.

117. When the data set has one or more extreme values, and when the mean is used to represent the whole data set, it provides a wrong impression of other values in the data set.

Thus, Option A is correct.

118. Monopsony is an imperfect market in which there is only one buyer. For example, a firm may be regarded as the sole buyer and price maker of labours in the factor market. On the other hand, under a monopoly, there is one seller who is the sole price maker in the product market. A bilateral monopoly is a combination of monopoly (a single seller) and monopsony (a single buyer).

Thus, Option C is correct.

119. The standard deviation along with several related measures like variance, coefficient of variance, coefficient of standard deviation etc. is used mostly in research studies and is regarded as a very satisfactory measure of dispersion in series.

Thus, Option C is correct.

120. Today's customers are smart, more price-conscious, more demanding and are approached by many competitors. So, they are harder to please. The challenge with marketers is to produce delighted and loyal customers and the key to customer loyal customers is value and equity. Thus, Both A and R are correct but R is not an appropriate explanation for A.

Thus, Option B is correct.

121. There are three types of behaviour of a consumer, pre-purchase, purchase, post-purchase. Post-purchase behaviour is very essential for marketer and company as it gives rise to more consumers. A well-satisfied consumer will spread a word of mouth giving rise to a more consumer base.

Thus, Option A is correct.

122. PERT is probabilistic in nature, CPM is deterministic in nature. PERT is a technique used for problems that occur once or relatively, a few times and that has a definite starting point and finishing point. It is not applied in continuous production like mining, oil refining.

Thus, Option B is correct.

123. • The financial viability of a project provides the following important information:

1) Full details of the assets as well as how liquid are those assets.

2) Funding potential of a project and repayment terms.

3) How easily can the assets be converted into cash.

• Resource Feasibility Study deals with the type and amount of resources required as

well as developmental procedures.

Thus, Option B is correct.

124. • IBRD loans are to be repaid in SDRs/principal currencies only while IDA loans are repayable in local currency as well.

• The interest rates on loans provided by IBRD are higher than IDA since IBRD loans are consistent with market-determined rates while IDA loans cover only administrative charges.

Thus, Option A is correct.

125. Planning-Routing-Scheduling-Dispatching-Expediting-Inspection is the correct step procedure of production planning and control.

Thus, Option A is correct.

126. Bandwagon Advertising is a type of advertising technique that tries to convince customers to join a group of people who already have bought a particular product. For example, a shampoo ad that says 10crore people are already using this shampoo, and you?

Thus, Option B is correct.

127. Following are the steps under Personal Selling:

1) Prospecting: The first step is to identify potential customers. Marketers can identify the prospects through emails, websites or other referral sources.

2) Pre-Approach: The next step is to decide how to approach prospective customers. Whether to make a visit, send a letter or make a phone call.

3) Approach: Under this stage, the salesperson properly approaches the customer, greets him/her and gives a start to the conversation.

4) Presentation and demonstration: Under this step, the salesperson gives detailed information about the product or service, it's use, benefits etc. and if required, demonstrates how to use the product.

5) Handling objections: After presentation and demonstration, customers may have objections relating to price, product features etc. Therefore, at this stage, the salesperson clarifies the doubts and tries to convince the customer to buy the product.

6) Closing the sale: The next step is to close the sale wherein the salesperson requests the customer to buy the product and place the order.

7) Follow up: Under this step, the salesperson ensures satisfaction and assures delivery at the right time, after-sales service etc.

Thus, Option C is correct.

128. • Grapevine is an internal informal person-to-person method of spreading information, gossip and rumours.

• Grapevine is undocumented and thus susceptible to interpretation and alteration.

• Proxemics is a form of non-verbal communication and used as a communication term for distance and personal space.

Thus, Option B is correct.

129. Usually, the method for the item selection from each stratum, resorted to is that of simple random sampling, but systematic sampling can also be used if it is considered more appropriate in certain situations.

Thus, Option A is correct.

130. A clinical interview is concerned with broad underlying feelings or motivations or with the course of an individual's life experience. While a focused interview is meant to focus attention on the given experience of the respondent and its effects.

Thus, Option A is correct.

131. a) Liability is the amount that is due to the outside parties from the company.

b) Reserve is the amounts that are kept aside for future endeavour. It's a type of savings kept aside for some particular purposes.

c) Provision is an amount set aside for uncertain obligations of the company.

d) A contingent liability is an obligation that may arise in future and the amount of losses can be reasonably estimated.

As bad debt provision is created as per the matching principle of accounting to match the related revenue with expenses in the same accounting year.

Thus, Option C is correct.

132. There are three types of blockchain

• Public

• Consortium

• Private

Thus, Option D is correct.

133. • Fiscal policy is defined as the means by which a government adjusts its spending levels and adjusts the tax rates to monitor and influence a nation's economy.

• So various tools used by the government for this purpose are taxation policy, government expenditure policy, public debt policy and deficit financing.

• Statutory liquidity ratio and direct action are the tools of monetary policy used by the Reserve Bank of India for controlling the money supply in the economy.

Thus, Option D is correct.

134. • Diffusion of Innovation Theory refers to the process by which an innovation is communicated among the members of the social system through certain channels.

• It attempts to identify the aspects that describe the rate at which innovations are adopted.

• According to the theory, the main aspects that affect the distribution of a new idea or Innovation are Time, Communication and Social Systems.

Thus, Option B is correct.

135. Input-Output technique is propounded by Prof. Wassily W. Leontief in 1951 to analyze the inter-industry relationship to understand conditions for maintaining equilibrium between supply and demand. It deals with the problems of production in an economy.

Thus, Option D is correct.

136. F-test is a small sample test given by Prof Snedicor. There is no such assumption as For two sets of populations there has to be a set of two samples. Rest three are correct assumptions.

Thus, option D is correct.

137. Print advertisement is a form of advertising that uses physically printed media, such as magazines and newspapers, to reach consumers.

Thus, Option C is correct.

138. In Quasi-strategic greening, a firm develops a green brand in addition to its other brands.

Thus, Option C is correct.

139. • Brand image is a combination of brand associations and brand personality. What consumers interpret and understand about the brand when they observe the brand name is referred to as the brand image.

• Brand identity is a unique set of brand associations.

• Brand position refers to the value proposition that is to be communicated to the target audience and explain the advantages of the brand over other competitive brands.

• Brand equity is the set of brand assets and liabilities linked to a brand.

Thus, Option A is correct.

140. • Chamberlin stated that in monopolistic competition there will be very few monopolists because of the availability of few commodities for which close substitutes do not exist.

• It is a form of market in which there are many sellers of a differentiated product.

Thus, Option D is correct.

141. • Convenience goods are a class of consumer goods that people buy frequently with minimum effort.

• The goods like milk, bread, newspaper, biscuits, etc. fall under convenience goods.

• These goods have a low unit price and are not affected by fashion trends.

Thus, Option B is correct.

142. • A comprehensive view of the influencing factors was provided by Webster and wind.

• Webster and wind divided the environmental influencing factors into four types. They are as follows:

1- Economic factors.

2- Infrastructural factors.

3- Social factors.

4- Political factors.

Thus, Option D is correct.

143. ● The ego defensive function protects consumers against internal and external anxieties and the environment.

● Marketing stimuli becomes an instrument in protecting the consumer.

● The positive consumer attitude serves as a mechanism of defense for these consumers.

Thus, Option A is correct.

144. Given,

Earnings before interest and tax (EBIT) = Rs 1,00,000

Debenture interest = Rs 8,00,000 * 10% = Rs 80,000

And, EAES = EBIT - Debenture interest

So. EAES = Rs 1,00,000 - Rs 80,000 = Rs 20,000

Thus, Option C is correct.

145. Given,

Net income (EAES) = Rs 20,000

Equity capitalisation rate = 10%

And, market value of equity = Net income / equity capitalisation rate * 100

So, Market value of equity = Rs 20,000 / 10 * 100 = Rs 2,00,000

Thus, Option A is correct.

146. Given,

Debt = Rs 8,00,000

Equity = Rs 2,00,000

And, value of company = Debt + Equity

So, value of company = Rs 8,00,000 + Rs 2,00,000 = Rs 10,00,000

Thus, Option D is correct.

147. Answer: Option A

According to Black Scholes model, purchaser can borrow fraction of security at risk free interest rate which is short term. Black-Scholes is a pricing model used to determine the fair price or theoretical value for a call or a put option based on six variables such as volatility, type of option, underlying stock price, time, strike price, and risk-free rate.

148. Answer: Option A

Input call parity relationship, put option minus call option in addition with stock is equal to exercise price present value. The exercise price is the price at which an underlying security can be purchased or sold when trading a call or put option, respectively.

149. Answer: Option C

Stocks which has lower book for market ratio are considered as less risky. A company whose stock is trading at a discount on its book value is not necessarily cheap. In particular, you should expect companies that have low returns on equity, high risk and low growth potential to trade at low price to book ratios.

150. Economic planning may be either comprehensive or partial plan. Comprehensive planning is a process that determines community goals and aspirations in terms of community development. The result is called a comprehensive plan and both expresses and regulates public policies on transportation, utilities, land use, recreation, and housing.

Paper-I

Q.1 Which model of communication is a one way process where sender is the one who sends the message but receiver does not give feedback or response?

A. Horizontal model   **B.** Transactional model
C. Linear model   **D.** Interactional model

Q.2 An individual stock required return is equal to risk free rate plus bearing risk premium is an explanation of:-

A. security market line
B. capital market line
C. aggregate market line
D. beta market line

Q.3 The timing of the action for parts of your car's engine. It is example of:-

A. Analog   **B.** Asynchronous
C. Synchronous   **D.** None of these

Q.4 Match the following List 1 with List 2 with correct responses.

List 1	List 2
a. Intrapersonal communication	(i) It is the communication where more than two individuals are involved in exchange of ideas, skills and interests.
b. Mass communication	(ii) It is a face to face communication between two persons.
c. Interpersonal communication	(iii) It uses mechanical devices that multiply messages and take it to a large number of people simultaneously.
d. Group communication	(iv) It is the communication within an individual, including talking to oneself.

A. a-iv, b-iii, c-ii, d- i   **B.** a-iii, b-ii, c-i, d-iv
C. a-iv, b-iii, c-i, d-ii   **D.** a-iv, b-i, c-ii, d-iii

Q.5 ___________ barriers to communication are related to the limitations of the human body and the human mind.

A. Psychological   **B.** Physiological
C. Social   **D.** Cultural

Q.6 Select the odd word from the given alternatives.

A. Stream   **B.** Rivulet   **C.** River   **D.** Valley

Q.7 Which number should come next in the series, 48, 24, 12, ...?

A. 4   **B.** 6   **C.** 5   **D.** 3

Q.8 RQP, ONM, _, IHG, FED, find the missing letters.

A. LKJ.   **B.** CDE   **C.** BAC   **D.** LKI

Q.9 Which word does not belong to others?

A. Inch   **B.** Kilogram
C. Centimeter   **D.** Yard

Q.10 Arrange the following words in a meaningful sequence.

1. Infection
2. Consultation
3. Doctor
4. Treatment
5. Recovery

A. 1, 2, 3, 4, 5   **B.** 2, 3, 5, 1, 4
C. 1, 3, 4, 5, 2   **D.** 1, 3, 2, 4, 5

Ques (11-15):Direction: Read the passage carefully and choose the best answer to each question out of the four alternatives.

It is not good manners to stop a person on the street or in a shop, or in the performance of any duty and to talk to him for ten, fifteen or twenty minutes just to pass the time of day. We can tell that a person is in a hurry to get somewhere, or he is doing something, and we know enough not to interrupt him for any length of time. Yet some of us think nothing of calling someone on the telephone, interrupting him without a thought about what he may be doing, and chattering away, forgetting about time or anything else. Perhaps we don't consider our telephone conversation an interruption because we don't see what we have interrupted. Naturally, we must observe the common courtesies over the telephone. But we must remember that one of the courtesies of telephoning is to be brief.

Never ask anybody to guess who you are. The person you are telephoning may not be in a guessing mood. If you know him, you may want to ask after the state of his health and that of his family, but as soon as you possibly can, go get on with your business. He certainly wants to know why you are telephoning him. When you are finished with your business, you might take moment to observe the natural courtesies of conversation, expressing your thanks before ending your call.

From the way the telephone is used in your home, you would hardly suspect that this is an instrument on which very important business transactions are conducted. There are times when even you are called upon to be business-like, brief, and effective on the telephone.

Q.11 How can we make the best use of a telephone?

A. By being elaborate.

B. By being brief, effective and business-like.

C. By observing the courtesies.

D. By not being business-like.

Q.12 We interrupt people in the telephone because:

A. we are thoughtless.

B. we enjoy doing it.

C. we forget about time.

D. we don't consider our telephone call an interruption.

Q.13 When we telephone, we must:

A. be business like.

B. ask people to guess who you are.

C. chatter away.

D. not bother about the time we spend.

Q.14 Which of the following statement/s is true?

(i) We know enough to interrupt someone.

(ii) We don't know enough to interrupt someone.

(iii) We can interrupt anyone on the telephone.

(iv) We can interrupt anyone anytime we want.

A. Only (i)   **B.** Only (ii)

C. (iii) & (iv)   **D.** Only (iv)

Q.15 It is not good manners to:

A. stop a person on the street to pass time.

B. stop a person in the shop to pass time.

C. stop a person during duty to pass time.

D. All of the above options.

Q.16 Which of the following statements is/are correct with respect to Internet and Intranet?

i. The number of users in Intranet is limited.

ii. Internet is a wide network of computers & open to all.

iii. Intranet uses internet protocols such as TCP/IP and FTP.

A. (i), (ii) and (iii)   **B.** (ii), (iii)

C. (i) only   **D.** All of the above

Q.17 _____ is the mechanical/electronic conversion of images of handwritten, typed, or printed text into machine-encoded text.

A. Digitizer

B. Optical Mark Reader

C. Optical Character Recognition

D. Bar Code Reader

Q.18 Which of the following initiatives has been implemented by MHRD under NMEICT Programme to incorporate Robotics into engineering education with the main objective of providing hands on application of Computer science, mathematics and engineering principles?

A. E-Kalpa   **B.** E-Yantra

C. E-Shodh Sindhu   **D.** E-Acharya

Q.19 Which of the following file extensions is used for the Bitmap Image File?

A. .btp   **B.** .bit   **C.** .bmp   **D.** .btm

Q.20 HTTP stands for:-

A. Hyper Text Transfer Protocol

B. Hyper Text Transition Protocol

C. Hyper Text Transfer Program

D. Hyper Text Transition Program

Q.21 Study the following statements carefully.

Statement I: Smog comprises of smoke & fog and soot comprises of soil, dust and smoke.

Statement II: Smog is the particulate matter whereas soot is the ground-level ozone.

A. Both Statements I and II are true

B. Only Statement I is true

C. Only Statement II is true

D. Both Statements I and II are false

Q.22 As a part of 'Go Green Initiative', Indian Railways has planned to set up a solar power plant of _____ by 2020-21?

A. 100 Mega Watt   **B.** 1000 Mega Watt

C. 150 Mega Watt   **D.** 1500 Mega Watt

Q.23 The Deccan Thorn Forests covers which of the following states in India?

A. Maharashtra   **B.** Andhra Pradesh

C. Karnataka   **D.** All of them

Q.24 Which of the following goals fall in the list of United Nations Sustainable Development Goals?

i. Good Health and Well Being

ii. Peace and Justice Strong Institutions

iii. Clean Water and Sanitation

iv. Partnerships to achieve the Goal

A. (i), (ii) and (iii) only

B. (ii), (iii) and (iv) only

C. (i), (iii) and (iv) only

D. All of the above

Q.25 What is Geeta's rank in the class?

I. There are 30 students in the class.

II. There are 10 students who scored less than Geeta.

A. Neither I nor II is sufficient

B. Both I and II are needed

C. Statement I alone is sufficient, but statement II alone is not sufficient

D. Statement II alone is sufficient, but statement I alone is not sufficient

Q.26 If in a certain language, NOIDA is coded as OPJEB, how is DELHI coded in that language?

A. CDKGH   **B.** EFMIJ   **C.** FGNJK   **D.** IHLED

Q.27 Identify if the statement given in the question is a conclusion, assumption, premise or none of these?

Statement: The team made a comparison of lifestyles of 450 people having benign brain tumours and 70 having a malignant brain tumour with a control group of 1200 people.

A. A conclusion

B. An Assumption

C. A premise

D. Not an Argument (None of these)

Q.28 According to Nyaya Sutra, which of the following is/are the kind of hetvabhasa according to Indian Logic?

(i) Savyabhichara

(ii) Viruddha

(iii) Badhita

(iv) Prakaranasama

A. (i), (iii) and (iv) only

B. (ii) ,(iii) and (iv) only

C. (i) , (ii) and (iii) only

D. All of the above

Q.29 Given below are three statements: a, b and c. From the given statements, four conclusions, I, II, III and IV are drawn. Select the correct option which states that conclusions logically follow from the given statements.

Statements:

a) Some chairs are tables.

b) Some tables are sofas.

c) All sofa is a bed.

Conclusions:

(i) Some beds are chairs.

(ii) Some tables are beds.

(iii) Some sofas are chairs.

(iv) All beds are sofas.

Code:

A. Only (4) follows

B. Only (2) follows

C. Only (1) and (2) follows

D. Only (1) and (4) follows

Q.30 A deductive argument is sound if it satisfies some conditions. Select the code which states these conditions.

(i) If the argument is valid.

(ii) Its premises are all true.

(iii) The argument may be valid or invalid.

Code:

A. (i) and (ii) only   **B.** (iii) only

C. (ii) and (iii) only   **D.** (ii) only

Ques (31-35): Study the following graph carefully to answer the given questions:

Human Resource Index of an organisation for the given years.

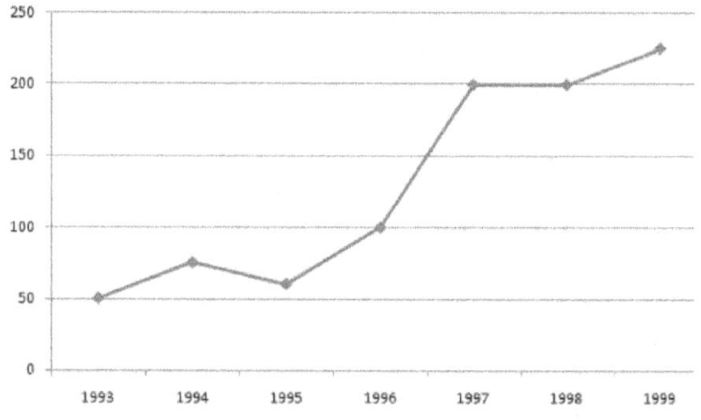

Q.31 What is the percentage increase from 1993 to 1999?

A. 260%   **B.** 350%   **C.** 280%   **D.** 275%

Q.32 The index in 1998 was what percent of that in 1996?

A. 100%   **B.** 380 %   **C.** 200%   **D.** 350 %

Q.33 Which of the following is true?

A. The growth is most remarkable after the year 1997.

B. Except for some spurts the index in general remained steady.

C. The index showed many ups and downs.

D. The index increased every year.

Q.34 What is the approximate average for the given years?

A. 133   **B.** 140   **C.** 155   **D.** 130

Q.35 In which year is the percentage increase the highest from its previous year?

A. 1994   **B.** 1996

C. 1999   **D.** None of these

Q.36 With respect to Research, which of the following variables is correct?

A. Intervening variable: is presumed to be the cause of another variable.

B. Independent variable: they establish a link between intervening and dependent variable.

C. Dependent variable: these are influenced by one or more independent variable.

D. Extraneous variable: these are variables which could not affect the results of the experiment.

Q.37 _______ considers the scientific and common-sense reasoning as one and the same thing.

A. Positivism   **B.** Post-positivism

C. Realism   **D.** Structuralism

Q.38 Match the set-I and set-II with correct responses.

Set 1	Set 2
(a) Ibid	(i) It is a footnote or endnote term u sed to repeat the title and page number for a give n work.
(b) Op. cit	(ii) It refers to the same author and source in the immediately preceding reference.
(c) Loc. cit	(iii) It refers to the reference listed e arlier by the same author.
(d) Et a l.	(iv) It is used when referring to a nu mber of people.

A. a-i, b-ii, c-iii, d-iv   **B.** a-iii, b-ii, c-i, d-iv

C. a-ii, b-i, c-iii, d-iv   **D.** a-ii, b-iii, c-i, d-iv

Q.39 An experimental research is often used for which of the following statements?

a) Where there is an involvement of two or more variables.

b) Where manipulation of one variable causes change in results.

c) Where the magnitude of correlation yields good results.

d) Where prediction of results in somewhat known.

A. a, b, c, d   **B.** a, b, c   **C.** a, b, d   **D.** b, c, d

Q.40 Which of these is true about ethnography?

a) Ethnography studies a group or culture of a group.

b) Participant's observation can be included while doing ethnography.

c) Ethnography as a method is appropriate for qualitative research as well as quantitative research.

d) It is not a holistic study.

e) It emerged as an important method in anthropology for studying the culture of 'other' subjects.

A. a, b, c and e   **B.** b, c, d and e

C. a, b, d   **D.** a, b, e

Q.41 MHRD works through which of the following departments?

(a) Department of School Education & Literacy.

(b) Department of Physical and Mental Health.

(c) Department of Higher Education.

A. (a) and (b)   **B.** (a) and (c)

C. (a), (b), (c)   **D.** (b) and (c)

Q.42 In the following table, Set-I mentions an apex level institution in India while Set-II indicates their establishment date. Match the two sets and give your answer.

Set - I	Set-II
(a) University Grants Commission (UGC)	(i) 1995
(b) All India Council of Technical Education (AICTE)	(ii) 1956
(c) National Council of Teacher Education (NCTE)	(iii) 1994
(d) National Assessment and Accreditation Council (NAAC)	(iv) 1945

A. a-i, b-iv, c-iii, d-ii   **B.** a-ii, b-iv, c-i, d-iii

C. a-ii, b-i, c-iii, d-iv   **D.** a-i, b-iv, c-ii, d-iii

Q.43 International Literacy day is celebrated every year on which of the following dates?

A. 8th September   **B.** 8th August

C. 10th July   **D.** 12th December.

Q.44 Fact 1: Jessica has four children.

Fact 2: Two of the children have blue eyes and two of the children have brown eyes.

Fact 3: Half of the children are girls.

If the first three statements are facts, which of the following statements must also be a fact?

I. At least one girl has blue eyes.

II. Two of the children are boys.

III. The boys have brown eyes.

A. II only

B. I and III only

C. II and III only

D. None of the statements is a known fact.

Q.45 Fact 1: Most stuffed toys are stuffed with beans.

Fact 2: There are stuffed bears and stuffed tigers.

Fact 3: Some chairs are stuffed with beans.

If the first three statements are facts, which of the following statements must also be a fact?

I. Only children's chairs are stuffed with beans.

II. All stuffed tigers are stuffed with beans.

III. Stuffed monkeys are not stuffed with beans.

A. II only

B. II and III only

C. I only

D. None of the statements is a known fact.

Q.46 The first death anniversary day of Sri Rajiv Gandhi was observed as the:

A. National Integration Day

B. Anti-Terrorism Day

C. Peace and Love Day

D. Secularism Day

Q.47 Complete the series.

QPO, NML, KJI, _____, EDC

A. HGF   **B.** CAB   **C.** JKL   **D.** GHI

Q.48 Which of the following statements is not true about teaching?

A. Classroom teaching is the most effective method of teaching.

B. Teaching is a comprehensive process.

C. Teaching can be made effective by making use of teaching aids.

D. Teaching requires expertise and experience.

Q.49 An effective assessment considers which of the following factors?

A. Checks the knowledge of the learners

B. Helps to take remedial measures

C. Acts as a motivation

D. All of them

Q.50 Which of the following is/are incorrect about the Reflective level of teaching?

(i) The student at this level understands the situation and uses his critical abilities to solve the problem.

(ii) The teacher presents subject matter before the students in a sequential and organized form.

(iii) The teacher explains the student about the relationship between principles and facts and teaches them how these principles can be applied.

(iv) Teaching is subject centred at this level.

A. (i) only

B. (i) and (iii) only

C. (ii), (iii) and (iv) only

D. (i), (ii) and (iii) only

Paper-II

Q.51 Revealed preference theory is also known as

A. Behaviourist Cardinal utility theory

B. Ordinal utility theory

C. Behaviouristic ordinal utility theory

D. None of the above

Q.52 Which of the following is a term used to describe the analysis of complex data from a data warehouse?

A. OLTP

B. OLAP

C. Big data

D. Data mining

Q.53 What is true with regard to Stagflation?

Statement - I: Stagflation is called the Inflationary Recession.

Statement - II: Stagflation is characterised by high unemployment and low levels of inflation.

Statement -III: The output increases during stagflation.

Choose the correct option from those below :

A. I only.　　　　　　　**B.** II only.

C. I , II and III　　　　　**D.** II and III only.

Q.54 Assertion (A): In Options trading, the clearing house acts as the counterparty in each contract.

Reason (R): The Option holder could close out his actual contract by selling it to a third party.

A. Both (A) and (R) are correct, and (R) is the correct explanation of (A).

B. Both (A) and (R) are correct, but (R) is not the correct explanation of (A).

C. (A) is correct., but (R) is not correct.

D. (A) is wrong, and (R) is correct.

Q.55 The strategy that helps employees to show compassion and respect towards different cultures in the workplace is:

A. Diversity Awareness

B. Diversity Knowledge

C. Diversity Sensitivity

D. Diversity Enlargement

Q.56 Which one of the following is wrong about HRD climate?

A. It results from the behaviour of members of the organizations but excluding the ones in top management.

B. It is perceived by the members of the organizations

C. It looks into interpreting situations

D. It acts as pressure for the activities that are to be carried out inside organizations

Q.57 Which of the following is not the correct depiction of Null Hypothesis under One -Tailed test?

a. $Ho > \mu$

b. $Ho = \mu$

c. $Ho < \mu$

d. $Ho \neq \mu$

Choose the correct option from those below:

A. a and d only.　　　　　**B.** b and c only.

C. a and c only.　　　　　**D.** b and d only.

Q.58 SWIFT was founded in _________ in the year _____.

A. London, 1975

B. Belgium, 1973

C. New York, 1982

D. Tokyo, 1984

Q.59 Which of the following Statements is correct?

A. Logistics is the operational framework within which SCM is performed

B. The main function of SCM is to make goods & services available to the customer at a place where there is demand for the product.

C. Process that is involved in logistics is from the procurement of raw materials till the outcome as finished products

D. The major functions involved in SCM are the procurement of raw materials, product development, marketing, operations, distribution, finance and customer services.

Q.60 Statement I: Institutional factors of Industrial relations include matters as state policy, labour legislation, social institutions and the system of industrial relations.

Statement II: Economic factors of Industrial relations include economic organizations, capital structure, technology, nature of labour force and attitudes to work.

Choose the correct option from those below:

A. Statement I is correct, Statement II is incorrect.

B. Statement I is incorrect, Statement II is correct.

C. Both Statement I and Statement II are correct.

D. Both Statement I and Statement II are incorrect.

Q.61 Which of the following is not a characteristic of Normal distribution?

A. Mean median and mode are the same.

B. Q.D.=(⅘) σ

C. All odd-order moments vanish.

D. Linear combination of independent normal variates is also a normal variate.

Q.62 Which model helps the marketer in the identification of stimulus which oversees the buying behaviour of the customer?

A. Psychological model

B. Black Box Model of consumer behaviour

C. Input, process, output model

D. Nicosia model

Q.63 Statement I: For mercantilists, the objective of foreign trade was considered to be achievement of surplus in the balance of payments.

Statement II: A nation's wealth depends upon its accumulated profits.

A. Statement I is correct., Statement II is incorrect.

B. Statement I is incorrect, Statement II is correct.

C. Both Statement I and II are correct.

D. Both Statement I and II are incorrect.

Q.64 Assertion (A): Competency mapping is identifying key competencies for a job and incorporating them via different processes

Reason (R): Competency is defined as a skill or ability

A. Both (A) and (R) are correct, and (R) is the correct explanation of (A).

B. Both (A) and (R) are correct, but (R) is not the correct explanation of (A).

C. (A) is correct, but (R) is not correct.

D. (A) is wrong, and (R) is correct.

Q.65 Which of the following is the part of 'Staff' in McKinsey 7'S Framework?

A. What are the core values that the employees possess?

B. Are there any gaps between the required competencies?

C. What is the company known for doing well?

D. What are the lines of communication that should be followed?

Q.66 A company having debtors Rs.20000 decides to keep 5% as a reserve for bad debts. What is the amount of debtors shown in the balance sheet if the company's reserve for discount is Rs.2000?

A. 17000   **B.** 17100   **C.** 18000   **D.** 19000

Q.67 Statement I: Whistleblowing extends till the activity of any employee of a public or private organization, and it has nothing to do with exposing government mismanagement.

Statement II: Whistleblower-protection acts generally provide adequate protection to whistleblowers.

Choose the correct option from those below:

A. Statement I is correct, Statement II is incorrect.

B. Statement I is incorrect, Statement II is correct.

C. Both Statement I and Statement II are correct.

D. Both Statement I and Statement II are incorrect.

Q.68 Assertion (A): Central banks' decision regarding monetary policy influences exchange rate determination.

Reason (R): Central banks' use its domestic currency to buy and sell foregin currencies in the forex market.

A. Both (A) and (R) are correct, and (R) is the correct explanation of (A).

B. Both (A) and (R) are correct, and (R) is not the correct explanation of (A).

C. (A) is correct., but (R) is not correct.

D. (A) is wrong, but (R) is correct.

Q.69 If Standard deviation = 4.8 and Mean = 120. Calculate the coefficient of variation.

A. 0.4%   **B.** 4.0%   **C.** 0.04%.   **D.** 44.0%.

Q.70 Which of the following statements are unrelated to the features of WTO are correct?

a. It is a set of rules and a multilateral agreement.

b. WTO members have to follow its rules and regulations.

c. It is applied on a provisional basis.

d. Rules are applicable to trade in goods, services and intellectual property rights.

e. Fast and efficient dispute settlement system.

Choose the correct option from those below:

A. a, c   **B.** b, d, e   **C.** c, e   **D.** b, c

Q.71 Statement I: Managers may work in various areas of management within an organisation, irrespective of their levels and are known as functional managers.

Statement II: Managers may work in various areas of management within an organisation based on their levels and are known as functional managers.

A. Statement I is correct., Statement II is incorrect.

B. Statement I is incorrect, Statement II is correct.

C. Both Statement I and II are correct.

D. Both Statement I and II are incorrect.

Q.72 Which of the following is not a work context stress-related hazard?

A. work pace

B. status and pay

C. work-life balance

D. role in the organization

Q.73 With respect to the customer life cycle in customer relationship management, which of the following is not a phase of the customer life cycle?

A. Customer acquisition

B. Customer retention

C. Marketing

D. Relationship management

Q.74 'Depreciation' is added in Cash Flow Statement despite being an expense because :

A. It is a non-cash expense and does not decrease the cash flow

B. It is a tax-saving expense

C. It is a source of funds

D. It increases the cash flow from operating activities

Q.75 Which one of these mentioned below aims at reducing transportation of in-process inventory from one section to another?

A. Lord Path Matrix method

B. Travel chart

C. Process flow charts

D. Correlation chart

Q.76 Which of the following is anything real or abstract about which a company wants to collect and store data?

A. Data packets   **B.** Data entity

C. Data virtualisation   **D.** Data silos

Q.77 Statement I: Group dynamics include democratic leadership, cooperation and participation

Statement II: Group dynamics are viewed from the external nature of groups, and it does not affect individual behaviour in any sense.

Choose the correct option from those below:

A. Statement I is correct, Statement II is incorrect.

B. Statement I is incorrect, Statement II is correct.

C. Both Statement I and Statement II are correct.

D. Both Statement I and Statement II are incorrect.

Q.78 Which of the following is not a part of the 3 sub-processes as emphasised by Dan Schendel and Charles Hofer model of strategic management?

A. Environmental analysis
B. Structural analysis
C. Resource analysis
D. Value analysis

Q.79 Which of the following are the effects of Share Repurchase?

a) Face value of the share remains the same.

b) No cash flow involved.

c) EPS increases.

d) PE ratio increases.

Choose the correct option from those below:

A. b and d only
B. a, c and d only
C. a and c only
D. a and d only

Q.80 Which statement out of the following is not correct wrt marketing mix in the international domain?

A. Marketing mix could be tailored as and when required according to the geographical requirements.
B. Tailoring in marketing mix is usually an easy to do task with no added costs incurred.
C. Specialization is one name that can be given to tailoring of marketing mix in international marketing
D. Any change in marketing mix is done according to the local marketing environment and customers specifically

Q.81 Assertion (A): When the investment policy of the firm is given, the dividend decision is of no significance in determining the value of the firm under MM Theory.

Reason (R): The value of the firm depends on the firm's earnings and the firm's earnings are influenced by its investment policy.

A. Both (A) and (R) are correct, and (R) is the correct explanation of (A).
B. Both (A) and (R) are correct, but (R) is not the correct explanation of (A).
C. (A) is correct, but (R) is not correct.
D. (A) is wrong, and (R) is correct.

Q.82 Assertion (A): An employee with more than one boss is as vulnerable as a pawn in the game of chess.

Reason (R): It is difficult to serve more than one superior as it will be difficult to prioritise work and may arise conflicts in the organisation.

A. Both (A) and (R) are correct, and (R) is the correct explanation of (A).
B. Both (A) and (R) are correct, but (R) is not the correct explanation of (A).
C. (A) is correct., but (R) is not correct.
D. (A) is wrong, and (R) is correct.

Q.83 Which of the following is not a key feature of a mixed economy?

A. Protection of labour
B. Absence of a central economic plan

C. Price mechanism
D. Dual objectives of both profit maximisation and social welfare.

Q.84 Which of the following statements are valid about Kanter's rules for stifling innovation?

a) To never regard any idea with suspicion and always be open to them from all employees

b) To never withhold your praise for your employees and tell them their ideas are always welcomed.

c) Ask departments to criticize each other's proposal

d) Never forget that your employees know everything important about the business

e) Treat identification of problems as signs of failure

Choose the correct option from those below:

A. a,b
B. c,e
C. e,d
D. a,c

Q.85 In Porter's Five Force Model, the 'threat of new entrants' relates to:

A. Substitutes
B. Buyer Power
C. Supplier Power
D. Barriers to entry

Q.86 Which level of management requires conceptual skills?

A. Lower level of management
B. Higher level of management
C. First-line managers
D. None of the above

Q.87 The task environment of marketing is not concerned about the factors of which of the following?

A. Production
B. After-sales service
C. Promoting
D. Distributing

Q.88 Assertion (A): Correlation techniques are reliable when a causal relationship has to be established between variables and sales

Reason (R): Correlation analysis cannot be used to develop demand functions for any kind of products.

A. Both (A) and (R) are correct, and (R) is the correct explanation of (A).
B. Both (A) and (R) are correct, but (R) is not the correct explanation of (A).
C. (A) is correct., but (R) is not correct.
D. (A) is wrong, and (R) is correct.

Q.89 Assertion (A): The geometric mean becomes zero when one of the items is zero.

Reason (R): Geometric mean of a set of n observations is the nth root of their product.

A. Both (A) and (R) are correct, and (R) is the correct explanation of (A).
B. Both (A) and (R) are correct, but (R) is not the correct explanation of (A).
C. (A) is correct., but (R) is not correct.
D. (A) is wrong, and (R) is correct.

Q.90 Which of the following is needed for the foremost step of Human Resource Planning?

A. Job Requirements

B. Work-Study

C. Human Resource Inventory

D. Recruitment and selection plan

Q.91 Statement I: Financial Break-Even Point is that level of EBIT where EPS remains the same.

Statement II: Point of Indifference is that level of EBIT which is just equal to pay the total finance charges.

Choose the correct option from those below:

A. Statement I is correct., Statement II is incorrect.

B. Statement I is incorrect, Statement II is correct.

C. Both Statement I and Statement II are correct.

D. Both Statement I and Statement II are incorrect.

Q.92 According to Robert Katz, which among the following skills is not essential for successful management?

A. Technical Skills

B. Physiological Skills

C. Interpersonal skills

D. Conceptual Skills

Q.93 Trading on Equity is also referred to as:

A. Financial Leverage

B. Operating Leverage

C. Composite Leverage

D. Working Capital Leverage

Q.94 Statement I: Trade Discount does not affect the original invoice because the adjustment is made post-sale.

Statement II: Rebate is reduced from the original value before the invoice is generated.

Choose the correct option from the following:

A. Statement I is correct, Statement II is incorrect.

B. Statement I is incorrect, Statement II is correct.

C. Both Statement I and Statement II are correct.

D. Both Statement I and Statement II are incorrect.

Q.95 Entry and exit of firm in monopolist market in the long run can

A. Earn normal profits

B. Earn supernormal profits

C. Incur losses

D. Any of the above

Q.96 Umbrella effect refers to

A. Demand set by the dominant competitor in a market.

B. Price set by the dominant competitor in the market.

C. Supply set by the dominant producer in a market.

D. Both A and B

Q.97 What does 'D' in RADAR Logic stand for?

A. Define

B. Design

C. Deploy

D. Determine

Q.98 Choose the correct sequence wrt Keller's Brand Equity Model.

A. Meaning, response, identity, relationships

B. Identity, meaning, response, relationships

C. Identity, response, meaning, relationships

D. Meaning, identity, response, relationships

Q.99 The formula for the computation of rate variance is:

A. (Standard Rate - Actual Rate) * Actual Quantity

B. (Standard Quantity - Actual Quantity) * Actual Price

C. Standard Rate - Actual Rate

D. (Standard Rate * Standard Quantity) - (Actual Rate * Actual price)

Q.100 Statement I: Greenfield investment happens when a company purchases or leases an existing facility.

Statement II: Greenfield investment is a type of foreign direct investment and involves companies and production facilities in different countries.

Choose the correct option from those below:

A. Statement I is correct., Statement II is incorrect.

B. Statement I is incorrect, Statement II is correct.

C. Both Statement I and Statement II are correct.

D. Both Statement I and Statement II are incorrect.

Q.101 Which of the following steps in the planning process involves the organization asking the question "in which environment – internal or external – will our plans operate"?

A. Formulating supporting plans

B. Comparing alternatives in the light of goals

C. Considering planning premises

D. Identifying alternatives

Q.102 Sakshi Pathak is considering the following questions as she approaches a planning period: (a) What industries should we get into or out of? (b) In which businesses should the corporation invest money? Which of the following levels would be appropriate to address the questions facing Ms. Pathak?

A. Corporate level

B. Business level

C. Operational level

D. Functional level

Q.103 Which of the following managers deal with the actual operations of an organization's units?

A. First level

B. Top level

C. Middle level

D. Administrative

Q.104 Which of the following is/are objectives of sensitivity training?

I. It helps individuals gain insights into their behavior and helps them analyze the way they appear to others.

II. It helps individuals develop the skills necessary for diagnosing and understanding of group processes.

III. It exposes managers to theories, principles and new developments in management.

A. Only (I) above

B. Only (III) above

C. Both (I) and (II) above

D. Both (II) and (III) above

Q.105 Growth in earnings per share is primarily resultant of growth in:-

A. dividends

B. asset value

C. fundamental value   **D.** yearly value

Q.106 The ___________ is a management strategy that aligns raw-material orders from suppliers directly with production schedules.

A. Mathematical model

B. Linear programming

C. Economic order quantity

D. JIT inventory system

Q.107 Which of the following ratios tests the relationship between the sales and the various assets of a firm?

A. Activity ratio

B. Current ratio

C. Inventory turnover ratio

D. Return on investment ratio

Q.108 Which model/theory of leadership does Kavita Ramakrishnan use, when she determines the effectiveness of decisions as measured by group performance/participation; quality and acceptance?

A. House's Path-Goal Theory

B. Fiedler's Contingency approach

C. Blake and Mouton's Managerial Grid

D. Vroom and Yetton's Normative Decision Model.

Q.109 The bargaining power of buyers, as described by Porter, is high when:-

A. There are only a few players in the industry

B. Their purchases form a large chunk of the sellers' total sales

C. There are no substitutes for products being purchased

D. Products or services are critical to the buyer's business

Q.110 According to General Financial Rules, 2005, loss of how many volumes per thousand volumes issued / consulted in a year is to be taken as reasonable.

A. Three   **B.** Four   **C.** Five   **D.** Six

Q.111 Managers at all three levels of management require different kinds of skills to perform the functions associated with their jobs. A major difference in skill requirements between middle level and top-level managers is that

A. Top managers must generally be more skilled than middle managers in every respect

B. Top managers require better interpersonal skills but less conceptual skills than middle managers

C. Top managers generally require better technical and interpersonal skills than middle managers

D. Top managers generally require higher level conceptual skills but less technical skills than middle managers

Q.112 The behavioral approach of management thoughts can be classified into:-

A. Contingency theory.

B. Group influences.

C. Hawthorne studies.

D. Both (II) and (III) above

Q.113 By studying the various approaches to management analysis, we can understand the concept of management and have a better understanding of managerial functions. Which approach to management emphasizes managing people by understanding their individual psychological needs?

A. Empirical approach

B. Decision theory approach

C. Management science approach

D. Interpersonal behavior approach

Q.114 Immoral management not only ignores ethical concerns, but also actively opposes ethical behavior. Organizations with immoral management is/are characterized by

I. Total concern for company profits only.

II. Laws are regarded as hurdles to be removed.

III. Less inclination to minimize expenditure.

A. Only (I) above

B. Only (II) above

C. Both (I) and (II) above

D. Both (I) and (III) above

Q.115 In expected rate of return for constant growth, capital gains is divided by capital gains yield to calculate:-

A. returning price   **B.** ending price

C. beginning price   **D.** regular price

Q.116 Practicing ethical guidelines enables managers to become followers of moral management approach. They facilitate ethical business decisions. Which of the following is not an ethical guideline for managers?

A. Upholding human dignity

B. Obeying the law

C. Non-allowance for participation of stakeholders in the decision-making process

D. Primum Non-Nocere

Q.117 Despite the many advantages of planning, there may be some obstacles and limitations in this process, since nothing is perfect on this earth, as a general rule of law. Which of the following would not be considered a potential advantage of planning?

A. It helps managers to be future oriented

B. It enhances decision coordination

C. It increases the amount of time available for other managerial functions

D. It emphasizes organizational objectives

Q.118 Which of the following would not be an accurate depiction of the differences between strategic and tactical planning?

A. Strategic planning is developed mainly by upper-level management and tactical planning is generally developed by lower-level management

B. Facts for strategic planning are generally easier to gather than facts for tactical planning

C. Strategic plans generally contain less details than tactical plans

D. Strategic plans generally cover a longer period of time than tactical plans

Q.119 Using the BCG matrix requires considering which of the following factors?

A. Types of risk associated with product development

B. Threats that economic conditions can create in future

C. Social factors

D. Market shares and growth of markets in which products are selling

Q.120 Proctor & Gamble (P&G) makes fourteen different laundry soap products and completely dominates the laundry detergent market. Through constant changes in packaging, it is trying to influence the perception of customers that its products are unique. Which of the following generic strategies is P&G using?

A. Cost leadership   **B.** Differentiation

C. Focus   **D.** Globalization

Q.121 Stock which has fixed payments and failure of payments which do not lead to bankruptcy is classified as:-

A. common stock   **B.** preferred stock

C. bonds equity   **D.** common shares

Q.122 The conflict-resolution approach that corresponds with a high level of assertiveness and a low level of cooperativeness, is referred to as:-

A. weak-form efficiency

B. strong form of efficiency

C. semi-strong efficiency

D. market efficiency

Q.123 Which approach to decision-making under conditions of uncertainty believes that individual attitudes toward risk vary with events, with people and positions?

A. Risk analysis

B. Risk communication

C. Decision trees

D. Utility theory

Q.124 Which of the following are characteristics of a closed system?

A. It is perfectly deterministic and predictable.

B. There is no exchange between the system and the external environment.

C. Both (I) and (II) above

D. It is a realistic view.

Q.125 Information that originates outside the organization is known as external information. Which of the following is an example of external information in an organization?

A. Daily receipts and expenditures

B. Salesperson quotas

C. Descriptions of customer satisfaction with products and services

D. Quantity of an item in hand or in inventory

Q.126 The major disadvantage of the divisional structure is:-

A. Diseconomies of scale

B. Requires people with general managerial capabilities

C. Managerial vacuum

D. Duplication of activities and resources

Q.127 Power-based upon identification with a person who has desirable resources or personal traits is called:-

A. Coercive power   **B.** Legitimate power

C. Expert power   **D.** Referent power

Q.128 Which of the following decision-making models emphasizes short-run solution of a problem rather than long-term goal accomplishment?

A. Rational model   **B.** Satisficing model

C. Incremental model   **D.** Garbage-can model

Q.129 Which of the following is usually the second step followed in the recruitment procedure?

A. Designing job description

B. Developing a job specification

C. Performing job analysis

D. Attracting a pool of applicants

Q.130 What is/are the steps in human resource planning?

A. Assessment of Supply of Human Resources

B. Analysis of Human Resource Planning Objectives

C. Matching Demand and Supply

D. All of these

Q.131 Which of the following is the four-step in formulating a career strategy?

A. Development of strategic career alternatives

B. Analysis of personal strengths and weaknesses

C. Consistency testing and strategic choices

D. Implementation of the career plan

Q.132 Forces/traits within the manager that determine effective leadership behavior include his/her:-

A. Values

B. Confidence in subordinates

C. Aggressiveness

D. All of these

Q.133 What is/ are the techniques of on the job training?

A. Organizational socialization

B. Creation of "assistant-to" positions

C. Job Instruction Training

D. Job enlargement

Q.134 What is/ are the features of human resource planning?

A. A Part Of Human Resource Management System

B. Related To Corporate Plan

C. Continuous Process

D. All of these

Q.135 Creativity is an important factor in managing people. Which of the following is not true with regard to the creativity process?

A. Creativity is the ability to develop new ideas

B. The creativity process starts with unconscious scanning

C. Intuition connects the unconscious with the conscious

D. Insight leads to intuition

Q.136 Which of the following is one of the leadership styles suggested by path-goal theory?

A. Instrumental leadership
B. Participative leadership
C. Supportive leadership
D. All of these

Q.137 Which of the following is/ are an effective listening technique?

A. Avoiding premature evaluation
B. Finding an area of interest in what the other person is saying
C. Exhibiting affirmative nods and appropriate facial gestures
D. All of these

Q.138 According to "Expectancy Theory", the probability of an individual acting in a particular way depends on:-

A. The personality of the individual and the likelihood that it will change.
B. The strength of that individual's belief that the act will have a particular outcome and on whether the individual values that outcome.
C. The company and it's potential to move in the right direction
D. None of these

Q.139 Corporations such as Citigroup, American Express and Fidelity are classified as:-

A. financial services corporations
B. common service corporations
C. preferred service corporations
D. commercial service corporations

Q.140 Financial corporations which serve individual savers and commercial mortgage borrowers are classified as:-

A. savings associations
B. loans associations
C. preferred and common associations
D. savings and loans associations

Q.141 A regulatory body which licenses brokers and oversees traders is classified as:

A. international firm of auction system
B. international association of network dealers
C. national firm of equity dealers
D. national association of securities dealers

Q.142 The Gantt Chart (invented by Henry L. Gantt), still used today in the production planning area of many organizations was the first simple visual device to maintain production control. It is essentially a bar graph with

A. Time on the horizontal axis; the activities to be scheduled on the vertical axis
B. Time on the vertical axis; project completion on the horizontal axis
C. Time on the horizontal axis; project completion on the vertical axis
D. Time on the vertical axis; the activities to be scheduled on the horizontal axis

Q.143 Controls can be classified based on timing or stage in the production process. Which of the following statements is not true about the various types of controls?

A. Steering controls are used following completion of activity
B. Preventive controls are used prior to the start of activity and feedback controls follow completion of activity
C. Concurrent controls are used during the performance of activity and feedforward controls prior to start of activity
D. Quality control tests of output are an example of concurrent control

Q.144 Which of the following arguments against a firm being socially responsible indicates the belief that businesses are being socially responsible when they attend only to economic interests?

A. Too much power
B. Violation of profit maximization
C. Excessive costs
D. Lack of social skills

Q.145 Practicing ethical guidelines enables managers to become followers of moral management approach. They facilitate ethical business decisions. Which of the following is not an ethical guideline for managers?

A. Upholding human dignity
B. Obeying the law
C. Non-allowance for participation of stakeholders in the decision-making process
D. Primum Non-Nocere

Q.146 The most general form of standing plans that specifies the broad parameters within which organization members are expected to operate in pursuit of organizational goals are called

A. Procedures
B. Programmes
C. Single-use plans
D. Policie

Q.147 Programmes and budgets are examples of:

A. Single-use plans
B. Standing rules
C. Procedures
D. Gantt chart components

Q.148 Management by Objectives (MBO) is a joint setting of goals and objectives by superiors and subordinates. If you were responsible for setting up an MBO program, which of the following steps would you need to complete before the others?

A. Establish specific goals for various departments, subunits and individuals
B. Formulate action plans
C. Clarify organizational roles
D. Implement and maintain self-control

Q.149 Which of the following is not true regarding programmed decisions?

A. They are made in well-structured situations
B. They are based on established policies and procedures
C. They require managers to exercise discretion
D. They are made mostly by lower-level managers

Q.150 Direct control is the control that is exercised after the deviations from plans have occurred. Which of the following is not the underlying assumption of direct control?

A. Performance can be measured
B. Personal responsibility is absent
C. The time expenditure is warranted
D. Mistakes can be discovered in time

// Smart Answer Sheet //

Correct Percentage of students who answered correctly.   **Skipped** Percentage of students who skipped.

Q.	Ans.	Correct / Skipped	Q.	Ans.	Correct / Skipped	Q.	Ans.	Correct / Skipped	Q.	Ans.	Correct / Skipped	Q.	Ans.	Correct / Skipped
1	C	50.0 % / 2.94 %	17	C	35.29 % / 35.3 %	33	A	17.65 % / 38.23 %	49	D	47.06 % / 35.29 %	65	B	20.59 % / 23.53 %
2	A	23.53 % / 29.41 %	18	B	47.06 % / 35.29 %	34	D	44.12 % / 38.23 %	50	C	26.47 % / 35.29 %	66	B	41.18 % / 23.53 %
3	C	47.06 % / 38.23 %	19	C	32.35 % / 35.3 %	35	D	26.47 % / 38.24 %	51	C	44.12 % / 11.76 %	67	B	26.47 % / 23.53 %
4	A	58.82 % / 35.3 %	20	A	61.76 % / 35.3 %	36	C	32.35 % / 38.24 %	52	B	26.47 % / 20.59 %	68	A	41.18 % / 23.53 %
5	B	32.35 % / 35.3 %	21	B	20.59 % / 35.29 %	37	B	23.53 % / 35.29 %	53	A	26.47 % / 23.53 %	69	B	44.12 % / 23.53 %
6	D	44.12 % / 35.29 %	22	B	35.29 % / 35.3 %	38	D	8.82 % / 35.3 %	54	B	29.41 % / 23.53 %	70	A	20.59 % / 26.47 %
7	C	17.65 % / 32.35 %	23	D	47.06 % / 35.29 %	39	B	32.35 % / 35.3 %	55	C	26.47 % / 23.53 %	71	A	23.53 % / 23.53 %
8	A	58.82 % / 35.3 %	24	D	20.59 % / 35.29 %	40	D	17.65 % / 35.29 %	56	A	44.12 % / 23.53 %	72	A	17.65 % / 26.47 %
9	B	64.71 % / 35.29 %	25	B	50.0 % / 35.29 %	41	B	52.94 % / 35.3 %	57	D	32.35 % / 23.53 %	73	B	23.53 % / 23.53 %
10	D	41.18 % / 35.29 %	26	B	55.88 % / 35.3 %	42	B	38.24 % / 35.29 %	58	B	41.18 % / 23.53 %	74	A	38.24 % / 26.47 %
11	B	52.94 % / 35.3 %	27	C	17.65 % / 35.29 %	43	A	47.06 % / 35.29 %	59	D	29.41 % / 23.53 %	75	A	29.41 % / 23.53 %
12	D	38.24 % / 35.29 %	28	D	17.65 % / 38.23 %	44	A	29.41 % / 38.24 %	60	A	35.29 % / 23.53 %	76	B	29.41 % / 29.41 %
13	A	32.35 % / 35.3 %	29	B	29.41 % / 38.24 %	45	D	26.47 % / 35.29 %	61	B	35.29 % / 23.53 %	77	A	55.88 % / 26.47 %
14	B	41.18 % / 35.29 %	30	A	38.24 % / 35.29 %	46	B	52.94 % / 35.3 %	62	B	41.18 % / 26.47 %	78	B	50.0 % / 23.53 %
15	D	44.12 % / 35.29 %	31	B	52.94 % / 35.3 %	47	A	52.94 % / 35.3 %	63	A	29.41 % / 23.53 %	79	C	17.65 % / 23.53 %
16	A	38.24 % / 35.29 %	32	C	52.94 % / 35.3 %	48	A	35.29 % / 35.3 %	64	C	11.76 % / 23.53 %	80	B	44.12 % / 23.53 %

Q.	Ans.	Correct / Skipped	Q.	Ans.	Correct / Skipped	Q.	Ans.	Correct / Skipped	Q.	Ans.	Correct / Skipped	Q.	Ans.	Correct / Skipped
81	A	44.12 % / 23.53 %	95	A	20.59 % / 23.53 %	109	B	52.94 % / 23.53 %	123	D	11.76 % / 26.48 %	137	D	38.24 % / 23.52 %
82	A	55.88 % / 23.53 %	96	B	41.18 % / 26.47 %	110	C	14.71 % / 29.41 %	124	C	29.41 % / 26.47 %	138	B	55.88 % / 23.53 %
83	B	52.94 % / 23.53 %	97	C	32.35 % / 23.53 %	111	D	50.0 % / 23.53 %	125	C	47.06 % / 23.53 %	139	A	38.24 % / 26.47 %
84	B	26.47 % / 26.47 %	98	B	44.12 % / 23.53 %	112	D	41.18 % / 23.53 %	126	D	29.41 % / 23.53 %	140	D	23.53 % / 26.47 %
85	D	23.53 % / 23.53 %	99	A	29.41 % / 23.53 %	113	D	35.29 % / 23.53 %	127	D	14.71 % / 23.53 %	141	D	35.29 % / 23.53 %
86	B	58.82 % / 23.53 %	100	B	38.24 % / 26.47 %	114	C	29.41 % / 23.53 %	128	C	17.65 % / 23.53 %	142	A	23.53 % / 26.47 %
87	B	44.12 % / 23.53 %	101	C	35.29 % / 23.53 %	115	C	20.59 % / 23.53 %	129	A	11.76 % / 23.53 %	143	A	32.35 % / 26.47 %
88	C	29.41 % / 23.53 %	102	A	38.24 % / 23.52 %	116	C	44.12 % / 23.53 %	130	D	47.06 % / 23.53 %	144	B	47.06 % / 26.47 %
89	A	44.12 % / 23.53 %	103	C	11.76 % / 23.53 %	117	C	47.06 % / 23.53 %	131	B	35.29 % / 23.53 %	145	C	41.18 % / 26.47 %
90	C	20.59 % / 23.53 %	104	C	47.06 % / 26.47 %	118	B	47.06 % / 23.53 %	132	D	41.18 % / 23.53 %	146	D	26.47 % / 26.47 %
91	D	11.76 % / 26.48 %	105	A	23.53 % / 26.47 %	119	D	52.94 % / 23.53 %	133	C	26.47 % / 23.53 %	147	A	26.47 % / 26.47 %
92	B	67.65 % / 23.53 %	106	D	41.18 % / 23.53 %	120	B	58.82 % / 23.53 %	134	D	58.82 % / 23.53 %	148	C	17.65 % / 26.47 %
93	A	50.0 % / 23.53 %	107	A	14.71 % / 23.53 %	121	B	38.24 % / 23.52 %	135	D	17.65 % / 23.53 %	149	C	14.71 % / 26.47 %
94	D	11.76 % / 23.53 %	108	D	14.71 % / 26.47 %	122	C	23.53 % / 23.53 %	136	D	32.35 % / 23.53 %	150	B	52.94 % / 26.47 %

//Hints and Solutions//

1. The linear model of communication is considered as a one-way process in which sender sends a message to the receiver but at that time receiver is not present to give feedback or any type of response.

Horizontal model of communication is the communication in which information is delivered to the people working at the same level of an organisational hierarchy.

Transactional model of communication is the communication in which the information is exchanged between the sender and receiver where each sender/receiver takes turn to send/receive the message.

Interactional model of communication is the communication where information is exchanged both ways between sender and receiver.

So, option C is correct option.

2. Answer: Option A

An individual stock required return is equal to risk free rate plus bearing risk premium is an explanation of security market line. The security market line (SML) is a line drawn on a chart that serves as a graphical representation of the capital asset pricing model (CAPM), which shows different levels of systematic, or market, risk of various marketable securities plotted against the expected return of the entire market at a given point in time.

3. Synchronous media takes place in real time and the audience is present when media is broadcasted or performed. This media helps to share the information at the same time i.e. information broadcasting and the audience is present at the same time to receive the information.

Example: Video conferencing.

The definition of synchronous is something that happens at the same time or has consistent timing between each occurrence. An example of something synchronous is swimmers that all start at the same sound. An example of something synchronous is the timing of the action for parts of your car's engine.

So, option C is the correct option.

4. Intrapersonal communication is a communication that takes place within an individual, including talking to oneself.

Mass communication is a communication that uses mechanical devices that multiply messages and take them to a large number of people simultaneously.

Interpersonal communication is a face to face communication between two persons.

Group communication is the communication where more than two individuals are involved in the exchange of ideas, skills and interests.

So, option A is the correct option.

5. Physiological barriers to communication are related to the limitations of the human body and the human mind. These barriers include poor listening skills, information overload, inattention, emotions, poor retention etc.

So, option B is the correct option.

6. Stream, Rivulet and River are all water bodies whereas Valley is a low area between hills or mountains. Thus, Valley is the odd word. So, option D is the right answer.

7. Answer: B

It is a simple division series in which each number is one-half of the previous number. We can also say that each number is divided by 2 to arrive at the next number;

On dividing 48 by 2, we get 24

On dividing 24 by 2, we get 12

So, on dividing 12 by 2, we will get 6 (option B).

8. The series consists of letters in reverse alphabetical order. Therefore, the missing letters are LKJ.

9. A kilogram measures weight and the other units are used to measure length.

10. Infection occurs first, then one visits a doctor, and after consultation, the doctor starts the treatment which is followed by recovery.

11. As per the last line of the passage, "There are times when even you are called upon to be business-like, brief, and effective on the telephone". We can say that the correct answer is option B.

12. The answer lies in the following lines of the passage, "Perhaps we don't consider our telephone conversation an interruption because we don't see what we have interrupted". So, option D is correct.

13. As given in the last line of the passage, "There are times when even you are called upon to be business-like, brief, and effective on the telephone." So, option A is the correct option.

14. Option A is incorrect as given in the following line of the passage, "We can tell that a person is in a hurry to get somewhere, or he is doing something, and we know enough not to interrupt him for any length of time".

Option B is correct as given in the above-mentioned lines.

Option C is incorrect as given in the following lines, "Yet some of us think nothing of calling someone on the telephone, interrupting him without a thought about what he may be doing, and chattering away, forgetting about time or anything else".

Option D is incorrect as it is suggested in the passage that we should not interrupt anyone just like that.

15. The answer lies in the following line of the passage, "It is not good manners to stop a person on the street or in a shop, or in the performance of any duty and to talk to him for ten, fifteen or twenty minutes just to pass the time of day". So, option D is the correct option.

16. Intranet

The number of users in Intranet is limited.

Intranet is safer than the Internet.

Intranet uses internet protocols such as TCP/IP and FTP.

Internet

Internet is a wide network of computers & open to all.

So, (i), (ii) & (iii) are true.

So, option A is correct.

17. Digitizer- It converts the analog data into digital form.

Optical Mark Reader- This device reads the marks made in on paper forms as responses to questions or tick list prompts by a pencil/pen.

Optical Character Recognition- It is the mechanical/electronic conversion of images of handwritten, typed, or printed text into machine-encoded text.

Bar Code Reader- It can read and output printed barcodes to a computer.

So, option C is the correct option.

18. E-Kalpa: It includes courses based on Design.

E-Yantra: Initiative has been implemented by MHRD under NMEICT Programme to incorporate Robotics into engineering education.

E-Shodh Sindhu: International e-journal and e-books are made available to all the higher educational institutions through this programme.

E-Archaya: It is the official repository of NMEICT e-content and all content produced under NMEICT.

So, option B is the correct option.

19. Bitmap image is stored as a series of tiny dots which are known as pixels. Each pixel is a very small square that is assigned a specific colour, and then these are arranged in a pattern to form the image. The file extension is .bmp.

So, option C is the correct option.

20. The Hypertext Transfer Protocol (HTTP) is an application protocol for distributed, collaborative, hypermedia information systems. HTTP stands for Hypertext Transfer Protocol, and is an application layer protocol. In simpler terms, it is the protocol over which information is sent from a user's web browser to the website they are visiting.

Note:- HTTP is the foundation of data communication for the World Wide Web. Hypertext is structured text that uses logical links (hyperlinks) between nodes containing text.

21. Smog and soot are the two kinds of air pollution.

Smog or ground-level ozone occurs when fossil fuels react with sunlight.

Soot or particulate matter is made up of tiny particles of chemicals, soil, dust, or allergens, in the form of gas or solids.

So, the only statement I is true.

So, option B is the correct option.

22. As a part of 'Go Green Initiative', Indian Railways has planned to set up a solar power plant of 1000 MW by 2020-21. The initiative will help Indian Railways to generate about 10 percent of its electrical energy from the renewable source. As of now, 71.19 MW of solar plants have already been installed over rooftops at service buildings and railways stations.

23. The Deccan Thorn Forests cover the arid region extending across Maharashtra, Tamil Nadu, Andhra Pradesh, Karnataka and Telangana.

24. There are 17 Sustainable Development Goals listed by the United Nations. Here is the list:

No Poverty, Zero Hunger, Good Health and Well-being, Quality Education, Responsible Consumption and Production Industry, Innovation and Infrastructure, Reduced Inequality, Sustainable Cities and Communities, , Climate Action, Life Below Water, Life on Land, Peace and Justice Strong Institutions, Partnerships to achieve the Goal, Gender Equality, Clean Water and Sanitation, Affordable and Clean Energy, Decent Work and Economic Growth.

So, option D is the correct answer.

25. From statements I and II, we conclude that out of 30 students 10 students scored less than Geeta. It means, 19 students scored more than Geeta. So, Geeta's rank in the class is 20th. Thus, both the statements are needed to answer the question.

26. Answer: B

Each letter in the word NOIDA is moved one step forward to form the code OPJEB. So, in DELHI, D will be coded as E, E as F, L as M, H as I, I as J. Thus, the code becomes EFMIJ.

27. The provided statement is a premise. Premise is a statement of fact which is supposed to set forth the reasons for believing a claim.

Assumption refers to something that is accepted as truth without question or proof.

Conclusion refers to a judgement or decision reached at the end by reasoning.

28. Hetvabhasa, means that a Hetu (reason) which appears to be real or appropriate but in fact is not. According to the Nyaya Sutra, there are five kinds of hetvbahasa:

    Savyabhichara (anaikanita),

    Badhita,

    Asidha

    Viruddha

    Prakaranasama

So, option D is the correct option.

29.

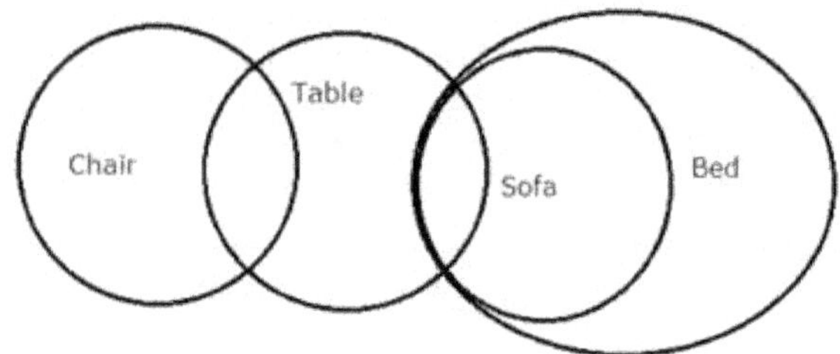

(i) Some beds are chairs does not follow as there is no direct relation between bed and chair.

(ii) Some tables are beds follows as from the diagram some part of the tables lies in bed.

(iii) Some sofas are chairs does not follow as there is no direct relation between sofa and chair.

(iv) All beds are sofas does not follow as some bed are sofa are true but not all.

Therefore, only conclusion 2 follows.

So, option B is the correct option.

30. A deductive argument: is an argument in which it is believed that the premises provide a guarantee of the truth of the conclusion.

A deductive argument is said to be sound if and only if the argument is both valid and all the premises are true.

Therefore, (i) and (ii) is correct.

So, option A is the correct option.

31. Required percentage increase

= (225 - 50)/50 * 100

= 350%

32. Answer: Option C

Required percent = 200/100 * 100

= 200%

33. Answer: Option A

The growth is most remarkable after the year 1997.

34. Answer: Option D

Average = (50 + 75 + 70 + 100 + 200 + 200 + 225)/7

= 130

35. Percentage increase from the previous year.

1994	1995	1996	1997	1998	1999
50%	NA	42.85	102%	0%	12.50%

36. Intervening variable: these are variables through which one variable affects another variable.

Independent variable: is presumed to be the cause of another variable.

Extraneous variable: There can be many factors or variables that may affect the outcome. They actually compete with the independent variable in explaining the outcome. So, they could affect the result of the experiment.

So, option C is the correct option.

37. The 20th century marked the shift from positivism to post-positivism. A post-positivist considers that the way scientist explore the everyday phenomenon is same as how we think about our everyday life. There is no difference between the two, but they are only a different in degree. Scientific reasoning is exactly same as common sense reasoning. However, positivism regards scientific knowledge as a thing par excellence.

So, option B is the correct option.

38. These are the main terms used in the context of footnotes and reference writing.

Ibid refers to the same author and source in the immediately preceding reference.

Op.cit refers to the reference listed earlier by the same author.

Loc.cit is a footnote or endnote term used to repeat the title and page number for a given work.

Et al. is used when referring to a number of people.

So, option D is the correct option.

39. Experimental research is conducted to study the cause and effect relationship of different phenomenon.

This involves manipulation of one or more variable to observe the change in effect. Correlation is the mutual relationship between the variables.

In experimental research, the magnitude of the correlation yields good results.

So, a, b, c is correct.

And, Option B is the correct answer.

40. Ethnography is a systematic study of people and culture.

It requires the researcher to immerse into the lives of individuals being studied, which is called Participant Observation.

Ethnographic studies are extremely important for a qualitative researcher for a detailed study of the cultural phenomenon.

The method was first introduced to the discipline of anthropology but later on, become popular in social sciences as well.

Ethnography is a holistic study.

So, a, b and e are true about ethnography.

So, option D is the correct option.

41. MHRD works through two departments:

Department of school education & literacy and Department of Higher Education.

While the Department of School Education and Literacy is in charge of improvement of school training and proficiency in the nation.

Department of Higher Education deals with what is one of the biggest Higher Education frameworks of the world, soon after the United States and China.

So, (a) & (c) are true.

So, option B is the correct option.

42. UGC (University Grants Commission) was established in the year 1956 as a statutory body through the Parliament Act for coordinating and maintaining the higher education standards in India.

AICTE (All India Council for Technical Education) was established in the year 1945 as an advisory body & as a statutory body through the Parliament Act for planning and development of technical education in India.

NCTE (National Council for Teacher Education) was established in the year 1995 to undertake and maintain the procedures and processes in the Indian Education System.

NAAC (National Assessment and Accreditation Council) was established in the year 1994 with the motive to evaluate the performances of universities and colleges in India.

43. International Literacy Day. 8 September. International Literacy Day, celebrated annually on 8 September, is an opportunity for Governments, civil society and stakeholders to highlight improvements in world literacy rates, and reflect on the world's remaining literacy challenges.

44. Answer: Option A

Since one-half of the four children are girls, two must be boys. It is not clear which children have blue or brown eyes.

45. Answer: Option D

None of the three statements is supported by the known facts.

46. May 21, the death anniversary of ex-prime minister of India, Shri Rajiv Gandhi is also observed as Anti-Terrorism Day in India.

47. Answer: Option A

This series consists of letters in a reverse alphabetical order.

48. Effective teaching can take place outside the classroom also. It is not important that learning and teaching can take place in classrooms only.

So, Classroom teaching is the most effective method of teaching is not correct.

Correct statements:

1. Teaching is a comprehensive process.

2. Teaching can be made effective by making use of teaching aids.

3. Teaching requires expertise and experience.

49. A good assessment process helps the learners to know their achievements, motivates them to do better and take corrective

measures by learners as well as teachers. So, option D is the correct option.

50. In Reflective level of teaching, the student understands the situation and uses his critical abilities to solve the problem. So, only (i) is correct about the Reflective level of teaching.

The teacher presents the subject matter before the students in a sequential and organized form, the teacher explains the student about the relationship between principles and facts and teaches them how these principles can be applied, and teaching is subject centred are the features of an Understanding level of teaching.

So, all (ii), (iii) & (iv) are incorrect with respect to Reflective level of teaching.

Therefore, option C is the correct option.

51. Samuelson's Revealed Preference Theory (1938) is also called the Behaviouristic ordinal utility theory. This theory is based on the concept of ordinal utility (preference) and explains consumer's demand from his market behaviour through price line and indifference curve.

Thus, Option C is correct.

52. ● Data warehouses and data marts are optimised for Online Analytical Processing(OLAP).

● OLTP(Online Transaction Processing) systems are designed to manage transaction data which are volatile and optimise transaction processing efficiency. DBMSs are referred to as OLTP systems.

Thus, Option B is correct.

53. Stagflation is called 'INFLATIONARY RECESSION'. It is characterised by high unemployment levels, high level of inflation and low output.

Thus, Option A is correct.

54. Under Options trading, clearing house acts as the counterparty. If the Option holder exercises his option, the clearing house chooses a writer randomly and the latter will be obliged to sell or buy the shares. The Option holder also has an alternate choice. He could execute the contract by selling the underlying asset to an outsider.

Thus, Option B is correct.

55. Diversity Sensitivity helps keep the employees sensitive towards different cultures. This will also help to maintain healthy communications and relationships in the workplace.

Thus, Option C is correct.

56. ● HRD Climate is concerned with an organization's internal environment, distinguishing it from other organizations.

● It results from the behaviour of members of the organizations including the ones in top management.

● It is perceived by the members of the organizations and looks into interpreting situations.

● It acts as pressure for the activities that are to be carried out inside organizations.

Thus, Option A is correct.

57. One-tailed tests use only $>.<$ signs to depict the null and alternative hypothesis.

signs like $\neq$, = are used under two-tailed tests.
Thus, Option D is correct.

58. SWIFT is the acronym for Society for Worldwide Interbank Financial Telecommunication, founded in Belgium in 1973. It is an international telecommunication network used by financial institutions to quickly and securely exchange information all over the world.

Thus, Option B is correct.

59. ● SCM is the operational framework within which logistics is performed. It is the effort of number of organizations working together as a supply chain that helps manage the flow of materials and ensure the finished goods provide value (customer satisfaction)

● The main function of Logistics is to make the goods & services available to the customer at a place where there is demand for the product.

● The major functions involved in SCM are the procurement of raw materials, product development, marketing, operations, distribution, finance and customer services.

Thus, Option D is correct.

60. ● Industrial Relations do not function in vacuum but are multi-dimensional in nature, and they are conditioned by two sets of determinants. The institutional factors and economic factors.

● The institutional factors of Industrial relations include matters such as state policy, labour legislation, social institutions, attitudes of work, system of power and status etc.

● The economic factors of Industrial relations include economic organizations, capital structure, technology, nature and composition of labour force and sources of supply and demand in the labour market.

Thus, Option A is correct.

61. - Normal distribution is a symmetrical distribution and for any symmetrical distribution mean, mode
and median are equal and all odd-order moments vanish.

● $M.D. = (4/s)\sigma$ and $Q.D. = (2/3)\sigma$

- The linear combination of independent normal variates is also a normal variate.
Thus, Option B is correct.

62. Black Box Model propounded by Michael Porter helps in identifying the stimuli which is responsible for the buying behaviour of the customer.

It has been divided into two parts-

● First, the buyer's characteristics influence how he or she perceives and reacts to the stimuli

● Second, the buyer's decision process itself affects the buyer's behaviour

Thus, Option B is correct.

63. According to mercantilists, the aim of foreign trade is to have surplus in BOP, and the nation's wealth depends upon the accumulated treasure, that is, gold and silver are currency of the trade.

Thus, Option A is correct.

64. ● Competency mapping is identifying key competencies for a job and incorporating them via different processes.

● A competency is defined as behaviour like communication rather than a skill or ability.

Thus, Option C is correct

65. Different areas of McKinsey Framework are associated to solve different issues of the firm. Following are the parts of Staff -

● Are there any gaps between the required competencies?

● What positions will be represented in the team?

● What positions need to be filled?

Thus, Option B is correct.

66. While calculating the amount of bad debts, the reserve for discount should be first deducted from the debtors. Thus, the equation for bad debts will be (20000-2000)* 5% =900.The amount of debtors = 18000-900=17100.

Thus, Option B is correct.

67. ● Whistleblower is an individual who reveals private information about an organization, usually related to wrongdoing or misconduct. It covers both governmental mismanagement and activities of public or private organizations.

● Whistleblower-protection acts generally provide adequate protection to whistleblowers because retaliatory behaviour may be successfully disguised as something else and may backfire for the whistle-blower.

Thus, Option B is correct.

68. Central bank utilizes its domestic and foreign currency reserves to buy and sell foreign currencies in the foreign exchange market. Monetary policy works on the basis of reserves and affects exchange rates indirectly.

Thus, Option A is correct.

69. Coefficient of Variation = [Standard Deviation/Mean]100

=[4.8 / 120] 100

= 4%

Thus, Option B is correct.

70. ● WTO is a permanent institution, unlike GATT, which was a set of rules and multilateral agreements applied on a provisional basis.

● Rules and regulations of WTO are applied on a full and permanent basis. Member institutions have to follow the rules and measures taken by the WTO to promote international trade.

Thus, Option A is correct.

71. Functional managers may work in different areas within an organisation, regardless of their level of management. Functional managers are Financial managers, Human Resource Managers and Administrative managers.

Thus, Option A is correct.

72. ● Stress-related hazards at work fall into two categories: work contents and work context.

● Work contents include job content, workload, work pace, working hours, control etc.

● Work context includes status and pay, work-life balance, role in the organization, culture in the organization etc.

Thus, Option A is correct.

73. There are four phases in a customer life cycle in CRM, which are:

● Marketing: It is the first phase of the customer life cycle wherein messages are sent to target markets to attract prospective customers.

● Customer Acquisition: This step deals with converting prospects into customers.

● Relationship management: In this step, a relationship is formed between the company and the customer and resell processes increase the value of existing customers.

● Loss/Churn: The last step concerns the inevitable loss of customers that happen to a company. The company should decide on the valuable lost customers and should try to win them back.

Thus, Option B is correct.

74. Depreciation is treated as an expense and is secured from profits in Profit and loss account. However, it does not involve actual cash expense, i.e. it is a non-cash expense and has to be adjusted in cash flow statement by adding it back to the profits in order to ascertain the exact cash position of the firm. All this implies that Depreciation is a non-cash expense and does not decrease the cash flow/reserves.

Thus, Option A is correct.

75. ● Lord Path Matrix method aims at reducing transportation of in-process inventory from one section to another.

● Travel charts help in deciding the position of one departement from another. It improves the existing plant layout.

● Process flow charts show how parts assemble to form sub-assemblies and sub-assemblies assemble to form assemblies.

● Correlation chart involves a grid of rows showing alternative solutions.

Thus, Option A is correct.

76. ● Data entity is anything real or abstract about which a company wants to collect and store data. Master data entities are the main entities of a company, such as customers, suppliers, employees and assets.

● Data silos are information systems that do not have the capability to exchange data with other Information systems.

Thus, Option B is correct.

77. ● Group dynamics is basically the interaction of group members in social situations.

● Group dynamics include democratic leadership, cooperation and participation.

● Group dynamics is viewed from the internal nature of groups, their structure and processes, and it does affect individual behaviour of members.

Thus, Option A is correct.

78. ● The strategic management model developed by Dan Schendel and Charles Hofer consists of the following steps:

○ Goal formulation

○ Environmental analysis

○ Strategy formulation

○ Strategy evaluation

○ Strategy implementation, and

○ Strategic control

● They emphasised on three sub-processes such as environment analysis, resource analysis and value analysis in the formulation of strategies.

Thus, Option B is correct.

79. Under share repurchase, cash flows out to the extent of the market value of share repurchased and PE decreases.

Thus, Option C is correct.organization, particularly when the objectives need to be changed.

80. ● Marketing mix could be tailored as and when required according to the geographical requirements.

● Tailoring in marketing mix results in higher costs but generally offset via profits made later.

● Specialization is one name that can be given to tailoring of marketing mix in international marketing.

● Any change in marketing mix is done according to the local marketing environment and customers specifically.

Thus, Option B is correct.

81. According to Modigliani and Miller theory, under a perfect market situation, the dividend policy of a firm does not affect the value of the firm and hence is irrelevant. Because the value of the firm depends on the firm's earnings and the firm's earnings are influenced by its investment policy.

Thus, Option A is correct.

82. According to the principle of unity of command, one subordinate should be accountable to only one superior. If this principle is violated it may create confusion and arise conflicts in the organisation.

Thus, Option A is correct.

83. • Unlike a Capitalistic economy, there is not a complete absence of a central economic plan in a mixed economy. The government interferes in areas which need regulation and for implementing policies for social welfare to ensure smooth functioning of the economy.

• In the private sector Price mechanism (market forces of demand and supply) fixes the price of goods and services.

• Whereas in the public sector, government regulation is there, and administrative pricing structure is used for government goods.

Thus, Option B is correct.

84. There are Kanter's 10 rules for stifling innovation, which are as follows:

• Regard any new ideas from below with suspicion.

• People who need your approval to act should go through various levels of management to get signatures.

• Ask departments and individuals to criticize each other.

• Withhold your praise and express your criticism.

• Treat identification of problems as signs of failure.

• Control everything carefully.

• Make decisions to change policies in secret.

• Make sure that requests for permission are fully justified.

• Lower level managers to cut back, lay off, move people to make them do work quickly.

• The higher ups or top management know everything.

Thus, Option B is correct.

85. • Porter's Five Force model includes Threat of new entrants, Power of Suppliers, Power of Buyers, Rivalry among Competitors and Threat of Substitution.

• Under the threat of new entrants, the easier it is for new companies to enter the industry, the more intense the competition will be. The factors that block or limit the threat of new entrants are known as Barriers to entry.

• The major barriers are the loyalty of customers to major brands, capital requirements, high fixed costs, scarcity of resources etc.

Thus, Option D is correct.

86. Conceptual Skills are the skills that represent persons' ability to provide solutions to complex situations. These skills are required at a higher level of management.

Thus, Option B is correct.

87. • The marketing environment consists of a task and a broad environment.

• Out of these, the task environment includes the immediate factors of producing, distributing and promoting the offering.

• The main factors involved are suppliers, distributors, dealers and target customers.

Thus, Option B is correct.

88. • Correlation analysis is used when a relationship is found between sales and other factors like income, expenditure etc.

• It is reliable when a causal relationship has to be established between variables and sales. It is used to develop demand functions for a number of products.

Thus, Option C is correct.

89. - The geometric mean becomes zero when one of the items is zero.

- The geometric mean of a set of n observations is the nth root of their product. $G = (x_1 x_2 \ldots x_n)^{\frac{1}{n}}$

In this, if one of the items is zero is that $x_i = 0$ for any is $1, \ldots n,$ then G becomes zero.

Thus, Option A is correct.

90. HRP is a continuous process and follows a clear stepwise method, which is as follows:

1. Objectives of HRP

2. Current Human Resource Inventory

3. Work-Study and Demand forecasting

4. Determine Job requirements

5. Recruitment plan

6. Selection procedure

7. Training & Development

8. Appraisal of HRP

Thus, Option C is correct.

91. • Financial Break-Even Point may be defined as that level of EBIT, which is just equal to pay the total financial charges, i.e., Interest and Preference dividend. At this point of earnings before interest and tax, the EPS equals Zero.

• Point of Indifference or Equivalence point refers to that EBIT level at which EPS remains the same irrespective of different alternatives of debt-equity mix.

Thus, Option D is correct.

92. Three kinds of management skills:

• Technical Skills- Person's knowledge and proficiency in any technique.

• Interpersonal Skills- Person's ability to interact and communicate effectively with people.

• Conceptual Skills-Person's ability to provide solutions to complex situations

Thus, Option B is correct.

93. • The use of long term fixed interest-bearing debt and preference share capital along with equity share capital is called financial leverage or trading on equity.

• A firm is known to have favourable leverage if its earnings are more than what debt would cost. If it doesn't earn as much as the debt costs then it will be known as unfavourable leverage.

Thus, Option A is correct.

94. • Rebate amount does not affect the original invoice because the adjustment is made post-sale.

• Trade Discount, on the other hand, is reduced from the original value before the invoice is generated.

Thus, Option D is correct.

95. Entry of new firms in a monopolistic market will result in a downward shift in the firm's individual demand curve. The supply will be divided among more sellers, and hence the factor prices will go up, that is, an upward shift in the cost curve. This adjustment squeezes out the supernormal profits. Thus, a monopolistic firm, in the long run, earns normal profit.

Thus, Option A is correct.

96.

Umbrella effect, also known as price umbrella, concerns with price set by dominant firms, and smaller competing firms can attract buyers only by lowering its price.

Thus, Option B is correct.

97. RADAR stands for Results, Approaches, Deploy, Assess and Refine. It is a significant managerial tool that provides a structured method of questioning the performance of the organisation.

Thus, Option C is correct.

98. • Keller's Brand Equity Model is also known as the Customer-Based Brand Equity Model.

• Concept behind the model is in order to build a strong brand; you must shape how customers think and feel about your product.

• The model illustrates four steps that are needed to be followed in order to build strong brand equity.

• The 4 steps follow the sequence: Identity, meaning, response, relationships.

Thus, Option B is correct.

99. • The rate variance is also known as price variance. The price variance is computed by deducting the actual price from the standard price and multiplying the amount by actual quantity.

• When we want the volume variance that is the usage, we deduct the actual quantity from the standard quantity and multiply the amount by actual price.

Thus, Option A is correct.

100. • Greenfield and brownfield investments are two types of foreign direct investment.

• In greenfield investment, a company will build its own brand new facilities from scratch and in Brownfield investment, company purchases or leases an existing facility.

• Both are a type of foreign direct investment and involves companies and production facilities in different countries

Thus, Option B is correct.

101. The question "in which environment – internal or external – will our plans operate" is asked in the stage/step when an organization is considering planning premises.

102. The puspose of the corporate level strategy is to identify the busines areas in which an organization will carry out its operations. Therefore, the corporate level strategy would be appropriate to address the questions facing Ms. Pathak

103. Middle-level managers deal with the actual operation of the organization's units. Hence, option C is correct.

104. Statements (I) and (II) are objectives of sensitivity training. Sensitivity training involves training in small groups in which people develop a sensitive awareness and understanding of themselves and of their relationships with others. Statement (III) is an objective of university management programs.

105. Answer: Option A

Growth in earnings per share is primarily resultant of growth in dividends. Earnings per share growth is defined as the percentage change in normalised earnings per share over the previous 12 month period to the latest year end. It gives a good picture of the rate at which a company has grown its profitability.

106. The just-in-time (JIT) inventory system is a management strategy that aligns raw-material orders from suppliers directly with production schedules. Companies employ this inventory strategy to increase efficiency and decrease waste by receiving goods only as they need them for the production process, which reduces inventory costs. This method requires producers to forecast demand accurately. One example of a JIT inventory system is a car manufacturer that operates with low inventory levels but heavily relies on its supply chain to deliver the parts it requires to build cars, on an as-needed basis. Consequently, the manufacturer orders the parts required to assemble the cars, only after an order is received.

107. The activity ratio tests the relationship between the sales and the various assets of a firm. Hence, option A is correct.

108. Kavita Ramakrishnan is using Vroom and Yetton's Normative Decision Model. In this model, the degree of participation of employees in the decision making process is important. Also the acceptance of the decision by subordinates is important.

109. The bargaining power of buyers is high when their purchases form a large chunk of the sellers' total sales. The remaining options are factors that make buying power of suppliers high. Hence, option (b) is the answer.

110. Loss of **five** volumes per one thousand volumes of books issued/consulted in a year may be taken as reasonable, provided such losses are not attributable to dishonesty or negligence.

111. The major difference in skill requirements between middle and top managers is that top managers generally require higher level conceptual skills but less technical skills than middle managers. Hence, from above discussion, we can infer that option (d) is correct.

112. The behavioral approach of management thoughts can be classified into:-

· Group influences

· Hawthorne studies.

113. Interpersonal Behavior Approach to management emphasizes managing people by understanding their individual psychological needs. Hence, from above discussion, we can infer that option (d) is correct.

114. Immoral management not only ignores ethical concerns, but also actively opposes ethical behavior. Organizations with immoral maangement are characterized by

· Total concern for company profits only.

· Laws are regarded as hurdles to be removed.

· Strong inclination to minimize expenditures.

Hence, option (c) is the correct answer.

115. Answer: Option C

In expected rate of return for constant growth, capital gains is divided by capital gains yield to calculate beginning price. Beginning market value (BMV) is the valuation at which a property or investment should exchange at the date of origination, and then at the beginning of each subsequent period.

116. Non-allowance for participation of stakeholders in the decision-making process is not an ethical guideline for managers. Hence from above discussion, we can infer that option (c) is correct. Options (a), (b), (d) are all ethical guidelines for managers.

117. Planning can be defined as the process by which managers set missions and objectives, assess the future, and develop courses of action to accomplish these objectives. However, it need not increase the amount of time available for other managerial functions. Hence, from above discussion, we can infer that option (c) is correct. Options (a), (b), (d) are all potential advantages of planning.

118. Strategic plan is used to establish overall objectives for the organization and position the organization in terms of its environment. Facts for strategic planning are generally more difficult to gather than facts for tactical planning. Hence, from above discussion, we can infer that option (b) is correct.

119. Using the BCG matrix requires considering market shares and growth of markets in which products are selling.

120. In the given example P&G uses the differentiation strategy. Hence, option B is correct.

121. Answer: Option B

Stock which has fixed payments and failure of payments which do not lead to bankruptcy is classified as preferred stock. Preferred stock refers to a class of ownership that has a higher claim on assets and earnings than common stock has.

122. Answer: Option C

An efficient market hypothesis states all public information which is reflected in current market prices is classified as semi strong efficiency. The semi-strong form efficiency is a type of efficient market hypothesis (EMH), which holds that security prices adjust quickly to newly available information, thus eliminating the use of fundamental or technical analysis to achieving a higher return.

123. The preference or utility theory is based on the belief that individual attitudes toward risk vary with events, with people and positions.

124. The following statements are characteristics of a closed system :

· It is perfectly deterministic and predictable.

· There is no exchange between the system and the external environment.

125. Descriptions of customer satisfaction with products and services are examples of external information in an organization. Hence from above discussion, we can infer that option (c) is correct. Options (a), (b), (d) are all examples of internal information in an organization.

126. Duplication of activities and resources is a major disadvantage of the divisional structure.

Disadvantages. The divisional structure does have disadvantages, including potentially dispersing technical competence and expertise or fostering unhealthy rivalries among divisions. The divisional structure also may increase costs by requiring functional specialists and better-qualified managers for each division.

127. referent power, hence, option D is correct.

 Power-based upon identification with a person who has desirable resources or personal traits is known as referent power.

128. Incremental model emphasizes short-run solution of a problem rather than long-term goal accomplishment. (a) Rational model is a model of managerial decision-making, which suggests that managers engage in completely rational decision process, ultimately make optimal decisions and process, and understand all information relevant to their decisions at the time they make them. (b) Satisficing model describe the way modern managers must, of necessity, make decisions with incomplete information by choosing from among the few most likely alternatives. (d) Garbage can model is a non-rational model of management decision-making stating that mangers behave in virtually a random pattern in making non-programmed decisions.

129. The Recruitment Procedure consists of the following steps :

· Performing Job Analysis.

· Designing Job Description.

· Developing a Job Specification.

·   Attracting a Pool of Applicants.

·   Selecting Best Recruits.

130. Top 5 Steps Involved in Human Resource Planning Process

Analysis of Organisational Plans and Objectives:

Analysis of Human Resource Planning Objectives:

Forecasting for Human Resource Requirement:

Assessment of Supply of Human Resources:

Matching Demand and Supply:

131. The steps in formulating a career strategy are as follows :

·   Preparation of a personal profile.

·   Development of long-range personal and professional goals.

·   Analysis of the environment.

·   Analysis of Personal Strengths and Weaknesses.

·   Development of Strategic Career Alternatives.

·   Consistency Testing and Strategic Choices.

·   Development of short-range career objectives and action plans.

·   Development of contingency plans.

·   Implementation of the Career Plan.

·   Monitoring Progress.

Hence, from above discussion, we can infer that option (b) is correct.

132. Forces/traits within the manager that determine effective leadership behavior include his/her

·   Values.

·   Confidence in subordinates.

·   Aggressiveness.

133. On-the-Job Training Methods – 6 Most Popular Training Methods: Job Instruction, Coaching, Mentoring, Job Rotation, Apprenticeship, and Committee Assignments

Job Instruction Training (JIT)

Coaching.

Mentoring.

Job Rotation.

Apprenticeship Training.

Committee Assignments.

134. The main Characteristics of human resource planning are as follows:

Future-Oriented.

Continuous Process.

Optimum Utilization Of Human Resources.

Right Kinds And Numbers. ...

Determination Of Demand And Supply.

Environmental Influence.

Related To Corporate Plan.

A Part Of Human Resource Management System.

135. Creativity is the ability to develop new ideas. The creative process comprises four phases: unconscious scanning, intuition, insight, and logical formulation. Intuition connects the unconscious with the conscious, and leads to insight. In the final phase of the creative process, insight is tested against organizational reality.

136. The original path-goal theory identifies achievement-oriented, directive, participative, and supportive leader behaviors: The directive path-goal clarifying leader behavior refers to situations where the leader lets followers know what is expected of them and tells them how to perform their tasks.

137. There are five key active listening techniques you can use to help you become a more effective listener:

Pay Attention. Give the speaker your undivided attention, and acknowledge the message.

Show That You're Listening.

Provide Feedback.

Defer Judgment.

Respond Appropriately.

Exhibiting affirmative nods and appropriate facial gestures.

Hence, option D is correct.

138. According to "expectancy theory", the probability of an individual acting in a particular way depends on the strength of that individual's belief that the act will have a particular outcome and on whether the individual values that outcome. Hence option (b) is the correct answer.

139. Answer: Option A

Corporations such as Citigroup, American Express and Fidelity are classified as financial services corporations. Financial services are the economic services provided by the finance industry, which encompasses a broad range of businesses that manage money, including credit unions, banks, credit-card companies, insurance companies, accountancy companies, consumer-finance companies, stock brokerages, investment funds, individual managers and some government-sponsored enterprises.

140. Answer: Option D

Financial corporations which serve individual savers and commercial mortgage borrowers are classified as savings and loans associations. Financial services are the economic services provided by the finance industry, which encompasses a broad range of businesses that manage money, including credit unions, banks, credit-card companies, insurance companies, accountancy companies, consumer-finance companies, stock brokerages, investment funds, individual managers and some government-sponsored enterprises.

141. Answer: Option D

A regulatory body that licenses brokers and oversees traders is classified as a national association of securities dealers. A regulatory body is like a professional body but it is not a membership organization and its primary activity is to protect the public.

142. A Gantt chart is essentially a bar graph with time on the horizontal axis and the activities to be scheduled on the vertical axis. Hence from above discussion, we can infer that option (a) is correct.

143. Steering controls are used during the performance of activity. So option (a) is the answer.

144. The belief that businesses are being socially responsible when they attend only to economic interests is known as "Violation of profit maximization" argument against a firm being socially responsible. Hence from above discussion, we can infer that option (b) is correct.

145. Non-allowance for participation of stakeholders in the decision-making process is not an ethical guideline for managers. Hence from above discussion, we can infer that option (c) is correct. Options (a), (b), (d) are all ethical guidelines for managers.

146. The most general form of standing plans that specifies the broad parameters within which organization members are expected to operate in pursuit of organizational goals are called policies.

147. Programmes and budgets are examples of single-use plans.

148. MBO (Management By Objectives) is the process of joint setting of goals/objectives by the superior and the subordinate, and clarifying on the objective itself.

The various steps in the MBO Process are:

Develop overall organizational goals.

Clarify organizational roles.

Establish specific goals for various departments, subunits and individuals.

Formulate action plans.

Implement and maintain self-control.

Do periodic review.

Do performance appraisal.

Hence, from above discussion, we can infer that option (c) is correct.

149. Programmed decisions require managers to exercise little discretion

150. The underlying assumptions of direct control are:

Performance can be measured.

Personal responsibility exists.

The time expenditure is warranted.

Mistakes can be discovered in time.

The individual who is responsible will take corrective steps.

Hence, from above discussion, we can infer that option (b) is not the underlying assumption of direct control. Options (a), (c), (d) are all underlying assumptions of direct control.

Paper-I

Q.1 Artifacts that arise and affect the internal validity in research are:

(a) History

(b) Randomisation

(c) Maturity

(d) Instrumentation

(e) Experimental mortality

(f) Matching

A. (a), (b), (c) and (d)   **B.** (a), (c), (d) and (e)

C. (b), (c), (d) and (f)   **D.** (d), (e), (f) and (b)

Q.2 The four major operations in scientific research are:

(a) Demonstration of co-variance

(b) Elimination of spurious relations

(c) Sequencing in terms of time-order

(d) Self-education

(e) Operationalization of personal choice

(f) Theorisation

A. (a), (b), (c) and (f)   **B.** (b), (c), (d) and (e)

C. (a), (b), (c) and (d)   **D.** (c), (d), (e) and (f)

Q.3 Which is the biggest advantage of giving regular homework to students?

A. Students keep busy and away from mischief

B. Students develop the habit of self-study

C. Parents are made aware of what the child is studying

D. Workload of teachers is reduced

Q.4 20th August is celebrated as:

A. Earth Day   **B.** Sadbhavana Divas

C. No Tobacco Day   **D.** None of these

Q.5 A ______________ attempts to establish the range and distribution of some social characteristics, such as education or training, occupation, and location.

A. Historical method

B. Descriptive survey method

C. Experimental method

D. Ex-post-facto method

Q.6 What is a Research Design?

A. A way of conduction research that is not grounded in theory.

B. The choice between using qualitative or quantitative methods

C. The style in which you present your research findings e.g. a graph

D. A framework for every stage of the collection and analysis of data.

Q.7 Sampling Cases means:-

A. Sampling using a sampling frame

B. Identifying people who are suitable for research

C. Literally the researcher's brief case

D. Sampling of people, newspapers, television programmes etc.

Q.8 Which of the following set of statements represents acceptable propositions in respect of teaching- learning relationships? Choose the correct code to indicate your answer.

i. When students fail in a test, it is the teacher who fails.

ii. Every teaching must aim at ensuring learning.

iii. There can be teaching without learning taking place.

iv. There can be no learning without teaching.

v. A teacher teaches but learns also.

vi. Real learning implies rote learning.

A. ii, iii, iv and v   **B.** i, ii, iii and v

C. iii, iv, v and vi   **D.** i, ii, v and vi

Q.9 A ______________ is a method for judging the worth of a program while the program activities are forming (in progress).

A. formative evaluation

B. A continuous and comprehensive evaluation

C. Summative evaluation

D. None of these

Q.10 Following are the main elements of the Choice Based Credit System. Identify the one which does not belong to Choice Based Credit System (CBCS).

A. The assessment is done twice in a year.

B. Students are given a choice to select from the available courses.

C. Each course is assigned a specific credit.

D. There are three main courses in CBCs-Main, Foundation and Elective

Q.11 Companies take savings as premium, invest in bonds and make payments to beneficiaries are classified as:

A. debit unions

B. life insurance companies

C. auto purchases

D. credit unions

Q.12 Which of the following are the characteristics of a seminar?

a) It is a form of academic instruction.

b) It involves questioning, discussion and debates.

c) It involves large groups of individuals.

d) It needs involvement of skilled persons.

A. b and c   **B.** b and d

C. b, c and d   **D.** a, b and d

Q.13 A, B and C can do a piece of work in 20, 30 and 60 days respectively. In how many days can A do the work if he is assisted by B and C on every third day?

A. 17 days   **B.** 25 days   **C.** 12 days   **D.** 15 days

Q.14 In the two sets given below Set – I indicates methods of teaching while Set – II provides the basic requirements for success/ effectiveness. Match the two sets and indicate your answer by choosing from the code:

Set – I	Set – II
1) Lecturing	i. Small step presentation with feedback provided
2) Discussion in groups	ii. Production of a large number of ideas
3) Brainstorming	iii. Content delivery in a lucid language
4) Programmed Instructional	iv. Use of teaching- aids
	v. Theme based interaction among participants

A. A-i B-ii C-iii D-iv   **B.** A-ii B-iii C-iv D-v

C. A-iii B-v C-ii D-i   **D.** A-iv B-ii C-I D-iii

Q.15 Which one of the following is considered a sign of motivated teaching?

A. Students asking questions
B. Maximum attendance of the students
C. Pin drop silence in the classroom
D. Students taking notes

Q.16 Anil played 8 cricket matches. The mean (average) of the runs was found to be 80. After playing four more matches, the mean of the runs of all the matches was found to be 70. The total runs made in the last four matches is

A. 400   **B.** 300   **C.** 200   **D.** 100

Q.17 5, 11, 21, 35, 53, ?, …is the next term in the series

A. 75   **B.** 90   **C.** 115   **D.** 125

Q.18 XY, ABC, FGHI, ? , … is the next term in the series.

A. MNPQO   **B.** MNOPQ   **C.** PQOMN   **D.** NMPOQ

Q.19 An alone can do a piece of work in 6 days and B alone in 8 days. A and B undertook to do it for Rs. 3200. With the help of C, they completed the work in 3 days. How much is to be paid to C?

A. Rs 300   **B.** Rs 400   **C.** Rs 500   **D.** Rs 700

Q.20 A man paid Rs. 160 while travelling 10 km in a taxi which has some initial fixed charges. Another man paid Rs. 276 for travelling 16 km and the taxi driver charged double of the initial fixed charges from him. The charges of the taxi per km is:

A. 10   **B.** 13   **C.** 11   **D.** 17

Q.21 Gopal walks 20 m North. Then he turns right and walks 30 m. Then he turns right and walks 35 m. Again, he turns left and walks 15 m. Then he again turns left and walks 15 m. The shortest distance between his original position and final one is:

A. 65 m   **B.** 55 m   **C.** 40 m   **D.** 45 m

Q.22 If two standard form categorical propositions with the same subject and predicate are related in such a manner that if one is undetermined the other must be undetermined, what is their relation?

A. Contrary   **B.** Sub contrary
C. Contradictory   **D.** Sub-altern

Q.23

How much time will it take for an amount of Rs. 450 to yield Rs. 81 as interest at 4.5% per annum of simple interest?

A. 3 years   **B.** 4 years   **C.** 5 years   **D.** 6 years

Q.24 Identify the type of reasoning shown in the following statements.

Statement 1: We see smoke coming out of the hills.

Statement 2: Wherever there is smoke, there is always a fire.

Conclusion: Therefore, hills have fire.

A. Pratyaksha   **B.** Upamana
C. Anumana   **D.** Arthapatti

Q.25 When the purpose of a definition is to explain the use or to eliminate ambiguity the definition is called:

A. Stipulative   **B.** Theoretical
C. Lexical   **D.** Persuasive

Q.26 A smart classroom is a teaching space which has:-

A. Smart portion with a touch panel control system.
B. PC/Laptop connection and DVD/VCR player.
C. Document camera and specialized software.
D. All of these

Q.27 The term 'grapevine' is also called:-

A. Downward communication
B. Informal communication
C. Upward communication
D. Horizontal communication

Q.28 A sum of Rs. 12,500 amounts to Rs. 15,500 in 4 years at the rate of simple interest. What is the rate of interest?

A. 9%   **B.** 8%   **C.** 7%   **D.** 6%

Q.29 Every type of communication is affected by:-

A. Reception   **B.** Transmission
C. Non-regulation   **D.** Context

Ques (30-34):The following line graph gives the percent profit earned by two Companies X and Y during the period 1996 - 2001.

Percentage profit earned by Two Companies X and Y over the Given Years

$$\% \text{ Profit} = \frac{\text{Income - Expenditure}}{\text{Expenditure}} \times 100$$

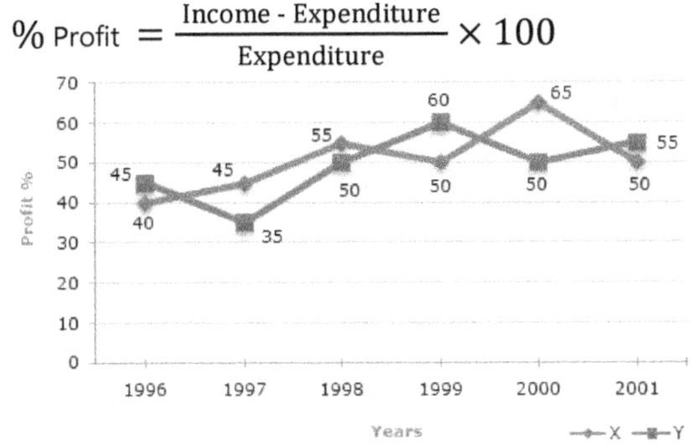

Q.30 The incomes of two Companies X and Y in 2000 were in the ratio of 3:4 respectively. What was the respective ratio of their expenditures in 2000 ?

A. 13:22　　　　　　　**B.** 17:22
C. 15:22　　　　　　　**D.** None of these

Q.31 If the expenditure for Company Y in 1997 was Rs. 220 crores, what was its income in 1997 ?

A. Rs. 297 crores.　　　**B.** Rs. 397 crores.
C. Rs. 298 crores.　　　**D.** Rs. 287 crores.

Q.32 If the expenditures of Company X and Y in 1996 were equal and the total income of the two Companies in 1996 was Rs. 342 crores, what was the total profit of the two Companies together in 1996 ? (Profit = Income - Expenditure)

A. Rs. 102 crores.　　　**B.** Rs. 103 crores.
C. Rs. 202 crores.　　　**D.** Rs. 104 crores.

Q.33 The expenditure of Company X in the year 1998 was Rs. 200 crores and the income of company X in 1998 was the same as its expenditure in 2001. The income of Company X in 2001 was?

A. Rs. 465 crores.　　　**B.** Rs. 365 crores.
C. Rs. 467 crores.　　　**D.** Rs. 495 crores.

Q.34 If the incomes of two Companies were equal in 1999, then what was the ratio of expenditure of Company X to that of Company Y in 1999?

A. 16:19　　　　　　　**B.** 16:18
C. 16:15　　　　　　　**D.** None of the above

Q.35 Which of the following are the demerits of globalization of higher education?

1) Exposure to global curriculum
2) Promotion of elitism in education
3) The commodification of higher education
4) Increase in the cost of education

A. 1 and 4　　　　　　**B.** 1, 3 and 4
C. 2, 3 and 4　　　　　**D.** 1, 2, 3 and 4

Q.36 What decimal of an hour is a second?

A. .0025　　　　　　　**B.** .000126

C. .00027　　　　　　　**D.** None of these

Q.37 _______ is used to send the same mail to different persons in MS Word.

A. Main join　　　　　　**B.** Mail copy
C. Mail insert　　　　　**D.** Mail merge

Q.38 In a Computer a byte generally consists of:

A. 4 bits　　**B.** 8 bits　　**C.** 16 bits　　**D.** 10 bits

Q.39 One of the anthropogenic sources of gaseous pollutants chlorofluorocarbons (CFCs) in air is:-

A. Cement industry　　　**B.** Fertiliser industry
C. Foam industry　　　　**D.** Pesticide industry

Q.40

If 2994 ÷ 14.5 = 172, then 29.94 ÷ 1.45 = ?

A. 17.2　　　　　　　　**B.** 17
C. 16.2　　　　　　　　**D.** None of these

Ques (41-45):Read the following passage carefully.

The last great war, which nearly shook the foundations of the modern world, had little impact on Indian literature beyond aggravating the popular revulsion against violence and adding to the growing disillusionment with the 'humane pretensions' of the Western World. This was eloquently voiced in Tagore's later poems and his last testament, Crisis in Civilization. The Indian intelligentsia was in a state of moral dilemma. On the one hand, it could not help sympathizing with England's dogged courage in the hour of peril, with the Russians fighting with their backs to the wall against the ruthless Nazi hordes, and with China groaning under the heel of Japanese militarism; on the other hand, their own country was practically under military occupation of their own soil, and an Indian army under Subhas Bose was trying from the opposite camp to liberate their country. No creative impulse could issue from such confusion of loyalties. One would imagine that the achievement of Indian independence in 1947, which came in the wake of the Allies' victory and was followed by the collapse of colonialism in the neighboring countries of South-East Asia, would have released an upsurge of creative energy.

No doubt it did, but unfortunately it was soon submerged in the great agony of partition, with its inhuman slaughter of the innocents and the uprooting of millions of people from their homeland, followed by the martyrdom of Mahatma Gandhi. These tragedies, along with Pakistan's invasion of Kashmir and its later atrocities in Bangladesh, did indeed provoke a poignant writing, particularly in the languages of the regions most affected, Bengali, Hindi, Kashmiri, Punjabi, Sindhi and Urdu. But poignant or passionate writing does not by itself make great literature. What reserves of enthusiasm and confidence survived these disasters have been mainly absorbed in the task of national reconstruction and economic development. Great literature has always emerged out of chains of convulsions. Indian literature is richer today in volume, range and variety than it ever was in the past.

Q.41 What was the impact of the last great on Indian literature?

A. It had no impact.
B. It aggravated popular revulsion against violence.
C. It shook the foundations of literature.

D. It offered eloquent support to the Western World.

Q.42 What did Tagore articulate in his last testament?
A. Offered support to Subhas Bose.
B. Exposed the humane pretensions of the Western World.
C. Expressed loyalty to England.
D. Encouraged the liberation of countries.

Q.43 What was the stance of Indian intelligentsia during the period of great war?
A. Indifference to Russia's plight.
B. They favoured Japanese militarism.
C. They prompted creativity out of confused loyalties.
D. They expressed sympathy for England's dogged courage.

Q.44 Identify the factor responsible for the submergence of creative energy in Indian literature.
A. Military occupation of one's own soil.
B. Resistance to colonial occupation.
C. Great agony of partition.
D. Victory of Allies.

Q.45 What was the aftermath that survived tragedies in Kashmir and Bangladesh?
A. Suspicion of other countries
B. Continuance of rivalry
C. Menace of war
D. National reconstruction

Ques (46-47): Which of phrases given below each sentence should replace the phrase printed in **bold** type to make the grammatically correct? If the sentence is correct as it is, mark 'D' as the answer.

Q.46 You need not come unless you want to.
A. You don't need to come unless you want to
B. You come only when you want to
C. You needn't come until you don't want to
D. No correction required

Q.47 The man **to who I sold** my house was a cheat.
A. to whom I sell
B. to who I sell
C. to whom I sold
D. No correction required

Q.48 ________________ is the practice of developing, cultivating and maintaining a corporate identity or brand image.
A. Horizontal communication
B. Vertical communication
C. Corporate communication
D. Cross communication

Q.49 Identify the important element a teacher has to take cognizance of while addressing students in a classroom.
A. Avoidance of proximity
B. Voice modulation
C. Repetitive pause
D. Fixed posture

Q.50 The choice of communication partners is influenced by factors of
A. Proximity, utility, loneliness
B. Utility, secrecy, dissonance
C. Secrecy, dissonance, deception
D. Dissimilarity, dissonance, deviance

Paper-II

Q.51 Xeta Electronics Ltd. is faced with the problem of allocating resources to its newly set up computer peripherals division, because of some practical constraints like limited availability of resources, time, man-hours etc. Which of the following decision-making techniques can help it solve the problem?
A. Linear Programming
B. Decision tree
C. Simulation
D. Waiting-line method

Q.52 The concept of span of management concerns:-
A. Seeing that managers at the same level have equal numbers of subordinates
B. Employee skill and motivation levels
C. Supervision of one less than the known number of subordinates
D. A determination of the number of individuals a manager can effectively supervise

Q.53 Who recommends the MSP (Minimum Support Price) to the Government?
A. Commission for Agricultural Costs and Prices
B. Department of Agriculture
C. Cabinet Committee on Economic Affairs
D. Department of Economics and revenue

Q.54 There are three major forms of divisional structures: product division, geographic division and customer division. Which of the following statements is not true about Customer Division or Departmentation?
A. It is set up to service particular types of clients or customers
B. It can address the special and widely varied needs of customers for clearly defined services
C. It is accompanied by the benefits of specialization
D. Coordination between sales and other functions becomes easier

Q.55 A matrix structure is a type of departmentalization that superimposes a horizontal set of divisional reporting relationships into a hierarchical functional structure. The major disadvantage of the matrix structure is
A. Duplication of resources
B. Lack of employee satisfaction
C. Lack of economies of scale
D. Its propensity to foster power, struggles

Q.56 Which of the following management information systems is an interactive computer system that provides managers with the necessary information for making intelligent decisions?

A. Transaction processing system
B. Decision support system
C. Office automation system
D. Executive support system

Q.57 Which of the following statements is not true of internationalization of organizations?

A. To reach organizational objectives, management may extend its activities to include an emphasis on organizations in foreign countries

B. In general, the larger the organization, the greater the likelihood that it participates in international activities of some sort

C. A manager's failure to understand different national sovereignties, national conditions, and national values and institutions can lead to poor investment decisions

D. Generally speaking, a multinational organization transcends any home country, whereas a transnational organization does not.

Q.58 Which of the following can be said to be an appropriate technique for line personnel in reducing the line-staff conflict?

A. Emphasize the objectives of the organization as a whole
B. Make proper use of the staff abilities
C. Obtain any necessary skills they do not already possess
D. Deal intelligently with resistance to change rather than view it as an immovable barrier

Q.59 From the delegator's aspect, all of the following are the factors affecting the delegation of authority except

A. Love for authority
B. Fear of exposure
C. Attitude towards subordinates
D. Fear of criticism

Q.60 The characteristic of an organization that describes the degree to which the organization monitors and responds to changes in the external environment is known as:-

A. Open-systems focus
B. Means-end orientation
C. Control
D. Unit integration

Q.61 Every organization structure, even a poor one, can be charted. Which of the following is false with respect to an organization Chart?

A. It is a vital tool for providing information about organizational relationships
B. It provides a visual map of the chain of command
C. Charting an organization structure can show up the complexities and inconsistencies, which can be corrected
D. It shows authority relationships as well as informal and informational relationships

Q.62 Modern organizations have been trying to create a corporate culture with a distinct identity by moulding the behaviours of their members. Which of the following is not a feature of organizational culture?

A. It is based on certain norms
B. It promotes dominant and stable values
C. It shapes philosophy and rules

D. It focuses on profit

Q.63 Manager Inventory Chart, also known as replacement chart, is used in Replacement Planning of human resource management in an organization. Which of the following is not an advantage of Manager Inventory Chart?

A. It gives an overview of the human resource situation of an organization
B. It shows the future internal supply of managers by indicating who is promotable in a year
C. It shows the position to which a manager may be promoted
D. Managers who are ready for promotion can be easily identified

Q.64 Federal government tax revenues if it exceeds government spending then it is classified as:

A. budget surplus
B. budget deficit
C. Federal Reserve
D. Federal Reserve

Q.65 Document in a corporation which consists of amount of stock, name and addresses of directors is classified as:

A. liability plan
B. stock planning
C. corporation paperwork
D. charter

Q.66 There can be different sources of resistance to change. For analytical purposes, they can be categorized as individual and organizational sources. Which of the following is an organizational source of resistance to change?

A. Habit
B. Structural inertia
C. Security
D. Fear of the unknown

Q.67 Creative thoughts are the result of hard work and there are various techniques to foster creativity. Which of the following is one of the best-known techniques for facilitating creativity, developed by Alex F. Osborn?

A. Brainstorming
B. Synectics
C. Delphi Technique
D. Nominal

Q.68 A price for equity is called:

A. interest rate
B. cost of equity
C. debt rate
D. investment return

Q.69 Risk in which value of the investment depends on what happens to foreign exchange rates is classified as:

A. preferred risk
B. exchange rate risk
C. country risk
D. foreign risk

Q.70 Communication can well be treated as the force that brings the organizational participants together. We cannot expect effective management without communication. Which of the following factors does not help in effective communication?

A. Consider the total physical and human setting whenever you communicate
B. Consult with others, when appropriate, in planning communications

C. Follow up your communication

D. Focus the communication primarily at meeting the demands of an immediate situation

Q.71 It is a normal practice to categorize management into three basic levels: top management, middle management and supervisory or first-level management. The managers at these three levels require different kinds of skills to perform the functions associated with their jobs. The major difference in skill requirements between middle and top managers is that

A. Top managers must generally be more skilled than middle managers in every respect

B. Top managers require better interpersonal skills but less conceptual skills than middle managers

C. Top managers generally require better technical and interpersonal skills than middle managers

D. Top managers generally require higher level conceptual skills but less technical skills than middle managers

Q.72 According to the Scientific Management School of Thought, which of the following is defined as the systematic, objective and critical examination of all the factors governing the operational efficiency of a specified activity to bring about improvement?

A. Work methods study

B. Micromotion study

C. Time study

D. Motion study

Q.73 Ability to trade at net price very quickly is classified as:

A. original trading   **B.** liquidity

C. offline trading   **D.** fixed price trading

Q.74 The process of estimating the optimum number of people required for completing a project, task, or goal within time. It is called:

A. Operations research

B. Human resources

C. Manpower planning.

D. Decision processes

Q.75 Which of the following is/are subsystem(s) that are frequently an integral part of 'Management by Objectives (MBO)'?

A. Manpower planning.

B. Compensation.

C. Organization design.

D. Both (I) and (II) above

Q.76 When decision makers construct simplified models that extract the essential features from a problem without capturing all the complexities of a problem, they are acting under which of the following?

A. Bounded rationality

B. Unbounded rationality

C. Uncertainty

D. Heuristics

Q.77 There are both advantages and disadvantages of group decision-making. Which of the following would generally not be considered an advantage of group decision-making?

A. Groups generally come up with more and better decision alternatives than an individual can

B. The members of the group tend to support the implementation of the decision more fervently than they would if the decision had been made by an individual

C. A group can bring much more information and experience to bear on a decision or problem than an individual acting alone

D. The group is more likely to use "groupthink" when coming to a decision

Q.78 Rate of change is one of the factors that determines effective span of management. Changes occur more rapidly in certain organizations than in others. This rate of change

A. Determines how efficient subordinates are without guidance from their superiors

B. Enables subordinates to clearly understand what is expected of them

C. Determines the degree to which policies can be formulated and the stability that can be achieved in the policies

D. Helps identify deviation in plans

Q.79 Which of the following are the generic strategies suggested by Porter that might adopt to make their organizations more competitive?

A. Focus.   **B.** Cost leadership.

C. Divestiture.   **D.** Both A and B

Q.80 Divisional structure is a type of departmentation in which positions are grouped according to similarity of products, services or markets. Which of the following is not an advantage of divisional Structure?

A. Each unit or division can respond or react quickly, when required, because they normally do not need to coordinate with other divisions before taking an action

B. Coordination is simplified as each division is similar to an organization, containing the various functions within it

C. Individuals are able to develop in-depth areas of specialization to the same extent as in a functional structure

D. It helps the organization to focus on serving a particular customer

Q.81 Delegate means to grant or confer on subordinates certain tasks and duties along with sufficient authority, to accomplish these. Which of the following points is most likely to increase the effectiveness of delegation?

A. Detail how the required tasks are to be completed for the subordinate

B. Predetermine the desired results and performance standards for the delegated task

C. Explain the relevance of delegated tasks to larger projects or to department or organization goals

D. Maintain the authority necessary to accomplish the main tasks

Q.82 If unprepared, what strategic pressures are recognized as key factors that can weaken the organization?

A. Competitive and environmental pressures

B. Control at the expense of flexibility

C. Lack of planners

D. Competitive and environmental pressures, and excessive control

Q.83 In modern times, organizations have been trying to create a corporate culture with a distinct identity by moulding the behavior of their members. The original source of an organization's culture is most strongly associated with

A. Overseas influences

B. Political factors in the external environment

C. General economic trends

D. The vision of the organization's founder(s)

Q.84 _____________are the resources, skills or other advantages a firm enjoys relative to its competitors.

A. Weakness   **B.** Strength

C. Threat   **D.** Opportunities

Q.85 The success of an organization greatly depends on the decisions that managers make. What are the three decision-making conditions, which managers deal with, in analyzing decision alternatives?

A. Certainty, uncertainty, risk

B. Certainty, uncertainty, maximax

C. Certainty, minimax, risk

D. Maximax, uncertainty, risk

Q.86 Apart from on-the-job training, there are many other approaches to manager development. Development of organizing and intervening skills in group processes, usually takes place in case of

A. Sensitivity training

B. Survey feedback

C. Team building

D. Process consultation

Q.87 Every organization makes minor structural adjustments in reaction to changes. The forces of change can be internal or external to the organization. Which of the following is not an internal force of change?

A. Organizational strategy

B. Technology

C. Employee attitude

D. Organizational culture

Q.88 A_____________ is a A a limitation or deficiency in resources, skills and capabilities that seriously impede effective performance.

A. Strength   **B.** Threat

C. Opportunities   **D.** Weakness

Q.89 Different behavioral scientists have developed different theories on motivation. One such behavioral scientist by the name of Herzberg gave the two-factor theory of motivation. According to Herzberg's motivation-hygiene theory, which of the following are hygiene factors?

A. Personal life, security, salary and recognition

B. Advancement, salary, status, company policy

C. Relationship with peers, status, supervision and security

D. Working conditions, relationship with subordinates, supervision and work itself

Q.90 The managerial grid identified five specific leadership styles. Which leader believes that thoughtful attention to the needs of people for a satisfying relationship leads to a comfortable, friendly organizational atmosphere and work tempo?

A. Task   **B.** Middle of the road

C. Country club   **D.** Team

Q.91 The Managerial Grid, propounded by Blake and Mouton, is based on a manager's concern for people and concern for production. The most effective management style as characterized by the Managerial Grid is:

A. High concern for people and low concern for production

B. High concern for people and high concern for production

C. Low concern for people and high concern for production

D. Low concern for people and low concern for production

Q.92 In an effective organization, information flows in various directions. Which of the following information flows takes place among persons at different levels, who have no direct relationships?

A. Downward   **B.** Upward

C. Horizontal   **D.** Diagonal

Q.93 Which of the following is a measure of how appropriate organizational goals are, and how well an organization is achieving those goals?

A. Competitor analysis

B. Environmental scanning

C. Situational effectiveness

D. Organizational effectiveness

Q.94 Financial ratios are particularly important to managerial control in an organization. One such financial ratio, viz., return on investment, is a ratio that attempts to measure a firm's

A. Leverage   **B.** Profitability

C. Liquidity   **D.** Reliability

Q.95 Robert Kalpan and David developed the balanced score card in the early as a performance measurement system:

A. 1991   **B.** 1990   **C.** 1992   **D.** 1995

Q.96 What is said to be the key factor in maintaining organizational growth (e.g., Hurst 1995)?

A. Entrepreneurial vision

B. Planning

C. Innovation

D. Flexibility

Q.97 Hazard Analysis and Critical Control Point Method (HACCP) is used in the food manufacturing industry to identify and prevent microbial and other germs from causing harm to food. Which of the following principles involves identification of preventive measures the manufacturing units can adopt, to control food safety hazards that arise during processing?

A. Hazard analysis

B. Identifying control points

C. Critical limits

D. Establish corrective actions

Q.98 Management Information System (MIS) helps the manager to discharge his/her managerial functions in a more efficient manner. The first necessary step to effectively operate an MIS is:-

A. Summarizing data

B. Analyzing data

C. Determining information needs

D. Gathering appropriate information

Q.99 Which of the following elements of strategy affect the process of strategy creation and implementation?

A. Synergy

B. The strategic leader???s perspective on strategy

C. Structure

D. Strategic paradoxes

Q.100 In which of the following orientations toward international business, does a firm analyze the needs of customers worldwide and then adopts standardized practices for all the markets it serves?

A. Ethnocentric

B. Polycentric

C. Geocentric

D. Regiocentric

Q.101 According to which of the following management approaches, does managerial practice depend on circumstances?

A. Systems approach

B. Contingency approach

C. Mc Kinsey's 7-S framework

D. Empirical approach

Q.102 Five different workers perform different tasks contributing to completion of one specific job for instance preparing a Big Mac at McDonald's. This division of labour refers to which of Fayol's principles of management?

A. Work specialization

B. Scalar chain

C. Order

D. Authority and responsibility

Q.103 Managers' making ethical decisions may belong to any of the three levels of moral development. Which of the following stages describes the pre-conventional level of moral development?

A. Following rules only when it is in one's immediate interest

B. Living up to what is expected by people who are close to oneself

C. Maintaining conventional order by fulfilling obligations to which one has agreed

D. Valuing rights of others, and upholding non-relative values and rights, regardless of the majority's opinion

Q.104 The only thing that is permanent in this world is change. A change is bound to occur in the internal environment or external environment, no matter what management does. Planning can't eliminate change, but managers usually plan in order to:

A. Decide what needs to be done when a change in environment takes place

B. Anticipate changes and develop the most-effective response to changes

C. Have the appropriate materials available when the demand for them comes about

D. Be prepared for when changes in management at the top occur

Q.105 Miles and Snow (1994) identify four main reasons for failure. Which of the following is one of those reasons?

A. Lack of competitive advantage

B. Lack of strategy competency

C. Lack of strategic resources

D. Poor judgement leading to poor, inappropriate strategic decisions

Q.106 In order to understand the opportunities and threats faced by an organization, managers should analyze their organization's environment. Various tools available for the purpose, what are the three most effective tools that managers can use to analyze the organization's environment?

A. Benchmarking, planning and evaluating

B. Environmental scanning, forecasting and benchmarking

C. Strategic planning, environmental scanning and TQM

D. Forecasting, budgeting and time management

Q.107 How does Checkland (1981) describe an organization?

A. A collection of people who are trying to act with purpose

B. Systems that comprise a collection of people who are trying to act with purpose

C. A collection of people that act with little purpose

D. A collection of systems and functions, inclusive of its people

Q.108 Major decisions in organizations are most often made by groups rather than a single individual. Group decision-making is the norm in most large and complex organizations. Which of the following would generally not be considered an advantage of group decision-making?

A. Groups generally come up with more and better decision alternatives than an individual can

B. The members of the group tend to support the implementation of the decision more fervently than they would if the decision had been made by an individual

C. A group can bring much more information and experience to bear on a decision or a problem than an individual acting alone

D. The group is more likely to use "groupthink" when coming to a decision

Q.109 How might an organization spot, create, and exploit new opportunities ahead of its rivals?

A. Through managers in the various businesses working together, sharing information and capabilities, helping each other, and creating synergy

B. Through managers in the various businesses sharing information, capabilities, and creating synergy

C. Through managers in the various businesses working together, sharing information, and sharing capabilities

D. Through managers in the various businesses working together to create strategic competencies for the organization in order to pursue opportunities

Q.110 Which of the following is not a competence recognized by Richardson and Thompson (1994)?

A. Strategic thinking
B. Managing paradoxes
C. Innovative climate
D. Providing excellent quality

Q.111 Departmentalization divides a large and complex organization into smaller and more flexible administrative units. A type of departmentalization in which similar specialists and people with common skills, knowledge and orientations are grouped together, is referred to as

A. Process departmentalization
B. Functional departmentalization
C. Product departmentalization
D. Customer departmentalization

Q.112 Which of the following statements is incorrect with respect to 'functional authority'?

A. Managing functional authority relationships is similar to managing dual-boss relationships
B. It should be restricted to the procedural aspects of a function
C. It is similar to line authority except that staff personnel with functional authority do not have a right to punish violations from the intended course of action
D. If unity of command were to be applied without exception, functional authority would be exercised only by staff managers.

Q.113 Every organization structure, even a poor one, can be charted. Which of the following is false with respect to Organization Chart?

A. It is a vital tool for providing information about organizational relationships
B. It provides a visual map of the chain of command
C. Charting an organization structure can show up the complexities and inconsistencies, which can be corrected
D. It shows authority relationships as well as informal and informational relationships

Q.114 Various selection devices are used to choose candidates who best meet the qualifications and have the greatest aptitude for the job. Asking a candidate for an automotive mechanic's position to assemble and disassemble part of an engine motor would be an example of what kind of selection device?

A. Psychological test
B. Personality test
C. Performance test
D. Intelligence test

Q.115 An excellent leader possesses the qualities of emotional and social maturity, along with it one more important quality, a leader has to be achieved is:

A. Formation of highly positive public opinion
B. Formation of high prestige in the group
C. Quick communication of his ideas and values in the whole group
D. Feelings of shamefulness when remained unsuccessful in his objectives

Q.116 Managers can adopt various methods to overcome initial resistance to change. In which of the following methods of overcoming resistance to change, management neutralizes potential or actual resistance by exchanging something of value for cooperation?

A. Facilitation and support
B. Manipulation
C. Negotiation and agreement
D. Explicit and implicit coercion

Q.117 The registered office clause of memorandum of association contains:

A. The name of the city/town only and not that of the state.
B. The complete postal address.
C. The name of the state in which the registered office of the company is to be situated.
D. The name of the registrar of companies.

Q.118 The manager of Master Products Ltd., a leading manufacturer of electrical components, instructed Tarun, Shreya, Aparna, and Sheila, who all worked together, to teach each other their job skills to be more effective. What is this called?

A. Cross-training
B. Role perception
C. Training
D. Simulation

Q.119 Senthil is a salesperson for Cloud 9 Corporation's Chennai office. If the salespersons meet their sales goals for the month, they are given an all-expense-paid trip to a Salgaonkar Club football game. Football is not one of Chennai's favorite sports, and the Salgaonkar Club is definitely not Senthil's favorite team. Which component of Vroom's expectancy theory influences Senthil's performance?

A. Effort-performance linkage
B. Performance-reward linkage
C. Effort-reward linkage
D. Valence

Q.120 The management should redress only those grievances that are

A. real
B. real or imaginary
C. imaginary
D. none of the above

Q.121 The managerial grid, propounded by Robert Blake and Jane Srygley Mouton, is a well-developed approach to defining leadership styles. It identifies five distinct leadership styles. According to this grid, the (9,9) manager:

A. Gives thoughtful attention to the needs of people, for a satisfying relationship leads to a comfortable, friendly atmosphere and work tempo
B. Believes that concern for people and tasks are compatible and that tasks need to be carefully explained and decisions endorsed by subordinates to achieve a high level of commitment
C. Believes in compromise, so that decisions are taken but only if endorsed by subordinates
D. Exerts minimum effort to get required work done

Q.122 Statement I: As per Section 125 of the Indian Contract Act, a contract of indemnity is a contract by which one party promises to save the other party from loss caused to him.

Statement II: The person who promises to indemnify or make good the loss is called the indemnity holder and the person whose loss is made is called indemnifier.

Which of the above statement (s) is/are true?

A. Only I

B. Only II

C. Both I and II

D. None of the above

Q.123 Which one of the following debt Service Coverage Ratio indicates?

A. Effective utilisation of assets.

B. A number of times fixed assets cover borrowed funds.

C. Excess of Current Assets over Current Liabilities.

D. A number of times surplus covers interest and installments of Term Loans.

Q.124 ___________ is a method of analyzing user needs in which a company works closely with its customers to design products that better meet their needs.

A. Uncovering

B. Benchmarking

C. Broadening

D. Customer partnering

Q.125 In which one of the following types of store retailers, large, low-cost, low margin, high-volume, self-service store attributes are designed to meet total needs for food and household products?

A. Supermarket

B. Superstore

C. Discount store

D. Convenience store

Q.126 Which of the following statements is/are true about investment centers?

I. The control system examines the role of assets in generating profit.

II. In investment centers, outputs are measured in monetary terms and directly compared with input costs.

A. Only (I) above

B. Only (II) above

C. Both (I) and (II) above

D. None of the above

Q.127 Operations Management is a tool by which management can create and improve upon its operations. Which of the following statements is true regarding Operations Management?

A. Operations managers are not found in the service sector

B. Operations Management is concerned with only the input stage of product development

C. The outputs of the operations system include both goods and services

D. Labour is part of the transformation stage and is not considered an input

Q.128 Which of the following controls is the cause of an unsatisfactory outcome traced back to the individual responsible for it, who is then made to correct the practice?

A. Preventive control

B. Cybernetic control

C. Direct control

D. Steering control

Q.129 Which one of the following attributes of advertising regarding the launching of a new product calls for spending all the advertising budget in a single period?

A. Pulsing

B. Continuity

C. Concentration

D. Flighting

Q.130 Which of the following management information systems aims at facilitating communication and increasing the efficiency and productivity of managers and office workers through document and message processing?

A. Transaction processing system

B. Decision support system

C. Office automation system

D. Executive support system

Q.131 Planning by a supervisor of a goods processing department to rearrange the location of several pieces of equipment so that the new order can begin on time, three months hence, would be an example of a/an:

A. Tactical plan

B. Operational plan

C. Tactical goal

D. Operational goal

Q.132 As the size of the organization increases the more sophisticated the organizational structure becomes. Hence management is categorized into three basic levels i.e. top-level management, middle level-management and supervisory-level management. Which of the following is false with regard to functions of supervisory management?

A. Making detailed, short-range operational plans

B. Reviewing performance of subordinates

C. Making specific task assignments

D. Counseling subordinates on production, personnel or other problems

Q.133 Which stage of the creativity process links the unconscious state of mind with the conscious state?

A. Unconscious scanning

B. Intuition

C. Insight

D. Logical formulation

Q.134 The span of management includes:

A. Determination of how many people working with each other report to a single manager.

B. Determination of the number of individuals a manager can effectively supervise.

C. Assessing employee skill and motivation levels.

D. Both (I) and (II)

Q.135 Who among the following has not given a model on Corporate Social Responsibility (CSR)?

A. Ackerman

B. Carroll

C. Friedman

D. Walker

Q.136 Which of the following is the best explanation of why Japanese companies tend to make decisions by consensus?

A. It is a reflection of the larger societal cultural value on groups

B. It is more efficient and timely than any other method

C. It is a carryover from Post-World War II influences from

Americans

D.   The Japanese government mandates it

Q.137 Systems that manage sales order entry, airline reservations are example of:-

A.   Management Information System

B.   Decision Support System

C.   Executive Support System

D.   Transaction Processing System

Q.138 Which of the following responsibility centers are also referred to as 'engineered expense centers?'

A.   Discretionary expense centers

B.   Standard cost centers

C.   Profit centers

D.   Revenues centers

Q.139 Lawrence is a new interviewer who just finished an interview with Pauline. Her professional style and her flawless grooming immediately struck him. Lawrence gave Pauline a very good evaluation although her previous work experience and educational background were not that exceptional. What rating error did Lawrence succumb to?

A.   Halo effect

B.   Rater prejudice

C.   Shifting standards

D.   Different Rater patterns

Q.140 Which of the following statements is false concerning Vroom's expectancy theory?

A.   It is based on self-interest where each employee seeks to maximize personal satisfaction

B.   Managers' must understand which rewards employees will positively value

C.   The employee must see the connection between performance and rewards

D.   The theory is concerned with reality, not perceptions

Q.141 Mark's Embroidery produces custom-made embroidery products. One department sells to retail customers, another department sells to catalog customers and a third department sells only to college bookstores. Mark's Embroidery is departmentalized by:-

A.   Product

B.   Customer

C.   Geographical location

D.   Process

Q.142 Who among the following bridges the gap between inventors and managers?

A. Investor

B. Entrepreneur

C. Industrialist

D. Intrapreneur

Q.143 In India, tripartite bodies of industrial relations began on the recommendations of which one of the following commissions?

A.   Law Commission of India

B.   Whitley Commission

C.   National Statistical Commission

D.   Kothari Commission

Q.144 The extrinsic properties of the product or service, including the ways in which the brand attempts to meet customers' psychological or social needs is known as:

A. Brand judgments

B. Brand resonance

C. Brand imagery

D. Brand performance

Q.145 Quantitative techniques are very useful in making decisions under conditions of varying degrees of uncertainty. Torque Engineering Co. Ltd. faces the problem of allocating resources to its newly set up hydraulic pumps division. Which of the following decision-making techniques can help solve the problem?

A.   Linear programming

B.   Decision tree

C.   Simulation

D.   Waiting-line method

Q.146 Blake and Mouton's Managerial Grid is an approach to defining leadership styles based on a manager's concern for people and concern for production. Which of the following styles of management assumes that exertion of minimum effort to get required work done is appropriate to sustain organization membership?

A.   Authority-obedience management

B.   Team management

C.   Country Club management

D.   Impoverished management

Q.147 Which of the following refers to the process that helps new employees adapt to the organization's culture?

A. Grapevine

B. Orientation

C. Socialization

D. Introduction

Q.148 The area of intellectual property includes:

1. Copyrights and related rights.

2. Trademarks including service marks.

3. Industrial designs.

4. The layout designs of integrated circuits.

Choose the correct codes.

A. Only 1

B. Both 1 and 2

C. 1, 2 and 3

D. All of the above

Q.149 Characteristics of Situational Leadership is/are:-

A.   Situational leadership will be high on the "directive" aspect when the juniors are not sufficiently developed and need continuous supervision.

B.   If the situation requires it, the leader will also coach their team.

C.   It takes a lot of courage for a leader to try out various leadership approaches and figure out which one is ideal.

D.   All of these

Q.150 ____________ refers to a leadership style where the leader of an organization has to modify his style to fit the progression level of the followers he is trying to influence.

A.   Competitor analysis

B.   Environmental scanning

C.   Situational effectiveness

D.   Organizational effectiveness

// Smart Answer Sheet //

Correct Percentage of students who answered correctly. **Skipped** Percentage of students who skipped.

Q.	Ans.	Correct / Skipped	Q.	Ans.	Correct / Skipped	Q.	Ans.	Correct / Skipped	Q.	Ans.	Correct / Skipped	Q.	Ans.	Correct / Skipped
1	B	19.44 % / 11.12 %	17	A	58.33 % / 36.11 %	33	A	16.67 % / 36.11 %	49	B	44.44 % / 38.89 %	65	D	11.11 % / 30.56 %
2	A	36.11 % / 36.11 %	18	B	63.89 % / 36.11 %	34	C	16.67 % / 38.89 %	50	A	25.0 % / 36.11 %	66	B	58.33 % / 30.56 %
3	B	63.89 % / 36.11 %	19	B	50.0 % / 36.11 %	35	C	36.11 % / 38.89 %	51	A	33.33 % / 22.23 %	67	A	41.67 % / 30.55 %
4	B	33.33 % / 36.11 %	20	C	16.67 % / 36.11 %	36	C	16.67 % / 38.89 %	52	D	44.44 % / 25.0 %	68	B	63.89 % / 30.55 %
5	B	44.44 % / 36.12 %	21	D	44.44 % / 38.89 %	37	D	30.56 % / 38.88 %	53	A	22.22 % / 27.78 %	69	B	50.0 % / 33.33 %
6	D	38.89 % / 36.11 %	22	C	11.11 % / 38.89 %	38	B	58.33 % / 38.89 %	54	D	19.44 % / 27.78 %	70	D	22.22 % / 33.34 %
7	D	22.22 % / 36.11 %	23	B	55.56 % / 36.11 %	39	C	25.0 % / 38.89 %	55	D	11.11 % / 27.78 %	71	D	36.11 % / 33.33 %
8	B	33.33 % / 36.11 %	24	C	22.22 % / 38.89 %	40	A	44.44 % / 38.89 %	56	B	55.56 % / 30.55 %	72	A	25.0 % / 33.33 %
9	A	25.0 % / 36.11 %	25	C	27.78 % / 36.11 %	41	B	38.89 % / 38.89 %	57	D	16.67 % / 36.11 %	73	B	41.67 % / 33.33 %
10	A	16.67 % / 36.11 %	26	D	47.22 % / 36.11 %	42	B	47.22 % / 38.89 %	58	B	30.56 % / 30.55 %	74	C	44.44 % / 33.34 %
11	B	50.0 % / 36.11 %	27	B	61.11 % / 36.11 %	43	D	16.67 % / 38.89 %	59	D	5.56 % / 30.55 %	75	D	38.89 % / 33.33 %
12	D	30.56 % / 36.11 %	28	D	27.78 % / 36.11 %	44	C	27.78 % / 38.89 %	60	A	19.44 % / 33.34 %	76	A	33.33 % / 33.34 %
13	D	22.22 % / 36.11 %	29	D	25.0 % / 36.11 %	45	D	19.44 % / 38.89 %	61	D	33.33 % / 33.34 %	77	D	11.11 % / 33.33 %
14	C	61.11 % / 36.11 %	30	C	11.11 % / 36.11 %	46	A	25.0 % / 38.89 %	62	D	38.89 % / 30.55 %	78	C	16.67 % / 36.11 %
15	A	52.78 % / 36.11 %	31	A	25.0 % / 38.89 %	47	C	52.78 % / 38.89 %	63	C	19.44 % / 33.34 %	79	D	36.11 % / 33.33 %
16	C	44.44 % / 36.12 %	32	A	5.56 % / 38.88 %	48	C	50.0 % / 38.89 %	64	A	27.78 % / 33.33 %	80	C	8.33 % / 33.34 %

Q.	Ans.	Correct / Skipped	Q.	Ans.	Correct / Skipped	Q.	Ans.	Correct / Skipped	Q.	Ans.	Correct / Skipped	Q.	Ans.	Correct / Skipped
81	C	22.22 % / 33.34 %	95	B	38.89 % / 36.11 %	109	A	13.89 % / 38.89 %	123	D	27.78 % / 36.11 %	137	D	19.44 % / 36.12 %
82	D	27.78 % / 33.33 %	96	D	8.33 % / 36.11 %	110	B	44.44 % / 36.12 %	124	D	22.22 % / 38.89 %	138	B	47.22 % / 38.89 %
83	D	33.33 % / 33.34 %	97	A	11.11 % / 38.89 %	111	B	58.33 % / 36.11 %	125	A	25.0 % / 36.11 %	139	A	22.22 % / 36.11 %
84	B	36.11 % / 33.33 %	98	C	52.78 % / 36.11 %	112	D	8.33 % / 38.89 %	126	A	2.78 % / 38.89 %	140	D	25.0 % / 38.89 %
85	A	16.67 % / 36.11 %	99	D	13.89 % / 36.11 %	113	D	30.56 % / 36.11 %	127	C	22.22 % / 36.11 %	141	B	58.33 % / 36.11 %
86	A	16.67 % / 33.33 %	100	C	27.78 % / 36.11 %	114	C	30.56 % / 36.11 %	128	C	19.44 % / 38.89 %	142	D	16.67 % / 38.89 %
87	B	58.33 % / 36.11 %	101	B	55.56 % / 38.88 %	115	C	27.78 % / 38.89 %	129	C	16.67 % / 38.89 %	143	B	36.11 % / 36.11 %
88	D	41.67 % / 36.11 %	102	A	33.33 % / 36.11 %	116	C	22.22 % / 38.89 %	130	C	11.11 % / 38.89 %	144	C	8.33 % / 38.89 %
89	C	11.11 % / 36.11 %	103	A	11.11 % / 38.89 %	117	C	16.67 % / 38.89 %	131	B	50.0 % / 36.11 %	145	A	27.78 % / 38.89 %
90	C	13.89 % / 36.11 %	104	B	50.0 % / 36.11 %	118	A	27.78 % / 38.89 %	132	D	8.33 % / 36.11 %	146	D	16.67 % / 36.11 %
91	B	61.11 % / 36.11 %	105	D	27.78 % / 38.89 %	119	D	16.67 % / 38.89 %	133	B	44.44 % / 36.12 %	147	C	2.78 % / 36.11 %
92	D	38.89 % / 36.11 %	106	B	47.22 % / 36.11 %	120	B	38.89 % / 38.89 %	134	D	36.11 % / 38.89 %	148	C	13.89 % / 36.11 %
93	D	22.22 % / 36.11 %	107	B	36.11 % / 36.11 %	121	B	47.22 % / 38.89 %	135	D	16.67 % / 36.11 %	149	D	25.0 % / 36.11 %
94	B	47.22 % / 36.11 %	108	D	11.11 % / 36.11 %	122	D	27.78 % / 38.89 %	136	A	19.44 % / 36.12 %	150	C	36.11 % / 33.33 %

//Hints and Solutions//

1. Confounds and artifacts are the two kinds of threats to the validity of socio-psychological research. The major threats to internal validity are history, maturation, testing, instrumentation, statistical regression, selection, experimental mortality, and selection-history interactions. Matching and randomization doesn't vary the treatment and outcome of the research.

2. The four major operations in scientific research is:

(i) Demonstration of co-variance: Covariance is the measure of the change of one variable with the change in the second variable. The scientific research demonstrates the effect of co-variance.

(ii) Elimination of spurious relations: It is a really important operation in scientific research. The relation between the variables should be valid and logically, nothing suspicious should be there.

(iii) Sequencing in terms of time-order: Every research should be in time order.

(iv) Theorisation: To provide relevant theory is the other operation of scientific research.

3. Giving regular homework to students allow students to revise content learned during the day with a fresh set of eyes and a fresh mind, hence developing their habit of self-study.

4. Rajiv Gandhi's birthday is celebrated as Sadbhawana Diwas on 20th August.

5. A descriptive survey attempts to establish the range and distribution of some social characteristics, such as education or training, occupation, and location, and to discover how these characteristics may be related to certain behavior patterns or attitudes. Descriptive research design is a scientific method which involves observing and describing the behavior of a subject without influencing it in any way.

6. Research Design is overall strategy to integrate various components and constitute the analysis of data. It is just a framework for collection and analysis of data at every stage.

7. 'Sampling Cases' means sampling of people, newspapers, television programmes etc. A sampling case is a small group that is generalised for the whole population.

8. Teaching is a series of principles and methods through which a teacher tries to bring modification in students behavior.so, according to the question various are the efforts of a teacher:

a) When students fail in a test it is the teacher who fails means it is the failure of a teacher's effort if he is unable to bring the improvement in students learning.

b) every teaching must ensure at learning means the aim and objective of teaching is to modify the student's behavior and ensures learning.

c) There can be teaching without learning taking place states that if teacher put all his/her efforts in teaching process even if a student doesn't want to learn then no teaching can make him learn but teaching is in the process.

d) During the process of teaching and learning it is not the students who is learning but it is the teacher also who learns a number of things like handling different types of student's behavior, discovering new ways for making teaching more effective etc.

9. A formative evaluation (sometimes referred to as internal) is a method for judging the worth of a program while the program activities are forming (in progress). They can be conducted during any phase of the ADDIE process.

Examples of formative assessments include asking students to:

draw a concept map in class to represent their understanding of a topic.

submit one or two sentences identifying the main point of a lecture.

turn in a research proposal for early feedback.

10. The assessment under CBCS is done twice in a year i.e. Semester wise. Students are given a choice to select from the available courses, each course is assigned a specific credit and there are three main courses in CBCs-Main, Foundation and Elective are the main elements of the Choice Based Credit System (CBCS).

11. Answer: Option B

Companies take savings as premium, invest in bonds and make payments to beneficiaries are classified as life insurance companies.

12. Seminar never includes large group of individuals. It can be a part of academic instructions, questioning or debates. It also involves skilled persons. So (a), (b) and (d) is correct.

13. Answer: Option D

A's 2 day's work $= \left(\frac{1}{20} \times 2\right) = \frac{1}{10}$

$(A + B + C)'s\,1$ day's work $= \left(\frac{1}{20} + \frac{1}{30} + \frac{1}{60}\right) = \frac{6}{60} = \frac{1}{10}$

Work done in 3 days $= \left(\frac{1}{10} + \frac{1}{10}\right) = \frac{1}{5}$

Now, $\frac{1}{5}$ work is done in 3 days.

∴ Whole work will be done in $(3 \times 5) = 15$ days.

14. •Lecturing – It is the process of delivering lectures in understandable languages.

•Discussion in groups -It is the action or process of talking about a theme in groups in order to reach a conclusion or to exchange ideas.

•Brainstorming - Brainstorming is a group creativity technique through which efforts are made to find a conclusion for a particular problem by colecting a list of relevant ideas contributed by its members.

•Programmed instruction - Programmed instruction is a method of presenting new subject matters to students in a graded sequence of controlled steps

15. B, C, D are not sign of motivated teaching as it doesn't indicate interest of students but student asking question clearly indicate that student are getting what is being taught to them and thus ask questions.

16. Runs after 8 matches = 80 * 8 = 640 and runs

after 12 matches = 70 * 12 = 840

Total runs made in the last four matches = 840 –640

= 200.

So, option C is correct option.

17. 5 11 21 35 53 75

_+6_ _+10_ _+14_ _+18_ _+22_

So, option A is correct.

18. XY (Z) ABC (DE) FGHI (JKL) = MNOPQ

+1   +2   +3

19. Answer: Option B C's 1 day's work $= \frac{1}{3} - \left(\frac{1}{6} + \frac{1}{8}\right) = \frac{1}{3} - \frac{7}{24} = \frac{1}{24}$

A's wages: B's wages: C's wages $= \frac{1}{6} : \frac{1}{8} : \frac{1}{24} = 4:3:1$

$\therefore C's$ share $(\text{for } 3 \text{ days}) = Rs. \left(3 \times \frac{1}{0.4} \times 3200\right)$

$= Rs. 400$

20. Let f be fixed charges and x be variable per km charge

276 = 2f + 16x --------- (i)

160 = f + 10x -------- (ii)

f = 160 – 10x --------- (iii)

Put (iii) in (i),

276 = 2 (160 – 10x) + 16x ------ (iv)

276 = 320 – 20x + 16x --------- (v)

x = 11

So, charges of the taxi per km = Rs. 11

21.

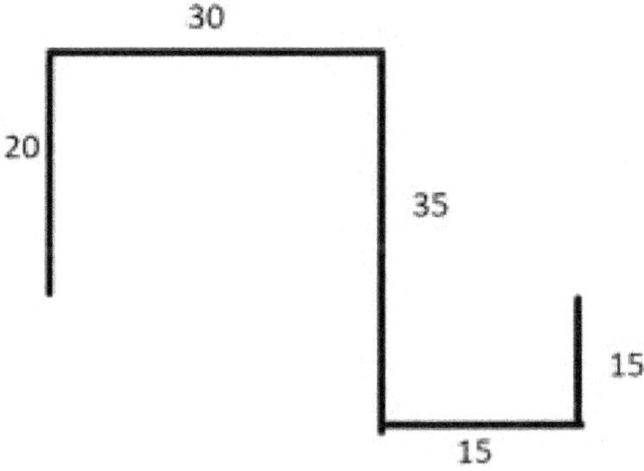

So, add 15m + 30m = 45m is the shortest distance.

22. If two standard form categorical propositions with the same subject and predicate are related in such a manner that if one is undetermined the other must be undetermined, then this phenomenon is called as contradictory.

23. Answer: Option B

Answer: Option BTime $= \left(\frac{100 \times 81}{450 \times 4.5}\right)$ years

$= 4$ years.

24. Anumana is a method by which knowledge is derived from another knowledge. On the basis of our perceptual knowledge, we know that wherever there is smoke there is fire (the opposite might not be true). After knowing the invariable relation between the two we can logically deduce the presence of fire whenever we see smoke. This is anumana.

25. A lexical definition is the meaning of the term in common usage or it simply reports the way in which a term is used within a language community. Lexical definition is descriptive, which report actual usage of language used by speakers and vary with the usage of the term, rather than prescriptive. When the purpose of a definition is to explain the use or to eliminate ambiguity the definition is called Lexical.

26. A smart classroom is a teaching space that has smart portion with a touch panel control laptop, it also has laptop connection and DVD player with camera and specialized software. A smart classroom is installed with projector and screen too.

27. Grapevine communication is also known as informal communication because communication is performed without maintaining the formalities/guidelines prescribed by the organization and moreover, there is no particular route for sharing the relevant information.

28. Answer: Option D

S.I. $= RS. (15500 - 12500) =$ Rs. 3000

Rate $= \left(\frac{100 \times 3000}{12500 \times 4}\right) \%$

$= 6 \%$

29. Every type of communication is affected by its context. Contexts can be similar, which sometimes might be confusing or overlapping. Communication will not be affected by reception or transmission.

30. Answer: Option **C**

Let the incomes in 2000 of Companies X and Y be $3x$ and $4x$ respectively.

And let the expenditures in 2000 of Companies X and Y be E_1 and E_2 respectively.

Then, for Company X we have:

$65 = \frac{3x - E_1}{E_1} \times 100 \Rightarrow \frac{65}{100} = \frac{3x}{E_1} - 1 \Rightarrow E_1 = 3x \times \left(\frac{100}{165}\right) \dots (1)$

For Company Y we have:

$50 = \frac{4x - E_2}{E_2} \times 100 \Rightarrow \frac{50}{100} = \frac{4x}{E_2} - 1 \Rightarrow E_2 = 4 \times x \left(\frac{100}{150}\right) \dots$ (ii)

From (i) and (ii), we get:

$\frac{E_1}{E_2} = \frac{3x \times \left(\frac{100}{165}\right)}{4x \times \left(\frac{100}{150}\right)}$

$$= \frac{3 \times 150}{4 \times 165}$$

$$= \frac{15}{22}$$

31. Profit percent of Company Y in $1997 = 35$

Let the income of Company Y in 1997 be Rs. x crores.

Then, $35 = \frac{x-220}{220} \times 100 \Rightarrow x = 297$

∴ Income of Company Y in $1997 =$ Rs. 297 crores.

32. Let the expenditures of each companies X and Y in 1996 be Rs. x crores.

And let the income of Company X in 1996 be Rs. z crores.

So that the income of Company Y in $1996 =$ Rs. $(342 - z)$ crores.

Then, for Company X we have:

$$40 = \frac{z-x}{x} \times 100 \Rightarrow \frac{40}{100} = \frac{z}{x} - 1 \Rightarrow x = \frac{100z}{140} \quad ......(i)$$

Also, for Company Y we have:

$$45 = \frac{(342-z)}{x} \times 100 \Rightarrow \frac{45}{100} = \frac{(342-z)}{x} - 1 \Rightarrow x = \frac{(342-z) \times 100}{145}$$

$$.........(ii)$$

From (i) and (ii), we get:

$$\frac{100z}{140} = \frac{(342-z) \times 100}{145} \Rightarrow z = 168$$

Substituting $z = 168$ in (i), we get: $x = 120$.

∴ Total expenditure of Companies X and Y in $1996 = 2x =$ Rs. 240 crores.

Total income of Companies X and Y in $1996 =$ Rs. 342 crores.

∴ Total profit $=$ Rs. $(342 - 240)$ crores

$=$ Rs. 102 crores.

33. Let the income of Company X in 1998 be Rs. x crores.

Then, $55 = \frac{x-200}{200} \times 100 \Rightarrow x = 310$

∴ Expenditure of Company x in $2001 =$ Income of Company x in 1998

$=$ Rs. 310 crores.

Let the income of Company X in 2001 be Rs. z crores.

Then, $50 = \frac{z-310}{310} \times 100 \Rightarrow z = 465$

∴ Income of Company X in $2001 =$ Rs. 465 crores.

34. Let the incomes of each of the two Companies X and Y in 1999 be Rs. x.

And let the expenditures of Companies X and Y in 1999 be E_1 and E_2 respectively.

Then, for Company X we have:

$$50 = \frac{x-E_1}{E_1} \times 100 \Rightarrow \frac{50}{100} = \frac{x}{E_1} - 1 \Rightarrow x = \frac{150}{100} E_1 \quad .... (i)$$

Also, for Company Y we have:

$$60 = \frac{x-E_2}{E_2} \times 100 \Rightarrow \frac{60}{100} = \frac{x}{E_2} - 1 \Rightarrow x = \frac{160}{100} E_2 \quad ......(ii)$$

From (i) and (ii), we get:

$$\frac{150}{100} E_1 = \frac{160}{100} E_2 \Rightarrow \frac{E_1}{E_2} = \frac{160}{150}$$

$$= \frac{16}{15}$$

35. Demerits of globalization of higher education are as follows:

• Promotion of elitism in higher education

• Commodification of higher education (It has become as saleable commodity)

• Increase in the cost of education (not affordable by everyone to study abroad)

36. Answer: Option **C**

Required decimal $= \frac{1}{60 \times 60}$

$$= \frac{1}{3600}$$

$$=.00027$$

37. Mail merge is used to send the same mail to different persons in MS Word. Mail merge is a way to create personalized letters and pre-addressed mailing labels. Microsoft Word can insert content from a database, spreadsheet into Word documents.

38. The byte is a unit of digital information that most commonly consists of eight bits.

1 Byte = 8 bits.

39. Chlorofluorocarbons released into the atmosphere since the 1930s in various applications like in air-conditioning, refrigeration, blowing agents in foams, etc.One of the anthropogenic sources of gaseous pollutants chlorofluorocarbons (CFCs) in air is in Foam Industry.

40. $\frac{29.94}{1.45} = \frac{299.4}{14.5}$

$$= \left(\frac{2994}{14.5} \times \frac{1}{10} \right) \left[\text{Here, Substitute } 172 \right.$$
in the place of $2994/14.5]$

$$= \frac{172}{10}$$

$$= 17.2$$

41. According to the first few lines of the passage, "The last great war, which nearly shook the foundations of the modern world, had little impact on Indian literature beyond aggravating the popular revulsion against violence and adding to the growing disillusionment with the 'humane pretensions' of the Western World."

This means that the last great war heightened the disgust against violence. Thus, option B is the correct answer.

42. The last great war had added "to the growing disillusionment with the 'humane pretensions' of the Western World." And this "was eloquently voiced in Tagore's later poems and his last testament, Crisis in Civilisation".

Hence, Tagore, in his last testament, articulated that the 'humane pretensions' of the Western World had been exposed. Option B is the correct answer.

43. According to the passage during the period of great war, the human intelligentsia, "could not help sympathising with England's dogged courage in the hour of peril". This means that they expressed sympathy towards England's courage during tough times. Thus, option D is the correct answer.

44. According to the given passage, "No doubt it (creative energy in Indian Literature) did, but unfortunately it was soon submerged in the great agony of partition, with its inhuman slaughter of the innocents..." Thus, the great agony of partition was responsible for the submergence of creative energy in Indian literature.

45. According to the latter half of the passage, "What reserves of enthusiasm and confidence survived these disasters (partition) have been mainly absorbed in the task of national reconstruction and economic development." Thus, option D is the correct answer.

46. Answer: Option A

You don't need to come unless you want to

47. Answer: Option C

The man to whom I sold my house was a cheat.

48. Corporate communication is the practice of developing, cultivating and maintaining a corporate identity or brand image. A solid corporate communications team provides initiatives to mold company image, communicate with internal and external audiences, and sustain a long-term positive reputation. Corporate communication is a management function that is committed to the dissemination of information to key constituencies, execution of corporate strategy and the development of messages for internal and external circulation.

49. Out of the given options, voice modulation plays an important while delivering the lectures. The voice modulation helps the students to understand the seriousness of that particular question or topic. So, voice modulation is an essential element a teacher has to take cognizance of while addressing students in a classroom.

50. The choice of communication partners is influenced by various factors - Proximity, utility, loneliness. Proximity means sense of closeness/connection to the partner. Utility means seeking benefit out of communication and loneliness means the person is alone and he needs to talk to some other person. Therefore, these factors play important role in influencing choice of communication partner.

51. Reason : Linear programming is a mathematical technique used in optimum allocation of resources in the organization.

(b) Decision tree is a graphical method for identifying alternative actions, estimating probabilities, and indicating the resulting expected pay-off.

(c) Simulation is the technique of developing a model that represents a real or existing system for solving complex problems that cannot be readily solved by other techniques.

(d) Waiting-line or queuing model is a mathematical model that describes the operating characteristics of queuing situations, in which service is provided to persons or units waiting in line.

(e) Game theory is a technique for determining the strategy that is likely to produce maximum profits in a competitive situation.

52. Reason : The concept of span of management concerns a determination of the number of individuals a manager can effectively supervise.

53. Commission for Agricultural Costs and Prices(CACP) is an expert body that recommends MSP by taking into account the cost of production, growing trends in domestic and international market prices.

- Commission for Agricultural Costs and Prices came into existence in 1965 as Agricultural Prices Commission.

- In 1985, Agricultural Prices Commission was renamed as Commission for Agricultural Costs and Prices(CACP).

- The commission comprises a Chairman, Member Secretary, One member (official), and two members (non-official).

- The Cabinet Committee on Economic Affairs (CCEA) approves the MSP.

Hence, the correct option is (A).

54. Customer Departmentation is done to service particular types of clients or customers.

Coordination between sales and other functions becomes difficult, as Customer-based Departmentation is applicable only to the sales function.

Hence from above discussion, we can infer that option (d) is not true about Customer Departmentation.

Options (a), (b), (c) all true about Customer Departmentation.

55. The major disadvantage of the matrix structure is its propensity to foster power struggles.

Hence, option D is correct.

56. A decision support system is an interactive computer system that provides managers with the necessary information for making intelligent decisions. Hence, option B is correct.

57. Reason : Generally speaking, a transnational organization transcends any home country, whereas a multinational organization does not.

58. Reason : Generally speaking, a transnational organization transcends any home country, whereas a multinational organization does not.

59. Reason : From the delegator's aspect, all of the following are the factors affecting the delegation of authority except Fear of criticism.

60. Reason : Open-system focus is characteristic of organization that describes the degree to which the organization monitors and responds to changes in the external environment.

61. Reason : Organization Chart is a vital tool for providing information about organizational relationships.

It shows authority relationships and neglects significant informal and informational relationships. Hence from above discussion, we can infer that option (d) is false with respect to Organization Chart. Options (a), (b), (c) and (e) are all true with respect to Organization Chart.

62. Reason : Organizational Culture is the collection of shared beliefs, values, rituals, stories, myths and specialized language that foster a feeling of community among organization members. It does not focus on profit. Hence, from above discussion, we can infer that option (d) is not a feature of Organizational Culture. Options (a), (b), (c) and (e) are all characteristics of Organizational Culture.

63. Reason: Manager Inventory Chart is a partial organization chart that shows managerial positions, current incumbents, potential replacements for each position, and the age of each person. However, it does not show the position to which a manager may be promoted. Hence, from above discussion, we can infer that option (c) is not an advantage of Manager Inventory Chart. Options (a), (b), (d) and (e) are all advantages of Manager Inventory Chart.

64. Answer: Option A

Federal government tax revenues if it exceeds government spending then it is classified as budget surplus. A budget surplus is a period when income or receipts exceed outlays or expenditures. A budget surplus often refers to the financial states of governments; individuals prefer to use the term 'savings' instead of the term 'budget surplus.'

65. Answer: Option D

Document in a corporation that consists of the amount of stock, name and addresses of directors is classified as charter. A charter plane or boat is one which is hired for use by a particular person or group and which is not part of a regular service.

66. Reason : Structural inertia is an organization's built-in mechanism to produce stability. e.g., formal rules and procedures for employees to follow. When an organization is confronted with change, this structural inertia acts as a counterbalance to sustain stability. Hence, from above discussion, we can infer that option (b) is correct. Options (a), (c), (d) and (e) are all individual sources of resistance to change.

67. Reason : Brainstorming is one of the best-known techniques for facilitating creativity, developed by Alex F. Osborn. Hence, from above discussion, we can infer that option (a) is correct.

68. Answer: Option B

A price for equity is called the cost of equity. The cost of equity is the return a company requires to decide if an investment meets capital return requirements.

69. Answer: Option B

Risk in which value of investment depends on what happens to foreign exchange rates is classified as exchange rate risk. Exchange rate risk, also known as currency risk, is the financial risk arising from fluctuations in the value of a base currency against a foreign.

70. Reason : According to L.A. Allen, communication involves a systematic and continuous process of telling, listening and understanding. Focusing the communication primarily at meeting the demands of an immediate situation is not a factor, which helps, in effective communication. Hence, from above discussion, we can infer that option (d) does not help in effective communication. All other options are factors, which help, in effective communication.

71. Reason : The major difference in skill requirements between middle and top managers is that top managers generally require higher level conceptual skills but less technical skills than middle managers.

Hence, from above discussion, we can infer that option (d) is correct.

72. Reason : According to the Scientific Management School of Thought, Work Methods Study is defined as the systematic, objective and critical examination of all the factors governing the operational efficiency of a specified activity to bring about improvement.

Hence, from above discussion, we can infer that option (a) is correct.

73. Answer: Option B

The ability to trade at a net prices very quickly is classified as liquidity. Liquidity describes the degree to which an asset or security can be quickly bought or sold in the market at a price reflecting its intrinsic value. In other words: the ease of converting it to cash.

74. Manpower planning is the process of estimating the optimum number of people required for completing a project, task or goal within time. Manpower planning includes parameters like a number of personnel, different types of skills, time period etc.

75. The following are subsystems that are frequently an integral part of 'management by objectives':

I. Manpower planning.

II. Compensation.

76. Reason : When decision makers construct simplified models that extract the essential features from a problem without capturing all the complexities of a problem, they are acting under bounded rationality.

77. Reason: Sometimes cohesive "in groups" let the desire for unanimity override sound judgment when generating and evaluating alternative courses of action.

Hence, from above discussion, we can infer that option (d) would generally not be considered an advantage of group decision-making.

Options (a), (b), (c) are all advantages of group decision-making.

78. Reason: Rate of change determines the degree to which policies can be formulated and the stability that can be achieved in the policies.

79. The generic strategies developed by Porter to illustrate the kind of strategies managers might develop to make their organizations more competitive are as follows:

I.   Cost leadership.

II.   Differentiation.

III.   Focus.

Hence, from above discussion, we can infer that option (d) is correct.

80. Reason: Divisional Structure is a type of departmentation in which positions are grouped according to the similarity of products, services or markets.

Individuals are unable to develop in-depth areas of specialization to the same extent as in a functional structure.

Hence from the above discussion, we can infer that option (c) is not an advantage of the divisional structure.

Options (a), (b), (d) are all advantages of divisional structure.

81. Delegate means to grant or confer. Thus, a manager grants or confers on subordinates certain tasks and duties along with sufficient authority, to accomplish these.

Explaining the relevance of delegated tasks to larger projects or to department or organization goals is most likely to increase the effectiveness of delegation.

Hence, from above discussion, we can infer that option (c) is correct.

82. Answer: Option D

If unprepared, Competitive and environmental pressures and excessive control strategic pressures are recognized as key factors that can weaken the organization.

83. Reason: The original source of an organization's culture is most strongly associated with the vision of the organization's founder(s).

Hence, from above discussion, we can infer that option (d) is correct.

84. Answer: Option B

Strengths are the resources, skills or other advantages a firm enjoys relative to its competitors. Strategic strength is your ability to set the right goals and to create action plans and follow them. Strategic strength is the foundation for success.

85. Reason : The three decision-making conditions, which managers face in analyzing decision alternatives are certainty, uncertainty and risk.

Hence, from above discussion, we can infer that option (a) is correct.

86. Reason: Sensitivity training is concerned with (i) better understanding of group processes, (ii) development of organizing and intervening skills in group processes and (iii) better insight into one's own behavior and the way one is viewed by others. Hence, option (a) is correct.

87. Reason: Technology is an external force of change.

Hence, option (b) is not an internal force of change.

Options (a), (c), (d)are all internal forces of change.

88. Answer: Option D

Weakness is a limitation or deficiency in resources, skills, and capabilities that seriously impede effective performance. The

organizational weaknesses that have the potential to lead the organization to inefficiency and ineffectiveness should be known and improved.

89. Reason: According to Herzberg's motivation-hygiene theory, relationship with peers, status, supervision and security are the four responses that are all hygiene factors.

Hence, option (c) is correct.

90. Reason: According to the managerial grid, the country club leader believes that thoughtful attention to the needs of people for a satisfying relationship leads to a comfortable, friendly organizational atmosphere and work tempo.

91. Reason: According to the Managerial Grid, propounded by Blake and Mouton, the most effective management style is characterized by high concern for people and high concern for production.

Hence, option (b) is correct.

92. Reason: Diagonal information flow takes place among persons at different levels who have no direct relationships.

Hence, option (d) is correct.

93. Reason: Organizational effectiveness is a measure of how appropriate organizational goals are, and how well an organization is achieving those goals.

Hence, option (d) is correct.

94. Reason: Return on investment is the ratio of earnings before taxes to that of total assets. So, it attempts to measure profitability.

Hence, option (b) is correct.

95. Answer: Option B

Robert Kalpan and David developed the balanced score card in the early 1990 as a performance measurement system. Performance measurement is the process of collecting, analyzing and/or reporting information regarding the performance of an individual, group, organization, system or component.

96. Answer: Option D

Flexibility is said to be the key factor in maintaining organizational growth (e.g., Hurst 1995). Strategic flexibility is the organization's. capability to identify major changes in the external environment, quickly commit. resources to new courses of action in response to those changes, and recognize and act. promptly when it is time to halt or reverse existing resource commitments.

97. Reason: Hazard analysis involves identification of preventive measures the manufacturing units can adopt, to control food safety hazards that arise during processing.

98. Reason: MIS (Management Information System) can be defined as an integrated, user-machine system for providing information to support managerial, operational and decision-making functions in an organization.

The first necessary step to effectively operate an MIS is determining information needs.

Hence, option (c) is correct.

99. Answer: Option D

Strategic paradoxes elements of strategy affect the process of strategy creation and implementation. The strategy paradox is a consequence of the conflict between commitment and uncertainty, i.e., strategic uncertainty. Commitments are what allow an organization to create and capture value. Uncertainty creates risk and opportunity

100. Reason: In the geocentric orientation toward international business, a firm analyzes the needs of customers worldwide and then adopts standardized practices for all the markets it serves.

101. According to contingency approach to management, managerial practice depends on circumstances.

102. Work specialization involves different people each doing a specific job.

103. Reason : Pre-conventional Level of Moral Development is influenced exclusively by personal interest. It is concerned with following rules only when it's of interest.

Hence from above discussion, we can infer that option (a) is correct.

104. Reason : Planning can't eliminate change, but managers usually plan in order to anticipate changes and develop the most-effective response to changes.

Hence from above discussion, we can infer that option (B) is correct.

105. Answer: Option D

Miles and Snow (1994) identify four main reasons for failure. Poor judgment leading to poor, inappropriate strategic decisions is one of those reasons. Miles and Snow suggest that business-level strategies generally fall into one of four categories: prospector, defender, analyzer, and reactor.

106. Environmental scanning, forecasting, and benchmarking are the three most effective tools that managers can use to analyze their organization's environment.

Hence from above discussion, we can infer that option (b) is correct.

107. Answer: Option B

Checkland (1981) describes an organization as Systems that comprise a collection of people who are trying to act with purpose.

108. Reason : Sometimes cohesive "in groups" let the desire for unanimity override sound judgement when generating and evaluating alternative courses of action.

Hence, from above discussion, we can infer that option (d) would generally not be considered an advantage of group decision-making.

Options (a), (b), (c) are all advantages of group decision-making.

109. Answer: Option A

Through managers in the various businesses working together, sharing information and capabilities, helping each other, and creating synergy an organization spot, create, and exploit new opportunities ahead of its rivals.

110. Answer: Option B

Managing paradoxes is not a competence recognized by Richardson and Thompson (1994). Paradox management describes how a great manager can successfully balance these paradoxes. By using paradox management, a business can simultaneously encourage both competition and collaboration, rather than being able to have only one of the two.

111. A type of departmentalization in which similar specialists and people with common skills, knowledge, and orientations are grouped together, is referred to as Functional departmentalization.

Hence, from the above discussion, we can infer that option (b) is correct.

112. If unity of command were to be applied without exception, functional authority would be exercised only by line managers. Hence, option (e) is incorrect and is the answer.

113. Reason : Organization Chart is a vital tool for providing information about organizational relationships.

It shows authority relationships and neglects significant informal and informational relationships

Hence from above discussion, we can infer that option (d) is false with respect to Organization Chart.

Options (a), (b), (c)are all true with respect to Organization Chart.

114. Reason : Performance Test or Work Sampling Test is used as a means of measuring practical ability on a specific job. The applicant completes some job activity under structured conditions.

Hence from above discussion, we can infer that option (c) is correct.

115. Emotional maturity is when someone can manage their emotions no matter their circumstances. They know how to respond to tough situations and still keep their cool. It's a skill set they can consistently work on overtime.

Social Maturity is the process of developing appropriate attitudes for the personal, interpersonal, and social adequacies of an individual, which are essential for functioning effectively in Society.

Leader:

- A leader is anyone who is recognized by individuals or by the group as an available source of help.

- Leadership is the process of influencing and supporting others to work enthusiastically towards achieving objectives.

- Leadership is closely linked to the level of emotional intelligence and social maturity that a leader owns. Equally, the leader who uses this will be followed easily.

- The mood of a leader influences the mood of followers and their performance at work. If people's emotions are channeled by enthusiasm, then it follows efficiency.

- People are made aware that bitterness and anxiety, reduce efficiency. Leaders generally can be found to be very social, intelligent, self-confident, and dominant. Furthermore, their knowledge and skills must be adequate to justify others following them.

Confusion Points:

- Formation of highly positive public opinion: This is not a quality of a leader because others' positive opinions can be influenced by the leader but cannot be formed by a leader.

- Formation of high prestige in the group: This is important in the group and can be formed by communicating ideas and values in the whole group.

- Feelings of shamefulness when remained unsuccessful in his objectives: Shamefulness cannot be the quality of a leader.

Therefore, we can conclude that an excellent leader possesses the qualities of emotional and social maturity, along with it one more important quality, a leader has to be achieved is quick communication of his ideas and values in the whole group.

Hence, the correct option is (C).

116. Reason : In negotiation and agreement method of overcoming resistance to change, management neutralizes potential or actual resistance by exchanging something of value for cooperation.

Hence, from above discussion, we can infer that option (c) is correct.

117. A Memorandum of Association contains the following clauses:

- Name Clause
- Registered Office Clause
- Object Clause
- Liability Clause
- Capital Clause

Registered Office Clause:

- This clause specifies the name of the state in which the registered office of the company is to be situated.

- It helps to determine the jurisdiction of the Registrar of Companies.

- The company is required to inform the Registrar of Companies about the registered office within 30 days from the date of incorporation or commencement of business.

Therefore, the registered office clause of the memorandum of association contains the name of the state in which the registered office of the company is to be situated.

Hence, the correct option is (C).

118. Tarun, Shreya, Aparna and Sheila all worked together, and to be more effective they taught each other their job skills. This process is called job rotation or cross-training. This is defined as a job design approach that involves periodically shifting workers through a set of jobs in a planned sequence. (b) Role perception is the individual's understanding of the behavior needed to accomplish a task or perform a job. (c) Training is the systematic development of knowledge, skills and attitudes required by an individual to perform adequately a given job or a task. (d) Simulation is a quantitative planning technique that uses mathematical models to imitate reality.

119. Senthil's performance is influenced by the component of valence. Hence option D is correct.

120. It is different to find a company where the employees do not have grievances of one kind or the other. **The grievances may be real or imaginary,** valid or invalid, genuine or false. A grievance produces unhappiness, discontent, indifference, low morale, frustration, etc. Ultimately, it affects employees' concentration, efficiency and productivity.

121. Reason : As per the managerial grid, the (9,9) manager believes that concern for people and tasks are compatible and that tasks need to be carefully explained and decisions endorsed by subordinates to achieve a high level of commitment.

Hence, from above discussion, we can infer that option (b) is correct.

122. Both statements are incorrect.

An explanation for Statement I:

Section 125: The promisee in a contract of indemnity, acting within the scope of his authority, is entitled to recover from the promiser-

- All damages which he may be compelled to pay in any suit in respect of any matter to which the promise to indemnify applies;

- All costs which he may be compelled to pay in any such suit if, in bringing or defending it, he did not contravene the orders of the promiser, and acted as it would have been prudent for him to act in the absence of any contract of indemnity, or if the promiser authorized him to bring or defend the suit;

- All sums which he may have paid under the terms of any compromise of any such suit, if the compromise was not contrary to the orders of the promiser, and was one which it would have been prudent for the promisee to make in the absence of any contract of indemnity, or if the promiser authorized him to compromise the suit.

However, As per Section 124 of the Indian Contract Act, a contract of indemnity is a contract by which one party promises to save the other party from loss caused to him.

An explanation for Statement II:

There are generally two parties in indemnity contracts:

- The Indemnity holder is the one who is protected from any liability.

- The Indemnifier is the one who promises to reimburse the Indemnitee for any claims.

Therefore, the person who promises to indemnify or make good the loss is called the indemnified, and the person whose loss is made is called the indemnity holder.

Hence, the correct option is (D).

123. A debt service coverage ratio of 1 or above indicates that a company is generating sufficient operating income to cover its annual debt and interest payments. A number of times surplus covers interest and installments of Term Loans. Hence option D is correct.

124. Customer partnering is a method of analyzing user needs in which a company works closely with its customers to design products that better meet their needs. The process is somewhat akin to using contextual inquiry and focus groups, but it provides much more detail about how the company can meet customers' needs and it involves the customer much more deeply in the design process. Rather than devoting one or two days to a site visit or a few hours to an interview or focus group session, company researchers engage customers in a series of working sessions over a period of weeks or months. This extended engagement allows both company researchers and customers to consider issues introduced at each new session in the context of perspectives developed in previous sessions.

125. Supermarkets sell food and household items at low prices, with low margins at large quantities.

Hence option A is correct.

126. The following statements is true about investment centers:

I. The control system examines the role of assets in generating profit.

127. Operations Management oversees the transformation process that converts resources such as labor and raw materials into finished goods and services.

Hence, from above discussion, we can infer that option (c) is tru e regarding Operations Management.

Options (a), (b), (d) are all false regarding Operations Management.

128. In direct control the cause of an unsatisfactory outcome traced back to the individual responsible for it who is then made to correct the practice.

Hence option C is correct.

129. The concentration of advertising regarding the launch of a new product calls for spending all the advertising budget in a single period. Hence option C is correct.

130. An office automation system aims at facilitating communication and increasing the efficiency and productivity of managers and office workers through document and message processing.

Hence option C is correct.

131. The given example is that of an operational plan. Operational plans help in day-to-day functioning and are developed by lower level managers. They consider time-frames of less than a year. Hence option B is correct.

132. Counseling subordinates on production, personnel or other problems is a function of middle level management.All other options are functions of supervisory level management. Hence option D is correct.

133. The intuition stage of the creative process links the unconscious state of mind with the conscious state. Intuition is the ability to acquire knowledge without recourse to conscious reasoning. Different fields use the word "intuition" in very different ways, including but not limited to: direct access to. Hence option B is correct.

134. The span of control refers to the number of subordinates a supervisor has. Simply a manager or a supervisor or a superior who has a group of subordinates, who can directly report him or her is called a Span of Management.

The span of management includes:

Determination of how many people working with each other report to a single manager.

Determination of the number of individuals a manager can effectively supervise.

Hence, option (d) is the answer.

135. Corporate social responsibility (CSR) is a self-regulating business model that helps a company be socially accountable—to itself, its stakeholders, and the public. By practicing corporate social responsibility, also called corporate citizenship, companies can be conscious of the kind of impact they are having on all aspects of society, including economic, social, and environmental. Corporate social responsibility is a broad concept that can take many forms depending on the company and industry. Through CSR programs, philanthropy, and volunteer efforts, businesses can benefit society while boosting their brands.

Walker has not given a model on Corporate Social Responsibility (CSR). Hence option D is correct.

136. Japanese companies tend to make decisions by consensus because it is a reflection of thelarger societal cultural value on groups. Hence option A is correct.

137. A Transaction Processing System is a set of information which processes the data transaction in database system that monitors transaction programs. The system is useful when something is sold over the internet. It allows for a time delay between when an item is being sold to when it is actually sold. Transaction processing systems consist of computer hardware and software hosting a transaction-oriented application that performs the routine transactions necessary to conduct business. Examples include systems that manage sales order entry, airline reservations, payroll, employee records, manufacturing, and shipping.

138. Standard cost centers are also referred to as engineered expense centers.

Hence option B is correct.

139. Lawrence has succumbed to Halo error, which is a common tendency to rate subordinates high or low on all performance measures based on one of their characteristics where as in rater

prejudice managers allow their personal biases to distort the rating they give to their subordinates. In shifting standards, managers rate each subordinate by different standards and expectations. In different rater patterns, managers differ in their rating styles. Some may rate harshly, others may rate easily. Whereas stereotyping is the process of categorizing or labeling people on the basis of a single attribute rating a person based on the characteristics of the group to which he or the she belongs. Hence option A is correct.

140. The theory is concerned with reality, not perceptions is false with regard to Vroom's expectancy theory. Vroom's expectancy theory is based on self-interest where each employee seeks to maximize personal satisfaction and holds that there are two crucial linkages among effort-performance-reward in this theory. Hence option D is correct.

141. Reason : Mark's Embroidery is departmentalized by customer, i.e. to say customer divisions are divisions set up to service particular types of clients or customers. Under this method, activities are grouped according to the customers the organization serves and service to the customers is of top priority. (a) Product divisions are divisions created to concentrate on a single product or service of at least a relatively homogeneous set of products or services. (c) Geographic divisions are divisions are designed to serve different geographic areas. Under this method, territory or location is taken as the basis for departmentation. (d) Process divisions are designed to departmentalize the activities through the different process which the organization follows. (e) In Functional departmentation activities are grouped according to their main functional or specialized area such as Production, Finance, Marketing, HR, etc.

142. Intrapreneurs bridge the gap between inventors and managers; they take new ideas and turn them into profitable realities." Hence option D is correct.

143. Tripartite Bodies:

It began as a statutory organization by the recommendation of the Whitey Commission to the ILO in 1931. Hence option B is correct.

144. Brand imagery deals with the extrinsic properties of the product or service, including the ways in which the brand attempts to meet customers' psychological or social needs. ... Brand feelings are customers' emotional responses and reactions with respect to the brand. Hence option C is correct.

145. Linear programming is a mathematical technique used in optimum allocation of resources in the organization.

Decision tree is a graphical method for identifying alternative actions, estimating probabilities, and indicating the resulting expected pay-off.

Simulation is the technique of developing a model that represents a real or existing system for solving complex problems that cannot be readily solved by other techniques.

Waiting-line or queuing model is a mathematical model that describes the operating characteristics of queuing situations, in which service is provided to persons or units waiting in line.

Game theory is a technique for determining the strategy that is likely to produce maximum profits in a competitive situation. Hence A is correct.

146. Blake and Mouton's Managerial Grid is an approach to defining leadership styles based on a manager's concern for people and concern for production. Impoverished management assumes that exertion of minimum effort to get required work done is appropriate to sustain organization membership. Hence option D is correct.

147. Socialization refers to the process that helps new employees adapt to the organization's culture.

Hence option C is correct.

148. Intellectual property (IP) is a category of property that includes intangible creations of the human intellect. There are many types of intellectual property, and some countries recognize more than others. The most well-known types are copyrights, patents, trademarks, and trade secrets.

- Copyright refers to the legal right of the owner of intellectual property. In simpler terms, copyright is the right to copy. This means that the original creators of products and anyone they give authorization to are the only ones with the exclusive right to reproduce the work.

- A trademark is a word, phrase, symbol, and/or design that identifies and distinguishes the source of the goods of one party from those of others. A service mark is a word, phrase, symbol, and/or design that identifies and distinguishes the source of a service rather than goods.

- Industrial design (ID) is the professional service of creating and developing concepts and specifications that optimize the function, value, and appearance of products and systems for the mutual benefit of both user and manufacturer.

A layout design of an integrated circuit refers essentially to the three-dimensional character of the elements and interconnections of an integrated circuit. An integrated circuit (IC) is an electronic circuit in which the elements of the circuit are integrated into a medium, and which functions as a unit.

Therefore, Intellectual property includes copyright, trademark, industrial designs but does not include layout designs of integrated circuits.

Hence, the correct option is (C).

149. Since situational leadership is based on a number of different situations, there are various traits and characteristics that a situational leader possesses. Below listed are some characteristics of situational leadership :

Supervising – Situational leadership will be high on the "directive" aspect when the juniors are not sufficiently developed and need continuous supervision. Here, the leader gives specific guidance about what the goals are, and exactly how the goals need to be achieved. It is similar to a parent supervising the actions of a newborn.

Coaching – If the situation requires it, the leader will also coach their team. This is an extension of the supervising approach; the leader still provides detailed instructions but they also focus on motivating the subordinates, seeking inputs, and explaining why they have made certain decisions.

Taking Part – The situational leader may try to advice a team to become more independent performing the tasks by letting them take routine choices. High-level problem-solving is still under their domain, but they allow team members to actively participate in the decision-making process.

Delegating – When dealing with a highly matured and competent team, the situational leader will slowly reduce their supervision and involvement in the daily activities of team members. The leader is involved while discussing the tasks and deciding on the goals to be achieved, but after that team members have total freedom on how they want to accomplish these goals.

It takes a lot of courage for a leader to try out various leadership approaches and figure out which one is ideal. Hence, option D is correct.

150. Situational leadership refers to a leadership style where the leader of an organization has to modify his style to fit the progression level of the followers he is trying to influence. In situational leadership, it is up to the leader to change his style, not the follower to accommodate to the leader's style. The style may change repeatedly to meet the needs of others in the organization based on the situation. As a leader you might wonder that you are not able to influence your employees in the organization and your approach does not work the same all the time.

Paper-I

Q.1 The type of research involves looking at variables over an extended period of time. It is called:-

A. Cross-sectional   **B.** Time series

C. Longitudinal   **D.** Latitudinal

Q.2 Large computer system typically uses:

A. Line printers

B. Ink-jet printers

C. Dot-matrix printers

D. Daisy wheel printers

Q.3 Which of the following statement/s about the Applied research is/are correct?

A. Applied research is used to solve a practical problem.

B. It can be used to solve problems of the education system of the developing countries.

C. Both A and B

D. Applied research is also called fundamental research.

Q.4 The format of thesis writing is the same as in:-

A. preparation of a research paper/article

B. writing of seminar presentation

C. a research dissertation

D. presenting a workshop / conference paper

Q.5 Which sequence of research steps is logical in the list given below?

A. Problem formulation, Analysis, Development of Research design, Hypothesis making, Collection of data, Arriving at generalizations and conclusions.

B. Development of Research design, Hypothesis making, Problem formulation, Data analysis, Arriving at conclusions and data collection.

C. Problem formulation, Hypothesis making, Development of a Research design, Collection of data, Data analysis and formulation of generalizations and conclusions.

D. Problem formulation, Deciding about the sample and data collection tools, Formulation of hypothesis, Collection and interpretation of research evidence.

Q.6 Arrange the list in correct order as per their usage in the article writing.

A. Abstract, Topic, Discussion, Method, Bibliography

B. Topic, Discussion, Method, Abstract, Bibliography

C. Topic, Abstract, Method, Discussion, Bibliography

D. Topic, Abstract, Discussion, Method, Bibliography

Q.7 In which of the following activities, potential for nurturing creative and critical thinking is relatively greater?

A. Preparing research summary

B. Presenting a seminar paper

C. Participation in research conference

D. Participation in a workshop

Q.8 Identify the learner characteristics which would facilitate the teaching-learning system to become effective.

A. Prior experience of the learner

B. Learner's family lineage

C. Learner's religious affiliation

D. All of these

Q.9 Which among the following is the best field of study to improve the ability of students to experiment and analyze?

A. Economics   **B.** History

C. Science   **D.** Languages

Q.10 Which of the following characteristics do not belong to an effective teacher/teaching. Identify the correct option.

A. A teacher is effective if he/she has full confidence of the subject

B. Teaching is always in a formal manner.

C. Teaching is a continuous process

D. Teaching is an interaction between teacher and students

Q.11 In which teaching method learner's participation is made optimal and proactive?

A. Discussion method

B. Buzz session method

C. Brainstorming session method

D. Project method

Q.12 Assertion (A) : Formative evaluation tends to accelerate the pace of learning.

Reason (R) : As against summative evaluation, formative evaluation is highly reliable.

Choose the correct answer from the following code:

A. Both (A) and (R) are true and (R) is the correct explanation of (A).

B. Both (A) and (R) are true, but (R) is not the correct explanation of (A).

C. (A) is true, but (R) is false.

D. (A) is false, but (R) is true.

Q.13 Suppose as a teacher you are training your students in public speaking and debate. Which among the following is most difficult to develop among the students?

A. Using/Selecting appropriate language

B. Control over emotions

C. Voice modulation

D. Concept formulation

Q.14 Which among the following reflects best the quality of teaching in a classroom?

A. Through the use of many teaching aids in the classroom

B. Through full attendance in the classroom

C. Through the quality of questions asked by students in classroom

D. Through observation of silence by the students in

classroom

Q.15 One of the most powerful factors affecting teaching effectiveness is related to the:

A. Social system of the country
B. Economic status of the society
C. Prevailing political system
D. Educational system

Q.16 In the series 1, 6, 15, 28, 45, ... the next term will be:
A. 66   **B.** 76   **C.** 56   **D.** 84

Q.17 The next term in the series
ABD, DGK, HMS, MTB, ... is :
A. NSA   **B.** SBL   **C.** PSK   **D.** RUH

Q.18 Ajay is a friend of Rakesh. Pointing to an old man Ajay asked Rakesh who is he? Rakesh said "His son is my son's uncle". The old man is related to Rakesh as:

A. Grandfather   **B.** Father-in-law
C. Father   **D.** Uncle

Q.19 A postman walked 20 m straight from his office, turned right and walked 10 m. After turning left he walked 10 m and after turning right walked 20 m. He again turned right and walked 70 m. How far he is from his office?
A. 50 m.   **B.** 40 m.   **C.** 60 m.   **D.** 20 m.

Q.20 The missing term in the series 1, 4, 27, 16,? , 36, 343, ... is:
A. 30   **B.** 49   **C.** 125   **D.** 81

Q.21 The next term in the following series, YEB, WFD, UHG, SKI, ? will be:
A. TLO   **B.** QOL   **C.** QLO   **D.** GQP

Q.22 In the series 3, 11, 23, 39, 59, ... The next term will be:
A. 63   **B.** 73   **C.** 83   **D.** 93

Q.23 In certain code, SELECTION is coded as QCJCARGML. The code of AMERICANS will be:

A. YKCPGAYLQ   **B.** BNFSJDBMR
C. QLYAGPCKY   **D.** YQKLCYPAG

Q.24 Two railway tickets from city A to B and three tickets from city A to C cost ₹177. Three tickets from city A to B and two tickets from city A to C cost ₹ 173. The fare for city B from city A will be ₹
A. 25   **B.** 27   **C.** 30   **D.** 33

Q.25 A is sister of B. F is daughter of G. C is mother of B. D is father of C. E is mother of D. A is related to D as:

A. Grand daughter   **B.** Daughter
C. Daughter-in-law   **D.** Sister

Ques (26-30):Read the following passage carefully and answer questions.

Singapore has long advocated for India to take up its role as an integral part of the region. It is gratifying to see how ASEAN – India relations have grown during the past 25 years. In 1991, when the Cold War ended and India began its economic liberalization, Singapore saw an opportunity to deepen ties and build on its historical and cultural links with the Asian region.

Singapore pushed for India to become a full ASEAN dialogue partner in 1995 and join the EAS in 1995 and since then, ASEAN – India ties have strengthened. All in all, around 30 platforms for co-operation exist, including seven ministerial dialogues and the Annual Leader Summit. However, there is scope for more and it is a must. For instance, there are tremendous opportunities in enhancing physical and digital connectivity between India and ASEAN. ASEAN is committed to strengthening land, air and sea linkages with India. These linkages will enhance people-to-people flows, as well as boost business, investment and tourism. The India-Myanmar-Thailand trilateral highway will connect India's Northeast to mainland Southeast Asia. While one can fly directly between India and several ASEAN countries, there is still much room to expand air links to support growing business and tourism. Beyond physical linkages, digital connectivity is the new frontier in the Fourth Industrial Revolution. India has made great progress in innovation, Start-ups and digital inclusion. There are opportunities to apply initiatives such as Aadhaar in our region. E-commerce and FinTech are two other areas of potential collaboration. As an economic hub, Singapore can serve as a springboard to lunch these ideas to Southeast Asia and beyond. India's role in ASEAN should be anchored by growing economic ties with Singapore. The economic integration involving 16 countries with one-third of global GDP and trade will create an integrated Asian market.

Q.26 The areas of collaboration between India and ASEAN are:
(a) FinTech
(b) Aadhaar
(c) E-commerce
(d) Digital backwardness
(e) Trilateral highways
(f) Fourth Industrial Revolution
A. (a), (c), (e) and (f)   **B.** (a), (b), (c) and (d)
C. (c), (d), (e) and (f)   **D.** (b), (c), (d) and (e)

Q.27 What prompted Singapore to opt for stronger ties with India?
A. End of Cold War
B. Economic liberalization in India
C. Historical past
D. Geo-political equations

Q.28 What is needed to encourage tourism between India and ASEAN?
A. Waterways   **B.** Air links
C. Innovation   **D.** Start-ups

Q.29 The commitment of ASEAN with India is:
A. Hold leadership summits
B. Offer political platforms
C. More and more dialogues
D. Improving transport links

Q.30 Who can be India's Launchpad for an integrated Asian market as per the passage?
A. Southeast Asia   **B.** Myanmar
C. Thailand   **D.** Singapore

Q.31 In which year Education Commission under the Chairmanship of Dr. DS. Kothari was set up?

A. 1960 **B.** 1955 **C.** 1952 **D.** 1964

Q.32 As per the latest data released by UGC, how many state universities are there in India?

A. 789 **B.** 123 **C.** 394 **D.** 260

Q.33 When was the University Education Commission constituted?

A. November 4, 1947 **B.** November 4, 1948
C. November 4, 1949 **D.** November 4, 1950

Q.34 Communicative abilities embrace which of the following skills?

A. Linguistic skills **B.** Semantic skills
C. Cultural skills **D.** Both a & b

Q.35 Non-verbal communication is considered as:-

A. Informal **B.** Precise
C. Culture-free **D.** Formal

Q.36 The rhetorical approach in classroom communication considers teachers as_____ agents of students.

A. Non-official **B.** Official
C. Influencing **D.** Academic

Q.37 The classroom communication should essentially be:

A. Contrived **B.** Empathetic
C. Abstract **D.** Non-descriptive

Ques (38-41):Direction: Study the following line graph and answer the question.

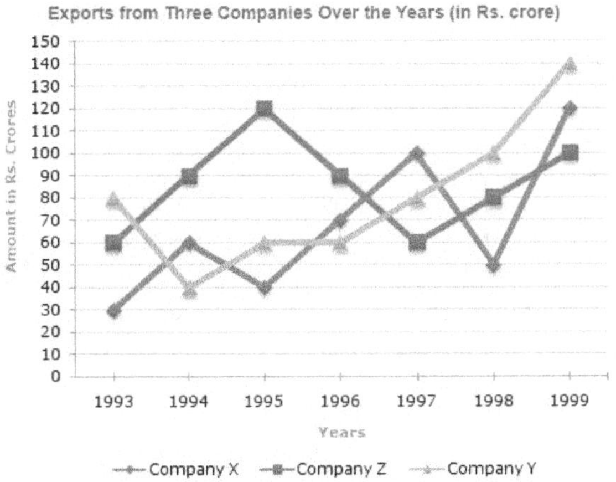

Q.38 For which of the following pairs of years the total exports from the three Companies together are equal?

A. 1995 and 1998 **B.** 1996 and 1998
C. 1997 and 1998 **D.** 1995 and 1996

Q.39 Average annual exports during the given period for Company Y is approximately what percent of the average annual exports for Company Z?

A. 87.12% **B.** 89.64% **C.** 91.21% **D.** 93.33%

Q.40 In which year was the difference between the exports from Companies X and Y the minimum?

A. 1994 **B.** 1995 **C.** 1996 **D.** 1997

Q.41 What was the difference between the average exports of the three Companies in 1993 and the average exports in 1998?

A. Rs. 15.33 crores **B.** Rs. 18.67 crores
C. Rs. 20 crores **D.** Rs. 22.17 crores

Q.42 A is two years older than B who is twice as old as C. If the total of the ages of A, B and C be 27, then how old is B?

A. 11 years **B.** 10 years
C. 13 years **D.** None of these

Q.43 What are the barriers to effective communication?

A. Moralising, being judgemental and comments of consolation.
B. Dialogue, summary and self- review.
C. Use of simple words, cool reaction and defensive attitude.
D. Personal statements, eye contact and simple narration.

Q.44 A small text file stored on user's computer by some websites in order to recognize and keep track of user's preferences is called:

A. Log **B.** Report **C.** Cookie **D.** History

Q.45 ______denotes an error in a computer program.

A. Bit **B.** Bug **C.** Spam **D.** Virus

Q.46 The output quality of a printer is measured by:

A. Digits per inch **B.** Dots per mm
C. Dots per inch **D.** Dots per cm

Q.47
Here are some words translated from an artificial language.
gorblflur means fan belt
pixngorbl means ceiling fan
arthtusl means tile roof
Which word could mean "ceiling tile"?

A. arthflur **B.** gorbltusl **C.** flurgorbl **D.** pixnarth

Q.48 Inside rural homes, the source/sources of Nitrogen Oxide Pollution may be:
1) Unvented gas stoves
2) Wood stoves
3) Kerosene heaters
Choose the correct code:

A. 1 and 2 only **B.** 2 and 3 only
C. 2 only **D.** 1, 2 and 3

Q.49 If 6 years is subtracted from the present age of Randheer and the remainder is divided by 18, then the present age of his grandson Anup is obtained, If Anup is 2 year younger than Mahesh whose age is 5 years, then what is the age of Randheer?

A. 96 years **B.** 84 years **C.** 48 years **D.** 60 years

Q.50 Negative Net Working Capital implies that:

A. Long-term funds have been used for fixed assets.

B. Short-term funds have been used for fixed assets.

C. Long-term funds have been used for current assets.

D. Short-term funds have been used for current assets.

Paper-II

Q.51 Susan is the General Manager at "Divine Corporation" and she is in charge of making sure that the IT department stays in close contact with the marketing department during the implementation of a new e-commerce effort with David as its Project Manager. Which managerial role described by Henry Mintzberg is Susan playing?

A. A figurehead role

B. A liaison role

C. A project manager role

D. An operational task role

Q.52 Which of the following is not upward communication?

A. Cost accounting report

B. Purchase order summary

C. Production report

D. Corporate policy statement

Q.53 There are various appraisal techniques used in an organization. A performance appraisal technique that makes use of feedback from supervisors, subordinates and co-workers, is called:-

A. Work-oriented appraisal

B. 360-degree appraisal

C. Informal appraisal

D. Graphic rating

Q.54 The BCG matrix was devised in the 1970's by the Boston Consulting Group, a leading management consulting firm. It is a widely used method of portfolio management and helps businesses evaluate their profitability. According to the BCG matrix, a strategic business unit comprising speculative products that entail high risks, would be referred to as:-

A. A question mark   **B.** A bull

C. A dog   **D.** A cash cow

Q.55 During the early 1900's, the mission of business firms was set exclusively in economic terms. After the 1960's, social activists began to question the singular objective of business enterprises. Managers' today continually encounter decisions that have a social dimension. Which of the following is defined as a business firm's obligation, beyond that required by law and economics, to pursue long-term goals that are good for society?

A. Social obligation

B. Social screening

C. Values-based management

D. Social responsibility

Q.56 Which of the following best describes line-staff conflict?

A. Conflict between two or more individuals with perceived differences in values, goals, or needs

B. Conflict among an individual's self values, goals, or needs

C. Intergroup conflict arising from perceived differences between those directly involved in producing or selling products and those that support functions such as information systems and human resources

D. Conflict on account of work delegated without conferring responsibility

Q.57 The Gantt Chart was invented by Henry L. Gantt. It is still used today in the production planning area of many organizations. It was the first simple visual device to maintain production control. The chart visually shows when tasks are supposed to be done and compares that with the______________.

A. Scheduled delivery of materials

B. Supervisor's estimate of completion

C. Customers' requested date of delivery

D. Actual progress on each task

Q.58 production manager of a manufacturing organization is trying to determine how to revise the production department, so that it can produce more units per day and achieve the targets in a specified time. Identify the managerial function.

A. Organizing   **B.** Leading

C. Controlling   **D.** Marketing

Q.59 Which of the following control systems is/are used by all levels of management?

A. Financial control system.

B. Quality control system.

C. Inventory control system

D. Budgetary control system.

Q.60 Every organization structure, even a poor one, can be charted. Which of the following is false with respect to an organization Chart ?

A. It is a vital tool for providing information about organizational relationships

B. It provides a visual map of the chain of command

C. Charting an organization structure can show up the complexities and inconsistencies, which can be corrected

D. It shows authority relationships as well as informal and informational relationships

Q.61 Managers need certain skills to perform the functions associated with their jobs. Which of the following skill implies the ability to solve problems in ways that will benefit the enterprise?

A. Design   **B.** Human

C. Conceptual   **D.** Technical

Q.62 Which of the following is defined as the possibility that individuals selected to participate in a study may show higher productivity only because of the added attention they receive from the researchers rather than any other factor being tested in the study?

A. Bank wiring observation

B. Hawthorne effect

C. Halo effect

D. Illumination effect

Q.63 The external environment of an organization consists of the mega environment and the task environment. Which of the following statement(s) is/are true regarding the task environment of a firm?

A. It consists of specific external elements such as customers and clients, competitors, suppliers, labor supply and government agencies, with which an organization interacts while conducting its business.

B. As it depends largely on the products and services offered by the firm and its business location, it may vary from firm to firm.

C. While a firm may not be able to directly influence its task environment, it can certainly influence its mega environment.

D. Both (I) and (II) above

Q.64 The major approaches utilized by managers to induce employees to accomplish the plannctions associated with implementation, should normally include all of the following except:-

A. Authority
B. Coercion
C. Persuasion
D. Feedback

Q.65 Two approaches can be used for setting objectives – the top-down approach and the bottom-up approach. There is often a conflict among management theorists as to which is the better method. Which of the following is not true with respect to the top-down and bottom-up approaches?

A. In the top-down approach, top-level managers determine objectives for subordinates to follow, while in the bottom-up approach, subordinates formulate objectives and present them to their superiors for approval

B. As per supporters of the top-down approach, the organization needs clarity in direction by way of corporate objectives set by the CEO and the board of directors

C. As per proponents of the bottom-up approach, top management should ascertain information from lower levels in the form of objectives

D. These approaches cannot be modified and there are hard and fast rules which indicate in which situation each approach should be used.

Q.66 In the strategic management process, any organizational skills or resources that are exceptional or unique to the organization are the organization's.

A. Potential external opportunities
B. Potential internal strengths
C. Core competencies
D. Bargaining power

Q.67 Which of the following involves a graphic representation of alternative courses of action and the possible outcomes and risks associated with each action?

A. Decision tree
B. Risk analysis
C. Utility theory
D. Incremental analysis

Q.68 A system comprises a set of interactive sub-systems. Which sub-system consists of jobs that require the interaction of personnel with the general environment?

A. Technical
B. Boundary spanning
C. Managerial
D. Feedback

Q.69 Matrix organization is also referred to as a grid organization or product management organization. Which of the following will not be a potential benefit in case of a matrix organization?

A. Strong project coordination
B. Improved environmental monitoring
C. Efficient use of support systems
D. Reduced prospects for interpersonal conflicts

Q.70 Which of the following is the process by which managers allocate a chunk of their work to subordinates along with sufficient authority to accomplish the work?

A. Delegation
B. Power
C. Motivation
D. Feedback

Q.71 It is essential that an organization clearly defines every managerial position. Which of the following is not a benefit of position descriptions?

A. They identify duties and responsibilities that are overlapping or neglected
B. They help in deciding upon the organization design
C. They provide guidance regarding candidate requirements, salary levels, and training needs of new employees
D. They help managers determine the tasks to be done and the employees who should do them

Q.72 From the viewpoint of staff personnel, the major reason(s) for line-staff conflict is/are that line personnel:-

A. Do not make proper use of staff personnel.
B. Resist new ideas.
C. Do not give staff personnel enough authority.
D. All of these

Q.73 According to the BCG matrix, which of the following business units do not hold out much economic purpose and as such the organization must either not invest in them or should consider selling them as soon as possible?

A. Question marks
B. Stars
C. Cash cows
D. Dogs

Q.74 Which of the following approaches to management emphasized the human element, thus viewing the organization from an individual's point of view?

A. Management science approach
B. Scientific approach
C. Administrative approach
D. Behavioral approach.

Q.75 There are different kinds of tests used in the selection process. Which of the followin selection tests explore alertness, comprehension and reasoning abilities of applicants?

A. Work Sampling tests
B. Knowledge tests
C. Personality tests
D. Intelligence tests

Q.76 Which of the following is not a corrective action resulting from the performance appraisal system?

A. Job performance
B. Incentives
C. Training
D. Penalties

Q.77 Which of the following is/are objective(s) of sensitivity training?

I. It helps individuals gain insights into their behavior and helps them analyze the way they appear to others.

II. It helps individuals develop the skills necessary for diagnosing and understanding of group processes.

III. It exposes managers to theories, principles and new developments in management.

A. Only (I) above
B. Only (III) above
C. Both (I) and (II) above
D. Both (II) and (III) above

Q.78 Which of the following is not a limitation of group discussion techniques to enhance creativity?

A. Members of a group may pursue only one idea, ignoring other alternatives

B. Members may hesitate to express their idea before the group due to fear of being ridiculed

C. Lower level managers may not be able to express their views openly in presence of top-level managers

D. Creativity is an individual phenomenon and cannot be discovered through groups.

Q.79 Herzberg's two-factor theory of motivation argues that hygiene factors are necessary to keep workers from being dissatisfied, but only motivators can lead workers to feel satisfied and motivated. Which of the following can be regarded as one of Herzberg's hygiene factors?

A. The work itself
B. Responsibility
C. Supervision
D. Career growth

Q.80 _______________ is a personality trait concerning the degree to which a person is generally agreeable in their relations with other people as opposed to aggressively self-centered and hostile.

A. Adaptability
B. Enthusiasm
C. Aggressiveness
D. Cooperativeness

Q.81 Listening is one of the most essential ingredients of effective communication. No message can be properly understood without intent listening. Which of the following is not an effective listening technique?

A. Avoiding premature evaluation
B. Avoiding eye contact
C. Exhibiting affirmative nods and appropriate facial gestures
D. Finding an area of interest in what the other person is saying

Q.82 Interpretation of messages plays a very important role in communication within or outside organizations. The interpretation of a message by an individual is called:-

A. Message interference
B. Perception
C. Noise
D. Semantics

Q.83 _______________ involve identifying and preventing problems in an organization as they occur.

A. Feedback
B. Interference
C. Precontrol
D. Concurrent

Q.84 "Debts are an important source of finance for a business". Which of the following ratios indicate the company's ability to pay long-term debts?

A. Asset Management
B. Leverage
C. Liquidity
D. Profitability

Q.85 "Operations management is a tool by which management can create and improve upon its operations". Which of the following statements is true regarding operations management?

A. Operations managers are not found in the service sector

B. Operations management is concerned with only the input stage of product development

C. The outputs of the operations system include both goods and services

D. Labor is part of the transformation stage and is not considered an input

Q.86 In which of the following controls is the cause of an unsatisfactory outcome traced back to the individuals responsible for it who are then made to correct the practice?

A. Preventive control
B. Cybernetic control
C. Direct control
D. Steering control

Q.87 "Management Information System (MIS) helps the manager to discharge his/her managerial functions in a more efficient manner". The first necessary step to effectively operate an MIS is:-

A. Summarizing data
B. Analyzing data
C. Determining information needs
D. Gathering appropriate information

Q.88 There are different orientations toward international business. One such orientation is geocentric orientation. The view associated with this type of orientation can be termed as:-

A. National **B.** Narrow **C.** Regional **D.** Global

Q.89 Which of the following is/are claim(s) that support self-appraisal?

A. It increases the personal commitment of employees.
B. It improves employees' understanding of job performance.
C. It provides a great deal of information about the appraisee.
D. Both A and B

Q.90 "The manager inventory chart is used in human resource replacement planning". Which of the following is not an advantage of the 'manager inventory chart'?

A. It gives an overview of the human resource situation of an organization

B. It shows the future internal supply of managers by indicating who is likely to be promoted in a year

C. It shows the position to which a manager may be promoted

D. Managers who are ready for promotion can be easily

identified

Q.91 Planning can be defined as the process by which managers set missions and objectives, assess the future and develop courses of action to accomplish these objectives. The amount of time spent in planning would be the greatest for which of the following levels of management?
- **A.** Lower-level management
- **B.** Middle-level management
- **C.** First-line supervisors
- **D.** Upper-level managers

Q.92 Which of the following is defined as management which conducts business by standards established, by facts or truths gained through systematic observation, experiment, or reasoning?
- **A.** Administrative management
- **B.** Behavioral approach to management
- **C.** Bureaucratic management
- **D.** Scientific management

Q.93 Today, many organizations are involved in social activities. Since the expectations of the society have changed, organizations have become more aware of their social responsibilities. A careful analysis of argument for and against the involvement of organizations in social welfare is necessary to determine whether an organization should implement social initiatives. Which of the following is an argument against Social Responsibility of Business?
- **A.** Avoidance of government regulations
- **B.** Balance of responsibility and power
- **C.** Weakened international balance of payments
- **D.** Favorable public image

Q.94 Problems are encountered at all levels in an organization, and managers at various levels have to solve them or manage them in the best possible way. Which of the following is a statement that spells out what should or should not be done in a particular situation?
- **A.** Rule
- **B.** Policy
- **C.** Budget
- **D.** Procedure

Q.95 Middle-level managers would engage in a setting which of the following objective(s)?
I. Division objectives.
II. Specific overall organization objectives such as those pertaining to key result areas.
III. Individual performance objectives.
- **A.** Only (I) above
- **B.** Both (I) and (II) above
- **C.** Both (I) and (IV) above
- **D.** Both (II) and (III) above

Q.96 What is/ are the steps in strategic planning?
- **A.** Gather and Analyze Information.
- **B.** Formulate a Strategy.
- **C.** Evaluate and Control.
- **D.** All of the above

Q.97 Shah Industries conducts its business in various industries, the hotel industry being one of them. Hetal Shah, who heads the hotel venture, is concerned about how her business in going to effectively combat the increasing competition. At this point, Ms. Shah has decided to identify ways and means to achieve a competitive advantage and respond to the changing environment and competitive situation. At which organizational level is Ms. Shah currently addressing her planning efforts?
- **A.** Corporate level
- **B.** Business level
- **C.** Functional level
- **D.** Operational level

Q.98 The characteristic of an organization that describes the degree to which the organization monitors and responds to changes in the external environment is termed as:-
A) Open-systems focus
B) Means-end orientation
C) Closed-system focus.
- **A.** Only A
- **B.** Only B
- **C.** Only C
- **D.** All of these

Q.99 Which stage of the decision-making process is either nonexistent or given little attention in programmed decision making?
- **A.** Analysis of alternatives
- **B.** Development of the alternatives
- **C.** Identification of decision criteria
- **D.** Identification of problem

Q.100 According to which of the following decision-making models, is the ability of managers to be completely rational in making decisions limited by certain factors?
- **A.** Rational model
- **B.** Satisficing model
- **C.** Incremental model
- **D.** Garbage-can model

Q.101 _______________ is a largely academic term for developing external relationships in order to accomplish your business objectives.
- **A.** Technical
- **B.** Boundary spanning
- **C.** Managerial
- **D.** Feedback

Q.102 The phenomenon in which individuals alter their behavior in response to being observed, and usually refers to positive changes. It is called:-
- **A.** Halo effect
- **B.** Hawthorne Effect
- **C.** Domino effect
- **D.** None of these

Q.103 The _______________ refers to the inclination of some people to work harder and perform better when they are being observed as part of an experiment.
- **A.** Halo effect
- **B.** Hawthorne effect
- **C.** Domino effect
- **D.** Sensitivity effect

Q.104 The manager inventory chart is used in human resource replacement planning. Which of the following is an advantage of the 'manager inventory chart'?
- **A.** It gives an overview of the human resource situation of an organization
- **B.** It shows the future internal supply of managers by indicating who is likely to be promoted in a year
- **C.** Managers who are ready for promotion can be easily

identified
D. All of these

Q.105 A career strategy should be designed to overcome weaknesses and utilize strengths so as to take advantage of career opportunities. There are various steps in formulating a career strategy. Which of the following steps will precede the others in formulating a career strategy?

A. Development of strategic career alternatives
B. Analysis of personal strengths and weaknesses
C. Consistency testing and strategic choices
D. Implementation of the career plan

Q.106 If a manager assesses the performance of an employee, who is one amongst a group, and mentors him explaining what the organization expects from him on a day-to-day basis, it is an example of:-

A. A halo effect
B. Hawthorne effect
C. Setting standards
D. Controlling

Q.107 A team consists of a set of people working together towards a common purpose. In an organization, there can be different types of teams. A work team comprised of experts from various specialties is most accurately referred to as:-

A. A functional team
B. A cross-functional team
C. An informal group
D. A self-managed team

Q.108 Read the assertion and reason carefully, choose the correct code:-

Assertion (A): Promotion is a move within the organisation to a higher position that has greater responsibilities and requires more advanced skills.

Reasoning (R): Promotion may not involve a raise in status but a hike in salary is a must.

Code:

A. (A) and (R) both are correct.
B. (A) and (R) both are incorrect.
C. (A) is correct whereas (R) is incorrect.
D. (A) is incorrect, whereas (R) is correct.

Q.109 Which of the following theories proposes that the factors that help prevent dissatisfaction on the job do not necessarily lead to satisfaction?

A. Vroom's expectancy theory
B. Adam's equity theory
C. Herzberg's motivation-hygiene theory
D. Mc Clelland's three-needs theory

Q.110 Lyman W. Porter and Edward E. Lawler III developed the expanded expectancy theory model. Which of the following is not true with regard to the Porter and Lawler model of motivation?

A) It's built on Vroom's expectancy theory
B) It means motivation is not a simple cause-and-effect matter
C) It assumes that satisfaction leads to performance

A. Only A
B. Only B
C. Only C
D. Both A and B

Q.111 Which of the following leadership styles is appropriate for a new entrant into an organization who is unable to solve task-related problems independently?

A. High-task/low-relationship
B. High-task/high-relationship
C. Low task/high-relationship
D. Low-task/low-relationship

Q.112 A well-known approach to defining leadership styles is the managerial grid, developed by Robert Blake and Jane Srygley Mouton. According to Blake and Mouton's managerial grid, which of the following managerial styles is also known as 'organization-man-management'?

A. Impoverished management
B. Middle-of-the-road management
C. Country club management
D. Team management

Q.113 "A message that is generated by the receiver in response to the sender's original message is known as feedback. It is a very important component of the communication process". Feedback returns the message to the sender and provides a check on:-

A. How well the receiver is doing
B. How well the sender is doing
C. Whether understanding has been achieved
D. What the sender should do the next time a message is sent

Q.114 ______________ is evident in all aspects of nature and technology. It occurs when a closed system regulates itself using a feedback loop.

A. Strategic control system
B. Tactical control system
C. Operational control system
D. Cybernetic control system

Q.115 What is the Formula for Calculating the Current Ratio?

A. Current ratio= $\frac{Current\ Assets}{Current\ Liabilities}$
B. Current ratio=Current Assets - Current Liabilities
C. Current ratio=Current Assets x Current Liabilities
D. None of the above

Q.116 Which of the following statement(s) about revenue centers is/are true?

A. Sales and marketing departments are examples of revenue centers.
B. In revenue centers, outputs are measured in monetary terms and directly compared with input costs.
C. A revenue center can be responsible for changes in profit levels.
D. All of these

Q.117 Capacity decisions are one of the key decisions included in an operations management program. Which of the following would most likely happen if a company was operating with insufficient capacity?

A. The company would have generally low production costs
B. The company would be able to minimize operating costs

C. The company would have a loss of sales and lower profits

D. The company would be able to maximize profits

Q.118 Which of the following controls is based on the idea that most of the negative deviations from standards can be overcome by applying the fundamentals of management?

A. Preventive control   **B.** Cybernetic control

C. Direct control   **D.** Steering control

Q.119 "Information is one of the important resources for managers. For information to be useful to managers, it must possess certain attributes". The information attribute which is prepared or presented to users often enough to be up-to-date is called:-

A. Information accuracy

B. Information timeliness

C. Information relevance

D. Information frequency.

Q.120 Firms with international business have several advantages over firms that operate only within the home country. Which of the following is not an advantage to a multinational corporation (MNC)?

A) Business opportunity in various countries and ability to raise funds for their operations throughout the world.

B) Developing countries have become more adept in international negotiations and have become aware of their resources.

C) Access to natural resources and materials that may not be available to domestic firms.

A. Only A   **B.** Only C

C. Both A and B   **D.** Only B

Q.121 Using a method called structured observation, Mintzberg isolated ten roles which he believed were common to all managers. According to him, maintaining self-developed networks of outside contacts and informers who provide favours and information can be best described as:-

A. The disseminator role

B. The liaison role

C. The monitor role

D. The entrepreneur role

Q.122 The managers at the different managerial levels require different kinds of skills to perform the functions associated with their jobs. The major difference in skill requirements between middle and top managers is:-

A. Top managers must generally be more skilled than middle managers in every respect

B. Top managers require better interpersonal skills but less conceptual skills than middle managers

C. Top managers generally require better technical and interpersonal skills than middle managers

D. Top managers generally require higher level conceptual skills but less technical skills than middle managers

Q.123 The term 'ethics' commonly refers to the rules or principles that define right and wrong conduct. Managers making ethical decisions may belong to any of the three levels of Moral Development, each composed of two stages. The Pre-conventional Level of Moral Development is concerned with which of the following stages?

A. Following rules only when it's of interest

B. Living up to the expectations of people close to managers

C. Maintaining conventional order by fulfilling obligations which managers have agreed to

D. Valuing rights of others, and upholding non-relative values and rights, regardless of the majority's opinion

Q.124 According to the Scientific Management School of Thought, which of the following is defined as the systematic, objective and critical examination of all the factors governing the operational efficiency of a specified activity to bring about improvement?

A. Work Methods Study

B. Micromotion Study

C. Time Study

D. Motion Study

Q.125 Max Weber, a German contemporary of Henri Fayol, coined the term "bureaucracy", based on the German word "buro" meaning office, to identify large organizations that operated on a rational basis. All of the following are characteristics of bureaucracy except:-

A) Centralized authority

B) Formalized rules and regulations

C) Wide spans of control

A. Only A   **B.** Only B

C. Both A and B   **D.** Only C

Q.126 "Planning is the first function of management and can be defined as the process by which managers set missions and objectives, assess the future, and develop courses of action to accomplish these objectives. However, there is no shortage of myths and misconceptions about planning". Which of the following statements is a common misconception about planning?

A. The end result of planning is only one of its purposes

B. Planning cannot eliminate change

C. Planning that proves inaccurate is a waste of management's time

D. The process of planning can, in itself, be valuable even if the results are inaccurate

Q.127 Problems are encountered at all levels in an organization, and managers at various levels have to solve them or manage them in the best possible way. A ______________ is a series of interrelated sequential steps that can be used to respond to a well-structured problem.

A. Rule   **B.** Policy

C. Budget   **D.** Procedure

Q.128 Assume that you have recently been assigned to a committee that is given the responsibility to review and institute a process for employees to use when requesting upgrades in computer equipment. Which type of objectives would you most likely be developing?

A. Intermediate-term objectives

B. Long-term objectives

C. Short-term objectives

D.   Organizational objectives

Q.129 Raj, Ramesh and Rajesh are all making decisions about how to approach the team project. They have only one week to write a 75-page analysis of the government's suit against Microsoft. In addition, they all work full-time. Which decision-making model will they probably rely on?

A.   Rational
B.   Break-even analysis
C.   Intuition
D.   Bounded rationality

Q.130 Keith Davis and William C. Frederick have worked on the concept of social responsiveness. According to them the social responsiveness of an organization can be measured on the basis of which of the following criteria?

A.   Contributions to profit-oriented projects
B.   Fair treatment of employees; fair pay and safe working conditions
C.   Unequal employment opportunity
D.   Unsafe and poor quality products to customers

Q.131 In the area of diversity, establishing task forces or committees to explore issues and provide ideas, carefully choosing work assignments to support the career development of all employees, and evaluating the extent to which diversity goals are being achieved would most likely be classified under which of the following managerial roles?

A. Planning   **B.** Staffing
C. Leading   **D.** Organizing

Q.132 In recent years, research has proved that culture has a tremendous impact on management practices. Which of the following is not a characteristic of Organizational Culture?

A.   It may vary in strength
B.   It is indistinct in nature
C.   It is based on certain norms
D.   It promotes dominant and stable values

Q.133 Organizations that have divisional structure but do not treat the divisions as autonomous businesses, so that they can have control over both the revenues and expenses, may opt to set up:-

A.   Standard Cost Centers
B.   Revenue Centers
C.   Profit Centers
D.   Investment Centers

Q.134 __________ is power you derive from your formal position or office held in the organization's hierarchy of authority.

A. Legitimate power   **B.** Coercive power
C. Expert power   **D.** Referent power

Q.135 A purchasing department may be created because the hospital administrator cannot effectively handle all purchasing. The purchasing department would evaluate the vendors and suggest the appropriate ones for purchasing the materials. What type of position authority has been created?

A. Accountability   **B.** Line authority
C. Staff authority   **D.** Responsibility

Q.136 Different behavioural scientists have developed different theories on motivation. One such behavioural scientist by the name of Herzberg gave the two-factor theory of motivation. Which of the following four responses are considered as Herzberg's hygiene factors?

A.   Personal life, security, salary and recognition
B.   Advancement, salary, status, company policy
C.   Relationship with peers, status, supervision and security
D.   Working conditions, relationship with subordinates, supervision and work itself

Q.137 Which of the following is not true with regard to the Porter and Lawler model of motivation?

A.   It is built on Vroom's expectancy theory
B.   It means motivation is not a simple cause-and-effect matter
C.   It assumes that satisfaction leads to performance
D.   It emphasizes reward structure

Q.138 The four phases of Creative process are:-
I. Logical formulation.
II. Intuition.
III.Unconscious scanning.
IV. Insight.
The order in which the process takes place is:-

A.   (I), (II), (III) and (IV)
B.   (II), (III), (IV) and (I)
C.   (III), (II), (IV) and (I)
D.   (IV), (I), (III) and (II)

Q.139 What is/ are the types of esteem needs?

A.   esteem for oneself
B.   desire for reputation or respect from others
C.   Both A and B
D.   None of these

Q.140 According to the Tannenbaum and Schmidt Leadership model, which of the following would be most accurate regarding someone exhibiting behavior toward right of the continuum of leader behaviours?

A.   He would be a boss-centered leader
B.   He would be more likely to ask the group to make a decision
C.   He would be more autocratic
D.   He would be more likely to "sell" the decision

Q.141 ________________ is a style of leadership in which all members of the organization work together to make decisions.

A.   Participative leadership style
B.   Benevolent-authoritative leadership style
C.   Consultative leadership style
D.   Exploitative-authoritative leadership style

Q.142 Democratic leadership is also called__________.

A.   Benevolent-authoritative leadership
B.   Participative leadership
C.   Exploitative-authoritative leadership
D.   None of the above

Q.143 For becoming a successful interpersonal communicator, a manager must be able to grasp all of the following except:-

A. How interpersonal communication works

B. The importance of verbal versus non-verbal interpersonal communication

C. How to get the most out of the grapevine

D. The relationship between feedback and interpersonal communication

Q.144 The basic method of ______ control is an improvement over feedback control because it tries to shorten or to eliminate the delay between performance and feedback about the performance.

A. Feedforward **B.** Concurrent

C. Unconcurrent **D.** None of these

Q.145 The Gantt Chart (invented by Henry L. Gantt), still used today in the production planning area of many organizations, is a method for comparing the actual and planned performances. It was the first simple visual device to maintain production control. It is essentially a bar graph with ________ axis and ________ axis.

A. Time on the horizontal; the activities to be scheduled on the vertical

B. Time on the vertical; project completion on the horizontal

C. Time on the horizontal; project completion on the vertical

D. Time on the vertical; the activities to be scheduled on the horizontal

Q.146 Fleet tracking is the example of which control?

A. Direct control

B. Indirect control

C. Preventive control

D. Concurrent control

Q.147 The principle of preventive control brings about a sharp distinction between analyzing performance reports and determining whether managers adopt the established principles in actual practice. Thus, the principle of preventive control can be stated as:-

A. The higher the quality of managers and their subordinates, the less will be the need for direct controls.

B. The higher the quality of managers and their subordinates, the less will be the need for preventive controls.

C. The higher the quality of managers and their subordinates, the less will be the need for concurrent controls.

D. Both (I) and (II) above

Q.148 What is/ are the steps in contingency planning?

A. Develop the contingency planning policy statement.

B. Ensure plan maintenance.

C. Implementation of the Career Plan

D. Both A and B

Q.149 Kanban is a subsystem of the ____________ involving a simple parts movement system that depends on cards and containers to pull parts from one work center to another.

A. ABC Analysis **B.** JIT Approach

C. Kaizen **D.** None of these

Q.150 Which of the following is/ are true with regard to DSS?

A. Executive decisions are the focal points in DSS

B. DSS specializes in easy-to-use software

C. DSS employs interactive processing

D. All of these

// Smart Answer Sheet //

Correct — Percentage of students who answered correctly. **Skipped** — Percentage of students who skipped.

Q.	Ans.	Correct / Skipped
1	C	30.61 % / 22.45 %
2	A	20.41 % / 38.77 %
3	C	44.9 % / 46.94 %
4	C	30.61 % / 40.82 %
5	C	42.86 % / 40.81 %
6	C	38.78 % / 40.81 %
7	C	22.45 % / 40.82 %
8	A	53.06 % / 38.78 %
9	C	51.02 % / 38.78 %
10	B	38.78 % / 42.85 %
11	D	32.65 % / 40.82 %
12	C	20.41 % / 38.77 %
13	B	44.9 % / 38.77 %
14	C	38.78 % / 38.77 %
15	D	36.73 % / 38.78 %
16	A	38.78 % / 38.77 %
17	B	44.9 % / 40.81 %
18	C	34.69 % / 40.82 %
19	A	36.73 % / 44.9 %
20	C	48.98 % / 36.73 %
21	B	51.02 % / 40.82 %
22	C	46.94 % / 38.77 %
23	A	53.06 % / 40.82 %
24	D	16.33 % / 42.85 %
25	A	36.73 % / 40.82 %
26	B	30.61 % / 38.78 %
27	B	40.82 % / 40.81 %
28	B	40.82 % / 38.77 %
29	D	32.65 % / 38.78 %
30	D	30.61 % / 38.78 %
31	D	32.65 % / 38.78 %
32	C	40.82 % / 40.81 %
33	B	26.53 % / 42.86 %
34	A	10.2 % / 28.58 %
35	A	36.73 % / 38.78 %
36	C	38.78 % / 38.77 %
37	B	48.98 % / 38.78 %
38	D	26.53 % / 38.78 %
39	D	24.49 % / 36.73 %
40	C	42.86 % / 38.77 %
41	C	24.49 % / 38.78 %
42	B	36.73 % / 40.82 %
43	A	44.9 % / 34.69 %
44	C	55.1 % / 34.7 %
45	B	59.18 % / 34.7 %
46	C	57.14 % / 34.7 %
47	D	26.53 % / 42.86 %
48	D	28.57 % / 38.78 %
49	D	22.45 % / 38.77 %
50	B	36.73 % / 38.78 %
51	B	42.86 % / 36.73 %
52	D	48.98 % / 32.65 %
53	B	55.1 % / 34.7 %
54	D	10.2 % / 34.7 %
55	D	32.65 % / 36.74 %
56	C	38.78 % / 38.77 %
57	D	24.49 % / 38.78 %
58	C	20.41 % / 36.73 %
59	B	30.61 % / 32.66 %
60	D	32.65 % / 36.74 %
61	A	12.24 % / 32.66 %
62	B	40.82 % / 36.73 %
63	D	28.57 % / 32.65 %
64	B	38.78 % / 32.65 %
65	D	28.57 % / 34.7 %
66	C	32.65 % / 32.66 %
67	A	36.73 % / 32.66 %
68	B	34.69 % / 36.74 %
69	D	30.61 % / 34.7 %
70	A	51.02 % / 30.61 %
71	B	32.65 % / 34.7 %
72	D	44.9 % / 32.65 %
73	D	40.82 % / 30.61 %
74	D	40.82 % / 30.61 %
75	D	36.73 % / 34.7 %
76	A	22.45 % / 36.73 %
77	C	48.98 % / 34.69 %
78	D	30.61 % / 30.61 %
79	C	20.41 % / 38.77 %
80	D	22.45 % / 34.69 %

Q.	Ans.	Correct / Skipped	Q.	Ans.	Correct / Skipped	Q.	Ans.	Correct / Skipped	Q.	Ans.	Correct / Skipped	Q.	Ans.	Correct / Skipped
81	B	36.73 % / 34.7 %	95	B	30.61 % / 40.82 %	109	C	36.73 % / 34.7 %	123	A	12.24 % / 36.74 %	137	C	22.45 % / 38.77 %
82	B	51.02 % / 32.65 %	96	D	42.86 % / 32.65 %	110	C	10.2 % / 36.74 %	124	A	32.65 % / 36.74 %	138	C	18.37 % / 36.73 %
83	D	24.49 % / 32.65 %	97	B	48.98 % / 34.69 %	111	A	18.37 % / 32.65 %	125	D	28.57 % / 34.7 %	139	C	38.78 % / 36.73 %
84	B	38.78 % / 28.57 %	98	A	36.73 % / 32.66 %	112	B	44.9 % / 36.73 %	126	C	26.53 % / 36.74 %	140	B	38.78 % / 40.81 %
85	C	32.65 % / 34.7 %	99	B	32.65 % / 36.74 %	113	D	6.12 % / 34.7 %	127	D	28.57 % / 36.74 %	141	A	34.69 % / 36.74 %
86	C	26.53 % / 32.65 %	100	B	24.49 % / 38.78 %	114	D	16.33 % / 38.77 %	128	C	18.37 % / 34.69 %	142	B	51.02 % / 36.74 %
87	C	44.9 % / 32.65 %	101	B	34.69 % / 34.7 %	115	A	32.65 % / 36.74 %	129	D	32.65 % / 34.7 %	143	C	32.65 % / 36.74 %
88	D	34.69 % / 40.82 %	102	B	36.73 % / 36.74 %	116	A	8.16 % / 38.78 %	130	B	53.06 % / 34.7 %	144	B	38.78 % / 34.69 %
89	D	40.82 % / 34.69 %	103	B	44.9 % / 32.65 %	117	C	40.82 % / 34.69 %	131	D	12.24 % / 32.66 %	145	A	20.41 % / 38.77 %
90	C	24.49 % / 40.82 %	104	D	26.53 % / 40.82 %	118	A	24.49 % / 40.82 %	132	B	32.65 % / 32.66 %	146	D	14.29 % / 38.77 %
91	D	32.65 % / 34.7 %	105	B	42.86 % / 34.69 %	119	D	10.2 % / 36.74 %	133	C	24.49 % / 32.65 %	147	A	14.29 % / 36.73 %
92	D	28.57 % / 32.65 %	106	C	28.57 % / 34.7 %	120	D	22.45 % / 36.73 %	134	A	34.69 % / 36.74 %	148	D	36.73 % / 36.74 %
93	C	16.33 % / 34.69 %	107	B	38.78 % / 36.73 %	121	B	34.69 % / 38.78 %	135	C	20.41 % / 36.73 %	149	B	34.69 % / 34.7 %
94	A	18.37 % / 32.65 %	108	C	22.45 % / 36.73 %	122	D	36.73 % / 32.66 %	136	C	20.41 % / 36.73 %	150	D	42.86 % / 38.77 %

//Hints and Solutions//

1. In longitudinal study, data is collected over a period of time ranging from weeks, months, years, decades etc. Firstly, the data is collected at the outset of the study, and may repeat over an extended period of time. By allowing this, the researchers can experience how the variables change over time within same strata.

2. A line printer prints one entire line of text before advancing to another line. Most early line printers were impact printers. Line printers are mostly associated with unit record equipment and the early days of digital computing, but the technology is still in use.

3. Applied research is used to solve a specific, practical problem of an individual or a group. This particular kind of research is used in business, medicine, and education in order to find solutions that may cure diseases, solve scientific problems, or develop technology.

4. The format of thesis writing is the same as in a research dissertation. The aim of the dissertation or thesis is to produce original piece of work on a clearly defined topic.

5. The correct sequence of research steps is as follows:

a) Formulation of Problem

b) Making of Hypothesis

c) Development of a research design,

d) Collection of data,

e) Data analysis

f) Formulation of generalizations and conclusions.

6. An article will generally have an order like: topic (name of the paper), abstract (brief of the study), method (tools used), discussion (research findings and other related research) and bibliography.

7. The research conference is a meeting for researchers to present and discuss their creative ideas and work at a large level. The conference inculcates creativity and critical thinking among the participants more than the seminars, workshop, research summary.

8. Following are the characteristics of learner which facilitates teaching-learning system to become effective are:

a) Prior or previous experience of the learner facilitates the teaching learning process a lot because without students' good previous knowledge or learning a good teaching learning process does not takes place.

b) Aptitude of a learner: Student talent, behaviour or aptitude facilitates the teaching learning process effectively.

c) Stage of development of a learner also affects the teaching learning process if the learners is in preschool level. His/her physical and intellectual development takes place very rapidly in comparison to other stage of development.

9. Although it is possible to carry out experiments in all the given field of studies, experiments in science offer more organized methods for analyzing the cause and effect relationship.

10. Teaching can be done in a formal as well as in an informal manner. Therefore, the option B is incorrect. Other options are correct.

11. Project method is a learning method where the participation of student is maximum in comparison to teacher and the students here is an active learner. Student here find the solution by themselves of assigned projects. Students learns how to solve real life problems with co-operation of each other.

12. Formative assessment accelerates the pace of learning because instant feedback is provided to the learner in turn of their performance. In this assessment learner makes changes in his behavior and learning within the time. This assessment occurs over a short period of time. But summative evaluation considered to be most reliable because through this assessment the whole performance of the student can be judged. And the results are used by the teacher and school to identify strength and weakness of the curriculum as well as of students.

13. As a teacher while preparing them for debate it is very difficult to develop in student how to control over emotions during debate because during debate activity student have to argue over opposite viewpoint and in this condition for proving correct for themselves student go deep inside the topic and sometimes divert from the topic which leads to arguments over the topic so, it is the biggest demerit of debate that student lost his control over their emotions.

14. The quality of teaching can be reflected in a best way through the quality of questions asked by the student. Quality of student's questions reflect the interest level and curiosity level of a student during teaching learning process.

The questions of the students give teacher an idea about how much their student is grasping the content taught by the teacher which further allows teacher to improve their teaching skills in order to make teaching more effective. Qualitied questions asked by the students ensures effective teaching learning process.

15. Teaching effectiveness can be affected by the education system of the country. Education system of the country is divided into three main categories i.e. primary, secondary and tertiary. Primary education covers the elementary prospects of the education system, secondary covers 10th and 12th level while tertiary level of the education covers graduate, post graduate and doctorate level courses. If all the three levels of education functions well then only education system should be improved in our country.

16. Solution :

2 * 3 = 6.

3 * 5 = 15.

4 * 7 = 28.

5 * 9 = 45.

6 * 11 = 66.

Answer = 66.

17. 1st letter- A +3 D +4 H +5 M +6 S

2nd letter- B +5 G +6 M +7 T +8 B

3rd Letter- D +7 K +8 S +9 B +10 L

Hence, option B is correct.

18.

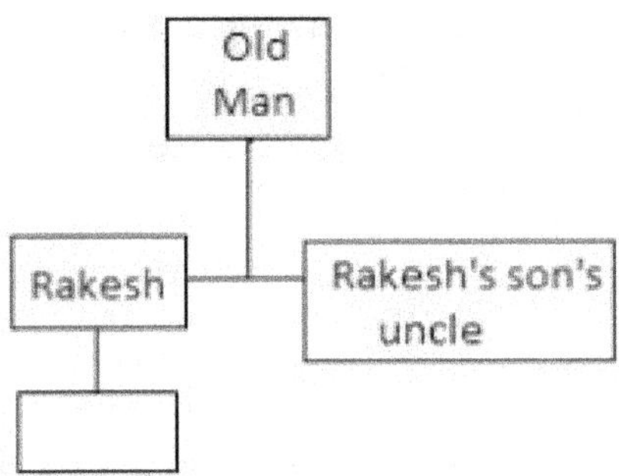

The old man is related to Rakesh as Father.

19.

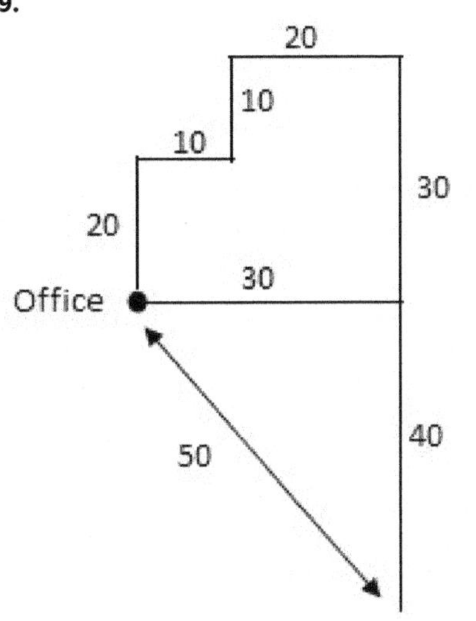

The distance between the postman and the office is 50 m.

20. There are two series:

1st series: 1, 27, 125, 343

(1^3, 3^3, 5^3, 7^3)

2nd series: 4, 16, 36

(2^2, 4^2, 6^2)

So, 125 is the missing option.

21. Y + 2 = W

E + 1 = F

B + 2 = D

W + 2 = U

F + 2 = H

D + 3 = G

U + 2 = S

H + 3 = K

G + 2 = I

S + 2 = Q

K + 4 = O

I + 3 = L

So, QOL is the next term in the series.

22. The pattern followed here is,

→ 3 + 8 = 11

→ 11 + 12 = 23

→ 23 + 16 = 39

→ 39 + 20 = 59

→ 59 + 24 = 83

Hence, "83" is the missing term.

23. SELECTION is coded as QCJCARGML

→ S − 2 = Q

→ E − 2 = C

→ L − 2 = J

→ E − 2 = C

→ C − 2 = A

→ T − 2 = R

→ I − 2 = G

→ O − 2 = M

→ N − 2 = L

Similarly,

→ A − 2 = Y

→ M − 2 = K

→ E − 2 = C

→ R − 2 = P

→ I − 2 = G

→ C − 2 = A

→ A − 2 = Y

→ N − 2 = L

→ S − 2 = Q

Hence, AMERICANS will be coded as "YKCPGAYLQ".

24. Two railway tickets from city A to B and three tickets from city A to C cost ₹ 177.

Three tickets from city A to B and two tickets from city A to C cost ₹ 173.

Let M:Ticket A to B

N: Ticket from A to C

2M + 3N = 177................. (eq1)

3M + 2N =173 .... (eq2)

By multiplying,

eq1 × 3 – eq2 × 2

6M + 9N = 531

6M + 4N = 346

⇒ 6M + 9N – 6M – 4N = 531 – 346 = 185

⇒ 5N = 185

⇒ N = 37

On putting N value in eq1,

⇒ 2M + 3 × 37 = 177

⇒ 2M = 177 – 111 = 66

⇒ M = 33

Hence, the fare for city B from A will be 33

25.

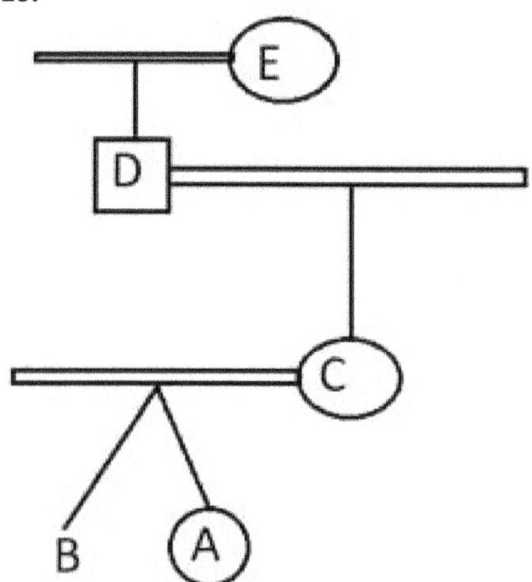

A is granddaughter of G

26. According to the passage, "Beyond physical linkages, digital connectivity is the new frontier in the Fourth Industrial Revolution. India has made great progress in innovation, Start-ups and digital inclusion. There are opportunities to apply initiatives such as Aadhaar in our region. E-commerce and FinTech are two other areas of potential collaboration. Thus, option B is the correct answer.

27. According to the passage, "In 1991, when the Cold War ended and India began its economic liberalization, Singapore saw on opportunity to deepen ties and build on its historical and cultural links with the Asian region." Note that the end of the Cold War prompted the economic liberalization in India, which in turn prompted Singapore to opt for stronger ties with India. So, the end of the Cold War did was not the reason behind Singapore to opt for stronger ties with India.

28. According to the passage, "While one can fly directly between India and several ASEAN countries, there is still much room to expand air links to support growing business and tourism." Thus, option B is the correct answer.

29. According to the passage, "ASEAN is committed to strengthening land, air and sea linkages with India." All these linkages can be categorized as transportation links; thus, option D is the correct answer.

30. According to the last few lines of the passage, "As an economic hub, Singapore can serve as a springboard (launchpad) to launch these ideas to Southeast Asia and beyond. India's role in ASEAN should be anchored by growing economic ties with Singapore. Thus, Singapore can be India's Launchpad for an integrated Asian market as per the passage.

31. In 1964, an education commission was set up under the Chairmanship of Dr. DS. Kothari. This commission laid down the principles and guidelines for the development of the education from the primary to higher level.

32. As per the latest data released by UGC, there are 892 universities comprising 394 state universities, 125 deemed universities and 325 private universities.

33. University Education Commission was constituted on November 4, 1948 under the chairmanship of Dr. Sarvapali Radhakrishnan. The commission was inaugurated by Abdul Kalam Azad on Dec 6, 1948.

34. Communicative abilities include those skills which are defined with reference to the manner and mode in which the system is realized in use. Communicative abilities embrace linguistic skills but not the reverse. Essentially, they are ways of creating or recreating discourse in different modes.

35. Non-verbal communication is considered as informal communication. Non-verbal communication includes the communication through facial expressions, gestures, tone and pitch of the voice.

36. The rhetorical approach in classroom communication considers teachers as influencing agents of students. It is the teacher who regulates his/her class upon the basis of his knowledge and that knowledge can only be delivered through the interaction between the teacher and students.

37. The classroom communication should be empathetic as it means showing an ability to understand and share the feelings of another.The other options are false as:

• Contrived means created or arranged in a way that seems artificial and unrealistic.

• Abstract means existing in thought or as an idea but not having a physical or concrete existence.

• Non-descriptive means lacking description.

38. Total exports of the three Companies X, Y and Z together, during various years are:

In $1993 = $ Rs. $(30 + 80 + 60)$ crores $= $ Rs. 170 crores

In $1994 = $ Rs. $(60 + 40 + 90)$ crores $= $ Rs. 190 crores

In $1995 = $ Rs. $(40 + 60 + 120)$ crores $= $ Rs. 220 crores

In $1996 = $ Rs. $(70 + 60 + 90)$ crores $= $ Rs. 220 crores

In $1997 = $ Rs. $(100 + 80 + 60)$ crores $= $ Rs. 240 crores

In $1998 = $ Rs. $(50 + 100 + 80)$ crores $= $ Rs. 230 crores

In $1999 = $ Rs. $(120 + 140 + 100)$ crores $= $ Rs. 360 crores

Clearly, the total exports of the three Companies X, Y and Z together are the same during the years 1995 and 1996.

Hence, the correct option is (D).

39. Analysis of the graph: From the graph it is clear that,

The amount of exports of Company X (in crore Rs.) in the years $1993, 1994, 1995, 1996, 1997, 1998$ and 1999 are $30, 60, 40, 70, 100, 50$ and 120 respectively.

The amount of exports of Company Y (in crore Rs.) in the years $1993, 1994, 1995, 1996, 1997, 1998$ and 1999 are $80, 40, 60, 60, 80, 100$ and 140 respectively.

The amount of exports of Company Z (in crore Rs.) in the years $1993, 1994, 1995, 1996, 1997, 1998$ and 1999 are $60, 90, 120, 90, 60, 80$ and 100 respectively.

Average annual exports (in Rs. crore) of Company Y during the given period,

$$= \frac{1}{7} \times (80 + 40 + 60 + 60 + 80 + 100 + 140)$$

$$= \frac{560}{7}$$

$$= 80$$

Average annual exports (in Rs. crore) of Company Z during the given period,

$$= \frac{1}{7} \times (60 + 90 + 120 + 90 + 60 + 80 + 100)$$

$$= \left(\frac{600}{7}\right)$$

$\therefore$ Required percentage $= \frac{80}{\left(\frac{600}{7}\right)} \times 100\% \approx 93.33\%$

Hence, the correct option is (D).

40. The difference between the exports from the Companies X and Y during the various years are:

In $1993 = $ Rs. $(80 - 30)$ crores $= $ Rs. 50 crores

In $1994 = $ Rs. $(60 - 40)$ crores $= $ Rs. 20 crores

In $1995 = $ Rs. $(60 - 40)$ crores $= $ Rs. 20 crores

In $1996 = $ Rs. $(70 - 60)$ crores $= $ Rs. 10 crores

In $1997 = $ Rs. $(100 - 80)$ crores $= $ Rs. 20 crores

In $1998 = $ Rs. $(100 - 50)$ crores $= $ Rs. 50 crores

In $1999 = $ Rs. $(140 - 120)$ crores $= $ Rs. 20 crores

Clearly, the difference is minimum in the year 1996.

Hence, the correct option is (C).

41. Average exports of the three Companies X, Y and Z in 1993,

$$= \text{Rs. } \left[\frac{1}{3} \times (30 + 80 + 60)\right] \text{ crores}$$

$$= \text{Rs. } \left(\frac{170}{3}\right) \text{ crores}$$

Average exports of the three Companies X, Y and Z in 1998,

$$= \text{Rs. } \left[\frac{1}{3} \times (50 + 100 + 80)\right] \text{ crores}$$

$$= \text{Rs. } \left(\frac{230}{3}\right) \text{ crores}$$

Difference $= \text{Rs. } \left[\left(\frac{230}{3}\right) - \left(\frac{170}{3}\right)\right] \text{ crores}$

$$= \text{Rs. } \left(\frac{60}{3}\right) \text{ crores}$$

$$= \text{Rs. } 20 \text{ crores}$$

Hence, the correct option is (C).

42. Let $C's$ age be x years. Then, $B's$ age $= 2x$ years. A's age $= (2x + 2)$ years.

$\therefore (2x + 2) + 2x + x = 27$

$\Rightarrow 5x = 25$

$\Rightarrow x = 5$

Hence, B's age $=> 2x = 10$ years.

43. Moralizing, being judgmental and comments of consolation are the restrictions or barriers to effective communication as these create hindrances in the communication. Rest all options such as summary, self-review, use of simple words, eye contact help in making the communication more effective.

44. A small text file stored on user's computer by some websites in order to recognize and keep track of user's preferences is called cookie. Cookie store some data that might be specific to a particular client.

45. Bug is a term used in a computer science to denote an error in a particular program that is used to run a software.

46. The output quality of a printer is measured by DPI. DPI stands for Dots per inch, in which the quality of the printer is being measured.

47. Answer: Option D

Gorbl means fan; flur means belt; pixn means ceiling; arth means tile; and tusl means roof. Therefore, pixnarth is the correct choice.

48. In rural homes, the main sources of Nitrogen Oxide Pollution can be unvented gas stoves, wood stoves or kerosene heaters.

49. Given:

Mahesh's present age $= 5$ years

Anup's present age $= 5 - 2 = 3$ years

Let the present age of Randheer be x.

Then, Anup's present age $= \frac{x-6}{18}$

Now, according to the question,

$$\frac{x-6}{18} = 3$$

$$\Rightarrow x - 6 = 54$$

$$\Rightarrow x = 54 + 6$$

$$= 60 \text{ years}$$

Hence, the correct option is (D).

50. Net WC = current assets - current liabilities

Net liabilities can only be negative when current liabilities exceed current assets,

Which means the entity is financing his "Fixed assets or non-current assets" from "short term or current liabilities".

51. Susan is playing a liaison role which is serving as a link in a horizontal chain of communication. In a figurehead role, the manager performs ceremonial and social duties as the organizations represented. A project manager is responsible for the success of the overall project. In operational tasking, the manager is directly responsible for a specific job task. Multi-tasking is the practice of assigning two or more comparably sized tasks to one. Hence, option B is correct.

52. Except for corporate policy statements, all the options given are examples of upward communication. Hence, option D is correct.

53. A performance appraisal technique that makes use of feedback from supervisors, subordinates and co-workers, is known as 360-degree appraisal. Hence, option (B) is correct.

54. A cash cow is one of the four categories (quadrants) in the growth-share, BCG matrix that represents a product, product line, or company with a large market share within a mature industry.

A cash cow is also a reference to a business, product, or asset that, once acquired and paid off, will produce consistent cash flows over its lifespan.

55. Social responsibility is defined as a business firm's obligation, beyond that required by law and economics, to pursue long-term goals that are good for society. Hence, option (d) is correct.

56. Line-staff conflict is intergroup conflict arising from perceived differences between those directly involved in producing or selling products and those that support functions such as information systems and human resources.

57. The Gantt chart visually shows when tasks are supposed to be done and compares that with the actual progress on each task. Hence, option (D) is correct.

58. When a planning exercise is implemented in production cycle, it is controlling and guiding the work schedules helps in reaching the desired goals. Hence, option (c) is the correct answer.

59. The quality control system is used by all levels of management. A quality management system (QMS) is defined as a formalized system that documents processes, procedures, and responsibilities for achieving quality policies and objectives. A QMS helps coordinate and direct an organization's activities to meet customer and regulatory requirements and improve its effectiveness and efficiency on a continuous basis.

60. Organization Chart is a vital tool for providing information about organizational relationships.

It shows authority relationships and neglects significant informal and informational relationships. Hence from above discussion, we can infer that option (d) is false with respect to Organization Chart. Options (a), (b), (c) are all true with respect to Organization Chart.

61. Design skill implies the ability to solve problems in ways that will benefit the enterprise. Hence, option D is correct.

62. Hawthorne effect is defined as the possibility that individuals selected to participate in a study may show higher productivity only because of the added attention they receive from the researchers rather than any other factor being tested in the study.

63. The following statements are true regarding the task environment of a firm:

It consists of specific external elements such as customers and clients, competitors, suppliers, labor supply and government agencies, with which an organization interacts while conducting its business.

As it depends largely on the products and services offered by the firm and its business location, it may vary from firm to firm. Hence, option D is correct.

64. The major approaches utilized by managers to induce employees to accomplish the planned actions associated with implementation should normally include all of the given options except coercion.

65. Both approaches are equally important and can be used according to the situation and can be modified depending on factors such as the size of the organization, the organization culture and the urgency of the plan. Hence, option (D) is not true.

66. In the strategic management process, any organizational skills or resources that are exceptional or unique are the organization's core competencies.

Hence from above discussion, we can infer that option (c) is correct.

67. The decision tree involves a graphic representation of alternative courses of action and the possible outcomes and risks associated with each action. Hence, option A is correct.

68. The boundary-spanning sub-system consists of jobs that require the interaction of personnel with the general environment. Hence, option B is correct.

69. A matrix organization is a type of departmentation that superimposes a horizontal set of divisional reporting relationships onto a hierarchical functional structure. But it might not result in reduced prospects for interpersonal conflicts.

Hence, from above discussion, we can infer that option (D) is correct.

70. Delegation is the process by which managers allocate a chunk of their work to subordinates along with sufficient authority to accomplish the work. Hence, option (A) is correct.

71. The following are benefits of position descriptions:-

They identify duties and responsibilities that are overlapping or neglected

They provide guidance regarding candidate requirements, salary levels, and the training needs of new employees.

They help managers determine the tasks to be done and the employees who should do them. They act as a means of control over the organization by furnishing standards against which the necessity of the position can be ascertained. Hence, option B is correct.

72. From the viewpoint of staff personnel, the major reason/s for line-staff conflict are that line personnel

I.   Do not make proper use of staff personnel.

II.   Resist new ideas.

III.   Do not give staff personnel enough authority.

Hence, option (D) is the correct answer.

73. Dogs are business units that do not hold out much economic purpose and as such the organization must either not invest in them or should consider selling them as soon as possible. Hence, option D is correct.

74. Behavioral approach to management emphasized the human element, thus viewing the organization from an individuals' point of view. Hence, option D is correct.

75. Intelligence tests explore alertness, comprehension and reasoning abilities of applicants. (a) Work sampling tests are a means of measuring practical ability of the candidate on a specific job. (b) Knowledge tests evaluate the applicant's knowledge about the company, its competitors and customers, its products, the target market and the like. (c) Personality tests are means of measuring characteristics such as patterns of thoughts, feelings etc., of an individual. (d) Performance tests are same as work sampling tests.

76. Job performance is an activity of the individual in a performance appraisal system and not a corrective action resulting from an appraisal. Hence, option B is correct.

77. Objectives of sensitivity training:- It helps individuals gain insights into their behavior and helps them analyze the way they appear to others. It helps individuals develop the skills necessary for diagnosing and understanding of group processes. Hence, option C is correct.

78. Creativity is an individual phenomenon and cannot be discovered through groups is not a limitation of group discussion techniques to enhance creativity. Hence, option D is correct.

79. According to Herzberg, hygiene factors help in maintaining the existing performance level but cannot by themselves motivate the employees to perform better.

Supervision is regarded as one of Herzberg's hygiene factors.

Hence, option (c) is correct.

Options (a), (b), (d) are all motivation factors.

80. Cooperativeness is a personality trait concerning the degree to which a person is generally agreeable in their relations with other people as opposed to aggressively self-centred and hostile. It is one of the "character" dimensions in Cloninger's Temperament and Character Inventory. Cloninger described it as relating to individual differences in how much people identify with and accept others. Cloninger's research found that low cooperativeness is associated with all categories of personality disorder. Cooperativeness is conceptually similar to and strongly correlated with agreeableness in the five factor model of personality. Hence, option D is correct.

81. Avoiding eye contact is not an effective listening technique. Effective listening requires eye contact.

Hence, option (b) is not an effective listening technique.

Options (a), (c), (d) are all effective listening techniques.

82. Perception is the process that individuals use to acquire and make sense out of information from the environment.

Hence, option (b) is correct.

83. Concurrent controls involve identifying and preventing problems in an organization as they occur. This means that systems are monitored in real-time. Concurrent controls begin with standards and all employee activity is measured against the standard. Usually, these include quality control standards.

The four steps are:

Establishing Performance Standards.

Measuring the Actual Performance.

Comparing Actual Performance to the Standards.

Taking Corrective Action.

Hence, option (D) is correct.

84. Financial leverage ratios (debt ratios) indicate the ability of a company to repay the principal amount of its debts, pay interest on its borrowings, and meet its other financial obligations. They also give insights into the mix of equity and debt a company is using.

Financial leverage ratios usually compare the debts of a company to its assets. The common examples of financial leverage ratios include debt ratio, interest coverage ratio, capitalization ratio, debt-to-equity ratio, and fixed assets to net worth ratio.

Financial leverage ratios indicate the short-term and long-term solvency of a company.

85. Operations Management oversees the transformation process that converts resources such as labor and raw materials into finished goods and services.

Hence, option (c) is true regarding Operations Management.

Options (a), (b), (d) are all false regarding Operations Management.

86. In direct control, the cause of an unsatisfactory outcome traced back to the individual responsible for it who is then made to correct the practice. Hence, option C is correct.

87. MIS (Management Information System) can be defined as an integrated, user-machine system for providing information to support managerial, operational and decision-making functions in an organization.

The first necessary step to effectively operate an MIS is determining information needs.

Hence, option (c) is correct.

88. The view associated with geocentric attitude can be said to be global. In such a situation, executives believe that a global view is needed in both the headquarters of the parent company and its various subsidiaries.

Hence, option (d) is correct.

89. The following are claims that support self-appraisal:-

· It increases the personal commitment of employees.

· It improves employees' understanding of job performance.

· It provides a great deal of information about the appraisee is a claim that supports multiple appraisals. Hence, option (d) is the answer.

90. Manager Inventory Chart is a partial organization chart that shows managerial positions, current incumbents, potential replacements for each position, and the age of each person.

However, it does not show the position to which a manager may be promoted.

Hence, option (c) is not an advantage of Manager Inventory Chart.

Options (a), (b), (d) are all advantages of Manager Inventory Chart.

91. The amount of time spent in planning would be the greatest for upper-level managers. Hence, from the above discussion, we can infer that option (d) is correct.

92. Scientific management conducts business or affairs by standards established, by facts or truths gained through systematic observation, experiment, or reasoning. Hence, option (D) is correct.

93. Weakened International Balance of Payments is an argument against the Social Responsibility of Business. Hence from the above discussion, we can infer that option (c) is correct. Options (a), (b), (d) are all arguments for the Social Responsibility of Business.

94. Rules are statements of actions that must be taken or not taken in a given situation.

· A procedure is a series of interrelated sequential steps that can be used to respond to a   well-structured problem.

· A policy is defined as a general guideline for taking action.

· A budget is a statement that outlines the expected results of a given future period in numerical terms. Norms are standards set by a group that regulates and foster uniformity in member behaviors.

95. Middle-level managers would specifically engage in setting (I) division objectives and (II) specific overall organization objectives such as those pertaining to key result areas. Hence, option B is correct.

96. The five stages of the process are goal-setting, analysis, strategy formation, strategy implementation and strategy monitoring.

Clarify Your Vision. The purpose of goal-setting is to clarify the vision for your business.

Gather and Analyze Information.

Formulate a Strategy.

Implement Your Strategy.

Evaluate and Control.

97. Ms. Shah is currently addressing her planning efforts at the business level. Hence, option B is correct.

98. Open-system focus is characteristic of an organization that describes the degree to which the organization monitors and responds to changes in the external environment. Hence, option A is correct.

99. Programmed decision making doesn't pay much attention to the development of alternatives as the solution already exists. Hence, option B is correct.

100. Satisficing model says, "the ability of managers to be completely rational in making decisions is limited by certain factors". Hence, option B is correct.

101. Boundary spanning is a largely academic term for developing external relationships in order to accomplish your business objectives. This can be accomplished in business by such acts as joining an industry association to help lobby for legislative changes or partnering with another small business to increase sales.

102. The Hawthorne Effect is a phenomenon in which individuals alter their behavior in response to being observed, and usually refers to positive changes. Workers participating in a study might, for example, temporarily become more productive as a result of being observed.

103. The Hawthorne effect refers to the inclination of some people to work harder and perform better when they are being observed as part of an experiment.

Description: Under the Hawthorne effect, it was observed that individuals being observed would change their behaviour and become more productive not because there was any change in any variable such as working conditions or new machinery, but solely because of the attention they were getting. It is also referred to as the study of employee productivity. It was named after one of the most famous experiments in industrial history. It involves the study of human behaviour, under a specific set of conditions (variables) which are changed to conclude the experiment.

104. Manager Inventory Chart is a partial organization chart that shows managerial positions, current incumbents, potential replacements for each position, and the age of each person.

Options (a), (b), (c) are all advantages of the Manager Inventory Chart.

105. The steps in formulating a career strategy are as follows:
(i) Preparation of a personal profile.
(ii) Development of long-range personal and professional goals.
(iii) Analysis of the environment.
(iv) Analysis of Personal Strengths and Weaknesses.
(v) Development of Strategic Career Alternatives.
(vi) Consistency Testing and Strategic Choices.
(vii) Development of short-range career objectives and action plans.
(viii) Development of contingency plans.
(ix) Implementation of the Career Plan.
(X) Monitoring Progress.
Hence, option (b) is correct.

106. Manager assess performance of an employee among a group and advises the employee the specific expectations of management on day to day basis. It is setting standards for that employee (c) is correct answer.

107. A work team comprised of experts from various specialities is most accurately referred to as a cross-functional team. Hence, option (b) is correct.

108. • Promotion is a vertical move/transfer within the organisation to a higher position/rank that has greater responsibilities and requires more advanced skills.

• Promotion commands a higher salary, privileges and status compared with the old position.

Thus, Option C is correct.

109. Herzberg's motivation-hygiene theory proposes that the factors that help prevent dissatisfaction on the job do not necessarily lead to satisfaction. Hence, option C is correct.

110. The Porter-Lawler model of motivation, which is an improvement of the expectancy theory, assumes that motivation does not equal satisfaction. It assumes satisfaction does not lead to performance. Rather, the converse is true: performance can, but does not always, lead to satisfaction through the reward process. It assumes that motivation is not a simple cause-and-effect matter. The model advocates that managers carefully assess their reward structures and also assumes that performance leads to intrinsic as well as extrinsic rewards. Hence, option C is correct.

111. A high-task/low-relationships is appropriate for a new entrant into an organization who is unable to solve task-related problems independently. Hence, option A is correct.

112. Leadership style (5,5) is known as 'organization-man-management' or 'middle-of-the-road management.' In this style managers show a moderate amount of concern for both people and production and have difficulty in bringing about innovation and change. Hence, option B is correct.

113. Feedback is receiver's response to the sender's message. The receiver communicates reaction to the sender through words, symbols or gestures. It is the reversal of communication process where receiver becomes the sender and sender becomes the receiver. Unless the receiver responds to the message, communication process is incomplete. Feedback helps the sender transform his message, if needed. It also allows the receiver to clear doubts on the message, ask questions to build his confidence and enables the sender to know efficiency of the message. Feedback of information makes the communication process complete.

114. Cybernetic control is evident in all aspects of nature and technology. It occurs when a closed system regulates itself using a feedback loop. Examples range from a body cooling itself through perspiration to a safety valve on a steam engine. Cybernetic control system is a self-regulating control system that once put into operation, can automatically monitor the situation.

115. The current ratio is calculated using two standard figures that a company reports in it's quarterly and annual financial results which are available on a company's balance sheet: current assets and current liabilities. The formula to calculate the current ratio is as follows:

$$\text{Current Ratio} = \frac{\text{Current Assets}}{\text{Current Liabilities}}$$

116. The following statements about revenue centers are true:

Sales and marketing departments are examples of revenue centers.

A revenue center cannot be responsible for changes in profit levels.

Hence, option A is correct.

117. The event that would be most likely to happen if a company was operating with insufficient capacity is that the company would have a loss of sales and lower profits. Hence, option (c) is correct.

118. Preventive control is based on the idea that most of the negative deviations from standards can be overcome by applying the fundamentals of management. Preventive controls attempt to deter or prevent undesirable events from occurring. They are proactive controls that help to prevent a loss. Examples of preventive controls are separation of duties, proper authorization, adequate documentation, and physical control over assets.

119. The information attribute which is prepared or presented to users often enough to be up-to-date is known as information frequency. Hence, option D is correct.

120. Developing countries have become more adept in international negotiations and have become aware of their resources is not an advantage to a multinational corporation, instead is a challenge for them. Hence, option D is correct.

121. The three general types of managerial roles identified by Mintzberg are: interpersonal, informational and decisional roles. According to him maintaining self-developed networks of outside contacts and informers who provide favours and information can be best described as liaison role.

122. The major difference in skill requirements between middle and top managers is that top managers generally require higher-level conceptual skills but less technical skills than middle managers. Hence, from the above discussion, we can infer that option (d) is correct.

123. The pre-conventional Level of Moral Development is influenced exclusively by personal interest. It is concerned with following rules only when it's of interest. Hence from the above discussion, we can infer that option (a) is correct.

124. According to the Scientific Management School of Thought, Work Methods Study is defined as the systematic, objective and critical examination of all the factors governing the operational efficiency of a specified activity to bring about improvement. Hence, from the above discussion, we can infer that option (a) is correct.

125. A bureaucracy is a highly structured, formalized and impersonal organization. It has narrow spans of control, as there are multiple hierarchical levels. Hence, from the above discussion, we can infer that option (D) is not a characteristic of bureaucracy. Options (A), (B), (C) are all characteristic of bureaucracy.

126. Planning is defined as the process by which managers set missions and objectives, assess the future and develop courses of action to accomplish these objectives.

Management that does a good job of planning will have direction and purpose, and planning is likely to minimize wasted effort. All of these can occur, even if the objectives being sought are missed. Hence, from above discussion, we can infer that option (c) is a common misconception about planning.

127. A procedure is a series of interrelated sequential steps that can be used to respond to a well-structured problem. (a) Rules are statements of actions that must be taken or not taken in a given situation. (b) A policy is defined as a general guideline for taking an action. (c) A budget is a statement that outlines the expected results of a given future period in numerical terms. Hence, option D is correct.

128. An objective is the aim of an action. It implies a specific work to be accomplished within a given period of time. A short-term objective is developed to accomplish work in a very short period of time. Hence, from above discussion, we can infer that option (c) is correct.

129. Raj, Ramesh and Rajesh are all making decisions about how to approach the team project and they will probably rely on Bounded rationality, which is defined as a concept that suggests that the ability of managers to be perfectly rational in making decisions is limited by such factors as cognitive capacity and time constraints. (a) In rational decision-making, managers possess and understand all the information that is relevant to their decisions at the time they make them. (b) Break-even analysis is a measure by which the level of sales, which is necessary to cover all fixed costs, can be determined. (c) Intuition is "direct perception of truth, fact, etc., independent of any reasoning process; immediate apprehension."

130. The social responsiveness of an organization can be measured on the basis of fair treatment of employees; fair pay and safe working conditions. Hence from above discussion, we can infer that option (b) is correct.

131. L.A. Allen defined organizing as "the process of identifying and grouping the work to be performed, defining and delegating responsibility and authority, and establishing relationships for the purpose of enabling people to work most effectively together in accomplishing objectives".

In the area of diversity, organizing involves establishing task forces or committees to explore issues and provide ideas, carefully choosing work assignments to support the career development of all employees, and evaluating the extent to which diversity goals are being achieved. Hence, from above discussion, we can infer that option (d) is correct.

132. Organizational Culture is the collection of shared beliefs, values, rituals, stories, myths and specialized language that foster a feeling of community among organization members.

It is distinctive in nature, as each organization has its own management philosophy, mission and objectives etc.

Hence from above discussion, we can infer that option (b) is not a characteristic of Organizational Culture. Options (a), (c), (d) are all characteristics of Organizational Culture.

133. Organizations that have divisional structure but do not treat the divisions as autonomous businesses, so that they can have control over both the revenues and expenses, may opt to set up Profit Centers. When Organizations treat the divisions as autonomous businesses they may opt to set up Investment Centers.

134. Legitimate power is power you derive from your formal position or office held in the organization's hierarchy of authority. For example, the president of a corporation has certain powers because of the office he holds in the corporation.

135. Staff authority is created when a purchasing department is created because the hospital administrator cannot effectively handle all purchasing. Staff authority is the authority to serve in an advisory capacity (the authority to advise). Managers whose role it is to provide advice or technical assistance are granted advisory authority.

136. According to Herzberg's motivation-hygiene theory, relationships with peers, status, supervision and security are the four responses, that are all hygiene factors. Hence, from above discussion, we can infer that option (c) is correct.

137. The Porter-Lawler model of motivation, which is an improvement of the expectancy theory, assumes that motivation does not equal satisfaction. It assumes satisfaction does not lead to performance. Rather, the converse is true: performance can, but does not always, lead to satisfaction through the reward process. It assumes that motivation is not a simple cause-and-effect matter. The model advocates that managers carefully assess their reward structures and also assumes that performance leads to intrinsic as well as extrinsic rewards.

138. Creative process is rarely simple and linear and usually comprises four overlapping and interacting phases. Phase (I): Unconscious scanning, Phase (II): Intuition, Phase III: Insight and Phase (IV): Logical formulation.

139. Esteem needs - which Maslow classified into two categories: (i) esteem for oneself (dignity, achievement, mastery, independence) and (ii) the desire for reputation or respect from others (e.g., status, prestige).

140. According to the Tannenbaum and Schmidt Leadership model, the statement that would be most accurate regarding someone exhibiting behavior toward right of the continuum of leader behaviours is option (b), i.e., He would be more likely to ask the group to make a decision.

141. Participative leadership is a style of leadership in which all members of the organization work together to make decisions. Participative leadership is also known as democratic leadership, as everyone is encouraged to participate. ... Implement decision: All members of the organization implement the decision.

142. Participative leadership is a style of leadership in which all members of the organization work together to make decisions. Participative leadership is also known as democratic leadership, as everyone is encouraged to participate. Implement decision: All members of the organization implement the decision.

143. The grapevine is an informal communication system and is popularly known as "rumour mill". It is not of relevance to interpersonal communication. Hence, from above discussion, we can infer that option (c) is correct.

144. Concurrent control takes place while operations are going on and is intended to minimize problems as they occur. Concurrent control is a control type based on timing that involves the regulation, monitoring and adjusting of ongoing activities that are part of the transformation process to ensure that they conform to organizational standards. Feedback control takes place after operations are finished and is intended to correct problems that have already occurred. A feedforward control is a control type based on timing that focuses on the regulation of inputs to ensure that they meet the standards necessary for the transformation process. Steering control is a technique used to detect deviations and allow corrective actions to be taken while the activity is being performed.

145. A Gantt chart is essentially a bar graph with time on the horizontal axis and the activities to be scheduled on the vertical axis. Hence from above discussion, we can infer that option (a) is correct.

146. With concurrent control, monitoring takes place during the process or activity. Concurrent control may be based on

standards, rules, codes, and policies. One example of concurrent control is fleet tracking. Fleet tracking by GPS allows managers to monitor company vehicles. Concurrent control takes place while an activity is in progress. It involves the regulation of ongoing activities that are part of transformation process to ensure that they conform to organizational standards. Concurrent control is designed to ensure that employee work activities produce the correct results.

147. The principle of preventive control can be stated as "The higher the quality of managers and their subordinates, the less will be the need for direct controls". Hence, option A is correct.

148. NIST's 7-Step Contingency Planning Process

Develop the contingency planning policy statement.

Conduct business impact analysis (BIA).

Identify preventive controls.

Create contingency strategies.

Develop an information system contingency plan.

Ensure plan testing, training, and exercises.

Ensure plan maintenance.

149. Kanban is a subsystem of the JIT approach involving a simple parts movement system that depends on cards and containers to pull parts from one work center to another. ABC analysis is a technique of inventory management, in which the inventory is distributed based on price and usage of the inventory. A JIT is an approach to inventory control that emphasizes having materials arrive just as they are needed in the production process. Kaizen is a Japanese term implying continuous improvement.

150. The following are the characteristics of DSS:-

(a) Executive decisions are the focal points in DSS.

(b) DSS specializes in easy-to-use software.

(c) DSS employs interactive processing.

Hence, option D is correct.

// Notes //

// Notes //